REFERENCE

The Illustrated Encyclopedia
of
Hinduism

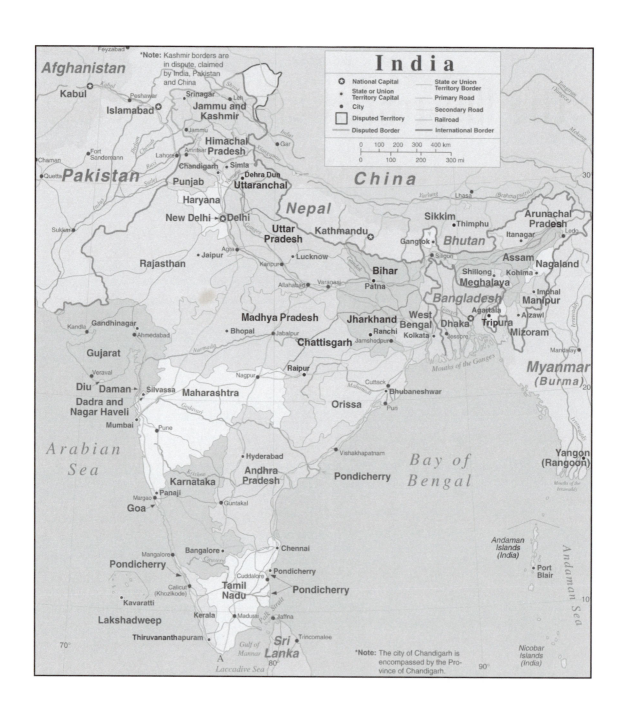

The Illustrated Encyclopedia
of
Hinduism

James G. Lochtefeld, Ph.D.

The Rosen Publishing Group, Inc.
New York

To teachers whose gift of learning I can never fully repay.
To students whose learning has taught me, and whose friendship has enriched me.
To Fiona, Vera, and Gavin, who put life back into perspective every day,
although they have yet to know this.
To Rachel, who has made all of this possible.

Published in 2002 by The Rosen Publishing Group, Inc.
29 East 21st Street, New York, NY 10010

Copyright © 2002 by James G. Lochtefeld

First Edition

Library of Congress Cataloging-in-Publication Data

Lochtefeld, James G., 1957–
The illustrated encyclopedia of Hinduism/James G. Lochtefeld.
  p. cm.
  Includes bibliographical references and index.
  ISBN 0-8239-2287-1 (set)
  ISBN 0-8239-3179-X (volume 1)
  ISBN 0-8239-3180-3 (volume 2)
  1. Hinduism Encyclopedias. I. Title.
BL1105.L63 2002
294.5'03—dc21
      99-27747
      CIP

Manufactured in the United States of America

Staff Credits

Editors: Margaret Haerens, Michael Isaac, Christine Slovey
Editorial Assistant: Rob Kirkpatrick
Book Design: Olga M. Vega
Cover Design: MaryJane Wojciechowski
Production Design: Erica Clendening, Beverly Fraser, Christine Innamorato,
    MaryJane Wojciechowski

Table of Contents

Volume One

Volume Two

Introduction

As you drive through the cornfields of northern Illinois, just north of the town of Aurora, you may see a massive brick building that seems out of place. It stands three or four stories high with an elaborate facade depicting pillars and cornices. Topped by towering spires with flapping banners, it looks as if it belongs to another world. In a sense it does—the architectural style comes from southern India, and the building itself is a Hindu temple.

I was there late on a Sunday morning, and the parking lot was about half full. There were cars from as far away as Michigan. The building's main entrance was a little below ground level, and as is common with Hindu temples outside of India, the lowest level had a lobby, a kitchen, and a large meeting room that was comparable to the "church basements" of its Christian counterparts. The lobby was furnished austerely, with folding tables and chairs. There were a few people sitting near the kitchen, drinking tea and chatting informally.

By the staircases leading upstairs to the temple room were rows of simple shelves, fronted by low benches. I removed my shoes, as is customary before entering a temple, both to preserve the temple and to signify that one is walking on holy ground. The staircase marked the threshold between two regions, the outer and the inner world. Upstairs, the temple was richly decorated. The presiding deity was Venkateshvara, a form of the god Vishnu, whose image was placed in the center of the temple, the most important space. Yet, as in most Hindu temples, there were images of deities from throughout the pantheon: Ganesh, Shiva, Subrahmanya, other forms of Vishnu, different forms of the Goddess, and various subsidiary deities. Most of the images were carved from black South Indian granite and polished to a mirrorlike finish. Many were housed in small shrines built out of white marble. The primary function of a Hindu temple is to serve as the home for the deities it contains, and it was clear that the people who had commissioned the temple had spared no efforts. The temple had been lovingly built and has been carefully maintained.

The worshipers in the temple took little notice of me, and I was allowed to roam as I wished. Even though Venkateshvara was the temple's presiding deity, the primary activity while I was there took place in front of one of the subsidiary shrines, an image of the Goddess in the form of Kumari ("virgin"). Seated around the image were about twenty members of an extended family. The young girls, who were clearly the focus of the rite, sat directly in front of the shrine. Brahmin priests took various offerings from the older women: plastic gallon jugs of milk, Ziploc bags of sugar, and Tupperware containers of yogurt and honey. Each offering was poured over the image in turn. A pitcher of water was poured over the image between each offering to wash it clean. The temple priests performing the rite were dressed traditionally, with white dhotis (garments worn around the waist, extending below the knees), bare chests, and the sacred thread over their left shoulders. They bore crisp red tilaks (sectarian identifying marks) on their foreheads, and intoned the rite in rapid-fire Sanskrit.

Although a Christian visitor might find the languages, deities, and rites completely alien, many of the other elements of the day would be soothingly familiar: a group of families coming for worship on a Sunday morning, dressed in their "Sunday best," with others chatting over coffee and sweets in the "church basement." Except for a few sari-clad older women, the people there were dressed no differently than anyone one might encounter on the street—the men in suits and jackets, the girls and women in long, flowing dresses.

Just as the Hindu temple in rural Illinois had introduced Indian customs to the local community, it was clear that the influence of American culture had set this temple apart from its traditional counterparts in India. Unlike in India, where temples serve mainly as places of worship, Hindu temples in America often serve as cultural centers for the Hindu community, sponsoring events such as dance, music, and drama performances, along with language study programs and festival celebrations.

In many cases, the membership of Hindu temples in America cuts across the traditional barriers that divide Indian society—social status, regional background, sectarian loyalty—giving these Hindu temples far more inclusive constituencies.

The cultural landscape of the United States has changed dramatically in recent years. Today it possesses a plurality of cultures that my grandparents and their generation probably would have found inconceivable. The Hindu temple outside of Aurora, Illinois, is but one small sign of the increasing visibility of Asian cultures in American society. Another sign of this pluralism is the growing number of ways that Americans are coming into contact with traditional Hindu culture—whether through practicing yoga, through alternative medical systems such as ayurvedic medicine, or through the piquant delights of Indian cuisine.

Despite the growing interchange between Indian and American cultures, Hinduism is still often stereotyped and misunderstood. On one hand are the remnants of an antiquated point of view that refuses to see the United States as anything but a Christian nation. Those holding this view either dismiss Hinduism as an alien or exotic set of rituals and beliefs or actively condemn it as idolatrous. On the other hand are people searching for an alternative spirituality who idealize Asian cultures as founts of ancient wisdom. At the very least, such an uncritical embrace ignores these cultures' genuine tensions, problems, and inequities; at the extreme it can result in a "designer religion," in which beliefs and practices from various religious traditions are selectively adopted, wrenching each of these elements from its roots in a living culture.

Outright condemnation and idealized acceptance overlook the richness and complexity of India's religious and cultural traditions. To gain a genuine understanding, it is important that we discern the cultural context behind Hindu beliefs, practices, and history. In learning about this context, one quickly encounters familiar ideas: hard work, thrift, education, and the importance of the family. Along with these general similarities to American cultural values, one finds equally profound differences. To examine the nuances of Hindu culture is to enter into a rich and complex world with its own inner logic and consistency. Encountering and understanding a different world view can throw one's own into sharper perspective, enriching it with new depth and understanding.

What Is Hinduism?

The very word *Hinduism* is misleading. The word was coined by the British as an umbrella term, referring to any and all forms of religion in India, many of which share few if any common features. It was used to describe all sorts of beliefs and practices, from simple nature worship to the most highly sophisticated ritual and philosophical systems.

Hinduism is a vast religious tradition, encompassing various and contradictory strands and ideas. It has usually defied all the usual strategies for categorization and classification. There is no founder, no definitive scripture, no centralized authority, no single supreme god, no creed of essential beliefs, and no heresy. Thus, it would be more accurate to think of the religion as *Hinduisms* rather than *Hinduism*, since this would reflect the rich diversity one encounters.

India is a land of contrasts and cultural variety. The subcontinent contains almost every type of environmental ecosystem, the inhabitants of each possessing their own local and regional culture. There are over a dozen distinct languages, each of which establishes and nourishes a regional identity that many Indians maintain with great care wherever they live. The combinations of language, regional identity, sectarian affiliation, and social status have given rise to overwhelming variation. For Hindus, diversity is a basic trait of Hindu life, and thus one person's practice may be very different from another's. This has given Hinduism little in the way of centralized doctrine or dogma, but its grounding in everyday life has made it extraordinarily resilient and adaptable.

Basic Beliefs

Hinduism is first and foremost a way of life. This means that Hinduism has tended to be orthoprax (stressing correct behavior) rather than orthodox (stressing correct belief). It tends to be woven through the differing elements of everyday life, rather than only performed as practices or rituals for certain days and times. Hindu religious expression is conveyed through every facet of society: music, dance, art and architecture, philosophy, politics, literature, and social life.

Some of the most important aspects of everyday life in the Hindu tradition are a person's family and social affiliations. Despite the incredible variety of Hindu belief and practice, each family and local community is tightly and carefully organized. Every individual, as a member of a particular family, has a well-defined role and an obligation to fulfill specific duties. As in any culture, one's individual identity is strongly shaped by the linguistic, regional, or sectarian characteristics of his or her family. This familial influence persists whether the family lives in its ancestral home or moves to a different region of India or a foreign country.

Families, of course, are members of a larger community. These communities share certain beliefs about a person's proper role in society based on status, age, and gender. Traditional Indian society was sharply hierarchical. According to the traditional social groupings, there should be four status groups: the brahmins, who are scholars and religious technicians; the kshatriyas, who are warriors and rulers; the vaishyas, who are artisans and farmers; and the shudras, who serve the others. Each person is born as a permanent member of a particular group. Society is seen as an organic whole, in which some parts have higher status than others, but every part is necessary for the whole to function smoothly. A common metaphor for social organization is the human body, which has many different parts performing many different functions, all of which are necessary for the body's maintenance and well-being. In actual practice, the picture was far more complex. Each of these four groups was split into hundreds of subgroups known as jatis. Jatis were most often identified with a certain hereditary occupation, and a jati's status in a particular place was subject to all kinds of local variables. These variables could include whether or not members of a jati owned land or the degree to which a jati's occupation was economically vital to its community.

These beliefs about social status are becoming less important in modern India, and have even less importance for Hindus who live abroad. In modern India, society is still functionally divided into four groups: brahmins; "forward castes," which tend to control land, money, or power; "backward castes," which have historically had very little influence, although the situation is changing rapidly; and Dalits ("oppressed"). Once called "untouchables," many Dalits live in poverty and oppressive social conditions. Except for the brahmins, these social divisions bear little relationship to the four groups in the earlier model.

Reincarnation is still a pervasive belief within Hinduism, as it is in other Indian religions such as Jainism, Buddhism, and Sikhism. Almost all Hindus have generally accepted that although our bodies are transient, our souls are immortal. After the death of a particular body, the soul will inhabit a different body. The nature of one's incarnation in a future life is determined by the quantity and quality of one's karma. Karma literally means "action," but it also can be generated by words or even thoughts. It is not produced only by the things one does or says, but also by one's underlying motives. An individual's good karma will bring a favorable rebirth in heaven as a god or on earth as a wealthy or high-caste human being. Bad karma will bring an unfavorable rebirth. A person's current social status reveals how properly he or she lived in the previous life. The notion of karmic rewards and punishments is a central justification for the traditional social hierarchy in India.

Karma is thought of as a purely physical process, like gravity, operating without any need for a divine overseer. An action one performs, for good or for ill, is seen as the cause, with the future reward or punishment as the effect. Some of these consequences occur in this life, while others occur in future lives. Since karma reflects the overall tone of one's life, it is comparable to the notion of a person's "character": Both are formed over a long period of time, both are measures of the whole person, and both reflect how our habitual ways of feeling, thinking, and acting tend to shape who we are.

It is tempting to envision reincarnation as an opportunity to rectify past mistakes or to learn lessons still unlearned. For Hindus, as for Buddhists, Sikhs, and Jains, nothing could be further from the truth; reincarnation is never seen as an opportunity, but invariably as a burden. This is because all states of being, both good and bad, are ultimately impermanent and thus provide no sure refuge. Even the gods, who are enjoying the rewards of their past actions, will be born elsewhere when their stored merit is exhausted. Others are enduring punishment for their sins, but when this is done they will be reborn elsewhere.

Although most Hindus would grant that liberation from reincarnation (moksha) is the ultimate goal, traditional Hindu culture has sanctioned three other goals, all of which are more compatible with a normal life in society: the search for pleasure (kama); the quest for wealth, fame, and power (artha); and, above all, the search for a righteous, balanced life (dharma). This stress on multiple goals reflects the flexibility of Hindu religious life. Each person can pursue different goals according to his or her inclinations, although certain goals are considered to be more appropriate for particular stages of life. In this way a person is free to express his or her individual religious identity, although that identity is inevitably shaped by forces arising from a larger familial, social, and cultural context.

The Roots of Hinduism

The influences and developments of Hinduism are as expansive as the roots and branches of a banyan tree. A banyan tree is unusual in that in addition to the tree's upward spreading branches, it also has branches that grow down, take root, and become trunks in their own right. An old banyan tree can be hundreds of feet in diameter, and it is often difficult to discern which is the original trunk. In the same way, the religion that we call Hinduism is constantly evolving. New religious forms arise from the older ones, while many of the older ones continue to exist. Despite Hinduism's complex origins, its religious history can be roughly divided into six periods, corresponding to the development of varying religious tendencies and ideas.

The earliest and most mysterious of these is the period of the Indus Valley Civilization, named for the large ruined cities found throughout the Indus Valley and beyond. The ruins of prominently placed storage granaries indicate that the civilization's economic base was agricultural, and the striking uniformity of the ruins of these cities leads one to believe that the people were bound by some strong central authority. Archaeologists have recovered a wealth of physical artifacts, revealing a great deal about the layout of the cities, what the inhabitants ate and wore, and the animals they domesticated. At the same time, nothing is certain about the religious life of these people, although certain artifacts have raised intriguing speculations. It is not even known whether the religion and culture of the Indus Valley Civilization have continued to affect Indian culture, although some scholars have been more inclined to infer this than others.

This culture seemed to lose its vitality sometime around 2000 B.C.E. Within a few centuries it had largely disappeared from the Indus Valley, although it remained vital for much longer in outlying regions, particularly Gujarat. According to some theories, its decline was the result of a prolonged drought. The latter part of its decline was marked by the arrival of the Aryans. This brought Hinduism into its second period of religious history. The Aryans were a nomadic cattle-herding people whose earliest religious text, the Rg Veda, is believed to have been preserved unchanged for almost four thousand years. The later strata of the Vedas were composed as the Aryans moved through the Punjab into the Ganges basin. These later parts of the Vedas included the Brahmana literature, which stressed the importance of sacrifice, and the later Aranyakas and Upanishads, which tended to focus on more speculative and philosophical questions. During the period in which the Aranyakas and Upanishads were composed, asceticism became an increasingly important element of Hinduism. Asceticism denotes the use of physical discipline and deprivation as a way to attain religious insight and liberate the soul from the cycle of reincarnation. Part of the reason for asceticism's prominence was the growth of competing groups, such as the Jains and the Buddhists, whose monks lived an ascetic life. Asceticism has had an important place in Indian religious life since that time.

The period after the composition of the Vedic literature is sometimes called the Epic period. Between roughly 300 B.C.E. and 500 C.E., many of the ideas most important to classical Hinduism were developed and codified. This time was marked by the initial composition of the two great Hindu epics, the Ramayana and the Mahabharata, although their final revisions came centuries later. The early part of this period also saw the composition of the religious literature known as the Kalpa Sutras. In theory, each Kalpa Sutra had three parts: a shrauta sutra, a grhya sutra, and a dharma sutra, but this neat ordering is belied by the scarcity of complete three-part collections, and the abundance of one or another of these sections without its corresponding parts. Shrauta sutras are manuals for Vedic sacrifice, which had become so complex that additional reference material was needed. The shrauta sutra is the only element of the three that has not retained great importance in modern Hindu life. The grhya sutras are manuals for domestic sacrifices, which include the life-cycle rites known as samskaras. Some elements of the grhya sutras still remain vital and vibrant parts of modern Hindu religious life, probably because of their connection with the central transitions in human life: birth, marriage, and death. The dharma sutras provide prescriptions for an organized and stable society by means of a rigid social hierarchy. The prescriptions in the dharma sutras were later expanded in the dharma shastras, which are the theoretical basis of the Hindu social structure.

Aside from the epics and the Kalpa Sutras, this period was also notable for the development of the six classical philosophical schools: the Nyaya, Vaisheshika, Samkhya, Yoga, Mimamsa, and Vedanta (although the defining figure in the Vedanta school, Shankaracharya, is generally dated in the early ninth century). The philosophical system developed by each of these six schools had a common goal: liberating the soul from the bondage of reincarnation. Each of the schools believed that the soul could be liberated by avoiding conceptual errors and apprehending universal truths, although there was considerable disagreement about the nature of these universal truths. The foundational texts for each of these schools laid out their basic philosophical position; in some cases, these texts buttressed their position by appealing to authoritative religious texts such as the Vedas. Over the following centuries these foundational texts received further elaboration through multiple layers of commentaries, which in some cases have continued to be written almost up until contemporary times.

This period is also marked by the rise in importance of the deities Shiva, Vishnu, and the Goddess, who are still the primary deities worshiped in modern Hinduism. These deities had a central place in the sectarian literature known as the puranas, another of the important types of text composed in this period. The puranas' most notable feature is their sectarian character, as they often exalt one particular deity over the others. They also include information on many other aspects of religious life, including sacred places, sacred times, instructions for various religious rites, and even descriptions of the heavens and hells. The final type of religious text first composed in this period were the tantras, which laid out esoteric and often hidden ritual traditions.

In later times, both the puranas and the tantras have been the subject of extensive commentaries. In addition, this period saw the development of new artistic and architectural styles. Many of the forces manifested or formed in this period remain integral parts of contemporary Hindu life.

The period following this was marked by the growth and flowering of the devotional (bhakti) tradition, which for more than a millennium has been one of the most powerful religious forces in Hindu culture. Bhakti stresses the necessity of a direct and personal relationship with God, in whatever form that deity is conceived. Its proponents tended to be contemptuous of the neatly constructed social order detailed in the dharma shastras, which stressed birth rather than devotional capacity as the most important criterion. Much of medieval Hindu thought was formed out of the tension between these two competing ideals, dharma and bhakti, and there was often no easy resolution of the conflict between their differing perspectives.

The growing presence of Europeans in India marked the next period in Hinduism's history. Although there had been a European presence in India since the mid-1500s, when the Portuguese colonized Goa, the introduction of British colonists presented the greatest challenge to Indian society. In the early 1600s, the British East India Company gained its first foothold with a trading station at Surat in modern Gujarat and gradually put down additional roots in Bombay, Madras, and the Bengal region. With the effective collapse of the Moghul empire in the mid-1700s, the nobility that ruled peripheral regions such as Bengal began to function independently. This allowed the British to displace the indigenous rulers as the political authorities and the recipients of land revenue. The East India Company was a commercial venture, and its primary goal was to make money for its shareholders. Yet the Indian body politic was so fragmented that the company encountered little effective resistance and aggressively expanded its sphere of influence from Bengal up the Ganges River valley and into central India. In some cases the company would simply absorb small kingdoms under the pretense of protecting law and order, especially when the leadership had no clear line of succession. In other cases it would make agreements with local nobility to create small princely states, some of which survived until Indian independence in 1947. General discontent with the company's aggressive expansion finally exploded in the rebellion of 1857–58, after which India was governed as part of the British Empire.

The company was primarily driven by economic motives, but it justified its paternal presence by portraying the Indians as unable to govern themselves effectively. Although the company's policy was not to interfere with its subjects' religious lives, since any such tensions would be bad for business, the company's board of directors in England was under strong domestic pressure to open up their dominions to Christian missionary activity. Contemporary missionary polemics against Hinduism usually stressed repugnant practices such as sati (the burning of a widow on her husband's funeral pyre), child marriage, the pitiable plight of many widows, or Hindu "idolatry." Such political and religious critiques assumed the implicit superiority of European Christian culture and provided the moral sanction for colonialism that Rudyard Kipling described as the "white man's burden."

Hindus responded to these critiques in several ways. The most violent response came in the rebellion of 1857–58, in which popular discontent led various groups to try to drive the British out of India. Although there was widespread opposition to British rule, it was never unified, allowing the British to defeat their adversaries one by one. A far more effective response came in religious terms, as progressive Hindus attempted to respond to the missionary critiques. One result of this was the formation of various societies, such as the Brahmo Samaj, Prarthana Samaj, and Arya Samaj. The first two of these attempted to reform Hindu religious life by removing certain offensive practices in response to criticism from outsiders. These practices included the caste system, child marriage, and the ban on widow remarriage. The Arya Samaj was formed to regenerate and revitalize Hinduism, with the explicit position that Hinduism was far superior to Christianity and Islam.

The end of the nineteenth century was also marked by the gradual establishment of Hinduism as a viable religious tradition in the West, as Hindu teachers arrived in Europe and America. Some of the early figures were Swami Vivekananda and Paramahamsa Yogananda, and the more recent ones are Prabhupada, Muktananda, Yogi Bhajan, Guru Maharaj Ji, Krishnamurti, and Shri Chinmoy. This recent group of teachers had an explicit missionary goal, aiming to gain followers among native-born Europeans and Americans.

The most recent period in the development of Hindu religious traditions is marked by the emigration of Indians to America. Many Indians have settled abroad seeking education or to pursue specialized careers. They have established centers of Hindu worship, like the temple Aurora, to serve the needs of the Indian community, including the need to pass on a sense of Hindu identity to their children. Yet despite their efforts to preserve their traditions and culture, their very presence in a different society is causing changes in their religious lives. American society has made certain traditions more difficult to preserve. For example, the community often celebrates religious festivals on the weekend following the traditional festival day, since this is when people have more spare time. Life in American society and the influence of American values have also made it difficult to conform to certain traditional patterns. The traditional requirement that Hindus marry within their jati has been assailed both by the American emphasis on the importance of a "love marriage" and by the potential shortage of suitable partners. In the same way, certain dietary restrictions become harder to maintain but have greater complexity. A Hindu in America must decide not only if he or she should simply avoid eating beef but also whether to avoid any place where beef is served.

In India, the twentieth century has been marked by the development of an assertive and militant Hindu nationalism. Hindu nationalism's "founding father" was V. D. Savarkar, but the most important body promoting this idea in the recent past has been the Rashtriya Svayamsevak Sangh (RSS). The RSS is the mother organization for many different affiliates, ranging from labor unions to student organizations to social relief bodies. Its two most important affiliates for promoting Hindu nationalism are the Vishva Hindu Parishad (VHP), a religious organization, and the Bharatiya Janata Party (BJP), a mass-based political party. In the early 1990s, both organizations were instrumental in radical Hindu politics, particularly in the destruction of a mosque alleged to have been built on the site of the god Rama's birthplace in the North Indian city of Ayodhya. Since that time, the VHP has retained its radical edge, but the BJP has not. The BJP has put greater distance between itself and the VHP, seeking to move toward the political center and thus expand its reach in electoral politics. It has begun stressing issues that are vital to a broader spectrum of Hindu voters, such as corruption and the rising cost of living.

This encyclopedia offers the student of religion a place to begin exploring the key elements of Hindu religious culture and practice. I hope that the entries will be a springboard for further study of this great, living religious tradition.

How to Use This Book

This encyclopedia includes the following features:

- The Contents by Subject lists related entries in the following categories: Art, Architecture, and Iconography; Astrology and Cosmology; Biographical Entries; Calendar and Time; Ceremonies, Practices, and Rituals; Communities, Groups, and Organizations; Dance; Dynasties; Geography; Literature, Language, and Drama; Medicine, Physiology, and Alchemy; Music, Hymns, and Prayers; Mythology and Beliefs; Philosophy and Logic; and Yoga and Tantra.

- Cross-referenced terms within entries are indicated in boldface type.

- Parenthetical citations are used to refer to selections from primary Hindu texts. For sources from the Vedas, the first number refers to the book and the second to the hymn. For later sources, including the Upanishads, the Bhagavad Gita, and all of the dharma literature, the first number refers to the chapter and the second to the verse.

- Lineage charts for characters in the Hindu epics the *Mahabharata* and the *Ramayana* appear on pages 401 and 556, respectively.

- Words with distinctive pronunciations are listed in the back of the book with diacritical marks—symbols above or below the letters to indicate their proper pronunciation.

- Abbreviated bibliographic citations appear at the end of some entries. The full citations are grouped together in the bibliography.

Note on Dates

In many cases, determining dates for the lives of Indian figures is problematic because there are not good records for many figures, even in comparatively modern times. The most definite dates tend to be from inscriptions, and thus this evidence is best for kings and others who were able to commission inscriptions. Philosophers, devotional poets, and writers often could not. In this book, a question mark follows dates that scholars have determined by inference (for example, based on internal evidence in texts, such as references to historical events) but are not backed up by documentary evidence.

Contents by Subject

Art, Architecture, and Iconography

Astrology and Cosmology

Biographical Entries

Calendar and Time

Ceremonies, Practices, and Rituals

Communities, Groups, and Organizations

Dance

Dynasties

Geography

Literature, Language, and Drama

Medicine, Physiology, and Alchemy

Music, Hymns, and Prayers

Mythology and Beliefs

Philosophy and Logic

Yoga and Tantra

Abhang

("unbroken") Poetic form characteristically used by the saint-poets of the **Varkari Panth**, a religious community centered around the **worship** of the Hindu god **Vithoba**. Each abhang is usually made up of four lines, with an *abbc* rhyme scheme. Although each abhang is a complete poem in its own right, they are often strung together in groups, to create either a longer narrative poem (in which each abhang stands as one segment) or a group of poems devoted to a common theme. Such versatility made it one of the dominant poetic forms in the Marathi language, just as the **doha** form is ubiquitous to medieval and modern **Hindi**.

Abhava

("[knowledge from] absence") Abhava is one of the two means of valid knowledge (**pramana**) unique to the **Purva Mimamsa** school of **philosophy**, the other being presumption (**arthapatti**). All Indian philosophical schools concern themselves with codifying pramanas, that is, the means by which human beings can gain true and accurate knowledge. Behind this concern lies the basic Hindu religious goal of learning to live, act, and think in a way that leads to the final liberation of the soul from the cycle of reincarnation (**samsara**). Almost all schools accept perception (**pratyaksha**), inference (**anumana**), and authoritative testimony (**shabda**) as pramanas. The Purva Mimamsa school claims that abhava, or perception of the absence of something ("there is no jug in this room"), is a means of knowledge that cannot be accounted for by the other pramanas.

Abhaya Hasta

In Indian **dance**, **sculpture**, and ritual, a particular hand **gesture** (**hasta**) in which the hand is held with the palm facing out, with the fingers together and pointing upward. The word *abhaya* means "without fear," and the gesture is meant to reassure the viewer that all will be well. This hand gesture can be found in most depictions of the Hindu gods and goddesses, particularly when the **deity** in question has multiple hands.

Abhijnanashakuntala

("Recognition of **Shakuntala**") Drama written by **Kalidasa** (5th c. C.E.), who is widely considered the greatest classical **Sanskrit** poet. The *Abhijnanashakuntala* describes the trials and troubles of the mythical heroine Shakuntala and is considered Kalidasa's greatest drama. In the story, Shakuntala, the **daughter** of the sage **Vishvamitra** and the celestial nymph **Menaka**, attracts the eye of King **Dushyanta** while he is away from his kingdom on a hunting trip. Shakuntala and Dushyanta marry by mutual consent, in what is known as a **gandharva marriage**. After their marriage, Dushyanta returns to his kingdom. Shakuntala remains at her home and has the misfortune to irritate the sage **Durvasas**, who **curses** her to be forgotten by her beloved. Shakuntala pleads with Durvasas, who is moved to mitigate the curse such that Dushyanta will remember everything if Shakuntala can show Dushyanta a sign of their union. Dushyanta had given Shakuntala his signet ring, but she loses it before she can see him. Denied by Dushyanta, Shakuntala endures numerous trials until she finds the ring in the belly of a fish. When Dushyanta sees the ring, he immediately recognizes Shakuntala (hence the play's name), and they live happily ever after.

The *Abhijnanashakuntala* has two features that characterize most classical Sanskrit plays. One is the preference for a happy ending, although this resolution

Dancers performing in the Kathak style. Most Kathak performances include dances in the abhinaya genre, in which performers use dance to act out a story from religious literature.

is usually preceded by trial and tribulation. The other is that the drama's dialogue is in two different languages. Characters from the higher classes speak Sanskrit, the language of high, learned culture. Characters from the lower classes (including many of the **women**) speak in **Prakrit**, an umbrella term for the grammatically simpler vernacular languages that developed from Sanskrit through natural linguistic change. This difference in dialogue doubtless reflected the social realities of the time in which the play was written, when Sanskrit would have been the elite language but was always learned as a second language after learning one's "natural" language. The play has been translated into English by Michael Coulson and published in an anthology titled *Three Sanskrit Plays*, 1981.

Abhimanyu

In the **Mahabharata**, the later of the two great Hindu epics, Abhimanyu is one of **Arjuna's sons** by his wife, **Subhadra**. Abhimanyu is known as a great warrior who fights with valor in the Mahabharata war. As he fights in battle, he enters the enemy's **chakravyuha** formation, a battle array that is widely believed to be virtually impenetrable. According to tradition, Arjuna is one of the few people who knows how to counter the chakravyuha. While Abhimanyu was in his mother's womb, he heard his father describe how to penetrate it. Once Abhimanyu is in, however, he realizes that he does not know how to get out, and although he kills a great number of the enemy, he is eventually slain.

Abhinavagupta

(10th c. C.E.) Kashmiri writer famous for his works on poetics and aesthetics. Abhinavagupta was a pivotal figure in the development of **Trika Shaivism**, a particular religious community devoted to the god **Shiva**. The writer's most famous religious work is the *Tantraloka*, a twelve-volume work elucidating the metaphysics and ritual of Trika Shaivism. His *Dhvanyaloka* gives similar attention to aesthetics and poetics. See also **Kashmir** and **Shaiva**.

Abhinaya

("bringing near") In Indian drama, the general name given to acting. Its ultimate purpose is to convey an emotion through a look or **gesture** and thus "bring" it to the audience. In Indian **dance**, this term refers to a piece in which the dancer acts out a story, with the aim to convey to the viewers the emotions of her character. Particularly with Indian dance, this sort of acting is not mere artistry, however refined, but carries explicit religious meaning. Not only is the story's content often drawn from religious literature, but most Indian dance forms were first performed in temples as entertainment for the resident **deity**.

Abhira

Sanskrit term for **Ahir**. See **Ahir**.

Abhisheka

("anointing") Ritual bathing (**snana**) or anointing with **water**, particularly of the image of a **deity** during **worship**. In earlier times this term referred to the ritual anointing of a king at his coronation (**rajabhiseka**). In modern times the term can also apply to anointing or sprinkling individuals with water during religious or life cycle rituals, particularly rites of **initiation** (**diksha**) involving a change of status for the initiate—such as the shift from householder to initiated **ascetic** or in the ritual tradition known as **tantra**, an initiation bestowing certain ritual and religious qualifications (**adhikara**). In both cases the anointing is intended to honor the initiate, to evoke images of royal coronation, and to suggest the importance of the occasion.

Abortion

Hindu views toward abortion have varied widely over the course of time. It is unequivocally condemned in the **dharma literature**, which prescribes loss of **caste** for a person procuring an abortion or for a **woman** having one. This prescription may have been based on the use of abortion to conceal illegitimate **births**, but it may well have been condemned because it entailed the loss of a potential son. In modern times attitudes have changed somewhat, in part because of family planning initiatives and in more recent times because of the technology available for sex determination. Abortion facilities are now more widely available in India due to the government's emphasis on family planning and population control, and there is less social stigma associated with the procedure. However, traditional proscriptions remain. With the advent of methods for prenatal sex determination, couples began selectively aborting female fetuses because **sons** are more highly valued in Hindu society. This practice was widespread and generated such concern that it was outlawed in 1995, although the law has reportedly only succeeded in driving this practice underground.

Achala Ekadashi

Festival falling on the eleventh **day** (**ekadashi**) of the dark (waning) half of the **lunar month** of **Jyeshth** (May–June). As are all of the eleventh-day observances, this is dedicated to the **worship** of the god **Vishnu**. The name Achala means "immovable"; another name for this ekadashi is *apara*, meaning "matchless." The name refers to the religious merit generated by observing this festival, which, according to tradition, cannot be nullified or overturned. Most Hindu festivals have certain prescribed rites, usually involving fasting (**upavasa**) and worship, and often promise specific benefits for faithful performance. Individual observance varies depending on a person's piety and inclinations. Fasting, for instance, can vary from abstaining only from certain foods to refraining from all foods during the day. Individuals may go to temples for worship, or they may worship in their homes. Faithfully observing this festival is believed to absolve one of the evil effects of one's past deeds, particularly deeds that would result in **birth** as a **pret**, or unquiet spirit, and also to increase one's fame, wealth, and religious merit.

Achamana

("sipping") The act of sipping **water** that has been poured or scooped into one's right hand. This is performed as a rite of purification. Achamana is a symbolic action that has been incorporated into many religious rituals. It is also part of the required early morning ablutions, the purpose of which is to remove any impurity (**ashaucha**) encountered while sleeping. In the Hindu tradition, human beings are considered impure upon waking for a number of reasons. Since sleep entails loss of consciousness, one may not know whether one has come into contact with impurity. Further, bodily functions that may occur while sleeping cause impurity. In addition, it is popularly believed that one's soul

(**atman**) leaves the body during sleep and then reenters it before the body awakens. While the soul is gone, the body is believed to be a **corpse**, which is an impurity that must be cleansed.

Achamaniya

("to be sipped") The fifth of the sixteen traditional **upacharas** ("**offerings**") given to a **deity** as part of **worship**, on the model of treating the god as an honored guest. In this upachara, the deity is offered **water** for rinsing and cleaning the mouth. The actual act of offering can be done in various ways and often depends on the worshiper's inclinations. In some cases the water vessel will simply be presented before the deity's image, with the understanding that the water has been taken, whereas in other cases the devotee (**bhakta**) will actually rinse the image's mouth. In either case the underlying motive is to show love for the deity and to minister to its needs.

Achara

("conduct") Appropriate or approved behavior according to customary law, which is established in the **dharma literature**. The **dharma** assumes that society is made up of different social subgroups known as **jatis**, which are usually defined (and hierarchically arranged) by the group's hereditary occupation. Each jati had its own customary code of appropriate behavior, and there were often sharp differences between them. For example, it was often acceptable for members of lower-status jatis to eat meat and drink **liquor**, whereas these practices were forbidden to higher-status groups. Aside from the customary rules of one's social group or subgroup, notions of appropriate behavior for a particular person would also be shaped by age and gender considerations: A young and sexually fertile **woman** would be subject to far greater restrictions than a postmenopausal woman, since any sexual scandal (or even the hint of it) could ruin a young woman's opportunities for a good marriage or produce an illegitimate child.

Acharya

Traditional term of respect for a religious leader or a spiritual teacher; the word connotes great learning as well as a religious life. The term literally means someone who knows or teaches about **achara**, the traditionally accepted way of life prescribed in the **dharma literature**. As a title in modern Hindu life, it indicates the respect and social standing conveyed by the English word *doctor*.

Achintyabhedabheda

("inconceivable identity and difference") Key philosophical concept of the **Gaudiya Vaishnava** school, which was founded by the Bengali saint **Chaitanya** (d. 1533) and is devoted to the **worship** of **Krishna** as the Supreme Being. The concept was first enunciated by Chaitanya's disciple **Jiva Goswami** (late 16th c.) and explains the relationship between God (Krishna) and the human soul, and between God and his **divine powers**. In both cases these relationships are described as simultaneously involving sameness and difference. On one hand, human souls are clearly different from God, as shown by their imperfections and their susceptibility to the action of **karma**, both of which contrast with God's utter transcendence and perfection. Yet since it is possible for human souls to gain ultimate liberation (**moksha**) from the action of karma, they must also share some part of God's nature, since liberation would be impossible if human souls were completely different. Even though human souls partake in the divine nature, their distinctness is upheld even after liberation, when the human soul does not merge with Krishna but remains separate.

This same concept is used to describe the second relationship, between God and his divine powers.

The divine powers are often conceived not just as attributes (e.g., the ability to create, preserve, and destroy the universe) but as actual embodied **deities**, particularly in the form of goddesses. These powers are both the same as God, since they come from Him, but also different since each of the embodied powers does not contain the glory of the whole. In both cases the precise nature of this simultaneous identity and difference is "inconceivable," which here carries a mystical sense. For further information see Sushil Kumar De, *Early History of the Vaishnava Faith and Movement in Bengal, from Sanskrit and Bengali Sources*, 1961.

Achyuta

("imperishable") Epithet of **Vishnu**, referring to the devotees' (**bhakta**) beliefs that nothing can stand against Vishnu and that his power will never wane. Hindu **deities** often have many names that sometimes denote unique form of the deity and at other times denote a special quality of the deity. No two deities will ever share the same epithet. The proliferation of names for deities may be related in part to the characteristics of the **Sanskrit** language, which is rich with synonyms. This allows words to fit into various poetic **meters**. See **Vishnu**.

Act of Truth

In Hindu mythology, a ritual action that is described as being able to neutralize poison, bring rain, make a river flow backward, or even compel the gods to grant one's wishes. The act of truth draws its effectiveness from the **power of truth** and is usually performed as a last resort when all other avenues have been blocked. The act of truth is a conditional statement: the first part is a true statement about one's past behavior, the second part a request for some specific result ("If I have always given to those who begged from me, may this **fire** not burn me"). The rite's success stems from the truthfulness of the first condition—that the power of truth in the condition actually causes the second part to come true. One example of the act of truth being used to compel the gods to grant a wish occurs in the story of the lovers **Nala** and **Damayanti**. Damayanti intends to choose Nala as her husband but finds that four of the gods have taken Nala's form, in an effort to foil her. Damayanti's act of truth affirms that she had chosen Nala as her husband and has never wavered in this choice, and it then directs the gods to take their true forms again. The gods take their true forms, and Nala and Damayanti are married.

As Sanskritist and Indologist W. Norman Brown observes, in cases where the act of truth is successful, the people making the act of truth have perfectly fulfilled their social roles, and this perfection allows them to make the conditional affirmation so central to the act of truth. Successful men have been either great kings, **ascetics**, or householders; successful **women** have usually been absolutely faithful to their husbands (fulfilling one idealized women's role). One story tells of a prostitute who affirmed that she had serviced all of her clients without partiality, thus perfectly fulfilling her particular social role. In any of these cases, perfection of one's role is believed to bring spiritual merit as well as the ability to unleash it by performing the act of truth. For further information see W. Norman Brown, "The Metaphysics of the Truth Act," in *Mélanges D'Indianisme à la Mémoire de Louis Renou*, 1968.

Adharma

In the **dharma literature**, this term designates the absolute opposite of **dharma**, the fundamental values that serve to uphold society. Although adharma can denote a particular unrighteous action, it more widely implies a state of affairs in which society has been completely corrupted; the values that uphold society have been subverted, overturned, or ignored and hence such particular unrighteous actions become possible, even likely.

Adhikamasa

See **Intercalary Month**.

Adhikara

("qualification") In any sort of Hindu **worship**, but particularly in **tantra**, adhikara indicates that one has the religious qualifications to perform certain ritual actions. This refers partly to knowing how to perform the ritual, and thus being "qualified" in that sense of the word. More importantly, it refers to having gained the ritual status that entitles one to perform the ritual. This status is usually conferred by some sort of formal **initiation** or initiations given by one's teacher, who decides what type of and how much adhikara to transmit based on an assessment of the student's abilities, temperament, and desire to learn.

Adhiratha

The foster father of **Karna** in the great Hindu epic, the *Mahabharata*. Karna is born when his mother, **Kunti**, uses a special **mantra** given to her by the sage **Durvasas**, which gives a **woman** the power to conceive and bear children by the gods. Kunti impulsively uses the mantra to invoke the **Sun**, by whom she conceives and bears Karna. In her panic at unexpectedly becoming a mother—she is still unmarried, and concerned about what people might think—she puts the child in a box and abandons him in the **Ganges**. When Adhiratha goes to the Ganges to bathe (**snana**), he finds the child, and since he and his wife are childless, they raise the boy as their own.

There are a number of interesting aspects to the story of Adhiratha. Although he is not of high status, he becomes the king of the country. He comes from a social group whose traditional occupation is driving chariots.

The Shri Channakeshara temple in Somnathpur, India. A traditional feature of Hindu temple architecture is the adhishthana, a raised base upon which the temple is built.

One can read this dissonance in the epic's recognition that the hierarchical, occupationally based social model is an idealized projection and not always the reality. It can also be argued that since Adhiratha is not fulfilling his particular religious duty (**dharma**) but has usurped that of the ruling class, both he and the country are destined for ruin. The reality of his family's lowly status and the uncertainty about his **birth** trouble Karna for most of his life.

Adhishthana

("foundation") In Hindu temple **architecture**, the raised base on which a temple was built. These are particularly high in the temples at **Khajuraho**, and their height accentuates the upward thrust of these temples. Whether high or low, the adhishthana is important as the temple's foundation, the stable base on which all else rests.

Adhvaryum

A type of sacrificial priest described in the **Brahmana** literature, one of the later strands of the sacred literature known as the **Vedas**. The Brahmanas largely functioned as manuals describing how to perform sacrificial rites—which primarily involved burning **offerings** in a sacred **fire**—and the care and attention devoted to detailing these **sacrifices**, which leads to the inference that these were the primary religious acts. These rites were so complex that they required specialized ritual technicians: the adhvaryum, the **hotr**, the **udgatr**, and the **brahman**. The adhvaryum was the sacrificial priest who chanted the hymns from the **Yajur Veda** that were used in the **sacrifice**. He was also responsible for preparing the sacred altar, assembling the sacrificial materials, kindling and feeding the sacred fire, and actually offering the sacrificial **animals**.

Adhyasa

("superimposition") In **Advaita Vedanta**, one of the **six schools** of classical Indian **philosophy**, this is a key concept used to explain the ultimate unreality of the world around us, despite its apparent reality. For the Advaita Vedanta school, there is ultimately only one real idea in the universe, namely **Brahman**. All things are in fact that one thing, and this never changes. Since Brahman is the all in all, it can never actually be an object of perception (**pratyaksha**). What the Advaitins then have to explain is how things in the world apparently change, or seem diverse and different. This is explained as stemming from our mistaken perception and under-standing. They call this notion adhyasa, which is rooted in the human tendency to "construct" a picture of world. According to this explanation, human beings superimpose a false understanding (that reality is diverse and differentiated) on top of the correct understanding (that all reality is nothing but undifferentiated Brahman). According to the Advaitins, the world is real because Brahman is real. What is not real is the world as most unenlight-ened people perceive it.

Advaitins illustrate this concept by two well-known errors in judgment: the case of a rope that one briefly mistakes for a snake, or a post that one imagines is a man. Although these judgments are erroneous—as one quickly discovers—they are not made up out of nothing. In each case, one is perceiving something real—the rope and post both actually exist—but "superimposing" a different and mistaken identity on these things, and thus "transforming" them into something they are not. In the same way, it is argued, human consciousness begins with the Supreme Reality (Brahman), which is actually there, but superimposes onto it something which is not (the judgment of a diverse world).

According to the Advaitins, the real problem is epistemological, that is, how human beings come to know things, rather than in the nature of the things themselves. One comes to a true understanding not when the things themselves change—to refer back to the example, the rope always was and always will be a rope—but with the destruction of the mistaken notions that led to the initial error, and their replacement by true understanding. For the Advaitins, adhyasa is a manifestation of **avidya** (lack of true knowledge); this avidya is reinforced and upheld by the **karmic** power of one's mistaken thoughts and actions. Adhyasa immediately disappears at the moment true understanding is gained, when one comprehends that the world (and oneself) are both nothing but Brahman. This moment of realization brings ultimate wisdom that can never be lost, just as that once one has recognized the piece of rope, it can never again become a snake. For further information see Karl H. Potter (ed.), *Advaita Vedanta up to Samkara and His Pupils*, 1981; and Sarvepalli Radhakrishnan and Charles A. Moore (eds.), *A Sourcebook in Indian Philosophy*, 1957.

Adi

Fourth month in the Tamil solar **year**, corresponding to the northern Indian solar month of Karkata (the zodiacal sign of Cancer), which usually falls within July and August. The existence of several different **calendars** is one clear sign of the continuing importance of regional cultural patterns. One way that the Tamils retain their culture is by preserving their traditional calendar. Tamil is one of the few regional languages in India with an ancient, well-established literary tradition. See also **Tamil months**, **Tamil Nadu**, and **Tamil language**.

Adigranth

("Primal Book") One of the names for the Sikh scripture, most often used by people outside the tradition. Sikhs themselves are more likely to use the honorific title *Shri Guru Granth Sahib*, which reflects the scripture's status as the spiritual leader (**guru**) of the Sikh community. This status was conferred by the tenth Sikh guru, Gobind Singh (d. 1708), who proclaimed that after his death the community would have no more human leaders, but only their scripture to guide them. The book's religious authority can be seen in the way that the Sikhs treat it. They accord the Adigranth the status of a living person. In Sikh temples the Adigranth is ceremonially put to bed at night and woken up in the morning. It is enshrined under a canopy (a sign of royalty) for **worship**, is fanned during hot weather and warmed during cold, and if it has to be taken anywhere, is carried on the bearer's head, considered the purest part of the body. In according this respectful treatment to a physical book, the Sikhs were probably influenced by Muslim practice with regard to the Qur'an, since in general Hindus pay little heed to a book itself, however important the text may be.

The Adigranth plays a central role in Sikh life: Children are named by opening the book at random and taking the first consonant on the upper-left-hand page as the first letter of the child's name; Sikh couples are married by circling the book, as Hindu couples circle the sacred **fire** (**agnipradakshinam**), and a commonly performed death rite is an unbroken reading (**akhand path**) of the entire text.

The text itself was compiled in 1603–1604 by Guru Arjan, the fifth Sikh guru. According to tradition he compiled the book in response to certain rivals contesting his authority, some of whom had compiled and were circulating books purporting to be the teachings of Guru Nanak, the Sikhs' founder and first guru. There may be some truth in this tradition, but it is now well established that Arjan himself was working from a compilation made a generation before. The text's opening verses are known as the mul **mantra**, which gives a collection of attributes and qualities ascribed to the Supreme Being. After this opening, the Adigranth has three main parts. The first is the Japji, a sequence of thirty-eight poems written by Guru Nanak that is considered the essence of the Sikh faith,

and which is recited by the faithful as the morning prayer.

The second section contains the hymns of the Sikh gurus, arranged by **raga**, or melodic mode. Within each raga the hymns are arranged according to poetic **meter**, and within each meter the hymns are arranged sequentially according to which of the gurus composed them. Since the Sikh tradition holds that all ten gurus contained the same divine spirit, they all identified themselves as "Nanak." But introductions to the songs differentiate between them by calling them *Mahala* (literally "house," but figuratively "body") followed by a number—from Mahala 1 for Guru Nanak to Mahala 5 for Guru Arjan.

The final section of the Adigranth contains hymns by various other devotees (**bhakta**), both Hindu and Muslim, whom the Sikh gurus believed to be propounding the essential Sikh message of monotheism and the need to serve God. Among the Hindu devotional (**bhakti**) poets whose works can be found in this section are **Trilochan**, **Jayadeva**, **Pipa**, **Ramananda**, **Sen**, **Namdev**, **Kabir**, and **Ravidas**, with significant collections for the last three. Even for those not interested in the Sikhs, this last section makes the Adigranth an extremely important document. Not only does this section provide manuscript tradition that can be precisely and accurately dated, but the sacred status of the text has ensured that it has remained unchanged since the beginning of the seventeenth century. Many other manuscript sources for these poets are far more recent and are made problematic by textual corruption and pseudonymous additions.

Adishesha
("Primal **Shesha**") Epithet of Shesha. See **Shesha**.

Aditi
In Hindu mythology, one of the wives of the sage **Kashyapa**, who also married

Adivasi man going to the market. The Adivasis consist of different tribal groups that are settled throughout the forest and hill regions of India.

Aditi's twelve sisters and through them begat all living creatures. Aditi is first mentioned in the **Rg Veda**, where she is one of the few female figures, although a minor one. The epic *Mahabharata* describes her as giving **birth** to twelve divine **sons**, the **Adityas**: Dhata, Aryama, Mitra, Shakra (**Indra**), **Varuna**, Amsha, Bhaga, Vivasvan (**Surya**), **Pushan**, Savitr (**Surya**), **Tvashtr**, and **Vishnu**. Both Hindu epics, the *Mahabharata* and the *Ramayana*, also describe how Aditi gave birth to the **Vamana avatar**, that is, the "divine descent" of the god Vishnu, in his form as a dwarf.

Aditya

In the Hindu epic the *Mahabharata*, a group of twelve divine **sons** born to the sage **Kashyapa** and his wife **Aditi**, from whom these sons get their collective name. The twelve are named Dhata, Aryama, Mitra, Shakra (**Indra**), **Varuna**, Amsha, Bhaga, Vivasvan (**Surya**), **Pushan**, Savitr, **Tvashtr**, and **Vishnu**. Several of these **deities** are important figures in the religious scriptures known

as the **Vedas**, and Vishnu later gained prominence as one of the primary Hindu gods. On one hand, the Adityas illustrate the Hindu concept that the divine beings (**devas**) have many similarities to humans, although they are more powerful and live in a different world, the **heavens**. On the other hand, they also demonstrate how the Hindu tradition changes over time. Among the Adityas, Vishnu is one of a number of divine beings who are all subject to **birth**, death, and the operation of **karma**, whereas in his later aspect as the Supreme Being, he is considered not only to be beyond all these forces, but to wield control over them.

The twelve Adityas are the sun in the twelve months of the year. In at least one of the Puranas these twelve Adityas are each connected with a particular sign of the **zodiac**.

Adivasi

("first inhabitant") General term for different groups of tribal peoples. They are usually associated with forests and other less developed areas, often making their living by hunting, woodcutting, gathering honey and medicinal plants, and through subsistence agriculture. The largest concentrations are in **Orissa**, **Madhya Pradesh**, and **Bihar**, on both sides of the **Vindhya Mountains** separating northern and southern India, but they are also found in regions such as the **Nilgiri Hills** in southern India. Adivasis are still largely unassimilated into **caste** Hinduism. Many are illiterate and desperately poor, despite programs giving them **reservations** for higher education and government employment. In recent years they have been the focus of intense missionary activity by both Christians and Hindu missionaries sponsored by the **Vishva Hindu Parishad**.

Adoption

One of the most important requirements for every Hindu male is to have at least one son, so that the funeral rites for himself and for his ancestors will be correctly performed and maintained. These rites are considered central for the well-being of the dead, particularly the recently departed. Even in modern times, only men are allowed to perform funeral rites. Given the importance of these ceremonies, men with no biological **sons** adopt a son to guarantee the performance of the ceremony. The ideal candidate is a blood relative, such as a brother's son, who is of equal social status with the adoptive father. Through adoption the boy becomes a member of another family, but the legal texts disagree on his continuing relationship with his natal family. Many sources claim that an adopted son has no right to the **inheritance** of his natal family and no entitlement to offer funeral rites for those ancestors, since by adoption he has become part of another family. Other texts speak of special arrangements by which an adopted son is considered to have two fathers, one biological, one adopted. He inherits from, and performs ancestral rites for both fathers.

Adultery

Given the traditional Hindu belief that **women** are the vessels and guardians of family status, rules about adultery outlined in the **dharma literature** are mostly concerned with the conduct of women, although these texts do prescribe a penance (**prayashchitta**) for a man who commits adultery with another man's wife. As outlined in the dharma literature, adultery is much more serious for women. It is notable that in most cases the dharma does not recommend the woman be driven from her home. An adulterous woman is to perform a rigorous penance until her next menstrual period—sleeping on the ground, wearing dirty clothes, and getting very little food; during this time she also loses her status as a lady of the house and whatever domestic authority she may have wielded. According to the dharma literature, all of this is to end with a bath at the end of her menstrual period, after which she is accepted back at her former status. Women who conceive as a result of adulterous liaisons are to be abandoned. In practice this often means being secluded and cut off from the family, although she still receives food. Abandonment is also recommended in certain other cases: in adulterous liaisons with a man's student or his **guru**, if a woman attempts to kill her husband, or if she kills her fetus. The reluctance to completely cast a woman away, and the willingness to bring her back to her former status after doing penance, both reflect the importance of marriage and family life in Hindu culture, as well as women's importance in the family.

Although these prescriptions in the dharma literature seem relatively humane, often there has been a considerable difference between these prescriptions and a particular group's actual practice. In general, the higher the group's social status (or the more a group is trying to improve its social status), the more harshly it treats such infractions, since these infractions injure its social standing. At present this disjunction is also affected by the differing attitudes toward sexuality between rural and urban contexts, with the latter tending to be more permissive and the former far more restrictive. These differences are illustrated by occasional reports of adulterous women being killed to restore the family's honor; this far exceeds even the harshest penalty prescribed in the dharma literature.

Advaita Vedanta

One of the branches of **Vedanta**, the philosophical school claiming to reveal the ultimate (anta) teaching of the ancient sacred texts known as the **Vedas**. The Advaita school upholds a philosophical position known as monism, which is the belief that a single Ultimate Reality lies behind all things. Advaita proponents believe that reality is nondual (advaita)—that is, that everything in the world is actually the formless, unqualified **Brahman**, despite the appearance of difference and diversity. To support this claim, the Advaitins provide a convincing explanation for the world one perceives to have many separate and diverse things.

Advaitans account for this apparent diversity by using the concept of **adhyasa** (superimposition), in which a false, mistaken understanding is projected upon a real object—in the classical Advaita example, seeing a rope in the twilight and mistaking it for a snake. For the Advaitins, the "snake" is not completely unreal, since it depends on the rope for its existence—one cannot see the snake unless the rope is there. At the same time, the "snake" is clearly not real since one does not persist in this error, and once the illusion of the snake has been dispelled, one can no longer see it.

In the same way, the Advaitins believe that our idea of the phenomenal everyday world is projected upon the one thing in the universe that is truly real—Brahman. Like the snake, the world is unreal as it is perceived but real insofar as it depends on Brahman. For the Advaitins, the roots of adhyasa are epistemological, that is, related to how human beings come to know things, but the results of adhyasa are both epistemological and ontological (related to how things actually are). On one hand, adhyasa obscures the Ultimate Reality and prevents one from accurately perceiving it, and on the other, its projective character creates our notions of the world. For the Advaitins, the source of all this confusion is ultimately rooted in **avidya**, or primal ignorance, under the influence of which one forms mistaken ideas about the world. The operation of this ignorance is said to have no beginning, but one of the things that keeps it going is one's **karma**, based on the continuing actions caused by this mistaken understanding. Another source of this ignorance is the power of illusion (**maya**) wielded by God (**Ishvara**), which bewilders human beings. For the Advaita Vedantin, God is identified as a qualified (**saguna**) form of Brahman—thus below the highest unqualified (**nirguna**) Brahman, and himself a product of superimposition.

Since the Advaita school believes that the source of bondage to karma results from mistaken understanding, the only way to destroy bondage is to gain the correct understanding. Although the Advaitans say that people must perform obligatory religious actions (**nitya karma**) as a matter of duty, actions can never bring about the understanding that is necessary for salvation, although they may aid the process by removing some of the karmic obstacles. To support this understanding, the Advaitins begin their analysis with an appeal to the knowing subject as the one thing that can never be doubted, and claim that this self-consciousness is evidence for the existence of the inner Self, or **atman**. Aside from this appeal to experience, they depend heavily on the authority of the sacred texts, particularly the **Upanishads**, to uphold their key doctrines: that Brahman is the source of all things; that the human soul is ultimately identical to Brahman, although hampered by obstructions based on past karma; and that gaining true knowledge is the basis of liberation.

The first and greatest Advaita thinker was the philosopher **Shankaracharya**; other significant figures were his two disciples, **Sureshvara** and **Padmapada**, as well as **Mandana Mishra** and **Vachaspati Mishra**. For further information see Karl H. Potter (ed.), *Advaita Vedanta up to Samkara and His Pupils*, 1981; and Sarvepalli Radhakrishnan and Charles A. Moore (eds.), *A Sourcebook in Indian Philosophy*, 1957.

Advani, Lal Krishna

(b. 1927) Modern Indian politician as well as past president and leader of the **Bharatiya Janata Party** (BJP), a party often considered the political wing of the **Rashtriya Svayamsevak Sangh** (RSS). Advani joined the RSS as a young man and was encouraged by the RSS to become active in politics, first in the **Jana Sangh** and later in the BJP. In the fall of 1990, Advani embarked on a tour of northern India to raise public support for building a **Rama** temple in **Ayodhya**, on a site which at the time was occupied by a Muslim mosque. The public response to this **rath yatra** ("chariot journey") was positive and brought great political benefits to the BJP; the BJP has since run the state governments in some of India's most important states and has become the largest opposition party in Parliament. During the 1990s the BJP's influence waxed and waned, but for much of this time, Advani has been one of the leading figures in the party. In the spring of 1996, however, he was one of many Indian political figures whose name was connected with a major bribery scandal. He immediately resigned his seat in Parliament and promised that he would not seek office until his name had been cleared. The allegation was found to be completely baseless, and Advani was reelected to Parliament in March, 1998. During the thirteen months of BJP government rule in 1998–99, Advani served as Home Minister (the Cabinet officer responsible for all domestic affairs) and

has continued in this position during the BJP-led National Democratic Alliance.

Aerial Cars

One of the standard images in Hindu mythology. The most famous of the cars is the **Pushpak Viman**, which is originally owned by **Kubera**, a minor **deity** associated with mountains and their mineral wealth. The Pushpak Viman is commandeered and stolen by **Ravana**, the **demon**-king of **Lanka**. In modern times, mythological references to such aerial cars are often cited as evidence that ancient Indians possessed the technology for flying machines, an assertion for which there is no historical evidence.

Aesthetics
See **Rasa**.

Agama

In its most general meaning, this refers to any authoritative text. In a philosophical context, this word designates one of the **pramanas**, the means by which human beings can gain true and accurate knowledge. As a pramana, the agama denotes testimony from a reliable source, particularly from scriptures such as the **Veda**. Within specific sectarian communities, such as the devotees (**bhakta**) of the gods **Shiva** (**Shaivas**) and **Vishnu** (**Vaishnavas**), the word also commonly designates the particular texts deemed most authoritative by that community.

Agastya

In Hindu mythology, Agastya is one of the **rishis** (sages) of ancient India and is attributed with various supernormal powers. As with many of the rishis, Agastya is marked as different even by his **birth**, which is far outside the normal manner. According to the story, Agastya is conceived when the **semen** of the **deities** Mitra and **Varuna** is placed in a pot and develops there into a baby boy. Agastya is described as preferring a detached, **ascetic** lifestyle, but he compromises in deference to his ancestors. The ancestors appear to Agastya in a vision, imploring him to marry and have children, so that his **sons** can continue performing the ancestral **offerings**; this is one of the **three debts** that every Hindu man must pay. Agastya consents and marries **Lopamudra**.

Agastya's ascetic lifestyle is said to have generated immense powers, which he demonstrates by performing many marvelous deeds. According to some accounts, he curses king **Nahusha** to become a giant serpent, in retribution for the insults Nahusha has heaped upon him. Agastya also curses King **Indradyumna** to become an **elephant**, and the **gandharva** named **Huhu** to become a crocodile; the two are released many years later through the god **Vishnu's** divine **grace**.

Not all of his exploits stem from his readiness to **curse**—a trait found in many of the sages—and some are performed for the benefit of human beings. He is reported to have humbled the **Vindhya Mountains** (here personified), which through envy of Mount **Meru** have grown so tall that the **sun** and **moon** are unable to get around them. Agastya does this by asking Vindhya to bow down to let him get through on his journey to southern India. Agastya promises that Vindhya can stand up again when he returns, which has yet to happen. In other cases Agastya is reported to have used his powers to help get rid of **demons**. On one occasion, when a group of demons is hiding in the sea by day and coming out to pillage at night, Agastya exposes them by drinking up the ocean and thus taking away their place of refuge. On another occasion he foils a demon who has been taking the form of a goat to be cooked and eaten by unsuspecting diners. The demon has been killing the diners by exploding out of their stomachs. Agastya eats the demon as usual, but it is then completely destroyed by Agastya's

prodigious digestive powers. See also **Gajendramoksha**.

Aghori

In one context this term refers to one of the two loosely organized groups of the **Jogi ascetics**, the other being the **Nathpanthis**. There are three major groups of ascetics devoted to the god **Shiva**; they are the Aghoris, Nathpanthis, and **Dashanami Sanyasis**. The difference between these is that the Dashanamis are said to have been founded by the philosopher **Shankaracharya**, while the Aghoris and Nathpanthis are believed to be descended from earlier **Shaiva** ascetic orders, particularly the **Kapalikas**, **Kalamukhas**, and **Pashupatas**. The term *aghori* also refers to ascetics whose reputed practices make them both respected and feared by the general population. The Aghoris draw their name from one of the names of the god Shiva, Aghora, which despite its literal meaning ("not terrifying"), designates one of the most frightful and powerful forms of Shiva. As devotees (**bhakta**) of this form of Shiva, the Aghoris are famous for their disregard of all social conventions and boundaries. They often eat from a vessel made of a human skull and are popularly reputed to eat anything, including dung and human flesh. Such behavior generates fascination and sometimes respect among the larger Hindu populace, but also considerable fear; Aghoris are so far outside the normal social boundaries that most people would rather avoid interaction with them.

Agni

("**fire**," cognate with Latin *ignis*) Hindu **deity** present in every fire. Agni is also one of the eight dikpalas, or **Guardians of the Directions**, with responsibility for the southeast quarter. As fire, Agni is also one of the five **elements** in classical Hindu **cosmology**.

Agni is important in the **samhitas** (hymns) of the **Rg Veda** and in the **Brahmanas**, a later strand of Vedic liter-

Depiction of the god Agni. Agni is identified with fire and is believed to be present in all fires, along with lightning and the sun.

ature emphasizing sacrificial rites. The Rg Veda opens with a hymn to Agni and describes him as "the household priest, the god and officiant of the **sacrifice**, [and]. . .the giver of blessings." Agni remained important in the Brahmanas since, as the sacrificial fire, he was essential to all ritual. Agni's importance in these texts stems from his presence in all three levels of the Vedic universe—on the **earth** as fire, in the middle atmospheric realm (**antariksha**) as lightning, and in the sky as the **sun**. This ability to move between these levels made Agni the intermediary between the gods and human beings. From above, Agni served as the messenger of the gods, while as the sacrificial fire on earth, Agni not only consumed the **offerings** but conveyed them in the smoke to the gods above. Because of his role in bringing about the sacrifice, another epithet for Agni is the "mouth of the gods."

Unlike many of the other Vedic deities, Agni has retained a certain prominence even in the present day. Although Vedic sacrifices are uncommon, sacrificial motifs have been incorporated into many contemporary rites.

Ceremonies often have a part in which offerings (often of clarified butter) are ladled into a sacrificial fire. Fire plays an important role in many rituals, particularly that of **arati**, in which lamps are waved before the image of a divinity as an offering of light. Agni also serves as the divine witness to the single action widely believed to seal a marriage. This is **agnipradakshinam**, in which the bride and groom make seven revolutions around a lamp or fire. Even on the most prosaic level, fire is still essential to daily life since most Indians continue to cook over an open flame—whether coal, wood, dung, or bottled gas. This everyday utility, combined with his abiding ritual presence, have assured Agni a continuing presence in Hindu life.

Agni Akhara

The name of a particular subgroup of the **Naga** class of the **Dashanami Sanyasis**, a particular type of renunciant **ascetic**. The Dashanami Nagas are devotees (**bhakta**) of the god **Shiva**, organized into different **akharas** or regiments on the model of an army. Until the beginning of the nineteenth century, the Nagas' primary occupation was as mercenary soldiers, although they also had substantial trading interests; both of these occupations have largely disappeared in contemporary times. The Agni akhara is a subunit of the **Juna akhara**, one of the largest and oldest of the Naga akharas.

The Agni akhara's membership is very different from that of the other established akharas. Whereas the other Naga Sanyasi akharas will accept men from all levels of society—in some cases even the lowest status group, the **shudras**—the Agni akhara admits only unmarried **brahmins** who have been lifelong celibates. Perhaps as a consequence of their more exclusive membership criteria, the Agni akhara is the only Dashanami Naga akhara that has no naked (naga) ascetics. All of its members remain fully clothed during the procession for their bath at the **Kumbha Mela**.

The Agni akhara was first established in **Benares**, and this remains their most important site. All of the akharas have particular features that define their organizational identity, including specific patron **deities**; the Agni akhara's patron deity is the **goddess** Gayatri, considered the embodiment of the **Gayatri Mantra**.

Agnihotra

("**fire sacrifice**") Religious rite in which **offerings** are made to the sacred fire, considered to be the god **Agni** in material form. The term can also refer to the maintenance and care of the sacred fire itself. The roots of **worship** based on a sacrificial fire go back to the **Vedas**, the oldest and most authoritative Hindu sacred texts. This type of worship is still present in modern times, although much diminished in emphasis.

Agnikula

("fire lineage") A collective name for the four main clans of **Rajputs** (warrior princes): the Pariharas, Chauhans, Solankis, and Pawars. According to tradition, this collective name refers to the Rajputs' descent from a single mythical king who had arisen from a sacrificial fire pit at Mount Abu in the state of **Rajasthan**. Although their historical origin is unclear, these four clans ruled over much of northwestern India, either as independent kings or feudal vassals, after their appearance at the end of the first millennium. The Pariharas ruled southern Rajasthan. The Chauhans ruled the region around Delhi. The Solankis ruled in **Gujarat**. The Pawars ruled in western **Madhya Pradesh**. Although their days as warrior princes have passed, they remain influential in politics, both as politicians and as constituent communities.

Agnipradakshinam

("circling the **fire**") A common rite in many modern Hindu **marriage ceremonies**, usually performed as part of the **saptapadi**, in which the bride and groom take seven steps to definitively seal their marriage. The saptapadi and the agnipradakshinam are combined so that the bride and groom make seven revolutions around a small fire. As the god **Agni**, the fire is the divine witness to the marriage bond between bride and groom, a bond often symbolized by tying the end of the groom's turban to the fringe of the bride's sari. The fire is also a sign that the celebration of marriage is a **yajna**, or sacrificial rite.

Agnipravesha

("entering **fire**") Death by fire, which could occur in several different contexts. This was often used to refer to the practice of **sati**, in which a **widow** would be burned on her husband's funeral pyre. Death by fire was also one of the mandated forms of religious **suicide**; this could be done either as a means of relief for someone afflicted by an incurable disease, or as part of certain rites of **sacrifice** such as the **sarvasvara**, which was performed to send the sacrificer to **heaven**. By the beginning of the eighteenth century, religious suicide had been condemned and had fallen into disuse. In the nineteenth century, British horror at the practice of sati led them to ban it wherever they were able to do so.

Agnishtoma

Particular rite of **sacrifice** prescribed in the later strands of the **Vedas**, the earliest Hindu sacred texts. The agnishtoma was most often performed in the early spring and was dedicated to the Vedic god **Agni** (**fire**). The rite's two central elements were the pressing and consumption of the mysterious sacrificial drink called **soma** (seen as a material form of the Vedic god Soma), and the slaughter of sacrificial **animals**, which were burned on the sacrificial fire (the god Agni in material form). A final chant during the sacrifice was addressed to Agni. During the Vedic period, this rite became largely the province of kings since they were the only people who could command the necessary resources for it. With the later reaction against **animal sacrifice**, the rite fell out of favor, although it is still performed occasionally in a modified fashion without sacrifice.

Agrahara

A **brahmin** residential enclave, usually established by a land grant from a wealthy land owner or royalty to a particular brahmin. Brahmins had the highest status in traditional Hindu society, based on the belief that they had higher ritual **purity**. The purpose of the agrahara was to protect this ritual purity since it could be compromised fairly easily. Agraharas were most common in southern India, where brahmins formed an extremely small percentage of the general population—on average, about four percent. As a small **minority**, southern Indian brahmins could maintain a more controlled environment, thereby reducing the possibility of having their purity tainted. In northern India, brahmins formed a significant part of the population and tended to live within the towns and cities, although they often inhabited particular sections of these places.

Ahalya

In Hindu mythology, Ahalya is the wife of the sage **Gautama**. She is turned into stone by Gautama's curse and later restored to life by being touched by the foot of the god **Rama**. Gautama's curse is brought on by the actions of the god **Indra**, who lusts for Ahalya. One day, when Gautama has gone to the river to bathe (**snana**), Indra takes Gautama's form and goes to Ahalya in a bid to make love to her. Accounts differ on whether Ahalya is aware of her lover's identity—in some she is flattered by Indra's attention, in others she is genuinely deceived. When Gautama discovers what has happened, he curses Ahalya to become a stone and Indra to have a thousand vaginas on his body, as a punishment for his lust. Gautama is later mollified into modifying the **curses**, so that Ahalya will remain a stone until she is touched by Rama's foot, and Indra will be covered instead with a thousand eyes. This story primarily illustrates the power of the sages to curse even the gods, but the different versions also reveal varying assumptions about the nature of **women**.

Aham Brahmasmi

("I am **Brahman**.") In the Hindu philosophical tradition, this is one of the four "great utterances" (**mahavakyas**) expressing an ultimate truth. The truth expressed in this utterance is the idea that **atman** (the individual Self) and Brahman (Ultimate Reality) are one and the same—identical; this truth is at the heart of the speculative texts called the **Upanishads**. The four mahavakyas, aside from their philosophical importance as capsulizing fundamental truths, were also appropriated by the four divisions of the **Dashanami Sanyasi ascetics** as identifying symbols. Each division had a different mahavakya, just as each had a different **Veda**, a different primary sacred center, and a different paradigmatic ascetic quality. Aham Brahmasmi is the mahavakya associated with the **Bhuriwara** division of the Dashanami Sanyasis.

Ahamkar

("I-making") In the **Samkhya** school of Hindu **philosophy**, ahamkar is one of the stages in the **evolution** of **prakrti** (primal matter) away from its initial undifferentiated unity toward differentiation of the Self and other things. The final result of this degradation is the world that we see around us, in which human souls are subject to

Temple to the goddess Durga in the city of Aihole.

reincarnation (**samsara**). Prakrti evolves first into **mahat** ("the great one") and then into ahamkar, which is the first stage in which there is a sense of self and subjectivity. This sense of subjectivity colors the entire devolution after that. Ahamkar then evolves further, forming the basis for both the subjective and objectice world: on one hand, the individual's organs of sense (**jnanendriya**) and organs of action (**karmendriya**) develop, and on the other hand, the five subtle **elements** (**tanmatras**), which are the basis of the gross material elements, evolve. In colloquial speech, *ahamkar* is used to mean "self-pride," invariably in a pejorative sense.

Ahimsa

("refraining from harm") Ahimsa refers to the conscious commitment to refrain from harming other living beings, either directly or indirectly. The emphasis on ahimsa originated with the Jains, for whom all actions carry karmic consequences, but who also believe that the karmic consequences generated by intentional evil acts are far more severe than those from unintentional ones. Jain and Buddhist commitment to ahimsa brought it further into Indian society, and it has been an important feature of Hindu practice for well over two thousand years. In the **Yoga Sutras**, **Patanjali** mentions ahimsa as one of the restraints (**yama**) and thus recommends it as one of the basic foundations for religious life. This commitment to ahimsa is believed to be one of the major forces responsible for the decline of **animal sacrifice**, which was one of the most important types of religious practice as described in the **Vedas**, the oldest Hindu scriptures. Far more recently, in the twentieth century, ahimsa was one of the guiding principles of **Mohandas Gandhi** during the struggle for Indian independence. Although Gandhi did not rule out the use of violence in principle, his commitment to ahimsa reflected his judgment that means and ends are karmically linked, and that the means one employs will determine both the nature and tone of one's ends. See also **karma**.

Ahir

The model for traditional Indian society was as a collection of **endogamous** subgroups known as **jatis** (**birth**). These jatis were organized (and their social status largely determined) by the group's hereditary occupation, over which each group had a monopoly. In traditional northern Indian society, the Ahiras were a jati whose hereditary occupation was herding and selling milk.

Aihole

Historical site in the state of **Karnataka**, just south of the modern city of Bijapur. Aihole was an important city during the **Chalukya dynasty** (4th–8th c. C.E.), and its surviving buildings are some of the oldest standing Hindu temples. These temples represent an early stage in the **evolution** of Hindu **architecture** from earlier architectural forms, such as the rock-cut cave temple (**chaitya**) or enclosed courtyard (**vihara**). One of the earliest temples (ca. 450 C.E.) is a simple square pavilion (**mandapa**) with a tower (**shikhara**) over the main image of the **deity**, one of the hallmarks of later Hindu temples. A temple to **Durga** built about a century later has the general plan of a chaitya, but a shikhara was also added. Although the temples at Aihole are related to the earlier forms, they also prefigure the mature development of medieval Hindu architecture.

Aims of Life

(purushartha) Four general goals that Hindu society has accepted as legitimate ends for all human beings: **artha** (wealth and power), **kama** (desire, especially sexual desire), **dharma** (righteousness or religious duty), and **moksha** (final liberation of the soul from the cycle of reincarnation). Hindus have affirmed that all of these are worthy ends, but have generally accepted that the last goal is qualitatively different from the other three, which are more strongly interrelated. There is nothing wrong with seeking money or pleasure, and Hindu culture affirms both of these aims with the understanding that their pursuit and enjoyment should ultimately be regulated by a commitment to dharma. Although there are paths to moksha that allow one to remain in the world, it is generally accepted that a person pursuing moksha will be less attentive to worldly desires because they are incompatible with this ultimate goal.

Aippasi

Seventh month in the Tamil solar **year**, corresponding to the northern Indian solar month of Tula (the zodiacal sign of Libra), which according to the Indian **calendar** usually falls within October and November. The existence of several different calendars is one clear sign of the continuing importance of regional cultural patterns. One way that the Tamils retain their culture is by preserving their traditional calendar. Tamil is one of the few regional languages in India with an ancient, well-established literary tradition. See also **Tamil months**, **Tamil Nadu**, and **Tamil language**.

Airavata

In Hindu mythology, the divine **elephant** who is the vehicle of **Indra**, king of the gods. The only significant role Airavata plays in any myth is as the ultimate cause for why the gods have to churn the Ocean of Milk. One day the powerful and irascible sage **Durvasas** gives a garland to Indra. Indra places the garland on Airavata, who throws it on the ground. The reasons for this differ— in one account Airavata is plagued by the bees gathering on it, and in another he is intoxicated by the scent of the flowers. Durvasas understands this as an insult and, in his anger, **curses** the gods to be subject to old age and death. The only way the gods can escape the effects of the curse is to obtain the nectar of immortality, which is done by churning the Ocean of Milk. See also **Tortoise avatar**.

Aiteraya Brahmana

Along with the **Shatapatha Brahmana**, the two most important texts in the

A shrine to Aiyanar, a regional deity in southern India who is the protector of villages.

Brahmana stratum of Vedic literature. The Brahmanas are primarily manuals describing the correct performance of Vedic ritual **sacrifices**. Because they were composed later than the actual **Vedas**, each Brahmana is connected in theory with one of the Vedas, to give it authority as a sacred Vedic text. According to tradition, the Aiteraya Brahmana is associated with the earliest of the Vedas, the **Rg Veda**.

Aiyanar

Southern Indian regional **deity**. In the state of **Tamil Nadu** Aiyanar is an important **village deity**, generally considered to be the guardian of the village tank, bringer of rain, and protector of the village. It is likely that he is an indigenous deity who has been assimilated into the Hindu pantheon. Aiyanar is sometimes identified with **Aiyappa**, although there are some discrepancies between the two—Aiyanar is a deity associated with the protection of villages, whereas Aiyappa is associated with the hills, the jungle, and the hunt. For further information see Louis Dumont, "A Folk Deity of Tamil Nad: Aiyanar, the Lord," in T. N. Madan (ed.), *Religion in India*, 1991.

Aiyappa

Hilltop **deity** of the southern Indian state of **Kerala**, who at the local level is often identified with **Aiyanar**, the Tamil **village deity**. The most important of Aiyappa's shrines is at **Shabari Malai** in the hills of central Kerala, to which there is an important pilgrimage each winter in December and January. Aiyappa's strong associations with the hills and the hunt make it likely that he was originally a local deity of the hills of Kerala, but in more recent times he has been assimilated into the larger Hindu pantheon as the **son** of **Shiva** and **Vishnu**. Although both of these gods are male, Aiyappa's conception is said to happen when Vishnu takes the form of the female enchantress **Mohini**, to beguile the **demons** into parting with the nectar of immortality. Because of his parentage, Aiyappa is also called Hariharaputra, "the son (putra) of Hari (Vishnu) and Hara (Shiva)."

Due to his unusual conception, Aiyappa is fated to kill a particularly troubling buffalo demoness, **Mahishi**, who has been given the boon that she cannot be killed by anyone born from the union of male and female. After his **birth** the infant Aiyappa is abandoned by a riverbank, and adopted by King **Rajashekhara**, who names him Manikanta. Manikanta's stepmother is very jealous of her stepson and wishes to clear the path to the throne for her own child. When Manikanta is twelve his stepmother feigns an illness that she says only **tiger's** milk can cure. Everyone is understandably reluctant to try to get the tiger's milk, but Manikanta finally agrees to do so.

On his way to get the tiger's milk, Manikanta is met by messengers of Shiva, who remind him that his life's ultimate purpose is to kill Mahishi. After a long struggle, Manikanta dispatches the demon, but while he is dancing on the she-buffalo's body, another female figure rises out of it. She identifies herself as **Lila**, and wants to marry Manikanta, but as a celibate student he does not desire this. He appeases Lila with the conditional vow that he will marry her the year that a celibate pilgrim does not come to visit him on Shabari Malai—a vow that will never come true since **celibacy** is the single most important requirement for the Shabari Malai pilgrimage. Manikanta then placates Lila by establishing a temple for her on a neighboring hilltop.

Returning to his original task of retrieving the tiger's milk, Aiyappa then bids Shiva to take the form of a tiger, upon which he rides back to his stepparents, inviting them to milk the tiger to their heart's content. This image of the young boy returning astride the tiger is one of the most common Aiyappa images. For further information see E. Valentine Daniel, *Fluid Signs*, 1984; Kunissery Ramakrishnaier Vaidyanathan, *Pilgrimage to Sabari*, 1978; and Lars Kjaerholm, "Myth and Fascination in the Aiyappu Cult: A View from Fieldwork in Tamil Nadu," in Asko Parpola and Bent Smidt Hansen (eds.), *South Asian Religion and Society*, 1986. See also **Tortoise avatar**.

Aja Ekadashi

Festival falling on the eleventh **day** (**ekadashi**) of the dark (waning) half of the **lunar month** of **Bhadrapada** (August–September). As are all of the eleventh-day observances, this is dedicated to the **worship** of **Vishnu**. Most Hindu festivals have certain prescribed rites, usually involving fasting (**upavasa**) and worship, and often promise specific benefits for faithful performance. The most important requirement for this festival is to pass the night in worship; taking part is believed to free one from all evil. The name Aja means "unborn" and is one of the epithets of Vishnu.

Ajamila

In Hindu mythology Ajamila is an example of a completely corrupted sinner, who is saved from Death by the boundless power of God's **grace**. Ajamila is a fallen **brahmin** who does all the things forbidden to brahmins—he eats meat, drinks **liquor**, takes a low **caste** woman as his mistress, and ignores all the **purity** laws which brahmins are supposed to keep. His only redeeming feature is his love for his **son Narayana**, which is also one of the names of **Vishnu**. As he lies dying, Ajamila sees the minions of Death coming for him, whose terrible forms portend a dire fate. In his terror at this vision and his longing for his son, Ajamila calls out "Narayana" with his dying breath, and because of this Vishnu sends his minions to rescue Ajamila. Ajamila is brought to **Vaikuntha**, Vishnu's dwelling place, where he lives happily.

Ajatashatru

("[he whose] enemy is unborn," 5th c. B.C.E.) King in the Magadha region in the modern state of **Bihar**. Ajatashatru deposed and murdered his father, **Bimbisara**, around 494 B.C.E., then expanded his father's territorial gains. Ajatashatru first annexed the area around the city of **Benares** and then conquered the city of **Vaishali**, capital of the kingdom of the Vrjjis. Ajatashatru and his father both aimed at building an empire in the **Ganges** River basin, and they were among the first Indian kings to conceive of a far-flung empire.

Ajatashatru

(2) In the **Brhadaranyaka Upanishad**, a great sage who was also the king of **Benares**. Ajatashatru is notable for instructing Gargya, a **brahmin** priest, on the nature of **Brahman**, even though this was inappropriate by contemporary standards since Ajatashatru was a **kshatriya** warrior king and thus should have been receiving instruction from Gargya. The **Upanishads** have several episodes in which, contrary to the norm, kshatriyas instruct brahmins. Such episodes reveal the nature of wisdom as conceived in the Upanishads—it is achieved by individual striving and realization and not conferred by **birth** or social position.

Ajita Keshakambalin

In classical Indian **philosophy**, the reputed founder of a **materialist** philosophical school and whose name reflects his usual garb—a hair blanket (kesha-kambal). Ajita was a contemporary of the Buddha, and information about him comes from the Buddhist scriptures. Ajita's materialist philosophy was that human beings are composed of four elements, that these elements disperse after death, and that the individual then ceases to exist. Given this philosophy, Ajita believed that one should enjoy life while one could, taking pleasure in the good and accepting the bad, and that all religious observances were a waste of time and a futile hope. Ajita was the first in a long tradition of materialists, and one finds evidence of this materialist perspective as late as the eighth century of the common era.

Ajivika

Ancient philosophical school traditionally believed to have been founded by **Gosala Maskariputra**, a contemporary of the Buddha. The Ajivikas were fatalists who believed that all things are inexorably predetermined by destiny (**niyati**). Since, according to this **philosophy**, all things are preordained, religious practice has no effect on one's future lives, and in doing such things people are only doing what they are already predetermined to do. The Ajivikas compared the process of reincarnation (**samsara**) to a ball of string, which would unroll until it was done and then go no further. The Ajivikas shunned clothing and lived a strict **ascetic** lifestyle, believing that this was the lifestyle preordained for them. The school had a significant presence in southern India well into the common era but finally disappeared around the fourteenth century. For further information see Arthur Llewellyn Basham, *History and Doctrines of the Ajivikas, a Vanished Indian Religion*, 1981.

Ajna Chakra

In many schools of **yoga** and in the esoteric ritual tradition known as **tantra**, the ajna chakra is one of the six psychic centers (**chakras**) thought to be in the **subtle body**. The subtle body is an alternate physiological system, believed to exist on a different plane of existence than gross matter but with certain correspondences to the material body. The subtle body is comprised of a set of six chakras, which are visualized as multipetaled lotus flowers running roughly along the course of the spine, connected by three vertical channels. Each chakra has important symbolic associations—with differing human capacities, different subtle elements (**tanmatras**), and different seed syllables (**bijaksharas**) formed from the letters of the **Sanskrit** alphabet, thus encompassing all sacred sound. Above and below the chakras are the bodily abodes of **Shiva** (awareness) and **Shakti** (power), the two divine principles through which the entire universe has come into being. The underlying assumption behind this concept of the subtle body is thus the homology of macrocosm and microcosm, an essential Hindu idea since the time of the mystical texts known as the **Upanishads**.

The six chakras are traditionally enumerated from the bottom up, and the ajna chakra is the sixth and highest of these. It is visualized as a two-petaled lotus located in the forehead just above the top of the nose. Its petals contain the bijaksharas Ham and Ksam, formed from the last two letters of the Sanskrit alphabet. The ajna chakra is associated with the capacity for thought, considered a distinctively human capacity and thus the most important human faculty. For further information see Arthur Avalon (Sir John Woodroffe), *Shakti and Shakta*, 1978; and Philip S. Rawson, *The Art of Tantra*, 1973.

Akasha

("**space**") One of the five **elements** in traditional Indian **cosmology**, the others being **earth**, **fire**, **water**, and **wind**. In some philosophical schools, each of the

Boys in Shri Shaku Khashbaug competing in the village akhara, or wrestling ground.
Training in wrestling and participating in competitions are considered religious disciplines.

elements is paired with one of the five senses; akasha is associated with hearing since it is believed to convey sound from place to place.

Akbar

(r. 1555–1605) Third and greatest ruler in the **Moghul dynasty**, a Muslim dynasty that controlled large parts of India between 1525 and 1707, existing in reduced form until 1857. Akbar's long reign was marked by generally good relations with his Hindu subjects, many of whom were put into positions of authority and for whom he seems to have had genuine sympathy and understanding. One of his most important gestures was to repeal a poll tax on non-Muslims, which had been customary but was highly unpopular among Hindus. Although more orthodox Muslims insinuated that Akbar was a closet Hindu, the goodwill and cooperation that he fostered helped keep things peaceful throughout his reign.

Akhand Path

("unbroken recitation") The unbroken recitation of an entire religious text, which is believed to bring religious benefits; individuals may perform such recitations for their own benefit, or they may hire another person to perform the recitation for them. The benefits of this action are believed to come from the perceived power of the sacred text itself. The recitation may be done as a pious act, simply for the merit in sponsoring it, or as part of a festival observance; it may also be a last resort in times of dire emergencies or a religious act performed after a death in the family. One of the texts often recited without a break is the ***Ramcharitmanas***, a retelling of the ***Ramayana*** by the sixteenth-century poet-saint **Tulsidas**; in the Sikh community, the **Adigranth** is recited.

Akhara

In its most basic meaning, an akhara is a "wrestling ground," a place in the village or city where young men come to train, tone, and compete. Such practices at an akhara are not merely physical exercise but also a form of religious practice, since wrestlers often begin by worshiping **Hanuman**, a **deity** associated with strength and power. Among the **Naga** class of the

Dashanami Sanyasis, the word *akhara* means something closer to "regiment." The Dashanami Nagas were **ascetics** devoted to the god **Shiva** and who formerly made their living as traders and mercenary soldiers. These Nagas were organized into different akharas based on the model of an army, and here the word primarily marks group affiliation, although it can also refer to the buildings in which the group lives. The Nagas are divided into seven main akharas—the **Juna** or Bhairava, **Agni**, **Avahana**, **Niranjani**, **Ananda**, **Mahanirvani**, and **Atala**. Among the **Bairagi Naga** ascetics—militant ascetics who are devotees (**bhakta**) of the god **Vishnu**—the largest division of forces is into **anis** ("armies"), which are then subdivided into akharas.

Akhyati

("nondiscrimination") **Theory of error** propounded by **Prabhakara**, a member of the **Purva Mimamsa** philosophical school, who lived in the seventh or eighth century C.E. All the theories of error aim to explain why people make errors in judgment, such as the stock example of mistaking the silvery flash of a seashell for a piece of silver. Prabhakara explains this error as rooted in the inability to make sharp distinctions. The person uncritically connects two simple judgments, "that object is silvery" and "silver is silvery." By themselves, both of these statements are true; what is false is their combination into the complex judgment, "that object is silver." According to Prabhakara, the problem lies not with the simple impressions given by perception (**pratyaksha**) or memory—both of which are true—but with their uncritical connection, in which the mind fails to recognize that other judgments are possible. For further information see Bijayananda Kar, *The Theories of Error in Indian Philosophy*, 1978; and Karl H. Potter (ed.), *Presuppositions of India's Philosophies*, 1972.

Akkadevi

Sister of King Jayasimha II (1015–1042 C.E.), a monarch in the **Chalukya dynasty** that ruled large parts of the **Deccan** peninsula. Akkadevi was important not only through her family connections but also because she served as a provincial governor in her brother's kingdom. Her example shows that **women** in powerful families have often been able to overcome the seeming social disadvantages imposed by their gender, a maxim proven most recently by Sonia Gandhi.

Akrura

In Hindu mythology Akrura is most famous as the envoy from the royal court at **Mathura**, who takes the god **Krishna** away from Krishna's childhood home in **Braj**, never to return. Krishna's wicked uncle, King **Kamsa**, instructs Akrura to lure Krishna and his brother **Balarama** to a festival, where they will be killed in a "friendly" bout with some wrestlers. Akrura sees through the plot and warns Krishna about it, but he remains indelibly associated with Krishna's departure from Braj, which for his devotees (**bhakta**) is the bitterest moment in all of Krishna's mythology. For a moving, dramatic account of this incident, see John Stratton Hawley, *At Play with Krishna*, 1981.

Akshakumara

In the Hindu epic the *Ramayana*, this is one of the **sons** of **Ravana** by his wife **Mandodari**. Akshakumara fights bravely and valiantly in the war against **Rama's** army but is eventually killed by Rama's servant, the monkey-**deity**, **Hanuman**.

Akshamala

A string of beads used to keep count when reciting prayers or **mantras**, sometimes translated by the accessible but misleading term "rosary." An akshamala is one of the most common religious articles, and the materials from which it is made can often reveal sectarian affiliations. **Shiva** is often depicted wearing beads made of the seeds of the *Elaeocarpus ganitrus* tree, which are known as **rudraksha** ("eye of **Rudra**"). Devotees (**bhakta**) of Shiva emulate this practice. Devotees of the god **Vishnu** often carry beads made of wood from the **tulsi** plant, which is considered a form of Vishnu's wife **Lakshmi**. Other commonly used materials are sandalwood and crystal, but akshamalas can also be made from expensive materials such as coral and amber. In Hindu iconography the akshamala is one of the items commonly held by the **goddess Saraswati**, in keeping with her identity as the patron **deity** of learning and, by implication, sacred sound. The akshamala is also one of the items commonly held by the god **Brahma**, but in his case it has less specific significance.

Akshar Purushottam Samstha

One of the prominent branches of the **Swaminarayan sect**, which split off from its parent body in 1906. The Swaminarayan movement is based on the teachings of Sahajananda Swami (1781–1830), an **ascetic** who was a devotee (**bhakta**) of the god **Vishnu**. Sahajananda's followers eventually revered him as a manifestation of **Krishna** (an incarnation of Vishnu), based on the idea that **avatars** of Vishnu appear on **earth** in times of extreme trouble. This same reverence is given to Sahajananda Swami's ascetic successors, who are known by the title **Pramukh Swami** ("President Swami"). At present the Akshar Purushottam Samstha has several million lay devotees (**bhakta**) who are mainly **Gujarati** merchants; their affluence has helped make the movement financially strong. The most important figures in the movement are the small number of ascetics who serve as teachers and spiritual advisers, headed by the Pramukh Swami. For further information see Raymond Brady Williams, *A New Face of Hinduism*, 1984.

Akshaya Trtiya

(also called Akha Teej) Festival celebrated on the third **day** of the bright (waxing) half of the **lunar month** of **Baisakh** (April–May). The festival's name reflects the belief that the religious merit from rites performed on this day is indestructible (akshaya). This is thought to be the day on which the **Treta Yuga** (a previous cosmic age) began, and as a transitional day is believed to be highly auspicious. This day is marked by **worship** of **Vishnu** and his consort **Lakshmi**; it is also believed to be the birthday of Vishnu's sixth incarnation, **Parashuram avatar**. Consistent both with the worship of Vishnu and the belief that this is a transitional day, on Akshaya Trtiya the temple doors are opened at the Four Himalayan Dhams (the holy towns of **Yamunotri**, **Gangotri**, **Kedarnath**, and **Badrinath**) after having been closed all winter, and worship in those places is resumed until after the festival of **Diwali** in the fall. See also **Four Dhams**.

Akshaya Vata

("indestructible banyan tree") In Hindu mythology, a particular banyan tree that existed before the creation of the universe and will be the only thing to survive the cosmic dissolution (**pralaya**) at the end of the cosmic cycle. According to one mythic account, the sage **Markandeya** saw a vision of pralaya in which the only thing remaining was this single tree, under which lay the god **Krishna** in infant form, sucking on his toes. The akshaya **vata** is identified with a particular banyan tree in **Allahabad** at the junction of the **Ganges** and **Yamuna** rivers, where it is now enclosed within the fort built by the Moghul emperor **Akbar**. Earlier writers report an enormous tree on the site, but in modern times the tree is quite small. In some stories it was cut down by one of Akbar's successors. According to the seventh-century Chinese pilgrim **Hsuan Tsang**,

The Alakananda River near Badrinath Garhwal.
As a tributary of the Ganges, its waters are considered sacred.

one of the preferred methods for committing religious **suicide** was to jump from the branches of the vata tree; this practice is also mentioned four centuries later by the Islamic scholar **Alberuni**.

Alakananda River

The longest and largest Himalayan tributary of the **Ganges** River; the Ganges forms at **Devaprayag**, where the Alakananda unites with a second major tributary, the **Bhagirathi** River. As with all the Himalayan tributaries of the Ganges, the Alakananda River is considered sacred. Important pilgrimage places (**tirtha**) along the river include the temple town of **Badrinath** near its headwaters, its junction with the **Pindara River** at **Karnaprayag**, its junction with the **Mandakini** River at **Rudraprayag**, and Devaprayag.

Alakhiya Akhara

The name of one subgroup of **ascetics** within the **Naga** class of the **Dashanami** order of **Sanyasis**. The Dashanami Nagas are devotees (**bhakta**) of the god **Shiva**, organized into different **akharas** or regiments that follow the model of an army. Until the beginning of the nineteenth century, the Nagas' primary occupation was as mercenary soldiers, although they also had substantial trading interests; both of these occupations have largely disappeared in contemporary times. The Alakhiya akhara is a subunit of the **Juna akhara**, one of the largest and oldest of the Naga akharas. The name *Alakhiya* comes from the word *alakh* ("without characteristics," a name for the Supreme Being), which many **Shaiva ascetics** utter when **begging** for alms.

Until the beginning of the nineteenth century, the Nagas were fighting ascetics, drawn largely from the ranks of the **shudras**, the lowest Hindu **varna**. According to tradition, these fighting ascetics were recruited to protect the learned ascetics who, because they were saintly and scholarly men, could not protect themselves. The Nagas also had substantial trading interests. Two and three hundred years ago, these akharas were very powerful, especially in parts of the country where the centralized government had broken down. The Naga akharas sold their services as mercenaries, lent money at interest, engaged in trade, and often owned large amounts of property. The one place where the divisions and subdivisions of the akharas are still quite important is at the celebration of the **Kumbha Mela**, a bathing (**snana**) festival. There is a strict order for bathing, and individuals get a place in line based on their affiliation. Two hundred years ago, being first in line signified political, economic, and/or military dominance. The present bathing order reflects each group's relative importance from that time.

Alambhusha

In Hindu mythology, a celestial **woman** who was the **daughter** of the sage **Kashyapa**. As with many of the celestial women, she was often sent by **Indra**, the king of the gods, to seduce sages whose spiritual merit was great enough to pose a threat to Indra's lordship. The assumption behind this is that **celibacy** builds spiritual power, through which one can become a rival to the gods themselves. Sexual activity quickly drains this accumulated power, although the release of such power usually has positive consequences. Alambhusha is best known for her dalliance with the sage **Dadhichi**, by whom she had a **son** named **Saraswat**.

Alamkara

("ornamentation") A term for figures of speech in **Sanskrit** poetry, of which there are more than one hundred types. Many of these are the same as those used in English poetics, such as metaphor, simile, contrast, hyperbole, alliteration, and puns. The Sanskrit literati distinguished these figures of speech even further into more specific types, such as a simile expressing wonder, a simile expressed by doubt, and poetic error, which is the inverse of a metaphor ("that's not the **moon**, but her face . . ."). Other forms are unique to Indian poetry, such as respective enumeration, an extended comparison in which one line mentions several referents and the following lines describe their attributes, always in the same order as the first line. Another form unique to Indian poetry is denial in which the speaker's real intent is expressed by denial, but is accompanied by enough suggestion to indicate the true meaning. The use of alamkara marked all kinds of Sanskrit poetry, both religious and nonreligious, and many of these forms were brought into the later devotional poetry in the vernacular Indian languages. For further information on Sanskrit poetics, see Daniel H. H. Ingalls, *Sanskrit Poetry*, 1968.

Alandi

Maharashtra village famous as the home of the poet-saint **Jnaneshvar** and the site of his **samadhi** (**burial**) **shrine**. Jnaneshvar was the first great figure in the **Varkari Panth**, a religious community centered around the **worship** of the Hindu god **Vithoba**. Varkari religious practice centers primarily around two annual pilgrimages, in which all the participants arrive in **Pandharpur** in the modern state of Maharashtra on the same day. Despite having been dead for over 700 years, Jnaneshvar still symbolically travels from Alandi to Pandharpur twice each year; a **palanquin** (palkhi) carrying his sandals is at the head of the procession bearing his name.

Alberuni

(973–ca.1050 C.E.) Anglicized version of the name of Abu Rayhan Biruni, a central Asian scholar-scientist who was one of the greatest intellectual figures of his time. Alberuni was a member of the court of King **Mahmud of Ghazni**—by most accounts, quite reluctantly—and was forced to accompany Mahmud on some of his pillaging raids in India. Alberuni used this involuntary "fieldwork" as an opportunity to study Hindu life, culture, and sciences, and his work shows him to be a perceptive, careful, and dispassionate observer. In 1030 C.E. he published his findings in his *Tahqiq ma li'l-Hind*, which was translated in 1888 by Edward Sachau as *Alberuni's India*. An abridged edition edited by Ainslee Embree was published in 1971.

Alchemy

Esoteric tradition that seeks to transform, transmute, and perfect the body through the use of various chemicals, with the ultimate goal of rendering the body immortal. Both Hindus and Buddhists have alchemical schools. The reported difference between the Buddhist **rasayana** school and the Hindu **dhatuvada** school is that the latter is solely materially based, whereas the former stresses meditation to gain final enlightenment. These two schools agree on many basic points of alchemy.

Hindu alchemists view the world as a series of bipolar opposites in tension with one another, and they are convinced that unifying these opposing forces brings spiritual progress and the end of reincarnation (**samsara**). Hindu alchemy shares this model of uniting or transcending opposing forces with Hindu **tantra**, an esoteric, ritually based system of religious practice, and with **hatha yoga**, which is based on a series of physical exercises that are also believed to affect the **subtle body**. Although all three traditions share a common assumption, they prescribe different forms of practice to effect the final goal: in tantra, ritual; in hatha yoga, physical exercises; and in alchemy, physical consumption of various substances.

In the alchemical tradition, the governing metaphor for this combination of opposites is the union of **sun** and **moon**. In Hindu tradition the sun and moon are connected to other opposing principles through an elaborate series of associations. The sun is identified with heat, drying power, **fire**, **Shakti**, and menstrual **blood**; the moon with coolness, healing power, **water**, **Shiva**, and **semen**. In alchemical practice the two essential chemical elements are **mercury** and **sulfur**—the former identified with Shiva's semen and the latter with Shakti's uterine blood. By properly mixing and consuming these elements, the aspirant's body is purified and refined, eventually rendering it immortal. Modern descriptions of this practice invariably warn that it should only be carried out under the direction of one's **guru** (spiritual teacher), since otherwise these combinations will be harmful. This warning is not surprising since mercury is a deadly poison. For further information see Shashibhushan B. Dasgupta, *Obscure Religious Cults*, 1962; and David Gordon White, *The Alchemical Body*, 1996.

Alidhasana

("shooting posture") Bodily posture (**asana**) characteristic of certain images in Hindu iconography. This position is like that of an archer drawing a bow, in which one knee is thrown forward, the other leg pushed back, and the trunk twisted in the direction of the front leg. The god **Shiva** in his manifestation as **Tripurari**, "the destroyer of the Triple City," is often shown in this posture. The god **Rama** is also portrayed in his warrior pose.

Allahabad

("City of Allah") City at the junction of the **Ganges** and **Yamuna** rivers. The city was named Allahabad by the Moghul emperor **Akbar**, who built a fort there in 1583 to signify Moghul control of the region. Traditionally, the place where the rivers meet is considered a sacred bathing (**snana**) place, and the city was called Prayaga ("place of **sacrifice**") by the Hindus. This name is still used to distinguish the sacred site (**tirtha**) from the city surrounding it. Another name for the junction is **Triveni** ("triple stream"), reflecting the traditional belief that the two visible rivers are joined at the confluence by a third underground river, the **Saraswati**. Near the bathing place is a banyan tree believed to be the **akshaya vata** ("indestructible banyan tree"), which despite its powerful name is at present very small.

As with all places where the Ganges makes some natural transition—here its confluence with another sacred river—Prayaga is considered especially holy, and bathing there is believed to confer even greater religious merit than a normal Ganges bath. This sanctity can be further amplified by bathing during particularly auspicious times in the **calendar**. For example, the annual **Magh Mela** is a bathing festival held during the **lunar month** of **Magh** (January–February). The holiest time for bathing is during a festival called **Kumbha Mela**, which is held approximately every twelve years when **Jupiter** is in Taurus. The Kumbha Mela is followed six years later by the **Ardha** ("half") **Kumbha Mela**, which carries less sanctity than the "full" Kumbha Mela but is still considered a highly propitious event. Allahabad's Kumbha Mela in 1989 was the largest religious festival on earth, attended by an estimated fifteen million people on a single day.

Allama Prabhu

(12th c. C.E.) Poet-saint and religious leader in the **Lingayat** community, a bhakti (devotional) community that **worships Shiva** as the single supreme god and rejects all **caste** regulations. The Lingayats formed in the southern Indian state of **Karnataka**, where they still have a considerable presence, and the collections of poetry that form their most important religious texts are composed in the **Kannada** language. According to legend, Allama was Shiva himself on **earth**, and the honorific title "Master" (Prabhu) indicates the respect that his Lingayat contemporaries granted him. In his poetry, Allama spoke from the perspective of one who had gained final liberation and had completely transcended all ritual and worldly ties. For further information see A. K. Ramanujan (trans.), *Speaking of Siva*, 1973.

Alvar

Collective name for twelve poet-saints devoted to the god **Vishnu** who lived in southern India between the seventh and tenth centuries. In conjunction with the **Nayanars**, who were devoted to the god **Shiva**, the Alvars spearheaded the revitalization of Hindu religion vis-à-vis the Buddhists and the Jains. Both the Alvars and the Nayanars stressed passionate devotion (**bhakti**) to a personal god and conveyed this devotion through hymns sung in the **Tamil language**. The earliest Alvars were a group of three seventh-century contemporaries: **Poygai**, **Pey**, and **Bhutam**, whose propitious meeting on a rainy night is described as sparking the devotional flame. The next group: **Tiruppan**, **Tirumalisai**, **Tondaradippodi**, **Kulashekhara**, **Periyalvar**, **Andal**, and **Tirumangai**, are believed to have lived in the ninth century. They were followed by **Nammalvar** and his disciple **Mathurakavi**, who can be reasonably placed in the beginning of the tenth century, as can **Nathamuni**, who collected all of the Alvars' hymns in the *Nalayira Prabandham*. Although the

Alvars described themselves only as human devotees (**bhakta**), by the tenth century they were revered by the **Shrivaishnava** religious community as **anshavatars**, or incarnations of Vishnu's attributes or companions. Their collected hymns were (and are) popularly known as the Tamil **Veda** and became a vital part of later **Vaishnava** piety in southern India. This is particularly true for the Shrivaishnava tradition, in which one of the major figures was Nathamuni himself.

Amalaka

In the **Nagara** style of Hindu temple **architecture**, the amalaka is a stone disk, usually with ridges on the rim, that sits on top of the temple's main tower. According to one interpretation, the amalaka represents a lotus and is thus the symbolic seat for the **deity** worshiped below. Another interpretation is that it symbolizes the **sun** and is thus the gateway to the heavenly world. The amalaka itself is crowned with a **kalasha** (finial), from which a temple banner is often hung. See also **heavens**.

Amalaki Ekadashi

Festival falling on the eleventh **day** (**ekadashi**) of the bright (waxing) half of the **lunar month** of **Phalgun** (February–March). As are all of the eleventh-day observances, this is dedicated to the **worship** of **Vishnu**. Most Hindu festivals have certain prescribed rites, usually involving fasting (**upavasa**) and worship, and often promise specific benefits for faithful performance. On this day, one should worship the amvala tree since this is one of the places in which Vishnu is believed to reside.

Amarkantak

Sacred site (**tirtha**) at the headwaters of the **Narmada River**, in the **Vindhya mountains** in the state of **Madhya Pradesh**. As with all the junctions of India's sacred rivers, Amarkantak is held to be an especially holy place for religious actions. Most pilgrims go there to perform common pilgrimage rites such as **snana** (bathing) and **shraddha** (memorial rites), but Amarkantak is also one of the places mentioned in **Sanskrit** texts as a site for religious **suicide**.

Amarnath

("The Undying Lord") Sacred site (**tirtha**) and pilgrimage place located high in the mountains of **Kashmir**, dedicated to the god **Shiva** in the form of Amarnath (The Undying Lord). The focus of the site is a limestone cave, where each year melting snow trickling through the limestone fissures naturally forms a pillar of ice. At its largest, this pillar can be more than seven feet tall, but this can vary significantly from year to year depending on the weather. The most common **aniconic image** of Shiva is the **linga**, a cylindrical form imperfectly described as a "phallic symbol." Hindus believe that the ice pillar in the Amarnath cave is a svayambhu, or "self-manifested," linga of Shiva. Such lingas are not made by human beings but are places where Shiva decides to reveal himself, out of love for his devotees (**bhakta**). Any **svayambhu image** is believed to be particularly holy because Shiva is thought to be uniquely present. These sites are often seen as places where prayers and **worship** are particularly efficacious.

The Amarnath cave is in a remote spot that is inaccessible for most of the year due to snow. The pilgrimage takes place during the month of **Shravan** (July–August), with travelers timing their trip to arrive on the day of the **full moon**. The pilgrimage officially begins at the **Dashanami Sanyasi akhara** in Shrinagar and is led by the akhara's leader (**mahant**), who carries a silver mace as an emblem of his authority. This preeminence is given to **ascetics** because they are living symbols of Shiva himself, who is the perfect ascetic. Most pilgrims start their journey at the town of Pahalgam. From there they walk almost thirty miles to

The outside entrance of the limestone caves at Amarnath.
This is a sacred site in which the god Shiva is believed to reside.

Amarnath, crossing two mountain ranges on the way. Although the region is thinly settled for most of the year, during the pilgrimage season, camps and businesses spring up along the route; many are run by local Kashmiri Muslims, for whom this is a major source of livelihood. The **offerings** at the shrine are evenly split between the mahant, the local **pandas** (Hindu pilgrimage priests), and a group of Muslims from a village near Pahalgam who traditionally maintained the road, although the state has done this since India has gained independence. During the early 1990s, parts of Kashmir were a war zone between Indian government forces and a variety of Kashmiri Muslim groups, some of which pressed for greater self-determination and others for unification with Pakistan. These problems have affected the pilgrimage, which passes through some of the most contested areas. In 1994 there were several attacks on travelers, reportedly prompted by pilgrims chanting anti-Muslim slogans, and in 1995 the pilgrimage took place under heavy security provided by the Indian army. The 1996 pilgrimage had no political turmoil, but several hundred people died of hypothermia caused by a sudden unseasonable snowstorm.

Amaru

(7th c.?) **Sanskrit** poet traditionally thought to be the author of the *Amarushatakam* ("Amaru's Hundred"), a collection of poems on the theme of **erotic** love. The text's name is doubly misleading since present editions contain almost 200 poems, and there is strong evidence that it was compiled from several earlier collections, making its authorship uncertain. Although Amaru's poetry explores the joys of carnal love and is thus not explicitly religious, the themes of lover/beloved and union/separation treated in this poetry later became standard themes in **bhakti** (devotional) poetry. In the *Shankaradigvijaya*, a legendary biography of the philosopher

Shankaracharya, Amaru is described as a king who becomes mythically connected with the great sage. In response to the challenge that he knows nothing about sexuality, Shankaracharya uses his yogic powers to animate Amaru's body immediately after the latter's death. In this form Shankaracharya experiences this facet of human life, although reportedly without desire on his part. Shankaracharya has sexual relations with Amaru's wives, enjoys the fruits of passion, and pens the *Amarushatakam* to record his deeds. Although this claim is highly doubtful, it helps to illustrate some important thematic connections between religious and erotic poetry. For further information see Lee Siegel, *Fires of Love—Waters of Peace*, 1983.

Amaruka

Another name for the legendary poet **Amaru**. See **Amaru**.

Amarushatakam

("**Amaru's** Hundred") Collection of poems on the theme of **erotic** love, traditionally ascribed to the seventh-century poet Amaru. The text's name is doubly misleading since present editions contain almost 200 poems, and there is strong evidence that it was compiled from several earlier collections, making its authorship uncertain. Although the poetry explores the joys of carnal love and is thus not explicitly religious, the themes of lover/beloved and union/separation treated in this poetry later became standard genres of **bhakti** (devotional) poetry.

Amba

In the Hindu epic the *Mahabharata*, Amba is the elder sister of **Ambika** and **Ambalika**. In the story she is abducted with her sisters by **Bhishma**, to be married to his stepbrother **Vichitravirya**. Ambika and Ambalika happily marry Vichitravirya, but when Amba confides that she has already given her heart to King Salva, Bhishma releases her to go to him. When Amba returns to Salva, he rejects her on the grounds that her virginity is suspect because she has been abducted by another man. Amba returns to Bhishma and demands that he marry her, since he is responsible for her plight. Bhishma refuses to do so because he has promised his father, King **Shantanu**, that he will never marry, to ensure that his stepbrothers will have no rivals for the throne. His refusal leaves Amba with no source of support, and she vows to get revenge. She is later reborn as the man-woman **Shikhandi**, behind whom **Arjuna** hides to shoot the arrows that eventually kill Bhishma.

Ambakeshvar

Another name for **Tryambakeshvar**, the presiding **deity** of a sacred site (**tirtha**) at **Trimbak**, in the **Nasik** district of the state of **Maharashtra**. Tryambakeshvar is one of the twelve **jyotirlingas**, the "**lingas** of light" that are considered especially sacred to **Shiva**. See **Tryambakeshvar**.

Ambalika

In the Hindu epic the *Mahabharata*, Ambalika is the **daughter** of the king of **Kashi** and one of the wives of King **Vichitravirya**. When Vichitravirya dies childless, his mother, **Satyavati**, calls upon her eldest **son**, **Vyasa**, to sleep with Ambalika and her sister **Ambika** in the hope that the **women** will conceive and continue the family line. According to tradition, Vyasa is very ugly, and each woman involuntarily reacts when Vyasa appears in her bed. Ambalika turns pale, causing her son **Pandu** to be born with an unnaturally pale complexion, and Ambika covers her eyes, causing her son **Dhrtarashtra** to be born blind.

Ambarisha

In Hindu mythology, a king of the **Ikshvaku** dynasty about whom various sources paint very differing pictures. In the *Ramayana*, the earlier of the two great Hindu epics, he is portrayed as a man who is willing to **sacrifice** a boy, Sunassepha, in place of a sacrificial **cow** that **Indra** has stolen. At the moment of the sacrifice, Sunassepha prays to the gods, and Indra appears to bless both Ambarisha and Sunassepha. In another story, from the ***Bhagavata Purana***, Ambarisha is portrayed as a fervent devotee (**bhakta**) of **Vishnu**. When the sage **Durvasas** tries to disrupt Ambarisha's **ekadashi** ("eleventh **day**") observances, Ambarisha calls for help from Vishnu's discus weapon, **Sudarshana**. At Ambarisha's prayer, the discus pursues Durvasas throughout the universe and gives him no place of refuge. In the end, a humbled Durvasas is forced to beg Ambarisha's forgiveness, and the latter informs Durvasas of the powers of ekadashi observance.

Ambedkar, Dr. Bhim Rao

(1891–1956) Thinker, writer, and social activist whose worldview always reflected his birth as a **Mahar**, a **caste** of **untouchables** in the state of **Maharashtra**. Ambedkar's father had joined the British army, which brought the family enough social mobility for Bhim Rao to get an education: a B.A. in Bombay, an M.A. and Ph.D. from Columbia University in New York City, and a D.Sc. from London University. He also passed the British bar exam. Ambedkar spent his life fighting for the rights of the untouchable classes, through both political lobbying and social action. In 1932, through his efforts, untouchables were given a separate electorate as a **minority** group. **Mohandas Gandhi** was bitterly opposed to removing untouchables from the larger Hindu body politic and began a fast unto death. In the end Ambedkar relented, but for the rest of his life he maintained that Gandhi had used the untouchables as pawns in India's political struggles with Britain. Ambedkar claimed that for untouchables there was no material difference between Gandhi's practices and traditional caste Hinduism, because rather than having any real political power, the untouchables had to continue relying on the "goodwill" of Hindus to look after their needs. Ambedkar played an important role in the formation of the Republic of India, including being called upon to author its constitution, but social inequality continued to rankle him. In 1956 he and many of his followers formally converted to Buddhism as a way to leave the caste system behind. These "neo-Buddhists" still exist, and despite their relatively small numbers, their militancy makes them an important group.

Ambika

("mother") Epithet of the **Goddess**. In many cases it refers specifically to **Shiva's** wife **Parvati**, but it is also used as the name of a powerful female **deity** in the ***Devimahatmya***, the earliest text in which a female divinity is presented as the Ultimate Reality in the universe.

Ambika

(2) In one of the great Hindu epics, the ***Mahabharata***, Ambika is the **daughter** of the king of **Kashi** and the wife of King **Vichitravirya**. When Vichitravirya dies childless, his mother, **Satyavati**, calls upon her oldest **son**, **Vyasa**, to have sex with Ambika and her sister **Ambalika** in the hope that the **women** will conceive and continue the family line. According to tradition, Vyasa is very ugly, and each woman involuntarily reacts when Vyasa appears in her bed. Ambika covers her eyes, causing her son **Dhrtarashtra** to be born blind, and Ambalika turns pale, causing her son **Pandu** to have an unnaturally pale complexion.

Ammonite

Spiral-shaped fossil shell of a prehistoric sea creature. The black stones in which these fossil shells are embedded are known as **shalagrams** and are found in great numbers in the **Kali Gandaki** River in **Nepal**. The name *ammonite* comes from the Latin expression meaning "horn of Ammon," which refers to a form of the god **Jupiter** that bears rams' horns. In India the ammonite's circular form is understood as a symbol of **Vishnu's** discus (**chakra**), and thus the shalagram is considered a **svayambhu** "self-manifested" image of Vishnu himself. As with all svayambhu forms of a **deity**, the shalagram is considered to be extraordinarily holy and is usually kept as an object of **worship**.

Amritanandamayi

(b. 1953, as Sudhamani) Modern Hindu teacher and religious leader, whose devotees (**bhakta**) **worship** her as an incarnation of the **Goddess**. She was born the **daughter** of a poor fisherman, and from her earliest childhood she focused on religious life. Her teachings stress the importance of devotion (**bhakti**), particularly to one's spiritual teacher (**guru**), and her devotees credit her with healing and spiritual awakening. The Mata Amritanandamayi **Math**, located in the city of Quilon in the state of **Kerala**, was formed to spread her teachings in India and abroad.

Amrta

("imperishable") In Hindu mythology this is the nectar of immortality, which is churned from the Ocean of Milk through the combined efforts of the gods and the **demons**. The word is also used metaphorically to describe anything believed to be especially purifying and powerful, such as **charanamrta** ("foot nectar"). Charanamrta are the liquids (milk, **water**, etc.) given to devotees (**bhakta**) to drink, which are often the fluids in which their **guru's** feet or the image of a **deity** have been bathed. See also **Tortoise avatar**.

Anahata Chakra

In many schools of **yoga** and in the esoteric ritual tradition known as **tantra**, the anahata chakra is one of the six psychic centers (**chakras**) believed to exist in the **subtle body**.

The subtle body is an alternate physiological system, thought to be on a different plane of existence than gross matter but with certain correspondences to the material body. It is comprised of a set of six psychic centers, which are envisioned as multi-petaled lotus flowers running roughly along the course of the spine, connected by three vertical channels. Each of these chakras has important symbolic associations—with differing human capacities, different subtle elements (**tanmatras**), and different seed syllables (**bijaksharas**) formed from the letters of the **Sanskrit** alphabet, thus encompassing all sacred sound. Above and below these centers are, respectively, **Shiva** (embodying awareness) and **Shakti** (embodying power), the two divine principles through which the entire universe has come into being. The underlying assumption behind this concept of the subtle body is thus the harmony of macrocosm and microcosm, an essential Hindu idea since the time of the mystical texts known as the **Upanishads**.

The six chakras are traditionally listed from the bottom up, and the anahata chakra is the fourth. It is visualized as a twelve-petaled lotus located in the region of the heart. These petals each contain a seed syllable formed from a letter of the Sanskrit alphabet, in this case the first twelve consonants. On a symbolic level, the anahata chakra is associated with the circulation of **blood** throughout the body. It is also identified as the bodily seat for the subtle element of **wind**, the action of which (through the operation of the five **vital winds** known as **pranas**) is believed to be responsible for circulating things through the body. For further information see Arthur Avalon (Sir John Woodroffe), *Shakti and Shakta*, 1978; and Philip S. Rawson, *The Art of Tantra*, 1973.

Analogy

In certain schools of Indian **philosophy**, analogy is considered to be one of the **pramanas**, the means by which human beings can gain true and accurate knowledge. See **upamana**.

Ananda

("bliss") One of the three traditional attributes of the Supreme Reality (**Brahman**), usually described as being-consciousness-bliss (**sacchidananda**). Ananda, or bliss, is heavily stressed in certain forms of **tantra**, an esoteric ritual tradition. In tantra, ananda is both an aspect of mundane physical enjoyment and a way of describing the ultimate realization. In this understanding, even ordinary pleasures are reflections of ultimate bliss. Ultimate bliss differs from ordinary pleasure both because it is permanent, and because you lose your sense of self and are aware only of bliss.

Ananda Akhara

The name of a specific group of the **Naga** class of the **Dashanami Sanyasis**, a particular type of renunciant **ascetic**. The Dashanami Nagas are devotees (**bhakta**) of the god **Shiva**, organized into six different **akharas** or regiments on the model of an army. Until the beginning of the nineteenth century, the Nagas' primary occupation was as mercenary soldiers, although they also had substantial trading interests; both of these occupations have largely disappeared in contemporary times.

For organizational purposes, the Ananda akhara is considered a subsidiary of the powerful **Niranjani akhara**, one of the other seven akharas. All of the groups have particular features that define their organizational identity, especially specific tutelary **deities**; the tutelary deity of the Ananda akhara is **fire**.

Ananda Marga Yoga Society

Modern Hindu organization founded by Shri Anandamurti. The Society emphasizes **yoga** and meditation, which are intended to set its practitioners on the path (marga) to bliss (**ananda**). The movement is the strongest in the state of **West Bengal**, and has been dogged by controversy in India, particularly after Anandamurti was indicted for the murder of two of his disciples. In the end he was acquitted of all charges, but the organization's legal troubles made its members withdraw from society. Many Indians view them with suspicion, if not outright hostility, and the movement is associated with ritual murder and black **magic**. In recent times, it has even been suspected of terrorism, after a large shipment of black-market arms was mysteriously parachuted into a nearby region in early 1995. Although it has never been proved that the arms were for the Society, this incident is one more element in the surrounding cloud of secrecy and suspicion.

Anandamath

Novel by the Bengali nationalist author **Bankim Chandra Chatterjee** (1838–1894). It is set in eighteenth-century Bengal during the so-called **Sanyasi Rebellion**, which invloved bands of Hindu and Muslim militant **ascetics**. Both groups fought with the British East India Company for control over the region.

Historical inquiry suggests that the roots of this conflict lay in the extreme social tensions in Bengali society, particularly changes in land ownership patterns and the havoc wreaked by the great famine of 1770–1771. Chatterjee was an ardent Indian nationalist and portrayed the Sanyasi Rebellion as a struggle by Mother India's loyal children to expel the parasitic British invaders from her shores.

Although the novel was set in an earlier era to avoid problems with the British authorities, *Anandamath* is clearly allegorical and nationalistic, and it is viewed by contemporary critics as Chatterjee's way to symbolize the need for continuing the struggle against British imperialism in the mid-nineteenth century.

Anandamayi Ma

(1896–1982) Hindu mystic and saint, who during her lifetime gained a wide following in all parts of Hindu society as a manifestation of the Mother **Goddess**. She was born in Dhaka in modern Bangladesh and from a very young age showed strong spiritual tendencies. These intensified after her marriage, when she would slip into blissful meditation, oblivious to her surroundings and the passage of time. The marriage was never consummated and her husband became one of her primary disciples. For some time she lived in an **ashram** in the city of **Benares**, which is famous as a sacred site (**tirtha**). Later she built an ashram just outside the city of **Haridwar**, where her **samadhi** ("**burial**") **shrine** can be found.

Anandapala

The last great king in the Pratihara dynasty, which ruled large sections of the northwestern part of the Indian subcontinent between the eighth and eleventh centuries. In 1001 C.E., Anandapala assembled a coalition of Hindu princes to do battle with **Mahmud of Ghazni** in a desperate attempt to halt the latter's expansion. Anandapala and his allies were annihilated in a battle near Peshawar in modern Pakistan, and the Pratihara dynasty's power was completely destroyed. With this powerful dynasty out of the way, there was no political force in northern India strong enough to stop Mahmud. He began making annual raids into India.

Anandawara

One of the four major groups of the **Dashanami Sanyasis**, renunciant **ascetics** who are devotees (**bhakta**) of the god **Shiva**; the other three divisions are **Kitawara**, **Bhuriwara**, and **Bhogawara**. Each of these groups has its headquarters in one of the four monastic centers (**maths**) supposedly established by the philosopher **Shankaracharya**. Each group also has particular religious associations: with one of the four **Vedas**, with a particular quarter of the Indian subcontinent, with one of the "great utterances" (**mahavakyas**) expressing ultimate truth, with a specific **ascetic** quality, and with several of the ten Dashanami divisions.

The Anandawara group is affiliated with the **Jyotir Math** in the Himalayan town of **Joshimath** and is thus connected with the northern quarter of India. Their **Veda** is the **Atharva Veda**, their mahavakya is **Ayamatma Brahman** ("This Self is **Brahman**"), and their ascetic quality is to be satisfied with whatever food they get without **begging**, since they are not attached to worldly pleasures. The particular Dashanami divisions associated with this group are **Giri**, **Parvata**, and **Sagara**.

Ananga

("bodyless") Epithet of **Kama**, a **deity** who is the personification of desire. Kama was given the name Ananga because his body was destroyed by the **fire** from **Shiva's** third eye. See **Kama**.

Ananta

("endless") Epithet of **Shesha**, the god **Vishnu's** serpent couch. See **Shesha**.

Anantadas

(late 16th c.) Poet and hagiographer who wrote "introductions" (parchais) for some of the best-known northern Indian devotional (**bhakti**) poet-saints, among them **Ravidas**, **Kabir**, **Namdev**, **Trilochan**, **Angada**, and **Pipa**. His era can be fixed with reasonable assurance since Anantadas himself gives 1588 C.E. as the date of composition for his *Namdev Parchai*. Anantadas was contemporary with another famous hagiographer, **Nabhadas**, whom Anantadas names as a "**guru** brother" to his own guru, making Nabhadas a "spiritual uncle" of Anantadas. Although both hagiographers provide valuable information, the descriptions by Nabhadas are quite brief, whereas Anantadas gives extended information about his subjects. Anantadas's works are by far the earliest detailed accounts of these literary figures, although the marvelous events included in the introductions render them suspect as historical sources. Because his collected works have never been published, he remains virtually unknown. For further information see David Lorenzen, *Kabir Legends and Ananta-Das's Kabir Parachai*, 1991; and Winand Callewaert and Peter G. Friedlander (trans.), *The Life and Works of Raidas*, 1992.

Anant Chaturdashi

Festival falling on the fourteenth **day** (chaturdashi) of the bright (waxing) half of the **lunar month** of **Bhadrapada** (August–September). This festival falls during the four-month period when the **deity Vishnu** is believed to be sleeping on **Shesha**, his serpent couch, while his wife **Lakshmi** massages his feet. The festival itself is named after Shesha, one of whose epithets is Anant ("endless"). On this day, devotees (**bhakta**) of Vishnu should **worship** and meditate on this particular image of Vishnu, with Shesha and Lakshmi.

Before beginning worship, devotees tie onto their forearm a string dipped in turmeric, an eastern Indian spice, in which fourteen knots have been made. Each of these elements is symbolic: The string is a symbol of Shesha, the color yellow is associated with Vishnu, and the fourteen knots signify the fourteenth day.

Aside from worshiping Vishnu, devotees should also fast (**upavasa**) on this day. Carefully observing the requirements for this festival is believed to ensure prosperity and freedom from exile. According to mythic tradition, keeping this vow enables the five **Pandava** brothers, the heroes of the epic *Mahabharata*, to escape from exile and regain their kingdom.

Anasuya

In Hindu mythology Anasuya is the wife of the sage **Atri**. On one occasion Anasuya is begged by the gods **Brahma**, **Vishnu**, and **Shiva** to help them. A woman named Silavati has cursed the **sun** not to rise, and the creatures on **earth** are very distressed. Anasuya succeeds in persuading Silavati to recall her **curse**, and in their gratitude the three gods tell her she can ask for whatever she wants. Anasuya requests that each be born as one of her **sons**, and this is granted: Vishnu is born as **Dattatreya**, Shiva as **Durvasas**, and Brahma as Chandra.

Ancestral Spirit

(pitr) This term is a translation of the word that literally means "fathers"; these ancestral spirits are seen as a collective group to whom every man has duties. One of these duties is to perform certain memorial rites for them, such as the rite of **sapindikarana**. Like most funerary rites (**antyeshthi samskara**), the major objective is to transform the recently deceased and potentially malevolent spirit into a benign and helpful ancestor. Another duty is to procreate **sons**, so that the rites may be performed without interruption. Both of these are weighty responsibilities, and Hindu mythology is replete with tales of lifelong **ascetics**, such as **Jaratkaru**, who are rebuked by their ancestral spirits for shirking their duty to procreate. By virtue of their stable ancestral status, these spirits are also well-defined and generally benevolent.

Andal

(9th c.) The only woman among the **Alvars**, a group of twelve poet-saints who lived in southern India between the seventh and tenth centuries. All the Alvars were devotees (**bhakta**) of the god **Vishnu**, and their stress on passionate devotion (**bhakti**) to a personal god, conveyed through hymns sung in the **Tamil language**, transformed and revitalized Hindu religious life.

Temple of Venkateshvara in the town of Tirupati in Andhra Pradesh.

As with many female bhakti figures, Andal had a particularly passionate relationship with her chosen **deity**, whom she considered her betrothed husband. This deity was **Ranganatha**, a particular form of Vishnu resident at the temple of **Shrirangam** in the state of **Tamil Nadu**. According to legend, Andal was an earthly manifestation of **Vishnu's** wife Bhudevi ("**Earth Goddess**") and appeared as an abandoned baby to her foster father, **Periyalvar**, another of the Alvars. When she came of age, she was adamant that she would have no human husband and merged into the image of Ranganatha at Shrirangam.

Although many of the details about her life are uncertain, Andal did compose two collections of poetry, the *Tirruppavai* and the *Nacciyar Tirumoli*, both of which are dedicated to Vishnu in his form as **Krishna**. For further information see Vidya Dehejia (trans.), *Antal and Her Path of Love*, 1990.

Andhaka
("blind") In Hindu mythology, a **demon** born from the darkness that arises when the **goddess Parvati** play-fully covers her husband **Shiva's** eyes with her hands. Shiva names him Andhaka because he arises from darkness. Andhaka lusts after Parvati and continues to pursue her, despite repeated remonstrances that approaching another man's wife is improper. Eventually he goes all the way to Shiva's home on Mount **Kailas**, where the god kills him.

Andhra
Brahmin subcommunity that is one of the five southern brahmin communities (**Pancha Dravida**). As their name would indicate, the core region for the Andhra brahmins is located in the modern state of **Andhra Pradesh**.

Andhra Pradesh
Modern southern Indian state. Andhra Pradesh is one of the so-called linguistic states formed after independence to unite people with a common language and culture (in this case, Telegu) under one state government.

In the case of Andhra Pradesh, this was done by combining the princely state of Hyderabad with the Telegu-speaking provinces of the former state of Madras. This merger did not happen without some drama; when independence arrived, the Nizam of Hyderabad, a Muslim ruler whose subjects were mainly Hindus, was initially reluctant to join the Indian union, although he acceded after troops were deployed by the Indian government. The state capital has remained at Hyderabad, which is the largest and most important city.

Andhra Pradesh is overwhelmingly agricultural, with fertile land in the **Krishna** and **Godavari** river deltas, but it is relatively undeveloped, and there is still a great disparity between the rich and the poor. In recent years it has become the home of an important regional political party, the Telegu Desam, as well as a base for the Marxist revolutionary group known as Naxalites, who are carrying on an armed struggle against the landlords.

Andhra is also home to India's richest temple, the temple of **Venkateshvara** at **Tirupati**, and to **Mallikarjuna**, one of the twelve **jyotirlingas**, a group of sites especially sacred to **Shiva**. For general information about Andhra Pradesh and all the regions of India, an accessible reference is Christine Nivin et al., *India*. 8th ed., Lonely Planet, 1998.

Anekantavada

One of the three **causal models** in Indian **philosophy**, along with **asatkaryavada** and **satkaryavada**. All three models seek to explain the workings of causality in the everyday world, particularly the relationship between causes and their effects, which has profound implications for religious life. Philosophical theory assumes that if one understands the causal process correctly and can manipulate it through one's conscious actions, it is possible to gain final liberation of the soul (**moksha**). Disagreements over differing causal models are grounded in varying assumptions about the nature of things.

The asatkaryavada model assumes that effects do not preexist in their causes; the satkaryavada model assumes that they do. The third model, Anekantavada ("the view that things are not single"), seeks to occupy the middle ground between these two.

Anekantavada stresses how one looks at things and the way that this can color a judgment. In viewing the transformation of milk to curds, butter, and clarified butter, an anekantavada proponent would claim that the substances in question were contained in the causes (supporting the satkaryavada notion), but that the qualities each of these substances possessed were newly created each time (supporting the asatkaryavada notion).

Thus, causes and effects are simultaneously both the same and different, depending on the lens through which one looks at them. This theory is an attempt to find a middle ground between the other two causal models by showing that each is possible, but it runs the risk of being seen as not taking any position at all. The major proponents of this position are the Jains, who are outside the scope of the present work. For further information see Karl H. Potter (ed.), *Presuppositions of India's Philosophies*, 1972.

Anga

The traditional name for the region and people of the border area in eastern India shared by the modern states of **West Bengal** and **Bihar**.

Angada

In the *Ramayana*, the earlier of the two great Hindu epics, Angada is the **son** of the monkey-king **Bali** and his wife Tara. Even though **Rama**, the seventh incarnation of **Vishnu**, has killed his father under questionable circumstances, Angada is one of Rama's loyal allies. Angada takes part in the search for **Sita**, and then in the battle in **Lanka** to free her, in which his major contribution is combat with **Ravana's** son Meghanada (an epithet of **Indrajit**).

After the conquest of Lanka, Rama appoints Angada as the crown prince of **Kishkindha**, a forest in southern India. Many of the characters in the *Ramayana* are paradigms for Indian cultural values. Angada exhibits bravery, loyalty, and sincere devotion to Rama, all of which bring their eventual rewards.

Angiras

In Hindu mythology, one of the six **sons** of **Brahma**, all of whom become great sages. All are "mind-born," meaning that Brahma's thoughts are enough to bring them into being. The others are **Marichi**, **Atri**, **Pulastya**, **Pulaha**, and **Kratu**.

Angkor

Temple complex built in northwestern Cambodia by the Khmer ruler **Suryavarman II** (1112–1153 C.E.). The Khmer people were indigenous to Kampuchea, but the temples at Angkor were dedicated to Hindu gods. This reflects the prodigious influence of Hindu culture, which by the end of the first millennium C.E. had been spread throughout Southeast Asia by Indian (primarily southern Indian) merchants and traders.

Ani

(according to tradition, a shortened form of the **Sanskrit** word *anika*, meaning "army") A major organizational division of the **Bairagi Nagas**, **ascetic** traders and mercenary soldiers who were devotees (**bhakta**) of the god **Vishnu**. At present there are three Bairagi anis: the **Digambara**, **Nirmohi**, and **Nirvani**. In earlier times these anis were actual fighting units, but in modern times these distinctions are mainly important to determine bathing (**snana**) order in the bathing processions at the **Kumbha Mela**. Of the three anis, the Digambaras are by far the most

important and at the time of the Kumbha Mela take precedence over the others.

Ani

(2) In the region of Tamil, which lies at the southern tip of the subcontinent on the Bay of Bengal, the month of Ani is the third month of the solar **year**. It corresponds to the northern Indian solar month of **Mithuna** (the zodiacal sign of Gemini), which usually falls within June and July. The existence of several different calendars is one clear sign of the continuing importance of regional cultural patterns. One way that the Tamils retain their culture is by preserving their traditional **calendar**. Tamil is one of the few regional languages in India with an ancient, well-established literary tradition. See also **Tamil months**, **Tamil Nadu**, and **Tamil language**.

Aniconic Image

A symbol that is meant to represent a **deity**. Although it is more common for human or **animal** likenesses to stand for deities, some deities are represented by symbols or non-pictorial images. Examples of this would be the **linga** or the **shalagram**, both of which are well-known symbolic forms of particular deities—**Shiva** and **Vishnu**, respectively.

Anima

("minuteness") One of the eight superhuman powers (**siddhi**) traditionally believed to be conferred as a result of high spiritual attainment. This particular power gives one the ability to become as small as an atom.

Animals

In the Hindu religion, it is believed that some human beings can be reincarnated as animals. According to generally held notions about **karma**, being born as an animal is an unfavorable rebirth in punishment for a previous grave sin. One is born as an animal to expiate, or atone for, one's evil deeds through suffering, in many cases by being born as a particular type of animal thousands of consecutive times.

Unlike the Jains, who see all matter (even stones) as possessing souls, most Hindus would consider this possible only for sentient, or fully aware, beings, including animal life. The conviction that animals have souls is one of the reasons why many Hindus are vegetarian, since this diet does the least harm to other living things.

For Hindus, the animal realm is considered a place of punishment. From a karmic perspective, being born as an animal is an unenviable state, since animal behavior is run entirely by instinct, and thus as animals they can make no conscious effort to better themselves. From a more concrete perspective, animals in India often lead very difficult lives—including, in many cases, the "sacred" **cow**.

As with all other unfavorable karmic states, one's animal life will eventually end, but only after one's sins have been fully expiated. This suffering and lack of control over one's destiny makes birth as an animal a state to be avoided.

Animal Sacrifice

The practice of animal sacrifice can be found in two different strands of the Hindu tradition. The first, and by far the earliest, is in the cult of sacrifice described in the later strata of the **Vedas**, particularly in the **Brahmana** literature. The cost of these rites virtually ensured that they could only be performed by royalty and nobility, since some entailed the slaughter of hundreds of **animals**.

Perhaps the most famous of these rites was the horse sacrifice (**ashvamedha**), which served to prove a king's great power. In the early centuries before the common era, these sacrifices grew less frequent—a trend often connected to the stress on **ahimsa** by the Buddhists and Jains, two groups that opposed the slaughter of any life—and by the early centuries of the common era, even Hindu commentators denounced the Vedic sacrifices because

they entailed animal slaughter. In modern times, these rites have largely fallen into disuse, and even when they have been revived and re-created, they usually do not involve animal slaughter but substitutions of some sort, such as vegetables or fruits.

The other context in which animal sacrifice can be found, and is still performed quite regularly, is in the **worship** of **village deities**, or certain powerful and terrifying forms of the **Goddess**. In this worship the animals (usually goats) are decapitated, and the **blood** is offered to the **deity**, often by smearing some of it on a post outside of the temple.

In Hindu culture, blood is considered a "hot" substance—highly impure, extremely powerful, and readily contaminating other things. Any deity that requires sacrifice is also "hot"—powerful enough to grant favors to their devotees (**bhakta**), but also marginal, potentially dangerous, and requiring frequent animal sacrifice to maintain their power.

The most extreme example is at the temple of the goddess **Kamakhya** in modern **Assam**, a region located in northeastern India. This is one of the few reported instances of **human sacrifice**, although the custom was halted by the British in 1832. When Kamakhya's present temple was consecrated in 1565, she was supposedly offered the heads of 140 men, all of whom had volunteered themselves as **offerings**.

Although such blood-drinking deities are often very powerful, many Hindus do not approve of the impurity (**ashaucha**) and slaughter connected with animal sacrifice. For this reason, one of the first ways to make a particular deity acceptable to a more cultured public is often to make the sacrifices vegetarian, by substituting a gourd or cucumber in place of the sacrificial animal.

Aniruddha

("unobstructed") In Hindu mythology, the **son** of **Pradyumna** and the grandson of **Krishna**.

Anirvachaniyakhyati

("indescribable discrimination") This is a particular **theory of error** that aims to explain why people make errors in judgment, such as the stock example of mistaking the silvery flash of a seashell for a piece of silver. This theory was advanced by the philosophical school of **Advaita Vedanta**, a group that would consider this judgment to be a false one; they would also believe, however, that until one realizes that the object is just a shell, one actually sees the silver there.

The Advaita theory of error is based on the fundamental concept of superimposition (**adhyasa**), in which one perceives something that is actually there (in this case, the shell). This real object is the basis for the illusory perception (the silver), which is a mistaken projection. The Advaitins claim that the "silver" is real insofar as it is based on the shell, and false insofar as one believes it to be precious metal.

Of course, according to the Advaitins, the shell and all the other "real" things of the world are themselves ultimately illusory since they are superimposed on **Brahman**, the only thing in the universe that is truly real. For further information see Bijayananda Kar, *The Theories of Error in Indian Philosophy*, 1990; and Karl H. Potter (ed.), *Presuppositions of India's Philosophies*, 1972.

Anjali Hasta

In Indian **dance**, **sculpture**, and ritual, the anjali hasta is a particular hand **gesture** (**hasta**) in which the palms of the two hands are joined together with the fingers pointing upward, often with the base of the thumbs resting against the chest. This gesture conveys respect and prayerful devotion.

In modern India this is also the most common gesture of greeting and salutation. Since traditional Indian society was (and to some extent, remains) so intensely conscious of **purity**, it is not surprising that this greeting can convey respect without requiring one to touch another person, which could transmit impurity (**ashaucha**) from one person to another.

Anjana

In the *Ramayana*, the earlier of the two great Hindu epics, Anjana is the mother of the monkey-**deity Hanuman**. In her previous birth, Anjana was a **goddess**, but as the result of a **curse**, she is born as a monkey. With the birth of Hanuman (fathered by **Vayu**, the god of **wind**), the curse was lifted and she returned to **heaven**.

Ankusha

("**elephant** goad") This is a weapon with a wooden or metal handle, with a point and a sharp hook that real elephant handlers use to coax and goad elephants—sometimes by poking them with the hook, sometimes by hitting them with the butt of the handle.

The ankusha is an important symbol in Hindu iconography and is primarily associated with the god **Ganesh**—perhaps partly because of his elephant head. This weapon also corresponds with Ganesh's stature as the Lord of Obstacles, since he can use the ankusha to poke and prod them out of the way.

Aside from Ganesh, the ankusha is also a symbol associated with certain powerful forms of the **Goddess**. This may originate with the myth that describes her as being formed from the collected radiance of all the gods, and receiving duplicates of their weapons from them.

Annakut

("Mountain of food") Northern Indian festival celebrated on the day after the festival of **Diwali** (October–November). This festival is more popularly known as **Govardhan Puja**.

A woman displays the anjali hasta hand gesture.
This gesture conveys respect and is a common greeting and salutation.

Annaprashana ("food-eating") Samskara

Traditionally, this is the seventh of the life-cycle ceremonies (**samskaras**) in which the young child is first given solid food. In many of the traditional texts on **dharma**, the **Dharma Shastras**, parents are directed to feed the child **animal** flesh. In modern times children are more commonly fed rice; as the most popular grain in much of India, rice can be considered a symbol for food in general.

As in any society, the introduction of solid food marks a major transition in the infant's young life, even though the infant may not wean for some time after that. Unlike many of the traditional samskaras, this is still an important **childhood rite** in modern India.

Anrta

In the **Vedas**, the earliest Hindu scriptures that are still the most authoritative religious texts, anrta is characterized as the opposite of **rta**, the cosmic order. Anrta is particularly associated with falsehood and untruth, and it involves acts of deliberate perversions of speech. Hindus believe that these mistruths undermine the established order of the cosmos.

Anshavatar

A "partial" (amsha) incarnation of a divinity, which is believed to have only part of the **divine power**. See also **avatar**.

Anshuman

In Hindu mythology, the grandson of King **Sagar**. After the death of his sixty thousand uncles, who because of their disrespect were killed by the sage **Kapila**, Anshuman was the sole surviving member of the royal line. Anshuman and **Dilip**, his **son**, labored mightily to bring the **Ganges** (the earthly embodiment of the **goddess Ganga**) from **heaven** down to **earth**, so that by her touch the souls of their relatives might find peace. Their efforts were unsuccessful, but Dilip's son **Bhagirath** was finally able to bring the Ganges to earth.

Antahpura

("inner city") In classical times, the name for the **women's** quarters of the palace, so designated because they were the most stringently protected. Although most Hindus had only one wife, in earlier times it was not uncommon for kings to have a number of wives and concubines, who would be housed in the antahpura. In such cases the king's first wife would generally have higher status, since this marriage would often be used to cement a political alliance.

Antarala

("intermediate space") The antarala was a transitional space between a temple's main hall and the inner sanctum (**garbhagrha**), where the image of the temple's primary **deity** would be housed. The antarala is characteristic of **Nagara architecture**, which is one of three primary styles of Hindu temples. This space was found only in the largest temples and in many smaller ones was omitted entirely.

Antariksha

In the **cosmology** found in the **Vedas**, the earliest Hindu scripture, the antariksha is the middle region of the sky between the **earth** and fixed stars; it corresponds to what might now be called the atmosphere. This region is considered the theater of activity for **Indra**, god of the storm and the most important Vedic **deity**; it is also home to one manifestation of the Vedic god **Agni** (**fire**), in his form as lightning.

Antaryaga

("internal **sacrifice**") In Hindu **worship**, but especially in the secret ritual tradition known as **tantra**, antaryaga refers to the internalization of worship. In this process, worship involving external actions is replaced by worship based on mental acts.

This is a later phase of the initiate's spiritual path, and is attempted only after the initiate has mastered the external forms of worship. The process of internalization becomes progressively more subtle and sophisticated. This step also demonstrates that the initiate has achieved more highly developed religious capacities, in which external objects are no longer needed.

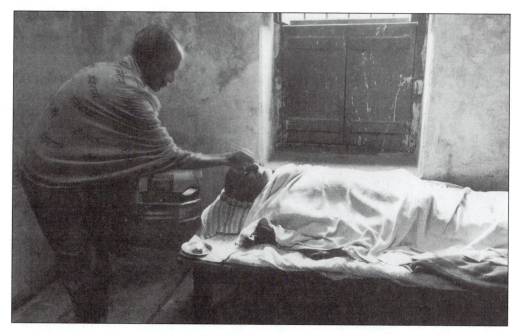

A woman prepares a deceased man for cremation.
This ritual is one stage of the antyeshthi samskara, the traditional Hindu funerary rites.

Antinomianism

This word has its origins in the convictions of an early Christian sect, whose members believed that the only thing needed for salvation was faith, and not obedience to moral rules. In an extended sense, this term describes an attitude in which people ignore accepted social rules.

In Indian society (as in all societies) most people uphold the accepted behavioral norms, but certain groups—particularly renunciant **ascetics** and practitioners of **tantra**, a secret ritual tradition—emphasize the breaking of society's normally held rules. For the ascetics, such intentional disregard was (and is) a symbol of their separateness from conventional society; they believe that such rules no longer apply to them. As a class, ascetics are well-known for their unpredictable and sometimes uncontrolled behavior.

The process is more controlled for practitioners of tantra and most often takes place in a formal ritual setting. The stereotypical pattern is to partake of the "five forbidden things" (**panchamakara**), thus consciously breaking societal norms by consuming **intoxicants** and nonvegetarian foods, as well as practicing illicit sexuality. Although tantric antinomianism deliberately breaks social taboos, in theory it is an attempt to make sacred what is normally forbidden. By doing this, tantric practitioners destroy embedded dualistic ideas that are exemplified by notions such as pure and impure.

From a tantric perspective, the entire universe is one principle—often the activity of a particular **deity**—which means that one must reject all concepts based on dualistic thinking. Such practices are also seen as proof that tantra is superior to other sorts of religious activities, since it uses things that are normally forbidden. For further information see Arthur Avalon (Sir John Woodroffe), *Shakti and Shakta*, 1978; Swami Agehananda Bharati, *The Tantric Tradition*, 1977; and Douglas Renfrew Brooks, *The Secret of the Three Cities*, 1990.

Antyeshthi ("last rites") Samskara

The sixteenth and last of the traditional life-cycle ceremonies (**samskaras**), comprising what can be described as funerary rites. These rites are not a single action, but a series: **deathbed rites** for the dying person, **cremation** for the **corpse**, **asthi-sanchayana** (gathering the ashes), **sapindikarana** (assimilation to the ancestors), various memorial rites known as **shraddhas**, and **asthi-visarjana** (immersing the ashes in a sacred river).

These rites have a twofold purpose. The first is to get rid of the corpse, which is a source of contagion and impurity (**ashaucha**), and thus to protect the living from the dead. The second is to ease the passage of the dead person's spirit into the next world. Aside from these functions, performing familiar and ceremonial rites for the dead undoubtedly gives psychological relief to the living and aids in the process of grieving. What follows is merely an overview of these rites; for more detailed information see the individual entries.

Ritual activities are the most concentrated during the first ten days after death, which is believed to be the period of greatest impurity. Cremation usually takes place on the day of death, not only to prevent decay and disease in a hot climate but also to destroy the body so it will not be reanimated by a wandering spirit. Gathering the ashes (asthi-sanchayana) is done on the second or third day. In earlier times they would have been kept in a safe place, sometimes for years, until a relative visiting a sacred river could perform asthi-visarjana (immersing the ashes); with the advent of modern transportation, this is generally performed a few days after death.

During this ten-day period, the spirit is given symbolic nourishment to help build a "new" body. On the eleventh day, the family performs the first of the memorial ceremonies known as shraddhas; in this case an **ekoddishta** shraddha is performed in which **brahmin** guests, considered surrogates for the ancestors, are fed. On the twelfth day after death, the family performs the rite of sapindikarana, through which the deceased is incorporated into the ranks of the **ancestral spirits** (pitr) and is thus no longer considered a restless spirit. This is followed by anniversary shraddhas at regular intervals during the first year; after this period there is an annual shraddha once a year during the **Pitrpaksha** ("fortnight of the ancestors"), the waning **moon** period in the **lunar month** of **Bhadrapada** (August–September), which is solely devoted to such memorials. For further information see Pandurang Varnan Kane (trans.), *A History of Dharmasastra*, 1968; and Raj Bali Pandey, *Hindu Samskaras*, 1969. For accounts of modern practice, see David M. Knipe, "Sapindikarana: The Hindu Rite of Entry into Heaven," in Frank E. Reynolds and Earle H. Waugh (eds.), *Religious Encounters with Death*, 1977; Lawrence Babb, *The Divine Hierarchy*, 1975; and Anne Grodzins Gold, *Fruitful Journeys*, 1988.

Anulepana

("smearing") The ninth of the sixteen traditional **upacharas** offered to a **deity** as part of **worship**, which are meant to treat the deity as an honored guest. In this **offering**, the deity is presented scented unguents, or ointments, such as sandalwood paste. These ointments are not only used for their fragrance but are also believed to be good for the skin.

Anuloma

("with the **hair**") See **hypergamous marriage**.

Anumana

("measuring after") In Indian **philosophy** this is the term for an inference, which is generally accepted as one of the **pramanas**, the means by which human beings can gain true and accurate knowledge. The word's literal meaning reflects the Indian conviction that any inference must be grounded in perception (**pratyaksha**), the most direct means of knowledge, and must ultimately appeal to perception for evidence.

A classic inference includes three terms: a hypothesis (**pratijna**), a reason (**hetu**), and examples (**drshtanta**), each of which is made up of parts. One part of the hypothesis is the idea to be proved (**sadhya**), which is predicated on a certain class of objects, called the **paksha**. In the statement "there is fire on this mountain," the sadhya is the assertion that there is fire, and the paksha is the particular mountain. The object mentioned in the paksha must also appear in the second term, the hetu, along with the stated reason. In the example cited above, the hetu could be "because there is smoke on this mountain."

As proof, it was necessary to cite positive and negative examples, known as the **sapaksha** and **vipaksha**, respectively. An appropriate sapaksha could be "like kitchen," since ancient kitchens had both fire and smoke; a vipaksha could be "unlike lake," since lakes contain neither of these.

This general form of an inference is subject to numerous tests for validity; one of the most important of these is **vyapti**, the requirement that the reason given must account for all cases of the idea to be proved. For further information see Karl H. Potter (ed.), *Presuppositions of India's Philosophies*, 1972.

Anushtubh

By far the most widely used **meter** in **Sanskrit** poetry, composed of two lines of sixteen syllables each with eight syllables per half line. The metric pattern for each half line is based on the distinction between "heavy" and "light" syllables. A heavy syllable is any syllable with a long vowel or consonant cluster; all other syllables are light. According to the prescribed pattern, the fifth syllable of each half line should be light, the sixth heavy, and the seventh alternately heavy and light. The anushtubh's simplicity makes it the meter of choice for many religious texts, including much of the **Bhagavad Gita**.

Anyathakhyati

("discrimination of something else") A **theory of error** that aims to explain why people make errors in judgment, such as the stock example of mistaking the flash of a seashell for a piece of silver. This particular theory of error originated with the **Naiyayika** philosophical school. Like the **Purva Mimamsa** philosopher **Prabhakara**, the Naiyayikas believe that the simple judgments "that object is silvery" and "silver is silvery" are both true and indisputable. Whereas Prabhakara explains the error as an error of omission, in which one fails to notice the non-relationship between these judgments, the Naiyayikas explain this as an error of commission, by projecting something that actually is not there.

In Naiyayikan metaphysics all objects and their attributes are connected by a dependent relationship known as **inherence** (**samavaya**), which in this case connects a silvery color with two different objects: elemental silver, and a shell. They believe that the perceiver is projecting a wrong inherence relationship (silver) onto the perceived object (shell).

The Naiyayikas can claim this projection is real because they accept the reality of nonexistent things (e.g., the nonexistence of a crocodile in my bathtub). For the Naiyayikas all such projections are rooted in karmic dispositions stemming from **avidya**, or primal ignorance, specifically the greed for silver that prompts people to look for such items of value. For further information see Bijayananda Kar, *The Theories of Error in Indian Philosophy*; 1978 and Karl H. Potter (ed.), *Presuppositions of India's Philosophies*, 1972.

Apabhramsha

("fallen away") An important northern Indian **Prakrit**, one of the vernacular languages that developed naturally from **Sanskrit**. Apabhramsha was the latest addition to the Middle Indo-**Aryan** languages and is considered a direct precursor of early modern **Hindi**, which was becoming established as early as the twelfth century. Although Apabhramsha has lesser status than **Sanskrit**, it was nevertheless an important regional literary language.

Apaddharma

Religious protocol that comes into effect in times of distress, disturbance, natural disaster, or social deterioration. The practical effect of apaddharma is to suspend most of the normal social rules, particularly those governing interaction and **commensality** between different social subgroups (**jatis**). In ordinary circumstances these rules are affected by concepts of **purity**, impurity (**ashaucha**), and relative social status.

The underlying message here is that the preservation of life is more important than such rules, and that they can be broken to save a life—as in the case of escaping a **fire** or flood, in which the usual concerns about physical contact with lower-status people are suspended.

Apana

One of the five bodily "winds" considered to be responsible for basic bodily functions, the others being **prana**, **vyana**, **udana**, and **samana**. The apana wind is believed to exist in the region of the anus and is associated with discharging material out of the body: urine, feces, gas, **semen**, menstrual discharges, and the **birth** of children.

Apastamba

(4th c. B.C.E.?) Sage, writer, and commentator. Apastamba is known for his influential work with the **Kalpa Sutra** form, a type of text that consists of three essential elements: instructions for **Vedic** rituals (**Shrauta Sutras**), for domestic rites (**Grhya Sutras**), and for suitable human behavior (**Dharma Sutras**).

He is one of three authors, along with **Baudhayana** and **Hiranyakeshin**, who wrote complete Kalpa Sutras with all three parts. All three of these men belonged to the same school, the Taittiriya school of the **Black Yajur Veda**.

Apastamba's Dharma Sutra is extremely significant, for it is considered one of the major sources for the law code attributed to **Manu**. This code was an important legal document even in the early twentieth century, since India's British rulers considered it a source of "traditional" Hindu law.

Appar

(7th c. C.E.) One of the earliest of the **Nayanars**, a group of southern Indian poet-saints who were devotees (**bhakta**) of the god **Shiva**. The Nayanars helped to revitalize the Hindu religion through their passionate devotion (**bhakti**) to a personal god, conveyed through hymns sung in the **Tamil language**.

Historians believe that Appar was born into a Shaivite family but became a Jain **ascetic** in his youth. The turning point came when he suffered a serious illness. Discouraged when Jain medicines were unable to cure his illness, he prayed to Shiva for help and was cured.

Along with his younger contemporary **Sambandar**, Appar actively confronted and opposed the heterodox sects of the times, particularly the Jains, with open defiance, debates, and miracles. His greatest achievement is reported to have been the conversion of King **Mahendravarman** (r. 600–630 C.E.), one of the greatest kings in the **Pallava dynasty**, from Jainism to Shaivism.

The collected hymns of the three most important Nayanars—Appar, Sambandar, and **Sundaramurtti**—comprise the **Devaram**, the most sacred of the Tamil Shaivite texts.

Appaya Dikshita

Sixteenth-century writer and commentator in the **Bhamati** branch of the **Advaita Vedanta** philosophical school.

Aprashasta ("reprehensible") Marriages

According to the texts on religious duty (**dharma**) known as the **Dharma Shastras**, these are the four forms of marriage subject to disapproval: the **asura marriage**, **gandharva marriage**, **rakshasa marriage**, and **paishacha marriage**. Although all of these are considered reprehensible, this disapproval comes in differing measures: the asura (paying money for a bride) and gandharva (betrothal by mutual consent) marriages are tolerated, while the rakshasa (forcible abduction) and paishacha (taking advantage of an insentient woman) forms are forbidden.

Despite such harsh condemnation, all of these marriages are held to be legally valid. It is generally agreed that this position was intended not to legitimatize unconscionable actions but to give the woman the legal rights of a wife, whatever the circumstances of her marriage. The asura marriage is the only one of these forms still practiced in modern times, although it is done only by people who are either very poor or of very low social status.

Apsara

In Hindu mythology, a class of celestial nymphs renowned for their beauty, **grace**, and irresistible attractiveness. One of their main mythic functions is to seduce **ascetics** and sages when they become too powerful. Because ascetics practice **celibacy**, and it is assumed that celibacy builds spiritual power, successful ascetics can become rivals to the gods themselves. Sexual activity will quickly exhaust the ascetic's power, although it can often bring other benefits to the world, including the **birth** of children, which always results from such intimate encounters.

The apsaras are sent on their missions by **Indra**, the king of **heaven**, since any ascetic who gains too much power will be able to claim Indra's divine throne. One famous apsara is **Menaka**, whose seduction of the sage **Vishvamitra** results in the birth of **Shakuntala**. Another is **Urvashi**, who is renowned for her dalliance with King **Pururavas**.

Apurva

According to the **Purva Mimamsa** philosophical school, apurva is an unseen force created by action—particularly ritual action. This unseen force exists from the beginning of the action to the result of that action, and it invariably brings the intended result into being. This doctrine was developed to connect actions with their results, particularly when the result came some time after the initial action, and is especially relevant to **karma**.

The Mimamsas developed the concept of the apurva because they wanted to support information found in the **Vedas**, which in many cases specifies that certain actions will eventually produce specific results. For further information see Sarvepalli Radhakrishnan and Charles A. Moore (eds.), *A Sourcebook in Indian Philosophy*, 1957.

Aranya Dashanami

One of the ten divisions of the **Dashanami Sanyasis**, **ascetics** who are devotees (**bhakta**) of **Shiva**. The Dashanamis were supposedly established by the ninth-century philosopher **Shankaracharya** in an effort to

An arati lamp is waved before an image of the god Ganesh before the statue is immersed in water.
The light from the flame is considered a religious offering.

create a corps of learned men who could help to revitalize Hindu life. Each of the divisions is designated by a different name—in this case, aranya ("forest"). Upon **initiation**, new members are given this name as a surname to their new ascetic names, thus allowing for immediate group identification.

Aside from their individual identity, these ten "named" divisions are divided into four larger organizational groups. Each group has its headquarters in one of the four monastic centers (**maths**) also established by Shankaracharya. The Aranya Dashanamis belong to the **Bhogawara** group, which is affiliated with the **Govardhan Math** in the city of **Puri**, on the Bay of Bengal.

Aranyaka

("Forest books") General designation for a type of literature contained in the sacred texts known as the **Vedas**. The Aranyakas are transitional in nature; in their content they move away from the focus on ritual and **sacrifice** found in the **Brahmana** literature and foreshadow the later, more speculative texts known as the **Upanishads**.

Because of their name, the Aranyakas are widely believed to have been composed in the forests, perhaps by **ascetics** who had left formal society. The tone in these texts is questioning and speculative, and in stylistic terms there is no clear break between the Aranyakas and the Upanishads: one of the earliest upanishads is named **Brhadaranyaka** ("Great Forest-Book") **Upanishad**, which reinforces the connection.

Arati

The act of waving a lighted lamp before a **deity**. The deity may be present in many forms, such as a picture, statue, symbol (**svayambhu image**) such as the **shalagram**, or even a natural phenomenon such as a river, as in the case of the **Ganges**.

The arati lamp usually is a shallow vessel holding a cotton wick soaked in oil or clarified butter, with a ring-shaped handle to protect one's hands. This is one of the sixteen traditional **offerings** (**upacharas**) presented to a deity as part of **worship**. This particular act is the offering of light.

Arati is arguably the single most common act of Hindu worship, performed daily in Hindu homes and temples throughout the world. Because of this fact, the word *arati* is sometimes used to refer to any act of worship, even singing panegyric hymns during worship. Before electric lights were invented, when the temples were much darker, arati also served to give the devotees (**bhakta**) in the temples a better view of the deity, which was very important.

Aravalli Hills

A range of hills running diagonally from the southwestern to the northeastern corner of **Rajasthan**. They are important for their physical characteristics, which have a profound effect on the environment. On the northern side of the hills, the land slopes gently into the Thar desert and is arid and thinly settled. On the southern side, the hills provide more protection. As a result the land is greener and comparatively richer than on the northern side.

Sacred sites (**tirthas**) in the Aravallis include the town of **Pushkar**, with its holy lake, as well as the temple devoted to **Balaji**, which is located in the village of **Mehndipur**.

Archana

("salutation") Rites of welcome and reverence, usually performed during formal **worship** of a **deity** in a temple. In a larger sense, this word can also refer to those rites of reverence and salutation performed for one's elders, superiors, or any honored guest.

Architecture

Hindu temple architecture in India has developed over time into several distinct, mature styles. The earliest phases are based on early Buddhist architectural forms, such as the rock-cut cave temple (**chaitya**) or enclosed courtyard (**vihara**). Some of these early Hindu rock-cut temples include those at **Ellora** and **Elephanta**; others are free-standing but based on this form, as at **Aihole**.

Later Hindu architecture has three basic styles: **Nagara**, **Dravida**, and **Veshara**, of which the first two are the most important. Each of these styles is found in a certain area of India: the Nagara in the north and east, the Dravida in the south, and the Veshara in the west and in **Deccan**. The basic differences between them can be simplified to the different styles of the temple towers.

The Nagara style emphasizes verticality, with the whole temple building culminating in a single highest point. Different emphases in the ways of treating the tower led to different substyles: In the temples at **Khajuraho**, the entire structure gradually leads up to the central tower, whereas the **Orissa** style stresses a single enormous tower surrounded by much smaller subsidiary parts.

In the Dravida style, the towers tend to be composed of horizontal tiers, with the visual emphasis on horizontal rather than vertical. In the later Dravida temples, the tallest structures are the **gopurams**, the central gateways in the walls enclosing the temples. A Dravida-style temple may have a fairly modest tower over the central shrine, but the area covered by the temple is often enormous, and many of them are cities in their own right.

The Veshara style has a barrel roof over the sanctuary, an architectural

An image of the deity Ardhanarishvara in Mahabalipuram. A form of the god Shiva, Ardhanarishvara is half male and half female.

feature with roots in the Buddhist chaityas (rock-cut cave temples). This architectural style is midway between the Nagara towers and the Dravida tiers.

Ardha ("Half") Kumbha Mela

A religious celebration secondary to the **Kumbha Mela**. The Kumbha Mela is a gigantic religious festival that entails bathing (**snana**) in sacred rivers. It is celebrated at four sacred sites (**tirthas**): **Haridwar**, **Allahabad**, **Ujjain**, and **Nasik**. It occurs approximately every twelve years, based on the position of the planet **Jupiter** in the **zodiac**.

The Ardha Kumbha Mela is celebrated six years after the full (purna) Kumbha Mela, when Jupiter has advanced halfway through the zodiac toward the next full Kumbha Mela. It is generally celebrated only at Allahabad and Haridwar, marking the greater importance of these two sites. Although the full Kumbha Mela is deemed more auspicious and gets much larger attendance, the Ardha Kumbha Mela is still attended by millions of pilgrims.

Ardhamandapa

("half pavilion") In the later **Nagara** style of temple **architecture**, the ardhamandapa was the entrance porch of the temple, which formed a transitional area between the outside world and the **mandapa**, or hall.

Ardhanarishvara

("the **deity** who is half woman") Particular form of the god **Shiva**, in which the left side of the image has female form, dress, and ornamentation, and the right side has male characteristics and dress.

The image has several possible interpretations. As a divinity one of Shiva's attributes is his ability to transcend all duality, and this half-woman, half-man image symbolizes that power over even the most basic human difference, sexual identity. In the context of the esoteric ritual tradition known as **tantra**, which describes the universe as the product of the interaction between the divine principles of awareness (Shiva) and power (**Shakti**), this image symbolizes not only the radically different natures of these two principles, but also their inseparability in action.

The Ardhanarishvara is sometimes referred to as the androgyne; this term seems inappropriate, however, since the image does not show the loss of sexual characteristics associated with androgyny but rather the full development of each on their respective sides.

Arghya

The fourth of the sixteen traditional **upacharas** ("**offerings**") given to a **deity** as a part of **worship**. The upacharas are based on the model of treating the deity as an honored guest. The word *arghya* literally means "to be respected"; in this offering the image is given a drink of **water** or some other beverage as a sign of respect.

The actual act of offering can be done in various ways and often depends on the worshiper's preferences. In some cases the water vessel will simply be presented before the deity's image, with the understanding that the deity has taken it, whereas in other cases the devotee (**bhakta**) will actually give some water to the image. In either case the underlying motive is to show love for the deity and to minister to its needs.

Arjuna

The third of the five **Pandava** brothers in the *Mahabharata*, the later of the two great Hindu epics. Arjuna is born when his mother, **Kunti**, uses a powerful **mantra** to have a **son** by **Indra**, the king of the gods.

Arjuna is the prototypical **kshatriya** warrior-king. He is described as peerless in battle, a hero ever ready to defend the truth, and a person always faithful to his word—but at times arrogant, egocentric, quick to anger, and inclined to use force to settle disputes.

Arjuna is most famous as an archer, as which he has no equal. When he and his brothers are studying archery with their teacher **Drona**, Arjuna outshines them all with his dedication and ability, but his spiteful side can be seen in the story of **Ekalavya**. Ekalavya is a tribal boy who wants to learn archery from Drona, the royal archery teacher, but is refused because of his low **birth**. Undaunted, Ekalavya makes a clay image of Drona, treats it as his teacher (**guru**), and through his assiduous practice and his devotion to his guru becomes the most skilled archer on **earth**. When Arjuna discovers this, he becomes jealous and complains to Drona, since the teacher has promised Arjuna that no one will surpass him as an archer. Drona asks Ekalavya how he has become so skillful, and when he learns that Ekalavya has worshiped Drona's image as his guru, Drona notes that he is entitled to a preceptor's fee (**dakshina**). As his fee he requests Ekalavya's right thumb, a gift that will considerably diminish Ekalavya's shooting abilities since its loss will impair his ability to draw a bow. Ekalavya fulfills Drona's wish without hesitation but from that day on he is no longer better than Arjuna.

Another instance of Arjuna's narrow-mindedness comes in his claim that another great rival, **Karna**, cannot compete in a royal shooting competition because Karna is a foundling, and his lineage is thus unknown. Karna is a close companion of Arjuna's cousin **Duryodhana**, and because of this insult the relations begin to deteriorate between the Pandavas and the **Kauravas**, the two branches of this extended family. The final result is the fratricidal civil war that is the climax of the epic.

Throughout the *Mahabharata*, Arjuna is associated with numerous heroic exploits. To fulfill a promise given to his teacher Drona, Arjuna defeats King **Drupada**, who has earlier insulted Drona. Through a feat of archery, he wins the hand of **Draupadi** by drawing a bow that others cannot even lift and then hits a target suspended in the air. He aids the **fire** god, **Agni**, in the burning of the **Khandava forest**. He shields Agni from the rain by creating a tent of arrows that keeps the forest covered. During the year that the Pandavas spend incognito, after twelve years of exile in the forest, Arjuna takes the guise of the eunuch **Brhannala** and in this guise wins a great battle against the Kauravas.

His greatest exploits occur during the epic's climactic eighteen-day war, in which he defeats the Kaurava armies, fights all their major figures, and finally kills his long-standing adversary Karna, who is actually his own half brother. After destroying the Kauravas in the Mahabharata war, Arjuna serves his elder brother, **Yudhishthira**, who becomes king; after the conflict, however, the need for such a warrior has passed.

Arjuna is also known as a listener. At the moment when the great war is about to begin, Arjuna has sudden doubts about the propriety of killing his friends and relatives, even during a just war. To allay his doubts and to help him regain his resolve, his charioteer **Krishna** recites the **Bhagavad Gita**, one of the single most influential Hindu religious texts. The Gita's advice on the nature of Self, struggle, and the search for God has served to counsel those fighting literal and metaphorical battles, most notably **Mohandas K. Gandhi** during the struggle for Indian independence.

Arranged Marriage

A marriage that is arranged by the parents of the bride and groom, although it has become fairly common for the prospective couple to meet beforehand to assess whether or not they are compatible.

Although this practice seems strange by mainstream American standards, proponents of arranged marriages see them as better and longer lasting than **love marriages**. It is assumed that with arranged marriages parents will be able to take a more detached and rational perspective. They will usually choose spouses who come from similar social and economic backgrounds, in many cases from the same **jati**, or social subgroup. Parents may compare their children's horoscopes for clues, and they may also try to match people with compatible personalities. Ideally, all of this is done with great care and with the understanding that their highest priority will be their children's long-term welfare. Marriage is widely seen as the most important event in a person's life since it is the basis of family life, and the family

is the foundation of society. Part of the marriage negotiations between the two sides includes whether or not the bride will have a **dowry**, and if she will, what this will be.

One of the assumptions with arranged marriages is that men and **women** will play fairly traditional roles. This gives the couple some idea of what to expect and what is expected of them, but it can also be confining for people who do not wish to fulfill such roles. At least in northern India, the adjustments often fall much more heavily on the new bride, since she will become part of her husband's family.

Arranged marriages are still extremely popular among modern Hindu families, and many young people would not dream of fixing their own marriages. A practical consideration supporting the popularity of arranged marriages is that it is often difficult for young people to meet and develop the friendships that could lead to love marriages. Indian society is still very sex segregated. Social interaction between unrelated single men and women is still uncommon in villages and smaller towns, although this pattern is breaking down in larger cities since more women are working outside the home.

In both contexts the biggest mixing place tends to be the college or university, but even there women and men tend to associate in groups rather than as individuals. In a society in which contact is limited, and formal dating even more unusual, an arranged marriage is often the best way to find a compatible spouse.

Arsha Marriage

One of the eight ways to perform a marriage recognized in the **Dharma Shastras**, the treatises on religious duty (**dharma**). In an arsha marriage, the bride's father receives a pair of cattle from the bridegroom with the understanding that the cattle are to be used for sacrifice.

This was regarded as one of the four approved forms of marriage (**prashasta marriages**) but fell out of favor because of the stigma of accepting any sort of gift for the bride, even one explicitly designated for sacrifice. The form was named after the **rishis** (sages) because of the implicit sacrificial rites. See also **marriage, eight classical forms**.

Artha

In Indian **philosophy** this is one of the four purusharthas, or **aims of life**, with the others being **kama** (desire), **dharma** (religious duty), and **moksha** (final liberation of the soul). The word *artha* has different shades of meaning in various contexts, but all of these meanings center on the definitions "aim," "goal," or "end." The word can thus refer to any goal of human life, but as one of these purusharthas, artha refers to riches, power, and worldly prosperity. These are the material things that allow one to fulfill one's temporal goals, and unless one gains them in some measure, any sort of worldly happiness becomes problematic.

Hindu culture has traditionally sanctioned wealth and power as a legitimate human goal, although this endeavor must be governed by a commitment to dharma. When controlled by an overall orientation to righteous action, the quest for wealth is part of an integrated life. Without this commitment the drive for wealth becomes an all-consuming desire that ultimately destroys a person.

Arthapatti

("presumption") All Indian philosophical schools concern themselves with codifying the **pramanas**, that is, the means by which human beings can gain true and accurate knowledge. Almost all schools consider perception (**pratyaksha**), inference (**anumana**), and authoritative testimony (**shabda**) as pramanas; the **Purva Mimamsa** school, one of the **six schools** of traditional Hindu **philosophy**, posited two others: **abhava** ("knowledge from absence") and arthapatti.

Arthapatti is an inference from circumstance in which a judgment is made about one case based solely on similarities to related cases. An example would be when a traveler is presumed to have reached her destination, since the train's arrival time has passed. According to Indian philosophy, this is not a true inference since the judgment must always be confirmed by direct perception, in this case that the train had actually reached its destination. The Purva Mimamsas justified this new pramana by arguing that this knowledge could not be accounted for by any of the existing pramanas and thus required this new one to explain it. The other schools were not inclined to accept it, since its presumptive nature could often lead to error.

Arthashastra

("Treatise on Power") Text on power and politics attributed to **Kautilya**, the Machiavellian prime minister said to have orchestrated the rise to power of **Chandragupta Maurya** (r. 321–297 B.C.E.), the founder of the **Maurya dynasty**. The *Arthashastra* was intended as a guidebook for the king, to help him control both the people in his kingdom and the surrounding states.

The *Arthashastra*'s fundamental assumption was that the king wanted to remain in power and should do whatever it took to retain it.

Within the kingdom, Kautilya advocated a strict and authoritarian government aided by an extensive network of spies to gather intelligence and assess the popular mood. These spies included men posing as wandering **ascetics**, who could move about without suspicion. The book also advised the king to assign special spies to his closest advisers to monitor their ambition, and to have these spies report only to the king himself.

In regard to neighboring countries, the *Arthashastra* assumed that each king wanted to increase his kingdom at the expense of his neighbors. Weaker neighbors were to be conquered and assimilated, whereas stronger ones were to be pacified or stalled with the eventual hope that these stronger states could be countered by making other alliances.

Although the *Arthashastra* was never the "Bible" of any ruling Indian dynasty, it detailed political **philosophy** and practices that existed in ancient and medieval India and can even be discerned in contemporary parliamentary politics.

Arundhati

The wife of the sage **Vasishtha**. In Hindu mythology Arundhati is a model of devotion to her husband, and during contemporary **marriage ceremonies**, she is invoked by the groom as a model of wifely fidelity. Arundhati is also personified as the minor star Alcor in the constellation known as the Big Dipper (known in India as the Seven Sages because of its seven main stars); here she accompanies the star personifying her husband.

Aryabhatta

Ancient astronomer and mathematician, whose major work was composed in 499 C.E. Among Aryabhatta's accomplishments were his theories that the **earth** was a sphere that rotated on its axis, and that **eclipses** were caused by the shadow of the **moon**. He also calculated the value of *pi* to four decimal places and the length of the **year** to seven decimal places. Both these feats show not only great facility with mathematics but also the use of the zero.

Although Aryabhatta is celebrated as a scientist, in the ancient world there was no differentiation between astronomer and astrologer. Given the assumption that the heavenly bodies influenced human affairs, his astronomical conclusions would have also been used in the field of astrology.

Aryan

This word is derived from the **Sanskrit** word *arya* ("noble"), which is used in the earliest Hindu sacred literature, the **Vedas**, to describe a certain group of people that believed the Vedas were sacred. In the beginning this word simply designated "our group" from "other people," whom the Veda names **Dasyus** ("slaves"). These provide a description of the slaves as having flat noses and curly **hair**. Throughout history Hindu writers have often described themselves as "Arya," although it is important to note that this need not be understood as a racial designation, since it could merely be intended to mean "noble."

Who were these Aryans? Nineteenth-century European philological research discovered structural relationships between Sanskrit and classical European languages and speculated that all these languages came from a common parent. Based on further analysis, these researchers hypothesized that people speaking this parent language originated in Central Asia, somewhere near the Caspian Sea. From there, some went west to Europe, some went southwest to Turkey, and some went south toward Iran and later to India. The conclusion that these Indian pilgrims came from Iran is based on comparisons between the Avesta and the Veda, the Iranian and Indian religious texts. These texts show broad linguistic similarities and indicate that the people speaking the languages were closely related. This entire theory is thus based solely on the observed similarities between languages and on how they changed.

For the nineteenth-century philologists, "Aryan" was a linguistic category used to designate people speaking certain languages and involved no assumptions about the speakers' racial identity. Despite this fact, the word quickly assumed a racial connotation in European discourse, with terrible consequences.

The Aryan movement was once described as an "invasion," but in recent years it has become more common to describe it as a "migration." According to the accounts in the Vedas, the Aryans were a pastoral people, and although some Vedic passages mention war chariots, the majority describe herds of cattle. Given this picture of nomads following their cattle to pasture, the image of an invading army seems improbable.

The Aryan migration theory accounts for the dissemination of various languages but is not universally accepted. Many modern Indians subscribe to the **Indigenous Aryan** (IA) **theory**, which maintains that the Aryans are the original inhabitants of India and as proof points to the artifacts found in the **Indus Valley civilization**. Some of the people that believe the IA theory may be reacting against the Aryan migration theory's perceived colonialist bias, since the theory was developed by Europeans and assumes that the dominant groups in modern India must have come from outside. Other supporters are the proponents of **Hindutva**, who claim that all Indians are "really" Hindus and thus one social group, whatever their particular religious beliefs.

This assertion has profound political implications in modern India, where Christians and Muslims are not only religious communities but social and political ones as well. By connecting Hindu identity with good Indian citizenship, Hindutva proponents are marginalizing Christians and Muslims as outsiders.

Arya Samaj

Reformist Hindu organization formed in 1875 by **Swami Dayanand Saraswati**. The Arya Samaj was formed in an era of sweeping social, economic, and religious change—the last particularly caused by Christian missionary evangelism—and represented an authentic Hindu response to these changes.

For some time, more traditional Hindus perceived this organization as a genuine religious threat. Swami Dayanand's fundamental assumption was that ultimate religious authority lay only in the ancient scriptures called the **Vedas**. This stance allowed him to attack many of the "social evils" plaguing nineteenth-century Hinduism, such as child marriages, **sati**, image **worship**, the **caste** system, and a ban on **widow** remarriage. He contended that these practices were corrupt and illegitimate since they could not be found in the Veda, and the Arya Samaj worked ceaselessly to get rid of such practices.

Unlike the **Brahmo Samaj**, an earlier reformist organization, the ideas of the Arya Samaj showed no Christian influence. It certainly addressed many concerns raised by Christian reformers, but the Arya Samaj was militantly anti-Christian. It was equally opposed to the "corruption" of contemporary Hinduism.

Although the Aryas claimed that they were simply getting back to the Veda, the ultimate aim was not to reclaim that long-gone era but to develop a form of Hindu religious life more compatible with "modern" times. The Aryas replaced image worship with a **fire sacrifice** based on the rituals in the Veda. The Arya Samaj was also notable for promoting the ceremony of "purification" (**shuddhi**), through which Hindus who had become members of other religious communities were received back into the Hindu community.

Dayanand and his followers were quite militant in espousing such reforms and saw themselves as developing the leadership for the future of Hinduism. To accomplish this the Arya Samaj strongly emphasized education, and one of its most lasting achievements has been establishing schools and colleges to educate its **women** and men.

Although the Arya Samaj was highly controversial for its first sixty years, by the late 1930s its revolutionary spirit had somewhat cooled; at present the Aryas have become a sectarian group more or less assimilated into larger Hindu

A man practices the fetus position.
This asana, or bodily posture,
is one of many that are used in yoga.

society. For further information see Ganga Prasad Upadhyaya (trans.), *Light of Truth*, 1960; Kenneth W. Jones, *Arya Dharm*, 1976; Daniel Gold, "Organized Hinduisms: From Vedic Truth to Hindu Nation," in Martin Marty and R. Scott Appleby (eds.), *Fundamentalisms Observed*, 1991; and Kenneth W. Jones, "The Arya Samaj in British India, 1875–1947," in Robert D. Baird (ed.), *Religion in Modern India*, 1998.

Asamanjasa

In Hindu mythology, the son of the celebrated King **Sagar** and his wife **Keshini**. Keshini has received a boon that she will bear a single son through whom the royal lineage will continue, whereas her co-wife **Sumati** will bear sixty thousand **sons** who will all die before they are married. Asamanjasa is that single son, but his character is so bad that his lineage, the **Solar Line**, seems to be in grave danger.

In the **Ramayana**, the earlier of the two great Hindu epics, the only mention of Asamanjasa describes how he throws children into the Sarayu River and then laughs as they drown. Fortunately for the Solar Line, which is one of the two great lineages, Asamanjasa's son **Anshuman** is very virtuous, and the line continues both unbroken and uncorrupted.

Asana

("bodily posture") In the **ashtanga** ("eight-part") **yoga** first codified by **Patanjali** (1st c. C.E.?), asana is the third of the eight elements of yoga practice and involves different body postures. In his text, Patanjali asserts that one's physical position should be stable and comfortable, since the ultimate end of these postures is to enable one to concentrate without physical distractions. A series of positions for developing and training the body evolved from this text. The most familiar of these is the lotus posture (**padmasana**).

These physical exercises are the best-known feature of yoga and are often confused with the larger practice of yoga itself. Although these postures have definite physical benefits, such as increased bodily flexibility, their ultimate purpose is to enable one to sit for long periods in meditation without physical distractions. As such, they are a necessary element for progress on the spiritual path but should not be confused with the end goal.

In a more general context, the word *asana* can refer to various ways of sitting, and by extension to the thing upon which one sits. In general the object upon which one sits—particularly for meditation or any sort of religious practice—is believed to be charged with power because of its association with spirituality. Many of these objects, especially **animal** skins, are believed to confer certain powers and thus have symbolic meaning as well.

In the context of **worship**, asana is the second of the sixteen **upacharas** ("**offerings**") given to a **deity** as a way of treating the god as an honored guest. In this case asana refers to offering the deity a place to sit, one of the most basic acts of human hospitality.

Asat

This word denotes a general category in Indian speculative thought and is often translated as "nonbeing." It is the absolute opposite of **sat** and is formed by the addition of the negative prefix. If sat is "that which (really and truly) exists," then its opposite is "that which does not exist." Since the word *sat* also carries connotations of Truth—that things that exist are both "real" and "true"—*asat* carries connotations of falseness.

Asatkaryavada

One of the three basic **causal models** in classical Indian **philosophy**, along with **satkaryavada** and **anekantavada**. All three models seek to explain the workings of causality in the everyday world, particularly the relationship between causes and their effects, which has profound implications for religious life. All of the philosophical schools assume that if one understands the causal process correctly and can manipulate it through one's conscious actions, it is possible to gain final liberation of the soul (**moksha**). Thus disagreements over differing causal models are not merely academic disputes but are grounded in varying assumptions about the nature of things.

The asatkaryavada model assumes that effects do not preexist in their causes; that is, they are completely and utterly distinct from them. In the classic examples for this model, one can create a clay pot by putting together the two halves of the pot, or one can weave a cloth from many strands of thread. Each of these acts creates a new object that did not previously exist, which came into being through certain material and instrumental causes.

Since each act of creation brings a new thing into being, this causal model tends to multiply the number of objects in the universe. It also admits that human efforts and actions are part of the causes influencing these effects, making it theoretically possible to act in a way that brings final liberation to the soul.

The disadvantage of this model is that it can lead to philosophical skepticism. As the world gets fragmented into more and more causes—most of which one cannot control—one can easily believe that one's actions will have no discernible effect, even over time. To counter this danger of skepticism, asatkaryavada proponents stress the conditions that govern the causal process and gear people's efforts accordingly.

This model is espoused by the **Nyaya Vaisheshikas** and the **Prabhakara** school of **Purva Mimamsa**, as well as by the Buddhists. For further information see Karl H. Potter (ed.), *Presuppositions of India's Philosophies*, 1972.

Ascetic

In the most general sense, this word denotes a person who has renounced regular society and conventional social life in a quest to seek religious insight and to gain final liberation of the soul (**moksha**). Such spiritual seekers sometimes emphasize **asceticism** or physical discipline, but this is not a necessary element.

Ascetics can be organized into different subgroups based upon organizational affiliation or the particular Hindu **deity** that they **worship**. The **Bairagis**, **Dashanami Sanyasis**, and **Nathpanthis** are all well-defined ascetic organizations into which one must undertake formal **initiation**; the Bairagis are devotees (**bhakta**) of the god **Vishnu**, and the other two are devotees of **Shiva**.

The **sadhu** ("straight") is the other major type of ascetic and the most difficult to define. Most sadhus are unaffiliated with any religious organization, have undertaken no formal ascetic initiation, and fall outside the other groups' sectarian boundaries. A sadhu is a solitary religious seeker, driven to attain religious goals by doing whatever seems best to him (or more rarely, to her).

Asceticism

In the most general sense, this word denotes physical discipline, most often the renunciation of regular society and conventional social life in a quest to seek religious insight and to gain final liberation of the soul (**moksha**).

Historically, **ascetic** practice has stressed several constant themes. One of the most common has been **celibacy**, for a variety of reasons. Not only does sexual enjoyment use the senses to trap a person, but the attachments caused by home and family are seen as a distraction to serious spiritual life. Yet the emphasis on celibacy is also motivated by the belief that **semen** is a man's concentrated essence, and thus it is something to be carefully hoarded. Although semen must be expended for procreation, it should not be spilled casually since this drains away a man's vitality. It is believed that energy gained from celibacy leads to greater spiritual accomplishment.

Another hallmark has been the practice of **tapas**, or physical asceticism, under the assumption that enduring physical hardship not only builds character but also generates spiritual power. At times tapas can assume grotesque forms of self-mutilation and mortification. At other times it may be a milder physical discipline, such as a form of **hatha yoga**, to train the body and mind for extended practice.

In general, ascetic spiritual development can proceed along a variety of different paths, which often reflect the abilities and inclinations of the ascetics following them. Some paths have stressed the importance of traditional learning, some have stressed **worship** and devotion, some have stressed physical asceticism, and some have stressed meditation and individual realization. In almost all cases, this spiritual training takes place under the direction of a religious preceptor (**guru**), who takes responsibility for the spiritual development of his disciples.

Asceticism in India has a long and venerable history, although there is considerable disagreement regarding how long and how venerable. The most ambitious claim is that the Indian ascetic tradition comes from the religion of the **Indus Valley civilization**. This claim is based on one of the **Indus Valley seals**, an ancient artifact that shows a figure sitting cross-legged as if in meditation.

Whether or not one accepts this claim, there is ample evidence of asceticism in the **Vedas**, the earliest Hindu scriptures. The Vedas mention renunciant figures, such as the **vratya**, **yati**, and **muni**, and also refer to ascetics living in the forest. Indeed, the very name of one stratum of the Veda, the **Aranyakas** or "Forest Books," suggests that it was composed by such ascetics. Buddhist and Jain literature clearly shows that ascetic life was well established by the fifth century B.C.E., as do some of the later upanishads. All of these ascetics, whether Hindu, Buddhist, or Jain, were designated under the umbrella term **shramana**, a word whose basic meaning is "to strive." It is generally accepted that there was religious tension between the two dominant religious paradigms, the **Brahmana** ideal connected with Vedic religion and the shramana ideal associated with asceticism. The Brahmana ideal was based on **sacrifice**, mastery of complex sacred texts, and hereditary priesthood; furthermore, it was so expensive that it virtually required royal patrons—all of these factors rendering it the "establishment religion." These concepts clashed with the shramana ideal, which was renunciant, individualist, and stressed inner experience.

By the time of the **Dharma Shastras** (treatises on religious duty), this tension had been somewhat resolved; asceticism had been relegated to the last of the four ashramas (**stages of life**), that of the **Sanyasi**. Yet even here the tension remains, since according to these texts, a **twice-born** man cannot become a Sanyasi until he has seen his children's children, which would make him well advanced in years. These texts restrict asceticism to twice-born men who have fulfilled their obligations as householders, but they deny it to **women** and low-**caste** men. Needless to say, the actual picture has never been quite as neat as the idealized society found in the Dharma Shastras.

Organizationally, initiated Hindu ascetics can be divided into several major groups. One division is based on the ascetics' patron deity; the **Shaiva** are devotees (**bhakta**) of **Shiva**, and the **Vaishnava** worship **Vishnu**.

The **Kapalikas**, **Kalamukhas**, and **Pashupatas** are Shaiva ascetic groups that have disappeared; the two Shaiva groups that still survive are the **Dashanamis** and the **Nathpanthis**. The Dashanamis are the most prestigious of all ascetics. They were supposedly organized by the great philosopher **Shankaracharya** and have traditionally emphasized learning. The Nathpanthis trace their origin to **Gorakhnath**, a miracle-working **yogi** about whom little is definitely known. The Nathpanthis are known for their stress on the transformation of the physical body through **yoga**.

Vaishnava ascetics are more recently organized, and in northern India they are broken into four groups (**chatuhsampradayi Nagas**), named after each group's reported founder: **Ramananda** for the **Ramanandis**, **Nimbarka** for the **Nimbarkis**, **Chaitanya** for the Madhva Gaudiyas (**Brahma Sampraday**), and **Vishnuswami** for the Vishnuswamis.

From at least the sixteenth century, and perhaps much earlier, both the Dashanamis and the Vaishnava ascetics organized bands of fighters known as **Nagas** ("naked"). These soldier-ascetics were commissioned to protect the other ascetics, but they also served as long-distance traders and mercenary soldiers. These Naga orders still exist today, although they are no longer prepared for battle. Another important sect is the **Udasis**, who worship the panchayatana ("five-fold"), a collection of five Hindu **deities**: Shiva, Vishnu, **Durga**, **Ganesh**, and **Surya**. Religiously speaking, the Udasis thus fall between the Shaivas and Vaishnavas.

In the past few centuries, reform-minded ascetics have organized their own ascetic bands, a process that still continues today. For further information see G. S. Ghurye, *Indian Sadhus*, 1964; Jadunath Sarkar, *A History of the Dasanami Naga Sanyasis*, 1958; Padmanabh S. Jaini, "Sramanas: Their Conflict with Brahmanical Society," in Joseph Elder (ed.), *Chapters in Indian Civilization*, 1970; Robert Lewis Gross, *The Sadhus of India*, 1992; and Peter van der Veer, *Gods on Earth*, 1988. See also **panchayatana puja**.

Ashadh

According to the lunar **calendar**, by which most Hindu religious festivals are celebrated, Ashadh is the fourth month in the lunar **year**, usually falling within June and July. In northern India, this is usually the hottest month of the year.

The major holidays celebrated in Ashadh are **Yogini Ekadashi**, the **Rath Yatra**, **Devshayani Ekadashi**, and **Guru Purnima**. Devshayani Ekadashi also marks the beginning of the **Chaturmas Vrat**.

This is a four-month (lunar) period generally coinciding with the rainy **season**. During this time the god **Vishnu** is believed to be "sleeping," and because of this the period is considered inauspicious.

Men wash the body of a deceased man to prepare it for cremation.
A dead body is considered to be a potent source of ashaucha, or impurity.

Ashaucha

("impurity") Name for the ritual impurity caused by contact with any source of pollution; these sources come in many different guises, both physical and social.

Purity and impurity are religious categories and thus fundamentally different from cleanliness and dirtiness, which are hygienic categories. For example, **cow dung** is considered a pure substance in traditional Hindu society and is smeared on patches of ground to purify it. It is also important to realize that impurity is a natural part of life—as just one example, everyone goes to the bathroom every day—and that becoming impure carries no sense of moral imperfection or lapse.

Most bodily fluids are considered polluting; one becomes impure through any activity involving them, such as urination, defecation, sexual activity, giving **birth**, or being born. One can become polluted through contact with people or things deemed impure, such as people of lower social status, **animals**, any sort of ordinary filth, or even the dust from the road.

Impurity can also be caused by social connections. The impurity from childbirth (**sutakashaucha**) obviously affects the mother and child because of the bodily fluids involved, but it also affects all other members of the immediate family.

If a person has come into contact with something polluting, the solution is to remove the source of impurity. The most common means of purification is to bathe in running **water**, which removes less virulent impurities by carrying them away with the water's flow. The purifying power of bathing (**snana**) makes it a prelude to many religious rituals, in which one of the general preconditions is scrupulous purity, both for the person performing the ritual and the place where it is performed.

The most polluting substance of all is a **corpse**, which is one reason why bodies are destroyed by **cremation** on the day of death. The impurity from death (**maranashaucha**) is the most violent impurity of all, and contact with a corpse affects the entire family for ten days after the death.

For further information see Pauline Kolenda, "Purity and Pollution," in T. N. Madan (ed.), *Religion in India*, 1991.

Ashirvad

("benedictory formula") General term used to denote words of blessing, whether formal or informal. One of the basic assumptions of Hindu religious life is that certain spiritually powerful people—in particular, **ascetics** and learned **brahmins**—can confer blessings and **curses** at will. Both the blessings and curses are believed to take effect immediately and without fail, which is why a prudent person will always treat ascetics and learned brahmins with the respect that they deserve.

Ashoka

(r. 269–232 B.C.E.) The greatest ruler in the **Maurya dynasty**, who reigned over a kingdom stretching from Afghanistan to southern India from his capital at **Pataliputra**. Ashoka's father, **Bindusara**, and his grandfather, **Chandragupta Maurya**, had created a centralized empire. Aside from the far south, the only area outside its influence was the region known as Kalinga (modern state of **Orissa**).

Early in his reign, Ashoka's armies conquered Kalinga in a bloody campaign, killing hundreds of thousands of people; the carnage had a profound effect on the young Ashoka. Several years later Ashoka formally adopted Buddhism and embraced the principle of nonviolence (**ahimsa**). As a result he formally renounced war as a means of conquest.

Early historians believed that Ashoka used his royal power to make Buddhism the state religion, but this position appears to misread the evidence. Ashoka did seem to be attracted to Buddhism, but his public pronouncements on "Dhamma," earlier identified with Buddhist teaching, seem to have been aimed at creating a cli-

mate of social responsibility, tolerance, nonviolence, and harmony. These were qualities that most reasonable people would endorse, and some historians have suggested that such vague guidelines indicate an attempt to unify a religiously diverse empire.

Ashoka is by far the best-known figure of his era, largely because he set up public **inscriptions** all over his kingdom. **Rock edicts** tended to be carved on rock faces close to the empire's borders, while **pillar edicts** were inscribed on pillars erected on the main roads.

The writing used for these inscriptions varied in different regions of the empire, although the language for all was a **Prakrit**, one of the grammatically simple vernacular languages that developed from **Sanskrit**. These inscriptions are the earliest written Indian documents of any historical significance; they reveal a great deal about Ashoka's public persona, his exhortations to his subjects, and even something about the man himself.

In modern India, Ashoka is the model for the enlightened ruler, and the Ashokan pillar capped with four **lions** has been adopted as the emblem of the modern republic of India.

Ashoka Tree

(*Jonesia ashoka*) Flowering tree traditionally associated with love and fertility. When in bloom, the Ashoka tree is covered with red flowers—a color typically associated with passion—that contrast with its green foliage. According to tradition, the ashoka tree will not bloom until it has been kicked by a young woman's foot, implying the transfer of her fertile energy to the tree.

The Ashoka tree is also famous in the *Ramayana*, the earlier of the two great Hindu epics. When **Sita** is kidnapped by **Ravana**, the **demon**-king of **Lanka**, she is imprisoned in a grove of Ashoka trees, where she pines away waiting to be rescued by her husband **Rama**.

Religious leader at an ashram in Puri.

Ashram

The abode of an **ascetic** or religious renunciant. The word is derived from a form of the verb "to strive" and has several different meanings: On one hand, an ashram is also a place where one gives up one's conventional worldly striving; on the other hand, it is a place at which one can seriously strive for spiritual goals that are often less emphasized in the material world.

In modern Hinduism (both in India and abroad) the word can refer to a full spectrum of living arrangements, from a simple hut or cave inhabited by one person to magnificent building compounds that can house thousands of people at a time.

Ashrama

("stages, abodes") See **stages of life**.

Ashrama Dashanami

One of the ten divisions of the **Dashanami Sanyasis**, renunciant ascetics who are devotees (**bhakta**) of **Shiva**. The Dashanamis were supposedly established by the ninth-century philosopher **Shankaracharya** in an effort to create a corps of learned men who could help to revitalize Hindu life. Each of the divisions is designated by a different name—in this case, *ashrama* ("hermitage"). Upon **initiation**, new members are given this name as a surname to their new ascetic names, thus allowing for immediate group identification.

Aside from their individual identity, these ten "named" divisions are divided into four larger organizational groups. Each group has its headquarters in one of the four monastic centers (**maths**) supposedly established by Shankaracharya, as well as other particular religious associations. The Ashrama Dashanamis belong to the **Kitawara** group, which is affiliated with the **Sharada Math** in the city of **Dwaraka**, located near the Arabian Sea.

The Ashrama division is considered an elite group because it is one of the few that will initiate only **brahmins** (the other such divisions are the **Saraswati Dashanamis**, **Tirtha Dashanamis**, and part of the **Bharati Dashanamis**.)

Ashtachap

("eight seals") A group of eight northern Indian **bhakti** (devotional) poets: **Surdas**, **Krishnadas**, **Parmananddas**, **Kumbhadas**, **Nanddas**, **Chaturbhujdas**, **Chitswami**, and **Govindswami**.

In the sectarian literature of the **Pushti Marg**, a **Vaishnava** community whose members are devotees (**bhakta**) of **Krishna**, all eight of these poets are named as members of the sect and associates of the Pushti Marg's early leaders. Surdas, Krishnadas, Parmananddas, and Kumbhadas are connected with the Pushti Marg's founder, **Vallabhacharya** (1479–1531); Nanddas, Chaturbhujdas, Chitswami, and Govindswami are associated with Vallabha's **son** and successor, **Vitthalnath** (r. 1566–1585). Evidence of their membership can be found in their poetry, which confirms this claim for many of the poets; for Surdas, however, this claim seems highly unlikely.

Ashtadhyayi

("Eight Sections") Text composed by the **Sanskrit grammarian Panini** (ca. 4th c. B.C.E.); the text's name stems from the eight sections it contains. Panini wrote the *Ashtadhyayi* as a descriptive account of contemporary Sanskrit, but in later generations the text was transformed into the prescriptive norm for the language. Each of the *Ashtadhyayi's* eight sections is composed of a series of brief aphorisms (**sutras**), which are usually only a few words long, and refers to a specific facet of Sanskrit grammar. Each sutra in a given section builds upon all the preceding sutras, and in turn provides the foundation and background for understanding those coming after it. This sequential description means that Panini began with Sanskrit's most general linguistic features and moved from there to more specific ones. This method allowed Panini to provide a complete account of the Sanskrit language as briefly as possible, and the text's condensed form facilitated memorization. As with most sutra texts, the *Ashtadhyayi's* terseness of expression presupposes a commentary, since the sutras themselves are so short and pithy that they are simply cryptic to the uninitiated. The *Ashtadhyayi's* most famous commentary is the *Mahabhashya*, written by the grammarian **Patanjali** in the second century B.C.E.

Ashtalakshmi

Eight different forms of the **goddess** named **Lakshmi**, representing her different aspects as the source of wealth and prosperity. The eight are often portrayed as a set, although one may also encounter them separately: **Vijaya** ("victory") Lakshmi, **Jaya** ("conquest") Lakshmi, Dhana ("wealth") Lakshmi, Dhanya ("grain") Lakshmi, Gaja ("**elephant**") Lakshmi, Aishvarya ("**divine power**") Lakshmi, **Vina** (a musical instrument) Lakshmi, and Raja ("royal") Lakshmi.

Ashtanga ("eight-limbed") Yoga

System of **yoga** (religious discipline) traditionally ascribed to **Patanjali** (1st c. C.E.?). This author is believed to be dif-

ferent than the **grammarian** Patanjali, who wrote the *Mahabhashya* commentary on **Panini's Sanskrit** grammar.

Patanjali's **Yoga Sutras** are the basis for the Yoga school of Indian **philosophy**, one of the **six schools**. By the early centuries of the common era (approximately 100–300 C.E.), the Yoga school had become paired with the **Samkhya** school. In this pairing, Samkhya provided the theoretical and metaphysical explanations for the bondage and liberation of the soul, while Yoga laid out the concrete path for ending bondage and gaining liberation.

Ashtanga yoga is made up of eight parts, known as "limbs" (**anga**): restraints (**yama**), observances (**niyama**), bodily postures (**asana**), restraint of breath (**pranayama**), withdrawal of the senses (**pratyahara**), concentration (**dharana**), meditation (**dhyana**), and trance (**samadhi**).

Patanjali's system is an eight-step program for self-transformation, which begins by cultivating certain wholesome behavioral patterns (yama and niyama). From there one progresses to development and control of the mind, which is considered a more subtle and internalized practice. It culminates in a mystic insight that brings liberation, which in its original articulation is described as yogic aloneness (**kaivalya**) because Samkhya is atheistic.

Patanjali's path shows general similarities to another well-known program for self-transformation, the Buddha's eightfold path. Although both Patanjali and the Buddha are credited with originating their particular paths, it is likely that they both drew from an existing yogic tradition and shaped it to fit their own assumptions.

Although Samkhya metaphysics have long been discredited, the techniques of the Yoga school are still vitally important in modern Hindu religious life. Many modern Hindu movements stress yoga practice as a means of spiritual discipline, purification, and self-awareness. For further information see Sarvepalli Radhakrishnan and Charles

A. Moore (eds.), *A Sourcebook in Indian Philosophy*, 1957.

Ashtavakra

("eight bends") In the **Mahabharata**, the later of the two great Hindu epics, Ashtavakra is a sage who is the **son** of Khagodara. According to tradition, Ashtavakra is an exceptionally precocious child, and this gets him into serious trouble. While he is still in his mother's womb, Ashtavakra corrects his father's pronunciation of a certain **mantra**. In response his father curses him to be bent, and when the child is born he has eight bends in his body.

Despite his unusual appearance, Ashtavakra becomes a learned sage and is widely believed to be the author of the *Ashtavakragita* ("Song of Ashtavakra"). This text describes the philosophical concept of monism, which is the belief that a single Supreme Reality (named **Brahman**) lies behind the entire universe, and that all things are merely differing manifestations of this reality.

Ashutosh

("quickly satisfied") Epithet of the god **Shiva**. This name reflects Shiva's relationship with his devotees (**bhakta**), as well as his ultimate nature. When his devotees approach him with sincerity, he demands neither expensive **offerings** nor prolonged **worship**, and he extends his favor immediately. See **Shiva**.

Ashvalayana

Sage and author of one of the **Grhya Sutras**, the manuals of domestic rites. Ashvalayana's work is one of the earliest to mention the various life-cycle ceremonies (**samskaras**) and is thus an important source on these rites.

Ashvamedha

("horse **sacrifice**") Vedic sacrifice performed to display and prove royal power. In this sacrifice a specially consecrated horse was released to roam as it wished, followed by an armed band of the king's servants. When the horse wandered into a neighboring ruler's territory, that king had two choices: He could either acknowledge subordinate status to the king who had released it, or he could attempt to steal the horse, and do battle with the king's servants.

After one year of wandering, the horse was brought back to the royal capital and killed by suffocation or strangulation, so that its **blood** would not be shed. After the horse had been killed, the chief queen would lie down next to it and simulate sexual intercourse. When the instructions for this ritual were first translated in the nineteenth century, this simulated intercourse generated considerable horrified interest among European scholars, even though it was clearly a subsidiary part of the ritual.

The rite's major emphasis was a celebration of royal power, since the king performing it was able to control the territory covered in a year by a free-roaming horse. The queen's role, in contrast, seems aimed at symbolically assuring the fertility of the land. Historical records indicate that the ashvamedha was performed until the tenth century C.E. As with all other cases of **animal sacrifice**, concerns about the karmic consequences of slaughtering a living being has been an important factor in its discontinuation. See also **karma**.

Ashvattha

The sacred fig tree, *Ficus religiosa*, which in modern times is more commonly known as the pipal. The ashvattha is especially noted for its aerial roots, which extend downward from some of the limbs until they touch the ground, at which point they take root themselves. Because their roots can become subsidiary trunks, ashvattha trees can grow to be enormous. They have traditionally been favored as places for **ascetics** to dwell, in part because of their sacred associations and in part because their dense foliage provides shelter from the elements.

Their unusual structure is noted in chapter fifteen of the **Bhagavad Gita**, in which the ashvattha is described as the tree of life. The ashvattha is also believed to be the type of tree under which the Buddha attained enlightenment.

Ashvatthama

In the *Mahabharata*, the later of the two great Hindu epics, Ashvatthama is the **son** of **Drona**. When Drona becomes the archery teacher to the **Pandavas** and the **Kauravas**, the epic's two central royal families, Ashvatthama also receives instruction along with the young princes. He absorbs his father's teaching well and masters the use of terrifying magical weapons. During the *Mahabharata's* climactic civil war, he fights on the side of the Kauravas and kills many of the Pandava allies; this includes **Dhrshtadyumna**, who has earlier killed his father, Drona. After the war is over, Ashvatthama retires to the forest with the sage **Vyasa**.

Ashvin

According to the lunar **calendar**, by which most Hindu religious festivals are determined, Ashvin is the seventh month in the lunar **year**, usually falling within September and October. In Ashvin the monsoon rains usually taper off, and the weather becomes a bit cooler.

The dark (waning) half of this month is the **Pitrpaksha**, one of the most inauspicious times of the year. The bright (waxing) half contains one of the most important festivals of the year, the fall **Navaratri**, culminating in **Dussehra** or Vijaya Dashami. Other festivals during this month are **Indira Ekadashi**, **Papankusha Ekadashi**, and **Valmiki Jayanti**.

Ashvins

Twin **deities** named Satya and Dasya, who are **sons** of the god **Surya** (the **Sun**) and the physicians to the gods. In the *Mahabharata*, the later of the two great Hindu epics, the Ashvins are the divine fathers of the **Pandava** twins, **Nakula** and **Sahadeva**. Nakula and Sahadeva are born when their mother, **Madri**, uses a powerful **mantra** enabling a woman to have a child by any one of the gods; as the sons of the divine physicians, the epic portrays these twins as having their fathers' ability to heal. In the Hindu lunar **calendar**, the month of **Ashvin** (October–November) is devoted to them.

Assam

Before Indian independence in 1947, this name designated the entire territory east of Bengal province in northeastern India; in the time since independence, it was divided into seven different administrative regions, one of which is the contemporary state of Assam.

Like all other states in the northeastern corner, much of modern Assam is culturally distinct from the rest of India. One marker of this cultural divide is language: whereas most Indians speak languages from the Indo-Aryan or **Dravidian** language families, many tribal people in Assam speak Tibeto-Burman languages. The bulk of modern Assam is in the Brahmaputra River valley, which is where most of the Hindus in the northeast reside.

Despite its remoteness from the rest of India, Assam does have one very important sacred place, the temple of the **goddess Kamakhya** just outside the capital of Gauhati. This is one of the **Shakti Pithas**, a network of sites connected with the **worship** of the Mother **Goddess** that were established at places where it is believed that body parts of the dismembered goddess **Sati** fell to **earth**. Kamakhya is considered the most powerful of all the Shakti Pithas since it is believed to be where Sati's vulva (a highly charged female body part) fell to earth.

In the asthi-visarjana funeral ceremony, after cremation
the remains of a body are gathered and immersed in sacred water.

Asthi-Sanchayana

("gathering the bones") Name for a particular ceremony performed as one of the last rites (**antyeshthi samskara**) connected with death. Asthi-sanchayana is usually performed on the second or third **day** after **cremation**. In this rite, some of the remains of the deceased—bits of bone and ash—are gathered from the site of the cremation pyre. These remains are collected and kept in a safe place until their final dispersal in the last of the death rites, **asthi-visarjana**.

Asthi-Visarjana

("scattering the bones") Name for a particular ceremony performed as one of the last rites (**antyeshthi samskara**) connected with death. In this ritual, bits of bone and ash collected from the **cremation** site in the rite of **asthi-sanchayana** are immersed in the **waters** of the **Ganges** or some other sacred river. This is the final ceremony for the dead, since in earlier times the collected remains might be kept for years before a family member was able to bring them to a pilgrimage place (**tirtha**) to perform this rite. Modern transportation has changed this pattern somewhat, making it more common for asthi-visarjana to be carried out immediately after death but before the **sapindikarana** ceremony on the twelfth day.

This rite is still widely performed in modern India and remains important for at least two reasons: On one hand, there is the symbolism of redemption for the dead through consigning their ashes to the sacred waters, and on the other, providing definitive ritual closure for the living.

Astrology
See **jyotisha**.

Asura
See **demons**.

Asura Marriage

One of the eight ways to perform a marriage recognized in the **Dharma Shastras**, the treatises on religious duty (**dharma**). It is named after the asuras, a class of powerful divine beings whose interests are often at odds with those of the gods (**deva**); thus, the name carries an unfavorable connotation.

An asura marriage takes place when a man gives money to the bride's family and the bride herself. This is one of the four reprehensible (**aprashasta**) forms of marriage because of the connotation that the bride is being sold, yet like all the other reprehensible forms, it is deemed to create a valid marriage.

Despite this general disapproval, it is one of the two classical forms that is still practiced (the other being the **Brahma marriage**), although because of the stigma attached to the implication of selling one's child, it is only done by people who are either very poor or of very low social status. See also **marriage, eight classical forms**.

Atala Akhara

The name of a subgroup of the **Naga** class of the **Dashanami Sanyasis**, a particular type of renunciant **ascetic**. The Dashanami Nagas are devotees (**bhakta**) of the god **Shiva**, organized into different **akharas**, or regiments, based on the model of an army. Until the beginning of the nineteenth century, the Nagas were known as mercenary soldiers, although they also had substantial trading interests; both of these occupations have largely disappeared in contemporary times. The Atala Akhara has traditionally been considered a subsidiary of the **Mahanirvani akhara**, at least for their marching order in the bathing (**snana**) processions for the **Kumbha Mela**. During the 1998 **Haridwar** Kumbha Mela, the Atala akhara demanded to be separated from the Mahanirvanis and to be allowed to march in their own procession; when this request was turned down, the Atala akhara boycotted the bathing processions in protest. The Atala akhara is one of the seven main Dashanami Naga akharas, although it is now the smallest and least important. All of the akharas have particular features that define their organizational identity, especially specific guardian **deities**; the guardian deity of the Atala akara is the god **Ganesh**.

Atharva Veda

The Atharva Veda is the last of the four **Vedas**, which are the oldest and most authoritative Hindu religious texts. In many ways the Atharva Veda is the most unusual. Whereas the other three—**Rg Veda**, **Sama Veda**, and **Yajur Veda**—focus mainly on sacrificial rituals, the Atharva Veda is largely a collection of spells and incantations that can be used to counter or correct misfortune, and also to bring about one's desired result. Its unusual contents make it very different from the other three, and since some early sources mention only the first three Vedas, it apparently gained authority as a Veda sometime later.

Atikaya

In the *Ramayana*, the earlier of the two great Hindu epics, Atikaya is one the **sons** of the great **demon Ravana** by his wife **Mandodari**. Like his father, Atikaya is described as a great devotee (**bhakta**) of **Shiva** and, because of his constant devotion, he gains many wondrous weapons and powers. Atikaya fights bravely and valiantly in the war with **Rama's** army but is eventually killed by Rama's brother **Lakshmana**.

Atita

("gone beyond") In its most general usage, this term denotes an **ascetic** who has completely renounced all things and thus "gone beyond" all the social boundaries that enmesh normal people. It is also the name of a particular low-**caste** community, some of whom are ascetics and some of whom are householders.

Atman

Reflexive pronoun in **Sanskrit** grammar, that can be used for all three persons in the singular and that carries the sense of "self" or "oneself." From the time of the mystical texts known as the **Upanishads**, the word *atman* has also been used to designate each human being's inner essence—which is eternal, unchanging, gives one continuing identity in one's different incarnations, and is ultimately identical to **Brahman**, the single source of all things in the universe.

Atranji Khera

Architectural site near the city of Aligarh that is located in the modern state of **Uttar Pradesh**. Excavations at Atranji Khera have revealed an ancient urban center dating back to the second millennium B.C.E. The settlements here were not as developed as those in the **Indus Valley civilization**, although they are believed to be distinct from it and thus another potential source for ancient Indian culture.

Atri

In Hindu mythology, Atri is one of the six **sons** of **Brahma**, all of whom become great sages. All are "mind-born," meaning that Brahma's thoughts are enough to bring them into being. The others are **Marichi**, **Angiras**, **Pulastya**, **Pulaha**, and **Kratu**.

Atri is also cited as one of the seven sages; the others are **Kashyapa**, **Bhrgu**, **Vasishtha**, **Gautama**, **Bharadvaja**, and **Vishvamitra**. All **brahmins** are believed to be descended from these seven sages, with each family taking the name of its progenitor as its **gotra** name.

In modern times, these gotra divisions are still important, since marriage within the gotra is forbidden. After her marriage the new bride adopts her husband's gotra as part of her new identity. See also **marriage prohibitions**.

Aughar

Name given to a novice in the **ascetic** community known as the **Naths**, who are devotees (**bhakta**) of the god **Shiva**. An aughar has been initiated as a member of the Naths and has taken up their ascetic way of life, but he has not yet received his final **initiation**. In this final ritual, the cartilage in the novice's ears is pierced in order to insert the large earrings that are one of the **Nath** community's defining characteristics.

Aurangzeb

(r. 1658–1707) The last of the great emperors in the **Moghul dynasty**, after whose reign the empire, which at its zenith stretched over most of the Indian subcontinent, was fragmented into smaller kingdoms. Aurangzeb was a very strict and pious Muslim who is generally painted as an enemy of Hinduism. He is the "bad" Moghul emperor, as opposed to his great-grandfather **Akbar**, the "good" Moghul emperor. Aurangzeb unquestionably ordered several notable acts of iconoclasm, the most renowned being the destruction of the **Vishvanath** temple in the city of **Benares**; however, the records from his reign also include orders that the Hindus of that city should not be hindered from practicing their religion.

One possible theory that reconciles these contradictions is that the destruction of the Vishvanath temple and other acts of iconoclasm were done for political rather than religious reasons, to punish local populations for rebellion and noncooperation. One piece of evidence for this theory is that the year before the destruction of the Vishvanath temple, the **Mahanirvani akhara** in Benares took part in a battle with Aurangzeb's soldiers.

Aurobindo Ghose

(1872–1950) Freedom fighter, philosopher, and **ascetic yogi**. He is perceived as a modern example of the concern for ultimate truth that always runs beneath the surface of Hindu life.

Until he was twenty, Aurobindo lived much of his life in England, to fulfill his father's desire to see his **son** get a "proper" English education. Upon his return to India, Aurobindo was more interested in politics than in working, and after a few years quit his job to take part in the political struggle against the British government. His political career lasted only four years, but his intellect and energy soon made him a leader in the Bengali language and national politics.

His life was transformed again by a stay in prison, during which he remembered the advice of an ascetic who had told him to focus on his inner self. Aurobindo later had a vision of **Swami Vivekananda**, who guided his **yoga** practice, and after he was released from prison, Aurobindo withdrew from political life. In 1910 he moved to the French enclave of Pondicherry in southern India, where he lived until his death in 1950. Aurobindo spent these years developing his spiritual life, and in his later years he was known as Shri Aurobindo.

His teachings focus on the insights found in the **Upanishads**, and stress the development of true knowledge, which leads to self-realization.

Auspiciousness

This is the general term for events or conditions that cause or promote life, prosperity, and overall well-being. Along with **purity** and impurity (**ashaucha**), auspiciousness and **inauspiciousness** are fundamental concepts in Hindu life.

The life-giving qualities connected with auspiciousness make it a state that Hindus pursue—whether through performing rituals, scheduling important events such as **marriage ceremonies** for astrologically favorable times, or avoiding people and things deemed to be inauspicious. For extensive information of auspiciousness and its importance in Hindu life, see Frederique Apffel Marglin, *Wives of the God-King*, 1985.

Avadhi

Avadhi is a language known in two different contexts. In a literary context, Avadhi is a dialect of medieval **Hindi** (and a sister language of **Braj Bhasha**) found in the eastern part of the state of **Uttar Pradesh**, in the region surrounding **Ayodhya** (Avadh). It is recognized as the language in which the poet-saint **Tulsidas** (1532–1623?) wrote his vernacular retelling of the *Ramayana*, the *Ramcharitmanas*.

In a linguistic context, Avadhi is one of the dialects of modern standard Hindi spoken throughout the same region. Although it shows similarities to the language of Tulsidas, it has evolved from that version.

Avadhuta

("one who has cast away [all attachments]") In its most general sense, an avadhuta is an **ascetic** who does not adhere to any social or religious rules but his (or far more rarely, her) own. Needless to say, their behavior is often unpredictable, seemingly capricious, and sometimes intentionally shocking.

As a more technical title, avadhuta is a term of respect for the senior members of the **Naga** class of the **Dashanami Sanyasis**, renunciant ascetics who are devotees (**bhakta**) of the god **Shiva** and who formerly made their living as traders and mercenary soldiers.

Avahana

("summoning") The first of the sixteen **upacharas** ("**offerings**") given to a **deity** as part of **worship**, which is done to treat the deity as an honored guest. Although the literal translation of this word ("summoning") seems inappropriate for interacting with a god, the true sense of the word is inviting the deity to become present for worship, just as one would invite a guest into one's house for hospitality.

Avahana Akhara

The name of a particular group of the **Naga** class of the **Dashanami Sanyasis**, which is comprised of renunciant

71

The ten avatars of the god Vishnu. In Hindu mythology, Vishnu has appeared on earth in different forms: Fish, Tortoise, Boar, Man-lion, Vamana (dwarf), Parashuram, Rama, Krishna, Buddha, and Kalki.

ascetics. The Dashanami Nagas are devotees (**bhakta**) of the god **Shiva**, organized into **akharas**, or regiments, on the model of an army. Until the beginning of the nineteenth century, the Nagas' primary occupation was as mercenary soldiers, although they also had substantial trading interests; both of these occupations have largely disappeared in contemporary times.

The Avahana akhara is one of the seven main Dashanami Naga akharas, but for organizational purposes it is considered a subsidiary of the **Juna akhara**. Its name, which means "summons," supposedly comes from its status as the first organized **ascetic** group, formed in response to the call from the philosopher **Shankaracharya** to revitalize Hindu society.

Avalon, Arthur

Pen name of **Sir John Woodroffe**.

Avani

Fifth month of the Tamil solar **year**, which usually falls within August and September. This month corresponds to the northern Indian solar month of Simha (the zodiacal sign of Leo). The existence of several different **calendars** is one clear sign of the continuing importance of regional cultural patterns. One way that the Tamils retain their culture is by preserving their traditional calendar. Tamil is one of the few regional languages in India with an ancient, well-established literary tradition. See also **Tamil months**, **Tamil Nadu**, and **Tamil language**.

Avatar

("descent") In Hindu mythology, the descent (of a **deity**), but more colloquially the incarnation, of a deity on **earth**. The concept of avatars has been best developed by the devotees (**bhakta**) of the god **Vishnu**, who perceive him as taking a specific form to help the world. Examples of avatars can be found for other divinities as well.

Hindus draw a distinction between full avatars, which have the complete power of the deity, and partial incarnations, or **anshavatars**. Vishnu has ten full avatars, each of whom has appeared to restore the cosmic balance when the world has fallen out of equilibrium. The root cause of such disequilibrium is usually a **demon** (asura) who has grown too strong and uses that power to oppress others. This imbalance prompts Vishnu to take form as an avatar, destroy the evildoers, and definitively restore the cosmic balance.

Although there is some variation in the list of Vishnu's avatars, the generally accepted list is as follows: **Fish**, **Tortoise**, **Boar**, **Man-Lion**, **Vamana** (dwarf), **Parashuram**, **Rama**, **Krishna**, **Buddha**, and **Kalki**. This list of avatars follows an "evolutionary" sequence—the first three are **animals**, the fourth a hybrid man-animal, and the ones after that mythic heroes and sages; the exception is the Buddha, a real person who has been incorporated into the Hindu pantheon. The tenth form, Kalki avatar, is yet to come, and his coming will herald the end of the age. Vishnu's partial avatars—as sages, saints, and gods—are countless and potentially limitless, providing a ready-made way for new Hindu movements to ascribe divine authority to their founders.

Although the avatar concept is most commonly associated with Vishnu, it has been applied to other Hindu gods as well. One example of partial avatars can be seen in the *Mahabharata*, the later of the two great Hindu epics, in which all five of the **Pandava** brothers are partial incarnations of various gods. In addition, devotees of the god **Shiva** have developed a list of his twenty-one avatars, who are saints, sages, and minor deities. This list was probably developed in response to the **Vaishnava** doctrine of avatars, but Shiva's forms are far less important than Vishnu's; Vishnu's avatars include Rama and Krishna, who are major objects of **worship** in their own right.

For the Vaishnavas, the avatar doctrine is generally seen as a way to assimilate existing cults into the pantheon by claiming that various deities are merely different manifestations of Vishnu. The **Shaiva** avatars were developed much later, essentially so that Shiva would also have these forms. See also **Jagannath** and **Balarama**.

Avidya

("lack of [true] knowledge") Avidya is the absence of true understanding and is the fundamental problem in almost all Hindu philosophical and religious thought. The presence of avidya leads people to misperceive the true nature of reality and to act based on these misperceptions.

The most fundamental of these false perceptions is to identify the eternal Self (**atman**) with the body. As a result of this misidentification, egoism leads one to try to protect and advance the Self (in its particular embodied state) and incites feelings and actions of greed, lust, and hatred. These feelings create bondage for the soul and entrap it in **samsara**, the cycle of rebirth.

In most Hindu philosophical schools, the avidya tends to be conceived in epistemological rather than metaphysical terms—that is, it is not an actual thing in its own right but exists as a function of how one comes to know things, insofar as that knowledge is inaccurate or incomplete. Once one's deficient awareness has been corrected, the cause of bondage is removed, resulting in the final liberation of the soul (**moksha**).

Avimukta

("unforsaken") The word *Avimukta* carries two shades of meaning: in a more general sense, it is a name for the city of **Benares**; in a more specific sense, it refers to the part of Benares considered to be the sacred heart of the city, in the region centered around the **Vishvanath** Temple.

Avimukta gets its name from the belief that **Shiva** never leaves this place, and because of this its proponents claim that it is the holiest spot on **earth**. See **Benares**.

Avvaiyar

Poet whose compositions appear in the **Sangam literature**, which are collections of Tamil poems written and compiled in the early centuries of the common era (approximately 100–300 C.E.). Avvaiyar is notable as a female poet, indicating that certain **women** at that time took an equal part in cultured and intellectual society. See also **Tamil language**.

Ayamatma Brahman

("This Self is **Brahman**") In the Hindu philosophical tradition, one of the "great utterances" (**mahavakyas**) expressing ultimate truth. The truth here is the identity of **atman** (the individual Self) and Brahman (Ultimate Reality); this identity is the heart of the mystical texts called the **Upanishads**.

Aside from their importance in a philosophical context as fundamental truths, four mahavakyas were also appropriated as symbols by the four divisions of the **Dashanami Sanyasi** ascetics. Each division had its own mahavakya, just as each had a different **Veda**, a different primary sacred center, and a different ascetic quality. Ayamatma Brahman is the mahavakya associated with the **Anandawara** division of the Dashanami Sanyasis.

Ayana

("going") In the estimation of the Hindu **calendar**, the word *ayana* refers to the movement of the **sun** during its yearly course, which is divided according to the direction of the sun's movement. The six months that the sun moves in a northerly direction is called the **uttarayana**, and its southward movement in the following six months is the **dakshinayana**. The transition points at which the sun changes direction do not fall on the solstices, as figured in the Gregorian calendar, but about three **weeks** later on **Makara Sankranti** (around January 14) and **Karka Sankranti** (around July 14).

The sun's northward journey is considered a more **auspicious** time than the southward journey, although many other factors can influence the judgment of a particular **day**.

Ayodhya

("unassailable") Sacred city (**tirtha**) on the Sarayu River, in the Faizabad district of the state of **Uttar Pradesh**, and one of India's **seven sacred cities**. Ayodhya is famous as the setting for much of the *Ramayana*, the later of the two great Hindu epics, whose principal character is the god **Rama**. In the *Ramayana*, Ayodhya is the capital city of Rama's father, King **Dasharatha**, the birthplace and childhood home of Rama and his brothers, and the city to which Rama returns in triumph after his exile is over.

Although historians have raised doubts about the *Ramayana*'s historical veracity and the reality of the events described there, Rama's devotees (**bhakta**) entertain no such doubts. For them the cult of Rama is deeply entrenched in Ayodhya, and various places in the city are associated with events in the epic that are believed to have actually occurred.

In most cases this has had no ill effects, with the exception of the **Ram Janam Bhumi**, the site identified as Rama's birthplace. Until 1992, this site was occupied by the **Babri Masjid**, a Muslim mosque supposedly built after the existing temple was demolished. On December 6 of that year, the mosque was destroyed by teams of activists from the **Vishva Hindu Parishad**, who tore it down in just over six hours. The destruction sparked Hindu-Muslim riots all over India, in which thousands of people were killed. For further information on Ayodhya, see Hans Bakker, *Ayodhya*, 1986; Peter van der Veer, *Gods on Earth*, 1988; Sarvepalli Gopal, *Anatomy of a Confrontation*, 1991; and Christophe Jaffrelot, *The Hindu Nationalist Movement in India*, 1996.

Ayudhapurusha

An ayudhapurusha is the personified form of a divine weapon or emblem, which is conceived as either masculine, feminine, or neuter according to the gender of the **Sanskrit** word. For example, the words **shakti** ("spear") and **gada** ("club") are portrayed as feminine, **chakra** ("discus") as neuter, and **khadga** ("sword") and **trishul** ("trident") as male.

Ayurveda

("knowledge of life") Ayurveda is the best known of the indigenous Indian medical systems and is primarily based on the two **Sanskrit** medical texts: the *Charaka Samhita* (1st c. C.E.) and the *Sushruta Samhita* (4th c. C.E.).

The underlying assumption in both of these texts and in ayurveda is the theory of the three bodily humors—**vata** (**wind**), **pitta** (bile), and **kapha** (phlegm). Each of these is composed of different elements, and although everyone has all three humors, their relative proportions are used to explain varying body types, metabolic dispositions, and personalities.

People in whom vata predominates are said to have quick minds, slender bodies, and to be full of energy, but they are also said to get run down more easily than others. Pitta-dominant people are said to be strong-willed and good leaders but also hot-tempered and bothered by heat. Kapha-dominant people are strong, healthy, and stable but also have tendencies toward lassitude and inertia.

Each of these humors can thus have both wholesome and unwholesome manifestations, but when the humors are in relative balance, the five bodily winds (**prana**) that are considered responsible for basic bodily functions will work effectively, and the person will be healthy.

According to ayurveda, disease is caused by an imbalance of these humors that usually has perceivable environmental roots. One possible cause is environmental circumstances, such as the stresses that the differing **seasons** (hot, cold, damp, etc.) put on varying constitutions. The other possible cause for an imbalance is the person's own behavior—improper diet, poor sleep habits, deficient or inappropriate bodily exertion, and other habitual stresses on the body.

In ayurveda, people are conceived as beings in interaction with their environment, and ayurveda's proponents recognize that many ailments may have multiple causes. The ultimate aim of any treatment, whether diet, exercise, or medicine, is to restore this lost equilibrium. The equilibrium being sought will be different for everyone, since it will necessarily reflect each person's individual makeup. For further information see Gopi Warrier, *The Complete Illustrated Guide to Ayurveda*, 1997; and Judith Morrison, *The Book of Ayurveda*, 1995.

B

Baba

In its literal meaning, an affectionate term of address meaning "father." Although this can be used to address any older man, it is most commonly applied to **ascetics**, either in speaking of them as a class or as a respectful way to address a particular one.

Babar's Mosque

See **Babri Masjid**.

Babri Masjid

("Babar's Mosque") Mosque built in 1528 on the outskirts of the city of **Ayodhya**, which was constructed at the order of Mir Baqi, a general of the Moghul emperor Babar (1483–1530). The site has long been a source of controversy between the Hindu and Muslim communities, and British sources recorded conflicts there in 1855 and 1934. Local tradition holds that the mosque was built on the birthplace of the Hindu **deity Rama**, and that it was constructed only after demolishing the Hindu temple there, although there is little hard evidence for the latter claim. A few months after India gained independence in 1947, several local Hindus surreptitiously installed images of the child Rama, his wife **Sita**, and his brother **Lakshmana**; they spread the tale that the images had miraculously appeared in a ball of light. The government had only recently quieted the Hindu-Muslim massacres that accompanied the division of British India into India and Pakistan, and it was reluctant to reinflame religious passions. Its solution was to padlock the compound's gates and

send the case to the courts for resolution, where it languished for almost forty years.

The early 1980s saw renewed controversy over the site, when the Hindu religious organization **Vishva Hindu Parishad** (VHP) first began calling for its "liberation" and proclaiming that the existing structure was an insult to all Hindus. This campaign portrayed the mosque as a symbol of Muslim iconoclasm. Moreover, it depicted government efforts to protect the mosque as an attempt to appease the Muslim community and retain their votes. In 1986 the VHP's drive to liberate the site was aided by the national government headed by Rajiv Gandhi, which in a patent attempt to claim Hindu support, unlocked the compound's gates so that Hindus could **worship** on the site.

The pressure intensified as the decade progressed, culminating in a series of campaigns to begin constructing a Hindu temple on the site. Many of these campaigns coincided with national elections, and the emotion they generated helped benefit the electoral fortunes of the **Bharatiya Janata Party**, a political party with close ties to the VHP. Eventually, on December 6, 1992, the mosque was demolished. The whole operation was carefully planned; the demolition teams were highly trained, and the first thing they did was to destroy all the television cameras there to prevent any media coverage by outsiders. It was carried out with the blessing of the state government, which made no attempt to protect the building. The demolition was followed by riots, particularly in the state of **Maharashtra**, in which over three thousand people were killed, most of them Muslims.

Even after the destruction of the Babri Masjid, the site remained a bone of contention. Immediately following the demolition, Prime Minister P. V. Narasimha Rao promised to rebuild the mosque on the same spot, but he did nothing to accomplish this during his time in office. Various Hindu groups,

Temple to the god Vishnu in the Himalayan town of Badrinath.
Parts of the temple's architecture suggest that it may have originally been a Buddhist temple.

including traditional religious leaders such as the **Shankaracharyas**, have been calling for the construction of the **Ram Janam Bhumi** temple at the site. Anticipating nothing but trouble ahead, the government again has sent the matter to the courts for resolution, where it remains to this day and may remain for four more decades. For further information see Sarvepalli Gopal, *Anatomy of a Confrontation*, 1991; and Christophe Jaffrelot, *The Hindu Nationalist Movement in India*, 1996.

Badarayana
(ca. 400–200 B.C.E.) Philosopher traditionally cited as the author of the **Vedanta Sutras**. This collection of 555 brief **sutras**, or aphorisms, is the basis of the philosophical school known as **Vedanta**, so named because it claims to reveal the ultimate meaning of the religious scriptures known as the **Vedas**. The sutras attempt to summarize and systematize the philosophic and religious ideas in the **Upanishads**, the speculative texts that form the latest stratum

in the Veda. Because the Vedanta Sutras are particularly concerned with the ideas about the Supreme Reality known as **Brahman**, they are also called the **Brahma Sutras**. The brevity of the individual sutras—many are only a few words—presupposes commentary, which was later provided by various writers. Badarayana himself considered the Upanishads the ultimate source for his teachings, although his text was judged equally authoritative by later Vedanta writers.

Badrinath
("Lord of Badri") Sacred site (**tirtha**) in the Himalayan area of Chamoli district in the state of **Uttar Pradesh**, near the headwaters of the **Alakananda River**, the largest tributary of the **Ganges**. Badrinath is high in the mountains at an altitude of over 10,000 feet. It is connected to Tibet by the Mana Pass, one of the traditional land routes by which Chinese goods have come into India. Badrinath's high altitude also means that it is only accessible between late April and

October, after which it is closed for the winter months; this pattern is echoed at **Yamunotri**, **Gangotri**, and **Kedarnath**, the three major Himalayan pilgrimage sites. The town's name comes from its presiding **deity**, **Vishnu**, whose temple is the reason for the site's existence. The main image in the temple is claimed to have miraculously emerged full-formed from a **shalagram**, a particular type of black stone containing fossilized **ammonite**, which is itself considered a "self-manifested" form of Vishnu.

Badrinath has a long history as a venerable sacred site. Scholars believe that it was occupied by a Buddhist temple until several centuries into the present millennium, based on the **architecture** of some of the temple's older parts. Local tradition reports that until the middle of the twentieth century when the Chinese sealed the Tibetan border, Buddhists came from Tibet for the temple's closing rites in the fall, bringing a hand-woven blanket to drape around the image. In Hinduism, Badrinath is one of the **four dhams** ("divine abodes") connected with the philosopher **Shankaracharya**. Shankaracharya reportedly chose one Hindu sacred center in each corner of the subcontinent to combat the spread of Buddhism and revitalize Hindu religion. At each center he established a **Dashanami Sanyasi** monastic center (**math**) to train learned monks. Badrinath is associated with the sacred center **Jyotir Math** in the Himalayan town of **Joshimath**, forty miles south. Each winter, the image at Badrinath is symbolically transported to the Narasimha temple in Joshimath.

According to Badrinath temple records, for several hundred years temple **worship** was performed by the **Dandi Sanyasis**; they were a group of **ascetics** devoted to the god **Shiva** who were also **Nambudiri brahmins**, the same **caste** into which Shankaracharya is supposed to have been born. When the last of these ascetics died without a successor in 1776, the local king who served as the protector of the shrine invited a non-ascetic Nambudiri brahmin to serve as the temple's priest. In deference to his ascetic predecessors, this priest was given the title **rawal** ("deputy"), and his extended family has run the shrine since then. The rawal is the only person allowed to touch the image, and as a consequence he is required to remain a bachelor, lest the ritual impurity (**ashaucha**) arising from the **birth** of a child (**sutakashaucha**) render him unable to attend to his duties. For a long time, the rawals had sole rights to the **offerings** given at the shrine, but since 1939 the temple has been managed by a committee, and the rawal has been restricted to ritual duties.

Bahi

("account book") Name for the pilgrim registers maintained by hereditary pilgrimage priests (**pandas**). Each panda family in any sacred site (**tirtha**) has the right to serve pilgrims whose ancestral homes are in a particular place, whether or not the pilgrims still reside there. For example, a family from the Marwar region of the state of **Rajasthan** will always be served by the **Marwari** panda, even if the family has not lived in Marwar for generations. Pilgrims make an entry in their panda's pilgrim register during each visit, in which they write down the date, the names of those who visited, and the reason or reasons for which they have come. These details are noted on a thick sheet of paper about ten inches wide and three feet long, and there may be multiple entries on a page. One of the page's narrow sides has holes punched in it, and a string can be threaded through these holes to tie a number of such sheets together. This allows the panda to compile registers for a particular village or specific family, and when not in use these bahis are rolled into a circle and tied.

These registers provide not only a record of pilgrim visits, but are also the unassailable evidence of the hereditary connection between a panda and a pilgrim family. Most pilgrims will demand to see the entries for their ancestors as proof that a particular priest is their hereditary panda. This usually happens when many years have elapsed between visits, and the pilgrims may never have met their panda in person. A panda's bahis are thus the sole proof of his rights to a particular pilgrim group, which makes these registers extremely valuable documents. Most pandas zealously safeguard their bahis, since anyone with a copy can claim the pilgrims therein. The bahis' importance also gives them a high market value. They may be used as collateral to gain a loan and can even be sold outright. This latter course is extremely unusual, since for working pandas their bahis are not only the source of their livelihood, but also their family **inheritance**.

Bahina Bai

(1628–1700) Poet and saint in the **Varkari Panth**, a religious community centered around the **worship** of the Hindu god **Vithoba** at his temple at **Pandharpur** in the modern state of **Maharashtra**. Bahina Bai ran counter to contemporary assumptions not only because she was a female religious figure, but also because she was a **brahmin** disciple of the **shudra** poet-saint **Tukaram**, an association that inverted the usual patterns of social status. This is because a brahmin is someone of high social standing while a shudra is of the lowest and least influential class in Hindu society. According to tradition, Tukaram initiated Bahina as his disciple in a **dream** because Bahina's husband— a learned brahmin who was highly conscious of brahmin status—had forbidden her to meet with him. Aside from her devotional poetry, Bahina also wrote an autobiography, whose content was heavily influenced by her religious beliefs. Bahina is notable as one of the only **women bhakti** (devotional) figures who was able to reconcile the demands of her marriage with her commitment to God, although these issues were not resolved without considerable trouble and heartache. For further information see Justin E. Abbott (trans.), *Bahina Bai*, 1985; and Anne Feldhaus, "Bahina Bai: Wife and Saint," in *Journal of the American Academy of Religion*, Vol. 50, 1982.

Bahiryaga

("external **sacrifice**") In Hindu **worship**, especially in esoteric ritual tradition known as **tantra**, bahiryaga refers to any type of religious practice involving actions, words, or the manipulation of concrete objects. This is the only kind of worship that most people perform. The ultimate goal in tantra, however, is to internalize these acts through repeated practice and to transform them into **antaryaga** ("internal sacrifice"), in which all external actions have been replaced by mental acts.

Bahudaka

("having much **water**") The name for one of four particular types of Hindu **ascetics**. Each of these four types reflects the ascetic's supposed means of livelihood, which in practice has been much less important for ascetic identity than organizational affiliation. The Bahudaka is an ascetic who begs for his food at sacred bathing places. The other three types are the **Kutichaka**, which has lower status than the Bahudaka, and the **Hamsa** and **Paramahamsa**, which have higher status.

Bahula Chauth

Religious festival celebrated on the fourth **day** (chauth) of the dark, or waning, half of the **lunar month** of **Bhadrapada**, the sixth month of the lunar **year**, which usually falls within August and September. On this day mothers perform duties for the welfare of their **sons**. They should refrain from all activity and from eating wheat or rice (the staple food grains). As a symbolic indication of allowing mothers to care for their children, on this day **cows** are not milked, and their calves are allowed to suckle as much as they want.

A baiga, or healer, uses spiritual techniques to remedy a person's physical or emotional troubles.

Such motherly concern for their sons reflects not only normal maternal instincts but the importance of male children in traditional Hindu life. According to the customary pattern, at least in northern India, **daughters** leave their natal homes to live with their husbands' families, whereas sons bring their brides into the family home. One's sons thus ensure the continuity of the family, in addition to taking care of the parents in their old age. Sons are also important because only they can perform the annual **shraddhas**, or memorial rites to the ancestors, although couples without any natural sons can satisfy this requirement through **adoption**.

Baiga

(probably a corruption of the word *vaidaga*, or "healer") A sorcerer, healer, and ritual technician connected with spirits at the lower levels of the pantheon; a baiga sometimes acts as a medium for **village deities** and at other times as an exorcist for witches, **bhuts**, and **prets**. A baiga's power is based on his command of **mantras**, sacred sounds either acquired from a relative as his hereditary birthright or bought from a knowledgeable person. Baigas minister to people's immediate troubles, whether caused by illness, misfortune, accident, or alleged **possession**. This pervasive connection with people's everyday concerns makes them important figures in urban as well as rural India. The most successful baigas are those who radiate the greatest air of authority, and thus instill in their patients the confidence that the baiga can and will alleviate their distress. For a short account of the baiga's work, see Lawrence Babb, *The Divine Hierarchy*, 1975; for a more developed perspective on Indian healers and healing, see Sudhir Kakar, *Shamans, Mystics, and Doctors*, 1991.

Baijnath

Sacred site (**tirtha**) and archeological area in the Himalayan foothills of the state of **Uttar Pradesh**, about forty-five miles north and west of the town of Almora. Baijnath contains a temple complex believed to date from the thirteenth century C.E. Many of the temples are quite well-preserved, although only one is still used as a place of **worship**. Although the name of the site is a vernacular form of **Vaidyanath**, a form of the god **Shiva**, the presiding **deity** in the temple is Shiva's wife **Parvati**. Her main image is over four feet tall and is a magnificent work of art, carved from a piece of rose-colored granite. Smaller figures carved into the image itself illustrate the mythic story of Shiva's wife **Sati**, her rebirth as Parvati, and Parvati's remarriage to Shiva. The statue is clearly the work of a master sculptor, and it far exceeds the quality of the artwork one normally finds in such isolated places. Another temple in a nearby village has a statue of **Vishnu** made from a similar type of stone and carved in a similar style. The simplest explanation for this correspondence is that a single sculptor was commissioned to create both images.

Bairagi

("dispassionate") This is the general name for any **ascetic** whose patron **deity** is **Vishnu**, but it is particularly applied to the fighting ascetics known as **Nagas**. See also **Chatuh-Sampradayi Nagas**.

Baisakh

According to the lunar **calendar** by which most Hindu religious festivals are determined, Baisakh is the second month of the lunar **year**, usually falling within April and May. This is established as one of the months of spring, but in northern India the weather is beginning to get quite warm at this time, especially in the middle of the day. The major holidays in Baisakh are **Shitalashtami**, **Baruthani Ekadashi**, **Parashuram Jayanti**, **Narasimha Jayanti**, **Baisakhi**, **Mohini Ekadashi**, and **Buddha Purnima**.

Baisakhi

Annual festival taking place in the **lunar month** of **Baisakh** (April–May), for which it is named. Baisakhi marks the **sun's** transition into Aries, which according to the Indian estimation occurs around April 14. This festival marks the beginning of the solar **year** on the traditional **calendar**. Baisakhi is celebrated mainly in the north, particularly in the state of **Punjab** and its surrounding regions. In the days when pilgrims still traveled through the **Himalayas** on foot, this festival marked the beginning of the Himalayan pilgrimage season; during the eighteenth and nineteenth centuries, Baisakhi was the occasion for a great trading festival in the town of **Haridwar**, the gateway to the Himalayan shrines. Although this fair has long been eclipsed, Baisakhi is still the climactic bathing (**snana**) day for the Haridwar **Kumbha Mela** and **Ardha Kumbha Mela**, each of which is a bathing festival that occurs about every twelve years when **Jupiter** is in the sign of Aquarius (for the Kumbha Mela) or Leo (for the Ardha Kumbha Mela).

Baithak

("seat") In the **Vaishnava** sect known as the **Pushti Marg**, a religious community whose members are devotees (**bhakta**) of the god **Krishna**, the baithaks are a group of 108 sacred sites (**tirthas**). Each site is somehow associated with the life and activities of the philosopher **Vallabhacharya**, the Pushti Marg's founder. Most of these baithaks are in well-established sacred areas that were considered holy long before Vallabhacharya's time, but the charter story for each baithak records some activity of the philosopher in that particular place, to further sanctify it for his followers. These baithaks create a sectarian network within the existing pilgrimage places and imbue each one with additional significance for the Pushti Marg.

Bajrang Dal

("**Hanuman's** Host") The Bajrang Dal is a modern Hindu organization that has strong connections with the Hindu nationalist **Vishva Hindu Parishad** (VHP), although both are nominally independent. The Bajrang Dal is sometimes characterized as the VHP's "youth wing," and its primary function is to aid the VHP in carrying out its religious, political, and social campaigns, particularly by supplying members to build a crowd. The god Hanuman is best noted for his prodigious strength, and it is this quality that the Bajrang Dal seems to have emphasized in choosing him as their symbol. Membership is open to young men from all social strata, but the organization reportedly draws much of its followers from lower-**caste** groups. Although local chapters of the Bajrang Dal often perform social services and philanthropic activities (as one might find with any organized group), as a whole the organization is widely seen as an instrument of the VHP, to be used when the situation calls for producing a crowd, intimidation, or violence.

Baka

In Hindu mythology, a **demon** killed by the god **Krishna** during Krishna's childhood in **Braj**. Baka is one of the demon assassins sent by Krishna's wicked uncle, **Kamsa**, to try to get rid of the god. He comes to Braj in the form of a giant crane (baka) and swallows Krishna and his companions, but he is killed when Krishna expands to such a giant size in Baka's stomach that the demon explodes.

Bakasur

In the *Mahabharata*, the later of the two great Hindu epics, Bakasur is a fero-

cious man-eating **demon**. To preserve their lives, the local villagers send Bakasur a daily sacrificial victim who is chosen by lot, along with a wagonload of food that the demon also eats. One day the lot falls to the **brahmin** who is hosting the **Pandavas**, the five heroic brothers who are the epic's protagonists. When the brothers' common wife, **Draupadi**, discovers what has happened, she asks one of the brothers, **Bhima**, to deliver the food in the brahmin's place. Bhima drives the wagon to the cave, goads the demon into battle by eating the food in front of him, and then slays Bakasur with one mighty blow.

Baksheesh

(from the Persian word *bakhshidan*, meaning "to give") A gift, usually of money, given to facilitate service. This is usually paid in advance but can also be given after the fact. In some cases this is unabashed bribery, but most often it is simply a way to ensure continuing service and attention, or a gratuity for services already rendered.

Balabhadra

Epithet of the mythic hero **Balarama**, the god **Krishna's** older brother. Although he is a fairly minor mythic figure, he is important for his connection with the temple of **Jagannath** in the city of **Puri**. The temple's presiding **deity** is Jagannath ("Lord of the World"), a tribal god who has been assimilated into the Hindu pantheon as a form of Krishna. The image of Jagannath appears together with two other images, Balabhadra and their sister **Subhadra**, and the three deities invariably appear as a group.

The poet **Jayadeva**, in his list of the ten **avatars** ("divine incarnations") typically associated with the god **Vishnu**, named Balabhadra as the eighth avatar, the place normally occupied by Krishna. According to Jayadeva, Jagannath/Krishna is not a form of Vishnu but the Ultimate Reality from whom all the avatars spring.

Balaji

Popular epithet of the god **Venkateshvara**, the presiding **deity** of the temple of the same name at **Tirupati** in the state of **Andhra Pradesh**. See **Venkateshvara**.

Balaji

(2) Presiding **deity** of the Balaji temple in **Mehndipur** village, **Rajasthan**, who is considered a form of the monkey-god, **Hanuman**. As an infant, Hanuman is continually hungry, and one day he attempts to eat the **sun**. **Indra**, the king of the gods and ruler of **heaven**, is incensed at Hanuman's action and strikes him with a thunderbolt, breaking his jaw (hanu). The **wind**-god, who is **Vayu**, Hanuman's father, goes on strike to protest this punishment. Since in traditional Indian physiology, winds are considered responsible for all internal functions, including digestion, respiration, and elimination, Vayu's strike means that no one can live a normal life. After a short time, the gods realize their predicament and beg Vayu for forgiveness; the deity is placated when each of the gods promises to give Hanuman a divine gift. By virtue of these gifts, Hanuman gains great power; not only is he immensely strong, but he is an expert healer, through both his skill in using herbs and natural medicines and his magical abilities to protect people from malevolent supernatural beings.

These powers and healing qualities make Hanuman a strong protective deity, and he is often worshiped on days and at times deemed inauspicious or unfavorable. These protective attributes have made him enormously important in contemporary Hindu life despite his theoretically intermediate place in the divine pantheon, and these qualities are especially evident in his form as Balaji. His temple has gained regional prominence as a healing center for people possessed by malevolent spirits known as **bhuts** and **prets**. The exorcisms proceed in a quasi-judicial fashion, with the spirits being hauled into the divine court, tried, and banished from the sufferer with the underlying assumption that these rites succeed through Balaji's irresistible healing powers. As Sudhir Kakar has masterfully shown, the language associated with **possession** and exorcism, when understood in the context of traditional Hindu culture, can be seen as a way of describing what modern psychiatrists might call the diagnosis and treatment of mental illness. See Sudhir Kakar, *Shamans, Mystics, and Doctors,* 1991.

Balakrishna

Figure of **Krishna** in the form of a child (bala). Devotees (**bhakta**) who **worship** this form of Krishna are partaking in the devotional relationship known as **vatsalya bhava**, which parallels the connection between parent and child. The unusual twist is that the devotee takes the role of the parent, lavishing love and care on the **deity** in its child form in a warm, protective, and intimate relationship.

Balarama

Krishna's older brother. According to most estimations, Balarama is a partial **avatar**, or incarnation, of **Shesha**, a serpent upon whom the god **Vishnu** reclines as on a couch. Shesha takes human form as Balarama, and Vishnu takes human form as Krishna, to destroy the evil king **Kamsa**. Kamsa has imprisoned their parents, **Vasudeva** and **Devaki**, because on their wedding day a disembodied voice has foretold that Devaki's eighth child will kill Kamsa. Kamsa kills Devaki's first six children at **birth** by flinging them onto stones, but Balarama is saved when the embryo in Devaki's womb is magically transplanted into the womb of Vasudeva's second wife, **Rohini**. Because of the unusual

Hindu temple in Bali, Indonesia. In the early centuries of the common era,
Hinduism was introduced to Bali by merchants and traders,
where it was transformed by the influence of both Buddhist and indigenous religious beliefs.

circumstances surrounding his development *in utero*, Balarama is also known as **Sankarshana** ("dragging away"). Balarama is raised with Krishna in **Nanda** and **Yashoda's** household and takes part in many of Krishna's adventures, including the slaying of Kamsa.

Balarama is usually portrayed as having a fair complexion, whereas Krishna is dark. According to one story, when the gods approach Vishnu to take form on **earth**, he plucks both a white **hair** and a black hair from his head. The former is born to Rohini as Balarama, the latter to Devaki as Krishna.

Jayadeva's *Gitagovinda* presents a different picture of Balarama. Jayadeva is closely linked to the **Jagannath** temple in **Puri**, whose presiding **deity** (Jagannath) has been assimilated into the pantheon as Krishna. For Jayadeva, Jagannath/Krishna is not a form of Vishnu but the Ultimate Reality from whom all the avatars spring. Jayadeva incorporates Balarama into the pantheon as the eighth avatar, to fill the place left by Krishna's promotion to supreme god.

Bali

In Hindu mythology Bali is a **demon** who is tricked by **Vishnu** into granting the god three paces of land of his own. Bali does this with little thought because Vishnu has come in the form of a dwarf (vamana), but when the gift has been given, Vishnu grows immensely large and claims the whole universe, relegating Bali to the **Patala** underworld. See also **Vamana avatar**.

Bali

(2) In Hindu mythology, a monkey-king in the *Ramayana*, the earlier of the two great Hindu epics. Bali and **Sugriva** are brothers who together rule the kingdom of **Kishkindha**, but enmity develops between them, and Bali drives away his brother and takes Sugriva's wife. After the abduction of the god **Rama's** wife **Sita**, Sugriva meets with Rama and the

god's brother **Lakshmana**, and they agree that Rama will help Sugriva regain his wife and kingdom if Sugriva and his monkey-subjects will help to search for Sita. Sugriva challenges Bali to battle but cannot compete with his superior strength. Although Rama has agreed to shoot Bali with an arrow, he is unable to tell which of the monkeys he is. In a second battle, when Sugriva is marked by a garland, Rama shoots Bali with an arrow from behind and kills him.

Bali

(3) Island in Indonesia that has the last surviving remnant of the Hindu-Buddhist culture that pervaded the region after the early centuries of the common era. Indian beliefs were first brought by traders and merchants, and **inscriptions** reveal that the Balinese kings patronized a variety of sects, both Hindu and Buddhist. In time, Indian sacred geography was transferred and transposed to Bali, native **deities** were gradually assimilated into the pantheon, and all the competing sects finally were fused into the new entity known as Balinese religion.

Bana

("arrow") One of the characteristic objects in Hindu iconography, which is associated with various **deities**—the **Goddess**, **Shiva**, and **Vishnu**—and is thus emblematic of no particular one. It is often found in images in which the figure carries a bow (**dhanus**).

Bana

(2) (7th c. C.E.) Poet and author who was a contemporary of the northern Indian emperor **Harsha** (r. 606–647), and one of the leading members of Harsha's court. Bana is widely acclaimed as one of the great **Sanskrit** writers, based on his two best works: the *Harshacharita*, a panegyric narrative of Harsha's deeds, and *Kadambari*, a romance left unfinished at his death. He is also famous for his *Chandishataka*, a collection of one

The bana linga, an egg-shaped stone, is believed to be a manifestation of the god Shiva.

hundred poems dedicated to the differing forms of the **Goddess**.

Bana Linga

An egg-shaped stone considered a svayambhu ("self-manifested") form of the god **Shiva**. As with all **svayambhu images**, the bana linga is considered to be extraordinary, since in it the god has spontaneously revealed himself. Bana lingas are only found in certain places, particularly on the banks of the Chambal River in the state of **Madhya Pradesh**, where they can be found in large numbers. They come in a wide spectrum of colors and can be several feet in width, although most are smaller. The smaller ones are movable and may even be carried by wandering **ascetics** as portable objects of **worship**. The larger ones are usually found only in temples, not only because of the limits on motion imposed by their greater size, but also because they are believed to be so powerful that they should be kept in a carefully maintained place.

Bania

(variant of Baniya) In traditional northern Indian society, a merchant or shopkeeper often but not exclusively belonging to the **vaishya varna**, which is the third of four social classes in Hindu culture. Aside from their merchant activities, the more prosperous ones often engaged in **moneylending**, sometimes at prodigious rates of interest, as a way to further increase their capital. In traditional lore, banias are invariably painted as greedy and avaricious people who care about nothing but money. Although they were often stereotyped as parasites, banias were a necessary part of the traditional agricultural economy, because they gave farmers goods on credit to be repaid after the harvest. They also lent farmers money to get started again after a bad harvest. Both groups thus depended on one another—the farmers for capital, the banias for continuing consumption and patronage. For a masterful reconstruction of the ethos in the northern Indian merchant family, in which Hindu piety was an important element, see C. A. Bayly, *Rulers, Townsmen and Bazaars*, 1983.

Banjara

The model for traditional Indian society was a collection of **endogamous** subgroups known as **jatis** ("birth"). These jatis were organized (and their social status determined) by the group's hereditary occupation. In traditional northern Indian society, the Banjaras were a jati whose hereditary occupation was driving pack **animals**, either as peddlers selling retail goods to people in more remote places or as transporters conveying commodities from one seller to another. They appear in poems by some of the **bhakti** (devotional) poets, particularly by **Ravidas**, as a symbol of human heedlessness or as a person who never stops moving to reflect on where he has been.

Banking

In traditional Hindu culture, banking was often an extension of a merchant family's economic life, particularly in times and places in which centralized banking did not exist. In most cases these families transacted their business using letters of credit known as **hundis**, which enabled them to conduct business over large distances without the risk of transporting gold and silver bullion. By the early 1800s, these hundis

functioned as virtual currency in much of India, since in some cases they were used in twenty or thirty transactions before eventually being returned to the issuing family for cashing. This system made a merchant family's creditworthiness its most valuable asset. Once this was lost, the family's hundis were no longer honored, and they were unable to conduct business. Since the evaluation of a family's credit was often tied to judgments about its character, merchant families strove to cultivate the image of seriousness, dependability, and thrift. In this ethos the only acceptable forum for lavish expenditures was for religious endowments, since these reinforced the family's pious image and thus enhanced their creditworthiness. With part of their surplus capital, these families would usually engage in **moneylending** as one way to increase their wealth; the largest families routinely lent money to royalty, which provided them with even greater status. For a masterful picture of the merchant family ethos in northern India, see C. A. Bayly, *Rulers, Townsmen, and Bazaars*, 1983.

Barahmasa

("twelve months") Poetic genre in which each of the poem's verses, or stanzas, is devoted to one month of the **year**, with the months treated in chronological order. This is a purely vernacular genre for which there are no known instances in **Sanskrit**. Barahmasa poems often reveal a great deal about everyday life and can be subdivided into several basic categories: an enumerative type, which describes appropriate activities for each month such as farming or religious practice; a narrative form, which recounts a woman's longing (**viraha**) for her absent lover; and a type describing a young wife's trial of chastity as she withstands various temptations during an extended separation from her husband. For further information see Charlotte Vaudeville, *Barahmasa in Indian Literature*, 1986.

Barat

One of the common elements in a modern northern Indian **marriage ceremony**, in which the groom is brought in a procession to the wedding site, escorted by his (mostly male) relatives and friends. The barat evokes the symbolism of a royal procession in which the groom is the king, at least for the day. The groom most commonly rides a gaily decorated white mare, although any means of transportation representing his importance is acceptable—from an **elephant** to a horse-drawn carriage to an automobile strung with garlands. In keeping with the royal imagery, the groom often wears a crown or ornaments made of tinsel. The entire procession is usually accompanied by a marching band, in the role of the heralds who march before the royal presence; the band will often stop along the way to play, at which time the participants will **dance** around them. Although the groom usually remains reserved throughout the barat—in keeping with the gravity of the occasion—for the rest of his companions, it is a time for joking, laughing, dancing, and celebration immediately before the wedding. The barat may also involve the consumption of **liquor**, although many more conservative Hindus frown upon this element.

Barsana

A village in the **Braj** region of the state of **Uttar Pradesh**, which is most famous as the birthplace of the god **Krishna's** loving companion, **Radha**.

Baruthani Ekadashi

Festival falling on the eleventh **day** (**ekadashi**) of the dark, or waning, half of the **lunar month** of **Baisakh**, which takes place within April and May. The festival is dedicated to the **worship** of **Vishnu**, especially in his **Vamana avatar**, which is his fifth incarnation. Most Hindu festivals have certain prescribed rites, usually involving fasting (**upavasa**) and worship, and often promise specific benefits for faithful performance. Those observing this ritual should abstain from anger and backbiting and eat food that is prepared without salt or oil. The name *Baruthani* means "armored" or "protected," and faithfully observing this festival is believed to protect one from all evil and grant enormous good fortune. In the charter myth, an **ascetic** whose foot has been chewed off by a wild beast regains the limb by performing this ritual.

Basavanna

(1106–67/68) Poet-saint and religious leader in the **Lingayat** community, a **bhakti** (devotional) group that worships **Shiva** as the single supreme God and rejects all **caste** regulations. The Lingayats were formed in the southern Indian state of **Karnataka** where they still have a considerable presence, and the collections of poetry that form their most important religious texts are composed in the **Kannada** language. According to tradition, from his youth Basavanna was a great devotee (**bhakta**) of **Shiva**, whose piety was so intense that he rejected all notions of ritual and caste. After spending much of his youth as a religious seeker, Basavanna became minister to a king named Bijjala. Basavanna used his position's wealth and influence to care for Shiva's wandering devotees (**jangama**), and Bijjala's court became a magnet for many important figures, including the poet and religious leader **Allama Prabhu**. Basavanna's patronage was vital in forming the Lingayat community, and as a token of his importance, the suffix *anna* ("elder brother") was attached to his name, Basava. As the Lingayat community grew stronger, their public opposition to ritual **worship** and caste distinctions generated intense hostility from more traditional groups. This conflict finally came to a violent head when the fledgling Lingayat community apparently arranged a marriage between an **untouchable** boy and a **brahmin** girl. Traditionalists became so enraged that they executed the bride and groom's fathers. The Lingayat community was dispersed, and Basavanna died soon afterward. For further information see A. K. Ramanujan (trans.), *Speaking of Siva*, 1973.

Basohli

A town west of **Jammu** in the state of Jammu and **Kashmir**, close to the border of **Himachal Pradesh**. Although it is an insignificant place in modern times, in the seventeenth century, Basohli was the capital of a small kingdom in the **Shiwalik Hills**. It was in Basohli that the **Pahari** style of **miniature painting** first appeared. The Basohli version of that style is characterized by highly defined profiles, sharply flattened perspective, and broad bands of a single intense color for backgrounds. It serves as a transitional style between the so-called **Rajasthani** and the more developed techniques of the Pahari schools.

Bath, Mohenjo-Daro

One of the most striking structures excavated at **Mohenjo-Daro**, the first city of the **Indus Valley civilization** to be discovered. This bath is an oblong pool, thirty-nine by twenty-three feet in area and eight feet deep. It is built of brick and sealed with pitch. The tank could be drained through an opening in one corner, and it was surrounded on all four sides by small rooms reminiscent of changing rooms. The Indus Valley cities gave great attention to plumbing, sanitation, and sewers, suggesting that bathing (**snana**) may have been connected with ritual **purity** as in modern Hindu life. With this in mind, the bath was probably not a swimming pool but rather had some deeper connection with religious life. For further information see Walter Ashlin Fairservis, *The Roots of Ancient India*, 1975.

Bathing

See **snana**.

Baudhayana

(6th–3rd c. B.C.E.) Sage, writer, and commentator. Baudhayana is the author of one of the three surviving religious texts known as the **Kalpa Sutras**. **Apastamba** and **Hiranyakeshin** wrote the other two Kalpa Sutras. Each of the surviving works contains the three elements dictated for a Kalpa Sutra: prescriptions for Vedic rituals (**Shrauta Sutras**), prescriptions for domestic rites (**Grhya Sutras**), and prescriptions for appropriate human behavior (**Dharma Sutras**). All three of the authors belonged to the same school, the Taittiriya school of the **Black Yajur Veda**. According to tradition, Baudhayana was the oldest, Apastamba was his disciple, and Hiranyakeshin was Apastamba's disciple. This relative chronology is supported by the texts themselves, since Baudhayana's work is much less organized than the others, his language is more archaic, and he is often less strict in his opinions. His texts gain their primary importance as a source for his successors.

Begampura

Fictional city named in one of the poems written by the poet-saint **Ravidas** (ca. 1500). The word *begam* can mean either "queen" or "without pain." The poem clearly shows the city as an idealized place far from the tribulations of ordinary human life, such as pain, sorrow, taxes, wrongdoing, and to a lesser extent, class distinctions. Although Ravidas was born a tanner (**chamar**), an occupation that was looked down upon, this is one of his only poems that speaks about social issues, however indirectly.

Begging

One of the recognized means of livelihood in traditional Hindu society that is a sign of either very low or very high

Beggars sitting outside of a religious fair in Allahabad.
When beggars receive alms, they are also believed to receive the giver's bad luck.

status, depending on the circumstances. Some beggars are simply people who are desperately poor, disabled, or unable to provide for themselves and their families and who must depend upon gifts (**dana**) to survive. Such beggars have extremely low social status, although they may make a fairly decent living, particularly if they live in a favorable environment such as a pilgrimage place (**tirtha**), where giving gifts is a common religious act. Aside from all of the obvious disadvantages—low social status, an uncertain income, and having to endure scorn and verbal abuse—these beggars also suffer the stigma of living on charity, rather than earning an income. This is karmically undesirable since giving gifts is one of the methods by which people get rid of **inauspiciousness**, which is transferred to the receiver along with the gift. In many cases such a beggar is considered nothing more than an instrument to be used, and the most common word for such a person is *patra* ("vessel").

Some **ascetics** also make their living by begging but fall into a completely different category. In the ideal case, these are people who have given up all visible means of support as part of an effort to renounce the world; this differentiates them from the poor, who are part of ordinary society, albeit at the lowest level. There is general social approval for supporting ascetics, at least the ones who are considered genuine spiritual seekers, and doing so is widely seen as a source of religious merit. Although it is sometimes difficult to distinguish poorer ascetics from ordinary beggars, in the case of the most respected ascetics the distinction is very clear. Such respected ascetics confer status on people by accepting their gifts, and consequently they tend to screen the donors and their motives very carefully to protect their reputations. See also **karma**.

Begram

Architectural site west of the city of Kabul in modern Afghanistan. Excavations there have revealed artifacts from Kushana culture, primarily relief carvings on ivory plaques.

Bel

Another name for the **bilva** tree. See **bilva**.

Belagave

Village in the Shimoga district of the state of **Karnataka**. Belagave was the most important center for the **Kalamukhas**, which was an **ascetic** sect of devotees (**bhakta**) of the god **Shiva**. The Kalamukhas had an important historical role in southern India between the tenth and thirteenth centuries, but they disappeared some time after that. Their ritual center in Belagave was the temple of Kedareshvara, which was Shiva in his form as the lord of Kedara. Although the Kalamukhas have disappeared, their presence and prominence in the region are confirmed by the **inscriptions** at this and numerous other temples.

Belur

Town in the state of **Karnataka**, about sixty miles northwest of the modern city of Mysore. As at its sister site, **Halebid**, Belur is known for a magnificent collection of temples built by the **Hoysala dynasty**, which ruled western Karnataka from the eleventh to thirteenth centuries C.E. At both sites the temples were built from a particular type of stone—variously described as chlorite schist, steatite, or soapstone—that was quite soft when newly quarried but gradually hardened with exposure to the air. This initial malleability made the stone easy to carve and facilitated the lush detail characteristic of Hoysala temples. Architecturally speaking, these temples have certain unique features: a central hall connecting three star-shaped sanctuaries, and temple towers (**shikharas**) composed of well-defined horizontal tiers rather than the continuous upward sweep characteristic of the northern Indian **Nagara** architectural style.

Belur Math

World headquarters of the **Ramakrishna Mission**, a modern religious organization. The Ramakrishna Mission was founded in 1897 by **Swami Vivekananda**, the most famous disciple of the nineteenth-century Bengali mystic **Ramakrishna**. The Mission is equally dedicated to both social service and spiritual uplift, based on Vivekananda's realization that India needed concrete development as much as religious teaching. Belur Math was constructed in 1899, two years after the Ramakrishna Mission was founded. It is located just north of Calcutta on the west side of the Hugli River, quite close to the **Dakshineshwar** temple where Ramakrishna lived for most of his adult life.

Benares

City and sacred center (**tirtha**) on the banks of the **Ganges** in the state of **Uttar Pradesh**. Benares is an anglicized form of **Varanasi**, one of the traditional Hindu names for the city, as well as **Kashi** and **Avimukta**. All three of these names are used to designate the entire city, but in a more specific context, they denote concentric sacred zones surrounding the **Vishvanath** temple; Avimukta is the smallest, then Varanasi, and finally Kashi. As with all other pilgrimage places on the Ganges, Benares is considered sacred because of its proximity to the river, particularly because at Benares the Ganges flows in a northerly direction, which is considered auspicious. The Ganges is an integral part of the identity of Benares, and much of the city's religious life centers around it.

The most important sacred presence in the city, however, is the god **Shiva**. Benares is the city of Shiva, his dwelling place on **earth**, and the site he never leaves, hence the name Avimukta ("never forsaken"). Temples to Shiva are scattered throughout the city—some old, some new, some nearly forgotten—but the most important is the Vishvanath ("Lord of the Universe") temple. Vishvanath is one of the twelve **jyotirlingas**, a group of sites deemed particularly sacred to Shiva. The original Vishvanath temple was destroyed by the Moghul emperor **Aurangzeb**, who built a mosque on the site; the present Vishvanath temple was rebuilt next to the original location. Shiva's eternal presence makes Benares one of the **seven sacred cities**, in which death brings liberation of the soul (**moksha**). At the moment of death, Shiva is believed to come to the dying person and impart his salvific wisdom. Shiva's presence is also evident at the **cremation ground** at the sacred site **Manikarnika Ghat**, which is in the very heart of the city rather than at the margin as in most other places. Here too Shiva teaches human beings a lesson; specifically, Shiva reminds them of their imminent death. This is not to distress or depress them, but to spur them on to serious religious life.

The presence of the Ganges and Shiva make Benares an ideal place to die, or to immerse oneself in spiritual life; what is often overlooked is that Benares is also an unusually vibrant place to live. It has a long history as a trading center and market town, and it remains so today even though the creaking wooden boats traversing the Ganges have been supplemented by other means of transport. Benares is famous for its artisans, particularly weavers and metalworkers, many of whom are Muslim. It has also been renowned as a cultural center for at least a thousand years. Benares is still one of the most important centers in India for all branches of traditional Sanskritic learning, from grammar to astrology to medicine. It is likewise a center for music, **dance**, and all of the arts and has been home to a galaxy of Indian religious figures, including the poet-saints **Tulsidas**, **Ravidas**, and **Kabir**. For a detailed exposition of the city and its life, see Diana Eck, *Banaras*, 1999.

Benares Hindu University

Indian educational institution founded in 1916 by the nationalist figure **Madan Mohan Malviya** (1861–1946). The World War I era marked a more activist orientation to the Indian independence movement. One of the ways this activism manifested itself was in founding educational institutions, which gave Indians greater control over the universities' mission, tone, and curriculum. Benares Hindu University was founded to uphold Hindu cultural and philosophical traditions, but also to educate its students in the sciences and thus prepare them for the modern world. This mission reflected the modernist thinking of its founders as well as their passionate commitment to traditional Hindu culture. It is still one of the finest universities in India, particularly for the study of classical Indian culture.

Bengali

Modern Indian language in the Indo-European language family, spoken in the region of modern Bengal, for which it is named. Like many of India's regional tongues, Bengali has a long history as a literary language in its own right. In the nineteenth century, Calcutta was the most important cultural center in India as well as a hotbed of resistance to British rule. As the vernacular tongue, Bengali was used in that era's revolutionary politics, particularly by **Bankim Chandra Chatterjee** and **Aurobindo Ghose**; it was also the language used by religious figures such as **Ramprasad** and **Ramakrishna**.

Betel

Common name for the small, hard nut from the areca palm tree, which is consumed by mixing slices of the nut with lime, tobacco, and spices and wrapping the whole thing up in a betel leaf. This is not eaten but lodged against the cheek and slowly chewed, to let the juices flow. This method of gradually absorbing the juice may be the reason for its most

Betel nuts wrapped in a leaf. These nuts are taken from acacia palm trees, dried, wrapped in betel leaves, and chewed to aid digestion.

common name, *pan* ("drinking"). The nut turns the saliva a bright red color, which is the reason for the distinctive crimson smears adorning many Indian buildings. Chewing betel is widely believed to be good for the digestive tract, a genuine concern in a country where intestinal upsets are still quite common. Chewing betel is such a deeply embedded part of sophisticated Indian cultural life that it even has its own aesthetic, and folding betel is one of the sixty-four arts mentioned in the *Kama Sutra*.

Bhadrakali

(from *bhadra*, meaning "blessed" in **Sanskrit**) In Hindu mythology, the epithet of a powerful and terrifying form of the **Goddess**. According to one version of the story, Bhadrakali's **birth** is associated with the death of **Shiva's** first wife, **Sati**. Sati goes to a great **sacrifice** sponsored by her father, **Daksha**. When Daksha intentionally and publicly insults her husband Shiva, in her anger and shame, Sati immolates herself in the sacrificial **fire**. When Shiva learns of Sati's death, he is so enraged that he plucks two matted locks (**jata**) from his head and

dashes them to the ground. The first takes form as **Virabhadra**, a wrathful and terrifying form of Shiva, and the second takes form as Bhadrakali. Just as Virabhadra represents Shiva's destructive aspect, Bhadrakali symbolizes the ferocious and dangerous side of the Goddess, in contrast with the gentle and loyal Sati. Shiva orders the two to destroy Daksha's sacrifice, which they do with great abandon.

Bhadrakali also appears in the stories connected with the birth of the god **Krishna**. While Krishna is developing in his mother, **Devaki's**, womb, Bhadrakali enters the womb of Krishna's foster mother, **Yashoda**. The two children are born on the same night, and under cover of darkness they are switched with one another. The next morning the baby girl is snatched from Devaki by her stepbrother, **Kamsa**, the wicked king of **Mathura**, who dashes out the child's brains on a rock; this is just as he has done with Devaki's six other children because it has been foretold that one of them will kill him. From the infant's **corpse** arises an eight-armed figure of the Goddess, who taunts Kamsa that his destroyer has already escaped and then disappears.

Bhadrapada

According to the lunar **calendar**, by which most Hindu religious festivals are determined, Bhadrapada is the sixth month of the lunar **year**, usually falling within August and September. This is one of the months associated with the **monsoon** rains. The major festivals in Bhadrapada are Kajari Teej (**Teej**), **Bahula Chauth**, **Janmashtami**, **Radhashtami**, **Aja Ekadashi**, Hartalika Teej (Teej), **Ganesh Chaturthi**, **Rishi Panchami**, **Parivartini Ekadashi**, **Anant Chaturdashi**, and in southern India, **Onam**.

Bhadrasana

("decent posture") In **yoga** practice this is one of the sitting postures (**asana**) described in commentaries to the **Yoga Sutras**. In this position the legs are crossed with the feet tucked under the thighs so that the crossed heels form a cavity around the scrotum. This is called the "decent posture" because the cupped hands are placed over the cavity made by the heels, covering the private parts. In Hindu iconography this is one of the common postures in which images of the **deities** are portrayed.

Bhagabhadra

Monarch in the Sunga dynasty, which was centered in the **Malwa** region in the western part of the state of **Madhya Pradesh**, in the centuries following the decline of the **Maurya dynasty** just before the turn of the common era. Despite the fragmentation of the Maurya state, rulers seem to have maintained contact with the Greek-speaking kingdoms to the west, since a pillar **inscription** records that Bhagabhadra received an ambassador named Heliodorus from the king of Takshasila, in modern Pakistan.

Bhagavad Gita

One of the best-known Hindu scriptures, which is itself a section in the *Mahabharata*, the later of the two great Hindu epics. The parts of the epic before the Bhagavad Gita chronicle the growing strife between the **Pandavas** and the **Kauravas**, the two branches of a royal family who are the epic's main characters. The parts following the Bhagavad Gita detail the battle that ultimately destroys the entire family. The Bhagavad Gita itself is set in that moment of calm just before the battle begins, and it is written as a dialogue between the **Pandava** prince **Arjuna** and the supreme divinity **Krishna**, here disguised as Arjuna's charioteer. Arjuna is the world's greatest archer and can decimate his enemies with ease. But as he looks at the faces of the enemy, he realizes that the people he is about to fight and kill are his relatives, teachers, and friends. Not surprisingly, the prospect leaves him cold, and it is up to Krishna to give him divine guidance.

The Gita's second chapter opens with Krishna trying to shame Arjuna into fighting (in essence, saying "everyone will think you were afraid and make fun of you"), but when this tactic fails, Krishna has to give more substantive advice, which makes up the rest of the text. Different parts of the Bhagavad Gita invoke all three of the generally accepted paths to liberation of the soul (**moksha**): the path of wisdom (**jnanamarga**), the path of action (**karmamarga**), and the path of devotion (**bhaktimarga**).

The path of wisdom is rooted in the teachings of the speculative texts known as the **Upanishads**. This path stresses the realization of one's essential nature as the eternal Self (**atman**). The atman is identical with the universal reality known as **Brahman**; once one has accepted this, all dualistic ideas and false knowledge disappear. The path of action stresses acting without selfish desire—performing one's duty as duty, but without attachment to the ultimate outcome. This path thus upholds and reinforces the rigid social structure propounded in the **dharma literature**. As a warrior in that social system, Arjuna's job is to kill people. At the same time, the path of action provides a way to transform socially sanctioned duty into religious practice. The path of devotion entails surrendering all one's actions to God and performing one's role as an instrument of divine will.

The Bhagavad Gita shows no clear preference for any of these paths, which implies that different writers reworked the text over time. Professor Arthur Llewellyn Basham has speculated that the "original" Bhagavad Gita ended with verse 2.38, after a section establishing the morality of fighting in a just war, thus giving Arjuna his rationale to fight. It is believed that this "original" text was then reworked by a philosopher of the upanishadic type, who conceived of the Ultimate Reality as the impersonal Brahman and of liberation in terms of mystical realization. The final sections were most likely added by a passionate devotee (**bhakta**) of **Vishnu**, particularly in his form as Krishna. According to Basham, this last author not only inserted verses in some of the earlier books but also added some completely new ones. One of these, Arjuna's vision of Krishna's cosmic form in the Gita's eleventh chapter, is considered among the most brilliant religious texts ever written. Although some scholars might take issue with specific points, Professor Basham's theory seems the most convincing explanation for a highly varied text.

In the roughly two thousand years since the Bhagavad Gita was compiled, different commentators have interpreted its message according to their own proclivities. The ninth-century philosopher **Shankaracharya** saw it as sanctioning the path of wisdom, while the eleventh-century philosopher **Ramanuja** was convinced that it stressed devotion. The most recent pivotal interpreter, **Mohandas Gandhi**, understood the text as commanding action. He saw in Arjuna's struggle a blueprint for his own time and work, urging him to labor for Indian independence but to do so without attachment or hope for personal gain. The text has become even more important as a "scripture" during the past two centuries, largely because of pressure from Christian missionaries. One sign of this is that in modern Indian courtrooms, the Gita is the text upon which Hindus take the oath of truthfulness when being called to take the stand. For an accessible translation of the text itself, see Barbara Stoller Miller (trans.), *The Bhagavad-Gita*, 1991; for Dr. Basham's analysis of the text, see Arthur Llewellyn Basham, *The Origins and Development of Classical Hinduism*, 1991.

Bhagavan

("Blessed One") Name denoting both respect and reverence. In different contexts this name can be used as an epithet of either the god **Krishna** (as in the **Bhagavad Gita**) or the god **Shiva**. In modern usage, at least in northern India, it is also the word that comes closest to expressing the notion of abstract divinity, much like the word "God" in English. It is often used to denote God by Hindus who are religious but who do not **worship** particular **deities**.

Bhagavata

("devotees of the Blessed One") General name for the earliest devotees (**bhakta**) of **Vishnu**, particularly the devotees of **Krishna**-Gopala, a deified cowherd hero who later became identified with Vishnu. Until the development of sectarian Vaishnavism in around the eleventh century C.E., the word *bhagavata* was a blanket term for all **Vaishnavas** except the Pancharatrikas, who were followers of the secret ritual tradition known as **Pancharatra**.

Bhagavata Purana

Sectarian religious text that is by far the most important text for the **worship** of the god **Krishna** as the single Supreme Being. Internal evidence hints that it was written in southern India in the ninth or tenth century, making it much later than many of the other **puranas**. The bulk of the text focuses on Krishna's early life in the village of **Brindavan**—infancy, childhood, and adolescence—but gives little attention to his later exploits as a king and hero. This purana's best-known section is the tenth book, which describes Krishna's amorous exploits with the local herd girls (**gopis**) as they pass the nights in a circle **dance** (**ras lila**) on the shores of the **Yamuna River**. The image of Krishna throughout the text is that of a god in constant play with the world. For Krishna's devotees (**bhakta**), the supreme felicity comes with the opportunity to take part in that divine play (**lila**).

Bhagirath

In Hindu mythology, the single person most responsible for bringing the celestial **Ganges** down to **earth**. The river Ganges and the **goddess** Ganges are the same, hence the river is considered holy. Bhagirath is the great-great-grandson of King **Sagar**, whose 60,000 **sons** have been burned to ash by the sage **Kapila's magic** power when they erroneously accuse Kapila of being a thief. The sage later tells **Anshuman**, King Sagar's grandson and sole surviving descendant, that the only way to bring peace to their souls is to bring the Ganges from **heaven** down to earth. Anshuman strives to do this for the rest of his life, as does his son **Dilip** after him, but both are unsuccessful. Dilip's son Bhagirath takes their efforts to heart and retires to the **Himalayas**, where he performs **asceticism** until the gods finally agree to send the Ganges down to earth. Yet Bhagirath's efforts are not over. He next has to appease the god **Shiva** so that the deity will agree to take the shock of the falling river on his head, since its force will otherwise destroy the earth. When all is finally in place, the Ganges falls to earth onto the head of Shiva. From there Bhagirath leads the river out of the

As a tributary of the Ganges, the waters of the Bhagirathi River are considered sacred and its banks contain several pilgrimage sites.

mountains to the sea, where she touches his ancestors' ashes, after which they find peace at last.

Bhagirathi

Epithet for the **Ganges** as both river and **goddess**. The word *Bhagirathi* is derived from the name **Bhagirath**, the single person most responsible for bringing the Ganges to **earth**. Bhagirathi is also the name for a Himalayan tributary of the river; the Ganges itself is formed when the Bhagirathi unites with the **Alakananda River** at **Devaprayag**. Although the Alakananda is longer and wider, the Bhagirathi flows through **Gangotri**, the sacred site (**tirtha**) celebrated as the source of the Ganges. As with all the Himalayan tributaries of the Ganges, the Bhagirathi is considered sacred. Important pilgrimage places along this tributary include Gangotri near its headwaters, **Uttarkashi**, and Devaprayag.

Bhairava

("terrible") A wrathful and powerful divine attendant of the god **Shiva** who is often identified as a form of Shiva himself. According to the *Shiva Purana*, a sectarian scripture, Bhairava is produced when the god **Brahma** insults Shiva, and Shiva's rage takes concrete form as Bhairava. After his **birth**, Bhairava's first act is to cut off one of Brahma's heads—the one whose mouth has uttered the insult—thus leaving the god with four remaining heads. Since Brahma is considered a **brahmin** priest, this act makes Bhairava guilty of brahmin murder, the most serious of the **four great crimes** (**mahapataka**). As a sign of the enormity of his act, Brahma's severed head sticks to Bhairava's hand; as penance (**prayashchitta**) Bhairava has to wander the countryside as a beggar, displaying Brahma's severed head as a continual advertisement of his crime. In his travels Bhairava visits many pilgrimage places (**tirtha**), but none of them have the power to cleanse him from the sin of brahmin murder. He finally obtains a pardon in the city of **Benares**, at a site named **Kapalamochana** ("releasing the skull"). As soon as Bhairava bathes there, Brahma's head falls from his hand into the **Ganges**—a sign that his crime had been expiated.

Although often seen as Shiva's attendant, Bhairava is important in several different contexts. He is often portrayed as the consort of powerful, independent **goddesses** such as **Durga** and **Kali**, although he is subordinate to them, befitting their status as supreme **deities**. Bhairava's associations with wrath and power have made him popular with practitioners of the secret ritual tradition known as **tantra**, who may invoke him for **magic** powers or other favors. Bhairava is also popular with the **Naga** class of the **Dashanami Sanyasis**, ascetic

devotees (**bhakta**) of Shiva who formerly made their living as traders and mercenary soldiers; this group sees him as a divine image of themselves. Some of the ambivalence associated with Bhairava is symbolized by his **animal** vehicle, the **dog**, which in Hindu culture is almost invariably a scavenger and considered highly impure.

Bhairava Akhara

Another name for the **Juna akhara**, a particular subgroup of the **Naga** class of the **Dashanami Sanyasis**, who are devotees (**bhakta**) of the god **Shiva**. See **Juna akhara**.

Bhairava Jayanti

Annual festival on the eighth **day** of the dark, or waning, half of the **lunar month** of **Margashirsha** (November–December), which is celebrated as the birthday of **Bhairava**. Bhairava is a wrathful and powerful form of the god **Shiva** and is actually the god's anger personified. He emerges from Shiva's forehead after Shiva has been insulted by the god **Brahma**, and Bhairava's first act is to cut off the head of Brahma that has uttered the insult, leaving the god with four heads. Bhairava's wrath gives him an aura of danger but also the power to help his devotees (**bhakta**), who **worship** him to attain success, remove obstacles, and recover from disease. On this festival people worship Bhairava, Shiva, and Shiva's wife, **Parvati**, as well as Bhairava's **animal** vehicle, the **dog**. People are encouraged to worship through the night and to pass this time by telling mythic stories of Bhairava, Shiva, and Parvati.

Bhairavaprakasha

("brilliance of **Bhairava**") Name given to the spear that is the symbolic weapon of the **Mahanirvani akhara**, a particular group of the **Naga** class of the **Dashanami Sanyasis**. The Dashanami Nagas are devotees (**bhakta**) of the god **Shiva** and are organized into different

akharas, or regiments, much like an army. Until the beginning of the nineteenth century, the Nagas' primary occupation was as mercenary soldiers, although they also had substantial trading interests; both of these have occupations largely disappeared in contemporary times. All of the akharas have particular features, including this spear, which signify their organizational identity.

Bhairavi

Feminine form of **Bhairava** and an epithet of the **Goddess**. Bhairavi is one of the ten **Mahavidyas**, a group of goddesses who are both extremely powerful and potentially dangerous.

Bhaiya Duj

Annual festival falling on the second **day** (duj) of the bright, or waxing, half of the **lunar month** of **Kartik** (October–November). This festival is celebrated to emphasize the bond between a brother (bhaiya) and sister. During Bhaiya Duj, married **women** invite their brothers into their homes, apply **tika** marks on their brothers' foreheads as a sign of respect, and feed them sweets and a hearty meal. Sisters also tie a string around their brothers' right wrists to symbolize the emotional bond between them and the brother's obligation to protect his sister throughout her lifetime. Unmarried women host their brothers in the same way in their natal homes. In either case, on this day women should pray that their brothers have long lives and that they themselves be happily married. The brothers, in turn, give presents to their sisters.

Aside from reaffirming the normal family love between brother and sister, this festival also emphasizes the protective role that brothers play in their sisters' lives, particularly after women are married. The traditional pattern in northern India is for married women to live with their husbands' families. Since women generally outlive their fathers, for most of her life a woman's primary protectors will be her brothers. A woman without brothers is in a position of relative weakness. If nothing else, these yearly visits give brothers the chance to assess their sister's happiness and the state of affairs in her married home. Such visits also notify the husband's family that they are still concerned with her welfare.

Bhajan

("sharing") General name for a religious or devotional hymn, which is almost always sung in a vernacular language. As an expression of personal devotion, bhajans have no prescribed forms and in contemporary times are often set to the melodies of film songs. As a genre, bhajans can have any or all of the following themes: detailing the deeds of a particular **deity**, praising the deity, addressing the god in a tone of complaint or humble supplication (vinaya), reminding the deity of the speaker's difficulties from internal or external sources, or warning the listeners to examine and reform their lives. Singing and listening to such hymns was, and remains, a major form of religious activity in the **bhakti** (devotional) movement. During these sessions, devotees (**bhakta**) "share" their songs and experiences with one another. Although one can find bhajans dedicated to all the gods in the pantheon, from a historical perspective this singing tradition has been strongest among the devotees of **Vishnu**. **Vaishnava** devotional literature is full of tales of Vishnu coming in disguise to take part in bhajan sessions, since the company of his devotees is said to be **heaven** on **earth**.

Bhakta

("sharer") In Hinduism, this word denotes a devotee of any particular **deity**. The word's literal meaning, "sharer," has a twofold sense. On one hand, the devotee shares in the deity's **grace** by virtue of his or her piety. On the

A family makes an offering in a burning tray.
Offerings are a sign of religious
devotion (bhakti) to a deity.

other hand, since most Hindu devotionalism involves a community of worshipers, the devotee also gets to share in the company and community of like-minded people.

Bhaktamal

("Garland of Devotees") Text written by **Nabhadas** (ca. 1600) in which he gives short (six-line) biographical accounts of over two hundred **bhakti** (devotional) figures. Although Nabhadas himself was a **Ramanandi**, and thus a devotee (**bhakta**) of the god **Rama**, his work not only includes devotees of all sectarian persuasions but is generally considered unbiased. The text is notably free of astonishing and miraculous events. Instead, the main emphasis is on the devotee's personal qualities, which serve as a model for others. In many cases the *Bhaktamal* gives the earliest reliable account of these figures, which makes it an extremely important source for northern Indian literary and religious history. It is all the more interesting that the text cannot be definitively dated,

although internal evidence suggests that it was completed early in the seventeenth century.

Bhaktavijaya

("Triumph of [God's] Devotees") Text written by **Mahipati**, an eighteenth-century writer and hagiographer of the devotional (**bhakti**) poet-saints. The stories in the *Bhaktavijaya* focus mainly on the saints connected with the **Varkari Panth**, a religious group centered around the **worship** of the god **Vithoba** at his temple at **Pandharpur**. This focus is understandable since Mahipati himself was a Varkari. In keeping with the trend toward unification often promoted by the devotional movement, he also included tales of other great devotees (**bhakta**), most notably **Kabir**, **Namdev**, **Jnaneshvar**, and **Narsi Mehta**. The stories in the *Bhaktavijaya* present each of these saints as a paradigm of devotion and stress the power of piety to overcome all obstacles. This theme also marks Mahipati's other major work, the *Bhaktililamrta*. The *Bhaktavijaya* has been translated by Justin E. Abbott and Narhar R. Godbole as *Stories of Indian Saints*, 1988.

Bhakti

("sharing") The most common word denoting devotion to God. This is one of the three traditional paths to gain final liberation of the soul (**moksha**), and it has been the most widespread type of religious practice for well over a thousand years. The word's literal meaning conveys the sense of relationship. On one hand, it refers to an intense and passionate love between devotee (**bhakta**) and **deity**, and on the other, it refers to separate communities of people bound together by their common love of God. Although references to bhakti can be found in such early texts as the **Shvetashvatara Upanishad** and the **Bhagavad Gita**, the bhakti propounded here is radically different from later usages. In both these texts, bhakti is presented as a form of **yoga** in which one contemplates God as part of a controlled and disciplined practice. This is a far cry from the abandonment and passionate involvement in later times.

The beginnings of this latter sort of bhakti arose in the Tamil country of deep southern India between the sixth and ninth centuries B.C.E. It had an intensity that was radically different from earlier notions, a devotional "heat" as opposed to the "coolness" of yoga. Tamil bhakti expressed, and continues to express, its devotion through songs sung in vernacular languages, conveying an intimate relationship with a personal god.

These characteristics basically held throughout history. The use of vernacular speech was especially significant, for this was the language of ordinary life and marked the egalitarianism that was one of the hallmarks of bhakti devotion. Bhakti devotees were men and **women** from all strata of society, from the highest to the lowest; here was an opportunity for religious life based solely on the depth and sincerity of one's devotion rather than on one's **birth**. Despite this religious egalitarianism, devotees rarely tried to restructure their hierarchical societies. The idea was that religious equality was supposed to transcend rather than reform human society.

Aside from egalitarianism and personal experience, bhakti worship also stressed community, based on the interconnections between devotees. Though each devotee was an individual (and indeed, bhakti poets had real personalities, as the many hagiographies bear witness), they also fell into "families," all of which were connected with each other. Many of the bhakti saints fell into recognizable groups: Some were centered around a particular sacred place, such as the temple at **Pandharpur** in the state of **Maharashtra**; some were connected as teachers and students, such as **Nammalvar** and his disciple **Nathamuni**; and some had long-term

associations, as with the **Lingayat** community. In all cases these devotees were keenly aware of those who had preceded them and their connections with one another. Such communities were both formed and reinforced through **satsang**, the "company of good people" whose influence over time was believed to have the power to transform. This was a type of "sharing" that bound devotees to each other and to their teacher, and through these two vehicles carried them to God.

These are general characteristics, and bhakti's regional manifestations often take on a distinct flavor marked by, if nothing else, the differing languages. The *Padma Purana* speaks of bhakti (a feminine noun) as a maiden who was born in southern India, attained maturity in the state of Maharashtra, and was rejuvenated in northern India. Although this is a metaphor, it accurately charts the historical diffusion of bhakti devotion, as well as its changes as it moved north. All forms of bhakti are shaped by specific times, places, and circumstances.

Bhaktililamrta

("Nectar of the Play of Devotion") Text written by **Mahipati**, an eighteenth-century writer and hagiographer of the devotional (**bhakti**) poet-saints. Mahipati belonged to the **Varkari Panth**, a religious group centered around the **worship** of the god **Vithoba** at his temple at **Pandharpur**. The *Bhaktililamrta* gives extended accounts of Varkari saints, such as **Eknath**, **Tukaram**, Ramdas, and Bhanudas. The text presents each of these saints as a paradigm of devotion and stresses the power of worship to overcome all obstacles. This theme also marks his other major work, the ***Bhaktavijaya***. Parts of the *Bhaktililamrta* have been translated by Justin E. Abbott as *The Life of Eknath*, 1981; and *The Life of Tukaram*, 1980.

Bhaktimarga

("path of devotion") Along with the path of action (**karmamarga**) and the path of wisdom (**jnanamarga**), this is one of Hinduism's three generally accepted ways to gain final liberation of the soul (**moksha**). The bhaktimarga seeks release of the soul through **bhakti**, or passionate devotion to God.

Bhaktirasabodhini

("Awakening the Delight in Devotion") Name of a commentary on the *Bhaktamal* of **Nabhadas**; this commentary was written by **Priyadas** in 1712. In the *Bhaktamal*, Nabhadas had given brief six-line biographies of over two hundred contemporary **bhakti** (devotional) figures. These biographies are notably free of astonishing and miraculous events and usually stress the devotee's personal qualities, to serve as a model for others. In the *Bhaktirasabodhini*, Priyadas gave greatly expanded accounts for each devotee mentioned by Nabhadas, often narrating amazing stories to which Nabhadas made no reference. In his biography of the poet-saint **Ravidas**, Nabhadas drew from the texts written by the biographer **Anantadas**, but in other cases his sources are not clear. The accounts in the *Bhaktirasabodhini* are suspect as genuine biographies of these saints, given Priyadas's penchant for miraculous events and his chronological distance from his subjects. Still, the text is extremely valuable as a mirror of his time, and careful analysis can reveal much about contemporary religious tensions and issues.

Bhamati Advaita

A later branch of the **Advaita Vedanta** philosophical school. The Advaita school upholds a position known as monism, which is the belief that a single Ultimate Reality lies behind all things and that everything is merely a differing form of that reality. Advaita proponents believe that reality is nondual (advaita), that is, that all things are nothing but the formless, unqualified **Brahman** despite the appearance of diversity. For the Advaitins, this assumption of diversity is a fundamental misunderstanding of the ultimate nature of things, or **avidya**. Although often translated as "ignorance," *avidya* is better understood as a lack of genuine understanding, which ultimately causes human beings to be trapped in karmic bondage, reincarnation (**samsara**), and suffering.

Bhamati Advaita is based on the ideas of **Mandana Mishra**, although the school takes its name from a commentary written by Mandana's disciple **Vachaspati Mishra**. Mandana was a contemporary of the philosopher **Shankaracharya**, Advaita Vedanta's greatest exponent, and took definitive stands on several philosophical points on which Shankaracharya had remained silent. One such point was the location of avidya, which Mandana claimed must be each individual Self because it was absurd to conceive of Brahman as subject to ignorance. For Mandana there were clearly multiple, separate selves, since one person's liberation did not bring liberation for all.

Mandana's comments presupposed the existence of a common, if illusory, world, which his followers explained as the activity of one primal ignorance; however, they also had to explain how a single primal ignorance could simultaneously affect multiple souls. This was done using philosophical models known as **limitationism** and **reflectionism**, although it is the former that has been more commonly associated with the Bhamati school. Limitationism assumes that there are some things (i.e., the color red) that we do not conceive of as divided, even when different red colors appear in different places. In the same way, the Bhamati school argued, avidya can be found in multiple souls at the same time but is complete and undivided in each of them. Reflectionism is based on the idea of a mirror's image, which is different from the original but made from it. Therefore the avidya found in any particular soul is a "reflection" of the original avidya. For further information see Karl H. Potter (ed.), *Presuppositions of India's Philosophies*, 1972.

Bhandara

("storehouse") A banquet given for large numbers of people—either by special invitation, restricted to certain classes of people (such as **ascetics**), or open to the general public. Sponsoring such a banquet is believed to generate considerable religious merit, but this is also a conspicuous opportunity for both the donor and attendees to enhance their status. Issues of status are also marked among the attendees. The most honored guests confer status on the donor simply by deigning to come, and accordingly such guests will be treated differently from the common lot. The rest of the guests generally get no such special treatment. They give status to the host by **eating** the food he (or she) has had prepared, but they get little in return other than the meal itself, which is usually of poor quality since the food is prepared in large quantities.

Based on these considerations, ascetics with sufficient resources of their own will usually avoid such banquets because of both the quality of the food and the concerns over status. To eat at a bhandara is not only to confer prestige on the donor, but to lower one's own status by appearing as though one needs to do this to survive. The main exception is when one has been invited as an honored guest, but even in these cases it is not unusual for such guests to eat little or nothing, thereby giving status by their presence but losing none through consumption.

Bhandarkar, R. G.

(1837–1925) **Sanskrit** scholar and intellectual who was the first Indian to serve as professor of Sanskrit at **Deccan** College, in Poona. Bhandarkar was one of the first Indian academics to combine the traditional mastery of Sanskrit texts with critical and objective research, a project that until then had been confined to European scholars. Bhandarkar is emblematic of Indian intellectuals in the late nineteenth century, who began by learning from the Europeans but were then able to work with the best of them. Bhandarkar authored two Sanskrit workbooks and numerous scholarly texts, but his most significant legacy is the **Bhandarkar Oriental Research Institute**; it was founded in 1917 by his students, friends, and admirers and is still a highly respected research institution.

Bhandarkar Oriental Research Institute

(BORI) Research institute founded in 1917 and named after the great scholar **R. G. Bhandarkar** (1837–1925). The Institute is devoted to the study and preservation of traditional Indian culture, and it is respected in scholarly circles throughout the world. Its two most important publications have been P. V. Kane's *History of Dharmasastra* and a multivolume critical edition of the *Mahabharata*, the later of the two great Hindu epics. Aside from its publications, the Institute is also noted for its vast collection of **Sanskrit** manuscripts, which makes it one of the finest research establishments in all of India.

Bhang

Paste or dough made from crushed marijuana (*Cannabis sativa*), which is often mixed with spices or other flavorings before being formed into a ball. It is taken as an **intoxicant**, either eaten, or mixed into a "cooling" milk-based drink called **thandai**. In general, **eating** bhang is disapproved of by respectable people, although it is fairly common in certain circles, particularly among ascetics. Despite this basic disapproval, bhang is widely consumed as part of the festival celebrations for **Shivaratri** and **Holi**, even by people who avoid it the rest of the year. The former festival is dedicated to **Shiva**, who is famous for his love of the **drug**, whereas Holi is associated with overturning social boundaries, giving greater license to do things normally proscribed. Aside from being consumed during certain celebrations, it can also be taken in special places, particularly when on a pilgrimage. Several of the most famous Hindu sacred sites (**tirthas**)—among them **Benares**, **Puri**, and **Haridwar**—have government-run bhang stands where pilgrims can fulfill their needs.

Bhanita

In poetry, particularly the vernacular form of the **bhakti** poets, a signature line in which the author is identified by name. This line has two major functions: to identify the poet and to provide a summation of the poem's message. The word *bhanita* comes from a verb meaning "to speak," and by adding a signature line the poet is stamping his or her authorship on the poem. Of course, there is nothing to prevent others from doing this as well. In a performance context, the poet's name comes at the beginning of the final line and alerts the audience to pay special attention to that line, which often sums up the entire poem's message.

Bharadvaja

In the *Ramayana*, the earlier of the two great Hindu epics, Bharadvaja is an important **ascetic** and sage. His **ashram**, or abode, is at **Chitrakut**; this is now a town in the southeastern area of the state of **Uttar Pradesh**, but the epic describes the place as a forest hermitage. When **Rama**, his wife **Sita**, and his brother **Lakshmana** are beginning their fourteen years of exile, they come to Bharadvaja to seek his blessings (**ashirvad**). In a broader mythological context, Bharadvaja is one of the seven sages whose names mark exogamous **gotra** ("lineages"); the others are **Kashyapa**, **Bhrgu**, **Vasishtha**, **Gautama**,

Atri, and **Vishvamitra**. All **brahmins** are believed to be descended from these seven sages, with each family taking the name of its progenitor as its gotra name. In modern times, these gotra divisions are still important, since marriage within the lineage is forbidden. After her marriage the bride adopts her husband's gotra as part of her new identity. See also **marriage prohibitions**.

Bharadvaja

(2) (5th c. B.C.E.?) Religious scholar named as the author of a **Shrauta Sutra** (manual on prescriptions for **Vedic** rituals) and a **Grhya Sutra** (manual on domestic rites). The period during which he flourished is uncertain but must precede **Panini**, since this grammarian mentions Bharadvaja in the *Ashtadhyayi*. Given their interest in strengthening the authority of their sacred texts, many Hindus identify this author with the legendary sage Bharadvaja, although there is no hard evidence for this claim.

Bharata

In Hindu mythology, the **son** of King **Dushyanta** and the maiden **Shakuntala**; Bharata is considered a partial incarnation of the god **Vishnu**. Dushyanta and Shakuntala are married in secret in a **gandharva marriage** executed by their mutual consent. Dushyanta must return to his capital and leaves Shakuntala at her home. While he is gone, she is cursed by the sage **Durvasas** that her lover will forget her. In time, Bharata is born and Shakuntala goes off to search for her beloved. She has to endure many trials before the **curse** is broken. Since Shakuntala and Dushyanta have been married in secret, it takes some time before Bharata is accepted as Dushyanta's legitimate son, and thus heir to the throne. When Bharata finally ascends the throne, he reigns for a long time. After his reign the land of India becomes traditionally known as Bharata.

Bharata

(2) In the **Ramayana**, the earlier of the two great Hindu epics, Bharata is the **son** of King **Dasharatha** by his wife **Kaikeyi** and the righteous younger brother of the god **Rama**, the epic's protagonist. Bharata's loyalty to his family has to endure several tests. The strictest one comes early in the epic when, through Kaikeyi's treachery, Rama is sent into exile in the forest for fourteen years, and Bharata is named king in his place. Despite the obvious temptations of wealth and power, Bharata refuses to assume the throne in place of his brother, **curses** his mother for her deceit, and sets off to live in exile with Rama. Rama commands Bharata to return to **Ayodhya** and rule during his exile, on the premise that the people will suffer without a king. Bharata reluctantly agrees to act as a temporary king, but with two symbolic adjustments: He moves the court from the capital city of Ayodhya to the village of **Nandigrama** as a symbol of **Rama's** exile, and throughout his rule sits at the foot of the royal throne; a pair of Rama's sandals are placed upon the throne as a symbol of the rightful king.

Many characters in the *Ramayana* are paradigms for Indian cultural values, and Bharata stands for the ideal younger brother. In the traditional joint household the brothers are the heart of the family, since it is they who remain at home their entire lives, whereas their sisters live with their husbands' families after they are married. The eldest brother in every generation eventually becomes the head of the joint family after the older members have passed away. He carries primary authority and responsibility for the family as a whole but cannot succeed without the cooperation of his younger brothers, who must acknowledge and support his authority. By refusing to usurp his elder brother's rightful leadership, Bharata is a paradigm for the ideal younger brother, who puts aside his own desires and opportunities to uphold and promote the welfare of the family as a whole.

A dancer performs in the classical Bharatanatyam form. She assumes the pose of Nataraja, the "Lord of the Dance."

Bharatanatyam

One of the classical **dance** forms of India; some of the others are **Kathak**, **Orissi**, **Kuchipudi**, **Kathakali**, **Chau**, and **Manipuri**. Bharatanatyam has its home in the temple towns of the state of **Tamil Nadu**, particularly **Tanjore** city's **Brhadeshvar** temple. This temple is dedicated to the god **Shiva**, whose most famous form is **Nataraja**, the "Lord of the Dance." According to tradition the name *bharata* comes not from the sage Bharata, the reputed author of the text on dance called the *Natyashastra*, but from an acronym of the dance's three most important elements: "bha" from *bhava* ("feeling"), "ra" from *raga* ("melodic mood"), and "ta" from *tala* ("rhythm"). The second word in the name, *natyam*, simply means "dance."

Bharatanatyam's historical roots are uncertain. The existence of dance can be dated to the early centuries C.E. since it is mentioned in the two **Tamil epic** poems, *Shilappadigaram* and *Manimegalai*. Carvings at the Shiva temple in **Kanchipuram** suggest that this dance was well developed in the **Pallava dynasty** (6th–9th c. C.E.), but hard evidence for structured temple dance, including the hereditary dancers known as **devadasis**, did not appear until the **Chola dynasty** (9th–14th c. C.E.). Although royal patronage was an important factor in its survival, Bharatanatyam was performed primarily in the temples until the twentieth century, when the dance began to be performed on stage.

As an artistic form, the dance's present technique was codified in the early nineteenth century by four brothers in the service of Raja Serfoji II of Tanjore. Stylistically, Bharatanatyam presents a sharply geometric line. The most characteristic posture has a stiff upper torso, with the knees flexed outward in line with the rest of the body, and the feet spread gently outward. This posture is a recurring motif in any performance. As in all the Indian dances, Bharatanatyam has a well-developed vocabulary of **gesture** and expression, which makes it possible for the dancer to tell complex stories. Like most other Indian dance forms, Bharatanatyam has been influenced by the shift from temple to stage as its primary theater. Although its roots lie in **worship** and devotion, the move to the stage has inevitably disrupted some of these religious connections. For further information see Mohan Khokar, *Traditions of Indian Classical Dance*, 1984.

Bharati Dashanami

One of the ten divisions of the **Dashanami Sanyasis**, renunciant **ascetics** who are devotees (**bhakta**) of **Shiva**. The Dashanamis were supposedly established by the ninth-century philosopher **Shankaracharya** in an effort to create a corps of learned men who could help to revitalize Hindu life. Each of the divisions is designated by a different name—in this case, *bharati* ("Indian"). Upon **initiation**, new members are given this name as a surname to their new ascetic names, thus allowing for immediate group identification. Aside from their individual identity, these ten divisions are divided into four larger organizational groups. Each group has its headquarters in one of the four monastic centers (**maths**) supposedly established by Shankaracharya, as well as other particular religious associations. The Bharati Dashanamis belong to the **Bhuriwara** group, which is affiliated with the **Shringeri Math** in the southern Indian town of **Shringeri**. The Bharati division is elite because it is one of the few that will initiate only **brahmins**. Other such divisions are the **Saraswati Dashanamis**, **Tirtha Dashanamis**, and **Ashrama Dashanamis**. The Bharatis are unusual, however, since only part of the division is restricted to brahmins.

Bharatiya Janata Party

(BJP) Modern Indian political party with a strong Hindu nationalist (**Hindutva**) orientation. The party was formed as the political wing of the Hindu nationalist organization known as **Rashtriya Svayamsevak Sangh** (RSS), and many of the BJP's leaders have been RSS members for decades. The BJP was formed in 1980 after the dissolution of its predecessor organization, the **Jana Sangh**. The latter was an RSS affiliate as well, several of the whose leaders, notably **Lal Krishna Advani** and Atal Behari Vajpayee, have also led the BJP. At first the BJP took a moderate political stance and fared quite poorly, winning only two seats in the 1984 elections. In the later 1980s it took a far more militant tone, stressing as its focal issue the campaign to build the **Ram Janam Bhumi** temple in **Ayodhya**. As the Indian electorate grew more religiously polarized, the BJP climbed to eighty-six seats in 1989 and 120 seats in 1991. In the 1996 elections it won 160 seats, becoming the largest single party in India's 535-seat Parliament.

The president of India invited the BJP to form a government, but this failed when it was unable to gain enough support from other parties to muster a majority of votes in Parliament.

The BJP's traditional constituency has been **brahmins** and members of the trading communities, both of whom tend to be religiously conservative and supportive of the Hindutva message. In the mid-1990s the BJP muted its Hindu nationalist rhetoric in an attempt to reach beyond these traditional constituencies and to gain more widespread support by moving closer to the political center. Despite these changes, many of the established secular parties still view the BJP with suspicion and have refused to ally themselves with the organization. The BJP's inability to mobilize such support among the larger body politic was a major factor behind the collapse of its short-lived government in 1996. The country was then run by a coalition of thirteen secular political parties, whose single binding commitment is their opposition to the BJP. However, since 1998 the BJP has succeeded in building coalitions to form a government. For further information see Walter K. Andersen and Shridhar D. Damle, *The Brotherhood in Saffron*, 1987; and Christophe Jaffrelot, *The Hindu Nationalist Movement in India*, 1996.

Bharat Mata

("Mother India") Modern Hindu "**deity**" whose primary image is a map of the subcontinent, often prominently marked with the network of India's sacred sites (**tirthas**). The presupposition behind most of these particular sacred sites is that the land itself is holy, but the idea of Bharat Mata takes this idea to a more abstract level, sanctifying the whole subcontinent. Although this map and its image of Mother India are usually not actual objects of **worship**, they carry important symbolic messages. In an abstract way, the holiness of Mother India unites all Hindus regardless of their sectarian affiliation.

Moreover, it suggests that India is one unified culture despite its striking regional diversity. These ideas can be found in specific areas, particularly in the networks of tirthas knitting the country together, yet in contemporary times this image's underlying purpose is often political rather than religious. At times it simply represents national pride, but at other times it has a more sinister hidden agenda. This identification of Indian culture with the motherland can be used as a way to marginalize religious **minorities**—primarily Muslims and Christians, whose holy places lie in other countries—as "foreigners," and people whose patriotism and connection to the Indian nation are potentially suspect.

Bharatmilap

("Meeting **Bharata**") A particular scene in the dramas known as the **Ram Lila**, which are reenactments of the *Ramayana*, the earlier of the two great Hindu epics. This scene records the meeting between the god **Rama** and his brother Bharata, which takes place after Rama has been in exile for fourteen years, during which Bharata has faithfully served as ruler in his brother's place. According to connoisseurs of the Ram Lila, this brief scene is filled with some of the most rapturous emotion in the play. Certainly there is the exaltation that the time of separation has ended, but the scene's popularity also comes from the way it reflects certain basic cultural values. The brothers are considered the heart of the traditional Indian joint family since they remain at home their entire lives, whereas their sisters become part of their marital families. The eldest brother in every generation eventually becomes the head of the joint household, but he cannot succeed without the support and cooperation of his younger brothers. Rama and Bharata are thus models for the brothers in a traditional joint family: Rama for treating his younger brother with love and care, and Bharata for obediently carrying out his

An image of the god Vithoba. Bharud poetry was composed by poet-saints in the Varkari Panth, a religious community devoted to Vithoba.

older brother's wishes for the good of the family as a whole.

Bharavi

(6th c. C.E.) **Sanskrit** dramatist who is best known as the author of the drama *Kiratarjuniya*. This play describes the meeting between the god **Shiva**, disguised as the tribal hunter Kirata, and the warrior-hero **Arjuna**. Arjuna is one of the five **Pandava** brothers, who are the heroes of the epic *Mahabharata*. In Hindu mythology, Arjuna is the world's greatest warrior, but he is also afflicted with pride. The play describes how the arrogant Arjuna becomes humbled at the hands of this tribal hunter, who in contemporary terms would be of very low social status. In the end, however, Shiva reveals his true form to Arjuna and blesses him for his valor.

Bhartrhari

(5th c. C.E.) **Sanskrit** poet-philosopher who authored the ***Shatakatrayam***

("Three Hundred"), a three-part collection of poems on political life, love, and renunciation. According to legend, Bhartrhari was born the **son** of the **brahmin** Vidyasagara and his **shudra** wife, **Mandakini**. Vidyasagara was the adviser to the king of Kalinga and was given the kingdom upon the ruler's death; after Vidyasagara's death Bhartrhari's brothers designated him as king. Bhartrhari was very happy until he realized that his wife was being unfaithful to him. When her secret was discovered she tried to poison him. Completely disillusioned, Bhartrhari renounced the world to live as an **ascetic**, during which time he reputedly composed his poetry.

Although this is a good story, since many of these poems stress the degradation inherent in courtly life, Bhartrhari was most likely a courtier. His poetry treats all of the conventional purposes of life. The first two sections are about power (**artha**), sensual desire (**kama**), and righteous action (**dharma**), whereas the final section is concerned with the ultimate end, or liberation of the soul (**moksha**). For further information see Barbara Stoller Miller (trans.), *The Hermit and the Love-Thief*, 1978.

Bhartrprapancha

(7th c. C.E.) In Indian **philosophy**, the first exponent of the **Bhedabhada** ("identity-in-difference") philosophical school. The period during which Bhartrprapancha flourished is uncertain, but he precedes the eighth-century Bhedabhada commentator **Bhaskara**. The Bhedabhada position identified three levels of being: the Ultimate Reality known as **Brahman**, the "witness" consciousness (**sakshin**) in the human being, and the world. This school paradoxically asserted that these three levels were identical, yet different. Thus the world is identical to Brahman but subject to change and decay, unlike Brahman. In the same way, while each human soul is identical to Brahman, it is also subject to bondage and reincarnation (**samsara**), unlike Brahman. The bondage of the soul was caused by the primal ignorance known as **avidya**, but it could be erased by a combination of action and awareness (**jnanakarmasamucchaya**). The basic philosophical problem for Bhartrprapancha and his followers came from their belief that Brahman was actually transformed into both the world and the Self, a philosophical outlook known as **parinamavada**. Since they believed that Brahman underwent real changes, it was subject to bondage and ignorance. This position was untenable and unacceptable from a religious perspective because Brahman was deemed to be perfect and unchanging. This difficulty may account for the school's relatively short life.

Bharud

The name for a specific genre of **bhakti** (devotional) poetry, found particularly among the **Varkari Panth**, a religious community centered around the **worship** of the Hindu god **Vithoba** at his temple at **Pandharpur**, in the modern state of **Maharashtra**. The bharud is essentially a dramatic poem in which the speaker takes on one or more roles to convey the message of devotion to God. It was especially favored by the poet-saint **Eknath**, who used the genre to adopt the personae of **women**, **untouchables**, Muslims, and other marginal people. In modern times these bharuds have become the basis for popular dramas, usually performed during the biannual Varkari pilgrimage to Pandharpur. While singing the songs of the earlier saints during a pilgrimage is an important religious act, these modern renditions are mainly for entertainment. The actors playing the roles in these bharuds frequently add in their own words and actions, which are often quite bawdy.

Bhashya

("commentary") Any commentary, whether on a text or an oral teaching.

The need for commentary was presupposed in most texts on Hindu **philosophy** as well as in the secret ritual tradition known as **tantra**. Philosophical works were often nothing more than collections of brief aphorisms, which were intentionally kept short to facilitate memorization but which clearly needed further explanation. In the case of tantra, commentary was essential because the texts were written using coded language to conceal their contents from the uninitiated. This may have been in the form known as **sandhabhasha**, which often uses **erotic** language to indicate religious practice, or it may simply have been a technical language in which everyday words had contextual meanings.

Bhaskara

In Indian **philosophy**, an eighth-century proponent of the **Bhedabhada** ("identity-in-difference") school. The Bhedabhada position identified three levels of being: the Ultimate Reality known as **Brahman**, the "witness" consciousness (**sakshin**) in the human being, and the world. They paradoxically asserted that these three levels were identical, yet different. Thus the world is identical to Brahman but subject to change and decay, unlike Brahman. In the same way, while each human soul is identical to Brahman, it is also subject to bondage and reincarnation (**samsara**), unlike Brahman. The bondage of the soul was caused by the primal ignorance known as **avidya**, but it could be erased by a combination of action and awareness (**jnanakarmasamucchaya**). The basic philosophical problem for the Bhedabhada school was that because they believed that Brahman was actually transformed into the world and the Self (**parinamavada**), it followed that Brahman was subject to bondage and ignorance. This idea was difficult to defend, since the transcendence of Brahman was well established by sacred texts such as the **Upanishads**, and this problem may account for the school's relatively short life.

Bhasmasur

In Hindu mythology, a **demon** with great power but limited intelligence. According to tradition, the god **Shiva** has given Bhasmasur the power to change anyone to ash (bhasma) simply by placing his hand on that person's head. Bhasmasur falls in love with Shiva's wife **Parvati** and attempts to place his hand on Shiva's head, and the god has to flee. Bhasmasur is destroyed when the god **Vishnu** tricks him into putting his hand on top of his own head, which instantly transforms him into ash. In metaphorical usage, the term *Bhasmasur* denotes any problem that has grown out of hand through lack of foresight.

Bhava

("being") Epithet of the god **Shiva**. See **Shiva**.

Bhavabhuti

(early 8th c. C.E.) **Sanskrit** dramatist and playwright noted for his ability to express and transmit emotions through language. His best-known play, the romance *Malatimadhava*, is famous not only in its own right, but because the primary villain is an evil **ascetic** believed to be a member of the defunct ascetic group known as **Kapalikas**. The Kapalikas were devotees (**bhakta**) of **Shiva**, and their reputed practices emulated Shiva in his wrathful form as **Bhairava**. They wore their hair long and matted, smeared their bodies with ash (preferably from the **cremation ground**), and carried a club and a skull bowl (**kapala**). According to some sources, they also indulged in forbidden behavior—drinking wine, **eating** meat, using cannabis and other **drugs**, performing **human sacrifice**, and orgiastic sexuality—which caused them to be avoided and feared. Bhavabhuti's

description of this evil ascetic and his disciples is one of the earliest datable references to the **Shaiva** form of **asceticism**, and therefore important from a historical perspective.

Bhavani

(feminine form of **Bhava**) Epithet of the god **Shiva's** wife, **Parvati**. See **Parvati**.

Bhavas

("states") In Indian aesthetics the bhavas are a set of nine states considered the most basic unadulterated emotions: sexual excitement, laughter, grief, anger, energy, fear, loathing, wonder, and peace. To these nine bhavas correspond the nine **rasas** ("tastes"), or moods transmitted by various types of artistic expression: the **erotic**, comic, compassionate, cruel, heroic, terrifying, loathsome, marvelous, and peaceful. Although these bhavas and rasas clearly correspond to one another, there is an important difference between them. A person's emotive states come and go in response to circumstances that are often beyond one's control. Because such naturally occurring emotions usually cannot be sustained, they are generally not objects of aesthetic satisfaction. This is not true in the case of rasa, since mood can be artificially generated by an artistic endeavor. Any particular rasa can thus be sustained and satisfying. The single most dominant aim in all the Indian arts, therefore, is to create such a mood or moods for the audience.

Bhave, Vinobha

(1895–1982) Social and religious reformer whose basic principles reflected his long association with **Mohandas K. Gandhi**, to whom Bhave came as a disciple in 1916. Bhave was one of Gandhi's close associates in the struggle for independence and was particularly absorbed with Gandhi's idea of village self-sufficiency. In the years after independence, he traveled around India on foot to meet the people. It was on one such tour that he started the Bhoodan ("land gift") movement, the purpose of which was to obtain donations of land for the poor. Much of Bhave's life after independence was devoted to village development, in particular through a movement called Sarvodaya ("welfare of all"), which sought to solve problems through collective involvement and service to one another.

Bhedabhada

("identity-in-difference") Philosophical school whose best-known figures were **Bhartrprapancha** and **Bhaskara**. The Bhedabhada position identified three levels of being: the Ultimate Reality known as **Brahman**, the "witness" consciousness (**sakshin**) in the human being, and the world. The school paradoxically asserted that these three levels are identical, yet different. Thus the world is identical to Brahman but is subject to change and decay, unlike Brahman. In the same way, while each human soul is identical to Brahman, it is also subject to bondage and reincarnation (**samsara**), unlike Brahman. The bondage of the soul was caused by the primal ignorance known as **avidya**, but it could be erased by a combination of action and awareness (**jnanakarmasamucchaya**). The basic philosophical problem for Bhartrprapancha and his followers was that because they believed that Brahman was actually transformed into the world and the Self (**parinamavada**), it followed that Brahman was subject to bondage and ignorance. Thus, if one must destroy avidya to gain liberation, one must also destroy part of Brahman. These were difficult ideas to defend since the transcendence of Brahman was well established by sacred texts such as the **Upanishads**, and this problem may account for the school's relatively short life.

Bhil

The name of a tribal (**adivasi**) group found in greatest numbers in the **Vindhya Mountains**, in the eastern part of the state of **Madhya Pradesh**. They are historically associated with the forest, particularly with hunting and gathering honey. As with many tribal groups, their homeland is often in marginal lands, and most of them are quite poor.

Bhima

The third of the five **Pandava** brothers who are the heroes in the *Mahabharata*, the later of the two great Hindu epics. Bhima is born when his mother, **Kunti**, uses a powerful **mantra** (sacred sound) to have a **son** by the **wind**-god, **Vayu**. Of all the Pandavas, Bhima is the largest and strongest, and his favorite weapon is the club, which requires great physical strength. This strength is one of the sources of enmity between the Pandavas and the **Kauravas** (cousins of the Pandavas), since during their adolescent training, Bhima can always draw on his superior power to outdo his cousins. His earthy and untamed nature is evident through his consumption of strange foods as well as from his liaison with the **rakshasi** (female **demon**) Hidambi, by whom he has a son, **Ghatotkacha**. Bhima's notable deeds tend to be feats of strength. In many cases this involves killing demons, such as **Bakasur** or Hidamba in hand-to-hand combat; but Bhima is also a major figure in the Mahabharata war, in which he uses his club to kill great masses of the Kaurava army.

Besides his strength and unusual appetites, which make him a figure subject to caricature, Bhima is also absolutely devoted to his brothers and to their common wife, **Draupadi**. Whenever her honor is at stake, Bhima is the person to whom she turns. When Draupadi is molested by **Kichaka** during the year that the Pandavas spend incognito at the court of King **Virata**, Bhima disguises himself as Draupadi, goes to meet Kichaka, and kills him. It is also Bhima who vows to kill the two Kaurava brothers, **Duhshasana** and **Duryodhana**, because of their behavior toward Draupadi after Bhima's brother

Bhima River at Pandharpur,
in the state of Maharashtra.

Yudhishthira loses an important game of dice. Duhshasana drags Draupadi into the hall by her **hair**, her garments stained with menstrual **blood**, and Duryodhana bares his thigh (a euphemism for the genitals) toward Draupadi and directs her to sit on his lap. Bhima vows that to avenge these insults he will rip open Duhshasana's chest so that Draupadi can wash her hair in his blood, and smash Duryodhana's thigh with his club. Although it takes thirteen years before he carries out these promises, in the end he avenges Draupadi's honor. After the Mahabharata war, Bhima aids his brother Yudhishthira in reigning as king. After Yudhishthira abdicates the throne, Bhima travels with him and their other brothers on a great journey to the **Himalayas**, where Bhima eventually dies of exposure.

Bhima River
A central Indian tributary of the **Krishna River**, rising in the state of **Maharashtra**, on the inland side of the western **ghats** and meeting with the Krishna in the state of **Karnataka**. At the Bhima's headwaters can be found **Bhimashankar**, which is one of the twelve **jyotirlingas**, a group of sacred sites (**tirthas**) deemed especially holy to the god **Shiva**. Aside from Bhimashankar, another important religious site on the Bhima is the temple of **Vithoba** at **Pandharpur**.

Bhimashankar
("**Bhima's Shiva**") One of the twelve **jyotirlingas**, a group of sacred sites (**tirthas**) deemed especially holy to the god **Shiva**. Bhimashankar is the name of both the place and the presiding **deity**. It is located in **Maharashtra's** Pune district at the source of the **Bhima River**, hence its name. Unlike many of the other jyotirlingas, Bhimashankar is visited little during the year since it is far from urban centers and relatively inaccessible. The major pilgrim traffic comes on the festival of **Shivaratri**, which usually falls within February and March.

Bhishma
In the *Mahabharata*, the later of the two great Hindu epics, Bhishma is the **son** of King **Shantanu** and an uncle and counselor to both warring factions, the **Pandavas** and the **Kauravas**. His name as a child is Devavrata; he receives the name Bhishma ("terrible") as an acknowledgment of his extremely difficult vow. King Shantanu has fallen in love with the maiden **Satyavati**, who agrees to marry him on the condition that her sons will rule instead of Devavrata, who has already been anointed the heir apparent. Bhishma not only agrees to give up the throne but takes the solemn vow that he will never marry, so that there will be no claimants from his lineage to compete for the throne. When Bhishma takes his dreadful vow, he is also given the option of choosing the time of his death.

Bhishma faithfully keeps this vow, and his adherence to it eventually costs him his life. It is Bhishma who abducts **Amba**, **Ambika**, and **Ambalika**, the **daughters** of the king of **Kashi**, to be married to his stepbrother **Vichitravirya**. Ambika and Ambalika happily marry Vichitravirya, but when Amba confides that she has already given her heart to King Salva, Bhishma releases her to go to him. Salva rejects Amba on the grounds that her virginity is suspect, since she has been abducted by another man. Amba returns to Bhishma and demands that he marry her since he is responsible for her plight, and when Bhishma refuses to break his vow, Amba is determined to get revenge. She is reborn as the man-woman **Shikhandi**, behind whom the **Pandava** prince **Arjuna** hides to shoot the arrows that eventually kill Bhishma.

Bhishma is a great man who is respected by all. His skill with arms makes him one of the finest warriors of his time, but he is most famous as a wise and generous counselor to both the Pandavas and the Kauravas. Although he ultimately sides with the Kaurava prince **Duryodhana** in the war between the two groups, before its outbreak Bhishma repeatedly advises Duryodhana to make peace with the Pandavas and share the kingdom with them. He fights valiantly in the Mahabharata war and destroys a large part of the Pandava armies, but finally he is hit by so many of Arjuna's arrows that he lays upon them like a bed. Although Bhishma is mortally wounded by Arjuna, he delays his death (through the boon given by his vow) until the **sun** resumes its more **auspicious** northern path (**uttarayana**). During this time he gives the victorious Pandavas copious instruction on state affairs and related topics. Bhishma's unswerving commitment to a vow that deprives him of the joys of family life, and his inability to avert the fratricidal conflict between his nephews, through which the family is ultimately destroyed, make him a lonely, somewhat tragic figure.

Bhishma Ashtami

Festival celebrated on the eighth **day** (ashtami) of the light, or waxing, half of the **lunar month** called **Magh** (January–February), marking the death of **Bhishma**. Bhishma is an uncle to both the **Kauravas** and the **Pandavas**, warring factions in the Hindu epic *Mahabharata*. He is well known for his bravery, continence, and truthfulness. He also has the power to choose the time of his death. Although he is mortally wounded in the great Mahabharata war, he remains alive until **weeks** later (delivering discourses and advice to the victorious Pandavas the entire time), delaying his death until the **sun** has resumed its northward course (**uttarayana**). On this day parents give **offerings** of food and **water** in Bhishma's name in the hope that their **sons** may have his good qualities.

Bhogamandapa

("food pavilion") The outermost entrance hall in the style of **architecture** found in the largest temples in **Orissa**. At the temple of **Jagannath** in Puri, the term *bhogamandapa* specifically refers to the area where the food offered to Jagannath as **prasad** ("favor") is cooked. Jagannath's temple is unusual in that the normal restrictions regarding **commensality** are suspended. Everyone eats together rather than being segregated by **caste**, signifying Jagannath's ultimate lordship over all beings. The prominence of this particular rite makes the bhogamandapa all the more important.

Bhogawara

One of the four major organizational groups of the **Dashanami Sanyasis**, renunciant **ascetics** who are devotees (**bhakta**) of the god **Shiva**; the other three groups are **Kitawara**, **Bhuriwara**, and **Anandawara**. Each of these divisions has its headquarters in one of the four monastic centers (**maths**) supposedly established by the philosopher **Shankaracharya**. Each group also has certain religious associations: with one of the four **Vedas**, with a particular quarter of the Indian subcontinent, with one of the "great utterances" (**mahavakyas**) expressing ultimate truth, with a specific ascetic quality, and with several of the ten Dashanami divisions. The Bhogawara group is affiliated with the **Govardhan Math** in the city of **Puri** on the Bay of Bengal, and it is therefore connected with the eastern quarter of India. Their Veda is the **Rg Veda**, their mahavakya is Prajnanam **Brahman** ("Knowledge is Brahman"), and their ascetic quality is to remain indifferent to worldly pleasures. The particular divisions associated with this group are the **Aranya Dashanamis** and **Vana Dashanamis**.

Bhoja

(r. 918–955 C.E.) Medieval Hindu king in the **Malwa** region of the modern state of **Uttar Pradesh**. Bhoja was famous both as a scholar and as a dam builder who created lakes for irrigation.

Bholanath

("simple lord") Common epithet of the god **Shiva**. In ordinary usage the word *bhola* carries a negative connotation: "simple," "guileless," and even "foolish." Yet in using this word to designate Shiva, his devotees (**bhakta**) are not intentionally insulting him but celebrating his boundless generosity to those with whom he is pleased. Shiva's devotees can give the simplest **offerings** (such as leaves, fruit, and **water**) and in turn ask for wealth, success, and power. Shiva's nature is considered "simple" because he willingly participates in such unequal exchanges, providing sharp contrast to the world economy, which demands equal value.

Bhramargit

("songs to the bee") Poetic genre in the devotional poetry of the god **Krishna**, which is set in the time after Krishna has gone to claim his kingdom in **Mathura**, never to return. The story tells how Krishna sends his companion **Uddhava** back to **Braj** with a message for the **gopis**, the cowherd **women** who are Krishna's dear companions, and who are virtually insane with longing because of his absence. Uddhava tries to reassure the gopis by telling them not to dwell on Krishna's physical absence. Uddhava further reminds them that since Krishna is the all-pervading divinity, he will always be with them even though he might not be visible. In the bhramargit poems, the gopis scornfully reject Uddhava's notions, asserting that this view of Krishna is abstract, lifeless, and suitable only for those who have never known Krishna in his embodied form. The genre's name comes from this story's earliest appearance, in the **Bhagavata Purana**. Here the gopis address their complaints about Krishna's absence to a large black bee, which in their passion and loneliness they mistake for Krishna.

Bhramari

("circling") Powerful form of the **Goddess**. Bhramari takes form to oppose the **demon** Aruna, who in his hubris is trying to compromise the chastity of the gods' wives. They implore the Goddess to help them, and in her form as Bhramari, she kills the demon and removes the threat. Bhramari is worshiped on the eighth night of **Navaratri**, a nine-**day** festival in which one goddess is appeased every night.

Bhrgu

In Hindu mythology, one of the **sons** of **Brahma** and one of the seven sages whose names mark exogamous clan "lineages" (**gotra**); the others are **Kashyapa**, **Bharadvaja**, **Vasishtha**, **Gautama**, **Atri**, and **Vishvamitra**. All **brahmins** are believed to be descended from these seven sages, with each family taking the name of its progenitor as its gotra name. In modern times these divisions are still important since marriage within the gotra is forbidden. After her marriage the bride adopts her husband's gotra as part of her new identity.

Bhrgu is most famous for testing the three major Hindu gods, which results in **Vishnu** being declared the greatest of the three. Bhrgu first goes to Brahma's house where the god does not pay Bhrgu appropriate respect, and in revenge Bhrgu **curses** Brahma to receive no **worship**. Next he goes to see **Shiva**, who refuses to meet with him because he is making love to his wife **Parvati** at the time. In turn, Bhrgu curses Shiva to be worshiped as the **linga**, the pillar-shaped symbol that has undeniable phallic associations. Lastly he visits Vishnu and, finding him asleep, gives him a sound kick in the chest. Vishnu wakes up, but shows no anger at this disrespect. Instead he massages Bhrgu's foot, gently inquires whether it has been hurt, and promises to retain its mark on his chest forever, where it appears as the **shrivatsa**. Vishnu's magnanimous behavior leads Bhrgu to proclaim him the best of all the gods. Not surprisingly, this version of the tale appears only in **Vaishnava** sectarian literature. See also **marriage prohibitions**.

Bhubaneshvar

Capital city of the modern Indian state of **Orissa**. Bhubaneshvar reportedly has over 500 temples, of which the most prominent is the **Lingaraja Temple**. It is dedicated to **Shiva** in his form as Tribhuvaneshvar ("Lord of the Triple World"), from which the city also gets its name.

Bhudevi

See **earth**.

Bhujangavalaya

("snake bracelet") In Hindu iconography, the name of a particular ornament worn by the god **Shiva**. The bhujangavalaya is a bracelet shaped in the form of a snake. In Hindu mythology Shiva is famous for wearing serpents, especially cobras, as ornaments around his arms and torso. This is just one of the attributes that marks him as different, powerful, and potentially dangerous. The prescriptive canons for the creation of Hindu images have followed up on this tradition, and Shiva is invariably shown wearing these bracelets.

Bhuriwara

One of the four major organizational groups of the **Dashanami Sanyasis**, renunciant ascetics who are devotees (**bhakta**) of the god **Shiva**; the other three groups are **Kitawara**, **Bhogawara**, and **Anandawara**. Each of these groups has its headquarters in one of the four monastic centers (**maths**) supposedly established by the philosopher **Shankaracharya**. Each division also has certain religious associations: with one of the four **Vedas**, with a particular quarter of the Indian subcontinent, with one of the "great utterances" (**mahavakyas**) expressing ultimate truth, with a particular ascetic quality, and with several of the ten Dashanami divisions. The Bhuriwara group is affiliated with the **Shringeri Math** in the southern Indian town of **Shringeri** and is thus connected with the southern quarter of India. Their **Veda** is the **Yajur Veda**, their mahavakya is **Aham Brahmasmi** ("I am **Brahman**"), and their ascetic quality is to renounce all wealth and to live on food growing wild in the jungles. The specific divisions associated with this group are **Saraswati Dashanami**, **Bharati Dashanami**, and **Puri Dashanami**.

Bhushundi

A character in the *Ramcharitmanas*, the version of the *Ramayana* written by the poet-saint **Tulsidas** (1532–1623?). Bhushundi is a crow who symbolizes the power of devotion to God to redeem even the lowest of creatures. One of the most pronounced differences between the original **Valmiki** *Ramayana* and the Tulsidas *Ramayana* is that Tulsidas puts

Women praying at a shrine in Bihar. This northern Indian state is home to many sacred sites.

far greater stress on devotion to **Rama**, of which Bhushundi is a perfect example. In Indian culture, crows are considered unclean birds since they are scavengers who will eat anything. Yet in one of the narrative levels of the *Ramcharitmanas*, it is the "unclean" crow Bhushundi who narrates the story to the "sacred" eagle **Garuda**—the vehicle of the god **Vishnu**. As part of his account in the *Ramayana*, Bhushundi relates the terrifying experience of being given an unmediated vision of Rama in all his majesty, and how he (as did the sage **Markandeya**) went into Rama's mouth and perceived the entire universe inside.

Bhut

("[someone who] was") The spirit of a person who has recently died, which is still inappropriately connected to the world of the living. This is often a troubling or malevolent presence, either to the departed's family or the general population. Bhuts and other malignant spirits, such as **prets** or **churails**, have generally either suffered an untimely or violent death or died with certain unfulfilled desires, particularly relating to marriage and family life. In cases where both these factors are present, the likelihood of the departed becoming a bhut is deemed much greater. Bhuts make themselves known to the living through either **dreams** or **possession**. In some cases they have specific requests and can be placated by **worship** and **offerings**. In such cases the dreams and possession are methods of communicating with the living, who can perform the necessary actions. Some bhuts resort to possession as an attempt to realize their unfulfilled desires by directly using a living person's body. These spirits are far more malevolent, and the only way to remove them is through exorcism. For further information on the care of restless family spirits, see Ann Grodzins Gold, *Fruitful Journeys*, 1988; for a masterful psychological interpretation of spirits, possession, and healing, see Sudhir Kakar, *Shamans, Mystics, and Doctors*, 1991.

Bhuta

Epithet of the god **Shiva**. See **Shiva**.

Bhutalingas

("elemental **lingas**") A network of five southern Indian sacred sites (**tirthas**), four in the state of **Tamil Nadu** and one in **Andhra Pradesh**, all dedicated to the god **Shiva**. In each of these centers, the most sacred object is the linga, a pillar-shaped form representing Shiva. What makes these sites unique is that the linga is supposedly composed of one of the five primordial **elements**. Thus the linga in **Tiruvannamalai** is formed from **fire**; the linga in **Jambukeshvar** is formed from **water**; the one in **Kanchipuram** is made from **earth**; that in **Kalahasti**, the sacred site in Andhra Pradesh, is formed from air; and the linga in **Chidambaram** is made from **space**. Between them, these five sites comprise a symbolic **cosmology** that encompasses all created things.

Bhutam

(7th c. c.e.) With **Pey** and **Poygai**, one of the first three **Alvars**, a group of twelve poet-saints who lived in southern India between the seventh and tenth centuries. All of the Alvars were devotees (**bhakta**) of the god **Vishnu**. Their stress on passionate devotion (**bhakti**) to a personal god, conveyed through hymns sung in the **Tamil language**, transformed and revitalized Hindu religious life. According to tradition, the three men were caught in a torrential storm, and one by one they took shelter in a small dry spot, with each making room for the next. As they stood together they felt a fourth presence, which was Vishnu. The Alvars were such great devotees that their combined energy was sufficient to provoke Vishnu's manifestation. Overwhelmed with ecstasy, the three burst into song, which formed the first of their compositions. For further information see Kamil Zvelebil, *Tamil Literature*, 1975.

Bhutayajna

("**sacrifice** to creatures") One of the five great sacrifices (**panchamahayajna**) that is prescribed in the texts on religious duty (**Dharma Shastras**). These five great sacrifices are daily religious observances for a "**twice-born**" householder, that is, a householder born into one of the three "twice-born" groups in Indian society—**brahmin**, **kshatriya**, and **vaishya**—who is eligible to receive the adolescent religious **initiation** known as the "second birth." Each sacrifice (**yajna**) is directed toward a different class of beings, from the Ultimate Reality down to **animals**, and is satisfied by specific actions. The bhutayajna is directed toward animals and outcasts (and in some understandings, **ghosts**), and it is satisfied by putting out food for them to eat. In the time since the Dharma Shastras were composed, Hindu life has undergone significant changes, and this particular sacrifice is rarely performed today.

Bidhai Samaroh

("farewell celebration") In northern India, the formal departure of a new bride for her marital home. This is a momentous event for several different reasons. A marriage is the start of a family, and through her marriage a young woman gets the opportunity to become a wife and mother; these roles are still seen as a woman's highest fulfillment and happiness. Yet according to the traditional model of the Indian joint family, after marriage a woman goes to live with and becomes part of her husband's family. Thus the act of seeing off a new bride carries bittersweet feelings—happiness for her marriage and hopes for her good fortune, but also the sense that things have irreversibly changed.

Bihar

One of the states in modern northern India, sandwiched between **Uttar Pradesh** and **West Bengal**, with **Nepal** on its northern border. Bihar has an incredibly rich history; it was the ancestral homeland of the **Maurya dynasty**, which ruled over much of the Indian subcontinent between the fourth and third centuries before the common era. The capital city was at **Pataliputra**, identified with modern Patna. Bihar also contains the town of Bodh Gaya, where the Buddha attained enlightenment, in addition to many other places associated with events in his life.

Despite this lush past, modern Bihar is an extremely difficult place to live; illiteracy and infant mortality rates are very high, life expectancy is fairly low, and social conditions can best be described as feudal. Most of its citizens can barely make a living and do so through agriculture, while a small percentage are fabulously wealthy. Bihar is also a textbook example of what modern Indians call the "criminalization of politics," in which known criminals are either agents for politicians or are themselves holding political office. Although Bihar has abundant mineral resources, its pervasive corruption virtually ensures that their benefits will reach only a few. Despite all of these disadvantages, Bihar does have well-known sacred sites (**tirthas**). One of these is the town of **Gaya**, famous as a place to perform funerary rites (**antyeshthi samskara**). Another sacred place is the temple at **Vaidyanath**, which is one of the twelve **jyotirlingas**, a group of sites especially sacred to the god **Shiva**. For general information about Bihar and all the regions of India, an accessible reference is Christine Nivin et al., *India*. 8th ed., Lonely Planet, 1998.

Bijak

("inventory") One of the three main collections of verse ascribed to the poet-saint **Kabir** (mid-15th c.?); the other two are found in the **Adigranth** and the manuscripts of the religious organization **Dadupanth**. Kabir is the best known of the **sants**, an umbrella term for a group of central and northern Indian poet-saints who share several concepts: stress on individualized, interior religion leading to a personal experience of the divine; disdain for external ritual, particularly image **worship**; faith in the power of the divine Name; and a tendency to ignore conventional **caste** distinctions. Of all the sants, Kabir is the most iconoclastic with regard to established religious practices and authorities. He invariably emphasizes the need for individual searching and realization.

Given the content of Kabir's message, it is notable that the *Bijak* is the scripture of the **Kabirpanth**, a religious community claiming to be his followers. Certainly Kabir himself would have condemned the notion of making him the founder of anything, or of his verses gaining the authority of a scripture. In content, the *Bijak* contains verses of varying types: short epigrams that have become proverbial wisdom, longer stanzas in the **chaupai** form, and shorter two-line verse (**doha**). Linguistic features identify the *Bijak* as belonging to the eastern part of the **Hindi** language region, hence its common name as the "eastern" recension. For translations of the text itself, see Linda Hess and Shukdev Singh (trans.), *The Bijak of Kabir*, 1983.

Bijakshara

("seed syllable") In the esoteric ritual tradition known as **tantra**, a bijakshara is a particular set of syllabic utterances that is believed to have an intimate connection with a **deity**—either as a way of gaining access to the god's power or as the subtlest form of the deity itself. These syllables are usually meaningless sounds (for example, *aum, hrim, klim*), although at times they may contain actual words. Bijaksharas are important not for their meaning but for the power inherent in the sounds themselves. The transmission of such seed syllables and the entitlement (**adhikara**) to use them is an important feature of tantric **initiation** (**diksha**). For further information see Swami Agehananda Bharati, *The Tantric Tradition*, 1977; and Douglas

Renfrew Brooks, *The Secret of the Three Cities*, 1990.

Bilva

The wood-apple tree (*Aegle marmelos*). Although this tree is known for its delicious fruit, its primary religious importance is its leaves. These are used in the **worship** of **Shiva** and are usually placed as an **offering** on the god's image or **linga** (pillar-shaped symbol). These leaves are believed to be dearer to him than any other offering. In everyday language this tree is also commonly known as the bel.

Bimbisara

(d. 494 B.C.E.) King of Magadha, the region corresponding to modern **Bihar**, whose reign ended shortly before the traditionally accepted date for the death of the Buddha. Bimbisara was an energetic administrator who had designs on ruling a much larger empire. To this end, he tried to conquer and control large parts of the **Ganges** basin. Bimbisara is believed to have been the first king to conceive of ruling a large empire, although he was deposed and murdered by his **son Ajatashatru** before he saw it become a reality.

Bindu

("drop") In the **Shrividya** school, a particular branch of the esoteric ritual tradition known as **tantra**, the bindu is the name for the dot in the very center of the **shrichakra**, which is a Shrividya symbolic diagram (**yantra**) used in **worship**. The shrichakra is composed of nine interlocking triangles—four pointing up and five pointing down—surrounded by a double series of lotus petals and exterior circular and angular walls. The bindu symbolizes the ultimate unity of the divine principles, **Shiva** and **Shakti**, and by extension the unity of all reality. For further information see Douglas Renfrew Brooks, *The Secret of the Three Cities*, 1990.

Bindusara

(3rd c. B.C.E.) **Son** of **Chandragupta Maurya**, the founder of the Mauryan empire, and father of **Ashoka**, the empire's greatest figure. At Bindusara's accession the Mauryans controlled the **Indus** and **Ganges** river basins. Bindusara not only consolidated his father's gains, but also expanded Mauryan control into the **Deccan** region as far south as Mysore. He was reportedly a man of universal tastes, since tradition holds that he asked Antiochus I, the Seleucid ruler of Syria, for sweet wine, dried figs, and a sophist. Antiochus apparently sent the first two items but declared that Greek philosophers were not for export. See also **Maurya dynasty**.

Birla, Ghanshyamdas

(1894–1983) Patriarch of the Birla industrial family. The Birlas made a fortune in opium in the early decades of the twentieth century and then diversified into a variety of other industrial ventures. Ghanshyamdas was a close friend of **Mohandas K. Gandhi** and the major financial supporter for Gandhi's political organization, the Indian National Congress, to which Birla had given an estimated 100 million rupees by the time of independence. In his later years, he devoted considerable money and attention to building temples, sponsoring religious and charitable trusts, and performing other honorable deeds.

Birth

At its most basic level, birth is a biological event, but it becomes a cultural event by virtue of the rites performed for and significance given to it. Different Hindu communities show considerable regional and sectarian variation in the ways that they mark a birth, but several themes remain fairly constant. Although the birth of a child is a highly **auspicious** occasion, it is also considered impure because of the various bodily tissues and fluids coming with it (**blood**,

Depiction of the god Vishnu's Boar avatar.
Vishnu appears on earth in the shape
of a boar to combat a demon.

membranes, amniotic fluid, placenta, etc.). Thus, birth rituals usually include rites of purification for both mother and child, to remove this birth impurity (**sutakashaucha**). For the mother this is fairly simple: a bath after the birth followed by baths during a period of seclusion (7–10 days). The final rite for the child, the head **shaving** known as the **chudakarana samskara**, may not come for years after the birth.

Aside from impurity (**ashaucha**), another constant theme is the threat of potential danger. Immediately after birth, both mother and child are seen as highly vulnerable, not only from environmental stresses such as cold, fatigue, or infection, but from ills brought on by **witchcraft** or the evil eye (**nazar**). Given this concern, it is not surprising that the placenta and all other childbirth byproducts are carefully collected and disposed of, lest they be used for spells. The period of seclusion after the birth is intended both to prevent contact with such malevolent forces and to ward them off through **rites of protection**. The mother is usually given massages and fed strengthening foods to bolster her resistance. The use of charms, or

amulets, is also quite common. For further information see Lawrence Babb, *The Divine Hierarchy*, 1975; and Doranne Jacobsen, "Golden Handprints and Redpainted Feet: Hindu Childbirth Rituals in Central India," in Nancy Falk and Rita M. Gross (eds.), *Unspoken Worlds: Women's Religious Lives in Non-Western Cultures*, 2000.

Black Yajur Veda
Along with the **White Yajur Veda**, one of the two major forms of the **Yajur Veda**, one of the oldest Hindu religious texts. The major difference between these two forms is in the placement of explanatory notes on the Vedic **mantras** (sacred sounds) and their significance. The four recensions of the Black Yajur Veda include these notes in the text itself. In contrast, the one recension of the White Yajur Veda gathers these notes into an appendix known as a **Brahmana**, which gives its name to the second major stratum of Vedic texts.

Blessing
See **ashirvad**.

Blood
As with all bodily fluids, blood is considered ritually impure and a source of pollution upon contact. Blood is also deemed a "hot" and powerful substance, not only by virtue of its impurity (**ashaucha**), but also because of its connection with life. Witches are popularly seen as deriving their nourishment from human blood. This highlights both their malevolent character, since they can only live by destroying others, and also their marginal, antisocial quality, since they feed on a substance considered violently impure. In another context, blood from **animal sacrifice** is often offered to **village deities** or to certain powerful and terrifying forms of the **Goddess**. Any **deities** taking blood sacrifice are considered "hot," meaning that they are powerful enough to grant favors to devotees but also marginal, potentially dangerous,

and requiring continual infusions of life-sustaining blood to maintain their powers. See also **witchcraft**.

Boar Avatar

The third **avatar**, or "incarnation," of the god **Vishnu**. Vishnu takes this form at the beginning of one of the cosmic ages, when the process of creation has been interrupted by the disappearance of the **Earth**. The source of this problem is the demon-king **Hiranyaksha**, who has kidnapped the Earth and hidden her in the depths of the cosmic ocean. Taking the form of a giant boar, Vishnu dives to the bottom of the ocean, where he slays Hiranyaksha, places the Earth on the tip of his tusk, and lifts her from the waters. With the reappearance of the Earth, the process of creation resumes.

It is generally accepted that the avatar doctrine provided a way to assimilate smaller regional **deities** into the larger pantheon by designating them as forms of Vishnu. This inference is supported by the Boar avatar, which seems to have absorbed an ancient cult in central India by making the boar an incarnation of Vishnu. In modern times the Boar avatar is worshiped little, although it had a significant following in the past, particularly in central India. This is partly supported by the sculptural record; the caves at **Ellora** and **Udayagiri** have particularly fine sculptural renditions of this avatar. For further information see Arthur Llewellyn Basham, *The Wonder That Was India*, 1968.

Bose, Subhash Chandra

(1896–1945) Bengali politician and freedom fighter. Before World War II, Bose had unsuccessfully contested with **Mohandas K. Gandhi** for the leadership of the Congress Party. Bose was more impatient than Gandhi for the British to leave, and he was more willing to expel them by force. During World War II, Bose used Japanese patronage to form the Indian National Army (INA), whose objective was to expel the British from India by armed force. Starting in Singapore the INA marched 5,000 miles through Southeast Asia, but they were ultimately defeated by the British army at the city of Kohima in eastern India. Although there is eyewitness testimony that Bose died from burns stemming from a plane crash in the final days of the Pacific war, even today many Bengalis believe that he is still alive and living incognito.

Brahma

Brahma is the first member of the **Trimurti**, the "three forms" of divinity made up of the dominant male **deities** in the Hindu pantheon: Brahma as the creator of the universe, **Vishnu** as the preserver or sustainer, and **Shiva** as the destroyer. Brahma is usually portrayed with four heads (the fifth having been cut off by **Bhairava**, a wrathful form of Shiva), and his **animal** vehicle is the **hamsa**, or Indian goose.

According to one widely held myth, during the time of cosmic dissolution between world cycles, Vishnu floats in the middle of the cosmic ocean, lying on the giant serpent **Shesha**. When the time for creation comes, a lotus sprouts from Vishnu's navel and opens to reveal Brahma inside. Brahma takes up the work of creation, and at the end of the world cycle, Brahma returns to the lotus, which is reabsorbed into Vishnu. Because of his spontaneous appearance at the beginning of every cosmic age, one of the names for Brahma is **Svayambhu** ("self-born"). Unlike the Judeo-Christian belief, the world is not created from nothing. Brahma merely arranges the existing elements of the universe into a coherent and ordered cosmos.

Brahma is a major figure in the pantheon and is prominent in many episodes in Hindu mythology. His mythic presence often obscures the fact that he is never worshiped as a primary **deity**. In fact, he has only one temple devoted to him in all of India, in

Pushkar. Some Hindus have attributed this lack of **worship** to his status as the creator. After all, since creation has been completed, why should one bother with Brahma, whose work is done? In the **puranas**, texts on Hindu mythology, this lack of worship is usually ascribed to a **curse**—sometimes by the god Shiva but in other stories by the sage **Bhrgu**.

Brahmacharin

("seeker of **Brahman**") A term with several possible meanings depending on the context. In the **dharma literature**, which gives instruction on religious duties, a brahmacharin is a person in a period of religious study. This period is the first of the four ashramas ("**stages of life**") of a **twice-born** man, that is, a man born into one of three groups in Indian society: **brahmin**, **kshatriya**, or **vaishya**. Such men are eligible to receive the adolescent religious **initiation** known as the "second birth." According to the ideal, after his initiation and adornment with the **sacred thread**—the most visible sign of a twice-born man—the brahmacharin shall live in his **guru's** household and study the **Veda**, the oldest Hindu religious text, in addition to performing other religious acts. Since brahmacharins are focused on gaining religious knowledge, this is supposed to be a very austere time of life marked by strict **celibacy**, hard work, service to the teacher, meticulous observance of all religious rites, and avoidance of luxuries such as beds, cosmetics, and bodily ornaments. Once this period of study is over, the student will marry and enter the second ashrama, that of the householder. The system described in the dharma literature is an idealized model, and one cannot be sure that it was ever strictly followed. Although many contemporary brahmin boys still undergo the "second birth," other elements—such as the **ascetic** lifestyle and emphasis on the study of the Veda—are largely ignored in contemporary times.

Some of the term's original meaning remains in an ascetic context.

Brahmacharin can also be defined as a novice or junior monk, whose duty is to serve and learn from the senior monks, or as the name of two particular ascetic groups. One of these groups is the prestigious **Swaminarayan sect**, whose members are recruited solely from the **caste** of brahmins. The other is an organization called the Brahmachari **Sanyasis**, devotees (**bhakta**) of the god **Shiva** who are distinct from the **Dashanami** Sanyasis. The Brahmachari Sanyasis have an **ashram** on Mount **Girnar** and in the bathing (**snana**) festival known as the **Kumbha Mela**, the Brahmachari **Naga** (fighting) Sanyasis have a recognized place among the other Naga groups. For further information see G. S. Ghurye, *Indian Sadhus*, 1964.

Brahmacharya

("going after **Brahman**") In its most traditional sense, this word refers to the lifestyle of a young man belonging to a particular class during his life as a student (**brahmacharin**). This period is the first of the four ashramas ("**stages of life**") of a **twice-born** man, that is, a man born into one of three groups in Indian society: **brahmin**, **kshatriya**, or **vaishya**. Such men are eligible to receive the adolescent religious **initiation** known as the "second birth." His life as a student will then commence, and he will move into his **guru's** household and study the sacred texts, the **Vedas**. This is conceived as a period of intense study, religious practice, and an austere lifestyle marked by the restraint of desires, for which the hallmark is **celibacy**. Although the model of the four ashramas is largely archaic in modern times, the word *brahmacharya* still connotes this sort of austere religious lifestyle, and it is often used as a synonym for celibacy.

Brahmahatya

("**brahmin** murder") In the **dharma literature**, which gives instruction on religious duties, brahmahatya is one of the

four great crimes that makes one an outcast from society. This crime's seriousness stems from notions of brahmin sanctity and status; with the exception of self-defense, the deliberate murder of a brahmin holds serious repercussions. Even the gods are subject to this act's negative karmic consequences. Hindu mythology records that the god **Bhairava** wanders the **earth** for years after cutting off one of the heads of the god **Brahma**. The skull sticks to his hand as a visible sign of his crime until it finally falls off at **Kapalamochana**. In the more lenient prescriptions in the dharma literature, the punishment for a brahmin murderer is parallel to that of Bhairava. The murderer has to carry the skull of the dead man for twelve years, wearing only a rough garment to cover his loins, and during that period he has to live on alms, **begging** at no more than seven houses per **day**. After twelve years he is deemed pure, unless the murder was intentional, in which case the term of punishment is doubled. According to several commentators, however, when a brahmin is intentionally murdered by a **kshatriya**, **vaishya**, or **shudra**, the only possible expiation (**prayashchitta**) is death.

Brahma Kumaris

Modern Hindu religious organization founded in the 1930s by a Sindhi jeweler named Dada Lekhraj. In 1947, after the partition of British India into India and Pakistan, the organization relocated its headquarters from Sindh (in modern Pakistan) to Mount Abu in the Indian state of **Rajasthan**. Although the sect has only about 100,000 members—minuscule by Hindu standards—it is noteworthy for several reasons. Unlike most Hindus, the Brahma Kumaris aggressively seeks out and converts new members, and thus it has a much higher profile than other religious sects. The organization preaches a doctrine foretelling the imminent end of the world, which must be prepared for by radical **asceticism**. It is also noteworthy that

since its beginning, the majority of its adherents have been **women**.

The movement began following a series of apocalyptic visions by Dada Lekhraj. These visions not only convinced him of the coming tribulation but also reinforced his conviction that a human being's real identity lay not in the body but in the soul. This latter realization resulted in the organization's adoption of complete **celibacy**. When this ideal was adopted by some of his young women followers, it initially led to a tremendous uproar, because they renounced their primary traditional roles as wives and mothers. The movement persisted despite these troubles, which bound the followers together even more tightly. By the time Dada Lekhraj died in 1969, the movement had developed a strong missionary bent. All of these factors make it unusual and, in the eyes of many ordinary Hindus, marginal and suspicious. For further information see Lawrence Babb, *Redemptive Encounters*, 1987.

Brahma Marriage

One of the eight ways to perform a marriage according to the **Dharma Shastras**, the treatises on religious duty (**dharma**). In a **Brahma** marriage the bride's father gives away his **daughter**, along with any ornaments he can afford, to a learned man of good character. This man is respectfully invited to accept her with absolutely no conditions or fees. This form is considered the most suitable for **Brahmans** because it is free from lust or any sort of financial inducements, hence the name *Brahma marriage*. For these reasons it is also deemed the best of the four approved (prashasta) forms of marriage.

The Brahma marriage is one of the two forms practiced in modern India. It is by far the more socially respectable, since the **asura marriage**—in which the groom gives money to the bride and her family—carries the connotation of selling the bride. Yet even with the Brahma

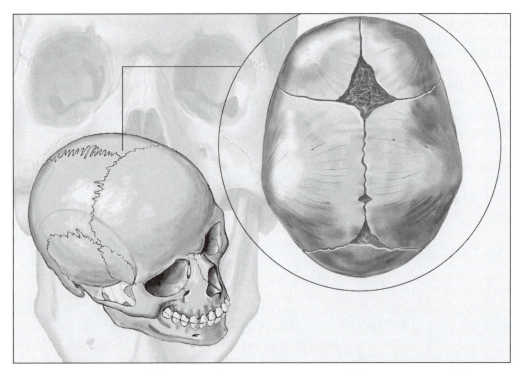

After death, a liberated person's soul is believed to escape through an opening in the skull called the brahmarandhra. This is thought to correspond to the fontanel, an opening in an infant's skull (right) that closes in adulthood (left).

marriage, there has been significant divergence from the classically mandated form. In many modern Indian weddings, it has become common for the bride's family to give the groom's family a **dowry** as a condition for the marriage, which can easily be interpreted as selling the groom. See also **marriage, eight classical forms**, and **prashasta marriages**.

Brahma Muhurta

("time of **Brahma**") The forty-eight-minute period (**muhurta**) immediately before sunrise, which is thought to be the most auspicious time of the **day**. This **auspiciousness** makes it the best time for **worship**, meditation, or any type of religious practice; serious spiritual aspirants rise before it begins so that they may take full advantage of the time.

Brahman

In its first appearances in the **Rg Veda**, the earliest text in the sacred literature known as the **Vedas**, the term *Brahman* both denotes the power inherent in, and gives potency to, the sacred word. In the **Brahmana** literature, one of the later strands in the Vedas, *brahman* was the name for one of the four types of priests who officiated at a **sacrifice** (the others being **hotr**, **udgatr**, and **adhvaryum**). In the **Upanishads** and afterward, *Brahman* is the generally accepted term for the highest reality in the universe, which is both the material cause and the final cause of all that exists. In the worldview of the Upanishads, the speculative and most recent texts in the Vedas, Brahman is the single binding unity behind the world's apparent diversity. These texts also affirm Brahman's identity with **atman**, the individual soul, and thus the identity of the essence of macrocosm and microcosm. As described in many of the Upanishads and later systematized by the philosopher **Shankaracharya** (9th c.), the ultimate form of Brahman is without qualities (**nirguna**), formless, nameless, indefinable, and grammatically a neuter noun. In contrast, particular **deities** are seen as lower, provisional, qualified (**saguna**) forms of Brahman. This understanding was modified by the influence of later devotional trends, in which ideas of the highest Brahman became identified with a particular deity, who was seen as the ultimate source of all things.

Brahmana

General name for the second literary stratum in the **Vedas**, the earliest and most authoritative Hindu religious texts. Although the composition of these differing parts of the Veda is not completely linear, the Brahmanas generally come after the hymns of praise to the gods known as **samhitas** and precede the speculative texts known as the **Aranyakas** and the **Upanishads**. In theory, each Veda has a Brahmana as an appendix, which is intended to give further explanation of the Vedic rituals. Although the **Yajur Veda** is the only one for which this is actually true, this understanding gives the Brahmanas the authority of revealed scripture (**shruti**) and thus makes them unquestionable. There are several different Brahmanas, of which the most important are the **Aiteraya Brahmana** and the **Shatapatha Brahmana**; the latter's tone and contents (including the **Isha Upanishad**) clearly mark it as the most recent of the Brahmanas.

The Brahmanas are primarily ritual manuals, and they give exacting, painstaking instructions for performing these Vedic rituals. These texts indicate a fundamental shift in religious practice, from the earlier emphasis on **sacrifice** as a means of invoking and pleasing the Vedic gods to an importance on the power of ritual itself. This new emphasis makes the sacrificial priests the most powerful people of all, since even the gods themselves are subject to the rituals. The power of correctly performed ritual paves the way for the Aranyakas and the Upanishads, which asks more speculative questions about the rituals themselves. At times these differing religious genres are juxtaposed—as in the Shatapatha Brahmana, in which the Isha Upanishad is embedded. Such juxtapositions indicate that although the stress varied in differing types of texts, there was some overlap during the time they were composed.

Brahmanda
See **cosmic egg**.

Brahmarandhra

("aperture of **Brahman**") In traditional mystical physiology, an opening in the crown of the head—perhaps corresponding to the fontanel in young children. Although this hole usually closes up, it is widely believed that if at the time of death the departing soul can be channeled through this aperture, it will bring final liberation of the soul (**moksha**). The earliest mention of this idea can be found in **Katha Upanishad** 6.16, and exercises to facilitate this practice are stressed in certain varieties of **yoga**. The desire to open this aperture is the reason behind one of the actions sometimes performed during **cremation**. In many cases the pyre's heat will itself split the skull, but when it does not, a long pole is used to break it open in an effort to release the soul.

Brahma Sampraday

One of the four branches of the **Bairagi Naga** class of **ascetics**. The Bairagi Nagas are devotees (**bhakta**) of the god **Vishnu**, organized in military fashion into different **anis**, or "armies." Until the beginning of the nineteenth century, their primary occupation was as mercenary soldiers, although they also had substantial trading interests; both of these occupations have largely disappeared in contemporary times. The Brahma Sampraday traces its immediate spiritual lineage through the **Gaudiya Vaishnava** sect, founded by the Bengali devotee **Chaitanya**, but claims ultimate descent from the southern Indian philosopher **Madhva**. This latter claim seems highly suspect, in part because the guardian **deities** of the two sects are different; Chaitanya and his followers **worship** the gods **Krishna** and **Radha**, whereas Madhva and his followers worship **Lakshmi**-Narayan. There are also differences in their observances. Although the Madhva ascetics have a long history in southern India, they have virtually no presence in the north, where the Chaitanyite ascetics are well represented. Ghurye speculates that this claim is based on the desire of the Gaudiya Vaishnavas to establish ties to an ancient lineage; this would give them an unassailable identity and thus a place in the bathing (**snana**) procession at religious festival **Kumbha Mela**. See G. S. Ghurye, *Indian Sadhus*, 1964.

Brahmasutra Bhashya

A commentary (**bhashya**) written by the philosopher **Shankaracharya** on **Badarayana's Brahma Sutras**, a collection of 555 brief aphorisms (**sutras**) that form the basis for the philosophical school known as **Vedanta**. This commentary is the defining text for the **Advaita Vedanta** school of Indian **philosophy**. Shankaracharya begins his investigation by establishing the Self as the basis of all knowledge, since the one thing that can never be doubted is the reality of the one who knows. He identifies this knowing consciousness as the eternal Self, or **atman**, which never changes over time despite the vicissitudes of the physical bodies it inhabits. According to Shankaracharya, the perceivable world is clearly subject to change and thus is not the Absolute Reality, which the philosopher identifies as the unqualified, unchanging **Brahman**. Following the **Upanishads**, Shankaracharya identifies atman as identical to Brahman. He states that for human beings the reason for both unhappiness and the bondage of the soul is the ignorance of this relationship, which causes one to mistake this perceivable reality for the Ultimate Reality. With the destruction of this mistaken understanding, all bonds are broken, and the person attains final liberation.

Brahma Sutras

Variant name for **Badarayana's Vedanta Sutras**, which date from the third to the fifth century B.C.E. This collection of 555 brief aphorisms (**sutras**) is the basis for the philosophical school known as **Vedanta**, so named because it claims to reveal the ultimate meaning of the religious scriptures known as the **Vedas**. They are given the name Brahma Sutras because they attempt to summarize and systematize the philosophic and religious ideas in the speculative texts known as the **Upanishads**, particularly the ideas about the Ultimate Reality known as **Brahman**. The sutras are so brief that they presuppose commentary, of which the most famous is the *Brahmasutra Bhashya*, written by the philosopher **Shankaracharya**.

Brahmayajna

("**sacrifice** to **Brahman**") One of the five great sacrifices (**panchamahayajna**) prescribed in the texts on religious duty (**Dharma Shastras**). These five great sacrifices are prescribed daily religious observances for a "**twice-born**" householder, that is, a householder who has been born into one of three groups in Indian society—**brahmin**, **kshatriya**, or **vaishya**. Such men are eligible for the adolescent religious **initiation** known as the "second birth." Each of the five sacrifices (**yajna**) is directed toward a different class of beings, from the Ultimate Reality down to **animals**, and is satisfied by different actions. The brahmayajna is directed toward the Ultimate Reality (Brahman) and is satisfied by teaching and studying the **Vedas**, the oldest Hindu religious texts. In the time since the Dharma Shastras were composed, Hindu life has undergone significant change, but many brahmins still study the Veda—if not daily, at some point in their youth.

Brahmi

The most commonly used script in the **inscriptions** of the emperor **Ashoka** (r. 269–232 B.C.E.), the greatest figure in the **Maurya dynasty**. Ashoka's empire encompassed all of the subcontinent except the deepest parts of southern India and went west into modern Afghanistan. Brahmi script was used in all regions of the Mauryan empire except in the northwest, where the **Kharoshthi** script was used. Ashoka's **rock edicts** and **pillar edicts** are the earliest significant Indian written documents and give invaluable information about contemporary social, political, and religious life. Brahmi is the ancestor of the modern Indian scripts, including **Devanagari**. It is also the ultimate source for all indigenous southeast Asian alphabets, which developed from trade with southern India in the early medieval period. Over the course of time, Brahmi was replaced by later scripts, was forgotten, and became unreadable. Although Ashoka's inscriptions ensured that Europeans were aware of Brahmi, their content was a mystery until 1837, when **James Prinsep** deciphered the Brahmi alphabet by working backward from later, known scripts.

Brahmin

In the traditional Hindu theory of the four major social groups (**varnas**), the brahmins are the group with the highest status, based on the belief that they are purer than all others. This belief is based on the creation story known as the **Purusha Sukta**, in which the brahmins are created from the Primeval Man's mouth. The mouth is part of the head and thus the highest part of the body, and it is also associated with speech, one of the definitively human faculties. From the earliest Hindu recorded history, brahmins have been associated with speech and the sacred word; they were the scholars, priests, ritual technicians, and protectors of sacred learning. This is still true in modern times, although there are also many brahmins who have other occupations, such as trade, business, and government service.

Aside from their traditional association with sacred learning, their other source of social status is their ritual **purity**, which is believed to be greater than that of all other human beings. This ritual purity is inherent, conferred by **birth**. According to tradition, even an uneducated brahmin should be considered a "god on **earth**," whereas a learned brahmin is more sacred still. This ritual purity makes brahmins preferable for service to many of the gods of the Hindu pantheon, since they are considered the best intermediaries to "insulate" the **deities** from ordinary people. Although brahmins as a whole have the highest status, within the brahmin community there are highly defined subgroups (**jatis**), which are often defined by region of origin.

Brahmo Samaj

The earliest of the Hindu reform groups, founded in Calcutta in the early nineteenth century by **Ram Mohan Roy** (1774–1833). His purpose was to purge contemporary Hinduism of its "corrupt" practices, such as **sati** (**widow** burning), the ban on widow remarriage, image **worship**, and **caste**. In his effort to find a traditional authority for such reforms, he chose the **Upanishads** as his key religious texts. After his death the movement was eventually headed by Debendranath Tagore (father of the Nobel laureate **Rabindranath Tagore**) and later by **Keshub Chander Sen**; disagreements over ritual matters split the movement under both leaders. By the late 1800s the Samaj's influence had largely passed, although in an interesting twist, it became the vehicle through which the mystic **Ramakrishna** met many of his disciples.

The Brahmo Samaj's social program reflected and responded to contemporary European critiques of popular Hinduism, some levied by Christian missionaries and others based on the rationalist emphasis of the Enlightenment. The Brahmo Samaj's openness put it at the forefront of legal reform—in particular, influencing the 1829 law banning sati. But at the same time, its members were mostly Westernized urban intellectuals, far removed from the life and religious concerns of Hindus. For further information see Spencer Lavan, "The Brahmo Samaj: India's First Movement for Religious Reform," in Robert D. Baird (ed.), *Religion in Modern India*, 1998.

Braj

Northern Indian region on the **Yamuna River**, south of the modern city of Delhi. According to Hindu tradition, Braj is the land where the god **Krishna** lived during his time on **earth**. The Braj region does not have clearly defined boundaries, and the name has never referred to an official administrative area. Instead it has been defined by popular piety. Krishna's devotees (**bhakta**) place great emphasis on visualizing his exploits as a way to attain communion with him, and thus places throughout the Braj region are associated with very specific incidents in Krishna's life. As it now stands, the southern and eastern borders of the region are just over five miles southeast of the city of **Mathura**, and its northern and western boundaries are nearly five times that distance. For extensive information on Braj and its culture, see A. W. Entwistle, *Braj*, 1987.

Braj Bhasha

The "language of **Braj**"; a dialect of medieval **Hindi** primarily spoken in the Braj region, south of the modern city of Delhi. Braj is the land associated with the god **Krishna**, and the devotion that flourished there between the fifteenth and eighteenth centuries made Braj Bhasha a major literary language. Aside from being the language of Krishna worshipers, it also functioned as a lingua franca—a common language used by diverse peoples—for religious devotees (**bhakta**) in a much larger area of northern India, although it varied at the borders.

Brhadaranyaka ("Great Forest Book") Upanishad

By general consensus, the oldest of the **Upanishads**, the speculative religious texts that form the most recent stratum of the **Vedas**. The Brhadaranyaka Upanishad's chronological priority is supported by at least four pieces of evidence: its length, its lack of organization, its archaic language, and its relationship to earlier Vedic texts. The opening passage gives an extended comparison between the world and the sacrificial horse, showing clear parallels with the earlier **Brahmana** literature. Moreover, by its very name ("great forest book"), the Brhadaranyaka Upanishad clearly points to a transition from the **Aranyaka** ("forest books") literature, which followed Brahmana literature. This upanishad first addresses many of the questions raised in later texts and is therefore an important source for the development of the tradition. Unlike most of the later Upanishads, it is written in prose rather than poetry, with the instruction often in the form of dialogue between various speakers.

Brhadeshvar

Temple built in the southern Indian city of **Tanjore** around the year 1000 B.C.E. by the Chola king **Raja Raja** (r. 985–1014). The temple is dedicated to the god **Shiva** in his form as Brhadeshvar (the "great lord"). It was built in the **Dravida** style characteristic of southern Indian temples, in which the buildings are of modest height but cover an immense area and are surrounded by a boundary wall with massive towers (**gopurams**) over each wall's central gateway. The Brhadeshvar temple is famous as a center for traditional arts and culture, particularly as a home for the **dance** style known as **Bharatanatyam**. It also contains some exceptional **murals**, an extremely unusual feature in Indian temples. See also **Chola dynasty**.

Brhannala

This was the identity assumed by **Arjuna**, one of the five **Pandava** princes, during the year they lived incognito after twelve years of forest exile. The Pandavas are the heroes of the *Mahabharata*, the later of the two great Hindu epics, which details the struggle for power between the Pandavas and their cousins the **Kauravas**. At one point in their struggle, Arjuna's older brother, **Yudhishthira**, has lost all the brothers' freedom and **possessions** to the Kauravas in a game of dice. As a penalty for this loss, the Pandavas have to go into exile for twelve years and spend the thirteenth year back in society, unrecognized. It is understood that if the brothers are discovered during that year, they will be banished again. Arjuna, the epic's most heroic warrior, disguises himself as a eunuch named Brhannala, knowing that no one will suspect him in such guise. He spends the year living in the women's quarters of the palace, singing and dancing as a eunuch. At the end of the year, still in his eunuch's garb, Arjuna takes part in a great battle in which he defeats the troops of the Kauravas.

Brhaspati

In Hindu mythology, Brhaspati is a sage chosen by the **deities** (**devas**) as their **guru**, or spiritual teacher. Brhaspati is also one of the names used to designate the planet **Jupiter**, since in Hindu astrology this planet is the most significant, and thus the symbolic "guru" among the **planets**.

Brideprice

The money the groom's family gives to the bride's family as a condition for marriage. This exchange of money for the bride is the defining feature of the **asura marriage**, one of eight recognized forms of marriage in the **Dharma Shastras**, the treatises on religious duty (**dharma**).

This form of marriage is considered **aprashasta** ("reprehensible") because of the implication of selling one's children. Even though it does take place in modern India, communities practicing this form have very low social status. In modern times, giving brideprice is an admission that the bride's family deserves compensation for the loss of a wage earner, implying that her labor is necessary for the family. In contrast, the higher-status type of marriage, the **Brahma marriage**, transfers both the bride and wealth (in the form of a **dowry**) to the groom's family with the understanding that both families have enough money that her paid labor is unnecessary.

Brindavan

("**tulsi** forest") Small town in the **Mathura** district of the state of **Uttar Pradesh**, which is the town in which the god **Krishna** is supposed to have lived during his childhood. Although every place in Brindavan is associated with the life of Krishna and is full of temples dedicated to him, one particularly important place is the **Chir Ghat**, at which Krishna stole the **gopis**' clothes as they were bathing (**snana**) in the **Yamuna River**. (The gopis were female cowherds who were companions to Krishna during his youth.) An interesting architectural site is the **Gobind Deo Mandir**, built in 1590, which has a vaulted ceiling. This latter temple is also notable for its lack of exterior ornamentation, perhaps to avoid antagonizing the nearby Moghuls. For a description of the sacred life in Brindavan, see John Stratton Hawley, *At Play with Krishna*, 1981. See also **Moghul dynasty**.

Bronzes

For most of Indian history, stone has been the preferred medium for creating images of the Hindu **deities** for **worship**. One of the significant exceptions to this trend can be found in southern India, primarily under the **Chola dynasty**

Depiction of the god Vishnu's Buddha avatar. Some Hindus claim that the Buddha was actually an incarnation of Vishnu.

(9th–14th c.), in which another important medium was bronze. The images were made using **lost wax casting**, which allows for great detail. They were cast in bronze with a high copper content, which tended to give them a greenish tinge as the metal oxidized. Some of the images are only a few inches high, albeit with exquisite detail, whereas the largest are over four feet tall and even today are the primary images worshiped in temples. These images were subject to the same established rules of construction (**shilpa shastra**) as stone **sculptures**. Despite this strict form, many of the bronzes are masterful works of art with a presence rarely found in the stone sculptures. Although images were made of all of the deities in the pantheon, among the best known bronzes are figures of the god **Shiva** as **Nataraja**, "the Lord of the **Dance**."

Buddha Avatar

The ninth **avatar**, or "incarnation," of the god **Vishnu**. As the only attested historical figure (and one who clearly differed with the Hindu orthodoxy of his time), the Buddha avatar shows how the avatar doctrine was used to envelop and assimilate existing religious figures. Although this designation as an avatar was an attempt to appropriate a significant religious figure by projecting him as an incarnation of Vishnu, this attempt's

transparency can be seen in the differing opinions over this avatar. In the opening chapter of his **Gitagovinda**, the poet **Jayadeva** claims that Vishnu incarnated as the Buddha to condemn the **animal sacrifices** prevalent in Vedic times. Other accounts portray him as misleading the wicked by instructing them to deny the authority of the **Vedas** (which the historical Buddha explicitly denied) and drive themselves into **hell**. Despite being named as one of the avatars, the Buddha was never worshiped by **Vaishnavas**, and Buddhists themselves have certainly never accepted this assertion.

Buddha Purnima

The **full moon** in the **lunar month** of **Baisakh** (April–May). Buddhists throughout the world celebrate this full moon as the anniversary of the Buddha's **birth**, enlightenment, and death. Although many Hindus respect the Buddha as a sage and religious teacher, he is not central to Hindu religion. Therefore, this is not a major festival, although this particular full moon is still named for him. More recently, the **day** of this full moon has been described as the best day of the **year** for bathing (**snana**) in sacred rivers, a practice that the Buddha would certainly have denounced. Given the **auspiciousness** connected with every full moon, this may be an effort to "take back" the day as a Hindu holiday by emphasizing a distinctively Hindu practice.

Buddhi

This word refers to the mental faculty often translated as "intellect," but it carries connotations beyond mere knowledge. The buddhi is the intellectual capability for awareness, mental perception, and decision-making, and as such it is the basis for all cognitive thought. In the account of **evolution** found in the **Samkhya** philosophical school, buddhi is one stage in the evolution of the human personality and the external world. In the Samkhya account, buddhi is the first faculty to emerge from **prakrti**, or "primal matter," and is also known by the name *mahat* (the "great one"). The mental processes facilitated by buddhi spur the development of the next stage of evolution, **ahamkar**, or "subjective consciousness." In more colloquial language, buddhi describes the overall quality of a person's mind, whether it is wholesome or unwholesome, sound or unsound.

Bull

Although the **cow** is the Hindu symbol for motherhood, with all of the emotional baggage that accompanies it, the associations connected with bulls are not nearly so important. In a religious context, the bull is associated with the god **Shiva** because his animal vehicle is the bull **Nandi**, who can invariably be found guarding the door at Shiva's temples. In pre-modern times, of course, adult bulls were a relatively small percentage of the total cattle population, since most young bulls were routinely castrated to become the oxen that were essential agricultural work **animals**.

Bundi

City and district in the southeastern part of the state **Rajasthan**, about 100 miles south of the state capital, Jaipur. Before 1947, when India gained independence, Bundi was a small kingdom. In the late seventeenth century, Bundi became a center for the **Rajasthani** style of **miniature painting**, perhaps by attracting artists from the Moghul court who were seeking outside patronage. Aside from the portraits and court groups characterizing this genre under the Moghuls, Rajasthani miniature painters portrayed Hindu religious themes, particularly incidents in the life of the god **Krishna**. Whereas some styles have flat, monochromatic backgrounds, the Bundi style shows an intense focus on nature, such as detailed depiction of the trees (usually banana trees) surrounding the subjects, in addition to flowers, birds, and lotus-filled ponds. For further information see

W. G. Archer, *Indian Painting*, 1957; or his *Indian Painting in Bundi and Kotah*, 1959. See also **Moghul dynasty**.

Burial

Although **cremation** is the most common means by which Hindus dispose of **corpses**, occasionally bodies are buried. One such case is with the bodies of very young children, as if it is recognized that they never developed into real individuals. The only other people usually buried are **ascetics**, for which there are varying interpretations. One idea is that they are not actually dead but in a state of deep meditation (**samadhi**). In such cases the ascetic is often buried in a sitting posture because he is considered still present. Another reason for burying ascetics may reflect the general assumption that renouncing the world had made them "dead" to it, making further ceremonies unnecessary. Indeed, one part of some ascetic **initiations** is to perform one's own funeral rites. Burial is often reserved for ascetics with disciples who will keep their graves as shrines. Those who are not buried are usually weighted down with rocks and thrown into bodies of water.

Busti

("settlement") In its literal meaning, anywhere people live—a settlement, village, or community. In modern usage it has come to denote an illegal settlement, such as one built by squatters who have put up dwellings on vacant land using whatever materials are available, from brick to cardboard to plastic. At first, such settlements have no civic amenities such as **water**, power, roads, or sewers, and in most cases the living conditions are abysmal. In many cases such "slums" become people's hereditary homes, particularly in Bombay, where real estate is exorbitantly expensive. These residents have usually gained access to electricity and water, typically via illegal hookups. In rarer cases squatters have gained title to the land through exerting political pressure, after which conditions have generally improved.

C

Calendar

One of the most fundamental Hindu religious beliefs is that different times carry different qualities. Whereas some times are considered more auspicious and propitious, others are more inauspicious and dangerous. These judgments may either describe the general qualities of specific times or determine the proper time for carrying out particular activities. Thus Hindus have given considerable attention to organizing time and predicting auspicious moments. Many modern Hindus simultaneously use several different calendars, although they may use them for different purposes. To begin with, everyday timekeeping is done with the Gregorian calendar of the common era, which may reflect the influence of the British empire or, more simply, the influence of modern commerce and communications. It is notable that the only holidays celebrated according to this calendar are national holidays such as **Independence Day**, **Gandhi Jayanti**, and **Republic Day**—all of which are fixed on particular **days**. Beyond this there are many other methods of measuring time, some of which overlap with each other and some of which are found only in certain regions of the country.

Several of these systems are based on the movement of the **sun**. The most basic unit, of course, is the solar day, which traditionally begins and ends not by the clock but by the rising of the sun. The **week** contains seven solar days. The movement of the sun divides the **year** into halves, with the **uttarayana** period occurring when the sun is moving northward and the **dakshinayana** period taking place when the sun is moving southward. There are also two separate versions of the solar year, each of which has twelve solar months. In northern India these months correspond to the twelve signs of the **zodiac** and mark the sun's passage through them. In southern India one finds an identical calendar, the Tamil solar year, in which the names of the months are drawn from the names of certain **nakshatras**, or signs of the lunar zodiac.

Whereas the solar calendar is usually used for astrological purposes, the lunar calendar is important for religious life. The lunar calendar is used to measure the two eras still used for dating history: the **Vikram era** (fifty-six or fifty-seven years later than the common era) and the **Shaka era** (seventy-eight years earlier than the common era). The lunar year is made up of twelve **lunar months**, each of which has thirty lunar days. Since the cycle of the **moon** is only about twenty-eight solar days, a lunar day is slightly shorter than a solar day. The lunar month is divided into two halves of fifteen days each: the "dark" (**krishna paksha**) half, when the moon is waning and that ends with the **new moon**; and the "light" (**shukla paksha**) half when the moon is waxing and that culminates in the **full moon**. In northern India the lunar month begins with the moon's dark half, and ends on the full moon, whereas in the south the reverse is often true. Since the solar year has about 365 days and the lunar year about 354, if left uncorrected each lunar year would begin eleven solar days earlier than the previous one. To correct this discrepancy, an **intercalary month** is added about every two and a half years. This helps to keep the lunar months falling at around the same time every year, although the celebration of a particular festival can vary by several weeks from one year to the next.

Almost all Hindu festivals are celebrated according to the lunar calendar. Some festivals' celebrations are associated with certain lunar days and thus occur twenty-four times in a twelve-month lunar year: The eleventh day (**ekadashi**) of each half of the lunar month is sacred to the god **Vishnu**; the eighth day (ashtami) is devoted to the **Goddess**, particularly in her form as **Durga**; the evening of the thirteenth day (trayodashi) and the fourteenth day (chaturdashi) are sacred to the god **Shiva**; and the fourth day (chaturthi) is dedicated to the god **Ganesh**. The time for celebrating annual religious festivals is set according to the lunar month, the half of the moon, and the particular lunar day. For example, the god **Krishna's** birthday is celebrated on **Bhadrapada** Krishna eight, the eighth day of the dark (waning) half of the lunar month of Bhadrapada. The birthdays of many important historical religious figures such as Guru Nanak, the founder of the Sikh community; the Buddha, and the devotional poet-saints are also celebrated according to the lunar calendar.

These overlapping calendars mean that any particular day can be designated by several different markers: the day of the week and the day in the common era (as in many societies), the day according to the traditional solar calendar, and the day according to the lunar calendar. Depending on the context—business, astrological, or festival—any one of these may be given preference. See also **auspiciousness**, **inauspiciousness**, and **Tamil months**.

Campantar

Tamil form of the name for the poet-saint **Sambandar**. See **Sambandar**.

Caste

The best-known term to denote the traditional Hindu social structure in which groups are arranged in a hierarchy of status, usually based on the perceived **purity** of each group's traditional occupation. The word "caste" is actually derived from the Portuguese word for "chaste." The Portuguese observed that different groups in Indian society kept themselves separate from each other, particularly when **eating** and in marriage.

They used the term "caste" to describe this social phenomenon.

Among Hindus themselves the most important concept for social ordering is known as the **jati** ("birth"). One becomes a member of a jati by being born into it. The jatis were usually divided according to traditional occupation, which (in theory) would be performed by that jati alone. A jati's social status generally stemmed from the status of its occupation, and jatis such as latrine cleaners and tanners were thought to be defiled by their trade. Society as a whole was conceived on the model of the body, with the different jatis comparable to different body parts. While each part had a differing status and role, every one was necessary for the whole to function smoothly. These differences in status were marked and reinforced by strict rules to keep each group distinct from the others. The strictest regulations were in regard to marriage, and in earlier times members of a jati would marry only within that group. It was almost as if the jatis were seen as separate "species" of human beings that had to be kept apart. Marrying within one's jati is still the ideal, although there is now considerably more intermarriage than in the past.

The best-known model for ordering Indian society is that of the four major social groups (**varna**) described in the **dharma literature**: **brahmin** (priest), **kshatriya** (warrior-king), **vaishya** (merchant), and **shudra** (servant). However, the number of different jati groups makes the social hierarchy far more complex. A small village might have dozens of jatis, all performing certain tasks, whereas a city might have hundreds of jatis, some highly specialized. Even within the brahmin varna, there are different brahmin jatis (for example, **Saraswat**, **Chitpavan**, **Kanyakubja**, and **Kanaujia**). For other varnas the picture is even more complex. For instance, some jati groups fall between the vaishya and shudra varnas, and jati groups of humble status who have achieved political success may claim kshatriya lineage. The same jati's social position can vary from region to region, depending on if they comprise a majority or a minority of the population or have status as a land-holding community. As in most of Hindu life, a group's status is usually influenced by local factors; in the past fifty years, such status determinations have also been affected by changes in Indian society, which have tended to relax social distinctions. For further information see McKim Marriot, "Hindu Transactions: Diversity Without Dualism," in Bruce Kapferer (ed.), *Transaction and Meaning*, 1976.

Castration

Castration of human beings has been almost completely absent in Indian history, with the notable exception of the **hijras**. Hijras are male cross-dressers who dress and behave as **women** and have usually undergone self-castration as a ritual renunciation of their sexuality. Hijras are often homosexual prostitutes, and they are an established part of the decadent underside of most Indian cities. Their most important ritual function is to sing and **dance** at the houses in which a male child has been born, but they may also be called to perform on other auspicious occasions. Despite the hijras' associations with certain auspicious occasions, they are marginal to society and have very low social status. For a reliable study of the hijras, see Serena Nanda, *Neither Man Nor Woman*, 1999. See also **auspiciousness**.

Causal Chains

The underlying ultimate concern in all Indian philosophical schools is to uncover and understand the causal forces that keep human beings enmeshed in **samsara**, the continual cycle of reincarnation. One of the ways that Indian philosophers attempted to do this was to formulate various chains of cause and effect detailing the process through which human beings become subject to the bondage of **karma**. By

understanding this process, they hope to be able to manipulate it, ultimately leading to the final liberation of the soul (**moksha**). The oldest causal chains were formulated by the Buddha and the Jains. In each of these theories, **avidya**, or lack of genuine understanding, starts the causal chain. In the Buddhist and Jain traditions, these causal chains can be broken by a religious discipline that begins with moral action and at more advanced levels involves meditation and wisdom.

Causal chains in Hindu **philosophy** have much in common with these beliefs, particularly the notion that avidya is the basic problem. In the **Nyaya Sutras**, the **Nyaya** philosopher **Gautama** propounded a five-fold causal chain: pain, **birth**, activity, defect, and wrong notion. Each of these elements is caused by the one succeeding it and is eliminated with the destruction of its cause. The **Vaisheshika** school, which was traditionally paired with the Nyayas, also used this model. The causal chain in the **Samkhya** philosophical school, as described by its founder, **Ishvarakrishna**, ascribes bondage to the process of **evolution**, stemming from the confusion between **purusha** (conscious spirit) and **prakrti** (primal matter). According to Samkhya, these two first principles are always separate from one another, but humans can confuse them. The **Yoga** school, traditionally paired with the Samkhya, used this model as well. The philosopher **Ramanuja**, founder of the **Vishishthadvaita Vedanta** school, proposes an evolutionary scheme similar to the Samkhya model, although instead of Samkhya's dualism, all things evolve from a single source, **Brahman**.

The only major Hindu philosophical school without a causal chain is **Advaita Vedanta**. All of the other schools explain the relationship between the Ultimate Reality (in most cases, Brahman) and the perceivable world with the doctrine of **parinamavada**. This philosophical perspective accepts the reality of the world as it is perceived and also assumes that the changes in the material world involve the genuine transformation (parinama) of one thing into another, which can be explained by cause and effect. The Advaita school upholds a philosophical position known as monism, which is the belief that a single Ultimate Reality lies behind all things, which are merely differing forms of that reality. For the Advaitins, this single reality is the formless, unqualified Brahman. Advaitins explain the appearance of difference and diversity in the everyday world as an illusory rather than a genuine transformation of Brahman, a philosophical outlook known as **vivartavada**. This illusory transformation is caused by a quality of the human mind, which leads to the mental superimposition (**adhyasa**) of a mistaken understanding in place of the real one. For the Advaitins, as for all of the other schools, the ultimate problem is still avidya, or mistaken understanding, which must be replaced by correct understanding. Whereas all of the other schools give some importance to actions, the Advaitins believe that avidya is the sole cause and its removal the sole solution. For further information see Karl H. Potter (ed.), *Presuppositions of India's Philosophies*, 1972.

Causal Models

In Indian **philosophy**, there are three different models describing the relationships between cause and effect: **satkaryavada**, **asatkaryavada**, and **anekantavada**. The first model, satkaryavada, assumes that effects preexist in their causes. Effects are thus transformations (real or apparent) of these causes. The classic example is the transformation of milk to curds, butter, and clarified butter. According to satkaryavada's proponents, each of these effects was already present in the cause and emerges from it through a natural transformation of that cause.

The second model, asatkaryavada, assumes that effects do not preexist in their causes—they are completely distinct. In the classic examples for this model, one creates a clay pot by putting together the two halves of the pot, or one weaves a cloth from strands of thread. According to asatkaryavada's proponents, with each of these acts, certain material and instrumental causes create an entirely new object.

The third model, anekantavada ("the view that things are not single"), seeks to occupy the middle ground between the other two models. Anekantavada stresses the importance of one's perspective and the way it can color a judgment. In viewing the transformation of milk to curds, butter, and clarified butter, an anekantavada proponent would claim that these substances were contained in the causes (supporting the satkaryavada notion) but that the qualities of these substances were newly created each time (supporting the asatkaryavada notion). Thus causes and effects are simultaneously both the same and different, depending on the way one looks at them.

All of these philosophical schools believe that if one understands the causal process correctly and can manipulate it through one's conscious actions, it is possible to gain final liberation of the soul (**moksha**). Each of these causal models thus has profound implications on religious life. Satkaryavada believes that causal relations are strong, but they may be so strong that humans cannot affect the **causal chain**; the asatkaryavada believes that causal relations are weak, with the danger that human action is too unreliable to bring about a desired effect; anekantavada purports to find a middle ground but can be construed as inconsistent or self-contradictory. For further information see Karl H. Potter (ed.), *Presuppositions of India's Philosophies*, 1972.

Cauvery

Southern Indian river rising at the base of the western **ghats** in the state of **Karnataka**, then flowing east through the state of **Tamil Nadu** before entering

The Kailasanatha Temple in the state of Maharashtra is surrounded by artificial caves sculpted into solid rock.

the Bay of Bengal. It is traditionally considered one of India's seven sacred rivers along with the **Ganges**, **Godavari**, **Indus**, **Narmada**, **Saraswati**, and **Yamuna**. Important sacred sites (**tirthas**) on the Cauvery include **Shrirangapatnam** and **Tiruchirappalli** as well as the Cauvery Delta in Tamil Nadu's **Tanjore** district, which is filled with temple towns. Since 1947, when India gained independence, the rights to the Cauvery's water have become a major dispute between Tamil Nadu and Karnataka. Farmers in Tamil Nadu have been demanding a more significant share of the waters impounded in reservoirs in Karnataka.

Caves, Artificial

This was a common architectural form in the western part of the state of **Maharashtra**, particularly in the early centuries of the common era. The earliest form was the **chaitya** or rock-cut cave temple, which is specifically associated with Buddhist architectural sites. A chaitya typically had a large chamber sculpted into the side of a hill, usually with a Buddha image at the far end and a window above the entrance to admit more light. These caves were excavated and sculpted from the top down so that no scaffolding was necessary. The sides and central pillars were carved to mimic wooden construction. Early Hindu **architecture** adapted the chaitya form but eventually moved beyond it to construct free-standing temples. The most impressive Hindu rock-cut temples are the caves at **Ellora**, particularly the **Kailasanatha** temple (late 8th c.), dedicated to the god **Shiva** in his form as the Lord of Mount **Kailas**. The Kailasanatha temple was sculpted out of solid rock but carved to look as if it were built of masonry. This temple marked the height of the artificial cave as an architectural type, although the temples at **Elephanta** were done later. After this period, the emphasis tended to be on free-standing temples.

Cekkilar

(12th c. C.E.) Author of the *Periya Puranam*, a hagiographical account of the sixty-three **Nayanars**. The Nayanars were a group of sixty-three **Shaiva** poet-saints who lived in southern India between the seventh and ninth centuries. Along with their **Vaishnava** counterparts, the **Alvars**, the Nayanars spearheaded the revitalization of Hindu religion in opposition to the Buddhists and the Jains. Both the Nayanars and the Alvars stressed passionate devotion (**bhakti**) to a personal god—**Shiva** for the Nayanars, **Vishnu** for the Alvars—and conveyed this devotion through hymns sung in the **Tamil language**. According to tradition, Cekkilar was a minister at the court of the **Chola dynasty**'s king Kullottunga II (r. 1130–1150 C.E.). Cekkilar was distressed by the king's admiration for a Jain epic poem and composed his own text to distract the king. His text portrays the Nayanars as models of devotion to Shiva, although they are sometimes extreme in their actions. Yet in every case, the love between devotee (**bhakta**) and **deity** manifests itself in the circumstances of everyday life, leading the saints to final liberation.

Celibacy

In traditional Indian culture, celibacy was widely seen not only as a sign of sanctity but also as a source of power. On one hand, since sexual desire is often the symbol for all types of desire, renunciation of sexual activity is thus a sign for the renunciation of the world in general. On a more literal level, retention of **semen** through celibacy is believed to prevent the loss of a man's vital energy. In traditional Indian physiology, semen is believed to be distilled from **blood** and is therefore the concentrated essence of a man's vitality. Although semen can and must be expended for procreation, all other losses should be carefully weighed. Thus there are strong taboos on masturbation. This vital energy, stored and conserved through celibacy, can then be used for spiritual advancement. The paradigm for the celibate **ascetic** is the god **Shiva**, one of whose symbols is the **linga**, a pillar-shaped

image with clear phallic associations. Shiva is the model husband and the consummate ascetic. The linga represents his stored celibate energy, as the product of his **tapas** (ascetic practices). In the same way, celibacy is a way for human men to conserve their vital energies, whether one is a lifetime celibate (**naisthika**), a student (**brahmacharin**), or—as in many cases—a married man who has already had children.

Chaitanya

(1486–1533 C.E.) Bengali saint, devotee (**bhakta**) of the god **Krishna**, and the founder of the **Gaudiya Vaishnava** religious community. Chaitanya was such a pivotal figure that there are many traditional sources for his life, although their hagiographic character makes them historically unreliable. According to one of these traditions, Chaitanya embodied Krishna himself. Krishna became Chaitanya to experience the longing of **Radha**, his beloved consort whom Chaitanya imagined himself to be. Thus, for his followers Chaitanya was conceived as Krishna and Radha in the same body.

Chaitanya was born in the town of **Navadvip** in the state of **West Bengal** and given the name Vishvambar. Traditional sources portray the young man as a gifted teacher but with no inclination toward Krishna. In 1508 he went to **Gaya**, a sacred site (**tirtha**) associated with rites for the dead, to perform rites for his dead father. In Gaya, Vishvambar met his teacher, **Ishvara Puri**, and something profound happened there, for he returned to Navadvip a passionate devotee of Krishna. On his return, Vishvambar began to hold the public **kirtan** (devotional chanting) that has become the hallmark of the Gaudiya Vaishnava school. Devotees sang and danced in the streets and wept uncontrollably. Through this ecstatic emotional **worship**, they sought to regain the devotional atmosphere associated with the **gopis**, Krishna's cowherd **women**, and thus share in the gopis' intimate relationship with Krishna.

In 1510 Vishvambar formally became an **ascetic**, taking the name Krishna Chaitanya, and for the rest of his life propagated the worship of Krishna. For much of that time, he resided in the sacred city of **Puri**. This was reportedly in deference to his mother, since she felt that Krishna's childhood home, **Brindavan**, was too far away. Despite his mother's wishes, Chaitanya did take several lengthy trips: a two-year tour of the holy places in southern India between 1510 and 1512, and in 1514, a trip to Brindavan, in which Chaitanya had frequent mystical experiences. After his return to Puri, he met the brothers **Rupa** and **Sanatana Goswami**. Chaitanya directed them to settle in Brindavan and re-establish the holy sites associated with Krishna's life. Driven by Chaitanya's charisma and ecstatic devotion, Rupa, Sanatana, and their nephew **Jiva Goswami** became pivotal figures in the development of the Gaudiya Vaishnava school. While Chaitanya was absorbed in his devotion to Krishna until his death, Rupa, Santana, and Jiva Goswami gave this devotion a systematic organization. For further information see Sushil Kumar De, *Early History of the Vaishnava Faith and Movement in Bengal*, 1961; and Janardana Chakravarti, *Bengal Vaishnavism and Sri Chaitanya*, 1975.

Chaitanya-Charitramrta

("nectar of **Chaitanya's** deeds") A name shared by at least three separate texts, all devoted to recounting the life of the Bengali saint Chaitanya (1486–1533). The earliest was written by **Murari Gupta**, an associate of Chaitanya. Most of this text focuses on Chaitanya's early life up to his southern Indian pilgrimage ending in 1513, but it also briefly mentions his pilgrimage to the town of **Brindavan** in 1514 and his final return to the sacred city of **Puri**, in which he lived until his death. The second account was written nine years after

Chaitanya's death by **Kavikarnapura**, who freely acknowledged his debt to Murari Gupta. The final account was written by **Krishnadas Kaviraj** about ninety years after Chaitanya's death. Kaviraj's account focuses mainly on Chaitanya's later life, particularly his time in Brindavan. This last version is marked by the philosophical influence of Chaitanya's most important disciples, the Goswamis (**Rupa Goswami**, **Sanatana Goswami**, and **Jiva Goswami**), whose ideas were a major influence in shaping the **Gaudiya Vaishnava** religious community. None of these texts gives an "objective" biography; the works are hagiographies written by passionate devotees (**bhakta**). See also **philosophy**.

Chaitra

According to the lunar **calendar**, by which most Hindu religious festivals are determined, Chaitra is the month in which the lunar **year** both begins (during the two weeks of the bright or waxing, half of the **moon**) and ends (during the two weeks of the dark, or waning, half of the moon, which precedes the bright half). Thus, the waning half of Chaitra ends one lunar year, while the waxing half that follows it begins the next lunar year. This month usually falls within March and April. This is one of the months of spring, and in northern India the weather is warm and pleasant at this time. The major festivals in Chaitra are **Papamochani Ekadashi**, the spring **Navaratri**, **Ram Navami**, **Kamada Ekadashi**, **Hanuman Jayanti**, and in **Tamil Nadu**, the **Chittirai** festival.

Chaitya

("place of **worship**") A rock-cut cave temple. This architectural form is closely associated with Indian Buddhism but was also used in early Hindu temple **architecture**. The earliest chaityas were simple caves, but these grew more elaborate as the form developed. In its later stages, the builders would not only cut out the side of the hill to make a cave; they would also sculpt pillars and other architectural details that mimicked free-standing construction. Another characteristic architectural feature was a ceiling carved into the shape of an arch. The true arch, built from the bottom up and used in Roman architecture, was not used in ancient India. A third common feature was a large window opening over the doorway to let in additional light. During the construction, the builders began removing stone at the top of the structure and worked their way down; this eliminated the need for any scaffolding during the building process, but it also meant that the builders had to work carefully to avoid mistakes. This construction method creates structures considered gigantic sculptures rather than buildings. The earliest examples are Buddhist caves carved into the side of the western **ghats** in **Maharashtra**. The form was later used to create Hindu temples, specifically at **Ellora** (in which the oldest caves are Buddhist) and on the island of **Elephanta**.

Chakora

The red partridge (*Perdrix rufa*). According to popular belief, the chakora bird eats nothing but moonbeams. It is thus happy and content during the night but tormented by hunger during the day. In court poetry the chakora bird often symbolized a cultured and discriminating person who appreciates the finer things in life. In **bhakti** (devotional) poetry the chakora is often a symbol for a devotee (**bhakta**), since the chakora bird is said to be in love with the **moon**. Thus it is joyful when the moon is out but pines for it during the day, just as a devotee is blissful in the **deity's** presence and in its absence is consumed with longing.

Chakra

("wheel") In Hindu iconography the chakra is the discus-weapon carried by several of the Hindu **deities**. It is often associated with the god **Vishnu** and is one of the four objects he invariably carries, along with the club (**gada**), lotus (**padma**), and conch shell (**shankha**). The discus was an actual weapon in the Indian military arsenal, and its sharp edges made it fearsome in close combat. Vishnu's discus (named **Sudarshana**) is even more fearsome in its power. According to tradition it was fashioned by the divine craftsman, **Vishvakarma**, from pieces trimmed off of the **sun**; thus it carries the power of the sun's blazing energy. The discus is also carried by certain powerful forms of the **Goddess**. In her charter myth, she was formed from the collected radiance of all the gods and received duplicates of all their weapons.

In the esoteric ritual tradition known as tantra, a chakra is a psychic center in the **subtle body**. The subtle body is an alternate physiological system that corresponds to the material body but is believed to reside on a different plane of existence. The subtle body is visualized as a set of chakras, or psychic centers, that are arranged in a column from the base of the spine to the top of the head and connected by three vertical channels. Each chakra is pictured as a multipetaled lotus flower. All tantric traditions speak of six chakras: **muladhara**, **svadhishthana**, **manipura**, **anahata**, **vishuddha**, and **ajna**; some traditions name additional ones. Each of these chakras has important symbolic associations—with a different human physiological capacity, subtle element (**tanmatra**), and with differing seed syllables (**bijakshara**) formed from the letters of the Sanskrit alphabet, together encompassing all sacred sounds. For further information see Philip S. Rawson, *The Art of Tantra*, 1973.

A shoemaker in Agra. Shoemaking and leather tanning are traditional occupations of the Chamar social group.

Chakravyuha

("circular phalanx") A circular military formation described in the *Mahabharata*, one of the two great Hindu epics (along with the *Ramayana)*. The Chakravyuha was widely believed to be unconquerable because each person in the formation was protected by those behind him. During a battle in the Mahabharata war, **Abhimanyu** becomes trapped in the chakravyuha by his enemy. Because his father, **Arjuna**, is the only person who knows how to get out, Abhimanyu is killed.

Chalukya Dynasty

(7th–8th c. C.E.) Central Indian dynasty whose capital was at Badami, in the **Deccan** plateau in modern **Karnataka**. The greatest Chalukya ruler was **Pulakeshin II**, who defeated the northern Indian emperor **Harsha**, stopping his southern advance. He also killed the **Pallava dynasty** ruler **Mahendravarman**, setting off a series of wars between the Chalukyas and the Pallavas in which each dynasty was able to defeat the other in battle, but neither was strong enough to retain control of the other's empire. Aside from the Chalukya dynasty based at Badami, there were two other smaller dynasties by the same name, both of which flourished between the tenth and thirteenth centuries. One of these later dynasties was in the **Gujarat** region, and the other was in the Karnataka region.

Chamar

In traditional northern Indian society, the chamars were a **jati** ("birth") whose hereditary occupation was tanning **leather** and making shoes. The jatis were subgroups of traditional Indian society whose social status was determined by their hereditary occupation. The chamars were traditionally considered among the lowest of the untouchables since their work brought them in continual contact with dead **animals** and their skins, which are considered extremely impure. The most famous chamar is the poet-saint **Ravidas**, whose poetry focuses on the difference between worldly status and devotion.

Champaran

Region in the northern part of the state of **Bihar**, between the **Gandaki** River and the border of **Nepal**. Now it is composed of two provinces, eastern Champaran and western Champaran. The Champaran region is famous as the place where **Mohandas K. Gandhi** engineered the first successful **satyagraha** (nonviolent resistance campaign) against British rule. At the time, the province was largely agricultural, as it remains today, and most of the inhabitants were very poor. The farmers had traditionally designated a portion of their land for growing indigo to give to the landlords as rent. This arrangement was disrupted by the invention of a much cheaper synthetic indigo. The landlords responded by ordering the tenants to stop growing indigo but proceeded to raise the rent on their land, based on the traditional agreement that allowed them to do so if a tenant grew no indigo. The trouble began in 1912, but Gandhi did not arrive until 1917. After a campaign lasting nearly a year, the tenants won concessions from the landlords guaranteeing no further rent increases and a 25 percent rebate on the previous increases. For further information see Mohandas K. Gandhi, *An Autobiography*, 1993; a more readable, though highly partial, account can be found in Louis Fischer, *Gandhi*, 1954.

Chamunda

Presiding **deity** of the Chamunda Devi shrine on the banks of the Bana Ganga in the state of **Himachal Pradesh**, and one of the nine goddesses whose shrines are scattered through the **Shiwalik Hills**. Although each of these goddesses has a separate identity, they are all ultimately seen as differing manifestations of a single **Goddess**. Chamunda's charter myth is drawn from events in the *Devimahatmya*, a **Sanskrit** text that describes the Goddess's several different forms and is the earliest and most important mythic source for the cult of the Goddess. The *Devimahatmya*'s seventh book tells how the goddess **Ambika's** anger takes material form as the terrifying goddess **Kali**, who

advances into battle against the **demon** generals **Chanda** and **Munda**, whom she eventually beheads. Since the shrine on the Bana Ganga marks the place where both Chanda and Munda were destroyed, the goddess is worshiped here as Chamunda.

The name Chamunda designates a fierce and dangerous goddess who has often been identified with the goddess Kali. In the poet **Bhavabhuti's** eighth-century drama *Malatimadhava*, the heroine, Malati, is kidnapped by devotees (**bhakta**) of the goddess Chamunda to be offered as a **human sacrifice** to her. The events in the drama reflect the ambivalence with which such powerful goddesses—and their devotees—have been seen. For further information see David R. Kinsley, *Hindu Goddesses*, 1986; and Kathleen Erndl, *Victory to the Mother*, 1993.

Chanakya

According to tradition, the chief minister of the founder of the **Maurya dynasty**, **Chandragupta Maurya** (r. 321–297 B.C.E.). As the king's counsel, Chanakya became famous for his skill in statecraft, and is believed to have been instrumental in establishing the dynasty. Under the name **Kautilya**, Chanakya is also celebrated as the author of the *Arthashastra*, the classic Indian treatise on the strategies and mechanics of ruthlessly efficient central government.

Chanda

A **demon** general killed by the **Goddess** in the *Devimahatmya*, the **Sanskrit** text that is the earliest and most important mythic source for the cult of the Goddess. This text describes the Goddess in several different manifestations. The seventh book tells how the goddess **Ambika's** anger takes form as the terrifying goddess **Kali**. Kali attacks the demon armies commanded by Chanda and his companion **Munda**, and after destroying the armies she beheads the two generals. As a memorial of this mythic deed, one of the names under which the Goddess is worshiped is **Chamunda**, as the slayer of Chanda and Munda.

Chandas

One of the six **Vedangas**. These were the auxiliary branches of knowledge intended to facilitate the use of the **Vedas**, the oldest Hindu religious texts. Chandas was concerned with the study of metrical forms and verse, which were central to the composition of the Vedas. One indication of the importance of **meter** is that in many sources (such as in **Panini's** grammar, the *Ashtadhyayi*) the word *chandas* is used to designate the Vedas themselves. Aside from chandas, the other Vedangas are **shiksha** (correct pronunciation), **vyakarana** (**Sanskrit** grammar), **kalpa** (ritual instructions), **nirukta** (etymology), and **jyotisha** (auspicious times for sacrifices).

Chandella Dynasty

(10th–14th c. C.E.) Northern Indian dynasty that in its heyday controlled much of the **Ganges** River valley and northern **Madhya Pradesh**. The Chandellas are famous for the magnificent temples that they built in the village of **Khajuraho**, largely between the eleventh and twelfth centuries. These temples have survived to the present, perhaps due to their remote and inaccessible location. They are excellent examples of the developed form of the **Nagara** architectural style and are world-famous for their astounding display of **erotic** sculptures.

Chandi

("fierce") Epithet used for the fierce and powerful goddesses **Durga** and **Kali**. A variant form of the name Chandi is **Chandika**, and under this name Chandi is identified as one of the **Navadurgas**, the "nine [forms of the **goddess**] **Durga**" worshiped during the nine nights of the **Navaratri** festival. Chandika is the goddess worshiped on the festival's ninth and final night and is thus the most powerful of these divine forms.

Chandidas

(15th c. C.E.) Bengali poet and devotee (**bhakta**) of the god **Krishna**. In his poems Chandidas uses the conventions of **Sanskrit** love poetry to express devotion to Krishna, most often through the figure of **Radha** as Krishna's favored devotee and lover. His poems are still recited in Bengal and according to tradition were admired by **Chaitanya**, the Bengali devotee who was the founder of the **Gaudiya Vaishnava** religious community. Despite his poetry's continuing acclaim, little is known about the life of Chandidas himself. This same name was used by a Bengali poet of the **Sahajiya** sect, who wrote several centuries later than the original Chandidas and whose poetry is clearly distinguished by doctrinal differences. For selections from the poetry of Chandidas, see Edward C. Dimock Jr. and Denise Levertov (trans.), *In Praise of Krishna*, 1981.

Chandika

A variant of the name **Chandi**, which designates a powerful and terrifying form of the **Goddess**. Chandika is one of the **Navadurgas**, the "nine [forms of the goddess] **Durga**" worshiped during the nine nights of the **Navaratri** festival. Chandika is the goddess worshiped on the festival's ninth and final night and is thus the most powerful of these divine forms.

Chandiprakasha

("effulgence of **Chandi**") Name given to the spear that is the symbolic weapon of the **Atala akhara**, a particular group within the **Naga** class of **Dashanami Sanyasis**. The Dashanami Nagas are devotees (**bhakta**) of the god **Shiva**, organized into different **akharas**, or regiments, on the model of an army. Until the beginning of the nineteenth century, the Nagas' primary occupation was as mercenary soldiers, although they also had substantial trading interests. These functions have largely disappeared in contemporary times. All of the akharas have certain symbols that signify their organizational identity, and the Atala akhara is represented by this particular spear.

Chandogya Upanishad

Along with the **Brhadaranyaka Upanishad**, one of the two earliest upanishads, the religious texts that form the most recent stratum of the **Vedas**. Internal textual factors indicate that the Brhadaranyaka Upanishad is the older of the two, and since large sections of both texts are the same, the Chandogya Upanishad is thought to be dependent on the Brhadaranyaka. Both texts are also much larger than the other upanishads and much less organized, rambling from topic to topic without an apparent focus. Both are written in prose rather than poetry, with the text itself often presented as a dialogue between various speakers. Their profoundly speculative discussions about the nature of the universe became important sources for the later upanishads.

Chandra Gupta I

(r. 320–35 C.E.) Founder of the **Gupta dynasty**, which like the **Maurya dynasty** had its capital in **Pataliputra**, identified with the modern city of Patna in the state of **Bihar**. The Gupta capital was later moved to **Allahabad**. At the height of the dynasty, under **Chandra Gupta II** (r. 376–415), the Guptas controlled all of northern India and modern Pakistan, as well as the **Coromandel** Coast all the way to modern Madras. The Gupta dynasty flourished between about 350 and 550 C.E., and its reign is associated with the development of Indian culture and a revival of Hinduism in northern India. Both were accomplished through the patronage of the Gupta kings, who are remembered both as patrons of high

Coins from the Gupta dynasty.

culture and ardent devotees (**bhakta**) of **Shiva**.

Chandra Gupta II

(r. 376–415 C.E.) Third in the line of great monarchs in the **Gupta dynasty**, after his father, **Samudra Gupta**, and his grandfather, **Chandra Gupta I**. The Gupta dynasty reached its territorial peak under Chandra Gupta II. During his reign the Shaka kingdom of the **Malwa** region was finally conquered, after which the Guptas controlled by conquest or tribute all of northern India and modern Pakistan, as well as the **Coromandel** Coast all the way to modern Madras. The Gupta dynasty flourished between about 350 and 550 C.E., and its reign is associated with the development of Indian culture and a revival of Hinduism in northern India. Both were accomplished through the patronage of the Gupta kings, who are remembered both as patrons of high culture and ardent devotees (**bhakta**) of **Shiva**. This is especially true of Chandra Gupta II, since one of the major figures associated with his court is **Kalidasa**, considered the greatest of the **Sanskrit** poets. See also **Shaka era**.

Chandragupta Maurya

(r. 321–297 B.C.E.) The founder of the **Maurya dynasty**. The young Chandragupta began his empire by overthrowing the last member of the **Nanda** dynasty and occupying the capital in **Pataliputra**, identified with the modern city of Patna in the state of **Bihar**. From there he took control of the **Ganges** River basin, moved south into the region of the **Narmada River**, and then turned his attention to northwestern India, taking advantage of the power vacuum left by the recent incursion of Alexander the Great. In 303 B.C.E. he defeated Alexander's general Seleucus Nicator in battle, then agreed to a treaty in which he received large parts of modern Afghanistan. Despite the battle, relations seem to have been friendly between the two, for Seleucus Nicator sent an ambassador to Pataliputra, **Megasthenes**, who lived there for many years. Chandragupta was reportedly advised by a brilliant **brahmin** minister, variously called **Kautilya** or **Chanakya**, who is considered the author of the *Arthashastra*. According to legend, Chandragupta renounced his throne to become a Jain monk and eventually died through ritual starvation.

Chandramati

In Hindu mythology, the long-suffering wife of King **Harishchandra**. Harishchandra is famous for his truthfulness and integrity; in modern Hindu culture he is also the paradigm for a person who patiently endures undeserved suffering. Harishchandra's suffering grows out of the competition between the sages **Vasishtha** and **Vishvamitra**. As his family priest, Vasishtha praises Harishchandra's virtue. Vishvamitra is determined to prove Vasishtha wrong and subjects Harishchandra to a series of trials in which he loses his kingdom, his **possessions**, and has to sell himself and his family into slavery. Through all of the trials he and Chandramati have to suffer, Harishchandra retains his integrity. After enduring many hardships, including the death of their only **son**, they are eventually restored to their original happy state, including the resuscitation of their son.

Chandrayana

("**moon's** path") Penitential rite (**prayashchitta**) lasting for one **lunar month** in which the penitent's food consumption mirrors the monthly course of the moon. A person observing this rite begins by **eating** fourteen mouthfuls of food on the first **day** of the waning moon, then one less mouthful on each successive day until the **new moon** day, when a complete fast (**upavasa**) is observed. On each successive day during the waxing moon, the penitent eats one more mouthful, finishing at fifteen on the day of the **full moon**. This is a fairly severe penance, given the scant amount of food allowed in the middle of the month. In the **dharma literature**, this penance was prescribed as an atonement for certain sorts of sexual misconduct: sexual intercourse with a woman belonging to the same **gotra** (mythic lineage), marrying a woman belonging to one's maternal grandfather's gotra, or marrying the **daughter** of one's maternal uncle or paternal aunt.

Charaka

(1st–2nd c. C.E.?) The attributed author of the *Charaka Samhita*, which along with the slightly later *Sushruta Samhita*, is one of the two major sources for **ayurveda**, a traditional school of Indian medicine. According to tradition, Charaka was the physician at the royal court in the city of Takshashila, in modern Pakistan.

Charaka Samhita

Along with the later *Sushruta Samhita*, one of the two major sources for the traditional Indian medical school known as **ayurveda**. Although its authorship is attributed to **Charaka**, it is more likely a compendium from earlier sources, given its reference to several different medical systems and approaches. The underlying medical framework of ayurveda is the theory of the three bodily humors—**vata** (**wind**), **pitta** (bile), and **kapha** (phlegm). Although everyone has all three humors, each of these is composed of different elements whose varying proportions are used to explain individual body types, metabolic dispositions, and personalities. Diseases result from an imbalance of these humors—caused by one's environment or personal habits—whereas equilibrium is the state of health. The *Charaka Samhita* has been edited and translated into various languages and has served as a source for secondary studies, such as Debiprasad Chattopadhyaya, *Science and Society in Ancient India*, 1977.

Charanadas

("slave of [God's] feet"; 1733–1782 C.E.) Founder of the **Charanadasis**, an **ascetic** religious community. Charanadas was born in the town of Dehra in the princely state of Alwar (in the modern state of **Rajasthan**). The Charanadasis are also known as the Shuka Sampraday because, according to tradition, Charanadas received **initiation** from the puranic sage **Shuka**. Charanadas formed his community in protest against the corruption and worldliness of the **Pushti Marg**, the religious community founded by **Vallabhacharya** (1479–1531 C.E.), whose members are devotees (**bhakta**) of the god **Krishna**. Like the Pushti Marg, the Charanadasis are **Vaishnavas**, but their patron **deity** is not Krishna alone but also his consort, **Radha**. Charanadas countered the Pushti Marg by stressing upright and appropriate behavior and an insistence on learning. His disciples translated and wrote commentaries on the **Bhagavad Gita** and the *Bhagavata Purana*, both important **Vaishnava** texts.

Charanadasi

Vaishnava ascetic sect founded by the reformer-saint **Charanadas** (1733–1782 C.E.). Charanadas formed his own community as a protest against the corruption of the **Pushti Marg**, the religious community founded by **Vallabhacharya** (1479–1531 C.E.) whose members are devotees (**bhakta**) of the god **Krishna**. Like the Pushti Marg, the Charanadasis are Vaishnavas, but their patron **deity** is not Krishna alone, but also his consort, **Radha**. The Charanadasis have stressed both learning and an upright way of life. Their main center is in Delhi, as is the **samadhi shrine** of Charanadas, their founder.

Charanamrta

("foot nectar") Literally, the **water** (or other liquid) in which the feet of one's **guru** or images of a **deity** are bathed. The disciple or devotee (**bhakta**) consumes it as a sign of subordinate status and as a way to receive **grace** and blessings. By extension, the word can refer to any liquid for devotees to consume as a symbol of the deity's grace, whether or not it has been used for bathing (**snana**).

Charas

Name for hashish. This is usually mixed with tobacco and smoked in a straight pipe called a **chillum**. Smoking hashish is typical in certain segments of the **ascetic** community. For many ascetics, smoking is a social activity and a rite of hospitality as well as a religious act that emulates the god **Shiva**, whose love for the **drug** is well known. In their travels many ascetics process the marijuana that grows wild throughout the **Himalayas** into hashish to use and sell. Drug use is forbidden for most people, but among ascetics—who are deliberately marginal members of society—it is a fairly common and tolerated behavior.

Charity

See **dana**.

Charvaka

One of the traditional names given to the **materialist** philosophical school. Its primary assertion was that a person is identical to his or her physical body and is destroyed with the body's demise. See **materialist**.

Vishnu sleeping on a serpent couch. According to Hindu tradition, during the four months that Vishnu sleeps, the world is denied his protective powers and the Chaturmas Vrat is observed during this time.

Chataka

In **Sanskrit** poetry and literature, the name for the **cuckoo** bird, usually invoked as a symbol of longing.

Chatterjee, Bankim Chandra

(1838–1894) Bengali writer and Indian nationalist who was one of the major figures in the nineteenth-century revival of Bengali literature and in making the area a hotbed of opposition to British rule. As a young man, Chatterjee perceived how the influence of English language and culture was superseding that of Indian culture among educated Indians. He sought to reverse this through his writing and political activism by encouraging Indian intellectuals to rediscover their classical culture. He became a seminal figure in both literature and politics, paving the way for the poet **Rabindranath Tagore** and political activists **Aurobindo Ghose** and **Subhash Chandra Bose**. Chatterjee's most famous novel, *Anandamath*, focused on the late eighteenth-century **Sanyasi Rebellion**, in which bands of militant **ascetics**, both Hindu and Muslim, fought with the British East India Company for control of Bengal. Although historical inquiry attributes this conflict to social and economic tensions in contemporary Bengal, Chatterjee portrays it allegorically as a struggle by Mother India's loyal children to expel the British invaders. Chatterjee also wrote the words to "Vande Mataram" ("Homage to Mother [India]"), a patriotic song often described as the unofficial Indian national anthem.

Chatti

A pilgrim shelter, particularly in the **Himalayas**. The word *chatti* is a variant form of the word for "umbrella" and was used because these shelters were often simply roofs supported by pillars, to keep the pilgrims dry in case of rain. Up until the middle of the twentieth century, many Himalayan pilgrims still traveled on foot and used a network of chattis along the pilgrimage routes. These chattis were eight to twelve miles apart, an easy day's walk for younger pilgrims, yet manageable for the elderly. Each chatti was maintained by a nearby family, which would sell the pilgrims wood and food grains and provide them with cooking utensils. This arrangement brought income to mountain families during the pilgrimage season and freed pilgrims to carry only their personal belongings. The advent of paved roads and bus transportation has largely rendered this network obsolete, although it survives in certain place names, such as Janaki Chatti and Hanuman Chatti.

Chatuh-Sampradayi Nagas

Collective name for four groups (**sampraday**) of militant (**Naga**) ascetics who are all devotees (**bhakta**) of the god **Vishnu**. They all trace their spiritual lineage to a different **Vaishnava** religious community, each of which is connected with a major Vaishnava figure. By far the most populous and powerful of these groups is the **Shri sampraday** of the **Ramanandi** ascetics, which traces its descent through the poet-saint **Ramananda** to the southern Indian philosopher **Ramanuja**, whom they claim as Ramananda's **guru**. The **Sanaka sampraday** of the **Nimbarki** ascetics traces its spiritual lineage to the philosopher **Nimbarka**. The **Rudra sampraday** of the **Vishnuswami** ascetics traces its lineage through the philosopher **Vallabhacharya** to an earlier figure, Vishnuswami. Finally, the **Brahma sampraday** of the **Gaudiya Vaishnava** ascetics traces its spiritual line through the Bengali saint **Chaitanya** to the southern Indian philosopher **Madhva**. Each of these sampradays is differentiated not only by its founder but also by its patron **deity** or deities. The Ramanandis **worship** the god **Rama**, whereas the others worship the god **Krishna** and, to different extents, his consort, **Radha**.

Scholars doubt that these groups were ever actually connected to the people whom they claim as their founders. The distinctions among the sampradays appear to be largely academic. Given that the overwhelming majority of these ascetics are Ramanandis, the others seem important only for representing the other great Vaishnava religious figures. The distinctions between groups are only significant during the bathing (**snana**) festival known as the **Kumbha Mela**, at which they determine the order of certain groups in the bathing processions. For more information see Peter van der Veer, *Gods on Earth*, 1988.

Chaturbhujdas

(late 16th c.) One of the **ashtachap**, a group of eight northern Indian **bhakti** (devotional) poets. The compositions of these eight poets were used for liturgical purposes by the **Pushti Marg**, a religious community whose members are devotees (**bhakta**) of **Krishna**. In the Pushti Marg's sectarian literature, all eight are named as members of the community and as associates of either its founder, **Vallabhacharya**, or his successor, **Vitthalnath**. Chaturbhujdas is claimed as an associate of Vitthalnath—an idea supported by references in his poetry—and is also said to be the **son** of **Kumbhadas**, one of the earlier ashtachap poets. In his poetry Chaturbhujdas presents himself as a companion to Krishna and his consort, **Radha**, giving latter-day devotees a picture of their daily routine.

Chaturmas Vrat

A period of time spanning four **lunar months**, beginning on the festival of **Devshayani Ekadashi** (June–July) and ending on the festival of **Devotthayan Ekadashi** (October–November). The four months in between these festivals are considered ritually inauspicious, since during that time the god **Vishnu** is considered to be sleeping, and the protective power in the universe is less attentive. Thus people generally do not perform auspicious life cycle rites such as weddings during this period. This time also coincides with the coming of the **monsoon**, which is essential for helping crops to grow but also brings danger from waterborne infections and venomous snakes. Chaturmas Vrat's inauspicious qualities and the difficulty of travel caused by the monsoon make this a time when wandering **ascetics** should stay in one place. Religious **worship** during this period tends to stress **rites of protection**, to shield one from these ritual and physical dangers. See also **inauspiciousness**.

Chau

One of the classical **dance** forms of India; some of the others are **Bharatanatyam**, **Kathak**, **Orissi**, **Kuchipudi**, **Kathakali**, and **Manipuri**. Different forms of Chau are found in the border areas shared by the states of **Orissa**, **Bihar**, and **West Bengal**. In all three regions, the dancers wear masks (chau), making this type different from other classical dance forms. The expressions on the masks set a mood and conceal the dancers' faces. Consequently, Chau performers use their bodies and **gestures** to develop the moods established by their masks. The prevailing themes in Chau dance are drawn from the mythical adventures of gods and heroes, particularly the mythology of the god **Shiva**. For further information see Mohan Khokar, *Traditions of Indian Classical Dance*, 1984.

Chaupai

("four-footed") Poetic form in northern Indian poetry. As its name suggests, the chaupai is made up of four lines. The rhyme scheme is *aabb*, which has led some to consider it a compound of two two-line segments. Based on the distinction between "heavy" and "light" syllables, each line contains sixteen metric beats arranged in a pattern of $6 + 4 + 4 + 2$. A heavy syllable contains a long vowel or a consonant cluster and is counted as two metric beats; all other syllables are light and count as one beat. The chaupai is one of the most important **meters** in medieval **Hindi** literature,

particularly for longer narrative works, and it is a significant meter in **bhakti** (devotional) poetry. Its most famous use appears in the *Ramcharitmanas*, the *Ramayana* retold by the poet-saint **Tulsidas**.

Chaurasi Vaishnavan Ki Varta

("account of eighty-four Vaishnavas") Sectarian hagiography supposedly composed by **Gokulnath**, the third **guru** of the **Pushti Marg**, a religious community of **Krishna** devotees (**bhakta**) founded by the philosopher **Vallabhacharya** (1479–1531). It is more likely that the text was written by Gokulnath's disciple **Hariray**, who also wrote a commentary on the work. The text describes the lives of eighty-four paradigmatic **Vaishnavas**, all of whom were allegedly associated with the sect's first two gurus, **Vallabhacharya** and **Vitthalnath**. The text's primary purpose is to illustrate the importance of the Pushti Marg, particularly the importance of the Pushti Marg's leaders on these eighty-four religious figures. This makes it an interesting sectarian work, but it is not historically reliable.

Chauri

A small whisk used to brush off flies and insects. The name is derived from the word for the long tail **hairs** of a yak (chamara), from which it was originally made. In ancient India the chauri was an emblem of royalty, and thus it is also often seen in statues of religious figures such as the **Didarganj Yakshi**.

Chayagrahi

("shadow grabber") A demoness in the *Ramayana*, the earlier of the two great Hindu epics. Chayagrahi lives in the ocean and catches birds flying overhead by grasping their shadows in the **water** and pulling the helpless creatures down to her waiting jaws. This method brings her a steady food supply, but her big mistake is trying to capture the monkey-god, **Hanuman**, in this way. Hanuman tries to leap over the ocean to **Lanka**, the capital of the **demon**-king **Ravana**, to search for his abducted mistress, **Sita**. Chayagrahi grabs him and drags him down, but he quickly kills her and continues on his way.

Chera Dynasty

Hindu dynasty that ruled much of the modern state of **Kerala** from the second century B.C.E. to the eighth century C.E. The Cheras were in continual conflict with the **Pandyas** and the Cholas, the two other dynasties in the deep south, and were eventually absorbed when the Cholas gained control in the ninth century C.E. See also **Chola dynasty**.

Chidambaram

("clothed in thought") Temple town in the South Arcot district of the state of **Tamil Nadu**, about 125 miles south of Madras. The town of Chidambaram is famous for the temple of the same name, dedicated to the god **Shiva** in his form as **Nataraja**, the lord of the **dance**. This temple is also renowned as containing the subtlest of the five elemental **lingas** (**bhutalingas**), the linga made from **space**. The temple is built in the classical **Dravida** style, with temple towers (**gopurams**) rising in each of the cardinal directions, and the walls enclosing the temple between them. The present temple was erected in the tenth century C.E., when Chidambaram was the capital of the **Chola dynasty**, and is reputed to be one of the oldest temples in southern India. As lord of the dance, Nataraja symbolizes the connection between religion and the arts. Nataraja is the primal dancer whose dance encompasses creation, destruction, and all things in between. Human dancers imitate him literally, by performing the dance positions he codified, and figuratively, by participating in a creative activity. The temple's eastern wall has relief carvings of the 108 basic dance positions (**karanas**) that are still central to classical Indian dance, particularly to the **Bharatanatyam** school, which is the major dance form in Tamil Nadu. Nataraja also has a group of hereditary servants, the **Dikshitars**. According to their tradition, the **Dikshitars** were members of Shiva's heavenly host (**gana**) and accompanied him down from **heaven** when he took up residence in Chidambaram.

Chidvilasananda

(b. Malti Shetty, 1955) Modern Hindu teacher and successor to Swami **Muktananda**. Muktananda taught a type of spiritual discipline called **siddha yoga**, the "discipline of the adepts," which stresses chanting, meditation, learning, and above all, devotion to one's spiritual master. Chidvilasananda is the current leader and preceptor of SYDA (Siddha Yoga Dham America), the organization founded by her teacher. During her childhood, her parents and other members of her family were Muktananda's disciples, and she spent much of her life in his service, eventually serving as his translator during his visits to America. She and her brother, Subhash (who later took the name Nityananda), were both designated by Muktananda as his successors, but her brother left the organization a few years after Muktananda's death. Chidvilasananda continues to travel between an **ashram** in Ganeshpuri, near Bombay, and ashrams and centers around the world.

Childhood Rites

A collective name for the **samskaras** of early childhood, as specified in the **Dharma Shastras**, or treatises on religious duty (**dharma**). These rites include the **jatakarma** (**birth** ceremonies), **namakarana** (naming), **nishkramana** (first outing), **annaprashana** (first feeding), **chudakarana** (tonsure), and **karnavedha** (piercing the ears). Virtually all Hindu communities have ceremonies for ritually marking births and childhood, but few people perform the rites prescribed by the Dharma Shastras other than **brahmins**. For further information see Pandurang Vaman Kane (trans.), *A History of Dharmasastra*, 1968; and Raj Bali Pandey, *Hindu Samskaras*, 1969. The former is encyclopedic and the latter more accessible; despite their age they remain the best sources for traditional Hindu rites.

Child Marriages

Until well into the twentieth century, in many families it was traditional to marry off their children before the onset of puberty. An early marriage was deemed particularly important for **women**, lest they come of age before they were married. Some apologists claim that this practice evolved as a way to preserve the honor of Hindu girls against the depredations of Muslim raiders. Though this may have been partially true, such depredations were not widespread enough to evolve such a well-accepted social practice. Traditional Indian culture ascribes a much stronger sex drive to women than to men, and an early marriage would ensure that they did not disgrace the family under the influence of their irresistible urges. These marriages were possible because **arranged marriages** were the norm, as they remain to this day.

Many of the Hindu reformist movements that began in the late nineteenth century considered child marriages one of the "corruptions" of contemporary Hindu life and lobbied vigorously to forbid it. Modern Indian law sets the minimum age for marriage at sixteen for women and eighteen for men. These guidelines are often flouted, particularly in rural areas, where one still hears of marriages between infants. Although child marriages still occur, it is a very low-status practice in modern Indian society, associated with poverty, backwardness, and a lack of education. In contrast, men and women from the upper classes often do not marry until their late twenties,

after pursuing advanced degrees. See also **marriage ceremonies**.

Child Widows

This term refers to girls who had been married as children and whose husbands (whether older men or boys their own age) died before the girls reached puberty and the marriage had been consummated. Although the lives of such child widows varied according to the status of their families, their lives were often quite grim, given the traditional prohibitions on widow remarriage and the strict behavioral codes mandated for widows. Reformers in the nineteenth century, such as **Ram Mohan Roy**, championed the drive to promote societal acceptance of second marriages for child widows. Due to the sharp decline in the frequency of **child marriages**, child widows are extremely uncommon in modern times. See also **marriage prohibitions**.

Chillum

Implement used for smoking. The chillum is a graduated cylinder of baked clay that is usually about six inches long, which is about an inch in diameter at the top and half that at the bottom. A pyramid-shaped piece of clay is wedged point-down in the cylinder to cut down on the airflow. The top part of the cylinder is filled with tobacco, cannabis, or a mixture of tobacco and hashish (**charas**). Smoking is a communal activity in which the chillum is passed from one person to another. The bottom of the chillum is covered with a cloth called a **safai**, which is sometimes changed from person to person and is often dipped in **water** to mellow the smoke. Chillum etiquette holds that one should not place one's mouth directly on the bottom of the implement, which would render it impure. Because of this, the chillum is generally held between one's fingers, often in highly elaborate and symbolic ways. Among many **ascetics**, smoking the chillum is a part of daily life, a congregational exercise, and also the act of emulating the god **Shiva**, the paradigmatic ascetic, whose love for **drugs** is well known.

Chinmayanand, Swami

(b. **Balakrishna** Menon, 1915–1993) Modern Hindu **ascetic** and teacher. Chinmayanand became an ascetic under the influence of **Swami Shivananda**, whose articles Chinmayanand had first read while serving a prison sentence for his involvement in the independence movement. For several years he devoted himself to the study of ancient texts and became one of the leading authorities of the **Vedas**. Part of his legacy is the Chinmayanand Mission, which carried the abstract, intellectual, and peaceful message of the **Vedanta** philosophical school to the world. Another part of his legacy is the **Vishva Hindu Parishad**, a modern militant Hindu organization. He was one of its founding members in 1964, and for some years he was the only ascetic on its governing council.

Chinmoy, Shri

(b. 1931) Modern Hindu teacher and missionary, who since 1964 has spent much of his life addressing Western audiences. His teachings are largely drawn from classical ideas on **yoga** and stress the importance of **vegetarianism**, discipline, and service to one's **guru**. His own lifestyle is austere and largely unostentatious, as an example to his followers. On one hand he is notable for his attention to the arts—painting, poetry, and music, particularly the bamboo flute—and on the other for performing prodigious feats of strength to demonstrate the power of mind over matter. He is based in New York City, although like many modern Hindu teachers, he travels throughout the world.

Chin ("consciousness") Mudra

In Indian **dance**, **sculpture**, and ritual, a particular symbolic hand **gesture** (**mudra**) in which the tips of the thumb and index finger are touching, with the rest of the fingers extended and the palm facing the viewer. This is the hand gesture used to signify explanation or exposition. For this reason it is also known as the **vyakhyana** ("teaching") **mudra** and the **sandarshana** ("expository") **mudra**.

Chinnamasta

("She whose head [masta] has been cut off [chinna]") Particular manifestation of the **Goddess**, one of the **Mahavidyas** (a group of ten powerful goddesses), and an important **deity** in the esoteric ritual tradition known as **tantra**. The image of Chinnamasta is one of the most striking in Hindu iconography: a naked headless woman often seated on a copulating couple, holding her head on a platter and gushing three streams of **blood** from her neck—two into the mouths of Chinnamasta's attendant deities and one into the lips of her own severed head. The story behind this figure is that Chinnamasta severs her own head to satisfy the demands of her attendants because they have not drunk their fill of blood in battle. This image graphically portrays the interconnections between nourishment, sex, and death and the power of the Goddess over all of these things. Although Chinnamasta is powerful, she does not have many temples dedicated to her. One of the most important is the temple of the goddess **Chintapurni**, identified as a form of Chinnamasta in the **Shiwalik Hills**. For further information see David R. Kinsley, *Hindu Goddesses*, 1986; and Kathleen Erndl, *Victory to the Mother*, 1993.

Chintapurni

("She who fulfills one's wishes") Presiding **goddess** of a temple in a village by the same name in the state of **Himachal Pradesh**. Chintapurni is one of the **Shiwalik goddesses**, a group of local deities in the **Shiwalik Hills** who are all considered to be manifestations

Depiction of Krishna having stolen the gopis' clothes while they were bathing.
This episode from Hindu mythology is believed to have taken place at Chir Ghat.

of a single feminine divine energy. Chintapurni is considered to be a form of the goddess **Chinnamasta**, and this temple is one of the few dedicated exclusively to her.

Chir Ghat

("Clothing **Ghat**") A bathing (**snana**) place on the **Yamuna River** in the town of **Brindavan**, which is identified as the site for one of the most famous stories about **Krishna**. The story tells how the **gopis**, Krishna's female companions, have taken a religious vow to bathe each morning in the Yamuna during the cold months and dedicate the religious merit from this vow toward gaining Krishna as their beloved. Although their austerity is laudable, they are also bathing naked, which is taboo in Hindu culture. Krishna spies them in the **water** and climbs up in a tree with their clothes. He then refuses to return the clothes until the mortified **women** come out of the water to ask for them, symbolically demonstrating the nakedness of the soul before God and humans' inability to control the divine. A gigantic tree still stands by the Chir Ghat, which is believed to be the same

tree from which Krishna humbled the gopis. As pilgrims recall the story, they tie strips of cloth to the tree to relieve the gopis' embarrassment and share in their feeling of communion.

Chitpavan

A **brahmin jati** that is a subset of the **Maharashtri** brahmins, who were themselves one of the five southern brahmin communities (**Pancha Dravida**). Jatis were **endogamous** subgroups of traditional Indian society whose status was determined by the group's hereditary occupation. This sort of differentiation applied even to brahmins, whose role has been to serve as priests, scholars, and teachers. The core region for the Chitpavan brahmins is in western **Maharashtra**, particularly the coastline and the region around Poona. Although never very numerous, they were historically significant both as the chief ministers (**peshwas**) to the **Maratha** kings and also for producing some of the great figures in the struggle for independence: **M. G. Ranade**, **G. K. Gokhale**, **B. G. Tilak**, and **V. D. Savarkar**. Because this group of brahmins was largely located on the

Konkan coastline, they are also known as Konkanastha.

Chitrakut

City in the Banda district of **Uttar Pradesh**, about sixty miles south and west of the city of **Allahabad**. In the *Ramayana*, the earlier of the two great Hindu epics, Chitrakut is the place in which **Rama**, the epic's hero, his wife **Sita**, and his brother **Lakshmana** live during the early part of their exile. It is here as well that Rama instructs another brother, **Bharata**, to rule as regent until the fourteen years of Rama's exile have ended.

Chitswami

(late 16th c. C.E.) One of the **ashtachap**, a group of eight northern Indian **bhakti** (devotional) poets. The compositions of these eight poets were used for liturgical purposes by the **Pushti Marg**, a religious community whose members are devotees (**bhakta**) of **Krishna**. In the Pushti Marg's sectarian literature, all eight are also named as members of the community and as associates of either the community's founder, **Vallabhacharya**, or his successor, **Vitthalnath**. Chitswami is traditionally associated with Vitthalnath, a link confirmed by his poems written in praise of this **guru**. Aside from such explicitly sectarian compositions, Chitswami also wrote poetry in praise of Krishna, which tends to be more elaborate and uses more **Sanskrit** than his contemporaries. To date, his works have not been translated, perhaps because interest in them is limited to a small sect.

Chittirai

First month in the Tamil **year**, corresponding to the northern Indian solar month of Mesha (the zodiacal sign of Aries, which by the Indian solar **calendar** usually falls within April and May). This name is a modification of Chitra, the fourteenth of the twenty-seven **nakshatras** in the lunar **zodiac**. See also **Tamil months**.

Chittirai

(2) Ten-**day** festival celebrated in the southern Indian city of **Madurai** during the **Tamil month** of Chittirai (March–April). Madurai is famous for its gigantic temple dedicated to the **goddess Minakshi**, and the Chittirai festival celebrates Minakshi's marriage to the god **Shiva** in his form as Sundareshvara. According to mythology, Minakshi is a fierce goddess who vows that she will marry only a man who bests her in battle. She fights and conquers all of the kings of the **earth**, but when she approaches Shiva, she is suddenly and spontaneously stricken with modesty. The powerful warrior is transformed into a shy and bashful girl, and she becomes his wife.

Although the wedding of a goddess normally marks her domestication and subordination to her spouse, in this case Minakshi remains the more powerful **deity**. She is the patron of Madurai, with a temple dedicated to her, whereas Shiva is merely her consort. The wedding is celebrated with great festivity throughout the city, and one of the high points is the public procession of the deities around the city in the temple chariots. For further information see Dean David Shulman, *Tamil Temple Myths*, 1980; the festival is also the subject of a film, *The Wedding of the Goddess*, produced by the South Asia Center of the University of Wisconsin at Madison.

Chokamela

(d. 1338 C.E.) Poet and saint in the **Varkari Panth**, a religious community centered around the **worship** of the Hindu god **Vithoba** at his temple at **Pandharpur** in the modern state of **Maharashtra**. Chokamela was born an **untouchable Mahar**, and he is the only untouchable among the Varkari saints. Despite Chokamela's deep devotion to Vithoba, his low social status prohibited him from ever entering the god's temple, since his very presence would have rendered it impure. The hagiographical literature tells many tales where Vithoba comes outside to meet him. Chokamela's memorial shrine is at the steps of the temple, the same steps that marked his boundary during his life. It seems that Chokamela accepted the restrictions that came with his social status, but some of his poetry expresses social protest. For further information see G. A. Deleury, *The Cult of Vithoba*, 1960; and Eleanor Zelliot, "Chokamela and Eknath: Two Bhakti Modes of Legitimacy for Modern Change," in *Journal of Asian and African Studies*, Vol. 15, Nos. 1–2, 1980.

Chola Dynasty

(9th–13th c. C.E.) Southern Indian dynasty whose ancestral homeland was the **Tanjore** district of **Tamil Nadu**. The earliest Chola capital was in the city of Tanjore itself, but was later moved to **Gangaikondacholapuran** under **Rajendra I** (r. 1014–1042 C.E.). The Tanjore district is in the **Cauvery** River delta and is extremely fertile rice-growing land. The Chola monarchs used this agricultural strength as the foundation for their empire. The Cholas were originally vassals of the **Pallava dynasty** but became independent late in the ninth century. In the tenth and eleventh centuries, the Cholas were the dominant power in southern India, controlling much of peninsular India and **Sri Lanka** and sending naval expeditions as far as Malaysia. The Cholas were noted for their public works, particularly the construction of massive temples in the Tanjore district and other parts of **Tamil Nadu**; one of the most impressive was the **Brhadeshvar** temple built by **Raja Raja** (r. 985–1014 C.E.). On a smaller scale, the Chola dynasty also patronized exquisite sculptures, especially **bronzes**. This dynasty's rapid rise was marked by an equally swift demise. By the middle of the thirteenth century, they had been attacked several times by the **Pandya dynasty** and were finally conquered in 1279.

Chudakarana ("tonsure") Samskara

The eighth of the traditional life cycle ceremonies (**samskaras**). In the chudakarana samskara, the **hair** is shaved off of the child's head, although frequently a tuft of hair (chuda) is left. This is the last of the childhood samskaras, marking the ritual end of infancy, and it is still often performed in modern India, particularly by **brahmin** families. The timing for this rite is usually determined by **family custom** (**kulachara**), although in many cases it is performed when the child's age is an odd number (most commonly at one, three, or five years old). Since most Indian babies are born with hair, and hair is commonly believed to trap impurities, the chudakarana is seen as a rite of purification where the last of the residual impurities from childbirth are removed. As in many other cultures, this cut-off hair is believed to retain a powerful connection with the child. Traditional belief holds that in the wrong hands, this hair could be used to work black **magic** against the child. Given this concern, the hair is usually carefully gathered and disposed of, most often by putting it into running **water**.

Chunar

Sandstone quarry about twenty-five miles south of modern **Benares**. This quarry is notable as the source of the stone for the pillars erected by the Mauryan king **Ashoka**. The pillars were set up on the major trade routes within his empire and were inscribed with royal proclamations known as the **pillar edicts**. See also **Maurya dynasty**.

Churail

(perhaps from the **Sanskrit** word *cur*, meaning "to steal") Feminine malignant spirit believed to be the **ghost** of a woman who dies childless, in childbirth, or with her desires somehow unsatisfied. These frustrated desires lead such spirits to seek revenge by harming others, particularly children, to destroy the happiness they were denied. For further information about churails and other unquiet spirits of the dead, see Lawrence Babb, *The Divine Hierarchy*, 1975; Ann Grodzins Gold, *Fruitful Journeys*, 1988; and Sudhir Kakar, *Shamans, Mystics, and Doctors*, 1991.

Cinnabar

Common name for mercuric sulfide, which takes the form of red crystals or clumps. Cinnabar is important in Indian **alchemy**, particularly that of the mercurial (**dhatuvada**) school because it is a chemical union of the two elements representing the god **Shiva** (**mercury**) and his consort, **Shakti** (**sulfur**). According to Hindu alchemy, the world is a series of bipolar opposites in tension with one another. By unifying these opposing forces, one may achieve spiritual progress and the end of reincarnation (**samsara**). In Hindu alchemy this is done by physically consuming various substances. In this case, mercury is said to be Shiva's **semen** and sulfur Shakti's uterine **blood**; their combination and consumption is believed to spur the aspirant's progress.

Collyrium

A salve for the eyes, traditionally made from soot, camphor, beeswax, and various fragrances. Part of its function is cosmetic—it is used to outline and define the eyes. It is also widely believed to have medicinal qualities that improve one's vision and heal various minor eye ailments.

Commensality

This word refers to patterns of social exchange, particularly those associated with **eating**. In traditional Hindu society, the hierarchical status distinctions between different social groups were both marked and maintained by strict rules on exchanges and sharing. Traditional marriage customs illustrate the role of social groups, in which people married those who belonged to their own particular **jati** ("birth"), or social subgroup. Another arena in which these concerns were quite visible was that of food. Cooked food is believed to be extremely susceptible to ritual impurity (**ashaucha**) and can transmit impurities to the person eating it. To shield themselves from this source of impurity, groups with higher social status would not accept cooked foods from groups with lower social status. In contrast, lower-status groups would accept cooked foods from groups with higher status.

These concerns over maintaining social status set up certain eating patterns whose influence is still evident. Higher-status groups, particularly **brahmins**, would generally eat with members of their own community and only when a brahmin had cooked the food. For groups highly concerned with ritual **purity**, the best meal is one cooked at home by a family member, because this ensures the food's purity. Even in modern times, the most orthodox brahmins will eat food cooked outside the home only when it cannot be avoided. It is always considered preferable to eat food brought from home, whether one is on a long journey or merely at lunch in the office. Although in earlier times, the groups with the highest status would generally not eat with others, this custom has changed. Thus brahmin office workers may eat lunch with colleagues from many different communities, but they would never think of inviting them for a meal at their homes. For further information on the way that exchanges reveal status differences, see McKim Marriot, "Hindu Transactions: Diversity Without Dualism," in Bruce Kapferer (ed.), *Transaction and Meaning*, 1976.

Conch Shell

With the end of its spiral removed, this was used as both a musical instrument and a weapon of war, since the sound of certain conch shells was believed to strike terror into people's hearts. This is

The architectural technique of corbelling was used to form the arched entrance to the Mukteshvar Temple in Bhubaneshvar.

one of the four objects invariably carried by the god **Vishnu** and thus one of his identifying markers. See **shankha**.

Consecration

This term can refer to two different rites performed in the creation of Hindu images. One of these is **devapratishtha**, or "establishing the **deity**," the rites by which an image of a deity is constructed and established as an object of **worship**. The word *consecration* can also be used to refer to **pranapratishtha**, the more important ritual, in which the image is infused with the breath of life and becomes the seat for the deity.

Coomaraswamy, Ananda

(1877–1947) Intellectual and art historian who was one of the first Indian scholars to address a predominantly Western audience. He was born in modern **Sri Lanka**, the son of a Hindu father and an English mother. Although he was trained as a geologist, by 1910 he had found his true vocation, the study of art.

Coomaraswamy was largely responsible for publicizing Hindu **miniature painting** as a genre distinct from the contemporary Muslim court painting. Due to the strength of this and other interpretive scholarly works, he became curator of Indian and Muslim art at the Museum of Fine Arts in Boston. He held this post from 1917 to 1931, and his catalog of the museum's collection shows painstaking and objective scholarship. In his later years, he began to publish works on aesthetics, myth, religion, and culture, focusing not only on India but also on traditional Europe.

Corbelling

In the realm of **architecture** this term refers to the creation of a dome or arch through overlapping masonry courses. This technique was widely used in Indian temples, particularly those constructed in the **Nagara** style of architecture in **Orissa** and the rest of northern India. Corbelling was the prevailing method of creating the shape of an arch, since the true arch—in which each part is supported in tension with the others—was unknown in classical Hindu architecture.

Coromandel

Traditional name for the southern Indian coastal region bordering the Bay of Bengal, in the modern states of **Tamil Nadu** and **Andhra Pradesh**.

Corpse

In the Hindu worldview, a corpse is the source of the most virulent possible ritual impurity (**ashaucha**). Although Hindus accept death as an inevitable part of life, the dangers caused by a corpse cannot be ignored. The dead body must be appropriately handled, both to protect the living from danger and to help the deceased make a smooth transition to the next life. For this reason the last rites (**antyeshthi samskara**) are begun on the day of death itself. Among the earliest of these rites is the **cremation** of the dead body, since the impurity will continue to affect those around the body until it has been consumed by **fire**. A second reason for immediate cremation is to get rid of a potential host for wandering spirits, who according to popular fears, can reanimate a corpse.

Coryat, Thomas

(1577–1617) English traveler in India popularly known as the English **faqir**. Coryat came to India from Persia and spent several years traveling around the Moghul empire in northern India as well as residing in the Moghul court at Agra. Although at times his need for patronage made him play the role of a buffoon and flatterer, Coryat was a careful observer who was full of curiosity. He is believed to have been the first European traveler to visit the pilgrimage city of **Haridwar**, and he was impressed with the rites performed there. He is also believed to have gone into the **Shiwalik Hills** all the way to the temple at **Jwalamukhi**. Unfortunately, Coryat died of dysentery before he could record these observations, and the only available references to these later journeys come from his companion, the Reverend Edward Terry. See also **Moghul dynasty**.

Cosmic Egg

(brahmanda) One of the traditional cosmological metaphors, which first appears in the *Markandeya Purana*. This text describes a single swollen egg floating on the **waters** of the sea of **pralaya**, or cosmic dissolution. When this egg is broken open by **Brahma**, its constituent parts (yolk, white, shell, and various membranes) form both the material universe and all the creatures in it. Although this account is clearly symbolic, it vividly expresses the Hindu conviction that all things have come from a single source, and thus the entire cosmos is an organic whole. For further elaboration see Cornelia Dimmitt and J. A. B. van Buitenen (eds. and trans.), *Classical Hindu Mythology*, 1978.

Cosmic Time

In traditional Indian **cosmology**, time has neither beginning nor end. Instead it proceeds in unceasing cyclic alternations between creation and activity, followed by cessation and quietude. The universe thus has neither an ultimate beginning nor an ultimate end—creation will always be followed by destruction and then destruction by a new creation. Within the confines of this assumption, there are several different and sometimes competing systems for measuring cosmic time.

The largest generally accepted measure of time, spanning 4.32 billion years, is the **kalpa**, or **day of Brahma**. This is the ultimate limit for the existence of the created world, although within this period the universe undergoes periodic renewals. At the conclusion of the day of Brahma comes the universal dissolution (**pralaya**), in which the universe is completely destroyed and reabsorbed into the god **Vishnu**. The day of Brahma is followed by a night of equal length, during which the only living thing is Vishnu; the god sleeps on the back of his serpent couch, **Shesha**, which floats on the surface of the cosmic ocean. When the night of Brahma is ended, a lotus sprouts from Vishnu's navel. This lotus opens to reveal the god **Brahma**, who takes up the work of creation, and the cycle of activity begins anew. Because of his spontaneous appearance at the beginning of every cosmic age, one of the names for Brahma is **Svayambhu** ("self-born"). Unlike the Judeo-Christian concept of creation, Brahma does not create the world from nothing but merely arranges and fashions existing elements into a coherent and ordered cosmos.

The day of Brahma is broken up into smaller units according to various systems. By far the most common system is that of the four **yugas**, or cosmic ages. According to this idea, the day of

Brahma is made up of one thousand **mahayugas** ("great cosmic ages"), each of which lasts for 4.32 million years. Each mahayuga is composed of four constituent yugas, named the **Krta yuga**, **Treta yuga**, **Dvapara yuga**, and **Kali yuga**. Each of these is shorter than its predecessor and ushers in an era more degenerate and depraved. The passage of the four yugas begins with a time of sudden and dramatic renewal at the onset of the krta yuga, followed by a steady and persistent decline. Although the kali yuga is the shortest of the four ages, it is also the time of the greatest wickedness and depravity, in which any evil is possible. It is also, not surprisingly, considered to be the period in which we are now living. By the end of the kali yuga, things have gotten so bad that the only solution is the destruction and recreation of the **earth**, at which time the next krta era begins. Even though the kali yuga is the shortest age, it still lasts for 432,000 years, and the preceding yugas are two, three, and four times the length of the kali age. The increasing degeneracy of each of the four yugas is symbolized by the metals associated with them: gold (krta), silver (dvapara), bronze (treta) and iron (kali). Another indication is the status of human beings, who are said to become shorter, more wicked, and shorter-lived in each succeeding age. The paradigm of the four yugas leaves little room in traditional Hinduism for the notion of progress, since according to this system, things will never be better than they have already been. It idealizes a lost and unattainable past rather than a utopian future.

An alternate system of measuring cosmic time connects the human and the divine calendars, with one human **year** equal to a single day for the gods. The six months when the **sun** travels toward the north (**uttarayana**) is the divine day, whereas the six months when it travels south (**dakshinayana**) is the divine night. Since an Indian **solar year** is 360 solar days, a divine year would thus last for 360 human years.

The life span of Brahma is one hundred divine years and thus 36,000 human years, after which the world is destroyed and created anew.

A third system is that of the Manvantaras, or ages of Manu. This system divides the day of Brahma into fourteen equal ages, with each one lasting a little less than 309,000 years. Each age is identified by the particular divine sovereign (manu) who rules during that age. None of these three systems correspond to one another, and there is no real effort to reconcile them. This lack of correspondence indicates that their function was primarily mythic, to establish a coherent cosmic chronology and pattern rather than to describe actual events.

Cosmology

Hindu culture has no single cosmology but rather several different systems, each of which is well established in its own right. The oldest model appears in the **Rg Veda** (10.90), the oldest Hindu religious text, and is known as the **Purusha Sukta** ("Hymn to the Primeval Man"). This hymn describes the **creation** of the world and all living beings as the result of the **sacrifice** of the primeval man (purusha). Different parts of his body become different parts of the physical universe and the traditional social groups. Another Vedic metaphor is that of the **Golden Embryo**, which is the only existing thing until it develops into **Prajapati**, the creator of the universe. A third version, that of the **Cosmic Egg**, is found in the later religious texts known as the **puranas**, which are compilations of mythology and lore. According to this image, the entire universe is originally contained in the Cosmic Egg. Once it is broken, the egg's constituent parts (shell, white, yolk, and membranes) become all of the things of the **earth**. The final cosmological image from the puranas, and perhaps the most common, begins with the god **Vishnu** floating in the sea of cosmic dissolution (**pralaya**), lying on the back of his serpent couch, **Shesha**. When the time for creation comes, a lotus sprouts from Vishnu's navel and opens to reveal the god **Brahma**, who begins the process of creation. This process reverses at the onset of the cosmic dissolution, with Brahma being reabsorbed into Vishnu's body. Despite their differing symbols, all of these models share the conviction that the universe has come from a single source and thus that the entire cosmos is an organic whole.

Although there are many models for the origin of the cosmos, there is wider agreement about its geography. The universe is generally considered to have three tiers, and each of these tiers can have multiple levels. The visible world is considered the middle tier, sandwiched between the **heavens** of the upper world (often numbered as seven) and the realms of the underworld. Some of the latter are **hells**, whereas some of these lower worlds are simply considered to be alternate realms of existence. The visible world is often described as a series of concentric landmasses (**dvipas**) separated from each other by seven oceans (the **saptasindhu**), each composed of a different substance. The innermost of these landmasses is **Jambudvipa**, whose center is the mythical Mount **Meru**, often identified with Mount **Kailas** in the **Himalayas**. In traditional cosmology Mount Meru stands at the center of the universe and is compared to the central calyx of a lotus. Mount Meru is surrounded by mountain ranges, with a different region in each of the cardinal directions. The region south of Mount Meru is the land known as **Bharata**, the traditional name for the Indian subcontinent. Bharata is said to be superior to the other three regions of Jambudvipa because only in Bharata are religious rituals correctly performed. In its mythic geography, therefore, India is considered the center of the universe and the best possible place to live to pursue religious life. For further information see Cornelia Dimmitt and J. A. B. van Buitenen, *Classical Hindu Mythology*, 1978. See also **cosmic time**.

Cow

Animal revered by almost all modern Hindus, although there is one small Hindu community in the state of **Kerala** that eats beef. Aside from this anomaly, reverence for the cow is one of the few unifying beliefs for almost all Hindu communities. Demands for a complete ban on **cow slaughter** have become a time-honored way for political groups to generate support from the orthodox Hindu community, although these demands carry far more weight in northern India, where a significant Muslim **minority** has few scruples about slaughtering and **eating** beef. Organized calls for such a ban began as early as the 1880s with the growth of tension between the Hindu and Muslim communities. This sentiment, generally called the **Cow Protection Movement**, has continued to the present day. Demands for a complete ban on cow slaughter have regularly surfaced since 1947, when India gained independence, and this is one of the loaded causes of Indian political life. Reverence for the cow goes to such lengths that one of the charitable acts performed by pious Hindus is to contribute to **goshalas**, institutions for old and infirm cows.

There is considerable speculation and some disagreement about the source of these feelings about the cow. Some arguments have stressed the cow's value in an agricultural society, as a source of both draft **animals** and reproducible wealth. Other arguments have stressed the cow's ability to transform agricultural waste into milk products and dung, a common fuel in much of northern India. Still others have noted the way that feelings about the cow are imbued with the symbolism of motherhood, since both are said to provide milk for a child's nourishment. This last point is probably the most important, since it is very clear that conservative Hindu feelings for the cow are based primarily on high emotional content rather than on rational considerations of costs and benefits.

Girls carry dried cow dung mixed with straw to be used as fuel.

Cow Dung

This is considered both ritually pure and purifying, perhaps because of its origin in the sacred **cow**. A piece of ground can be purified (as when preparing a site for a ritual) by smearing it with cow dung. Cow dung is one of the ingredients in the "five products of the cow" (**panchagavya**), which is drunk as a means of purification from sin. In addition to its spiritual significance, cattle dung is very important for daily life in the villages of India. When mixed with clay it forms a hard, dustless, and easily cleaned surface that is preferable to an earthen floor. It is also a reliable source of fuel available to even the poorest people.

Cow Protection Movement

General term for a grassroots conservative Hindu effort to ban the slaughter of cattle, particularly the **cow**. The traditional Hindu devotion to the cow has been articulated in calls for a ban on **cow slaughter** for more than a century. The call was first raised in 1875 by **Swami Dayanand Saraswati**, the founder of the reformist **Arya Samaj**. It continued to be a basic demand of later conservative Hindu-oriented groups, including the **Hindu Mahasabha**, the **Ram Rajya Parishad**, and the **Vishva Hindu Parishad**. The call for this ban occasionally surfaces even in contemporary times, since it carries strong support from many religiously conservative Hindus.

The cow protection demand continues to have profound political implications. Swami Dayanand Saraswati's work in the late nineteenth century coincided with the awakening of Indian political consciousness and the beginnings of the struggle to regain power from British imperial rule. Under British power, overt political dissent was subject to heavy government restrictions, and outright rebellion was impossible. Since the British did not generally interfere with "religious" issues, the demand for a ban on cow slaughter was a way for Hindus to assert and define their identity and by implication affirm that India was a Hindu land.

The Cow Protection Movement also caused friction between the Hindu and Muslim communities, since Hindus worship cows, whereas Muslims eat them. Hindus saw Muslim beef consumption as a flagrant violation of their religious sensibilities, and Muslims saw the demand for a ban on cow slaughter as a thinly veiled attempt to reinforce Muslim status as second-class citizens. Communal relations were often particularly volatile around the annual Muslim festival of Id, at which it is traditional for each family to **sacrifice** an **animal** and in which many of the more affluent Muslim families would sacrifice cattle. As the relationship between these two communities deteriorated in the 1930s, cow slaughter (or rumor thereof) was often cited as the spark for communal riots in which hundreds of people were killed.

This tension persists in modern India, although it has rarely erupted into violence since the partition of the subcontinent in 1947. Modern India was founded as a secular state where the government does not favor any particular religious community. This founding ethos has made the Indian government reluctant to pass legislation banning cattle slaughter, despite continued calls from traditional Hindus. The Indian Muslim community, facing the reality of its **minority** status in a Hindu majority state, has had to be far more discreet about when and how such cow slaughter takes place.

Cow Slaughter

A complete ban on cow slaughter has been one of the more durable issues taken up by Hindu interest groups, from before India gained independence in 1947 all the way up to the present day. Although debate on this issue has continuously emerged and faded, it remains a reliable hot button for stirring Hindu passions. This issue has predictably carried far more weight in northern India, where there is a significant Muslim **minority** with no religious objection to slaughtering and **eating** beef. The first widespread demand for such a ban came during the **Cow Protection**

Movement in the 1930s. This movement aggravated tense communal relations between the Hindu and Muslim communities, resulting in significant bloodshed. Since independence it has been a perennial demand by religious leaders and **ascetics**, and it has been an issue in the platform of Hindu political organizations such as the **Jana Sangh**, **Shiv Sena**, **Vishva Hindu Parishad** (VHP), and **Bharatiya Janata Party** (BJP). In the past, such demands had little effect since the proponents did not have the power to implement them. As the BJP and the Shiv Sena have gained control of state and local governments, they have tried to implement this policy. In late 1995 the VHP initiated a national drive to ban cow slaughter completely. Like many of the VHP's campaigns, this was undertaken just before upcoming elections, in this case at the national level. This campaign was seen as an attempt to polarize the Hindu electorate in an effort to influence the national election.

Creation

See **cosmology** and **cosmic time**.

Creation Hymn

Popular name for a hymn in the **Rg Veda** (10.129), which is one of the most unusual hymns in the **Vedas**. The four Vedas are the oldest Hindu religious texts, and based on its style and content, the Rg Veda is the oldest of these. Most of the hymns in the Rg Veda are invocations addressed to various divinities. These hymns are sung to invoke and propitiate these divinities so that human beings may enjoy the good things in life. In marked contrast to the confidence and optimism found in the earlier hymns, the Creation Hymn takes a far more speculative tone. In the Creation Hymn, the poet begins by imagining a time before the existence of Being and Nonbeing, and he speculates on the origin of the world. In the end the poet ascribes all creation to a single impersonal agent, "That One" (**Tad**

Hindu cremation on the Ganges River. Although cremation is the religiously preferred way to dispose of a corpse, the relatively high cost of wood makes this difficult for poorer families.

Ekam). However, the poem concludes with the thought that even That One may not know the secrets of the cosmos. In its speculative tone and its admission that the ultimate answer may be unknown, it foreshadows the final stratum of the Vedic literature, the **Upanishads**.

Cremation

For most Hindus cremation is the approved method for disposing of a dead body, although one finds **burials** in certain circumstances and subcommunities. The body is usually cremated on the day of death, often only a few hours after the person has expired. Although one could see this as a hygienic measure in a hot climate, for many Hindus the religious reasons are even more compelling. First, a **corpse** is considered to be a source of violent impurity (**ashaucha**) that is removed by destroying the body by **fire**. A second reason for immediate cremation is to get rid of a potential vehicle for wandering spirits, who according to popular fears, can reanimate a corpse.

The rites leading to cremation begin immediately after death. As for all Hindu rituals, there is great variation in different regions and communities, but the following description gives a general picture of these rites, at least in northern India: The body is bathed, laid on a bier (often made from bamboo, which is cheap, strong, and readily available), and covered with a cloth (white for a man or a **widow**, a colored sari for a married woman). In many cases the big toes are tied together with a thread, due to the belief that this prevents an alien spirit from reanimating the body. The mourners carry the bier to the **cremation ground**, chanting the traditional dirge *Ram Nam Satya Hai, Satya Boli Gati Hai* ("God's name is Truth, Truth spoken is Passage"). On the way, the mourners will often halt several times, not only to rest but also on the chance that the deceased was merely unconscious. When they arrive at the cremation ground (which is often by a river or source of **water**), the corpse is bathed again and set on a pyre. The chief mourner (traditionally the eldest **son**) circles the pyre, pouring water from a clay pot, which is then broken. Since poetic images often compare the ephemeral quality of human bodies to that of clay pots, this action clearly signifies the final destruction of the body. The chief mourner then ignites the pyre and remains there while the body burns. If the skull does not crack from the heat of the fire, he is given a long bamboo stick to pierce the skull. This is believed to release the **vital winds** (**prana**) of the deceased, which have collected in the head. The chief mourner's final duty is to collect bones and ash from the pyre (**asthi-sanchayana**), often on the following day, and to immerse these remains in the **Ganges** or some other sacred river (**asthi-visarjana**).

The wooden pyre is the traditional means for cremation and remains the preferred method, despite the development of more efficient and cheaper electric crematoria. This has led to an unusual ecological problem in modern India, particularly in the big cities. Many poor people cannot afford to buy enough wood to cremate the body with a pyre but, because of tradition, are unwilling to use electric crematoria. They will perform incomplete cremations in which part of the body is left unburned. This is a bad state of affairs, both from a religious and a public health perspective, because the bodies are a source of religious impurity and contribute to the contamination of the rivers. For further information see Pandurang Vaman Kane (trans.), *A History of Dharmasastra*, 1968; and Raj Bali Pandey, *Hindu Samskaras*, 1969. For accounts of modern practice, see Lawrence Babb, *The Divine Hierarchy*, 1975; and Ann Grodzins Gold, *Fruitful Journeys*, 1988.

Cremation Ground

Literally a place where bodies are cremated, but in Hindu culture it also has a significant symbolic meaning. The cremation ground is pervaded by associations with death and impurity (**ashaucha**), making it an intensely inauspicious place that is often believed to be inhabited by malevolent wandering spirits. The cremation ground is usually located at the boundary of a community, both to remove any contact with this source of **inauspiciousness** from everyday life and perhaps to symbolically deny the reality of death by relegating the cremation ground to the margins of the "settled" world.

One well-known exception to this rule occurs in **Benares**, where the cremation ground at **Manikarnika Ghat** is in the middle of the city. This prominence symbolically forces the inhabitants to confront the reality of death, but since Benares is also the home of the god **Shiva**, it also raises the hope that death will bring final liberation of the soul (**moksha**). Similarly, although most people avoid the cremation ground as inauspicious, certain religious adepts voluntarily choose it as their place of residence and religious practice. This may include certain types of **ascetics** who are simply emulating terrifying forms of Shiva who are said to reside in cremation grounds. Practitioners of the esoteric ritual tradition known as **tantra** may live in a cremation ground to assert the radical unity of all reality and transcend the concepts of **purity** and impurity, which they consider artificial. See also **cremation**.

Cuckoo

(*Cuculus melanoleucus* or *jacobinus*) Indian songbird intimately connected with both love and the **monsoon** rains. The cuckoo's mating season comes during the monsoon, when its piercing calls are fancifully interpreted as *piu, piu* ("beloved, beloved"). These cries are said to excite the hearts of human lovers—either to passion if they are together or to bitter pain if the monsoon is keeping them apart. The cuckoo's behavior in the rainy season is supposed to reflect its love for the monsoon. According to popular belief, the cuckoo drinks only raindrops, which means that for much of the year, it is tormented by thirst. In devotional (**bhakti**) poetry, the cuckoo is often used as a symbol for the devotee (**bhakta**), who is tormented by the **deity's** absence but who waits patiently for the divine presence. In **Sanskrit** poetry this bird is called the **chataka**; in modern dialects it is known as the kokila or koil.

Cunningham, Sir Alexander

(1814–1893) First director of the Archeological Survey of India and the father of modern Indian archeology. Cunningham first came to India in 1831 as an officer in the Royal Engineers, but his hobby was the study of ancient India's material artifacts. This passion eventually resulted in the formation of the A.S.I., which Cunningham headed until his retirement in 1885. By surveying sites, cataloging their contents, and translating **inscriptions**, his work was fundamental to preserving India's heritage.

Cuntarar

Tamil form of the name for the poet-saint **Sundaramurtti**.

Curses

In Hindu mythology, one of the standard devices either to advance the story's plot or to account for some inexorable event. Such curses are often the work of sages and other spiritual adepts, but they can also be levied by any person who has perfectly fulfilled his or her social role, such as a faithful wife, loving **son**, or devoted parent. Making a curse expends the spiritual powers that a person has accumulated. At least in mythical tales, such curses invariably come true no matter what a person might do to try to prevent them. For example, in a mythic story, King **Parikshit** secludes himself on a high pillar to escape death by snakebite but is killed when a divine serpent conceals itself as a worm in a piece of fruit. Once pronounced, a curse cannot be simply nullified, although it can be modified to blunt its overall effect. For a consideration of the function of curses in Indian mythology, see Robert Goldman,

"Karma, Guilt, and Buried Memories: Public Fantasy and Private Memory in Traditional India," in the *Journal of the American Oriental Society*, Vol. 105, No. 3, 1985.

D

Dabistan-I-Mazahib

("School of Manners") An outside source for the religious life of the times, and gives the earliest detailed description of the Sikhs, as well as many other contemporary religious communities. The text traditionally is ascribed to **Muhsin Fani**. Fani was a Persian who traveled through much of northern India, apparently motivated only by his intense curiosity to encounter the country's different forms of religious life. The text is also notable for the seeming absence of authorial bias—Fani reports that he had simply translated what his friends and informants had told him, and the *Dabistan's* tone seems to maintain this claim. The text has been translated by David Shea and Anthony Troyer as *The Dabistan, or School of Manners*, 1843.

Dadhichi

A sage in Hindu mythology who is a paradigm for self-sacrifice. The gods (**devas**) and the **demons** (supernatural beings) are engaged in a long-running war, in which neither side can prevail. **Indra**, the king of the gods, finally decides to seek advice from the god **Brahma**. Brahma advises Indra that if he obtains a bone from Dadhichi's body, it can be made into a weapon that will defeat the demons. Indra is understandably uncertain that his request will be granted, but when he appears before Dadhichi, he not only gives his consent, but immediately abandons his body through yogic powers. Indra takes Dadhichi's bones, fashions a weapon from them, and successfully defeats the demons.

Dadhikra

A divine war horse described in a few of the hymns in the **Vedas**, the oldest Hindu religious texts. The Vedas were the religious hymns of a group known as the **Aryans**, and hymns throughout the Vedas clearly show the importance of horse-drawn chariots as weapons of war. Given this importance, it is not surprising that one finds a divinized horse in these hymns, even if it is only a minor figure.

Dadu

(1554–1603) **Sant** poet-saint and founder of the religious organization known as the **Dadupanth**. The sants were a group of central and northern Indian poet-saints who share several general tendencies: a stress on individualized, interior religion leading to a personal experience of the divine; disdain for external ritual, particularly image **worship**; faith in the power of the divine Name; and a tendency to ignore conventional **caste** (social order) distinctions. According to tradition, Dadu was born into a family of cotton-carders, a fairly low-status occupation. He is also reported to have been born a Muslim, although based on his poetry he seems to have been relatively unaffected by Islam. His songs highlight many of the aforementioned sant themes. His poems also stress nonviolence (**ahimsa**), and as a practical application of that principle, **vegetarianism**. Another prominent theme is the religious value of work, since despite his fame he is said to have carded cotton until his death.

Some of Dadu's poems give lists and categories, as if systematizing his ideas for instruction. This suggests that he envisioned an established community of disciples. According to legend, Dadu met with the Moghul emperor **Akbar**, who was so impressed by Dadu's charisma that he ceased his harming of living beings. The tale is probably fictitious, since there are similar stories for many of the sant poets, which all illustrate the well-established theme of the temporal ruler bowing to the spiritual adept. For further information on traditional sources, see Winand Callewaert (trans.), *The Hindi Biography of Dadu Dayal*, 1988. See also **Moghul dynasty**.

Dadupanth

Religious organization founded by the **sant** poet-saint **Dadu** (1554–1603). The Dadupanth is strongest in **Rajasthan**, the desert state in which Dadu is believed to have lived. The Dadupanth stresses religious themes common to the sant poet-saints: the rejection of ritual and image **worship** in favor of an internal search for a formless **deity**, stress on the power of the divine Name, and a belief in the relative unimportance of conventional **caste** distinctions. It also emphasizes certain points that were particularly important to Dadu himself, among them nonviolence (**ahimsa**), **vegetarianism**, and the religious value of work. The Dadupanth has always been a numerically small organization, but they are historically important because of their manuscript collections. These collections are known as the "five voices" (*panchvani*), because they contain the works of five different devotional (**bhakti**) poets: Dadu, **Kabir**, **Namdev**, **Ravidas**, and Hardas. Rajasthan's desert climate has helped to preserve these manuscripts, some of which date from the early seventeenth century. The Panchvani manuscripts are among the earliest sources for all of these poets, which makes them an important resource for the historical study of northern Indian devotional poetry. For further information on the literary resources of the Dadupanth, see Winand Callewaert (trans.), *The Sarvangi of the Dadupanthi Rajab*, 1978; and *The Sarvangi of Gopaldas*, 1993.

Dadupanthi Nagas

Particular group of **Naga** (fighting) **ascetics** associated with the religious community (**panth**) established by the western Indian poet-saint **Dadu**. The Nagas are renunciant ascetics organized into different **akharas**, or regiments based on the model of an army. Until the beginning of the nineteenth century the Nagas' primary occupation was as mercenary soldiers, although they also had substantial trading interests; both of these have largely disappeared in contemporary times. In the bathing (**snana**) processions at the **Kumbha Mela** festivals ("Festivals of the Pot"), the Dadupanthi Nagas march with the **chatuh-sampradayi Nagas**, who are devotees (**bhakta**) of the god **Vishnu**, but are considered independent of them. According to tradition, the Naga section of the **Dadupanth** was established by Sundardasa, one of Dadu's direct disciples.

Daita

Tribal (**adivasi**) community in the modern state of **Orissa**. The Daitas are hereditary temple servants at the temple of the god **Jagannath** in the city of **Puri**. Jagannath has been brought into the larger Hindu pantheon by identifying him as a form of the god **Krishna**, but he is originally believed to have been a local, tribal **deity**. This history is partly inferred from Jagannath's relationships with the Daitas themselves, who are considered Jagannath's relatives, even though their social status is very low. This relational connection gives the Daitas several unique roles. During the annual **Rath Yatra**, a ceremonial procession in which Jagannath, his brother **Balabhadra**, and their sister **Subhadra** are processed around the city in giant wooden chariots, the Daitas convey the deities' giant wooden images from the temples to the chariots and pull the ropes that draw the carts. An even more important role comes when new images of the deities are constructed, usually every twelve or nineteen years. The Daitas carve the new images, each from a single massive log. When the new image has been completed, the oldest Daita removes a wooden plug in the old image that seals an interior cavity. He then transfers a mysterious substance called the "life substance" to a corresponding cavity in the new image, which is sealed with another wooden plug. The Daita chosen to make this transfer is blindfolded and has his hands wrapped in layers of cloth, so he is unable to tell exactly what is transferred, and this "life substance" is considered so sacred that the person who makes this transfer reportedly dies soon afterward. After the "life substance" has been removed, the old image is considered a "**corpse**." The Daitas bury it, observe a ten-day period of ritual death impurity (**maranashaucha**), and the heirs of the deceased claim his "belongings"—primarily clothes and resin, which they sell to pilgrims. Jagannath's continuing relations with the Daitas point to his origins as a local, tribal god, and this relationship gives the Daitas continuing special privileges.

Daiva Marriage

One of the eight ways to perform a marriage recognized in the **dharma literature**, the treatises on religious duty (**dharma**). In a Daiva marriage the father of the bride gives away his **daughter** with her ornaments to a **brahmin** (priest). The priest then officiates at a **sacrifice** sponsored by the father. According to some interpretations, the girl is given as the **dakshina**, or fee for these sacrificial services. This form of marriage was named after the gods (**devas**), and was one of the four approved (**prashasta**) forms of marriage. Even though a daiva marriage was considered an approved form, it fell out of favor because of the hint that the bride had been given as a payment for services, rather than without any conditions whatsoever. See also **Marriage, eight classical forms**.

Daksha

In Hindu mythology, one of the **sons** of the god **Brahma**, and the father of the

Image of the Hindu god Daksha. His head was replaced with the head of a goat as the result of a conflict with the god Shiva.

goddess Sati. Sati has been given in marriage to the god **Shiva**, and Daksha's most famous mythic story has to do with this divine pair. According to legend, when Daksha feels that Shiva has not shown him proper respect, he wants to put Shiva in his place—even though in this mythic story Shiva is clearly identified as the supreme **deity**. Inflated with pride, Daksha plans a great **sacrifice** to which he invites all the other gods, but as an insult purposely excludes Shiva. When Sati learns about the sacrifice, she insists on going to it, despite Shiva's warning that it is unwise to go without an invitation. When she arrives at the sacrificial ground, and asks why her husband has been excluded, Daksha responds with a stream of abuse denouncing Shiva as worthless and despicable. Humiliated by these public insults, Sati commits **suicide**—in some versions, by leaping into the sacrificial **fire**, in others by withdrawing into a yogic trance and giving up her life. Shiva becomes furious when he hears of Sati's death, and in his rage creates the fierce deities **Virabhadra** and **Bhadrakali**. He comes storming with his minions (**gana**) to the sacrificial ground, destroys the sacrifice, and cuts off Daksha's head. Daksha is eventually restored to life, but with the head of a goat rather than a human being. He repents of his arrogance and worships Shiva as the highest god. In this story, Daksha is a symbol for the foolish pride that eventually causes one's destruction.

In another mythic story, Daksha is portrayed in a more sympathetic light. Chandra (the **moon**) has married Daksha's twenty-seven **daughters**, but was paying attention to only one of the daughters, named **Rohini**. Daksha remonstrates with Chandra to give each of his wives equal time, and when Chandra ignores this advice, Daksha curses him to lose his luster. As Chandra begins to wane, the other gods intercede with Daksha, and implore him to modify the **curse**. At their urgent prompting, Daksha decrees that Chandra will only wane for half the month and then wax for the other half. He then directs Chandra to take a bath at the **Somnath** temple in **Gujarat** state, which will heal him from the original curse. Here Daksha is still powerful and imperious, but his actions are rooted in his concern for his daughters.

Dakshina

("preceptor's fee") Gifts or fees given to one's teacher in return for the services rendered. The paradigm for this goes back to the **dharma literature**, or the texts on religious duty (**dharma**), which propose an idealized doctrine for the four stages (**ashramas**) of a man's life. The first of these stages is as a celibate student (**brahmacharin**), in which the young man will live in his teacher's household and commence studying the **Vedas**, the oldest Hindu religious texts. At the conclusion of his studies, the student will give his teacher dakshina as a sign of appreciation. In modern times this pattern has been extended to other contexts, particularly the arts, and it has become customary for students to give gifts to their teachers on various occasions, particularly on the **full moon**

known as **Guru Purnima**, which usually falls in June or July. Dakshina is always given in exchange for services, and is thus essentially payment that is "owed" for these services. In this aspect it is a very different mode of exchange from **dana** (charitable giving). Dana generates religious merit, but the donor receives nothing tangible in return.

Dakshinachara

("right-hand practice") In the secret ritual tradition known as **tantra**, this is the term for a type of tantric practice that does not avail itself of any forbidden substances or promote any behavior that the orthodox would consider scandalous or objectionable. It stands in opposition to the **vamachara**, or "left-hand practice," which uses such forbidden substances in its ritual, and shows no such regard for conventional sensibilities. The most common forbidden substances are the Five Forbidden Things (**panchamakara**), so called because they all begin with the letter "m" (in the sacred language of **Sanskrit**, *makara*) **madya** (wine), **matsya** (fish), **mamsa** (meat), **mudra** (fermented or parched grain), and **maithuna** (copulation). In left-hand tantra these forbidden things are used in their actual forms, whereas right-hand practitioners substitute other more socially acceptable things for them. This is one more instance of the pervasive Hindu polarity between right and left, which carries inherent value judgments. In this case, the left-hand practitioners are seen as impure and dangerous, because they intentionally violate social boundaries, whereas the right-hand are socially respectable. For further information see Arthur Avalon (Sir John Woodroffe), *Shakti and Shakta*, 1978; Swami Agehananda Bharati, *The Tantric Tradition*, 1977; and Douglas Renfrew Brooks, *The Secret of the Three Cities*, 1990.

Temple in Dakshineshwar dedicated to the goddess Kali.

Dakshinayana

The six months of the solar **year** in which the **sun** is reckoned as moving southward. In the Gregorian **calendar**, this is the period between the summer solstice and the winter solstice (roughly December 20 to June 20) and is based on the actual motion of the sun with respect to the **earth**. The Indian reckoning is based on the motion of the sun through the **zodiac**, which is calculated differently than in western astrology. The Dakshinayana begins on **Karka Sankranti** (the **day** the sun is thought to enter Cancer, usually July 14), and ends the day before **Makara Sankranti** (the day the sun enters Capricorn, usually January 14). The Dakshinayana is considered less auspicious than the **Uttarayana**, the six months in which the sun travels north, because the southern direction is associated with the **Yama**, the god associated with death, judgment, and punishment for evildoers.

Dakshineshwar

Temple site about four miles north of modern Calcutta, on the eastern bank of the Hugli River. Dakshineshwar's primary **deity** is the powerful and dangerous **goddess Kali**, although like most Hindu temples it also has images of most of the deities in the pantheon. Dakshineshwar's importance comes not from its age—the primary image was consecrated in 1855, and it is thus a relatively recent site—but through its association with the Bengali saint **Ramakrishna**, who lived there for most of his life.

Dalit

("oppressed") Modern name for the social groups that have the lowest social status, groups that in earlier times would have been called **Harijan** or **untouchable**. This term is significant because it is the name used by low-status groups to designate themselves as members of a disadvantaged group. Adoption and popularization of this term reflects their growing awareness of the situation, and their greater assertiveness in demanding their legal and constitutional rights. In certain parts of the country, particularly in the state of **Maharashtra**, the Dalits have formed a militant organization called the Dalit Panthers, modeled after the Black Panthers in America.

Damaru

Hourglass-shaped hand drum, which has membranes stretched over the top and bottom of the hourglass, and at the middle, two strings with a bead at the end. The drum is played by holding it by its narrow middle and rotating the hand back and forth so that the beads strike the drumheads. The pace of the rhythm (**tala**) is determined by the speed of hand movement. In Hindu iconography, this drum is almost invariably associated with the god **Shiva**. In his form as **Nataraja**, the Lord of the **Dance**, the drum signifies the rhythm by which Shiva undertakes the creation of the universe. Another iconic motif is to show the damaru hanging from Shiva's trident. In modern times this drum is often carried by **ascetics**, either because of its association with Shiva, its portability, or both. See also **iconic image**.

Damayanti

In Hindu mythology, the **daughter** of the king of Vidarbha and the wife of King **Nala**. The story of Nala and Damayanti appears as a story within the *Mahabharata*, the later of the two great Hindu epics. It is recounted to the five **Pandava** brothers, the epic's protagonists, during a twelve-year exile in the forest as a way to keep up their spirits by telling how others had transcended misfortune.

In the story, when Damayanti comes of marriageable age, her father sends invitations to the kings of the **earth**, announcing her **svayamvara**, a rite in which Damayanti will choose her own husband. The kings of the earth come to the svayamvara to seek her hand, as do the gods (**devas**) themselves. Yet Damayanti has already decided, with the help of a swan who has praised King Nala to her, to choose Nala. The gods try to foil this by taking on physical bodies identical to Nala, so that Damayanti will not be able to tell the difference between them. As a last resort, Damayanti makes an **act of truth**, a ritual action whose efficacy is based on the **power of truth** itself. In her act of truth, Damayanti declares that she has never loved anyone but Nala, and directs the gods to resume their true forms to prove that this statement is true. The gods immediately do as she commands, compelled by the power of truth. Nala and Damayanti are married, and as a reward for her fidelity the gods give Nala various divine gifts. Hearing of the marriage, two of the rejected suitors curse Nala to lose his kingdom, and like all **curses** in Indian mythology, this eventually comes to pass. Because of the curse, Nala and Damayanti are separated and suffer long tribulations, including Nala having his body magically changed so that no one would be able to recognize him. In the end Damayanti recognizes him by his divine gifts, which could not be hidden, and the lovers are happily reunited.

Damodara

(*dama* "rope" + *udara* "waist") Epithet of the god **Krishna**, given in memory of a particular incident in his childhood. In an effort to curb Krishna's mischief by restricting his movements, Krishna's foster mother, **Yashoda**, uses a rope to tie her toddling boy to the heavy stone mortar used in grinding grain. The mortar's weight is more than sufficient to restrain any normal child, but for Krishna it proves no hindrance, and he proceeds to crawl about, dragging the mortar after him. At one point the mortar becomes wedged between two trees growing closely together, and Krishna pulls so hard that the trees are uprooted. After the trees fall to the ground, they immediately disappear, and in their place stand two young men. These are **sons** of the god **Kubera** who have been cursed to take the form of a tree until Krishna comes to save them.

Dampati

("husband and wife") In Indian art and **architecture**, the figure of a married couple. These are usually portrayed as standing next to one another and are usually devoid of any sexual connotation. This is unlike the more famous **mithuna** figures, which are engaged in sexual activity.

Dana

("giving") Charitable giving. This is a common religious practice, for it is believed to be a pious act that generates religious merit. Dana is especially prevalent at pilgrimage places and other sacred sites (**tirthas**), since the sacredness of these places is believed to magnify the consequences of any act, whether good or bad. Dana is one of the traditional paradigms for exchange, the other being **dakshina** (preceptor's fee). The difference between them is that dakshina is a fee for services, whereas dana is given freely and brings one no tangible benefits. Aside from the intangible religious merit generated by dana, it is also a common way to get rid of any **inauspiciousness** or ill fortune, which is transferred to the receiver along with the gift. This assumption makes receiving dana karmically risky, whereas there are no such stigmas associated with dakshina. People who live solely by receiving gifts, such as beggars at pilgrimage sites, are thus in an unenviable position, since they are commonly described as "vessels" (patras) for the depositing of ill fortune. Yet this transfer of inauspiciousness is a pervasive pattern in regular society, and even within the family there are means to transfer inauspiciousness through well-established gift-giving patterns, particularly the **kanyadan**, or gift of a bride in marriage. For further information on dana and gift-giving patterns, see Gloria Goodwin Raheja, *The Poison in the Gift*, 1988.

Danava

("descendants of Danu") In Hindu mythology, the **sons** of Danu with her husband, the divine sage **Kashyapa**. Kashyapa is the chief of the **Prajapatis**, a class of semi-divine beings, and Danu herself is the **daughter** of the demigod **Daksha**, so their children have divine **blood** from both sides of their lineage. The name Danava is a general term for all the families of **demons** (supernatural beings), or more properly, **asuras**. The asuras are powerful divine beings, who have legitimate interests of their own, but whose interests often run counter to those of human beings as well as those of the gods (**devas**). Asuras are thus usually opposed to the gods—a sense of opposition carried by the English word "demon"—but they are not perceived as inherently evil.

Dance

In traditional Hindu culture, all of the performing arts had intimate connections

Dancers performing in the Manipuri style.

with religious life, and dance was no exception to this pattern. In their art, dancers merely follow the divine model, since in Indian mythology **Shiva** is the preeminent dancer; indeed, in his dancing he first creates the universe and later destroys it. Several classical dance forms can be directly tied to specific Hindu temples. The **Bharatanatyam** form developed in the temples of **Tamil Nadu** beginning at the **Brhadeshvar** temple in **Tanjore**, and is immortalized in the sculptures of the Shiva temple at **Chidambaram.** The **Orissi** style came from the temple of **Jagannath** in the city of **Puri**, on the Bay of Bengal. Some of the other classical styles were traditionally performed only in temples, or had their beginnings in religious festivals: the **Kathakali** form in the state of **Kerala**, the **Kuchipudi** form in **Andhra Pradesh**, the **Chau** form in eastern India, and the **Manipuri** form in Manipur. The only exception is the northern Indian **Kathak** form, whose birth and performance lay in a court rather than a temple setting, but which in its subject matter often treated religious themes, particularly ones drawn from devotion to the god **Krishna**.

All of these styles share a highly articulated language of **gesture** (**mudra**) and expression, through which the dancer can tell a story to the audience. As in all the classical arts, the dancer's aim is not only to entertain, but to create and convey a particular aesthetic mood (**rasa**),

which will evoke a corresponding emotion (**bhava**) from the audience. Beyond these general similarities, each form has a certain characteristic and stylistic quality. Bharatanatyam, Kuchipudi, and Orissi are the most clearly related forms, but where Bharatanatyam presents a sharply geometric line, with a stiff upper body, the lines presented by Kuchipudi and Orissi are progressively softer, rounder, and more fluid. Kathakali is characterized by elaborate costumes and stage makeup, and also by its particular stress on developing and controlling facial mobility. These things facilitate ease and power of expression. Manipuri and Chau are both highly athletic forms, clearly showing the influence of folk dance, and Chau is unusual in that the dancers always wear masks, which sets a prevailing mood. Kathak is the only dance form in which the legs are kept straight; this form stresses intricate footwork in which the bells on the dancer's ankles serve as a complement and counterpoint to the drum, combined with dramatic turns and spins.

As mentioned above, all the dance forms except for Kathak developed in some sort of religious context. In many of these latter cases, dance was an **offering** presented to the **deity**, and was primarily performed for the deity's entertainment, although the other spectators could enjoy it, as well. Although different schools have different typologies, the most pervasive distinction is between "pure" dance (**nrtya**), conveying nothing beyond the dancer's skill in movement, and "acting" dance (**natya** or **abhinaya**), in which the dancer tells some sort of story. Until the twentieth century, the dancers were usually temple servants known as **devadasis**. The devadasis were officially married to the temple's deity and performed various ritual services in the temples as his "wives," but they could have liaisons with other men as they wished. Any children from these liaisons would also be in the service of the temple—their **sons** as musicians, and their **daughters** as dancers. At times this arrangement degenerated into common **prostitution**, but in many cases it was recognizably different. These **women** had status and property of their own, even though their status was unusual, and thus marginal. In the twentieth century the dance performance site has moved from the temple to the stage, which has had a number of effects on transforming it from a form of **worship** to a performing art. For further information on the history of the dance and its particular manifestations, see Mohan Khokar, *Traditions of Indian Classical Dance*, 1984. For a masterful analysis of the devadasis, see Frederique Apffel Marglin, *Wives of the God-King*, 1985.

Danda

("stick") A symbol of authority in traditional Hindu culture. On one hand, this stick referred to royal authority and was visibly evident as a scepter or mace, but was considered emblematic of the king's obligation to maintain social order by inflicting punishment on evildoers. This rule through punishment (**dandaniti**) was the king's role and duty in traditional Indian ideas of kingship, for without such rule normal social life would be impossible. In a different context, the staff can be a symbol of **ascetic** authority. Among the **Dashanami Sanyasis**, a group of **ascetics** who are devotees (**bhakta**) of the god **Shiva**, the ascetics with the highest status carry a staff as a sign of their authority, and are known as **Dandi Sanyasis**.

Danda Hasta

In Indian **dance**, **sculpture**, and ritual, a particular hand **gesture** (**hasta**), in which the arm and hand are extended straight forward, like a stick (**danda**).

Dandakaranya

A particular forest (aranya) in the *Ramayana*, the earlier of the two great Indian epics. This is where the god **Rama**, the epic's protagonist; his wife **Sita**; and his brother **Lakshmana** live during the latter part of their fourteen years in exile, in their **ashram** (abode) in the village of **Panchavati**. Many of the epic's pivotal events take place in this forest: Rama and Lakshmana's humiliation and mutilation of the demoness **Shurpanakha**, their destruction of the **demon** army led by her brothers **Khara** and **Dushana**, and Sita's abduction by Shurpanakha's third brother **Ravana**, the demon-king of **Lanka**. The Dandaka forest's actual location is uncertain, since many of the events in the *Ramayana* cannot be set in any particular place. One traditional location for Panchavati, however, is just outside of the city of **Nasik** in the state of **Maharashtra**.

Dandaniti

("rule through the stick") In the **dharma literature**, or the texts on religious duty (**dharma**), dandaniti is the preservation of social order by inflicting punishment on evildoers. This rule through punishment was the king's role and duty in traditional Indian ideas of kingship, for without such rule it was believed that normal social life would be impossible.

Dandasana

("staff-posture") One of the sitting postures (**asana**) described in commentaries to the **Yoga Sutras** (aphorisms on yoga). In this position, the upper body is erect, the arms are straight with the hands flat on the ground and pointing forward, and the legs are outstretched with the big toes, ankles, and knees touching one another.

Dandavat ("stick-like") Pranam

Type of reverential salutation in which the person lies prostrate on the ground with the arms extended (hence the comparison between the body and a stick). This shows the highest reverence of all greetings, since one's entire body is in contact with the ground.

Dandi Sanyasi

Among the **Dashanami Sanyasis**, or the **ascetic** devotees (**bhakta**) of the god **Shiva**, the Dandi Sanyasis are the most prestigious of the three general ascetic types; the others being the **Paramahamsa** and the **Naga Sanyasis**. Dandi Sanyasis take their name from the staff (**danda**) that they are given at their ascetic **initiation** and that they carry for the rest of their lives as a sign of ascetic restraint. The danda is always kept off the ground to maintain its **purity**. The Dandi Sanyasis tend to put the highest stress on the importance of **Sanskrit** (sacred language) learning and uphold the traditional social and cultural values it propounds. Of the ten Dashanami divisions, Dandis tend to belong to those divisions that will only initiate **brahmins**—that is, the **Saraswati**, **Ashrama**, and **Tirtha** divisions, and also some sections of the Bharati division. In many cases, Dandi Sanyasis are initiated as ascetics only after having completed the other three **stages of life** (**ashramas**), fulfilling the idealized pattern in the **dharma literature**, the texts on religious duty. Thus, their ascetic status does not come only from the strictness of their ascetic observance, for which

they are rightly famous. It also reflects the continuing influence of their former "worldly" status, which was supposedly left behind upon ascetic initiation, and their adherence to traditional idealized cultural patterns. The philosopher **Shankaracharya**, traditionally named as the Dashanami order's founder, was himself believed to be a Dandi Sanyasi. This pattern of leadership still continues, since even now Dandi Sanyasis are invariably chosen for the **Shankaracharyas**, the religious leaders who preside over the four monastic centers (**maths**). These centers supposedly were established by the philosopher Shankaracharya, and in many cases these present leaders have been lifelong ascetics, as Shankaracharya is believed to have been. For further information see Dana Sawyer, "Monastic Structure of Banarsi Dandi Sadhus," in Bradley R. Hertel and Cynthia Ann Humes (eds.), *Living Banaras*, 1993.

Dan Lila

One of the types of divine play (**lila**) between the god **Krishna** and his devotees (**bhakta**). In this lila, the adolescent Krishna intercepts the **gopis**, his **cow**-herding female friends, who are on their way to the city of **Mathura** to sell their butter and curds. Krishna refuses to let them pass until they give him some as a gift (**dana**). The story of this lila is often presented in religiously oriented theatrical presentations, which are themselves known as lilas ("plays"), since their function is to reveal the work of the divine. This lila is but one instance in a long history of butter thievery. For further information see John Stratton Hawley, *Krishna: The Butter Thief*, 1983.

Dantavaktra

In the *Mahabharata*, the later of the two great Hindu epics, Dantavaktra is an **asura** or **demon** king who is the rebirth of **Vijaya**, one of the gatekeepers of the god **Vishnu**. Vijaya has been cursed to be reborn three times as an asura and to be killed each time by Vishnu. In his previous incarnations Vijaya is born as **Hiranyakashipu**, who is killed by the **Man-Lion avatar** (one incarnation of the god Vishnu) and as **Kumbhakarna**, who is killed by Vishnu's **Rama avatar**. When Dantavaktra is killed by **Krishna**, the **curse** is broken, and Vijaya returns to his rightful place.

Darshan

("seeing") By far the most common religious act in popular modern Hinduism, darshan designates direct eye contact between the devotee (**bhakta**) and the image of a **deity**, which is considered to be a conscious, perceiving being. Such intimate interaction is a way to communicate with the deity on a personal basis, which is similar to the stress on the individual found in **bhakti** (devotional) religiosity. For further information see Diana Eck, *Darsan*, 1985.

Darshan

(2) ("perspective") In the context of Indian **philosophy**, this is the word most often used to designate a philosophical "school." The word itself comes from the verb "to see," and thus can be loosely translated as a "point of view," "perspective," or [way of] seeing." In a diverse and competitive philosophical culture, this is a neutral way to describe a philosophical position, whether or not one agrees with it.

Dasa ("servant") Bhava

The second of the five **modes of devotion** (system of devotion to a **deity**) to God that were most prominently articulated by **Rupa Goswami**, a devotee (**bhakta**) of the god **Krishna** and a follower of the Bengali saint **Chaitanya**. Rupa used differing types of human relationships as models for differing conceptions of the link between deity and devotee. These five modes showed growing emotional intensity, from the peaceful (**shanta**) sense that comes from realizing one's complete

identity with **Brahman**, or Ultimate Reality, to conceiving of God as one's master, friend, child, or lover. The Dasa Bhava is the second of these, in which devotees considered themselves as servants and the deity as their master. This second mode of devotion should be understood in light of the relationship between masters and servants in Indian society, which goes far beyond that of employer and employee in modern American society. A family's servants will often stay with a family for many years and in some cases, such service becomes hereditary. Longtime servants become virtual members of the family; they are respected, trusted, and sometimes regarded as advisers.

Dashamukha

("ten-faced") In the *Ramayana*, the earlier of the two great Indian epics, this was one of the epithets of **Ravana**, the **demon**-king of **Lanka**. This name is descriptive, since Ravana has ten heads.

Dashanami

("ten names") Collective name for the ten divisions among the **Sanyasis**, an **ascetic** order supposedly founded by the great philosopher **Shankaracharya**, whose members are devotees of the god **Shiva**. These ten divisions are each distinguished by a different name, which is taken as a surname by an ascetic after his **initiation** in the division. These ten names are **Giri** ("mountain"), **Parvata** ("mountain"), **Sagara** ("ocean"), **Saraswati** (the **goddess** of learning), **Bharati** ("India"), **Puri** ("city"), **Aranya** ("forest"), **Vana** ("forest"), **Tirtha** ("crossing-place"), and **Ashrama** ("hermitage").

Although all of the ten divisions are Dashanami Sanyasis, there are internal status differences based on the distinction between three ascetic classes: **Dandi**, **Paramahamsa**, and **Naga**. The **Dandi Sanyasis**, named for the staff (**danda**) that they must always carry, have the strongest connection with classical **Sanskrit** (sacred language) learning, are the strictest in their ascetic practices, and tend to be the most conservative in their social views. Dandi Sanyasis often follow ascetic initiation only after having completed the other three **stages of life** (ashramas), and thus fulfill the idealized pattern in the **dharma literature**, the texts on religious duty. Dandi Sanyasis were virtually always **brahmins** (priests) before becoming ascetics, and almost all Dandis belong to the Dashanami divisions that will only initiate brahmins—that is, the Saraswati, Ashrama, Tirtha, and some sections of the Bharati divisions. The remaining Dashanami divisions will admit members from all four of the traditional social classes: brahmins, **kshatriyas**, **vaishyas**, and **shudras**. Members from the first three groups, known as "**twice-born**" because they are eligible for the adolescent religious initiation known as the "second birth," are initiated as Paramahamsa Sanyasis, whereas shudras are initiated as **Naga**, or militant ascetics. Thus, despite the supposed loss of identity among ascetics after formally "renouncing" the world, one can see the continuing influence of a person's former worldly status.

These ten divisions are collected into four larger organizational groups: **Anandawara**, **Bhogawara**, **Bhuriwara**, and **Kitawara**. Each of these groups has two or three of the ten Dashanami orders, and each is centered in one of the four sacred centers (**maths**) supposedly established by Shankaracharya. Each of these four groups is also associated with one of the four **Vedas**—the oldest Hindu sacred texts, a different geographical quarter of India, a different "great utterance" (**mahavakya**), and a different ascetic quality.

Dasharatha

In the *Ramayana*, the earlier of the two great Indian epics, Dasharatha is a king of the **Ikshvaku** dynasty and the father of **Rama**, the epic's protagonist.

Dasharatha is generally portrayed as a good king, but like many characters in Indian mythology, his ultimate destiny is governed by the result of a **curse**, whose effects he is unable to avoid. As a young man, Dasharatha is very fond of hunting. On one occasion, he blindly sends an arrow to the spot where he hears the sound of an **animal** drinking at a stream. When he investigates, he is horrified to discover a young man struck by his arrow, with the water pot he had been filling by his side. With his dying breaths the young man informs Dasharatha that he is the sole source of support for his blind parents and commands Dasharatha to inform them of his death. Dasharatha is a man of honor and fulfills the boy's last request. When the boy's father hears the story, he angrily curses Dasharatha to die in similar grief, bereft of his **sons**.

For many years it seemed as if this curse would not come true, since Dasharatha had no sons, even though he had three wives: **Kausalya**, **Kaikeyi**, and **Sumitra**. Dasharatha sponsors various religious rites for the **birth** of sons, and finally commissions the sage **Rishyashringa** to perform a great **sacrifice**. At the rite's conclusion, a shining figure emerges from the sacrificial **fire**, places a pot of milk-rice before Dasharatha, and directs him to feed it to his wives. Dasharatha divides the contents of the pot between Kausalya and Kaikeyi, each of whom give some to Sumitra. In due time Kausalya bears Rama, Kaikeyi gives birth to **Bharata**, and Sumitra (by virtue of receiving a share from each of her co-wives) bears the twins **Lakshmana** and **Shatrughna**.

As his sons grow into manhood Dasharatha is blissfully happy, and the memory of the curse fades from his mind. As a young man, Rama shows his prowess and goodness, and Dasharatha decides to anoint him as the heir-apparent. Yet the night before this ceremony, the curse finally comes to fruition. During the preparations preceding Rama's investiture, the mind of his stepmother Kaikeyi has been slowly poisoned by the whisperings of her maid **Manthara**. Manthara convinces Kaikeyi that she and her son Bharata will be mere slaves after Rama is crowned the heir-apparent. This prompts Kaikeyi to take drastic action. Many years before, Dasharatha promised Kaikeyi two blessings as reward for her help in winning a great battle. She has never asked for these, but she now requests that Rama spend fourteen years in forest exile, and that her own son, Bharata, shall rule in his place. Dasharatha pleads with Kaikeyi to change her mind, but she is adamant that her wishes have to be granted if Dasharatha will retain the unbroken family honor. Dasharatha later pleads with Rama to disobey him and take over the kingdom by force, but Rama refuses this as it is an unrighteous action. Rama leaves for the forest, thus upholding the family honor, but in his sorrow at being separated from Rama, Dasharatha dies of a broken heart.

Dashavatar

("ten descents") Collective name for the ten **avatars** (incarnations on **earth**) of the god **Vishnu**. In each case, Vishnu takes form to restore the cosmic equilibrium when it has been thrown out of balance by the action of a particular **demon**. See also **avatar**.

Dashavatara Stotra

("Hymn to the Ten **Avatars**") The opening canto of the *Gitagovinda*, a twelfth-century lyric poem written by the poet **Jayadeva**. The *Gitagovinda* is an allegory of the union of the human soul with the divine, described through the story of the god **Krishna** and his human lover **Radha**. At the narrative level, this tale describes the couple's initial passionate lovemaking, followed by jealousy, anger, and estrangement. It concludes with their reconciliation and an even more passionate reunion.

Although it is preceded by a short introduction, the Dashavatara Stotra is the text's true beginning. The

The Dashavatara Stotra is the opening song in the *Gitagovinda*, a twelfth-century lyrical poem that tells the story of the god Krishna and his human lover Radha.

Dashavatara Stotra is a hymn paying homage to the ten avatars or earthly incarnations of the god Krishna, each of whom has been responsible for preserving the cosmos in a time of crisis. Jayadeva uses this opening hymn to remind his readers that the Krishna of his story is no mere mortal lover—even though the story employs the language and images commonly found in **Sanskrit** love poetry—but rather the lord and master of the universe, who has saved it from destruction again and again. The context supplied by the images in this opening hymn alert the reader that this text is not merely a love story.

Jayadeva is unusual in describing the god Krishna as the source of the ten avatars, since Krishna is more commonly considered an avatar of the god **Vishnu**. This theological difference stems from Jayadeva's connection with the **Jagannath** temple in the city of **Puri**. Jagannath is said to be a form of Krishna, but it is generally accepted that

Jagannath was originally an autochthonous ("of the land") **deity** who happened to be Puri's local deity. Identifying him with Krishna was a way to assimilate Jagannath into the Hindu pantheon. For Jayadeva, Jagannath-Krishna is thus the supreme deity, not an avatar, and the place usually occupied by Krishna in Jayadeva's enumeration of the avatars is taken by Krishna's brother, **Balarama**. For the text of the Dashavatara Stotra and the *Gitagovinda*, see Barbara Stoller Miller (ed. and trans.), *The Love Song of the Dark Lord*, 1977.

Dasyu

("slave") The name used for non-**Aryan** peoples in the **Vedas**, the earliest Hindu sacred texts. The words Aryan and Dasyu are an "us" and "them" opposition—in essence, the people who composed the Vedas called themselves Aryans, and referred to the "outsiders" as Dasyus. Although one cannot be certain whether these names refer to a particular group of people, or any group of all, one theory is that the Aryans were a people who had migrated from outside of India, and the Dasyus were the indigenous people in northern India. The Vedas describe the Dasyus as living in fortified cities, some of which were destroyed by the god **Indra**. Some readers have interpreted this image as the Aryans' destruction of the **Indus Valley** cities, but there is little historical record for such spectacular conquests.

Other hymns in the Vedas describe the Dasyus as dark-skinned and noseless, which is generally taken to mean flat-nosed. This has led some to identify the Dasyus with the **Dravidian** language speakers who now live in southern India, since some of them share these characteristics. According to this belief, the Dravidian language speakers would have been gradually displaced toward the south as the Indo-Aryan language speakers—in short, the Aryans—came into India from the north. One piece of linguistic evidence for this comes from modern Pakistan, in which a small group of people speak Brahui, which is a member of the Dravidian language family. This Brahui-speaking community is entirely surrounded by people speaking Indo-Aryan languages, and the simplest theory for this anomaly is that these Brahui speakers are an isolated linguistic fragment of that earlier time. These theories are intriguing, but it is naive to read the Vedas as an objective historical account, or even to assume that any of its references correspond to events outside the sacred world to which they were the key.

Dattatreya

In the religious texts known as the **puranas**, Dattatreya is a famous **ascetic** and is considered to be a partial **avatar** (incarnation) of the god **Vishnu**. Many modern ascetics consider him a paradigm for **asceticism**, and Dattatreya has actually been installed as a **deity** in certain places associated with ascetics, such as Mount **Girnar**. Dattatreya's mother is **Anasuya**, and he is born after she has done a great favor to the gods. According to the story, a faithful wife named Silavati curses the **sun** not to rise, and in consequence the creatures of the **earth** are greatly troubled. Anasuya succeeds in persuading Silavati to recall her **curse**, and in their gratitude, the gods **Brahma**, Vishnu, and **Shiva** inform her that she may ask for whatever she wants. Anasuya requests that each be born as one of her **sons**, and this is granted: Vishnu is born as Dattatreya, Shiva as **Durvasas**, and Brahma as Chandra.

Datura

(from **Sanskrit** word *dhattura*) Name for a genus of plants known as the thornapple, which is a distant relative of the potato. The datura plant contains poisonous alkaloids, which when consumed in small quantities produce intoxication, and in larger quantities, sickness and death. Devotees (**bhakta**) of the god **Shiva** eat the datura plant's swollen

Seed of the datura, or thorn-apple.
Devotees of the god Shiva eat the
intoxicating seedpods, which can be lethal
if consumed in large amounts.

seedpods as **intoxicants**, in imitation of
their patron divinity's narcotic revels.
Needless to say, because of its danger,
datura must be consumed with great
care, and under the direction of someone who knows its nature.

Daughters

The status of female children varies
widely in Hindu society, based on
regional customs, the position of the
social subgroup (**jati**/**caste**) to which a
family belongs, and the particular circumstances of individual families. In
general, although the **birth** of a daughter is a welcome event, it brings greater
responsibility than the birth of a son.
Parents have a religious duty to arrange
a daughter's marriage, and this is still
taken very seriously, since her marriage
is seen as the key to her continued material prosperity, as well as her fulfillment
as a human being. The gift of a daughter
(**kanyadan**) in marriage brings the parents immense religious merit, but also
an onerous economic obligation.
Arranging a marriage in modern India
usually involves considerable time,

anxiety, and expense. The last comes not
only from the expenses of the wedding
ceremonies, but also from the practice
of giving a **dowry** (gift to the groom's
family) with the bride, which is still quite
common. In many poor families, the
birth of multiple daughters is often seen
as a disaster, since their families will be
unable to marry them properly.

Aside from the expense and trouble,
in many parts of India daughters are
often seen as "temporary" members of
their natal families. After their marriages
they will live in their marital homes and
become part of their marital families,
whereas their brothers will bring their
brides into their natal home and will live
there for the rest of their lives. It is upon
these **sons** and their wives that the parents will depend for support in their old
age, as well as for the performance of
ancestral rites after their deaths. This is
the traditional pattern throughout
much of India; although as the forces of
modernity have changed the joint family,
it has become more common for husbands and wives to live separately from
their parents. This pattern also shows
considerable local variation. For example, because the **brahmin** community in
southern India is so small, cross-cousin
marriage is fairly common there, and in
this circumstance a woman is actually
moving from one branch of her family
to another.

These economic and social factors
have sometimes led to unfortunate consequences. Consciously or uncon-
sciously, one often finds that sons are
favored over daughters in many significant ways: in their access to education;
in their opportunities, which are
deemed more important for men
because of their need to support a family;
in Hindu **inheritance** laws (in which
sons get a much larger share, under the
presumption that they will be supporting a family); and in poorer families, in
which sons are favored for even more
basic needs such as food and access to
medical care. Despite these general patterns, it must be emphasized that many
families treat all their children with

equal love and care. This is particularly true in contemporary times, and given the trend toward smaller families, the birth of a daughter is cause for just as much rejoicing as the birth of a son. See also **arranged marriage**.

Day, Structure of

In some sense, most divisions of time are arbitrary, which is a feature that appears in several different dimensions of the traditional Indian divisions of the day. The twenty-four hours of the solar day can be divided using several different measures of time, some of which do not exactly correspond with one another, and these differing times can also be subject to judgments about their symbolic values. In one system, the day is divided into eight equal periods (**prahars**) of three hours each. These eight periods mark the general progress during the day and night, with the first of these prahars ending at sunrise. Shorter units of time are reckoned in periods of about twenty-four minutes called **ghatikas**, of which there are sixty in every twenty-four hours. The ghatika supposedly takes its name from the clay pots (ghata) that were used to make water-clocks; these pots measured time by the amount of water that dripped through a small hole. Two ghatikas make a **muhurta**, of which there are thirty during each twenty-four hours. The reckonings of the day in prahars and ghatikas thus do not exactly correspond to one another, since each prahar has 7.5 ghatikas. Based on this, it would seem that the former marks the more general divisions of each day and the latter more specific time periods.

The other way in which the times of day can be viewed is with regard to their symbolic value. The most auspicious time of day is the "Time of **Brahma**" (**Brahma muhurta**), the period immediately before sunrise. This is reckoned the best time of the entire day for **worship**, meditation, or any type of religious practice. Although this is named a muhurta, and thus should be limited to

forty-eight minutes, the Brahma muhurta is often thought to encompass the entire three hours in the day's first prahar. Hence, it is not unusual for devout religious people to arise around 3 A.M., to take advantage of this period. In contrast, the immediately preceding prahar (roughly midnight to 3 A.M.) is the most inauspicious in the day, a time when spirits and **demons** are loose. Sleep is the most appropriate activity for this time; other activities are appropriate only when absolutely necessary. The only time religious practices are done during this time is when they are part of an all-night ceremony (jagaran), or a continuous reading (**akhand path**) of a religious text. In following the most inauspicious and chaotic period with the most auspicious, the cycle of the day (as well as the **year**) mirrors that of the cosmos, whose gradual and continuing degeneration are suddenly replaced with complete renewal and regeneration. See also **Cosmology** and **Cosmic Time**.

Dayabhaga

("division of **inheritance**") Pivotal legal text, written by the Bengali scholar **Jimutavahana** (early twelfth century). As its name would indicate, the *Dayabhaga* was concerned with matters of inheritance, partition, and the division of property, and it eventually became the primary legal code for the entire Bengal cultural region. The inheritance pattern in the *Dayabhaga* stresses succession, which is very different from the predominant Hindu pattern of survivorship. Survivorship vests all surviving males in the male line with equal shares of the family property, but gives no inheritance to **women**. Under this arrangement, the death of a male heir automatically increases the share of all the other surviving males, whereas their share decreases when another male is born. Under the succession model in the *Dayabhaga*, **sons** do not become shareholders of the family property at **birth**, but upon the death of their father. If a son happens to die before his father, the son's heirs (including his wife and **daughters**) become inheritors, not in their own right, but as representatives of the deceased heir. Under the *Dayabhaga*, **widows** and daughters can thus have a share in family property, and they are allowed to act as agents in their own right. In theory this arrangement seems far more advantageous to women, but in fact it had some gruesome consequences. When the British first settled in Bengal in the late eighteenth century, they were horrified by the prevalence of **sati**, the rite in which a widow would be burned on her husband's funeral pyre. It seems that sati was not nearly so common in many other parts of India, and one theory is that this rite was the family's way to ensure that their daughter-in-law—who was an outsider to the family—would not be able to gain control over any of their ancestral property.

Dayanand Saraswati

(1824–1883) Nineteenth-century reformist **ascetic** and founder of the **Arya Samaj**, a reformist Hindu organization. The late nineteenth century was an era of sweeping social, economic, and religious change in northern India, and the Arya Samaj was an authentically Hindu response to these forces. Dayanand's mission for the Arya Samaj was to reform and revitalize Hinduism by purging it of the "false practices" that had gradually crept in. Swami Dayanand's fundamental assumption was that ultimate religious authority lay only in the ancient scriptures called the **Vedas**, and that any contemporary religious practices not found in the Vedas were mistaken, odious, and deserved to be abandoned. This stance allowed him to attack many of the "social evils" plaguing nineteenth-century Hinduism, such as child marriages, **sati** (the rite in which a **widow** would be burned on her husband's funeral pyre), "idolatrous" image **worship**, untouchability, a ban on widow remarriage, and the unequal status of **women**. In claiming that such practices were "corrupt," Dayanand had found not only a viable strategy for reform, but a way to undercut the claims of Christian missionaries, who pointed to such evils as evidence that Hindu religion was inferior to Christianity.

Unlike its predecessor, the **Brahmo Samaj**, which was heavily influenced by Christianity, the Arya Samaj was a Hindu response drawing from purely Hindu sources. Dayanand belonged to the first generation of Hindus aiming to reassert the greatness of Hinduism as opposed to the Christian missionary challenge, and much of his writing is militantly anti-Christian. One sign of his crusading spirit is his support for the ceremony of purification (**shuddhi**), through which Hindus who had become members of other religious communities were received back into the Hindu community. Although the Arya Samaj claimed that they were simply getting back to the **Veda**, the ultimate aim was not to reclaim that long-gone era, but to develop a form of Hindu religious life more compatible with "modern" times. Thus, even though Dayanand was "traditionalist" in his emphasis on the Vedas, he was radical in insisting that the Vedas should be accessible to all people, including groups such as women and the **shudras**, or the lowest social group, both of whom had traditionally been forbidden to read or even hear it. During his ministry Dayanand spoke throughout India, attacking any and all religions not rooted in the Vedas, including contemporary Hinduism. His eloquence, charisma, and commitment brought him considerable success, but also many enemies, and he was eventually assassinated by poisoning. For further information see Dayanand Saraswati, *Autobiography of Swami Dayanand Saraswati*, K. C. Yadav (ed.), 1978; Ganga Prasad Upadhyaya (trans.), *Light of Truth*, 1960; and Arvind Sharma, "Swami Dayananda Sarasvati," in Robert D. Baird (ed.), *Religion in Modern India*, 1998.

Day of Brahma

The Day of Brahma, or **kalpa**, is the largest generally accepted measure of time in Indian **cosmology**, and spans 432 million years. This time period is the ultimate limit for the existence of the created world, although within it the universe undergoes periodic renewals. At the conclusion of the Day of Brahma comes the universal dissolution (**pralaya**), in which the created universe is completely destroyed and reabsorbed into **Vishnu**. The Day of Brahma is followed by a night of equal length, during which the only living thing is the god Vishnu, who sleeps on the back of his serpent couch, **Shesha**, and floats on the surface of the cosmic ocean. When the Night of Brahma is ended, a lotus sprouts forth from Vishnu's navel, which opens to reveal the god **Brahma**, and with the new Day of Brahma the universe begins anew.

The Day of Brahma can be divided into smaller units based on two different methods. One of these divides the Day of Brahma into fourteen equal ages, in which each age is identified by the particular divine sovereign (**Manu**) who rules during that age. Another divides the Day of Brahma into one thousand **mahayugas**, each of which has four constituent **yugas** (units of **cosmic time**), each shorter than the last. See also **Cosmic Time**.

Deathbed Rites

General term for the rites done for a dying person. These rites have a twofold purpose: to purify the person's body, and, more importantly, to calm the mind. The first is generally done by applying holy substances, such as **Ganges water** or a **Tulsi** leaf. In some cases, the dying person will also hold the tail of a **cow**, since according to popular mythology this will enable the person to cross the **Vaitarani River**, the river leading to the afterlife. The emphasis on calming the dying person's mind comes from the belief that one's dying thoughts have enormous karmic ramifications for

future lives. Ideally, the dying person should be calm and composed, since any sort of fear or agitation is believed to have negative consequences. One method to help promote such calmness is to read passages from religious texts, whether to remind the hearer of the body's impermanence, or to have the last thing one hears be the name of God. At the moment of death the dying person is often placed on the **earth**—perhaps so that the earth can absorb the impurity (**ashaucha**) of the **corpse**, or perhaps as a symbol that whatever a person's status in life, all human beings eventually share the same fate. After death the rites associated with **cremation** begin, which are the next set of rites in the series known as the **antyeshthi samskara** ("last rites").

Death Rites

See **antyeshthi samskara**.

Deccan

A region of the Indian subcontinent. In its broadest usage, this word can refer to all of India south of the **Vindhya Mountains**, the range that divides northern and southern India. More specifically, this term denotes the dry and hilly plateau in the northern and eastern parts of the region south of the Vindhyas, bounded on the east and west by the highlands known as the Eastern and Western **Ghats**. In Hindu cultural terms, the Deccan is a transitional cultural area between the northern Indian plain and the deep south.

Deer

In Hindu iconography, an **animal** strongly associated with the god **Shiva**, particularly in his form as **Pashupati**, the "Lord of Beasts." In many of the four-armed images of Shiva, one of the upper arms will have the figure of the deer emerging from it, symbolizing his control over all life. In Hindu **bhakti** (devotional) poetry, the musk deer is often used as a symbol for an ignorant, unenlightened person. According to this image, just as the deer does not recognize that the heady scent of musk comes from its own body, but rushes all over the forest in search of it, so are human beings ignorant of God inside and ever close to them, but looking outside themselves in search of the divine.

Dehu

Town in the Pune district of **Maharashtra** state, sixty-five miles east and south of Bombay. It is most famous as the home of the poet-saint **Tukaram**, one of most important figures in the **Varkari Panth**. The Varkaris are a religious community centered around the **worship** of the Hindu god **Vithoba**, at his temple at **Pandharpur** in modern Maharashtra. Varkari religious practice centers primarily around two annual pilgrimages in which all the participants arrive in Pandharpur on the same day. Tukaram still symbolically travels to Pandharpur twice each year; a **palanquin** (palkhi) bearing his sandals is at the head of the procession bearing his name.

Deities

This is a word with various possible meanings in different contexts. On one hand, it can refer to the gods (**devas**). These are beings who live in one of the heavenly realms, by virtue of their past good **karma** (actions), but who are still subject to the law of karma and who therefore must someday be reborn in a lower state. This word can also refer to the Supreme Reality, which can best be designated as "God," although the Hindu imagination has given it various names: **Brahman**, the **Goddess**, **Vishnu**, **Shiva**, **Ganesh**, and a host of other deities in the pantheon, including **village deities**.

Demons

The Hindu mythic universe has various classes of supernatural beings, some of which are perpetually at odds with one another. The most prominent conflict is between the suras ("gods") and another class of divine beings called asuras ("not-gods"). Aside from the asuras, there are other powerful beings such as **rakshasas**, **pisacas**, and **vetalas**, which have greater or lesser malevolence toward the gods and human beings. The English word most often used to denote all these divine adversaries is the word "demon." Although this is a convenient label and avoids the need for unfamiliar **Sanskrit** terminology, it also carries inappropriate and misleading associations. The word "demon" carries connotations of absolute and radical evil, as well as willful opposition to a single supreme divinity. Neither assumption is appropriate in the Hindu mythic universe, which is polytheistic, or believing in more than one god. This polytheistic universe has a host of divine beings, whose individual interests may well conflict with those of the gods, and whose mutual opposition may spill over into open war. This does not make such opponents, or "demons," inherently evil, but rather the opponents of the Hindu gods, from whose perspective Hindu mythology is clearly recounted. These "demons" may also be ill-disposed toward humans, but they are not necessarily or inherently so. Perhaps the clearest recognition of their status is that despite their occasional opposition to the gods, they are never completely destroyed, but simply demoted to a more appropriate status. For example, when the "demon" **Hiranyakashipu** is destroyed by **Vishnu's Man-Lion avatar**, he is succeeded by his **son Prahlada**. In the same way, after the god **Rama** kills **Ravana**, the "demon" king of **Lanka**, Rama appoints as successor Ravana's brother **Vibhishana**. Asuras and other supernormal beings thus have a legitimate place in the Hindu mythic world, and as long as they do not overreach themselves and throw the world into imbalance, they are allowed to remain.

Deogarh

Small town in the extreme southern part of the state of **Uttar Pradesh**, seventy miles south of the city Jhansi, in a part of Uttar Pradesh almost completely enclosed by the state of **Madhya Pradesh**. It is famous as the site for one of the few surviving temples from the **Gupta dynasty**, a fifth-century temple dedicated to **Vishnu** as the **Dashavatar** ("Ten Incarnations"). The temple itself is a masonry cube about twenty feet on each side, topped by a ruined tower that would have originally been about forty feet high. In its modest size and square construction, this temple shows little resemblance to the Hindu temples of a later age. However, it prefigures later **architecture** in its magnificent carvings: in the images carved in panels on the side walls, around the temple's single door, and on friezes at the top of the walls. The portrayal of the divine figures in these carvings is identical to that done centuries later, which indicates that the images used to represent these **deities** were already fixed at the time the temple was built.

Deoghar

("God's home") Sacred site (**tirtha**) in the southeastern corner of the modern state of **Bihar**, about 130 miles southeast of the city of Patna. Deoghar is famous throughout India as the site for a temple to the god **Shiva**, in his form as **Vaidyanath**, the "Lord of Physicians." Vaidyanath is one of the twelve **jyotirlingas**, a group of sacred sites deemed especially holy to Shiva, and at which Shiva is believed to be uniquely present. Deoghar hosts an enormous religious gathering on the festival of **Shivaratri** (February—March) and during the **lunar month** of **Shravan** (July—August), both of which are times deemed particularly sacred to Shiva. On both occasions, pilgrims draw **water** from the **Ganges** at Sultanganj, more than sixty miles from Deoghar, and then walk to Deoghar to present the water as an **offering** to Shiva. This particular observance combines devotion to God with the willingness to suffer hardship; it is often performed to fulfill a vow made when asking for some divine favor. As in many Hindu holy places, pilgrim traffic peaks at Deoghar at certain festival times and at other times of the **year** drops off to almost nothing.

Deoras, Balasaheb

(1915–1996) Third sarsanghchalak ("Supreme Leader") of the **Rashtriya Svayamsevak Sangh** (RSS), a conservative Hindu organization whose express purpose is to provide the leadership cadre for a revitalized Hindu India. The RSS is a highly autocratic organization that lays great stress on obedience to authority, thus the sarsanghchalak wields virtually complete power over it. During Deoras's tenure from 1973 to 1994, he took a much more activist stance than his predecessor, M.S. **Golwalkar**, particularly in promoting the growth of the RSS's affiliate organizations, in giving the RSS an orientation to social service, and in actively seeking to recruit members and establish **shakhas** (branches) in all parts of the country. For further information see Walter K. Andersen and Shridhar D. Damle, *The Brotherhood in Saffron*, 1987; Tapan Basu et al., *Khaki Shorts and Saffron Flags*, 1993; and Christophe Jaffrelot, *The Hindu Nationalist Movement in India*, 1996.

Deshastha

The model for traditional Indian society was as a collection of **endogamous** subgroups known as **jatis** ("birth"). These jatis were organized (and their social status determined) by the group's hereditary occupation, over which each group had a monopoly. This sort of differentiation applied even to **brahmins**, whose role has been to serve as priests, scholars, and teachers. The Deshastha brahmin jati is a subset of the **Maharashtri** brahmins, who were themselves one of the five southern brahmin communities

(**Pancha Dravida**). The core region for the Deshastha brahmins is in the **Deccan** region in **Maharashtra**, whereas the other major subcommunity, the **Chitpavan** or Konkanastha, is found on the coast.

Deshnok

Small village in the Bikaner district in the state of **Rajasthan**, roughly twenty miles south of the city of Bikaner. Deshnok is famous for the temple to the **goddess Karni Mata**, in which thousands of **rats** have been given sacred status and are treated as **deities**, in the belief that they are Karni Mata's **sons**.

Deul

(probably a form of *deva*, "**deity**") In the temple **architecture** of the state of **Orissa**, this is the name for the beehive-shaped tower under which the image of the temple's primary deity resides. Unlike the architecture in other parts of northern India, in which a series of towers (**shikharas**) gradually led up to the tallest tower, Orissan temples tend to have a fairly long and low entrance porch (**jagamohans**) and an extremely high deul, with this difference in visual forms accentuating the contrast between the two.

Deva

The word deva literally means "shining one," although the most common (and often most appropriate) translation is "god." This word is an epithet for any superhuman being, although it can also be used figuratively for any person of high status, such as a king or a **brahmin** (priest). The notion of "gods" in Hinduism must be understood in light of the generally assumed context of reincarnation (**samsara**), which assumes that a person can be reborn in many different realms of reality. Some of these are realms of punishment where people atone for the effects of their bad **karma**, while others are realms of pleasure (the **heavens**) where people enjoy the results of their good karma. The devas are the inhabitants of these heavens, and are thus "gods," since gods, by definition, live in heaven.

Yet all these gods are still subject to the vicissitudes of reincarnation—even **Indra**, the ruler of heaven. **Birth** in heaven is based on one's good karma, which is inevitably diminished by enjoying the rewards of life in heaven, just as a savings account is depleted by continuing withdrawals. When their good karma has been exhausted, even the gods are subject to rebirth in other realms. So even though these gods are superhuman, they are still subject to the law of reincarnation. There is thus a qualitative difference between these gods (the devas) and the so-called Great gods, such as **Vishnu**, **Shiva**, and the **Goddess**. These latter **deities** are seen by their devotees (**bhakta**) as totally outside the realm of **space**, time, and the causes and effects of karma, and thus correspond more directly to the Judeo-Christian notion of "God," as the ultimate power in the universe.

Devadasi

("[female] servant of the lord") Name for a class of **women** kept in temples as singers and dancers in the service of the temple's presiding **deity**, to whom they were usually considered to be "married." Their special status prevented them from marrying human husbands, although in many cases they would form long-term liaisons with prominent local men. Any **daughters** born from such liaisons would in turn be dedicated to the temple, while **sons** would be trained as musicians. In many cases, devadasis had unusual legal rights, such as the ability to own, manage, and transfer property, which for most women were vested only in their husbands. At best, these devadasis were literate and cultured women, whose talents brought them considerable status, while at worst (as was often the case in the nineteenth century) they were prostitutes whose services enriched the temple. The latter situation prompted the British to formally ban this practice, despite their general reluctance to interfere in Hindu religious affairs.

Devaki

In Hindu mythology, the god **Krishna's** mother. Krishna is considered the eighth **avatar** (incarnation) of the god **Vishnu**, and like all of the avatars, he comes down to **earth** to restore the cosmic balance by destroying the forces of evil that are upsetting it. Devaki is the niece of King **Kamsa**, the evil king of **Mathura**, and on the day she is married a heavenly voice proclaims that her eighth child will kill Kamsa. Kamsa seeks to destroy this prophecy by imprisoning Devaki and her husband, **Vasudeva**, killing each of their children as they are born. Devaki's seventh child is magically transferred to the womb of her co-wife, **Rohini**, and is born as **Balarama**. At the **birth** of the eighth child, **Krishna**, the locked gates magically open, and a deep sleep falls over all the guards, allowing Vasudeva to spirit the infant child to his foster parents, **Nanda** and **Yashoda**.

Devanagari

Name for the most common northern Indian script, in which the sacred **Sanskrit**, modern **Hindi**, and Marathi languages are commonly written to this day. It is a descendant of the ancient **Brahmi** script, and from it developed the scripts used for the modern **Bengali**, **Gujarati**, Oriya, and Punjabi languages. Its most characteristic feature is that the top element of most letters is a horizontal line, which, when the letters are written together, causes the letters to "hang," like laundry from a clothesline. Its name literally means "[script of the] city of the gods," and according to one theory, it was given this name because it was developed in **Benares**, one of the holiest cities in India.

Devapratishtha

("establishing the **deity**") Rite by which the image of a deity is established in a temple and consecrated for **worship**. The image itself must be constructed according to carefully defined sculptural and artistic canons that date back to the early centuries of the common era, as the sculptures at the **Deogarh** temple clearly show. The image, temple site, and the performers must be purified before the rite begins, and this **purity** must be maintained throughout the entire rite—which can last for days—to ensure that the image remains pure. All parts in the transmission and physical **installation** of the image are carefully done, but the climactic rite is the **pranapratishtha**, in which the image is infused with the breath of life and becomes the seat for the deity. After this point, the image is considered to be ritually "alive," and must receive regular worship and ministrations.

Devaprayag

("divine confluence") Sacred town (**tirtha**) in the northern part of the state of **Uttar Pradesh**, in the **Himalaya** Mountains about sixty miles up the **Ganges** from the city of **Haridwar**. Devaprayag is sacred because it is at the confluence of the **Bhagirathi** and **Alakananda** rivers, the largest Himalayan tributaries of the Ganges. Devaprayag is the final such river confluence in the Himalayas, and it is at this confluence that the Ganges is definitively formed as one indivisible sacred stream.

Devar

In the northern Indian joint family, the term designating a husband's younger brother. The traditional Indian joint family is headed by a husband and wife. The couple's **sons**, the sons' wives, and unmarried **daughters** live with them. The married daughters live with their husbands' joint families. The joint family is not just a group of people living together. The good of the family is given higher value than any individual's desires. Traditional Indian society was highly status-conscious, a trait reflected not only in the traditional hierarchical conception of society, but also in similar conceptions within the family. Based on these assumptions, there are different words for all sorts of relationships in the Indian family. These words are based partly on a person's age in relation to the speaker, whether he is related by blood or by marriage, and whether blood relatives come from the mother's or the father's side of the family. Since a woman's devar is younger than her husband, he is considered a person of less exalted status, and thus someone with whom she may have a more familiar "**joking relationship**."

Devara Dasimayya

Tenth-century devotee (**bhakta**) of **Shiva**, who was much admired by **Basavanna** and the other **Lingayat** leaders. According to tradition Dasimayya earned his living as a weaver, but spent most of his energies propagating the **worship** of Shiva. He encountered particular opposition from the Jains and the **Vaishnavas**, about which there are many miraculous tales, but he also served as a missionary to jungle tribes. For further information see A. K. Ramanujan (trans.), *Speaking of Siva*, 1973.

Devaram

Name for the collected hymns of the poet-saints **Appar**, **Sambandar**, and **Sundaramurtti**. These were the most important of the **Nayanars**, a group of sixty-three **Shaiva** poet-saints who lived in southern India between the seventh and ninth centuries. Along with their **Vaishnava** counterparts, the **Alvars**, the Nayanars spearheaded the revitalization of Hindu religion versus the Buddhists and the Jains. Both the Nayanars and the Alvars stressed passionate devotion (**bhakti**) to a personal god—**Shiva** for the Nayanars, **Vishnu** for the Alvars—

The town of Devaprayag. It is considered sacred because it lies at the confluence of the Bhagirathi and Alakananda Rivers, the two largest tributaries of the Ganges in the Himalayas.

and conveyed this devotion through hymns sung in the **Tamil language**. Appar and Sambandar were the first of the Nayanars, and Sundaramurtti was the last. Although the hymns in the Devaram are devotional, they form the basis for the philosophical school known as **Shaiva Siddhanta**, and are thus considered the holiest of the Tamil Shaivite texts. The hymns are also marked by opposition and hostility to non-Hindu traditions, particularly the Jains, with whom the Nayanars were apparently contesting for influence and patronage.

Devasena

In southern Indian mythological tradition, Devasena is the wife of the god **Skanda**, in his southern Indian form as **Murugan**. Following the pan-Indian custom of **arranged marriage**, Devasena is given in marriage to Skanda by **Indra** (king of the gods) and the other

Hindu gods. After his marriage, Skanda contracts a "love-marriage" with the tribal girl **Valli**. Skanda's two wives thus symbolize both sides of his identity—Valli bears witness to his connection with the land, and his ultimate roots as a tribal **deity**, while Devasena shows his assimilation into the larger Hindu pantheon.

Devayajna

("**sacrifice** to the gods") One of the Five Great Sacrifices (**panchamahaya-jna**) that is prescribed in the texts on religious duty (**dharma literature**). These Five Great Sacrifices are pre-scribed daily religious observances for a "**twice-born**" householder, that is, a householder who has been born into one of the three twice-born groups in Indian society—**brahmin**, **kshatriya**, or **vaishya**—and who has received the adolescent religious **initiation** known as the "second birth." Each of the five sacrifices (**yajna**) is directed toward a different class of beings—from the Absolute Reality down to **animals**—and is satisfied by different actions. The devayajna is directed toward the gods and is satisfied by **homa**, the **offerings** of clarified butter into the sacred **fire**. In the time since these texts were composed, Hindu life has undergone significant changes, and since most Hindu homes no longer maintain a sacred fire, this particular rite has been largely omitted.

Devimahatmya

("Greatness of the **Goddess**") The earliest and most important mythic source for the cult of the Goddess as the supreme divine power. The *Devimahatmya* is itself a section of a larger **Sanskrit** (sacred language) text, the *Markandeya Purana*, and is gener-ally accepted to have been composed in the **Narmada River** region in the fifth or sixth century. The *Devimahatmya* is most notable for its assertion that God is female. This notion has no clear source in the earlier Hindu tradition, in which female **deities** exist but are insignificant. This conviction must have existed at some level, because it emerges fully developed in the *Devimahatmya*, and the idea must have spent some time developing before its full fruition in this text.

The *Devimahatmya* itself is a text of 700 verses, hence its other common name, the *Durgasaptashati* ("700 verses to **Durga**"). The text begins with a frame story, in which a king and a merchant, each beset by worldly trials, seek refuge in the peace of the forest. There they meet a sage, who listens to each of their stories, and explains that all of their troubles are due to Mahamaya (an epi-thet of the Goddess). This is an epithet for the Goddess as the wielder of illu-sion, who is the sole power behind the universe. When pressed for further details, the sage tells three mythic sto-ries, each describing the salvific activity of the Goddess. These three tales form the bulk of the text and the basis for the **worship** of the Goddess.

The first story retells the myth of the **demons Madhu** and **Kaitabha**, who are born from the god **Vishnu's** earwax dur-ing the period of cosmic dissolution (**pralaya**). As the creation of the world begins anew, a **lotus** sprouts from Vishnu's navel. It opens to reveal the cre-ator-god **Brahma**, who is immediately menaced by Madhu and Kaitabha. The story of these two demons also appears in the mythology connected with Vishnu, but there are significant differ-ences in this version. In all versions of the myth, Brahma appeals for help, and Vishnu eventually slays the demons. But in the *Devimahatmya*, Brahma's hymn of praise is to the Goddess, who in her form as **Yoganidra** ("sleep of **yoga**") has lulled Vishnu into a cosmic stupor, rendering him unable to come to Brahma's aid. Pleased by Brahma's praise, the Goddess withdraws her influence over Vishnu, he awakens and slays the demons.

The second story centers around the buffalo-demon **Mahishasura**, who is so powerful that none of the gods can conquer him. One day, when the gods are recounting their defeats at the demon's hands, each of the gods begin to give off a great radiance. This radiance collects into a single glowing mass, and from it the figure of the Goddess emerges. This myth portrays the Goddess as the concentrated essence of all the gods, and thus superior to any one of them. This motif is accentuated by each of the gods giving her a copy of their weapons, so that symbolically she wields all of their **divine powers**. The Goddess takes up arms against Mahishasura and his army, and after a terrifying battle, slays him.

The third story also portrays the Goddess as a warrior-queen. In this episode, she fights and destroys the demon armies of **Shumbha** and **Nishumbha**, along with their minions **Chanda**, **Munda**, and **Raktabija**. This story is notable for the first appearance of the fierce goddess **Kali**, who springs forth from the forehead of the Goddess as her anger personified. Kali helps the Goddess to defeat the demon armies by stuffing them into her mouth and consuming them. Kali is also instrumental in destroying the demon Raktabija, who has been granted the wish that whenever a drop of his **blood** falls to the ground, it will be transformed into another full-sized copy of himself. This makes him impossible to kill by conventional means. Kali is able to thwart this special power by drinking Raktabija's blood before it reaches the ground. As with the second book, this story has extended descriptions of battlefield carnage.

All of these stories describe the Goddess as the supreme divine power, far superior to the male gods in the pantheon. The frame story ends with an extended hymn of praise to the Goddess, and descriptions of the benefits gained from her worship. Both the king and the merchant begin to worship her, and after three years both are granted their desires. The king asks for a larger and unconquerable kingdom, alluding to the Goddess's power to bestow worldly wishes. The merchant,

however, requests final liberation, showing his awareness of her power over illusion, and the ultimate spiritual goal. For further information see Thomas B. Coburn, *Devi Mahatmya*, 1984.

Devotee
See **bhakta**.

Devotthayan Ekadashi
Festival falling on the eleventh **day** (**ekadashi**) of the bright (waxing) half of the **lunar month** of Kartik (October–November). This is celebrated as the day on which the god **Vishnu** awakens from his four-month slumber, having fallen asleep on **Devshayani Ekadashi** ("eleventh day festival") in **Ashadh** (June–July). When Vishnu has arisen from sleep, the ritually dangerous **chaturmas** ("four-month") period is over, and auspicious life-cycle rites such as weddings and the **sacred thread** ceremony ("adolescent **initiation**") may be performed again.

Devshayani Ekadashi
Festival falling on the eleventh **day** (**ekadashi**) of the bright (waxing) half of the **lunar month** of Ashadh (June-July). This is celebrated as the day on which the god **Vishnu** falls asleep on his serpent couch **Shesha**, and remains sleeping for four lunar months, waking up on **Devotthayan Ekadashi**. This four-month period (**chaturmas**) is considered unlucky and ritually dangerous, since it is a period when the god is considered to be insensible. Weddings are generally not performed during this period, nor is any other life-cycle rite that can be postponed. This festival coincides with the advent of the rainy **season**, and the ambivalence connected with the rains can be seen here. On one hand, the rains are essential to the crops, and thus foster life and fertility. On the other hand, the rains also bring all too real dangers from snakes, scorpions, and gastrointestinal infections.

Dhanga

(d. 1003) A monarch in the **Chandella dynasty**, most famous for committing religious **suicide** by drowning himself at **Allahabad**, at the confluence of the **Ganges** and **Yamuna** rivers. The **inscription** that records this event mentions that Dhanga did this at the end of his life—when he had lived more than one hundred years—while meditating on the god **Rudra**, a form of **Shiva**, and further notes that by committing suicide Dhanga gained final liberation of the soul (**moksha**). This description clearly shows that religious suicide was a highly structured religious act, the object of which was to help the performer die in a calm and composed state of mind, ideally with one's last thoughts focused on a **deity**. A crucial element in this ritual was the statement of purpose (**samkalpa**), in which the performer would state the benefit desired from his performance. Dhanga's statement of purpose is almost certainly the basis for his assertion that he attained final liberation, since this claim is not verifiable in any other way.

Dhangar

The model for traditional Indian society was a collection of **endogamous** subgroups known as **jatis** ("birth"). These jatis were organized (and their social status determined) by the group's hereditary occupation, over which each group had a monopoly. In traditional central Indian society, the Dhangars were a Hindu jati whose hereditary occupation was herding sheep and goats. They are particularly associated with the state of **Maharashtra**.

Dhanus

("bow") In Hindu iconography, the bow is a weapon associated with several Hindu **deities**. It has strong mythic associations with the god **Shiva**, who in one of his mythic exploits destroys the Three Cities (**tripura**) with a single arrow. It is also commonly associated with the god **Rama**, whose unfailing arrows slay **Ravana**, the **demon**-king of **Lanka**. Aside from these, it is also one of the weapons commonly carried by powerful forms of the **Goddess**, such as **Durga**. The reason for this can be found in her charter myth in the **Devimahatmya**, in which the Goddess is formed from the collected radiance of all the gods and receives duplicates of all their weapons.

Dhanvantari

In Hindu mythology, Dhanvantari is the physician of the gods and is credited as the founder of **ayurveda**, a traditional system of Indian medicine. Dhanvantari is born when the **gods** and **demons** (supernatural beings) churn the Ocean of Milk to produce the nectar of immortality. In the course of their churning, many precious things are produced, including the **goddess Lakshmi**, the wishing-**cow Kamadhenu**, and the **Kaustubha** jewel. As the churning reaches its climax, Dhanvantari himself emerges from the ocean bearing the pot of **amrta**, the nectar of immortality that has been the ultimate product of the whole endeavor. See also **Tortoise avatar**.

Dharamshala

("abode of **dharma**") A no-frills rest house for pilgrims. Dharamshalas were often built by pious donors (this was endowed as a religious act), to provide pilgrims not only with a basic place to stay during their pilgrimage, but also a place with a wholesome religious atmosphere. The facilities at a dharamshala are generally quite basic, and well below the standard set by a hotel—in many cases it is a nearly bare room in which the pilgrims cook, eat, and sleep, often on their own bedding. Until well into the twentieth century, pilgrims were under no obligation to pay anything for staying, although on departing they were expected to leave a donation according to their means and inclination. In most cases dharamshalas now have set rates for lodging, but they are always cheaper than hotels since the amenities tend to be less. There is also a marked difference in their general atmosphere and clientele. Most dharamshalas still strive to promote and maintain a wholesome religious atmosphere: by having a temple in the building; by holding **worship** in the morning, evening, and on special occasions; and by sponsoring scriptural readings, lectures, and other religious activities. These activities help to create a religious community, and those who are seeking this during their journey will strive to stay in such places.

Dharana

("concentration") In the **ashtanga yoga** (system of religious discipline) first codified by the philosopher **Patanjali**, dharana is the sixth of the eight elements of yoga practice. Along with **dhyana** and **samadhi**, dharana is one of the three parts known as the "inner discipline" (**samyama**), the culmination of yogic training. Dharana is described as steadfastness of mind. It is the ability to focus on any object, whether a part of the body or an external object, and to keep the mind steadily focused there. This is training for one's mind and one's awareness and is an essential prerequisite for focused meditation.

Dharma

One of the four **purusharthas**, or **aims of life**, the others being **artha** (wealth, power, and prosperity), **kama** (desire), and **moksha** (liberation). The concept of dharma is so fundamental to Hindu culture that it cannot be adequately translated by any single English word—possible translations are "religious law," "religious duty," "duty," "religion," "law," or "social order." The root meaning for the word dharma comes from a verb meaning "to support" or "to uphold." Dharma is thus that which supports or upholds society, which shows why all

Kama, the god of desire. He is one of many gods who carry a dhanus, or bow. The five different arrows in Kama's arsenal each produce a different emotion in the people they strike.

the aforementioned translations could make sense in context. Dharma provides the overall regulatory framework for life in the world and gives a sense of ultimate purpose to keep one's life in balance. Although Hindu culture sanctions the pursuit of both power (artha) and pleasure (kama), it is always assumed that both of these will be regulated by an underlying commitment to dharma, to keep one's life integrated and balanced.

The **dharma literature**, primarily the **Dharma Sutras** (aphorisms on religious duty) and **Dharma Shastras** (treatises on religious duty), was largely concerned with laying down guidelines for an organized and orderly society, and these guidelines take into account many possible factors. Although these texts spoke of an eternal (**sanatana**) dharma, and of certain common duties (**sadharana dharma**) incumbent on all human beings, the most important thing for any person was one's personal dharma (**svadharma**). One's svadharma provided a well-defined social status and role, based on one's social status (**varna**), **stage of life** (ashrama), and gender (the particular dharma for **women** was **stridharma**). These texts were almost certainly composed by **brahmin** (priests) men, and reveal everything about how these men thought things should be, but are far less reliable with regard to actual social practices. The men who composed this literature presupposed an unequal society, in which **birth** into high or low status groups was determined by the nature of one's **karma** (actions), whether good, bad, or mixed. Although various groups had unequal status, they were all necessary for society to function harmoniously, and true virtue lay in meticulously fulfilling one's prescribed social role. Doing so faithfully was not only a source of religious merit, but if one did one's obligations dispassionately from a sense of duty, it was also described as one of the three paths for liberation of the soul, the path of Action (**karmamarga**). For further information see Pandurang Vaman Kane (trans.), *A History of Dharmasastra*, 1968; and K. S. Mathur, "Hindu Values of Life: Karma and Dharma," in T. N. Madan (ed.), *Religion in India*, 1991.

Dharma

(2) A **deity**, seen as the personification of dharma as religious duty. In the *Mahabharata*, the latter of the two great Hindu epics, the five **Pandava** brothers, who are the epic's protagonists, all have divine fathers, and the eldest brother **Yudhishthira** is the **son** of Dharma. Yudhishthira and his brothers belong to a kingly (**kshatriya**) family, but Yudhishthira himself shows great concern for truth, righteousness, and compassion. None of these are proverbial kshatriya qualities, which tend to stress courage and martial valor, and Yudhishthira's qualities are usually explained by invoking the influence of his divine father. A different sort of Dharma cult arose in medieval Bengal, from the commingling of Buddhist, Muslim, and Hindu ideas. In this cult Dharma was worshiped as the formless single supreme Lord (probably reflecting the influence of Islam), but the **worship** of Dharma contained many similarities with Bengali Hindu rituals. For further information see Shashibhushan B. Dasgupta, *Obscure Religious Cults*, 1962.

Dharma Literature

Many texts are explicitly or implicitly concerned with the question of **dharma**, or religious duty. These begin with the **Vedas**, the oldest Hindu sacred texts, which are believed to articulate the eternal (**sanatana**) dharma. The first major texts explicitly devoted to dharma are the **Dharma Sutras**, texts written in an aphoristic (**sutra**) style between the seventh and second centuries B.C.E. At least in theory, the Dharma Sutras were all connected with particular schools of the Veda, and were thus primarily intended as a manual for behavior for members of that school alone. The Dharma Sutras were followed by the **Dharma Shastras**, in which the material in the Dharma Sutras was expanded and put into verse; these latter texts included instructions for all members of society and were thus intended to be "legal" in their import. Among the earliest was the Manava Dharma **Shastra** (**Manu Smrti**), which was composed around the turn of the common era. The process of rethinking and expanding this legal tradition through commentary has continued until present times, although the most significant works were completed by the sixteenth century.

Dharmaputra

("son of **Dharma**") One of the epithets of **Yudhishthira**, the eldest of the five **Pandava** brothers. The Pandavas are the protagonists in the *Mahabharata*, the later of the two great Hindu epics. In the epic, Yudhishthira and his brothers are the **sons** of various **deities**, magically born when their mothers use the power of a **mantra** (sacred sound). Yudhishthira's father is the god Dharma, the guardian of righteousness. His paternity is used to explain

Yudhishthira's concern with truth and righteousness, which are defining qualities in his character. These are not usually considered to be kingly (**kshatriya**) values, which stress courage and martial valor.

Dharmaraja

("King of Righteousness") Colloquial name for **Yama**, god of death and presiding **deity** of the underworld. Yama is responsible for judging and punishing the dead, and this threat of punishment, at least in popular belief, makes people avoid committing evil. This name is also one of the epithets of **Yudhishthira**, the eldest of the five **Pandava** brothers, since his father is the god **Dharma**, the guardian of righteousness.

Dharmashastra

A general term to denote the study of **dharma** (religious duty), whether referring specifically to the actual texts (**Dharma Shastras**), or the treatises on religious duty or more generally to the extensive commentary-like literature on these texts. Although the Dharma Shastras are generally believed to have been written between the second century B.C.E. and the early centuries of the common era, this literature continued to be written until modern times. The literature detailed views on legal matters, such as crime and punishment, civil law, contracts, and rules of evidence. It also concerned matters of social order. The most extensive catalog of all these sources is a five-volume set by Pandurang Vaman Kane (trans.), *A History of Dharmasastra*, 1968.

Dharma Shastras

("Treatises on **Dharma**") In its most particular sense, this word refers to a particular set of **Sanskrit** texts. These texts were explicitly written to give guidelines for the organization of society, and for correct human behavior in that society. The Dharma Shastras were written soon after the **Dharma Sutras** (aphorisms on

religious duty) and are clearly modeled on them, but have several important differences. With regard to form, the Dharma Sutras are written in prose, whereas the Dharma Shastras are written in simple verse. The language of the Dharma Shastras is close to classical Sanskrit, and the writers were trying to make their texts clear and easy to understand. In their content, the Dharma Shastras treat the same general subjects as the Dharma Sutras, but they place far more emphasis on working out the practical details of a social life, particularly the duties and functions of the king.

The final difference is their connection with the earlier Vedic literature. The Dharma Sutras were conceived as the final element of a **Kalpa Sutra** (complete handbook of religious practice), along with the **Shrauta Sutras** (prescriptions for Vedic rituals) and the **Grhya Sutras** (prescriptions for domestic rites). Each Kalpa Sutra was associated with one of the **Vedas** (the oldest sacred Hindu texts), and thus the "family property" of the particular **brahmins** (priests) connected with that Veda. A particular Dharma Sutra was thus associated with a particular group of brahmins, and was primarily intended as a manual for their behavior. In contrast, the Dharma Shastras purported to lay down rules for all members of society. They show little concern for ritual matters, and no connection with any particular Vedic school, but rather profess to lay down universal truths. In keeping with this emphasis, the surviving Dharma Shastras are all attributed to mythical sages—**Manu**, **Yajnavalkya**, and **Narada**—whereas the Dharma Sutras are given human authorship. The Dharma Shastras thus mark the study of dharma (**dharmashastra**) as a discipline distinct from the earlier Vedic literature, and applied to society as a whole.

Dharma Sutras

("aphorisms on **dharma**") The earliest texts specifically devoted to dharma—

rules of conduct for various social groups, moral duties, rights, and obligations. These were composed as collections of aphorisms, some so brief that they virtually presuppose commentary, and were written between the seventh and second century B.C.E. According to theory, the Dharma Sutras were the third and final part of a **Kalpa Sutra** (complete handbook of religious practice), which would also contain prescriptions for Vedic rituals (**Shrauta Sutras**) and domestic rites (**Grhya Sutras**). Each Kalpa Sutra was theoretically connected with one of the four **Vedas**, the oldest Hindu religious texts, and was thus the "family property" of the **brahmins** (priests) connected with that Veda. A particular Dharma Sutra was associated with a particular group of brahmins and was primarily intended as a manual for their behavior.

The real picture is far more complex, since more than twenty collections of Dharma Sutras have been identified, although the most important are attributed to sages and writers **Apastamba**, **Gautama**, **Vasishtha**, **Baudhayana**, and the god **Vishnu**. These Dharma Sutras were an attempt to provide an ordered way of life by delineating each person's rights and duties depending on his or her social status (**varna**) and **stage of life** (ashrama). These texts were the basis for the later **Dharma Shastras** (treatises on religious duty), which expanded the sutras, put them into verse, and were intended to serve as an actual code of law for the members of the community.

Dharna

Name for a rite intended to compel another party to address one's grievances; the rite is usually adopted when all other options have failed. The word *dharna* comes from the **Sanskrit** (sacred language) verb that means "to hold" or "to maintain." One element in the dharna rite is just that—the persistent public presence of the supplicant in proximity to the people to whom he or she is appealing. Thus, an aggrieved civil servant in modern India may hold a dharna near the Parliament building in Delhi, and in some cases people have camped there for months in an effort to publicize their plight and mobilize public opinion. In the same way, people may hold a dharna at the temple of a **deity** to seek guidance or help; the most prominent example of this is at the **Tarakeshvar** temple in the state of **West Bengal**.

Aside from persistent presence, dharna's other common characteristic is self-inflicted suffering, usually done through fasting (**upavasa**) or other forms of **ascetic** self-denial. Pilgrims to Tarakeshvar refrain from **eating** or drinking until the god **Shiva** grants them a vision, although in practice the temple priests often limit such exertions to three days. On the political level, **Mohandas K. Gandhi** perfected the "fast unto death" as a tool to help attain his political ends. One of the cultural assumptions that helps make such self-inflicted suffering persuasive is the ancient Hindu belief that by voluntarily enduring physical suffering (**tapas**) one can generate spiritual and magical power. The other working assumption that makes the dharna effective comes from the declaration at the rite's beginning. On the human level, dharnas are usually undertaken to address very specific perceived injustices, which are made public at the start. It is generally believed that should the person performing dharna die, then the person against whom the dharna had been held will be assessed the karmic demerit for causing that person's death. Such dharnas are generally only undertaken when one has no other alternative. Because of this assumption, they remain a powerful resource, even in contemporary times.

Dhatuvada

Hindu branch of the Indian tradition of **alchemy**, which seeks to transform, transmute, and perfect the body through the use of various chemicals with the ultimate goal of rendering the

Dhobis, or washermen, cleaning clothes by beating them on stone slabs.

body immortal. Just as both Hindus and Buddhists appropriated the idea of **yoga** (act of discipline), both traditions also have alchemical schools. The Dhatuvada school stressed seeking bodily perfection solely through consuming **drugs** and potions, particularly ones compounded from **mercury** and **cinnabar**. This is theoretically different from the Buddhist **Rasayana** school, since the latter is said to use such material means only to prolong life until the body can be transmuted through meditation, ritual, and yoga. The conceptual foundation for Hindu alchemy is its analysis of the world as a series of bipolar opposites, and the conviction that unifying these opposing forces brings spiritual progress and the end of reincarnation (**samsara**). The governing metaphor for this combination of opposites is the union of **sun** and **moon**. In keeping with this bipolar symbolism, both the sun and the moon are connected to other opposing principles through an elaborate series of associations. The sun is identified with heat, drying power, **fire**, the **goddess Shakti**, and menstrual **blood**; the moon with coolness, healing power, **water**, the god **Shiva**, and **semen**. In alchemical practice, the two essential chemical elements are mercury and **sulfur**—the former identified with Shiva's semen, and the latter with Shakti's uterine blood. Through properly mixing and consuming these elements, the impure body is purified and refined, eventually rendering it immortal.

Modern descriptions of this practice invariably warn that it should only be carried out under the direction of one's **guru** (spiritual teacher); otherwise these combinations will be harmful. This warning is not surprising, since by itself mercury is a deadly poison. For further information see Shashibhushan B. Dasgupta, *Obscure Religious Cults*, 1962; and David Gordon White, "Alchemy: Indian Alchemy," in Mircea Eliade (ed.), *Encyclopedia of Religion*, 1993.

Dhenuka

In Hindu mythology, a fierce **demon** (supernatural being) who appears in the form of a **cow** (dhenu). Dhenuka is only one of the demons slain by the god **Krishna**—this time in concert with his brother **Balarama**—during Krishna's childhood in the village of **Brindavan**. In these episodes, Krishna dispatches the most ferocious demons as if it were child's play, which in one sense it is. Krishna's presence in the world, and his interaction with his devotees (**bhakta**), is considered to be a **lila** ("play"), and the ease with which he handles these demons attests to this playful revelation of his divine nature. For further consideration of this theme, see David R. Kinsley, *The Sword and the Flute*, 1975.

Dhobi

A washerman, traditionally one who has cleaned clothes by getting them wet and then beating them on a stone slab. As with all the occupations in traditional India, this was a hereditary occupational group (**jati**), although the names used to designate them are different from region to region. They were typically believed to be of low status, since they habitually handled clothes rendered impure by sweat and other bodily fluids.

Dhrshtadyumna

In the *Mahabharata*, the later of the two great Hindu epics, Dhrshtadyumna is the **son** of King **Drupada** and the brother of **Draupadi**, King Drupada's **daughter**. Dhrshtadyumna and Draupadi are magically born by emerging from a sacrificial **fire**. Their father sponsors this rite of **sacrifice** to give **birth** to a hero who will kill **Drona**, who has taken away half of Drupada's kingdom after being insulted by Drupada. Drona accepts the boy as a pupil and teaches him the martial arts. Even though a heavenly voice has announced that the boy will eventually kill him, he does this under the conviction that fate cannot be avoided. Dhrshtadyumna is instrumental in arranging Draupadi's marriage to the five **Pandava** brothers, the epic's protagonists, and he fights on their side during the Mahabharata war. Dhrshtadyumna fights fiercely in the war and eventually kills Drona by cutting off his head, thereby avenging his father's defeat. Yet his triumph is short-lived, for that very night Dhrshtadyumna is killed by Drona's son **Ashvatthama**, who secretly gains entry to the Pandava camp and kicks Dhrshtadyumna to death.

Dhrtarashtra

In the *Mahabharata*, the later of the two great Hindu epics, the **son** of the sage **Vyasa** and queen **Ambika**. Dhrtarashtra and his stepbrother **Pandu** are the result of a desperate attempt to preserve the royal line of King **Shantanu**, after Shantanu's son **Vichitravirya** has died without heirs. Upon Vichitravirya's death, his mother **Satyavati** calls upon her oldest son, Vyasa, to sleep with Ambika and her sister, **Ambalika**, in the hope that the **women** will conceive. According to tradition Vyasa is very ugly, and each woman involuntarily reacts when Vyasa appears in her bed. Ambika covers her eyes, causing her son Dhrtarashtra to be born blind, and Ambalika turns pale, causing her son **Pandu** to be born with an unnaturally pale complexion. Despite his disability, Dhrtarashtra assumes the throne after Pandu's abdication; the latter renounces the world after being cursed by the sage **Kindama**. Pandu's two wives have five **sons**, known as the **Pandavas**, and Dhrtarashtra and his wife **Gandhari** have one hundred sons, collectively known as the **Kauravas**. The ultimate source of conflict in the *Mahabharata* stems from the conflict between these two royal lines, each of which has a legitimate claim to rule.

Dhrtarashtra does little to forestall this struggle. Although he is generally portrayed as a good person, he is also weak and unable to contain the ambitions of his eldest son, **Duryodhana**. Here Dhrtarashtra's blindness is not just literal, but also symbolic, as he lacks the vision and clarity that would have allowed him to recognize the breakdown between these two families and to therefore take steps to avoid it. His disability not only keeps him on the margin of daily life, but is also a sign of his inability to influence the course of events, whatever his feelings about them. One of the few times that he actually shows force is when he offers boons to **Draupadi** (**daughter** of King **Drupada**) after her humiliation by Duryodhana and his brother **Duhshasana**, through which she regains freedom for herself and her husbands.

Because of his blindness, Dhrtarashtra does not actually fight in the **Mahabharata** war, but receives regular reports from his bard **Sanjaya**, who has the ability to see events at a distance. After the Kauravas are defeated, he goes with Gandhari and several others to live in

Ascetics gather around a dhuni, a smoldering fire used to stay warm and perform ascetic rituals.

seclusion in the forest. Six years later he is killed in a forest **fire**.

Dhruva

("fixed") In Hindu mythology, a boy who is a symbol for the unrelenting pursuit of a goal. Dhruva is a king's **son**, but for some unknown reason his father favors Dhruva's half-brother over Dhruva. Distressed by this insult, Dhruva takes a vow to attain a place above all others, and goes off to the forest to perform austerities (**tapas**). After enduring bodily mortifications for eons, the god **Vishnu** appears to Dhruva to grant him a boon. In response to Dhruva's request for a place above all others, Vishnu promises Dhruva that after his death he will be installed as the **Pole Star**, the pivot around which all the other stars in the sky will turn. Even now this star is known by that name in India.

Dhuni

(from **Sanskrit** *dhu*, "to ignite") A smoldering **fire** that is kept burning by ascetics. This fire serves multiple purposes in **ascetic** life: It is a means to stay warm in cold climates, a means to perform physical **asceticism** by withstanding heat, particularly in the summer, and its care and tending is also a form of religious observance. The dhuni is a natural gathering place, and for many ascetics it is the center of ascetic life, providing heat for warmth, a fire for cooking and making tea, and coals for lighting the **chillum**, a straight pipe used to smoke tobacco mixed with hashish (**charas**). The fire itself is seen as the **deity Agni** in material form. Agni is a witness to the conversation around the dhuni, which should be of a serious and spiritual nature. The dhuni's sacred character can be seen by certain restrictions that were designed to maintain its **purity**: one should not blow directly on the fire (lest some saliva should contaminate it), but through a tube used for this purpose; one should keep clean the boundary around the dhuni (usually of made of hardened clay); and one should not touch this boundary with one's feet. Certain ascetic centers have a long history of a continuous fire. One such example is the sacred village **Triyuginarayan** in the **Himalayas**, where a fire is claimed to have been burning for the past three cosmic ages (**yugas**).

Dhupa

("incense") The eleventh of the sixteen traditional **upacharas** ("offerings") given to a **deity** as part of **worship**, which follows the model of treating a deity as an honored guest. In this offering, the deity is offered incense to enjoy the scent. The underlying motive here, as for all the upacharas, is to show one's love for the deity and minister to the deity's needs.

Dhushmeshvar

Another name for the form of the god **Shiva** known as **Ghrneshvar**. This is one of the twelve **jyotirlingas**, a group of sacred sites (**tirthas**) deemed especially holy to Shiva, and at which Shiva is believed to be uniquely present. This site is located in **Maharashtra** state. See **Ghrneshvar**.

Dhvani

("echo") In poetics—whether secular or sacred—the suggestion or connotation brought out by the poet's language. Indian literary theorists paid great attention to this notion, since attention to it allowed the poet to exercise much greater emotive depths than the surface meanings of the words would indicate and pack a much deeper range of images and associations into even a very short verse.

Dhyana

("meditation") In the **ashtanga yoga** (eight-point discipline) first arranged by the philosopher **Patanjali**, dhyana is the seventh of the eight elements of yoga practice. Along with **dharana** ("concentration") and **samadhi** ("trance"), dhyana is one of the three parts known as the "inner discipline" (**samyama**), the culmination of yogic training. Dhyana is described as an extension of dharana, in which the fixed concentration upon an object acquired in dharana is continued and extended without break. In more colloquial modern usage, the word dhyana can be used to describe any sort of focused meditation.

Dhyanashloka

("meditation verse") A verse or verses specifying the physical attributes of a **deity** to give the worshiper a mental image upon which to meditate. Dhyanashlokas are particularly important in the esoteric ritual tradition known as **tantra**, in which one of the aims is to replace all outward acts of **worship** with mental activities. In this highly ritualized context, the dhyanashlokas provide both a form and a focus for one's interior worship.

Diaspora Populations

Although the vast majority of Hindus live in their traditional homeland of South Asia, particularly in India and **Nepal**, there is also a long history of Hindus settling in other lands. By about the fourth century C.E., Hindu traders had spread Indian influence throughout Southeast Asia, where the monuments at the **Angkor** temple complex and the culture of **Bali** bear witness to its presence. In the past century, poverty and overcrowding in certain parts of India (especially **Bihar**) led many of these traders to sign up as agricultural contract laborers in **Fiji**, **South Africa**, East Africa, the **West Indies**, **Mauritius**, and even **Sri Lanka**. All of these places have substantial Hindu communities, although their local status differs. In some of these places Indians are considered equal citizens with the indigenous peoples, and in others, such as Fiji, they suffer legal obstacles. Aside from agricultural labor, another possibility for mobility and advancement came through serving in the British army or civil service in other parts of the British Empire, such as Singapore or Hong Kong. Finally, the liberalization of immigration and nationalization laws since the end of World War II has led to the formation of a substantial Hindu community in North America, both in Canada and the United States.

Didarganj Yakshi

Statue found in 1919 in Didarganj, a village near Patna in the state of **Bihar**. The image is believed to date from the third century B.C.E. and is thus a product of the **Maurya dynasty**. The statue is of a voluptuous female figure, bare to the waist, wearing abundant jewelry and bearing a yak-tail whisk (**chauri**), which was a contemporary sign of authority. It is believed to be a statue of a **yakshi**, a class of nature-spirits connected with fertility and prosperity. It is notable as one of the earliest known stone statues, and there is speculation that this may have come through contact with the Greeks. The figure itself is masterfully rendered in highly polished **Chunar** sandstone from the sandstone quarries near **Benares**; the sharply detailed rendering of her clothing and jewelry conveys the illusion of softness and swelling of the bare flesh.

Digambara

("**space**-clad," i.e., naked) In a general **ascetic** context, this can refer to any ascetic who is completely naked, which is a sign of having renounced all **possessions** and all worldly conventions. Among the **Bairagi Nagas**, or renunciant ascetics who are devotees (**bhakta**) of **Vishnu** and who formerly made their living as traders and mercenary soldiers, the Digambaras are one of the three **Naga anis** ("armies"), the others being the **Nirmohis** and **Nirvanis**. In earlier times these anis were actual fighting units, but in modern times are mainly important for determining bathing (**snana**) order in the bathing processions at the **Kumbha Mela** ("Festival of the Pot"). Of the three, the Digambaras are by far the most important, and at the time of the Kumbha Mela take precedence over the others.

Diksha

("**initiation**") A religious initiation involving the reception of secret religious teachings; the term is said to be derived from the verb *dis*, "to point out." The word diksha carries a different sense from the life-cycle rite known as **upanayana**, the adolescent religious initiation that is the ritualized "second birth" conferred on young men from the three "**twice-born**" groups—that is, **brahmin** (priestly), **kshatriya** (martial), or **vaishya** (mercantile). Both are religious initiations, and both involve the creation of new capacities and entitlements. Yet diksha is not a rite usually seen as a transition point in the life cycle, but a religious initiation in which the initiate gains secret knowledge from a religious teacher (**guru**), usually given in the form of the verbal formulas known as **mantras**. Whereas upanayana takes place while a boy is an adolescent, the time for diksha is based not on physical age, but on a person's willingness and readiness. Diksha is a particularly important concept in the ritual tradition known as **tantra**, in which such personalized initiations are the way of transmitting the tradition from master to student.

Dikshanama

("**diksha** name") Name given to a person after receiving **initiation** (diksha), as a way of acknowledging and reinforcing the new identity created by the act of initiation. Sometimes, as in the case of **ascetic** initiation, the initiate's former name will be replaced with the dikshanama. In other cases the name will be kept secret, as a source of hidden power.

Dikshitar

Southern Indian **brahmin** (priest) sub-community. The Dikshitars are an extremely small community and are found mainly in the temple-town of **Chidambaram** in the state of **Tamil Nadu**. They are the hereditary servants at the temple of **Nataraja**—the god **Shiva** in his form as the "Lord of the **Dance**." According to their own mythic understanding, the Dikshitars were members of Nataraja's heavenly host (**gana**) when he lived in **heaven**. They accompanied Nataraja when he came down to **earth**, where they still serve him.

Dilip

In Hindu mythology, one of the figures in the charter myth describing how the river **Ganges** descended from heaven to **earth**. Dilip is the great-grandson of King **Sagar**, and the father of the sage **Bhagirath**, who finally accomplishes this task. The story begins with King Sagar, whose 60,000 heroic **sons** made the mistake of insulting the sage **Kapila**, and have been burned to ash by the **fire** of Kapila's yogic powers. Kapila tells Sagar's grandson **Anshuman** that the souls of his dead uncles will find peace only when the Ganges River (which is considered to be the material form of the **goddess Ganga**) comes down from heaven and touches their ashes. After this, the family labors unceasingly to do this; Anshuman and Dilip die with this goal unrealized, but Bhagirath finally brings it to fruition by performing **asceticism** until the gods agree to send the Ganges to earth.

Dindi

Pilgrim group in the **Varkari Panth**, a religious community that is centered around the **worship** of the god **Vithoba** at his temple at **Pandharpur** in modern **Maharashtra**. The primary Varkari religious practice is taking part in two annual pilgrimages, in which all the participants arrive in Pandharpur on the same day. On this pilgrimage, pilgrims travel in groups called dindis. Dindis are often made up of people from the same neighborhood or area and are usually formed along **caste** lines. During the pilgrimage, members of a dindi travel as a unit, walking and singing devotional hymns together during the day, and cooking and camping together at night. These dindis thus create smaller subcommunities within the larger pilgrim body.

Di Nobili, Roberto

(1577–1656) Jesuit priest and missionary who spent much of his life in **Madurai** in southern India. Di Nobili came to India to convert Indians to Catholicism and to facilitate his attempt at following the Jesuit pattern of learning the local languages, in this case **Sanskrit** (sacred language) and Tamil. He also strove to understand local culture and to gain the ritual authority that came with **brahmin** (priestly) status by emulating brahmin practices (**vegetarianism**, modes of dress, etc.), as a way to spread the Gospel more effectively. He was a perceptive and careful observer, but his writings remained unpublished during his lifetime. They have only been recently rediscovered. See also **Tamil language**.

Dipa

("lamp") The twelfth of the sixteen traditional **upacharas** ("offerings") given to a **deity** as part of **worship**, following the model of treating the deity as an honored guest. In this action, the deity is given an offering of light by waving a lighted lamp before it. This rite more commonly goes by the name of **arati**, a word that is often used to denote worship in general. The underlying motive here, as for all the upacharas, is to show one's love for the deity, and to minister to the deity's needs.

Directions

In traditional Hindu reckoning, each of the primary and intermediate directions

A man performs the dipa ritual, offering a lamp before the image of a deity.

is associated with a particular divinity, which is believed to rule over this direction and to be the guardian associated with it. See **Guardians of the Directions**.

Divine Life Society

Religious organization founded in 1936 by **Swami Shivananda**. It is headquartered at the Divine Life **Ashram**, just outside the holy city of **Rishikesh** on the river **Ganges** in the state of **Uttar Pradesh**. Although Shivananda himself died in 1963, the society is still quite active in spreading the ways of Hindu life: through **yoga** (self-discipline) training programs at the Divine Life Ashram; through publishing religious texts, both traditional scriptures and the teachings of Swami Shivananda; through establishing religious centers throughout the world; and through various social service projects in India itself. Swami Shivananda was a **Dashanami Sanyasi** (**ascetic**) in the **Saraswati** division, which is one of the divisions that admits only **brahmins** (priests). The Swami's brahmin background comes through in

the organization's teachings, which stress **vegetarianism**, rigorous spiritual development, an emphasis on learning, and a strict moral code. For all these reasons the organization is widely respected in Indian society, despite having a significant number of foreign practitioners.

Divine Powers

When a single divinity is deemed to be the supreme power in the universe, he or she is generally said to wield five overarching divine powers: creation, ordering and maintaining the cosmos, destruction, concealment, and giving **grace** (divine self-revelation). The first three powers describe the relationship between the **deity** and the physical universe, whereas the fourth and fifth focus on the deity's relationship with individual devotees. By using the power of concealment, the deity becomes hidden in creation, and thus human beings are kept in ignorance. This power of concealment is often also described as the deity's **maya**, or the power of illusion that keeps human beings from perceiving the divine reality that lies behind all things. This power of illusion is so strong that the only way human beings can break through it is through the deity's grace, the final power. This grace is an act of divine self-revelation, in which the deity shreds the concealing veil of illusion and reveals himself or herself to human beings.

Divorce

Until the twentieth century, formal divorce did not exist in traditional Hindu society. This absence was undoubtedly rooted in the Hindu perspective on marriage. Marriage was seen as a permanent binding of husband and wife (or more precisely, assimilating her identity to his), in a way that ruled out a dissolving of the marriage while both members were still living. When a wife failed to bear children, the husband would sometimes take a second wife, but the original marriage would remain intact. Among the lower social classes, who were often less concerned with maintaining group status through appropriate behavior, husbands and wives would simply abandon their spouses for other partners, but this was strictly forbidden among "respectable" people.

Divorce is legally available in modern India, but social and cultural factors continue to weigh against it. Various factors make many **women** in unhappy marriages reluctant to sue for divorce: lack of support from their natal families, who are often more interested in trying to make the marriage work; the inability to earn a living on their own; and the near certainty that their husband's families will be awarded custody of their children, if they have any. Although attitudes are slowly changing, it is also still difficult for divorced women to remarry.

Divya Prabandham

("Divine Composition") Shorter name for the *Nalayira Divyaprabandham*, the collected hymns of the **Alvars**. The Alvars were a group of twelve **Vaishnava** poet-saints (devotees of the god **Vishnu**), who lived in southern India between the seventh and tenth centuries. In conjunction with their **Shaiva** (devotees of the god **Shiva**) counterparts, the **Nayanars**, the Alvars spearheaded the revitalization of Hindu religion vis-à-vis the Buddhists and the Jains. Both the Alvars and the Nayanars stressed passionate devotion (**bhakti**) to a personal god—Vishnu for the Alvars, Shiva for the Nayanars—and conveyed this devotion through hymns sung in the **Tamil language**. In the southern Indian religious community known as the **Shrivaishnavas**, the collected hymns of the Alvars have such high status that they are known as the "Tamil Veda"—that is, the religious texts in the Tamil language which carry the authority of the **Veda**, the oldest Hindu religious texts.

Diwali

One of the most important festivals in the Hindu religious **year**, which falls on the **new moon** in the **lunar month** of **Kartik** (October–November). This festival is dedicated to **Vishnu's** wife **Lakshmi**, a **goddess** who represents wealth, prosperity, and good fortune. According to popular belief, on this night of the new moon Lakshmi roams the **earth**, looking for households in which she will be welcomed, and which she will render prosperous by her presence. People spend the days before Diwali cleaning, repairing, and whitewashing their homes to make them suitable for welcoming the goddess. On the evening of Diwali people open all their doors and windows to facilitate her entry and place lights on their windowsills and balcony ledges, as an invitation to the goddess. In earlier times these lights would be clay lamps or candles, but today strings of electric lights are also widely used. It is from these lights that Diwali gets its name, as a shortened form of Dipavali (*dipa* "light" + *avali* "series"). The charter myth for

Bright, spinning lights decorate homes and streets during the festival of Diwali.
According to Hindu tradition, these lights welcome Lakshmi, a goddess who embodies good fortune.

displaying these lights describes how a poor old woman somehow gained a royal boon that all houses but hers would remain unlit on the night of Diwali. When Lakshmi wandered the land she went to the only house that was lit to welcome her. Because of Lakshmi's presence, the old woman's troubles quickly ceased.

Lakshmi's strong associations with money and good fortune account for several other practices often found on Diwali. For many traditional merchant families, Diwali is observed as the beginning of the fiscal year. All outstanding debts and obligations must be cleared up beforehand, for on Diwali new account books are begun. In some cases the account ledgers are themselves ceremonially worshiped on this day and are seen as material manifestations of Lakshmi. Another common practice is **gambling**, although in most cases it is done within the family, and for small stakes. During the rest of the year gambling is condemned as a potential drain on one's wealth, but doing so on Diwali reaffirms the connection between money and Lakshmi's favor, here in the guise of Lady Luck. Diwali is also an occasion for **eating** sweets—the more the better—and celebrating the advent of the new year by shooting off fireworks. India's loose regulation of fireworks gives celebrants access to rockets and crackers of truly impressive size, and in the larger cities people celebrate the holiday with such zeal that it sounds like an artillery barrage.

Dog

In general, the dog is considered an extremely unclean and impure **animal**. Today, keeping dogs as pets in India is a practice that is gaining favor. Traditionally, however, Indian dogs roamed the streets as scavengers, eating whatever they could find, including each other. Such promiscuous eating habits render them ritually impure, even aside from the vermin and disease that they often harbor, particularly rabies. Aside from their practical importance as scavengers, the dog is also the animal vehicle of **Bhairava**, a wrathful form of the god **Shiva**. Bhairava's symbolic association with an unclean animal clearly shows his marginal status in the pantheon—he is powerful, but also feared, because he is not bound by normal rules.

Doha

Metrical form in northern Indian **bhakti** (devotional) poetry, made up of two lines of twenty-four metric beats, divided unevenly after the thirteenth beat. The metric pattern for the first line is 6 + 4 + 3, with the second line being 6 + 4 + 1. The method of counting the metric beats is based on the distinction between "heavy" and "light" syllables. A heavy syllable is any syllable with a long vowel or a consonant cluster and is reckoned at two metric beats; all other syllables are reckoned as light, and reckoned as one. Aside from the metric pattern, there are rules about how each half line should end—that the three metric beats ending the first line cannot be a heavy syllable (two beats) followed by a light one (one beat)—which means that it must either be a light syllable followed by a heavy one, or three light ones—and that the line's final syllable must be light. These conventions still leave a great deal of fluidity, and the doha is one of the most important poetic forms for poets writing in **Braj Bhasha** (the language of **Krishna** devotion) and **Avadhi** (a dialect of medieval **Hindi**). At times the doha can stand alone, as in the epigrams of the poet-saint **Kabir**, which have become proverbial sayings in much of modern India. The doha was also used in conjunction with verses in other meters, as in the *Ramcharitmanas*. In this vernacular rendition of the epic *Ramayana*, written by the poet-saint **Tulsidas**, the doha usually comes after four verses in the **chaupai** (four-line) **meter**, and serves to sum up what has transpired in the preceding verses.

Dom

The model for traditional Indian society was as a collection of **endogamous** subgroups known as **jatis** ("birth"). These jatis were organized (and their social status determined) by the group's hereditary occupation, over which each group has a monopoly. In traditional northern Indian society, the Doms are a jati whose hereditary occupation was cremating **corpses**. They have extremely low social status because of their habitual contact with dead bodies, considered the most violently impure objects of all. Despite their low status, some of the Doms are unbelievably wealthy, particularly the ones who control the **cremation ghats** in the city of **Benares**, for without their cooperation, a body cannot be burned. The word *ghat* refers to any flat area on the bank of a river. In most cases ghats are used as places for bathing (**snana**), but in some other cases they are also places for burning bodies, so that the ashes can be placed in the river to ritually "cool" them.

Dorasamudra

Capital city of the **Hoysala dynasty**, who ruled the region in southern part of the state of **Karnataka** from the eleventh to the thirteenth centuries. Today Dorasamudra is known by the name of **Halebid** and is a village about sixty miles north and west of the city of Mysore. Although largely uninhabited, the site is known for a magnificent collection of temples, in particular the **Hoysaleshvar Temple**, dedicated to the god **Shiva** in his form as Lord of the Hoysalas. The Hoysala temples were built out of a particular type of stone—variously described as chlorite schist, steatite, or soapstone—that was quite soft when newly quarried, but gradually hardened with exposure to air. This initial malleability made the stone easy to carve, and facilitated the lush detail that characterizes these temples.

Dowry

In the strictest terms, this word is used in modern Indian society to designate any wealth transferred from the bride's family to the groom's as a condition for the marriage to occur. As with most marriages around the world, Hindu marriages often involve giving gifts to the couple, but Indians themselves draw distinctions between different categories of gifts. It is customary for the bride's parents to give her gifts of clothing and jewelry for her wedding, according to their means. This practice is attested in the **dharma literature's** (text on religious duty) description of the **Brahma marriage**. This is one of the eight recognized ways to perform a marriage and describes the bride as richly adorned. These gifts are her personal property, and serve both to give the bride some wealth of her own and as a last resort for the family. It is also common for the bride's family to give gifts to the groom and his family, of which the greatest is the "gift of a virgin" (**kanyadan**), i.e., the bride herself. In many cases, the newlyweds also receive gifts from other relatives, particularly when they are setting up a household. Both of these sorts of gifts carry no stigma in Indian society and in the popular mind are not considered "dowry."

Unfortunately, not all wedding "gifts" fall into these categories. Most marriages in India are still arranged by the parents, who are operating under differing imperatives. For the bride's parents, marrying off their daughter is a religious duty, which is over and above their natural inclination to provide for their daughter. This gives the groom's parents a distinct advantage, since they "take" the bride, and this advantage can give rise to ugly and even tragic situations. The parents of a young man with a promising career can usually expect larger and richer gifts from the bride's family, since her future will be more secure. In many cases these gifts are neither asked for nor negotiated, but simply given as part of the exchange between two families of equal status. In the worst cases, the groom's family presents a list of demands, which the bride's family is expected to fulfill as a condition for the marriage. Given the pressure to marry off their **daughters**, the bride's parents may promise more than they are actually able to "deliver." One consequence of this failure is the much-publicized **dowry deaths**, in which the bride is killed.

Most decent people in India recoil at the notion of "selling" their **sons** to the highest bidder, or of using his marriage as an opportunity for the family to get rich. At the same time, it is generally accepted that marrying one's daughter will entail considerable effort and expenditure, and that at her wedding one should give appropriate gifts. It is from these assumptions that the evils of dowry stem, and can be exploited by unscrupulous people.

Dowry Death

Name given to a particular type of violent crime against **women**. According to the much-publicized pattern, it is the killing of a new bride by her in-laws, either for failing to bring enough **dowry** with her into the marriage, or when her parents could not deliver the dowry that had been promised. In many cases these women were killed by being doused with kerosene and lit, since this could be passed off as an accidental death suffered while cooking. These murders received great publicity in India and abroad in the mid-1980s, in part because of their calculated and horrific nature. The aforementioned pattern simplifies the issues, however, by reducing it to a question of money. It is true that there have been many cases in which women have been killed solely for financial reasons—that is, for not bringing enough dowry. Yet many of the victims of these so-called dowry deaths had been married for years, and their deaths are better explained as the result of an escalating pattern of domestic violence, rather than a calculated extortion and murder.

Draupadi

In the *Mahabharata*, the later of the two great Hindu epics, Draupadi is the **daughter** of King **Drupada**, and the wife of all five **Pandava** brothers, the epic's protagonists. This literary reference to **polyandry** (the marrying of one woman to several brothers) is interesting, since it seems to have been extremely rare throughout Indian history, and the epic has to give an explanation for how this happened. Draupadi's father vows that he will give his daughter in marriage only to the man who can lift a giant bow, and then hit a target suspended in the air. This feat is child's play for **Arjuna**, one of the Pandava brothers and the world's greatest archer, and he wins Draupadi as his wife. The wedding party returns home, but while they are still outside, their mother **Kunti** calls out that whatever they have won must be shared between them. To obey their mother, each of the brothers marry Draupadi. They agree that each will live with her for a year, during which time the others shall not attempt to see her.

Draupadi's most famous scene in the epic comes after her husband **Yudhishthira** has wagered and lost her in a game of dice. Yudhishthira has been **gambling** with his cousins **Duryodhana** and **Duhshasana**, who seize Yudhishthira's gaming ineptitude as an opportunity to win the kingdom all to themselves. After the loss, Duhshasana comes to Draupadi's chamber and drags her by her **hair** back to the gambling hall. Her pain and humiliation are compounded by the fact that she is in the middle of her menstrual period and is not allowed to change her stained robe. In the gambling hall Draupadi is paraded and humiliated before the crowd like an **animal** at auction, and her property status is emphasized when Duryodhana offers her his thigh (the euphemism for the genitals) as her place to sit. The final

insult comes when Duhshasana tries to disrobe Draupadi by unwinding her sari. Here the god **Krishna** enacts a miracle: No matter how much cloth Duhshasana pulls away, Draupadi remains fully clothed. Stunned and confused, he finally gives up.

Shocked by her humiliation, Duryodhana's father **Dhrtarashtra** asks Draupadi to choose a boon. She chooses freedom for her husbands, although they eventually agree to spend a period in exile. Even before this incident there has been tension between the Pandavas and their cousins. With these insults to Draupadi, however, the seeds of discord are more deeply sown. Because Duhshasana has dragged her by the hair, Draupadi vows to leave her hair unbound until she can wash it in Duhshasana's **blood**, while her husband **Bhima** takes an oath to avenge Duryodhana's insult by smashing Duryodhana's "thigh." Draupadi's hunger for revenge and uncompromising hatred for these two are a major force driving the remainder of the epic, pushing all the parties toward the inevitable fratricidal war.

Dravida

One of the three developed styles in medieval Hindu temple **architecture**; the others being the **Nagara** and the **Veshara**. The Dravida style is primarily found in southern India, particularly in the modern state of **Tamil Nadu**. Whereas the temple tower in the Nagara style stresses an unbroken verticality, culminating in one high peak, towers in the Dravida style are composed of a series of horizontal tiers, emphasizing the successive layers. Although earlier southern Indian temples have as their focus one central tower, as at the **Rajrajeshvar Temple** in the city of **Tanjore**, the focus shifted in about the twelfth century to the building of walls around the temple's complex perimeters. These walls had enormous **gopurams** or central gateways at the cardinal points, which were usually the temple's tallest structures by far. The enclosed area inside the temple complex was often enormous, as in the estimated 500 acres at the temple of **Shrirangam**, but most of the construction was only a single story. (There would be taller towers over the temple's primary images, however.) In the developed examples of the Dravida style, this lessened emphasis on soaring height was compensated by its enormous horizontal spread. The best examples of this later type are the Ranganathaswamy temple in Shrirangam, and the **Minakshi** temple in **Madurai**.

Dravida

(2) **Brahmin** (priestly) group that is one of the five southern brahmin communities (**Pancha Dravida**). As their name would indicate, the core region for the Dravida brahmins is in deep southern India, in the modern states of **Tamil Nadu** and **Kerala**. The most illustrious of the Dravida subcommunities are the **Nambudiris**, among whom the great philosopher **Shankaracharya** is believed to have been born.

Dravidian

In the strictest linguistic sense, the word Dravidian is the name for a particular family of languages in which the primary members are the four southern Indian languages: **Tamil**, Telegu, **Kannada**, and Malayalam. Aside from these four languages, all located in the southernmost part of the subcontinent, another language in the Dravidian family is Brahui. This is spoken by a small and fairly isolated population in modern Pakistan, far from any other Dravidian language speakers, and completely surrounded by people speaking Indo-**Aryan** languages. One theory to explain this irregularity is that the Dravidian languages were originally spoken all over the subcontinent, but were gradually displaced toward the south as Indo-Aryan language speakers—better known as the Aryans—came into India. According to

Built in the Dravida architectural style, the Minakshi Temple contains enormous gopurams, the gateways to the temple grounds.

this theory, the Brahui-speaking community is an isolated remnant of that earlier time, which somehow managed to remain intact.

This notion also affects how southern Indians form their identities. The word *Dravidian* can be used to denote a southern Indian or any person whose mother tongue is one of the four primary Dravidian languages. For southern Indians with a strong regional identity, it is a way for them to distinguish themselves from northern Indians and the "imperialism" of northern Indian culture. It is also used with an underlying tone of pride, that as Dravidians they are descendants of the subcontinent's original inhabitants.

Dreams

As symbol and reality, dreams have multiple uses in Hindu thought. Philosophically, dreams are often used as examples to illustrate the illusory nature of the world as it is perceived. Just as a dream disappears when one wakes up and is perceived to have been unreal the entire time, so does the everyday understanding of the world disappear when one has perceived the ultimate truth. In quite a different understanding, the dream state is the second of the states of consciousness mentioned in the **Mandukya Upanishad**, or one of the religious texts known as the **Upanishads**. In the Upanishads, the dream state is the first step in turning one's awareness away from the outside world and into one's Self, where all sense of ego is lost. Waking consciousness is further away from one's Self than the dream state. The four-step pattern in this upanishad, and in others as well, is from waking consciousness, to dreams, to deep sleep, and from there to the realization of the eternal Self.

On quite another level, dreams are an important part of religious life in popular Hinduism. They are often believed to give **omens** for the future, which may be interpreted as favorable or unfavorable, according to the dream's content and context. Dreams are also seen as providing a channel for communicating with spirits, **ghosts**, **village deities**, and other nonhuman spiritual beings. Unquiet spirits of the dead will often appear to family members in dreams to reveal what they need to find peace. The same process is often found with village deities, who usually manifest themselves to specific people in the village, either to give warnings or to make demands.

Drona

In the *Mahabharata*, the later of the two great Hindu epics, Drona is famous as a teacher of all the arts of war, but particularly for teaching archery. He is the martial preceptor to both the **Pandavas** and the **Kauravas**, the two royal factions whose battle for power is at the heart of the *Mahabharata*. Drona is the **son** of the sage **Bharadvaja**, born through an involuntary seminal emission when the sage sees a celestial nymph (**apsara**). Drona's skill in weapons is gained from the god **Vishnu's Parashuram avatar**, who bequeaths both his weapons and his skills to Drona as a boon. Drona's skill as an archer is legendary, as is his prowess as an archery teacher. Among his pupils he has a particular fondness for **Arjuna** (a **Pandava** brother), whose commitment and concentration so outstrip his peers that Drona promises Arjuna that he will be the world's greatest archer. This support for Arjuna can be seen in the story of **Ekalavya**, a tribal boy whom Drona refuses to teach because of his low status, but who becomes Arjuna's equal as an archer by worshiping a clay statue of Drona. When Drona discovers this, he demands that Ekalavya give him his right thumb as a preceptor's fee, to ensure that no one will be Arjuna's equal.

During the Mahabharata war, Drona fights valiantly on the side of **Duryodhana** (eldest son of **Dhrtarashtra**), but is finally killed by King **Drupada's** son **Dhrshtadyumna**. In the epic, Drupada and Drona have a long history of conflict. They have lived together as students, but after their student life ends Drupada becomes the king of **Panchala**, whereas Drona is so poor he cannot afford to feed his family. On one occasion, when Drona asks Drupada for alms, Drupada upbraids him most insultingly. Drona vows revenge, and after teaching the arts of war to the Pandavas and Kauravas, Drona demands Drupada's kingdom as his teacher's fee (**dakshina**) from his students. When Drupada is defeated, Drona takes half of his kingdom; Drupada vows to get revenge on Drona. Drupada subsequently performs a great **fire sacrifice** to give **birth** to a son who will kill Drona. Out of the fire come two luminous children, one of whom is Dhrshtadyumna, and the other his sister, **Draupadi**.

Dropsy

Bodily condition in which the body retains excess **water**, and in consequence swells up. In several hymns in the **Vedas**, the oldest Hindu religious texts, dropsy is described as the punishment levied by the god **Varuna** for speaking falsehood. Varuna was conceived as the guardian of cosmic order (**rta**), and intentionally false speech was considered the paradigm of **anrta**, the destructive force that ran counter to the ordering force of rta. In this case the punishment was seen as fitting the crime, as if one had been metaphorically inflated by the lies one had told.

Drshtanta

("example") In Indian **philosophy**, the examples that are one of the required elements in the accepted form of an inference (**anumana**). These examples were provided as further evidence to prove the reason (**hetu**) given to support the hypothesis. As a rule, there had to be two such examples. One was a positive example (**sapaksha**) to show that similar things happened in comparable cases, and the other was a negative example (**vipaksha**) to show that this did not happen in other cases. In the most common example of an inference, "There is **fire** on the mountain, because there is smoke on the mountain," the sapaksha could be "like kitchen" (a place with both fire and smoke), and the vipaksha "unlike lake" (a place without fire or smoke). The purpose of both examples is to support the reason given, by showing that this reason gives sufficient cause to support the theory.

Drugs

The attitude toward drugs in Hindu society shows the incredible variation for which the Hindu religion is famous. In general, the use of drugs is zealously condemned among "respectable" people, as is anything leading to a potential loss of control. Yet Hindu mythology also portrays the god **Shiva** as regularly consuming **intoxicants**, particularly **bhang**, a preparation made primarily from marijuana, and **datura**, a genus of plants containing poisonous alkaloids. Given this mythic example, some of Shiva's devotees (**bhakta**) do the same as a variety of religious practice. Many ascetics regularly spend much of their day smoking hashish (**charas**) mixed with tobacco, although this is not always viewed as normal **ascetic** practice. There are also particular times and places when consumption of drugs is more accepted, even among "normal" people. Consuming bhang is a fairly common element in the celebration of certain festivals, such as **Shivaratri** ("Night of Shiva") and **Holi** (the festival of reversal). It is also sometimes consumed when people are on pilgrimage, and government-regulated stands selling bhang can be found at several important pilgrimage places (**tirtha**), including **Benares**, **Puri**, and **Haridwar**. Despite this more widespread use in particular specialized contexts, there are many people who do not use drugs under any circumstances and would never consider doing so. Such rigid refusal is still only one part of the "orthodox" picture, in which one can find many different attitudes.

Drupada

In the *Mahabharata*, the later of the two great Hindu epics, Drupada is the king of the **Panchala** region, and the father of **Dhrshtadyumna** and **Draupadi**. Much of Drupada's life is absorbed by his struggle with **Drona**, who has been one of Drupada's fellow students. After their course of studies is finished, Drupada assumes his throne and lives quite lavishly, whereas Drona is so poor that he cannot even afford to feed his family. In distress, Drona approaches Drupada for help, reminding him of their past connection. Drupada arrogantly dismisses him, telling him that such ties are of no consequence. Drona swears that he will get revenge, and after teaching the arts of war to the **Pandavas** and **Kauravas**, the two royal factions whose battle for power is at the heart of the *Mahabharata*, demands Drupada's kingdom as his preceptor's fee (**dakshina**). After Drupada is defeated, Drona takes half of his kingdom, whereupon Drupada swears revenge. He performs a great **sacrifice** to give **birth** to a **son** who will kill Drona. Two children emerge from the sacrificial **fire**: Dhrshtadyumna, who eventually kills Drona; and Draupadi, who becomes the wife of all five **Pandavas**. During the Mahabharata war, Drupada fights on the side of the Pandavas, his sons-in-law. He is eventually killed in battle by Drona but is later avenged by his son Dhrshtadyumna, who kills Drona.

Duhshasana

In the *Mahabharata*, the later of the two great Hindu epics, Duhshasana is one of the hundred **sons** of **Dhrtarashtra**, who are collectively known as the **Kauravas**. The heart of the *Mahabharata* is the struggle for power between the Kauravas and their cousins the **Pandavas**, and the latter are the epic's protagonists. Duhshasana is most infamous for his misbehavior toward the Pandavas' common wife **Draupadi** after the eldest Pandava, **Yudhishthira**, loses everything—including Draupadi—in a game of dice. Duhshasana drags Draupadi into the **gambling** hall by her **hair** and with her garments stained by her menstrual **blood**; he also attempts to disrobe Draupadi by pulling off her sari, but is frustrated here by the god **Krishna**, who miraculously makes Draupadi's sari infinitely long.

Duhshasana's behavior in this incident only fans the enmity between the two families. Draupadi's husband **Bhima**, the Pandava brother renowned for his physical strength, vows to avenge this insult by ripping open Duhshasana's chest and drinking his blood, whereas Draupadi vows that she will leave her hair unbound until she can wash it in Duhshasana's blood. During the Mahabharata war Duhshasana fights with his brother **Duryodhana** and is eventually killed by Bhima, after which both Bhima and Draupadi fulfill their dreadful vows. As an extra measure of revenge before killing Duhshasana, Bhima tears off the hand that had held Draupadi's hair and beats Duhshasana with his own severed limb.

Durga

("inaccessible, impassable") A particular form of the Hindu Mother **Goddess**, although the name is often used as a more general title for the mother goddess in her fierce and powerful form. As depicted in images and pictures, Durga rides on a **lion** and holds in her eight hands the weapons of all the gods. Both of these features correspond to the description of the great goddess in the *Devimahatmya*, the earliest and most important mythic text used for the **worship** of the Goddess as the supreme **divine power**. The general identification of Durga with this great Goddess is underscored by the *Devimahatmya*'s other common name, the *Durgasaptashati* ("The 700 [verses] on Durga"). As a form of the great Goddess, Durga is a major divinity in the Hindu pantheon and in modern Hindu life. The eighth **day** in the waxing and waning halves of the **lunar month** are considered sacred to her, and her rites are practiced on those days. Her most important festivals are the Nine Nights (**Navaratri**), which occur in both the spring and the fall. In each of these festivals Durga is worshiped in her nine forms (**Navadurga**), one on each consecutive night. The variety of goddesses as which she is worshiped again shows us how Durga is conceived as the embodiment of the Goddess in all her forms.

Durgasaptashati

("700 [verses in praise of] **Durga**") Another name for the *Devimahatmya*, the earliest and most important mythic text for the **worship** of the **Goddess** as

Worshipers immerse an image of the goddess Durga in the Yamuna River, near New Delhi.
Durga is depicted riding a lion and holding a weapon in each of her eight hands.

the supreme **divine power**. It has this name because the text is 700 verses long, and Durga is one of the common names designating this powerful goddess. The *Devimahatmya* is well-known for its assertion that God is female. This is a notion with no clear source in the earlier tradition, where female **deities** were insignificant. The text begins with a frame story, but the bulk of the work is three stories describing the salvific activity of the Goddess, who is portrayed as far superior to the pantheon's male gods. See *Devimahatmya*.

Durvasas

In Hindu mythology, a sage who is a partial incarnation of the god **Shiva**. Durvasas is the son of **Anasuya**, who for her influence in persuading another woman to remove a curse has been given boons by the gods **Brahma**, **Vishnu**, and Shiva. Anasuya requests that each be born as one of her **sons**, and Vishnu is born as **Dattatreya**, Shiva as Durvasas, and Brahma as Chandra. As a mythic figure, Durvasas is noted for his **magic** powers, which are not surprising given his background. He is also known for his bad temper and for his tendency to curse anyone who makes him angry. One victim of his wrath is the maiden **Shakuntala**, who in her reverie on her newfound love with King **Dushyanta** does not notice and pay homage to Durvasas. She is cursed that her love would completely forget her. In another case Durvasas curses all the gods to be subject to old age and death. This is provoked by an "insult" from **Indra's elephant Airavata**, which had flung a garland given by Durvasas to the ground. As with most **curses** in Hindu mythology, neither of these curses can be withdrawn, but their severity is reduced by mitigating conditions. Shakuntala is told that King Dushyanta will remember her if she shows him some sign of their relationship, which she does. The gods can avoid old age and death by obtaining and consuming the nectar of immortality (**amrta**).

As with all the sages, Durvasas can also grant wonderful boons to people with whom he is pleased. One such beneficiary was **Kunti**, one of the heroines in the epic *Mahabharata*. Durvasas gives Kunti a powerful **mantra** (sacred sound), which will allow her to have a child by any of the gods simply by thinking about him. As soon as Kunti receives this mantra, she tests it while looking at the **sun**, and immediately bears the golden child **Karna**. In her panic at unexpectedly becoming a mother—she is still unmarried, and understandably concerned about what people might think—she puts the child in a box and abandons him in the **Ganges**. After her marriage to **Pandu** (son of the sage **Vyasa** and queen **Ambalika**), this mantra is the only way that she is able to have children, since Pandu has been cursed to die the moment he sleeps with one of his wives. She uses this mantra to bear **Yudhishthira**, **Arjuna**, and **Bhima**, then teaches it to her co-wife **Madri**, who bears **Nakula** and **Sahadeva**. Thus, through the gift of Durvasas, all the **Pandava** brothers—the epic's protagonists—are children of the gods.

Duryodhana

In the *Mahabharata*, the later of the two great Hindu epics, Duryodhana is the eldest **son** of King **Dhrtarashtra**, and thus the leader of the **Kauravas**, one of the two royal factions whose struggle for power is at the heart of the epic. Duryodhana and ninety-nine brothers are born in an unusual manner. Their mother **Gandhari** gives **birth** to a great lump of flesh, which is divided and put into one hundred pots of clarified butter. In these pots the lumps develop into infants. At the moment Duryodhana is born there are a host of evil **omens**, and when the court astrologers are asked to interpret these, they conclude that Duryodhana will be the ruin of the country and his family, and that it will be better to abandon him to the elements. Fatherly feelings prevent Dhrtarashtra from doing this, which sets the stage for the final conflict. Even though the major force driving the epic's plot is the animosity between Duryodhana and his cousins, the **Pandavas**, and this ends with the Kauravas being utterly destroyed, it would be inaccurate to paint Duryodhana as an unredeemable villain. He is less evil than ill-starred—proud, stubborn, unwilling to admit his mistakes, and after a certain point, unwilling to grant his cousins any advantage. These character flaws are magnified by the lack of strong guidance from his father Dhrtarashtra, and eventually spell his doom.

The rift between the cousins develops early, inflamed in part by the fact that the Pandavas are more heroic than Duryodhana and his brothers. As a child, **Bhima**, the Pandava brother best noted for his prodigious strength, used to whip all hundred Kauravas at once. Needless to say this does not endear him to them. Later in adolescence, when their archery teacher, **Drona**, requests the capture of King **Drupada** as his preceptor's fee, the Pandava brother **Arjuna** succeeds in doing this, whereas Drupada defeats Duryodhana in battle.

Another rift grows when the Pandavas contest the right of Duryodhana's friend **Karna** to take part in an archery match, claiming that Karna's unknown parentage makes him unfit to compete with kings. Duryodhana skirts that issue by proclaiming Karna as the King of **Anga**, but by then the bad **blood** between the cousins is well-established.

This bad blood becomes apparent in many different plots. Duryodhana first tries to kill the Pandavas by building a flammable **house of lac** for them, which is then set on **fire**. The Pandavas, however, are able to escape unharmed. Duryodhana later entices **Yudhishthira** (a Pandava brother) into a game of dice. Yudhishthira wagers and loses everything that he has, including himself, his brothers, and their common wife **Draupadi**. After this loss Duryodhana and his brother **Duhshasana** publicly humiliate Draupadi, after which Bhima swears a solemn oath to kill them both. Dhrtarashtra gives the Pandavas their freedom, which they promptly lose in yet another game of dice. The outcome of this loss is that the Pandavas agree to spend twelve years in exile in the forest, and live incognito for the thirteenth, with the condition that if they are discovered in the thirteenth year the cycle will begin anew.

Despite the best efforts of Duryodhana's spies, the Pandavas manage to escape detection during the thirteenth year, and at its conclusion send envoys to Duryodhana to claim their share of the kingdom. Perhaps emboldened by Yudhishthira's comment that he and his brothers will be satisfied with a mere five villages, Duryodhana replies that he will not give them enough land to put under the point of a needle. In the face of such stubbornness and injustice, the Pandavas prepare for war to claim what is rightfully theirs. During the war Duryodhana fights valiantly, but in the eighteen days of battle sees his forces disintegrate around him. His final battle is with Bhima, who in exchange for Duryodhana's earlier insult to Draupadi (he had directed her to sit on his thigh, which was a euphemism for the genitals), smashes Duryodhana's thigh with his mace, killing him.

Dushana

In the *Ramayana*, the earlier of the two great Indian epics, Dushana is one of the brothers of the demon-king **Ravana**. Together with his brother **Khara**, Dushana tries to avenge the honor of their sister **Shurpanakha**, whose ears and nose have been cut off by **Rama's** brother **Lakshmana**. In a fierce battle with their **demon** (supernatural being) army, Rama destroys the army and kills Khara and Dushana. Seeing the failure of her two brothers, Shurpanakha goes to Ravana to beg for vengeance. Ravana realizes he cannot kill Rama in battle but resolves to avenge his sister by kidnapping **Sita**, wife of Ravana. This sets in motion the plot of the latter part of the epic.

Dushyanta

In the *Mahabharata*, the later of the two great Hindu epics, Dushyanta is a king of the **Lunar Line** and the husband of **Shakuntala**. Their romance is also described in **Kalidasa's** drama *Abhijnanashakuntala*. Dushyanta meets Shakuntala, who is living in a forest **ashram** (abode of an **ascetic**), while he is hunting in the forest. They fall in love and are married by their mutual consent. After a short time Dushyanta has to return to his kingdom, with Shakuntala to follow soon after. In the meantime, Shakuntala has been cursed by the sage **Durvasas** that her beloved will completely forget her, although Durvasas later modifies the **curse**, and says that Dushyanta will remember everything if Shakuntala can show him any proof of their union. The bulk of the story in both episodes is concerned with Shakuntala's trials and tribulations as she strives to regain her rightful place as queen. In both versions, Dushyanta is a minor character, but clearly an essential one.

In Kulu, people celebrating the festival of Dussehra carry temple images in procession through the streets.

Dussehra

(variant of Dashahara, "ten days") Festival celebrated on the tenth **day** of the bright (waxing) half of the **lunar month** of **Ashvin** (September–October), and one of the most important celebrations in the **year**. The festival celebrates the victory of good over evil, and is also known as Vijaya Dashami ("Victory Tenth"). The festival has two charter myths, both of which mark the ultimate triumph of good over evil. One charter comes from the mythology of the **Goddess**, and marks this as the day on which **Durga** (form of the Hindu Mother Goddess) slays the buffalo-**demon Mahishasura**. This episode comes from the *Devimahatmya*, and is the central theme of the text—the goddess is born

to destroy Mahishasura when the gods cannot, and the struggle between the two is the climax of the text. Since the nine days preceding Dussehra are the fall **Navaratri**, the "nine nights" spent in **worship** of the Goddess, it seems reasonable that the tenth and concluding day would be marked by the climactic moment in the *Devimahatmya*, the most important source of mythology for the Goddess.

The other charter myth for this festival comes from an entirely different source, the mythology of **Rama** (the seventh incarnation of **Vishnu**). This is celebrated as the day on which Rama slays **Ravana** (demon-king of **Lanka**) and regains **Sita** (wife of Rama) from captivity. This victory is symbolized by burning huge effigies of Ravana and his **son**

Meghanada (an epithet of **Indrajit**) on the night of Dussehra, and these effigies often contain fireworks to enhance their pyrotechnic capacity. This time of year is often celebrated with dramatic enactments of the *Ramayana* (the **Sanskrit** epic), known as the **Ram Lila**. In some cases this lasts for ten days, ending on Dussehra; in other cases (as in the Ram Lila in **Benares**, the sacred city on the banks of the **Ganges** River) it will last an entire month, with Dussehra marking the death of Ravana.

Dussehra is a highly auspicious day, and popular tradition holds that anything begun on this day will succeed. Dussehra is thus a favored occasion for initiating any important projects, beginning endeavors, or forming organizations, even if it is only a token beginning. Dussehra also marks the beginning of the cool **season**, when the end of the hot weather and the monsoon rains bring better conditions for military action. Both charter myths have connections with battle and conquest, and in earlier times Dussehra was particularly celebrated by the royal and martial classes. On Dussehra it was customary for soldiers to worship their weapons. Given the festival's martial associations and the guarantee that all things initiated on that day would be successful, it was also the day of choice for rulers to send out their armies to invade neighboring territories. Even today one of the most spectacular celebrations is in Mysore, where the ruler presides over this festival in his ritual position as king, even though he no longer rules. The other great celebration is in **Kulu**, where all the **deities** in the region journey to Kulu to celebrate this festival (along with hordes of their human retainers).

Dvadashakshara Mantra

("[the] twelve-syllable **mantra**") Twelve-syllable mantra (sacred sound) used in parts of the **Vaishnava** community. The mantra is "**Om** *namo bhagavate narayanaya*" ("*Om*, Homage to the blessed **Narayana**").

Dvaitadvaita Vedanta

One of the branches of **Vedanta**, the philosophical school claiming to reveal the ultimate (anta) teaching of the ancient sacred texts known as the **Vedas**. Dvaitadvaita Vedanta's founder and most important figure was the fourteenth-century philosopher, **Nimbarka**. Nimbarka stressed the **worship** of the god **Krishna** and his companion **Radha** as a divine couple, but on a philosophical level he was attempting to find some middle ground between the monism of the **Advaita Vedanta** school and the dualism of the **Dvaita Vedanta** school. The former claimed that a single Ultimate Reality—called **Brahman**—lay behind all things, and that all things were merely differing forms of this single reality. The latter emphasized the utter distinction between God as Ultimate Reality on the one hand, and the world and human souls on the other. Nimbarka stressed that the world and souls were dependent on God, in whom they exist and with whom they had a subtle connection. Nimbarka thus supported the philosophical doctrine called **parinamavada**, which stressed the real transformation of the divine and the capacity of human beings to transform themselves back to their divine status.

Dvaita ("dual") Vedanta

One of the branches of **Vedanta**, the philosophical school claiming to reveal the ultimate (anta) teaching of the ancient sacred texts known as the **Vedas**. Dvaita Vedanta's founder and most important figure was the philosopher **Madhva**, who lived in southern India in the thirteenth century. Madhva's basic theory is the utter transcendence of God, and this conviction leads him to suggest a philosophical position known as dualism. Dualism asserts a qualitative difference between God in his transcendence and the corruptions of material things. According to Madhva, God is completely different from human Selves and the material world, even though both of these come from God and depend on Him for their continuing existence. In this dualism, Madhva differs sharply from the major school of Vedanta, **Advaita Vedanta**. The Advaita school upholds a philosophical position known as monism, which is the belief that a single Ultimate Reality—called **Brahman**—lies behind all things, and that all things are merely differing forms of this single reality. Whereas Advaita collapses all things into one thing, Madhva firmly insists on maintaining differences.

Madhva's stress on dualism leads him to clarify these differing types of things, which is known as the "fivefold difference": the difference between God and the Self, between God and the world, between individual Selves, between Selves and matter, and between individual material things. Even though each Self is believed to contain an aspect of God, this fundamental difference gives the Self only a limited capacity for religious life. This limited power means that final liberation of the soul comes solely through the **grace** of God, who alone has the power to effect it. Final liberation is conceived both as freedom from rebirth and as the soul's opportunity to remain in the divine presence forever.

With its stress on God's utter transcendence and the emphasis on grace as the sole vehicle for salvation, Madhva's Dvaita Vedanta has often been compared to the theology of John Calvin. Madhva even stated that the world had three classes of beings: those eventually destined for liberation (**muktiyogas**), those destined for eternal rebirth (**nityasamsarins**), and those destined for eternal damnation (**tamoyogas**). Like Calvin, Madhva did not see these categories as promoting **fatalism**, but rather that the prospect of never attaining liberation could urge one to the faith necessary to pursue an active religious life. For further information see Karl H. Potter (ed.), *Presuppositions of India's Philosophies*, 1972; and Sarvepalli Radhakrishnan and Charles A. Moore (eds.), *A Sourcebook in Indian Philosophy*, 1957.

Dvapara Yuga

Particular age of the world in one of the reckonings of **cosmic time**. According to traditional belief, time has neither beginning nor end, but alternates between cycles of creation and activity, followed by cessation and quietude. Each of these cycles lasts for 4.32 billion years, with an active phase known as the **Day of Brahma**, and the quiet phase known as the Night of Brahma. In one reckoning of cosmic time, the Day of Brahma is divided into one thousand **mahayugas** ("great cosmic ages"), each of which lasts for 4.32 million years. Each mahayuga is composed of four constituent **yugas** (units of cosmic time), named the **Krta Yuga**, **Treta Yuga**, Dvapara Yuga, and **Kali Yuga**. Each of these four yugas is shorter than its predecessor, and ushers in an era more degenerate and depraved. By the end of the Kali Yuga, things have gotten so bad that the only solution is the destruction and recreation of the **earth**, at which time the next Krta era begins.

The Dvapara Yuga is thus the third of the four yugas contained in a mahayuga, and lasts for 864,000 years. The metal associated with the Dvapara yuga is **bronze**—less valuable than the gold and silver associated with the earlier ages, but better than the iron of the Kali yuga. This is popularly believed to be the cosmic age in which the god **Krishna** appeared on earth.

Dvarapala

("door-protector") Guardian images placed on either side of the entrance to a Hindu temple. These figures are usually portrayed as minor celestial beings and conceived as the protectors of the sacred space inside. Since any Hindu temple is first and foremost the home for the **deity** within, and since both kings and gods often used the same symbols to display and reinforce their status, it is not surprising that the deities would have some "servants" guarding theirs door and restricting access to them, in the same way as their human counterparts.

Dvija

("**twice-born**") Name for a member of the three "twice-born" groups in Indian society, that is, a **brahmin** (highest in status), **kshatriya** (second in status to brahmins), or **vaishya** (third in status to brahmins). This name exists because these groups are ritually eligible to receive the adolescent religious **initiation** called **upanayana**, which is often described as the "second birth." See **twice-born**.

Dvipas

According to traditional mythic geography, the visible world is composed of a series of seven concentric dvipas, a word that literally means "islands," but can be translated to "landmasses." All but one of these are named after particular plants. At the center is **Jambu** ("Rose-apple") **dvipa**, followed by **Plaksha** ("fig-tree") **dvipa**, **Salmala** ("silk-cotton tree") **dvipa**, **Kusha** ("kusha grass") **dvipa**, **Krauncha** ("curlew") **dvipa**, **Shaka** ("Teak") **dvipa**, and at the outermost edge, **Pushkara** ("blue lotus") **dvipa**. Each of these lands is separated from its neighbors by one of the seven oceans (the **saptasindhu**), with each ocean composed of a different substance. The innermost ocean, as experience shows, is composed of salt **water**, the ones beyond this are of sugar cane juice, wine, ghee, yogurt, milk, and sweet water, respectively. At the center of Jambudvipa (and thus the world) is Mount **Meru**, which is compared to the central calyx of a lotus, and is surrounded by the dvipas as its petals. The physical world is thus seen as a symmetrical whole, with the land of India (in the southern part of Jambudvipa) positioned at the symbolic center.

Dvarapala, or gatekeeper, statue at the entrance of the Brhadeshvar Temple in Thanjavur. These statues depict minor deities that protect the space inside.

Dwara

("door" or "gateway") Among the **Bairagis**, renunciant ascetics who are devotees (**bhakta**) of the god **Vishnu**, the word *dwara* is used to denote a branch or subsect of a particular order. Each dwara is named after its **ascetic** founder, who was himself usually a noted disciple of the larger order's founder. For example, the **Nimbarki** ascetics are one of the four established orders among the militant **Vaishnava** ascetics known as the **chatuh-sampradayi Nagas**, along with the **Ramanandis**, the **Vishnuswamis**, and the Madhva Gaudiya (**Brahma sampraday**) ascetics. The Nimbarkis themselves are divided into nine dwaras, or subsects, each named after the dwara's founder. The division of ascetics by means of dwaras is another means of subdividing ascetic orders, and creating even more sharply defined ascetic identities and loyalties.

Dwaraka

Sacred city (**tirtha**) on the western coast of **Gujarat**, on the shore of the Arabian Sea. In mythic terms, Dwaraka is most famous as the capital city for the god **Krishna's** kingdom, at which he is believed to have lived in the years following the **Mahabharata** war. Dwaraka's most important site is the Dwarakanath Temple, dedicated to Krishna in his form as the "Lord of Dwaraka." Dwaraka is also one of the **four dhams** ("divine abodes"), sacred centers that approximately define the geographic boundaries of India; the three others are **Badrinath**, **Puri**, and **Rameshvaram**. Dwaraka is also the site of the **Sharada math**, one of the four **Dashanami Sanyasi maths** (monastic centers) supposedly established by the philosopher **Shankaracharya**. The Sharada math is the headquarters of the **Kitawara** group of the Dashanami Sanyasis, one of the four major organizational groups, with each one centered at one of the maths. As with many other Hindu sacred sites, Dwaraka is sanctified by a network of mythic and religious associations.

Dyaus

A minor **deity** in the **Vedas**, the oldest and most authoritative Hindu religious texts. Dyaus is a god associated with the sky, but his character is not well-developed, since even at the time of the Vedas he had been largely eclipsed by other gods. Dyaus is part of the oldest layer of Indo-**Aryan** deities, as evidenced by the Greek form of his name, Zeus.

E

cosmology, the others being **water**, **fire**, **wind**, and **akasha**. In some philosophical schools, each of the elements is paired with one of the five senses; in this case earth is associated with smell. The element earth is also associated with certain bodily functions, especially the elimination of solid wastes.

Earth

In Hindu mythology, Earth is considered a **goddess**. The notion that India is a sacred land is one of the most deeply rooted elements in Hindu life, and many of India's mountains, rivers, and other geographical features are considered gods and goddesses. This belief extends to Earth itself. In the **Vedas**, the oldest Hindu sacred texts, Earth appears as the goddess **Prthivi**, who is lauded for her fertility, her nurturing capacity, and her firmness in supporting all things. Prthivi almost always appears in conjunction with **Dyaus**, a male **deity** associated with the sky, whose name is a cognate form of the Greek god Zeus. Sky and Earth thus form the divine couple, with the rain from the sky fertilizing and energizing the earth.

In later mythology the figure of Prthivi is supplanted by the goddess Bhudevi ("Earth Goddess"), who is considered to be one of the wives of the god **Vishnu**. Bhudevi is less frequently associated with fertility and nurturing; her primary function is as a supplicant to galvanize the world-rescuing activity of Vishnu. When the wicked become too oppressive, or a **demon** becomes too powerful and disrupts the cosmic order, Earth cries out to Vishnu for help, and Vishnu obligingly restores the cosmic balance. One example of this is the **Boar avatar**, in which Earth herself is rescued from bondage by Vishnu. For further information see David R. Kinsley, *Hindu Goddesses*, 1986.

Earth

(2) In its material form, one of the five **elements** in traditional Indian

Eating

Throughout the world the act of eating is imbued with cultural significance and cultural messages, and Hindu culture makes no exception. Given the strong emphasis on **purity**, Hindus pay significant attention to the preparation and consumption of food. Factors such as whom one eats with, who may prepare one's food, and what types of food one will eat and how it should be prepared all send messages about the social status of an individual or a community. The groups with the highest status, particularly **brahmins**, are the strictest with regard to their dining habits. For the most part, such high-status groups adhere to a principle known as **commensality**—that is, only eating food cooked by members of their social group. With regard to the content of one's diet, the great divide is between vegetarian and nonvegetarian. An exclusively vegetarian diet indicates higher status, and among nonvegetarians there are status gradations depending on what types of meat one eats. For orthodox Hindus, every meal is a potential source of ritual contamination and must be carefully monitored. Food cooked in water is seen as far more susceptible to pollution (**ashaucha**) and greater care is taken in accepting it, whereas food fried in oil or ghee is believed to be much more resistant to pollution and thus a lesser source of ritual danger. From a religious perspective, the safest meal of all is the meal that is cooked and eaten at home. See also **Vegetarianism**.

Eclipses

Without exception, eclipses are considered highly inauspicious and ritually dangerous times. As in many other cultures, Indian astronomers were able to figure out the motion of the **moon**, and thus could predict both solar and lunar eclipses fairly accurately. The traditional mythic explanation for eclipses comes from the story of the **Tortoise avatar**, in which the **gods** and **demons** agree to join forces to churn the Ocean of Milk into the nectar of immortality, which they will then share. The gods manage to trick the demons out of their share, but as the gods divide it among themselves, the demon **Sainhikeya** slips into their midst in disguise. As Sainhikeya begins to drink, the **sun** and moon alert the god **Vishnu** to Sainhikeya's presence, and Vishnu quickly uses his discus to cut off the demon's head. Yet since the demon drank some of the nectar, both his head and trunk become immortal, with the head becoming **Rahu** and the trunk becoming **Ketu**. Rahu has particular enmity for the sun and moon, the **deities** responsible for his demise, and tries to swallow them whenever he meets them in the **heavens**. He always succeeds, but since he no longer has a body to digest them, they escape unharmed through Rahu's severed neck.

This association with Rahu makes eclipses inauspicious and ritually dangerous times, and in popular culture eclipses are believed to emit malevolent rays that have a physical quality. Many people respond to this danger by remaining indoors for the duration of an eclipse. During an eclipse, people will often perform **rites of protection**, including giving donations (**dana**) as a way to give away potential bad luck. Pregnant **women** must take particular care, lest the **inauspiciousness** of the time affect the growing child. Some believe that pregnant women should lie completely motionless during an eclipse, fearing that the child will be born missing the body part corresponding to the one that the woman moved. After the eclipse, people bathe (**snana**) and perform other rites of purification to remove any possible lingering taint of impurity (ashaucha) or bad luck.

Eighteen Minor Works

(Padinenkilkanakku) Name given a collection of early Tamil works of literature, which was complete by the late fifth century C.E. All of these works have a moral emphasis and aim to inculcate ethical or religious values in the hearers. The two most famous examples in this collection are the *Tirukkural* and the *Naladiyar*.

Ekadashi

(eleventh **day**) Hindu religious life is primarily based on the lunar **calendar**, in which the **year** contains twelve **lunar months**, each of which is divided equally into "dark" (waning) and "bright" (waxing) halves. Ekadashi is the name of the eleventh day in both the waning and the waxing half of the lunar month. Certain days during each half of the lunar cycle are deemed sacred to particular gods and goddesses, and these are days for special **worship**. The ekadashi or eleventh day in each half of the lunar month is deemed sacred to the god **Vishnu**. With one exception, each of the twenty-four ekadashis has a separate name, charter myth, prescribed rites, and promised result for fulfilling it. Pious Vaishnavas observe each of these twenty-four festival days. In their order of occurrence throughout the year, the ekadashis are: **Papamochani** Ekadashi and **Kamada** Ekadashi during the lunar month of **Chaitra**, **Baruthani** Ekadashi and **Mohini** Ekadashi during the lunar month of **Baisakh**, **Achala** Ekadashi and **Nirjala** Ekadashi during the lunar month of **Jyeshth**, **Yogini** Ekadashi and **Devshayani** Ekadashi during the lunar month of **Ashadh**, **Kamika** Ekadashi and **Putrada** Ekadashi during the lunar month of **Shravan**, **Aja** Ekadashi and **Parivartini** Ekadashi during the lunar month of **Bhadrapada**, **Indira** Ekadashi and **Papankusha** Ekadashi during the lunar month of **Ashvin**, **Rambha** Ekadashi and **Devotthayan** Ekadashi during the lunar month of **Kartik**, **Utpanna** Ekadashi and **Mokshada** Ekadashi during the lunar month of **Margashirsha**, **Saphala** Ekadashi and **Putrada** Ekadashi during the lunar month of **Paush**, **Shattila** Ekadashi and **Jaya** Ekadashi during the lunar month of **Magh**, and **Vijaya** Ekadashi and **Amalaki** Ekadashi during the lunar month of **Phalgun**. Of these ekadashis, some are more important to the general populace than others, particularly Devshayani and Devotthayan Ekadashis, which mark the rainy **season** "sleep" of Vishnu during the **chaturmas** period. The only ekadashi to appear twice is Putrada ("son-giving") Ekadashi. This promises that faithful observance will bring the **birth** of a son, and its reappearance clearly points to the traditional preference for **sons** over **daughters**.

Ekalavya

In the *Mahabharata*, the later of the two great Hindu epics, Ekalavya is a figure who illustrates the pervasive reach of the **caste** system. Ekalavya is a tribal boy who wants to learn archery from **Drona**, the royal archery teacher, but is refused because of his low **birth**. Undaunted, Ekalavya makes a clay image of Drona, treats it as his teacher, or **guru**, and through assiduous practice and devotion to his guru becomes the most skilled archer on the earth. When **Arjuna**, a young warrior-king and Drona's best student, discovers this, he becomes jealous and complains to Drona, since Drona has promised Arjuna that no one will surpass him as an archer. Drona asks Ekalavya how he has become so skillful. When he learns that Ekalavya has worshiped Drona's image as his guru, Drona notes that he is entitled to a preceptor's fee (**dakshina**). As his fee he requests Ekalavya's right thumb, a gift that will considerably diminish Ekalavya's shooting abilities. Ekalavya fulfills Drona's wish

without hesitation, but from that day is no longer better than Arjuna.

Ekmukhi Rudraksha

A particular type of **rudraksha**, which is a bead made from the dried seed of the tree *Elaeocarpus ganitrus*. The rudraksha is considered sacred to the god **Shiva**, and is often strung into garlands and worn by his devotees (**bhakta**). The seed itself is typically round, with a knobby pitted surface and a natural channel in the middle through which a thread can be easily drawn. It has natural divisions running from top to bottom, which divide the seed into units known as "faces" (mukhi). The Ekmukhi Rudraksha is one in which the dividing lines running from top to bottom are completely absent, making the whole seed a single and undivided piece. Such a rudraksha is extremely rare, as well as holy, for it is believed to be a manifestation of **Shiva** himself in material form. Their rarity also makes them extremely valuable, and street sellers routinely counterfeit them by carving reproductions out of pieces of wood, often with the symbol *Om* on one side.

Eknath

(1533–1599) Poet and saint in the **Varkari Panth**, a religious community that worships the Hindu god **Vithoba**, at his temple at **Pandharpur** in the modern state of **Maharashtra**. Eknath was a **brahmin** who lived most of his life in the city of **Paithan**, which was an important trading and political center. Today, there is a shrine to Eknath in Paithan. In keeping with his birth as a brahmin, Eknath was highly learned in traditional Sanskritic lore. His best-known work is a translation into Marathi of the eleventh chapter of the **Bhagavata Purana**, a sectarian religious text that is the most important for the **worship** of the god **Krishna**. Yet Eknath also seems to have been intensely conscious of the spiritual capacities of the lower **castes** and the way in which social boundaries could be leveled by devotion. In short poems known as **bharuds** he speaks in a variety of voices, including those of untouchables, Muslims, and **women**. Traditional accounts of his life describe him as treating **untouchable** devotees (**bhakta**) as his equals, and even **eating** and drinking with them. Such flagrant transgression of social boundaries brought trouble from more orthodox brahmins—who are portrayed as the villains in these traditional accounts—but on each occasion Eknath managed to escape being outcasted by them, often through divine intervention. For further information see G. A. Deleury, *The Cult of Vithoba*, 1960; Justin E. Abbott, *The Life of Eknath*, 1981; and Eleanor Zelliot, "Chokamela and Eknath: Two Bhakti Modes of Legitimacy for Modern Change," in *Journal of Asian and African Studies*, 1980, Vol. 15, Nos. 1–2, 1980. See also **Sanskrit**.

Ekoddishta

"Intended for one [person]." A particular type of **shraddha** or memorial service for the dead, which is performed for the benefit of a single person. An ekoddishta shraddha can be performed as a series of sixteen **offerings** performed during the first **year** after the person's death. These sixteen offerings are more commonly collapsed into a single rite performed on the eleventh **day** after death, the day after the ten-day period of ritual impurity (**maranashaucha**) has come to an end.

Elements

Traditional Indian **cosmology** holds that there are five basic elements, four of which are similar to those found in medieval European conceptions: **earth**, **fire**, **water**, and **wind** (as moving air that is perceptible to human beings). The fifth element, **akasha**, has no readily understandable correlate to European ideas. It is generally translated as "**space**" and is considered to pervade the environment around us, filling the

empty spaces. An unusual feature in Indian cosmology is that each of these elements is associated with a particular sense: earth with smell, fire with sight, water with taste, wind with touch, and akasha with hearing.

Elements, Subtle

The subtle elements (**tanmatras**) are one of the stages in the **evolution** of the world and the human being in the **Samkhya** philosophical school. The subtle elements are the basis for the formation of the five gross elements: **earth**, **air**, **fire**, **wind**, and **akasha**. See **tanmatras**.

Elephant

In ancient India, one of the emblems of royalty, in part because an elephant's prodigious appetite would soon bankrupt any individual pretending to have the wealth of royalty. Elephants also appear in the Hindu pantheon: The divine elephant **Airavata** is the **animal** vehicle of **Indra**, and the god **Ganesh** has an elephant's head on a human body, a souvenir of his conflict with **Shiva**.

Elephanta

Island in the harbor outside the city of Bombay, most famous for its temple to **Shiva** by the same name. The date of the temple's construction is disputed, but is generally ascribed to the seventh or eighth century C.E. Elephanta is a rock-cut cave temple, in which the sandstone hillside was carved away to form the temple itself, and the images of the **deities**. This follows the general pattern of the rock-cut temples at **Ellora** in **Maharashtra** and required careful planning, since carving errors could not be corrected. The Elephanta shrine displays images of Shiva in his various forms: as Lord of the **Dance** (**Nataraja**), as the Lord of **Asceticism** (Yogishvara), as Bearer of the **Ganges** (Ganghadhara), as the pillar-shaped form known as the **linga**, and as the combination of male

Stone columns carved into the entrance of a cave in Ellora.

and female known as **Ardhanarishvara**. The central image, and by far the most famous, is the three-headed, eighteen-foot-tall image of Shiva as **Maheshvar**, the "great Lord." The face on the left shows his horrific and destructive facet as **Bhairava**, the face on the right his benevolent, creative facet as **Uma**, whereas the center face shows him as Tatpurusha—blissful, eternal, and transcending the ephemeral affairs of the world. Although the primary image is virtually untouched, many of the others sustained damage from Portuguese imperialists who considered the images idolatrous and used them for target practice. For further information see Pramod Chandra, *Elephanta Caves, Gharapuri*, 1970.

Ellora

Historical site in modern **Maharashtra**, about twenty miles north of Aurangabad. It is world famous for a group of thirty-three rock-cut temples, which were sculpted between the fourth and tenth centuries C.E. Twelve of the caves have Buddhist images, and these tend to be the oldest; four of the caves are Jain, and the remaining seventeen are Hindu. In each case, the caves were created by excavating into the volcanic stone outcrop of the hillside, carefully cutting away the stone to leave finished images. Several of the Hindu caves have images of exceptional artistic quality. The most famous is the eighth century **Kailasanatha** Temple for which the entire hillside was cut away, leaving the temple behind, looking as if it had been built there from the ground up.

Endogamy

In an anthropological sense, a marriage pattern in which members of a particular social group marry only members of the same group. In northern India, traditional marriages tend to be endogamous with regard to the **jati** (hereditary occupational group), and exogamous with regard to the village community and the **gotra** (mythic family lineage).

Eroticism

Although Hindu religious life is often associated with detachment and

Erotic sculptures decorate the facade of the Kandariya Mahadev Temple in Khajuraho.

renunciation, Hindu culture has also fostered considerable eroticism, which has a recognized place in everyday life. One example of this is the ***Kama Sutra***, a well-known "manual" on the art of love, which is but one example of a literary genre called ratishastra, or "treatises on [sexual] pleasure." Other examples of eroticism in the culture can be seen in the sculptures carved on the temples **Konarak** and **Khajuraho**, and in the amount of attention given to poetry on love. In Hindu culture **kama** ("desire," particularly sexual desire) is one of the purusharthas, or **aims of life**, with the others being **artha** (wealth), **dharma** (religious duty), and **moksha** (final liberation of the soul). Erotic pleasure is thus recognized as a legitimate goal, as long as it is kept in proper perspective. Although renunciation is one of the great themes in Hindu life, nonrenunciation has been stressed at least as strongly.

In modern popular Hindu culture, eroticism is expressed through the esoteric ritual tradition known as **tantra**, in which sexual union is a symbol for liberation. Sexual intercourse is sometimes incorporated as an actual element in tantric ritual, as the most notorious of the **panchamakara** or "Five Forbidden Things." Although tantric practice has strong popular associations with illicit sexuality, such acts are always performed within a strict ritual context. In tantric practice, the ultimate aim is not to satisfy one's carnal desires, but to demolish the dualism between sacred and profane that is ultimately a sign of ignorance. The act of ritualizing normally taboo behavior is one way to destroy this duality, as well as a way to emphasize the superiority of tantric practice over other forms of religious life. In such practice, the adept is also imitating **Shiva**, who is himself both the perfect **yogi** and the model husband.

Erotics, Texts on

One of the established genres in Indian literature was ratishastra, or "treatises on [sexual] pleasure," of which the best-known is the *Kama Sutra*. Sexual pleasure was seen as an established part of human life, which did not have to be hidden, and for which no excuses were necessary. **Kama** (as both "desire" and "sexual desire") was one of the purusharthas or **aims of life**. Satisfying one's desires was seen as a legitimate goal and considered a good thing, insofar as the pursuit did not interfere with other ends. The texts on erotics analyzed and classified sexuality in terms of aesthetic experience, as well as a vehicle for physical pleasure. For its sophisticated practitioners, such well-defined sexuality was intended to provide fulfillment for both partners, and here the literature is unusual for giving **women** equal desire and equal pleasure.

Error, Theories of

Indian philosophical schools give serious consideration to the questions of how and why people make errors in judgment. Although these schools may cite seemingly mundane examples, such as mistaking the silvery flash of a seashell for a piece of silver, investigating judgment errors is ultimately rooted in religious goals. Specifically, the religious goal is to gain true awareness of the actual nature of things, and through this to bring about final liberation of the soul (**moksha**) from the karmic cycle of reincarnation (**samsara**). Each school's answers to the question of truth and falsity reveal fundamental differences about the understanding each has of the inherent nature of things, which have clear implications for bondage and liberation. Although the differing schools disagree on the mechanics of "how" one sees silver instead of a shell, there is general agreement about why such a mistake takes place. This and other errors are rooted in the karmic predispositions stemming from **avidya**, most specifically the greed that prompts human beings to look for items of value. Far more explanation can be found in the individual entries, but in brief there are six major theories of error.

In the **Prabhakara** branch of the **Mimamsa** school, the theory is **akhyati** or "nondiscrimination," in which the source of error is the inability to make sharp distinctions. The theory in the **Naiyayika** school is **anyathakhyati**, the "discrimination of something else," in which the mind projects an erroneous perception (**pratyaksha**) onto another object. The Mimamsa philosopher **Kumarila** explains error as **viparitakhyati** or "contrary discrimination," in which the source of error is a bad assessment of an object's similarities and differences. The **Samkhya** school propounds the theory of **sadasatkhyati**, or "discrimination of the unreal as the real," in which the source of error is merely an extension of the original error to distinguish between the two basic realities, **purusha** and **prakrti**. **Ramanuja**, founder of the **Vishishthadvaita** Vedanta school, propounds the theory of **satkhyati**, "discrimination of the real," in which one correctly perceives the silvery flash, but makes an incorrect assumption based on this. The final theory of **anirvachaniyakhyati** or "indescribable discrimination," is advanced by the **Advaita Vedanta** school; according to this, one illusory perception is superimposed on another conventionally true but ultimately illusory perception. For further information see Bijayananda Kar, *The Theories of Error in Indian Philosophy*, 1978; and Karl H. Potter (ed.), *Presuppositions of India's Philosophies*, 1972.

Ethics
See **dharma**.

Evil Eye
See **nazar**.

Evolution
Fundamental doctrine of the **Samkhya** school of Indian **philosophy**. The Samkhya school uses a theory of evolution to explain the human perception of

an inner world of subjective experience and the objective outer world, which it argues are not true aspects of the real, or essential, world. Samkhya metaphysics posits two principles as the essence of the universe, **purusha** and **prakrti**. Purusha is pure awareness, which is conscious but inactive and unchanging. Prakrti is primal matter which, in its most basic form, is an equilibrium of three different unconscious forces (**gunas**): **sattva** (goodness), **rajas** (passion), and **tamas** (decay). According to the Samkhya, the conflation and confusion of purusha and prakrti is the basic cause for the bondage of the soul to the cycle of reincarnation (**samsara**)— where purusha is seen as if it is acting, and prakrti is seen as if it is conscious. While this misunderstanding does not effect purusha, it causes prakrti to undergo an evolutionary process, in which this primal matter becomes increasingly differentiated, leading to further confusion of the nature of the universe. The first stage of evolution is called **mahat** ("great one") and occurs when the original equilibrium between the three gunas has been disturbed; mahat is also known as **buddhi**, which is conceived as the cognitive faculty necessary for thought. The mental processes facilitated by buddhi spur the development of **ahamkar** ("I-making"), in which one finds the first feelings of ego-consciousness. With the rise of this subjective feeling comes the division into subjective and objective worlds: on one hand, ahamkar evolves the five subtle elements (**tanmatras**), the precursors of the gross **elements**, and on the other it evolves into the eleven faculties: five **jnanendriyas** or sense organs, five **karmendriyas** or organs of action, and the mind as the eleventh. At liberation this process of evolution happens in reverse, with the many successively devolving into the one. As in most Indian philosophical systems, liberation comes when correct understanding has replaced a mistaken one. For further information see Gerald Larson and Ram Shankar Bhattacharya (eds.) *Samkhya*, 1987; and Sarvepalli Radhakrishnan and Charles A. Moore (eds.), *A Sourcebook in Indian Philosophy*, 1957.

Expiation
See **prayashchitta**.

Fables
See *Panchatantra*.

Fallacies
In defining the parameters for what is and is not a valid argument, certain types of arguments have been dismissed outright by Indian logicians, since these arguments are held to be based on invalid premises. The key flaw shared by these objectionable arguments is the fallacy known as **self-residence**, in which the cause and its effect are the same thing. Varieties of this fallacy include **reciprocal dependence**, a **vicious circle**, and an **infinite regress**. The presence of any of these fallacies is sufficient grounds to dismiss an argument as invalid.

Fallacies of Inference
See **Hetvabhasa**.

Family Custom
(**kulachara**) Hindu religion is fluid enough that a family's customary practices can heavily influence a person's individual religious life. For example, family custom plays an important role in **worship**. The Hindu pantheon contains many different gods, and the one that an individual worships as "God" is often strongly influenced by the family's practice, although other factors such as personal inclination can also play a role. Family custom also plays an important role in setting parameters for religious practice, both in everyday religious life, and in setting rules for performing the rituals of the life cycle. For example,

many families have a customary age for performing the **chudakarana samskara**, the "tonsure" or head-**shaving** rite of passage that marks the definitive end of infancy. Some families perform this in the first year, others in the third, or the fifth, or even the seventh. Religious practice varies widely among families, although it tends to be very stable within families, since this is one of the ways in which families create a distinctive identity for themselves.

Family Deity
See **kuladevata**.

Family Relationships
Hindus consider the family the basis of society. The idealized Hindu family is a multigenerational joint family, composed of elderly parents, their adult **sons**, and their sons' families. The sons are considered the core of the family, since the **daughters** will live with their husbands' families after marriage and are considered to belong to them. When the families become too large, or tensions between brothers develop to an unbearable level, these joint families divide into smaller households, upon which the general pattern continues. Hindu families have different names for all possible family relationships. These differing names reveal the exact nature of the relationship and the person's precise relationship in the family—as one example, although in English the word "aunt" can designate the sister of either one's father or one's mother, there are different names for both in northern Indian languages. Some of this is related to the higher status connected with the father's or the husband's side of the family, and some of it has to do with proximity, since these relatives are more likely to be living with one another in a joint family or close by. These differences mark the lines of importance in Indian families, which give greater emphasis to the father's side. One noteworthy term is the word for the wife's

brother (**sala**), which in modern times often serves as a term of abuse.

Fani, Muhsin

(ca. mid-17th c.) Traditionally thought to be the author of the ***Dabistan-i-Mazahib*** ("School of Manners"), which was probably written about 1665. The Dabistan is an invaluable outside source for the religious life of the times and gives one of the earliest descriptions of the Sikhs, as well as many other contemporary groups. Fani was a Persian, and a Parsi by birth, who came to India because of his intense curiosity about religious life, and his desire to see whatever he could. He is believed to have been a careful observer and relatively objective. He states that he had simply translated (into the Persian in which the text was written) what his friends and informants had told him, and the text seems to support this claim.

Faqir

(variant of *fakir*, from the Arabic *poor*) In the strictest sense of the word, this refers to a Muslim **ascetic**, as is hinted by the Arabic origin of the word. Colloquially, the word has been used much more broadly, as an appellation for any ascetic (witness Winston Churchill's characterization of **Mohandas Gandhi** as a "half-naked faqir"). Both usages are still current in modern India. Although since the partition of India in 1947 the word more commonly designates a Muslim, Hindu ascetics still describe someone who is detached from all things and dependent on God for support as a "faqir **baba**."

Fasting

See **upavasa**.

Fatalism

Philosophical position attributed to the **Ajivika** school. The Ajivikas believed that all things were preordained by an impersonal destiny (**niyati**), and therefore that one's conscious actions had no effect on one's future. Although this position would seem to undercut any reason for religious practice, the Ajivikas were also noted for performing strict **asceticism**, in the belief that they were only doing what had been predetermined for them. For further information see Arthur Llewellyn Basham, *History and Doctrines of the Ajivikas*, 1981.

Fathers, World of the

The earliest reference to the transmigration of souls, which is found in both the **Brhadaranyaka Upanishad** (6.2) and the **Chandogya Upanishad** (5.10), makes a qualitative distinction between two different paths for the soul. The path to the **world of the gods** ultimately led to the **sun**, and the person traveling it did not return again; the path to the world of the fathers led to the **moon**, and the person traveling it was eventually reborn on **earth**. The leitmotiv running through all the **Upanishads** is the need for individual spiritual realization, and this is the key to getting on the path to the world of the gods. Those who gain such realization attain the final and ultimate end, whereas those who simply do good deeds will return to earth, although their good deeds will give them karmic benefits.

Festival Calendar

Since few festivals are celebrated by all Hindus, establishing a single festival calendar is problematic. Festival celebrations are subject to the same differing forces that drive the rest of Hindu life. On one hand, there are significant regional differences in the celebration of festivals, and on the other there are major sectarian variations. Some of the sectarian festivals may be celebrated within particular regions or they may be celebrated across the nation. It is also true that the general public is aware of most festivals—by virtue of these days being public holidays, or being marked on the calendar—but far fewer people celebrate any particular festival as a religious holiday. Finally, some holidays are so significant that they are celebrated by almost everyone, although here too some people will observe them with far greater energy. For example, although the **Goddess** festival known as the fall **Navaratri** is celebrated throughout the country, it is kept with particular gusto in Bengal, where the cult of the Mother Goddess is particularly important.

With these considerations in mind, the festival calendar for the lunar **year** is given below, with the holidays given in order during the successive **lunar months**. The purpose in this entry is only to lay out the order of these festivals during the year; further details for the lunar months and each festival can be found in the individual entries.

- **Chaitra** (March–April)
  Papamochani Ekadashi, Spring Navaratri, **Ram Navami, Kamada Ekadashi, Hanuman Jayanti, Chittirai.**

- **Baisakh** (April–May)
  Shitalashtami, Baruthani Ekadashi, Akshaya Trtiya, Parashuram Jayanti, Narsingh Jayanti, Baisakhi, Mohini Ekadashi, Buddha Purnima.

- **Jyeshth** (May–June)
  Achala Ekadashi, Savitri Puja, Ganga Dashahara, Nirjala Ekadashi.

- **Ashadh** (June–July)
  Yogini Ekadashi, Rath Yatra, Devshayani Ekadashi, Guru Purnima, Chaturmas Vrat.

- **Shravan** (July–August)
  Nag Panchami, Kamika Ekadashi, Tulsidas Jayanti, Putrada Ekadashi, Raksha Bandhan, Shravan Vrat.

- **Bhadrapada** (August–September)
  Kajari Teej (**Teej**), **Bahula Chauth, Janmashtami, Radhashtami, Aja Ekadashi**, Hartalika Teej (Teej), **Ganesh Chaturthi, Rishi Panchami,** **Onam, Parivartini Ekadashi, Anant Chaturdashi.**

- **Ashvin** (September–October)
  Pitrpaksha, Indira Ekadashi, Fall Navaratri, **Dussehra** (Vijaya Dashami), **Papankusha Ekadashi, Valmiki Jayanti.**

- **Kartik** (October–November)
  Karva Chauth, Rambha Ekadashi, Narak Chaturdashi, Diwali, Govardhan Puja (Annakut), **Devotthayan Ekadashi, Tulsi Vivah, Kartik Purnima.**

- **Margashirsha** (November–December)
  Bhairava Jayanti, Utpanna Ekadashi, Mokshada Ekadashi.

- **Paush** (December–January)
  Saphala Ekadashi, Putrada Ekadashi.

- **Magh** (January–February)
  Sakata Chauth, Shattila Ekadashi, Mauni Amavasya, Vasant Panchami, Bhishma Ashtami, Jaya Ekadashi, Ravidas Jayanti, Pongal, Magh Mela, Float Festival.

- **Phalgun** (February–March)
  Janaki Navami, Vijaya Ekadashi, Shivaratri, Amalaki Ekadashi, Holi.

The festival calendar is further complicated by the fact that the lunar year begins on the first **day** of the bright (waxing) half of the lunar month of Chaitra. This creates an unusual situation since, at least in northern India, the lunar months end on the **full moon**, making the two weeks of the waning moon the first half of the lunar month. The waning fortnight in Chaitra comes at the end of the lunar year, and the waxing fortnight that follows is the first fortnight of the following year. Thus, the month of Chaitra is both the first and the last month of the lunar year.

Depiction of the god Vishnu's Fish avatar.
Vishnu takes this form to protect living
creatures from floods that engulf the earth.

Feticide

This refers to selective **abortion** of female fetuses, which was made possible by the advent of reliable prenatal sex determination technology. This practice is driven by the desire for **sons** in Hindu culture, a desire spurred by economic, social, and religious concerns. Selective abortions were outlawed in India in 1995.

Fiji

One of the countries with significant Hindu **diaspora populations**. Indians were first brought to Fiji in 1879 as indentured laborers to work in the sugarcane fields. In the 1990s Indians comprised about 45 percent of Fiji's population. Despite their near parity in terms of population, Indians in Fiji have been legally relegated to a **minority** role and for the most part have been prohibited from owning land. The split between the Indian and Fijian communities became transparent in 1987, when

a military coup ousted a Parliament dominated by Indians, and installed a native Fijian as prime minister. Because of these restrictions, many Indians still work as tenant farmers for Fijian landlords, but they also play an important role as shopkeepers and professionals.

Fire

One of the five **elements** in traditional Indian **cosmology**, the others being **earth**, **wind**, **water**, and **akasha**. In some philosophical schools, each of the elements is paired with one of the five senses. Fire is associated with sight, since the eye's action in apprehending a visual object is compared to flame darting out and scorching something. Within the body, fire is also associated with digestion, which is generally conceived of as "cooking" the foods in the digestive system.

Fish Avatar

The first of **Vishnu's** ten full **avatars** or "incarnations" on **earth**. Each avatar appears when the cosmos is in crisis, usually because of a **demon** (asura) who has grown disproportionately strong, and whose power is throwing the universe out of its natural balance. According to the doctrine of the avatars, Vishnu takes material form when the earth has fallen out of equilibrium, to destroy the source of evil and restore the cosmic balance.

The tale of the fish avatar begins in the distant past, when the righteous king **Manu** discovers a small fish in the **water** he holds between his cupped hands as he performs the **tarpana** or water-**offering** rite for his ancestors. The compassionate king puts the tiny fish into a pot of water, but the fish soon outgrows it. As the fish keeps growing, Manu transfers it to larger and larger vessels, and finally puts the fish into the **Ganges**. When the fish grows too large for the Ganges and has to be put into the ocean, Manu realizes that the fish is

Vishnu himself, and begins to sing Vishnu's praises.

The fish then informs Manu that the destruction of the world is imminent—first through blazing fire that will scorch all life, then through floods that will turn the entire earth into a single cosmic sea. Vishnu informs Manu that the gods have built a boat from the **Vedas**, and directs Manu to collect all the creatures of the earth and put them on the boat for safekeeping. He promises Manu that all the creatures on this boat will survive the coming destruction, and when the world returns to normal with the advent of the **Krta Age**, Manu will be the ruler of the earth.

Manu does as he has been directed, and when the destruction of the world is imminent, Vishnu appears in the form of a great horned fish. Manu ties the boat to the fish's horn and, protected by Vishnu's power, all the beings on the boat survive to repopulate the earth.

Five Forbidden Things
See **panchamakara**.

Float Festival
Festival celebrated in the city of **Madurai** in the southern Indian state of **Tamil Nadu**, on the **full moon** in the **lunar month** of **Magh** (January–February). This is the birthday of King **Tirumalai Nayak** (r. 1623–1659), during whose reign large parts of Madurai's **Minakshi** Temple was built. During the festival the **goddess** Minakshi and her consort Sundareshvara (an epithet of **Shiva**) are taken in procession to an artificial lake east of Madurai, where they are put on richly decorated floats and drawn back and forth over the lake's waters.

Flood, Legend of
See **Fish avatar**.

Four Dhams
("[divine] abodes") Four major pilgrimage sites in the four geographical corners of India, which lay out the boundaries of India's sacred geography: **Badrinath** in the **Himalayas**; the city of **Puri** in the east, on the Bay of Bengal; **Rameshvaram** in the south; and **Dwaraka** in the west. Each site is associated with one of the four **Sanyasi maths** all supposedly founded by the great philosopher **Shankaracharya**: Badrinath has the **Jyotir math** in the town of **Joshimath** (about thirty-five miles south of Badrinath), Puri has the **Govardhan math**, Dwaraka has the **Sharada math**, and Rameshvaram has the **Shringeri math** (in Shringeri). The first three of these maths are close to their associated sacred sites (**tirthas**), but Shringeri is about 450 miles away from Rameshvaram.

Four Great Crimes
In the **dharma literature**, four actions are deemed such heinous offenses that the person performing them becomes an outcast from society. These four actions are murdering a **brahmin** (**brahmahatya**), stealing a brahmin's gold (**steya**), drinking **liquor** (**surapana**), and **adultery** with the wife of one's **guru** (**gurutalpaga**). Aside from expulsion from society, another indication of the gravity of these acts was that their penalties were so severe that they normally ended in death, and in some cases this outcome was specifically prescribed. In addition to prescribing such punishments for the actual offenders, the dharma literature also prescribed expulsion for anyone who knowingly associated with such people for a period longer than one **year**.

Four States of Consciousness
A hierarchy of states of experience that is first outlined in the **Mandukya Upanishad**. In its description, the upanishad moves from greatest duality to utter nonduality; these four states are

229

also correlated with the phonetic elements of the sacred sound *Om*. *Om* symbolizes the four states of consciousness and is the sum and quintessence of them all. The first stage of consciousness is waking consciousness, in which one perceives both subject and object; then dreaming, in which one's experience is totally subjective; then deep sleep, in which (until waking) even consciousness of oneself as subject has been lost. The final state is so removed from human experience that it cannot be designated by language, and so is simply called "the fourth" (**turiya**). In the Mandukya Upanishad, this fourth state is clearly identified as the ultimate truth, the **atman** or inner Self, knowledge of which brings final liberation of the soul.

Friday

(Shukravar) The fifth **day** of the Hindu **week**, whose presiding **planet** is **Venus** (**Shukra**). Friday is also the day of the week dedicated to the **Goddess** and is thus potentially a powerfully auspicious day. Although the Goddess can be worshiped in many forms, one of the most popular in northern India is **Santoshi Ma**. **Worship** of Santoshi Ma has spread dramatically since its origin in the mid-1970s.

Full Moon

(Purnimasa or Purnima) In northern India, the full moon is the final **day** of the **lunar month**, whereas in southern India it is often considered the midpoint. In either case, the full moon carries associations of fullness, completion, and abundance and is always an auspicious time. One sign of its **auspiciousness** is the commonly accepted belief that the religious merit generated from rites performed on the day of a full moon is equal to rites performed for an entire month. There are festivals associated with the full moon of each lunar month, but the most important are in **Baisakh** (**Buddha Purnima**), **Ashadh** (**Guru Purnima**), **Shravan** (**Raksha Bandhan**), **Kartik** (**Kartik Purnima**), and **Phalgun** (**Holi**).

Funerary Rites

See **deathbed rites**, **antyeshthi samskara**, and **shraddha**.

G

Gada

("club") In Hindu iconography, one of the identifying objects carried by the god **Vishnu**, along with the conch shell (**shankha**), lotus (**padma**), and discus (**chakra**). In the *Mahabharata*, the later of the two great Hindu epics, the gada is also the weapon of choice for **Bhima**, one of the five **Pandava** brothers who are the epic's protagonists. Of these five brothers, Bhima is noted for his prodigious size and strength, which gives him obvious advantages in wielding the gada.

Gadge Maharaj

(1876–1956) Modern **ascetic** teacher and religious preceptor in the **Varkari Panth**, a religious community centered around the **worship** of the Hindu god **Vithoba** at his temple at **Pandharpur** in the modern state of **Maharashtra**. Gadge Maharaj got his name from the clay pot (gadge) that was his only **possession**, signifying his rejection of all wealth and worldly entanglements. Gadge had been born into a **caste** of washermen, who are considered a low status group since their everyday work brings them in contact with other people's soiled garments. In his teachings, Gadge not only stresses the importance of devotion to God—the hallmark of the **bhakti** (devotional) movement—but also advocates temperance, poverty, and **vegetarianism**.

Gahadavala Dynasty

(r. 1089–1194) Northern Indian dynasty whose core region was the western and central parts of the Gangetic plain. The Gahadavalas were a short-lived and transitional dynasty who filled a political vacuum during the tumultuous years following the turn of the first millennium. During this period the Gangetic plain was plagued by political instability and was regularly subjected to Muslim raids. The Gahadavalas supplanted the **Rashtrakutas**, whom they conquered in 1089, and consolidated their power through the middle **Ganges** basin. In 1194 the Gahadavalas were defeated by the Ghurids, an Afghani Muslim dynasty. Following their defeat, most of the Gahadavala territory became part of the Ghurid empire.

Gaja Hasta

A particular hand **gesture** (**hasta**) used in Indian **dance**, **sculpture**, and ritual. In the gaja ("elephant") hasta, the arm is extended straight out, with the hand gently curving down; the curved arm is fancifully compared to the trunk of an **elephant**.

Gajendramoksha

("release of the **elephant**-king") The name of a particular incident in Hindu mythology involving a battle between king **Indradyumna**, in the form of a giant elephant, and a **Gandharva** (celestial musician) named **Huhu**, in the form of a giant crocodile. Both Indradyumna and Huhu have assumed these forms as the result of a **curse**. Indradyumna has been cursed by the sage **Agastya**, who becomes angry when the meditating king fails to greet him with proper respect. Huhu has been cursed by the sage Devala, when the amorous **water** play between Huhu and some celestial damsels has disturbed the sage's meditation.

The struggle between the two **animals** begins when the elephant comes to the water to drink and the crocodile grabs him by the leg. The crocodile attempts to pull the elephant into deeper water while the elephant struggles to break free. The pair are so evenly matched that neither can best the other. After the battle has raged for a thousand years the god **Vishnu** appears, kills the crocodile, and restores Indradyumna to his previous form. The story thus takes its name, the "release of the elephant king," because Indradyumna was freed from the crocodile's grasp and the effects of the curse.

Galta

A village in the state of **Rajasthan**, a few miles east of Jaipur, the capital. Galta is most famous for its connection with the **Bairagi Naga** ascetics, renunciant trader-soldiers who were devotees (**bhakta**) of the god **Vishnu**. According to Bairagi tradition, in 1756 a conference took place at Galta in which the different groups of Bairagi Naga ascetics were welded into one cohesive military unit called the **Ramanadis** or "army of Ram" under the leadership of a Bairagi named Balanand. Balanand organized the Ramanandis into three **anis** or armies—the **Digambara** Ani, **Nirvani Ani**, and **Nirmohi Ani**—which are still the major Bairagi divisions. According to tradition, this unification was necessary because of continual attacks by the Naga class of the **Dashanami Sanyasis**, a competing group of renunciant trader-soldiers who were devotees of the god **Shiva**. The dispute occurred during the festival **Kumbha Mela**, ostensibly over precedence in the bathing (**snana**) procession, which was a sign of relative status. However, an underlying cause may have been power and control of an area's resources.

The exact circumstances under which the armies of Ram were formed are difficult to determine. Independent sources clearly show that the Bairagis became more cohesively organized during the late eighteenth century and that some of these bairagi bands were using their mobility, resources, and power to engage in long-distance trading. However, the decentralized nature of **ascetic** life makes the summary formation of such an army highly unlikely, unless this was the final fruition of an already existing trend.

Gambling

A practice with a long history in Indian culture, but that has almost always been portrayed in a negative light by Hindu texts. The earliest reference appears in the **Rg Veda**, the oldest Hindu religious text, in a hymn often described as "The Gambler's Lament." The hymn is a gambler's first-person account of the ways in which his obsession with gaming ruined his life. It ends with a warning to the listener not to be seduced by gambling's siren song. Gambling is also negatively portrayed in the *Mahabharata*, the later of the two great Hindu epics. A passion for gaming is the only fault afflicting **Yudhishthira** (the eldest of the five **Pandava** brothers who are the epic's protagonists), but it brings disastrous results. In a dice game with the kingdom's most skillful player, **Shakuni**, Yudhishthira loses his kingdom, his brothers, and even himself; as a result of the game, he and his brothers have to go into exile.

These mythic models mirror the attitudes toward gambling in Hindu society. Sober and upright Hindus have generally avoided games of chance, since they are not a stable or respectable way to risk one's capital or earn a living. The only time that prudence and caution can be legitimately disregarded is on the festival of **Diwali**, which is sacred to **Lakshmi**, the **goddess** of wealth and prosperity. Gambling is a traditional part of the Diwali celebrations, used to pay homage to Lakshmi in her guise as Lady Luck. Diwali is most often celebrated in people's homes, and thus any gambling will take place with one's family and close associates, and with purely nominal betting. Aside from Diwali, gambling is strictly proscribed in polite society, and even on Diwali its disruptive capacities are strictly contained.

Gana

("host") In Hindu mythology, a collective term for a group of minor gods who are the god **Shiva's** servants and attendants. The members of this gana are often represented in frightening forms—smeared with ash, bearing skulls and weapons, physically malformed, and grinning and laughing horribly. The members of the gana are Shiva's followers, supporters, and minions, who are ready to do his bidding when commanded. The leader of the gana is the god **Ganesh** ("Lord of the Host").

Ganapati

("Master of [**Shiva's**] host") Another name for the god **Ganesh**. See **Ganesh**.

Gandaki River

One of the tributaries of the **Ganges**, it flows southward from **Nepal**, joining the Ganges at the city of Patna in the state of **Bihar**. Although the river's source is now extremely poor, in the time of the Buddha it contained major urban centers, particularly the city of **Vaishali**.

Gandhari

A character in the *Mahabharata*, the later of the two great Hindu epics. Gandhari is the wife of the blind king **Dhrtarashtra** and the mother of the **Kauravas**, a group of boys who are the epic's antagonists. Gandhari shows her devotion to her blind husband by always covering her eyes with a blindfold, thus sharing his sightlessness. As is often the case in Hindu mythology, her **sons** are born in an unusual manner. Gandhari receives a blessing (**ashirvad**) from the sage **Vyasa** that she will give **birth** to one hundred sons. Soon after, she becomes pregnant. However, her pregnancy lasts for more than two years. When she grows impatient and tries to hasten the delivery, she gives birth to a great lump of flesh. Vyasa advises Gandhari to divide the lump and place each piece in a pot of clarified butter (ghee). Eventually the pots break open, revealing one hundred handsome boys and a single **daughter**, Dussala.

All of Gandhari's children are killed by her nephews the Pandavas in the Mahabharata war. Just as Gandhari is about to **curse** the Pandavas, Vyasa reminds her that her sons' deaths are the result of their own misconduct. After the war, Gandhari retires to the forest with her husband and a few others. They live in retirement for six years before they are killed in a forest **fire**.

Gandharva

In Hindu mythology, a class of demigods who are celestial singers and musicians. The gandharvas occasionally interact with humans. One of their divine gifts is the ability to bestow good singing voices to girls. Since the Gandharvas are always watching from above, they are considered to be the witnesses in a Gandharva marriage, one of the eight forms of marriage recognized in the **dharma literature**. The gandharva marriage was a marriage contracted by consensual sexual intercourse. See also **Marriage, eight classical forms**.

Gandharva Marriage

One of the eight forms of marriage recognized in the **dharma literature**, the treatises on religious duty. A **Gandharva** marriage takes place when a man and woman have sexual intercourse by mutual consent, but without consulting anyone else. The marriage is so named because gandharvas, who are demigods and celestial musicians, are said to be the witnesses. Although the gandharva rite created a valid marriage, it was considered one of the four reprehensible (**aprashasta**) forms of marriage because it was done without parental consent, performed without religious rituals, and was rooted in lust. These marriages were recognized not to sanction and legitimize promiscuous behavior, but to provide the woman with the legal status of a wife. Although **Sanskrit** literary sources are replete with Gandharva marriages—perhaps the most famous being the marriage of King **Dushyanta** and **Shakuntala**—it is doubtful that this form was ever widely practiced. See also **marriage, eight classical forms**.

Gandhi, Mohandas K.

(1869–1948) Leader of the Indian National Congress, one of the architects of the struggle for Indian independence, and one of the best-known Indians in history. Gandhi was born in **Gujarat**, where his father was a minister to one of the native princes. Shortly after Gandhi's father died, the British ousted the ruling prince for mismanagement, and the family lost their position. Gandhi was sent to London to study law, and during this time he came into contact with a variety of new ideas that would strongly influence his future. Ironically, one of these influences was the **Bhagavad Gita**, an important Hindu religious text from which he drew continuing inspiration in his later life. After returning to India in 1891, Gandhi failed in his attempt to set up a law practice in Bombay, and he went back to Gujarat. In 1894 Gandhi traveled to **South Africa** to do some work for a Muslim trading firm. He intended to be gone only a short time, but ended up staying in South Africa for twenty years. During this time he discovered his true calling, political activism. This was sparked by his own experience of racial discrimination—being thrown out of a railway car reserved for "whites only"—and was fueled by the social, political, and legal disadvantages suffered by South Africa's 40,000 Indians, most of whom were illiterate agricultural workers. During his time in South Africa, Gandhi developed and refined his basic tactics: mass noncooperation, nonviolent resistance, willingness to face imprisonment, and skillful use of the print media to influence public opinion. In 1914 he returned to India, where he soon became one of the leading figures in the struggle against the British—first for home rule, and finally for outright independence.

Gandhi's deeply held moral principles shaped his entire career. He saw his political activism not as a vehicle for personal advancement, but as a means for selfless action for the welfare of the world. This stress on selfless action drew heavily on the message of the Bhagavad Gita, in which the god **Krishna** recommends a similar path to his friend and devotee (**bhakta**), **Arjuna**. Throughout his life Gandhi remained committed to nonviolence. Gandhi felt strongly that the nature of any goal would be influenced by the means by which it had been attained. Another of his fundamental principles was truth, as seen in his insistence that evil and injustice had to be resisted, even by violence when all other means had failed. A third essential tenet was self-control, which he considered the prerequisite to leading others. His commitment to his principles gave him the strength to endure imprisonment, injury, and more than thirty years of struggle with the British government; it also moved him to campaign against many other injustices, particularly the notion of untouchability.

When independence finally arrived in 1947 it was tainted by the partition of British India into India and Pakistan, fueled in part by Muslim concerns about their **minority** status in an independent Hindu India. The partition sparked a massive exodus, in which fifteen million people migrated from one country to the other. It also sparked unspeakable communal violence, in which an estimated one million people died. Despite his best efforts, Gandhi was unable to prevent partition or to create good relations between the two countries. Within six months of independence, Gandhi was assassinated by **Nathuram Godse**, a Hindu nationalist who felt that Gandhi was being too soft on Pakistan.

Gandhi had critics and opponents throughout his career, many of whom felt that he did not deserve the sainthood that people attributed to him.

Mohandas K. Gandhi in 1931.

A sculpture of the god Ganesh from the village of Khajuraho. As "Lord of Obstacles," Ganesh has the power to remove or bestow difficulties.

Among his critics were **B. R. Ambedkar**, who felt that Gandhi had used the untouchables as pawns in negotiations with the British because he opposed letting the untouchables separate from the larger body politic. His critics also included **Subhash Chandra Bose**, who advocated an armed struggle against the British, and **Vinayak Damodar Savarkar**, a Hindu nationalist who was Godse's inspiration. For further information see Mohandas K. Gandhi, *An Autobiography*, 1993; Louis Fischer, *Gandhi*, 1954; Mark Juergensmeyer, "Saint Gandhi," in John Stratton Hawley (ed.), *Saints and Virtues*, 1987; and Sudhir Kakar, "Gandhi and Women," in *Intimate Relations*, 1990.

Gandhi Jayanti

Indian national holiday falling on October 2, celebrating the **birth** of **Mohandas Gandhi**. Perhaps because Gandhi is a relatively recent figure, or because the event is a national holiday, this celebration is one of the few that is marked according to the common era **calendar**, rather than the lunar calendar that is used to determine most Hindu festivals.

Gandiva

In the *Mahabharata*, the later of the two great Hindu epics, Gandiva is the name of the bow carried by **Arjuna**. Arjuna is the world's greatest archer and the third of the five **Pandava** brothers, the *Mahabharata*'s protagonists. Gandiva was originally fashioned by the god **Brahma** and is given to Arjuna by the god **Varuna** (identified with the ocean) at the request of another **deity**, **Agni** ("**fire**"). Agni makes this request because he wants to "eat" (burn) the **Khandava forest**, but is afraid of interference in the form of rain from the god **Indra**, ruler of the storm. Arjuna uses the bow to create a canopy of arrows that shields the forest from Indra's storms, thus allowing Agni to consume the forest in peace. Arjuna uses this bow for many years. At the end of his life he returns it to Varuna by throwing it into the sea.

Ganesh

("Lord of [**Shiva's**] Host") **Elephant**-headed god who leads Shiva's horde of divine followers; another name for Ganesh is Ganapati. Ganesh is usually portrayed as short and fat, with a bowl of sweets and his **animal** vehicle, the **rat**, close by. Among the items most often portrayed in his hands are a lotus (padma) and his own broken tusk. He also often holds a noose and an elephant goad (**ankusha**), which symbolize his power to restrain or move obstructing forces.

Although Ganesh is worshiped as a primary **deity** by a small sectarian community, the **Ganpatyas**, most Hindus **worship** him as a subsidiary deity along with their principal divinities. Ganesh's importance in Hindu life, however, is far greater than his relatively minor place in the pantheon. Hindus consider Ganesh as "Lord of Obstacles" (Vighneshvar), who has the power both to remove and to bestow difficulties, depending on whether or not a person has pleased him. Hindus invoke Ganesh at the start of any important undertaking—whether it is performing a religious ritual, starting a business, performing a marriage, building a home, or even taking a school examination—so that through his **grace**, potential obstacles may be removed or avoided and the undertaking will proceed smoothly and successfully. This power over obstacles is symbolized both by his elephant head and his animal vehicle, the rat. The elephant's strength allows it to break down any impediments, while the rat is able to slip through the smallest cracks to gain access to locked places. Ganesh's **aniconic image** is the threshold, the transitional strip dividing and separating different spaces, which further symbolizes his power to control transitions from one state to another.

Ganesh is considered to be the **son** of the god **Shiva** and his wife **Parvati**, but he is born in an unusual manner. One day when Parvati is bathing (**snana**), she forms a child from the dirt from her body, animates him, and directs him to permit no one to enter her bathing place. When Shiva comes to the door Ganesh bars his way, and in the ensuing battle Shiva cuts off Ganesh's head. Parvati is so upset that Shiva promises to replace the missing head with the head of the first animal he encounters, which happens to be an elephant. Upon reviving Ganesh, Shiva appoints him as the leader of his troop of followers. As a further boon, Shiva tells Ganesh that he will be worshiped before any other deity.

Ganesh's elephant head has a broken tusk, and there are differing myths recounting how this happened. In one story it comes from an altercation with the **Parashuram avatar**, who tries to enter Shiva's chambers while Ganesh is guarding the door. According to another account, the injury is self-inflicted. In a fit of rage at the **moon**, Ganesh breaks off his tusk and throws it at the moon. According to tradition, Ganesh uses this tusk as a pen to write down the text of the epic ***Mahabharata*** as it is dictated by the sage **Vyasa**. For further information on Ganesh and his cult, see Paul Courtright, *Ganesa*, 1985; other information can be found in works on Hindu mythology.

Ganesh Chaturthi

Festival falling on the fourth (chaturthi) **day** of the bright or waxing half of the **lunar month** of **Bhadrapada** (August–September), dedicated to the **worship** of the god **Ganesh**. This festival is observed throughout India, but is particularly celebrated in **Maharashtra**. During this festival clay images of Ganesh are consecrated and worshiped. At the festival's end the images are carried in procession for ceremonial immersion in bodies of **water**—whether the sea, a river, or the village pond.

Although Ganesh is a relatively minor **deity** in the Hindu pantheon, his role as the Lord of Obstacles (Vighneshvar) makes him important in everyday life, since his involvement can either further or hinder one's efforts. For this reason, Ganesh is always worshiped at the start of any endeavor and at the beginning of all religious ceremonies. While Ganesh plays an important role in people's everyday lives, the festival Ganesh Chaturthi gained prominence in Maharashtra for political reasons. **Bal Gangadhar Tilak**, one of the most important figures in the nineteenth-century Hindu renaissance, promoted the celebration of Ganesh Chaturthi as a visible way to assert and celebrate a Hindu nationalist identity during the time of British imperial rule. Given the power of British rule, outright rebellion was simply impossible, and the British government heavily restricted all forms of political dissent. The Ganesh festival provided a way to circumvent these restrictions, since the British had a long-standing policy of not interfering with religious observances. The celebration of this festival in Maharashtra, particularly the processions to immerse the images in the sea, became an important theater to demonstrate and affirm Hindu cultural and political identity.

Ganga

In Hindu mythology, the **goddess** whose material form is the **Ganges** River. The Ganges is sacred because the river is considered to be a goddess who has the power to take away the sins of those who bathe (**snana**) in her. There are numerous legends to explain her origin. The best-known is the tale of King **Bhagirath**, who by his **ascetic** practice succeeds in bringing the Ganges down from **heaven** to **earth**. Bhagirath is the great-great-grandson of King **Sagar**, whose 60,000 **sons** had been burned to ash by the sage **Kapila's magic** power after they had erroneously accused Kapila of being a thief. Kapila later tells **Anshuman**, King Sagar's grandson and sole surviving descendant, that the only way to bring peace to the souls of Sagar's sons is to bring the Ganges down from heaven to earth. Anshuman strives unsuccessfully to do this, as does his son **Dilip** after him. Dilip's son Bhagirath takes their efforts to heart and retires to the **Himalayas**, where he performs **asceticism** until the gods finally agree to send the Ganges down to earth. Yet Bhagiratha's efforts are not yet over. Next, he has to gain the favor of the god **Shiva**, so that Shiva will agree to take the shock of the falling river on his head. Otherwise, its force will destroy the earth. When all is finally in place, the Ganges falls to earth onto the head of Shiva. Bhagirath leads Ganga out of the mountains to the sea, where she touches his ancestors' ashes and they finally find peace. This myth highlights both the salvific touch of the Ganga and her intimate association with the last rites (**antyeshthi samskara**) for the dead.

According to another story, the Ganges comes down to earth because of a curse pronounced during a family quarrel between **Vishnu** and his wives Ganga, **Lakshmi**, and **Saraswati**. When one day Ganga and Vishnu begin exchanging lustful glances in public, Saraswati gets angry and begins to beat Ganga. As Lakshmi tries to stop her, Saraswati let loose a string of **curses**: that Vishnu will be born as a stone (the **shalagram**), that Lakshmi will be born as a plant (the **tulsi** plant), and that Ganga will be born as a river and take the sins of the world on her. In the struggle, Saraswati is cursed to become a river. Vishnu sweetens Ganga's curse by telling her that she will be considered very holy on earth and have the power to remove people's sins. Vishnu also tells her that she will fall from heaven onto the head of the god **Shiva** and become his consort.

Ganga Dashahara

Festival celebrated on the tenth **day** of the bright or waxing half of the **lunar month** of **Jyeshth** (May–June), which marks the day that the **goddess Ganga** is believed to have descended from **heaven** to **earth** to become the **Ganges** River. The primary religious rite performed on this day is bathing (**snana**) in sacred rivers, particularly the Ganges.

Ganga Dynasty

(11th–15th c.) Eastern Indian dynasty that ruled the coastal strip on the Bay of Bengal in the modern states of **Orissa** and **Andhra Pradesh**. Although the Ganga dynasty was never more than a regional power, it left an artistic legacy in a series of stunning temples in modern Orissa. The Ganga dynasty was responsible for the temple to the god **Jagannath** in the city of **Puri** and the **Sun Temple** at **Konarak**, built by king Narasimhadeva (r. 1238–1264). The dynasty also built temples scattered throughout the modern city of **Bhubaneshvar**, including the temple to the god **Shiva** as Tribhuvaneshvar, "the Lord of the Triple World," from which the city takes its name.

Street fair in Ganga Sagar.

Gangaikondacholapuran

Temple town in the eastern part of **Tamil Nadu**, about forty-five miles north and east of the city of **Tanjore**. This was one of the temples in the Tanjore region built by the Chola kings during their era of preeminence between the ninth and thirteenth centuries. The temple at Gangaikondacholapuran was built in 1025 by King **Rajendra I** (r. 1014–1042) to commemorate his march to the **Ganges** in 1023 after vanquishing the king of Bengal. One of the images outside the temple door shows the kneeling Rajendra being garlanded by the god **Shiva** and his wife **Parvati**, doubtless intended to give Rajendra divine support for his entitlement to rule. See also **Chola dynasty**.

Ganga Sagar

Sacred site (**tirtha**) on **Sagar** Island, which is located at the outer edge of the Hugli River delta in the Bay of Bengal. Ganga Sagar is where the **Ganges** River merges with the sea (sagar). As with all the places where the Ganges makes some natural transition, this spot is considered especially holy. Ganga Sagar's biggest festival comes on **Makara Sankranti**, the **day** in January when the sun resumes its northward course. On this day, hundreds of thousands of pilgrims come to bathe (**snana**). The site is also famous for a temple to the irascible sage **Kapila**, whose fiery power incinerates the 60,000 **sons** of King Sagar and sets in motion a series of events leading to King **Bhagirath** bringing the Ganges down to **earth**.

Ganges

Northern Indian river that has its source in various small rivers in the Himalaya Mountains. It comes onto the northern Indian plain at the city of **Haridwar**, flows east across the state of **Uttar Pradesh** to the city of **Allahabad**, where it unites with the **Yamuna River**, and then flows east through the states of **Bihar** and **West Bengal** before joining the sea at **Ganga Sagar**. At 1,560 miles in length, the Ganges is shorter than many other major rivers, but for Hindus no river carries greater religious significance. To pious Hindus the Ganges is not merely a river, but the **goddess Ganga** come down from **heaven**, and by whose touch they are purified of all sin and defilement. For the Ganges no superlatives are spared—every drop is sacred, every inch along its banks is

Temple in Gangotri. Located in the Himalayas,
Gangotri is traditionally considered the source of the Ganges River.

holy, and one gains great religious merit by seeing it, drinking from it, touching it, or merely by thinking about it. It is also considered the best place to perform certain rites for the dead.

Hindu devotion to and reverence for the Ganges has established it as a place of unique importance. The religious importance of the Ganges is reflected in the religious practices connected with it and the many well-known pilgrimage places (**tirtha**) that are found on its banks, particularly the city of **Benares**. The Ganges is considered the paradigm for the sacred river. Other Indian sacred rivers, such as the **Godavari** and the **Cauvery**, are claimed to "be" the Ganges—that is, one can gain the same religious benefits from bathing (**snana**) in them that one gains by bathing in the Ganges.

Gangotri

Sacred site (**tirtha**) in the **Himalayas** at the headwaters of the **Bhagirathi** River, one of the Himalayan tributaries of the **Ganges**. Ritually speaking, Gangotri is considered to be the source of the Ganges, although the river's actual source is the glacier at **Gaumukh**, another twelve miles upstream. Its high altitude also means that it is only accessible between late April and October, after which it is closed for the winter months. One ritual center in Gangotri is the river itself, in which pilgrims bathe (**snana**), braving the frigid waters. The other center is the temple to the **goddess Ganga**, first built about 250 years ago by the Gurkha monarch Amar Singh Thapa and restored in the late nineteenth century by the royal house of Jaipur. By the side of the river is a large stone slab, on which the sage **Bhagirath** is said to have performed his austerities to bring the Ganges down to **earth**. As with all the places where the Ganges makes some transition, Gangotri is considered particularly holy. Its sanctity is amplified because it is difficult to get to and is only accessible during the summer months.

Ganika

("harlot") In Hindu mythology, a figure who serves as an example of the boundless power of God's **grace** and the ease with which one can be saved by even unconscious devotion. Ganika is a notorious prostitute who devotes little time or attention to religious life. Her only pious act is to teach her pet parrot to repeat the name of the god **Vishnu**, and in trying to teach it she repeats the divine name over and over again. This continual repetition of the name is enough to gain Vishnu's grace. Upon Ganika's death, Vishnu's servants rescue her from the minions of Death and convey her to his celestial realm, **Vaikuntha**.

Ganpatya

Sectarian Hindus who **worship** the god **Ganesh** as their primary **deity**. Most Hindus pay considerable homage to Ganesh, in part because his status as "Lord of Obstacles" (Vighneshvar) gives him power to help or hinder human endeavors. However, he is usually worshiped as a secondary deity. The Ganpatyas, in contrast, venerate Ganesh as their primary deity and worship no other deities. Most of the Ganpatyas live in the state of **Maharashtra**, where a network of shrines centered around the city of Pune and the nearby village of Chinchvad serves as their sacred center. The Ganpatya sect was founded by the sixteenth-century figure Moraya Gosavi, whose spiritual **initiation** came through a series of visions of Ganesh. One of his visions revealed that partial incarnations of Ganesh would be born in Moraya's family for seven generations. For further information see Paul Courtright, *Ganesa*, 1985.

Garbhadhana Samskara

The first of the sixteen traditional life-cycle ceremonies (**samskaras**) performed at important moments throughout one's life. The Garbhadhana Samskara was performed to ensure the conception of a child. This rite was performed on a specific **day** following the onset of the wife's menstrual period, although different sources specify different days. Although part of this rite obviously involved sexual intercourse between husband and wife, as a whole it was meant to create a sacred context for the act of procreation.

Garbhagrha

("womb-house") In traditional Hindu **architecture**, the garbhagrha is the inner sanctum of a temple, which contains the image of the temple's primary **deity**. In the **Nagara** architectural style found in northern and eastern India—in which the whole temple building culminates in one highest point—the garbhagrha was located directly below the summit of the highest tower (**shikhara**). In the **Dravida** style found in southern India—in which the temples are shorter, but tend to sprawl over vast areas—the garbhagrha's location is marked by a tower higher than the rest of the roof.

Garhmukteshvar

Sacred site (**tirtha**) on the **Ganges** River in the Ghaziabad district of the state of **Uttar Pradesh** about sixty miles due east of Delhi. Garhmukteshvar's primary temple is dedicated to the god **Shiva** in his form as the "Lord of Liberation" (mukteshvar), but the site's major importance comes from its location on the Ganges as a place for bathing (**snana**) and performing memorial rites (**shraddhas**) for the dead. Large crowds gather there to bathe on festival days, particularly on **Kartik Purnima**, the **full moon** in the **lunar month** of Kartik (October–November).

Garhwal

In the most technical sense, Garhwal is the name of a particular hill district in the northern Indian state of **Uttar Pradesh**. Garhwal is more commonly used as the name for a cultural region in the Uttar Pradesh hills, made up of the districts of Garhwal, TehriGarhwal, Dehra Dun, Chamoli, and **Uttarkashi**. The Garhwal region contains all the major tributaries of the **Ganges**: the **Bhagirathi**, the **Mandakini**, the **Pindara**, and the **Alakananda**. It also contains many of the holiest sacred sites (**tirthas**) in the **Himalayas**, including **Yamunotri**, **Gangotri**, **Kedarnath**, and **Badrinath**. In the eighteenth and nine-teenth centuries, under the patronage of the king of the state of Tehri, the region was also one of the centers for the **Pahari** school of **miniature painting**.

Garibdas

(early 18th c.) Founder of the **Garibdasi** religious community. Garibdas was born in the Rohtak district in what is now the state of **Haryana**. Garibdas did not have a human **guru**. Instead, he claimed to have received his religious **initiation** from the poet-saint **Kabir**, who appeared to him in a **dream**. Garibdas was a householder, as were his immedi-ate disciples. Under one of their later leaders the Garibdasis renounced their **possessions** and became an **ascetic** community. Garibdas preached and taught on a number of subjects and was a well-respected and influential reli-gious reformer.

Garibdasi

Religious community founded by the religious reformer **Garibdas** (early 18th c.). The Garibdasi community was originally made up of household-ers, but was fundamentally altered by one of the later leaders, Swami Dayaludasa. Under his direction, the community renounced their **posses-sions** and became an **ascetic** sect. The Garibdasis have more than one hun-dred centers in northern India, mainly concentrated in the regions of **Uttar Pradesh** and **Haryana** around pre-sent-day New Delhi, where Garibdas lived during his life.

Garuda

A mythical bird, often portrayed as an Indian kite or eagle. All of the Hindu **deities** have **animal** "vehicles," who are their symbols and their associates. Garuda is considered the vehicle for the god **Vishnu**. As Vishnu's vehicle, Garuda reflects some of the protective, life-affirming qualities associated with Vishnu. Garuda is the **son** of the sage **Kashyapa** and the divine maiden **Vinata**. The most famous story associated with Garuda explains the proverbial antipathy between eagles and snakes. Vinata has given **birth** to a line of eagles, whereas her sister **Kadru** has engendered a line of serpents. One day the sisters get into an argument about the tail color of a certain celestial horse—Vinata argues that it is white and Kadru asserts that it is black. They finally agree that the person who is wrong will become a slave to the other. To ensure her victory, Kadru persuades a number of her children to hang from the back of the horse, which from a distance makes the white tail appear to be black. When Vinata sees the black snakes, she accepts her defeat and has to serve Kadru under extremely harsh conditions for many years. When Garuda learns what has happened, he embarks on an endless program of killing snakes.

Gauda

One of the five northern **brahmin** com-munities (**Pancha Gauda**); the other four are the **Kanaujias**, the **Maithilas**, the **Utkalas**, and the **Saraswats**. Gauda brahmins are most numerous in the western half of northern India, particu-larly in the western parts of the states of **Uttar Pradesh** and **Madhya Pradesh**, in the state of **Haryana**, and in the state of **Rajasthan**.

Gaudapada

(5th c.?) Philosopher and textual commentator traditionally said to be the grand-teacher of the philosopher **Shankaracharya**. Shankaracharya maintained that Gaudapada was a proponent of **Advaita Vedanta**, one of the **six schools** of classical Hindu **philosophy**, despite Gaudapada's similarities to certain Buddhist positions. Gaudapada's most famous work is a commentary on the sacred text called the **Mandukya Upanishad**.

Gaudapada

(2) (5th–8th c.) Philosopher and commentator in the **Samkhya** school, one of the **six schools** of classical Hindu **philosophy**. Gaudapada is best known for his commentary on the *Samkhyakarikas*, the foundational text of the Samkhya school, which is ascribed to the philosopher **Ishvarakrishna**.

Gaudiya Vaishnava

Religious community founded by the Bengali saint **Chaitanya** (1486–1533). It takes its name from the ancient name for Bengal (**Gauda**), and its stress on the **worship** of the god **Vishnu**. The community's religious practices and beliefs are founded in Chaitanya's ecstatic devotionalism. He asserted that the path to religious ecstasy is the repetitive recitation of **Krishna's** name, often while singing and dancing in the streets. Chaitanya's religious charisma gained him many followers, of whom the most important were the **Goswamis**—the brothers Rupa and **Sanatana**, and their nephew **Jiva**. At Chaitanya's command the Goswamis went to live in **Brindavan**, the village where Krishna is believed to have grown up. The Goswamis' descendants live there to this day. In Brindavan, the Goswamis set about organizing and systematizing the philosophical foundation of Chaitanya's ecstatic experience. Although they conceived of themselves as Chaitanya's servants, they are equally important in the community's development. The Goswamis' key philosophical doctrine was **achintyabhedabheda**, the idea that there was an "inconceivable identity and difference" between the Supreme Divinity (Krishna) and the human being that renders the soul simultaneously identical to and different from the divinity. The Gaudiya Vaishnava community is also famous for its exhaustive analysis of devotion (**bhakti**) as an emotional experience. They enumerated the different ways to experience the love of god as five **modes of devotion**. For further information see Sushil Kumar De, *Early History of the Vaishnava Faith and Movement in Bengal*, 1961.

Gaumukh

("cow's mouth") Sacred site (**tirtha**) high in the **Himalayas**. It is located at the glacier that is the actual source of the **Bhagirathi** River, one of the tributaries of the **Ganges**. Gaumukh is twelve miles upriver from **Gangotri**, the place that is ritually celebrated as the source of the Ganges. In popular Hindu belief, the Ganges is believed to issue from the mouth of a **cow**, hence the name.

Gauna

This is the name for the ceremony of taking a new bride into her marital home for the first time. The addition of a new bride marks an important change for a family and is a time of both opportunity and danger. On one hand, it carries the potential for great blessings, since it is assumed that the bride and groom will soon begin a family. On the other hand, it also carries the threat of danger since the addition of a new person to the family brings the potential for disruption. The bride and her new family perform various rituals to ensure that her addition to the family will be auspicious and harmonious.

Gaura

Festival celebrated in central India that climaxes on the first **day** of the bright or waxing half of the **lunar month** of **Kartik** (October–November), the day after the festival of **Diwali**. The Gaura festival celebrates the marriage of the god **Shiva** and the **goddess Parvati**.

The Gauri-Shankar is a bead that is formed when two seeds grow together naturally. Worn by devotees of the god Shiva, it is believed to be a manifestation of the union of Shiva and his wife Parvati.

Gaurava

("[needless] complexity") In Indian logic, one of the faults to be avoided in constructing and pursuing an argument. According to the principle of "simplicity" (**laghava**), when one is presented with two equally plausible theories, one should choose the theory that is easier to understand and makes the fewest assumptions. The primary criterion in evaluating any argument is the validity of the argument itself, and it is only after this has been satisfied that one may raise objections based on complexity or simplicity.

Gauri

("fair") Epithet of the **goddess Parvati**, wife of the god **Shiva**. According to a story from the *Shiva Purana*, a sectarian text recounting the mythology of Shiva, Parvati takes offense when Shiva refers to her as **Kali** ("black"). She performs harsh physical austerities (**tapas**) to accumulate the power to rid herself of her dark complexion. When this is accomplished, she receives the epithet Gauri to signify her new and lightened complexion. This story illustrates the pervasive religious belief that physical hardship can give one spiritual and even magical powers, a conviction that is still found in contemporary India. This brief story also reveals the stigma that Indian society attributes to people with dark complexions—a prejudice that persists in modern times.

Gaurikund

Village and sacred site (**tirtha**) in the **Himalaya** Mountains of the state of **Uttar Pradesh**. Gaurikund is located about ten miles downstream from the headwaters of the **Mandakini** River, which is itself one of the Himalayan tributaries of the **Ganges**. Gaurikund is the end of the motorable road on the way to **Kedarnath**, and after this pilgrims must travel on foot. Gaurikund's mythic charter is connected with the god **Shiva** and his wife **Parvati**. Parvati is said to have performed harsh **asceticism** at Gaurikund in order to gain Shiva as her husband; after a long time Shiva is pleased with Parvati, reveals himself to her, and the two become lovers in that place. According to local geography, the place at which Parvati lived during this time is marked by a group of hot springs, which are another of Gaurikund's attractions.

Gauri-Shankar

A particular variety of **rudraksha**, a bead made from the dried seed of the tree *Elaeocarpus ganitrus*, which is considered sacred to **Shiva**. The rudraksha is often strung into garlands and worn by Shiva's devotees (**bhakta**). The Gauri-Shankar rudraksha is made when two seeds grow together naturally. Although the Gauri-Shankar is not as rare as certain other beads, it is unusual enough to command a fairly good price. The Gauri-Shankar is revered as a natural manifestation of the divine couple, the **goddess Parvati** (Gauri) and the god Shiva (Shankar). It thus represents the total presence of divinity in its eternal and its dynamic aspects: Shiva as knowledge and Parvati as **Shakti** or power.

Gautama

(6th c. B.C.E.) In Hindu mythology, one of the seven sages whose name marks a clan "lineage" (**gotra**); the others are

Kashyapa, **Bharadvaja**, **Vasishtha**, **Bhrgu**, **Atri**, and **Vishvamitra**. All **brahmins** are believed to be descended from these seven sages, with each family taking the name of its progenitor as its gotra name. In modern times, these gotra divisions are still important, since marriage within the gotra is forbidden. A new bride adopts her husband's gotra after her marriage as part of her new identity.

Gautama is most famous as the husband of **Ahalya**. When he discovers that the god **Indra** has slept with Ahalya, he curses his wife to turn into stone and curses Indra to have a thousand vulvas on his body. Both **curses** are later modified to reduce their severity. Ahalya is turned to stone, but returns to life when touched by the god **Rama's** foot, whereas Indra's body becomes covered with a thousand eyes. See also **marriage prohibitions**.

Gautama

(2) (3rd c. B.C.E. ?) Indian philosopher who is traditionally cited as the author of the **Nyaya Sutras**, the foundation of the **Nyaya** philosophical school. The Nyaya school is one of several schools that seek to explain the cause of human bondage in the cycle of reincarnation (**samsara**) and how it can be overcome.

Gaya

Sacred site (**tirtha**) and city in the modern state of **Bihar** and capital of a district by the same name. According to Hindu mythology, this is the place where the god **Vishnu** sacrifices a powerful **demon** named **Gayasura**, having promised the demon that the space covered by his body will be the holiest spot on **earth**. Gaya is best known as a site to perform various rites for the dead, particularly the memorial rites known as **shraddhas**. Its sanctity is so well known that it draws people from all over the eastern part of India.

Gayasura

In Hindu mythology, the name of a very powerful asura (**demon**). Gayasura performs harsh **asceticism** (**tapas**), spurred by the traditional Indian assumption that to voluntarily endure physical suffering brings one spiritual and magical powers. Gayasura's powers grow so large that all the gods become concerned that he might become powerful enough to overthrow them. As the gods' fears grow, the god **Vishnu** advises the god **Brahma** to convince Gayasura to allow his body to be sacrificed. Vishnu promises Gayasura that the place where he dies will become holier than all the sacred sites (**tirthas**) in the world. The spot where Gayasura's body lies becomes the holy place known as **Gaya**, which by virtue of Vishnu's boon is claimed to be holier than all other places on earth. See also **magic**.

Gayatri Mantra

A particular verse from the **Rg Veda** (3.62.10), the oldest Hindu religious text; this verse is written in the poetic **meter** named gayatri, hence its name. The verse itself is an invocation to the **sun** and can be translated "let us meditate on the sun, most excellent of all the **deities**, may he inspire our minds." Reciting the Gayatri mantra is part of the morning and evening **worship** (**sandhya**) prescribed for every "**twice-born**" man who has received the adolescent religious **initiation** known as the "second birth." An important part of this initiation is the transmission of this **mantra** to the young man. Although the Gayatri must be recited every **day**, it should not be recited over **water**; in earlier times this was one reason why many orthodox Hindus were reluctant to travel abroad.

Gayawal

Endogamous group of pilgrimage priests (**pandas**) who live in **Gaya**, a pilgrimage place (**tirtha**) famous as a site for rites for the dead. Each Gayawal family has exclusive hereditary rights to serve all the pilgrims whose ancestral homes lie in a particular region or regions, regardless of where those pilgrims may be living at the time. As at all pilgrimage sites, pilgrims are supposed to be served only by their hereditary family priest. This monopoly gives the Gayawals greater leverage in negotiating fees with their pilgrim clients, who are in a vulnerable position since most of them have come to perform rites for dead relatives. The Gayawals are notorious for their rapaciousness, greed, and general lack of learning. These qualities render them somewhat debased by **brahmin** standards, as does the fact that they make much of their income from the dead, which is considered inauspicious. In fairness to the Gayawals, the relative power derived from this monopoly is also balanced by a sense of hereditary obligation to their clients—the perennial issue is never whether the clients will be served, but how much they will have to pay.

Gemstones

In Hindu astrology, gemstones are used to strengthen, neutralize, or counteract the celestial influence of certain **planets**. Hindu astrology recognizes nine planets, each of which is associated with a particular gemstone: **sun** (ruby), **moon** (pearl), **Mars** (coral), **Mercury** (emerald), **Jupiter** (topaz), **Venus** (diamond), **Saturn** (sapphire), **Rahu** (agate), and **Ketu** (turquoise). Each of these nine planets is considered to be a minor **deity** and to have a distinct personality and characteristics. When deciding which gemstones to wear, one must make certain astrological considerations, particularly the position of the planets in one's **natal horoscope** (janampatrika), which is believed to reveal each planet's influence. These gemstones are worn in rings, with the base of the stone in contact with the skin to give the gemstones their efficacy over their planetary counterparts.

Gesture, in Dance and Drama

Gestures in Hindu **dance** and drama are divided in two categories: **hasta**, which are broad positions of the arms and hands; and **mudra**, which are stylized hand gestures, usually with specific meanings.

Ghanta

A handbell. These bells typically have a long straight handle projecting upward from the top and are usually rung with the bell part projecting from the bottom of the closed hand. Ringing bells is an important element in Hindu **worship** (**puja**) and its pleasing sound is one of the sixteen traditional **offerings** (**upacharas**) given to the **deity** as part of worship. Many different deities are pictured with bells in Hindu iconography, but it is particularly associated with the **goddess Kali**, whose roaring voice is equated with a tolling bell.

Ghat

In its broadest meaning, a ghat is a bathing (**snana**) place by a body of **water**, such as a river, lake, or pond. The word ghat is also commonly used to refer to the permanent structures that have been built at these bathing places. They usually include a flat area at the water's edge, where people can walk, stand, or sit. A set of steps leads from the platform into and below the surface of the water. Constructing a ghat is often considered a pious act that generates religious merit. This is particularly true in pilgrimage places (**tirtha**), where ghats are often centers for public religious life.

Ghatika

In traditional Indian timekeeping, a ghatika is a period of twenty-four minutes. There are sixty in each twenty-four hour **day**. The ghatika gets its name from the clay pots (ghata) that were used to make **water**-clocks; these water-clocks measured the time by allowing water to drip out from the pot through a small hole.

Ghatotkacha

In the *Mahabharata*, the later of the two great Hindu epics, Ghatotkacha is a **son** of **Bhima**, one of the five **Pandava** brothers who are the epic's protagonists. Ghatotkacha's mother is a **rakshasi** (female **demon**) named Hidambi; Bhima's carnal relations with a nonhuman being are one sign of his earthy and unsophisticated personality. As the offspring of a rakshasi and the strongest Pandava, Ghatotkacha is a massive physical specimen. He is a staunch ally to the Pandavas all his life and fights valiantly on their behalf during the war between the Pandavas and their cousins the **Kauravas**, destroying large parts of the Kaurava army. He fights several times with the hero **Karna**, but is finally killed when Karna uses a **magic** weapon known as **Vaijayanti Shakti**.

Ghora

("terrifying") Term used to refer to Hindu **deities** in their frightful, terrifying, and powerful aspects, as opposed to their benevolent (**saumya**) manifestations. This distinction is particularly applicable to the god **Shiva** and the forms of the **Goddess**, both of whom can appear in either form, and devotees (**bhakta**) can focus their **worship** on either aspect.

Ghosts

Popular Hindu culture generally accepts the existence of ghosts and spirits, particularly of people who have died a violent or untimely death. Despite the virtually universal belief in reincarnation (**samsara**), it is generally accepted that the spirits of people who have died such deaths linger near where they lived during their lives. Ghosts will usually reveal themselves through disturbances, misfortunes, or by appearing to family members in visions or dreams. The family will then take measures to appease the spirit. Sometimes this is done by sponsoring rituals or ceremonies. Other times a family may prepare a shrine for the ghost to inhabit. Such ghosts are usually believed to have unsatisfied desires—either they died prior to getting married or having children, or they started major enterprises they were unable to finish. People who have lived long lives and fulfilled all the major human goals will not become ghosts.

Ghrneshvar

("Lord of Compassion") One of the twelve **jyotirlingas**, a group of images of the god **Shiva** that are deemed particularly holy and powerful. Shiva is believed to be uniquely present at these places. This particular jyotirlinga is located in the village of **Velur** in the state of **Maharashtra**, and is also known as Dhushmeshvar. This site is unusual because the form of Shiva that resides here is known by two different names and has no unequivocal charter myth. At none of the other jyotirlingas is there any doubt about the presiding **deity's** form or how it came to be there. This indicates that Ghrneshvar is a minor site, perhaps one simply filling out the catalog of the jyotirlingas to get the number up to twelve. Despite this apparent lack of importance, Ghrneshvar is arguably the most-visited of the jyotirlingas. It is only a few miles from the world famous cave temples at **Ellora** and is a regular stop on the local tourist circuit. The temple is fairly small but is well kept and very impressive. Male visitors are required to remove their shirts before entering Shiva's presence.

Giri Dashanami

One of the ten divisions of the **Dashanami Sanyasis**, renunciant ascetics who are devotees (**bhakta**) of **Shiva**. The Dashanamis were supposedly established by the ninth-century philosopher **Shankaracharya**, in an effort to create

Jain temple in Girnar. Settled atop a hill, Girnar is an ancient site that is sacred to both Hindu and Jain religious communities.

a corps of learned men who could help to revitalize Hindu life. Each of the divisions is designated by a different name—in this case, giri ("mountain"). Upon **initiation**, new members are given this name as a surname to their new **ascetic** names, thus allowing for immediate group identification.

Aside from their individual identity, these ten "named" divisions are collected into four larger organizational groups: **Anandawara**, **Bhogawara**, **Bhuriwara**, and **Kitawara**. Each group has its headquarters in one of the four monastic centers (**maths**) supposedly established by Shankaracharya. Each of the four groups is also associated with one of the four **Vedas**—the oldest Hindu sacred texts, a different geographical quarter of India, a different great utterance (**mahavakya**), and a different ascetic quality. The Giri Dashanamis belong to the **Anandawara** group, which is affiliated with the **Jyotir math** in the Himalayan town of **Joshimath**.

Giridhara

("mountain-lifter") In Hindu mythology, a youthful and heroic form of the god **Krishna**. According to the story, as a young man Krishna observes that the village elders make yearly **offerings** to **Indra**, the god of the storm. After some persuasion, Krishna manages to convince the elders that instead of making offerings to Indra, who is too far off in **heaven** to do them any good, they should offer them instead to Mount **Govardhan**. This mountain looms over their village as a symbol of their prosperity, and since Krishna's devotees (**bhakta**) consider this mountain to be another form of Krishna, he is actually persuading the elders to make offerings to him. Indra is furious when he discovers what has happened, and unleashes a violent storm that threatens to wash away the village and destroy all the inhabitants. To protect the villagers and their cattle from harm, Krishna lifts up Mount Govardhan, and holds it over their heads as an umbrella to protect them from the rain. After seven days, Indra admits defeat, and Krishna emerges as the hero of the village. This story illustrates the gradual eclipse of the older Vedic **deities**. The figure of Krishna as Giridhara is widely worshiped in **Rajasthan** and is particularly noteworthy as the "chosen deity" (**ishtadevata**) of the poet-saint **Mirabai**.

Girnar

Sacred site (**tirtha**) on a hill outside the city of Junagadh in the state of **Gujarat**. Girnar has been a holy site for at least 2,000 years and remains an important place for several religious communities. The hill's summit is an important pilgrimage site for the Jains and has a cluster of Jain temples, some of them dating back to the twelfth century. It also has a long history as a center for Hindu ascetics—the Brahmachari **Sanyasis** (**Brahmacharin**) have an **ashram** there, and the summit is said to have a set of footprints left by **Dattatreya**, a famous mythic figure who is considered a partial **avatar** of the god **Vishnu** and a paradigm for **asceticism**. Girnar is the site of a large Hindu **ascetic** gathering on **Kartik Purnima**, the **full moon** in the **lunar month** of Kartik (October–November).

Gitagovinda

("Govinda's Song") Lyric poem written in the twelfth century by the poet **Jayadeva**. Written in an era when vernacular languages were becoming the prevalent vehicle for devotional religiosity, the *Gitagovinda* is one of the last great devotional (**bhakti**) texts composed in **Sanskrit** and is an exquisite example of Sanskrit poetry. According to tradition, Jayadeva was associated with the temple to **Jagannath** in the eastern Indian city of **Puri**, and his wife Padmavati was a dancer at the same temple. The *Gitagovinda* is a devotional poem to the god Jagannath. The text was obviously meant to be sung, since its twenty-four cantos are set in various differing musical modes (**ragas**), each of which conveys a different emotion. The text has also been expressed through

dance for at least 500 years in the **Orissi** dance style that originated in the Jagannath temple. The *Gitagovinda* is still used in the daily **worship** of Jagannath and occupies a position held by no other literary text.

The *Gitagovinda* is an allegory of the union of the human soul with God. This union is described through the story of the love between the god **Krishna** and his human consort **Radha** as they experience an initial flush of passion, followed by jealousy, separation, reconciliation, and reunion. Although Jayadeva's text lavishly employs the images from Sanskrit love poetry, it is far more than a romantic novel. The poem was written to show that Krishna is the lord of the entire universe. The first cantos after the introduction, the **Dashavatara Stotra**, pay homage to Krishna in his ten avatars or earthly incarnations (**Dashavatar**), each of whom is instrumental in preserving the cosmic equilibrium. Although Krishna is considered an **avatar** of the god **Vishnu** in many parts of the Hindu tradition, Krishna is the supreme **deity** for Jayadeva. The place usually occupied by Krishna in the enumeration of the avatars is taken by Krishna's brother, **Balarama**. The song that follows continues this theme, giving the divine attributes of Krishna as Vishnu, and further emphasizing that the entire *Gitagovinda* describes the deity's divine play (**lila**).

Having set the appropriate context in the opening songs, Jayadeva's text returns to a more conventional tale of romantic love. The next chapter describes the symbols of spring, which are intended to evoke a mood of love. Yet this mood is marred by Radha's jealousy when Krishna sports with a troop of cowherd girls, for she desires Krishna for herself alone. She withdraws and sits apart, sulking and despondent, only to burst into rage when Krishna comes to meet her, bearing the signs of another **erotic** liaison. Her anger and dismissal make Krishna realize what he has done. He eventually succeeds in dispersing her anger, and convinces Radha of his love. They reconcile and make passionate love. The text ends by describing their love play in the afterglow, in which Radha orders Krishna to ornament her as she wishes, showing her complete power over him.

As a text, the *Gitagovinda* can be read on many different levels simultaneously. The themes of love, betrayal, and reconciliation speak easily to everyday human experience, but the theological and mystical levels are always present. In the end, deity and devotee (**bhakta**) are described as needing and loving one another. Neither is complete without the other. Radha's demand for exclusive love is at first denied, but in the end her persistence and conviction are rewarded. The *Gitagovinda* has been masterfully translated by the late Barbara Stoller Miller as *The Love Song of the Dark Lord*, 1977.

Goa

One of the smallest states in modern India. It lies between the states of **Maharashtra** and **Karnataka** on the shore of the Arabian Sea. Goa was a Portuguese colony for more than 400 years and did not become a part of the Indian union until 1961, when India engineered a nearly bloodless takeover. Goa still retains much of its Portuguese influence—in its food, easygoing pace, and the continuing presence of Roman Catholicism—which makes it one of the most unusual cultural areas in India. For general information about Goa and all the regions of India, an accessible reference is Christine Nivin et al., *India*. 8th ed., Lonely Planet, 1998.

Gobind Deo Mandir

A temple built in 1590 in **Brindavan**, the town believed to be the god **Krishna's** childhood home. The temple is dedicated to **Krishna** in his form as the "Divine Cowherd." From an architectural perspective, the temple is unique for its vaulted ceiling, which is seldom found in Hindu temples. The temple's interior

and exterior are also notable for their almost complete lack of figural ornamentation, which is extremely unusual. The temple is close to the major road connecting Agra and Delhi. These are the two major political centers of the Moghul empire (1525–1707), whose rulers were Muslims. Since many orthodox Muslims believe that figural representations are idolatrous, particularly in places of **worship**, the temple's austere style may have been an attempt to avoid inciting Muslim iconoclasm. There is evidence of conflict between Hindus and Muslims at this site since the few figures inside the temple, carved into the lintels of door and windows, have had their heads broken off. See also **Moghul dynasty**.

Godana

("gift of a **cow**") In Hindu religious practice, gift giving (**dana**) is common and believed to be a pious act that generates religious merit. Godana is the gift of a cow, usually to a **brahmin**. Traditional religious texts highly laud the gift of a cow, both as a charitable act and as a way to expiate one's sins. However, since many of these texts were written by brahmins, one can detect a hint of self-interest.

Godavari

River running from west to east in central India. The Godavari's headwaters lie in the state of **Maharashtra** on the inland side of the western Ghats. It meanders through that state to **Andhra Pradesh**, where it enters the Bay of Bengal. The Godarvi is traditionally considered one of India's seven sacred rivers, along with the **Ganges**, **Yamuna**, **Cauvery**, **Saraswati**, **Narmada**, and **Indus**. The Godavari has special status in central India, where it is often referred to as the "Ganges"—the most sacred river for Hindus. Although its entire length is considered sacred, the Godavari's most important religious sites are all in the west: **Nasik**,

A shrine in the Godavari River near the riverbank of Nasik.

Tryambakeshvar, and **Paithan**. See also **ghat**.

Goddess

India is home to a host of different goddesses. Although goddesses differ greatly in demeanor and character, they are all generally seen as expressions of a single underlying female **deity**. This vision of the goddess coincides with the characteristic Hindu practice that allows for multiple manifestations of a divinity, while at the same time asserting his or her underlying reality as a single entity. Many of India's goddesses are the deities of a specific site, who might be worshiped only in that specific place. Yet as these local goddesses are all mythically linked as differing forms of a single great Goddess, the sacred sites (**tirthas**) are also connected with this great Goddess. The sites, called **pithas** or "benches," form a sacred network stretching throughout the entire subcontinent.

The origins of the goddess cult in India are uncertain. Excavations of cities of the **Indus Valley civilization** have unearthed female figures with enormous breasts, hips, and buttocks. These figures resemble the Venus of Willendorf found in Bronze Age Europe and suggest that there was some kind of cult associated with **women's** fertility. Some interpreters have seen the Indus Valley figures as proof that the cult of the Mother Goddess originated in the Indus Valley civilization, but hard evidence supporting this claim is slim. Another reason some interpreters believe that goddess **worship** must have come from the indigenous Indian culture is that the deities mentioned in the **Vedas**, the oldest Hindu religious texts, are almost exclusively male. The female goddesses in the Vedic hymns are infrequent and unimportant—**Ushas** (the dawn), **Prthivi** (the **earth**), and **Nirriti** (death and destruction). But somehow female divinities were elevated from virtual obscurity and became conceived as the reigning power in the universe.

The cult of the great Goddess appears fully formed, seemingly out of nowhere, in about the fifth century. She first appears in the text known as the *Devimahatmya* ("greatness of the Goddess"), which is itself a section of the

Markandeya Purana. The depth and subtlety of her characterization in this text leads scholars to infer that this cult had existed for some time, perhaps as a secret religious community open only to initiates. The goddess in the *Devimahatmya* is a powerful, independent female force and is able to do what the gods cannot. She is created from the collected radiance (tejas) of all the gods, and comes into the world to kill a demon against whom the gods have struggled in vain. The *Devimahatmya*'s three different episodes portray her in three different divine personas: as **Mahasaraswati** in the slaying of the **demons Madhu** and **Kaitabha**, as **Mahalakshmi** in slaying a demon named **Mahishasura**, and as **Mahakali** in the battle against the demon generals **Shumbha** and **Nishumbha**.

Many of India's goddesses are the patron deities of particular locales, and are considered unique to that place. The **Shiwalik goddesses**, for example, are unique to particular sites in the **Shiwalik hills**. At the same time, all of these goddesses are considered different manifestations of the same divine energy. According to the sites' charter myth, each site is associated with a particular body part of the primeval goddess. The myth tells of the death of **Sati**, who commits **suicide** when her father **Daksha** insults her husband **Shiva**. Shiva picks up Sati's body and wanders the earth, carrying her on his shoulders. In his grief Shiva neglects his divine duties, and the world begins to fall into ruin. The other gods beg **Vishnu** for help, lest the world be destroyed. Vishnu uses his razor-sharp discus to cut off pieces of Sati's body, until finally there is nothing left. When the body is completely gone, Shiva goes to the mountains, where he becomes absorbed in meditation. Wherever a part of Sati's body falls, that place becomes a **Shakti Pitha** ("seat of the Goddess"), sanctified to the Goddess in a particular form. The number of these places differs from source to source—some list fifty-one, and others 108. Whatever the number, the sites are spread throughout the subcontinent, from Baluchistan in modern Pakistan, to **Assam** in the far east, to deep in southern India. Each Shakti Pitha is associated with a particular body part of the great Goddess, has a particular presiding female deity, and has a particular **Bhairava** as a consort to that goddess. From this perspective, the entire subcontinent is seen as a single cohesive unit, with the network of sites connected to one another as are the parts of the body. Different places may claim the same body part, the result of the drive to establish a site and to give it prestige. For example, Sati's vulva, the most powerfully charged part of the female body, is usually accepted to have fallen at **Kamakhya** in Assam, but the same claim is made at **Kalimath** in the **Himalayas**. There is no single authoritative list of sites and competing claims are not uncommon. Many Hindus seem unconcerned with the seeming inconsistency of having the same body parts claimed by different sites; perhaps this reflects the conviction that the Goddess is behind them all, and that the specifics are therefore less important.

While some goddesses are only worshiped in their particular locale, such as the goddesses found in the Shiwalik hills, other goddesses have become more widely worshiped, and some have become pan-Indian. In the pantheon, the Goddess generally appears in two widely differing types of manifestations. At times she appears as a wife and mother, in forms such as **Parvati**, **Lakshmi**, and **Saraswati**. Although these married goddesses are not completely powerless, they tend to be benign, benevolent, and auspicious. Her other manifestation is in forms such as **Durga** and **Kali**, whose male consorts are considered subordinate to them. These independent manifestations of the Goddess have the power to help their devotees (**bhakta**), but they are also volatile and potentially dangerous, since their power is sometimes unleashed without control. Cultural observers have suggested that this dual perspective represents cultural perspectives on Indian women, particularly the belief that women's procreative capacities should be channeled through the safe, confining bounds of marriage. Married women, as wives and mothers, are auspicious, life-giving, and life-sustaining because their creative power has been regulated under male control. Unmarried women remain a source of danger, particularly to the family's prestige, since the quickest way to ruin a family's good name is through the corruption of its women.

Godman

Colloquial name for a particular type of charismatic Hindu **ascetic**. As religious figures, godmen are generally characterized by a high-profile presence, by their ability to attract attention and support from the larger Indian society, and by their claims to advanced spiritual attainments. They sometimes claim to possess **magic** powers—such as the ability to heal, read minds, foretell the future, or to influence future events—which are exhibited to prove the godman's spiritual attainments. Godmen often come from outside the established ascetic orders and may have never even taken formal ascetic **initiation**. They are able to flourish in the Indian religious "free market," which recognizes and rewards religious charisma. Godmen typically dwell in their own **ashrams** rather than one belonging to an order. Although most of them acknowledge a **guru** or religious preceptor, their success stems more from their personal qualities than the strength of their spiritual lineage. In recent years a number of these godmen have cultivated large numbers of foreign disciples, which can bring both wealth and enhanced prestige. One contemporary example of such a godman is **Sathya Sai Baba**, whose ashram is in **Puttaparthi** in the southern state of **Andhra Pradesh**. For an example of one person's encounters with a variety of these figures, see Peter Ludwig Brent, *Godmen of India*, 1972.

Gods, World of the

The earliest reference to the transmigration of souls is found in both the **Brhadaranyaka Upanishad** (6.2) and the **Chandogya Upanishad** (5.10). These texts make a qualitative distinction between two different paths. The path to the world of the gods ultimately led to the **sun**, and the person traveling it did not return again, whereas the path to the **world of the fathers** led to the **moon**, and the person traveling it was eventually reborn on earth. The leitmotiv of the **Upanishads** is the need for individual spiritual realization, which is the key to getting on the path to the world of the gods. Those who gain this realization attain the final and ultimate end, whereas those who simply do good deeds will return to earth, although their good deeds will give them karmic benefits. See also **karma**.

Godse, Nathuram

(1912–1948) Hindu nationalist figure who is most famous as the assassin of **Mohandas Gandhi**. Godse was a devoted follower of **Vinayak Damodar Savarkar**, whose articulation of Hindu nationalism equated Hindu identity and Indian patriotism. Savarkar and his followers saw the partition of India in 1947 as the "vivisection" of Mother India, dividing her into India and Pakistan. Like many of Savarkar's followers, Godse was enraged by Gandhi's post-partition efforts to protect Indian Muslims and to influence the Indian government's policy toward Pakistan, particularly his hunger strike to force the Indian government to transfer to Pakistan a large sum of money that had been promised. Filled with the conviction that Gandhi had to be stopped, Godse intercepted Gandhi on the way to a prayer meeting, touched his feet as a sign of respect, and then shot him three times. Godse was tried and executed for his action and is sometimes cited as a martyr by the most ardent contemporary nationalists.

Gokarna

("**cow's** ear") Sacred site (**tirtha**) in the state of **Karnataka** on the shore of the Arabian Sea, just south of Karnataka's border with the state of **Goa**. Gokarna is most famous for a temple to the god **Shiva** in his form as Mahabaleshvara, the "exceedingly powerful Lord." According to the site's charter myth, Shiva intends to perform the work of creation, but before he begins he becomes rapt in meditation in the depths of the earth. The god **Brahma** grows impatient with the delay and carries out the work of creation himself. Shiva is enraged when he discovers what has happened and is about to force his way up through the earth, which will create a terrible cataclysm. The earth appears to Shiva in the form of a cow, who begs him to rise to the surface through her ear. It is claimed that a cave at Gokarna is the remnant of that passage through which Shiva rose.

Gokhale, Gopal Krishna

(1866–1915) College professor, legislator, and reformist Hindu, who worked for much of his life with his older contemporary, **Mahadev Govind Ranade**. Unlike Ranade, whose position as a judge barred him from active political involvement, Gokhale spent the last fifteen years of his life as a legislator. Thirteen of these years were spent as Bombay's Indian representative to the Imperial Legislative Council, the highest lawmaking body in India. Like Ranade, Gokhale sought to influence British policy by working within established institutions, in this case through the British colonial government. This willingness to compromise brought him opposition from leaders such as **Bal Gangadhar Tilak**, who advocated stiffer, even violent opposition to British rule.

Gokulnath

(1551–1640) The third **guru** of the religious community known as the **Pushti Marg**. Gokulnath inherited the mantle of leadership from his father **Vitthalnath**, who was the successor to his father **Vallabhacharya**, the community's founder. During his tenure Gokulnath helped solidify the religious community and paid particular attention to its organization. He is best known for compiling several hagiographic works describing the careers of his father and grandfather, to provide an appropriately reverent picture for their followers. Gokulnath was also the moving force behind a text named the *Chaurasi Vaishnavan ki Varta* ("Account of eighty-four Vaishnavas"), although the actual text was probably compiled by Gokulnath's disciple **Hariray**. This text is a sectarian hagiography describing the lives of eighty-four paradigmatic **Vaishnavas**, all of whom—at least according to the text—were associates and disciples of Vallabhacharya and Vitthalnath. The text's real purpose is not to provide a biography, but to illustrate the importance of the Pushti Marg and its leaders.

Golden Embryo

One of the earliest cosmological myths. It first appears in the **Rg Veda** (10.121), the oldest Hindu religious text. According to this account, the universe originally consisted of the Golden Embryo (Hiranyagarbha). The Golden Embryo stirred and evolved into **Prajapati**, the creator of all things and ruler over all creatures. In this story, as with most other accounts of Hindu **cosmology**, the cosmos originates from a single source and is thus an organic whole.

Golwalkar, Madhav Sadashiv

(1904–1973) Second sarsanghchalak ("Supreme Leader") of the **Rashtriya Svayamsevak Sangh** (RSS). The RSS is a conservative Hindu organization whose express purpose is to provide the leadership cadre for a revitalized Hindu India; for most of its history it has characterized its mission as cultural, rather than religious or political. Golwalkar is a pivotal figure in RSS history. He took office in 1940 upon the death of its founder, **Dr. K. B. Hedgewar**, and guided it through the tumultuous years surrounding India's independence. After **Mohandas Gandhi's** assassination by the Hindu nationalist **Nathuram Godse** in 1948, the RSS and several other organizations were briefly banned. Despite initial suspicions, the RSS has never been implicated in Gandhi's death. During the ban the RSS continued to function underground, and many of its leaders became more politically active, a trend that Golwalkar had earlier discouraged. When the ban was rescinded in 1949, the RSS began to exercise greater influence by forming and sponsoring affiliated organizations, such as trade unions, student organizations, charitable institutions, and political parties. This trend continued throughout the rest of Golwalkar's tenure, although he was far less activist than his successor, **Balasaheb Deoras**. For further information see Walter K. Andersen and Shridhar D. Damle, *The Brotherhood in Saffron*, 1987; and Tapan Basu et al., *Khaki Shorts and Saffron Flags*, 1993.

Gond

Tribal (**adivasi**) community in central India. The Gonds are concentrated in the state of **Madhya Pradesh**, particularly in the hills on both sides of the **Vindhya Mountains**, in the Kaimur Range at the eastern border of Madhya Pradesh and **Uttar Pradesh**, and in the **Ramgarh** Hills on the border of Madhya Pradesh, **Orissa**, and **Bihar**. Like most tribal peoples, they tend to be quite poor and eke out a living from subsistence agriculture.

Gopala

("protector of cows") Epithet of the god **Krishna**, reflecting his childhood occupation as a cowherd. See **Krishna**.

Gopi

(feminine of *gopa*, "**cow**-keeper") In Hindu mythology, the gopis are the cow-keeping **women** who are the god **Krishna's** companions in **Braj**, the region south of Delhi in which Krishna is believed to have spent his early life. The gopis are the simple village women of Braj, who keep the village cows, churn the milk into butter for sale, and provide Krishna with an adoring and familiar presence as he grows up. They exclaim over his beauty as an infant and they endure his boyhood pranks—particularly his continual theft of their hard-earned butter. When he becomes an enchanting adolescent, they respond to the nightly call of his flute to join him in the circular **dance** (**ras lila**) on the shores of the river **Yamuna**. Although the gopis are completely devoted to Krishna and love him above all else, their relations with him are also devoid of any affectation or awe. The gopis are simple country women, and they treat Krishna as one of their own. For example, they feel no qualms about scolding him when he has stolen their butter. Their intimate but unaffected relationship with Krishna makes them paradigms for the ideal devotee (**bhakta**). For his part, Krishna is said to prefer this sort of natural and spontaneous relationship to any sort of calculated **worship**. Krishna loves Braj more than any other place on **earth** because the people there treat him as one of their own.

Gopichand

Princely protagonist of *The Song of Gopichand*, an allegorical adventure that is much beloved throughout northern India and has even spread to Bengal where it is called ***The Song of Manik Chandra***. The story tells of the trials of Gopichand, who loses his kingdom through the vicissitudes of fate but eventually regains it after numerous trials and setbacks. Aside from the song's story, it is also embedded with the ideas of the **Nathpanthis**, an **ascetic** community supposedly founded by

Towering gopurams mark the gateways to the Brhadeshvar Temple in Tanjore.

Gorakhnath. Some members of this community believed that perfecting their bodies through **yoga** would make them immortal. This idea appears in the song through its description of Gopichand's mother Mayana, who has power over Death himself. In some versions of the story Mayana's religious preceptor is identified as a low-**caste** sweeper, while in others it is the sage Gorakhnath himself. Two versions of this song have been translated by G. A. Grierson in the *Journal of the Asiatic Society of Bengal*, the first published in 1878 and the second in 1885.

Gopuram

In the **Dravida** style of temple **architecture**, which was mainly prevalent in southern India, gopurams are the ornate temple gateways in the center of the temple's perimeter walls. Temples built in the Dravida style tend to be shorter than temples built in the northern Indian **Nagara** style, but compensate for this by stretching over vast areas, often forming towns in their own right. There are usually four gopurams, one for each

of the cardinal directions; in some cases these gopurams are ten stories tall and can be seen for miles from the surrounding countryside. The gopurams were originally fortified gateways built to restrict access to the temple, but in present times their function is more decorative. By dominating the skyline around the temple—much like spires of Gothic cathedrals—gopurams are a pronouncement about the power of the resident **deities** (and their client rulers); they have also helped to educate the faithful, since they are usually covered with sculptures detailing mythological themes.

Gora

(1267–1397?) Poet and saint in the **Varkari Panth**, a religious community centered around the **worship** of the Hindu god **Vithoba** at his temple at **Pandharpur** in modern state of **Maharashtra**. According to tradition, Gora was a potter, which by the standards of the time was a very low-status occupation; Gora's inclusion as one of the Varkari saints helps underscore the devotional (**bhakti**) conviction that **birth** status was less important than genuine love of God. Gora is reported to have lived most of his life at Teradhoki village in the state of Maharashtra, but since he is a minor Varkari figure, little is known about his life. For further information see G. A. Deleury, *The Cult of Vithoba*, 1960; and Justin E. Abbott and Narhar R. Godbole (trans.), *Stories of Indian Saints*, 1982.

Gorakhnath

(13th c.?) Medieval **yogi** and wonder-worker who is the founder of the **Nathpanthi ascetics**. There is little doubt that Gorakhnath was a historical person, and his teacher was named **Matsyendranath** (also known as Minanath). However, the accounts of his life tell of him performing so many miracles and wonders that they cannot be taken as factual. He is generally believed to have lived early in the thirteenth century, since the Maharashtrian poet-saint **Jnaneshvar** (1275–1296?) described his own spiritual preceptor as one of Gorakhnath's disciples.

Tradition regards Gorakhnath not only as a magician and a wonder-worker, but also as the author of the *Gorakhshatakam*. This text is a religious manual that gives instruction on a specific type of **yoga** practiced by Nathpanthi ascetics. The ultimate goal of this yogic practice is to transform the perishable elements in the physical body into immortal elements. Whether or not Gorakhnath authored this text, the spiritual instructions therein are consistent with those of the Nathpanthi ascetics who claim to be his disciples. According to legend, Gorakhnath and his most accomplished followers have never died, and their victory over death is a sign of their spiritual accomplishment. The most complete source on Gorakhnath and his followers, despite its age, is George Weston Briggs, *Gorakhnath and the Kanphata Yogis*, 1973; and Shashibhushan B. Dasgupta,

Obscure Religious Cults, 1962. See also **Maharashtri**.

Gorakhnathi

Ascetic community who claim to be the disciples of sage **Gorakhnath** and claim to have conserved his teachings. These ascetics are also known as the **Nathpanthis**. See **Nathpanthi**.

Gorakhshatakam

("Gorakh's Hundred") Text attributed to the sage **Gorakhnath**. Although his authorship is ultimately unprovable, its teachings are consistent with those of the **Nathpanthi ascetics** who claim to be his disciples. In at least one of its forms, as translated by Briggs, the text has 101 verses, not 100 verses as the title suggests. The *Gorakhshatakam* gives instruction on the type of **yoga** practiced by the Nathpanthi ascetics in which the major motif is the union of polar opposites. It begins with instruction on the structure of the **subtle body**, an alternate physiological system that resides on a different plane of existence than gross matter, but possesses certain correspondences to the material body. The subtle body is visualized as a set of six psychic centers (**chakras**) running roughly along the course of the spine. Above and below these centers are the bodily abodes of the two divine principles, **Shiva** (awareness) and **Shakti** (power). The aspirant aims to awaken a latent spiritual energy residing in the shakti called **kundalini** and move it to union with the Shiva principle at the crown of the head. The ultimate aim of this practice is to gain control over the forces that affect the body, allowing one to become purified and immortal.

Gosain

Vernacular form of the **Sanskrit** word *goswami* ("master of the senses"). Although this epithet could be used to refer to any **ascetic**, during British colonial rule in the eighteenth and nineteenth centuries it was most commonly used to denote certain subgroups among the **Sanyasis**, the ascetic devotees (**bhakta**) of the god **Shiva**. The name was particular to Sanyasis at the low end of the ascetic status scale, such as the **Nathpanthis** or the **Naga** (militant) Sanyasis, who were often recruited from the lower classes of society.

Gosala Maskariputra

(5th c. B.C.E.?) According to tradition, a philosopher who was a contemporary of the Buddha. Gosala is believed to be the founder of the **Ajivikas**, an extinct religious community whose philosophical position is generally described as **fatalism**. In the Buddhist and Jain literature he is generally referred to as Makkhali Gosala ("**cow**-shed"), referring to his lowly birth.

Goshala

("abode of cows") In modern India, a goshala is a rest home for aged, infirm, and unproductive cows, where they can live for the rest of their lives in peace and happiness. Goshalas are usually established and supported as acts of religious merit, to provide for cows that would either be slaughtered or abandoned. These institutions are built as a sign of respect for cattle, which is one of the most pervasive ideas in Hindu culture.

Goswami, Jiva

(ca. late 16th c.) A pivotal figure in the **Gaudiya Vaishnava** religious community, along with his uncles **Sanatana Goswami** and **Rupa Goswami**. Although the Gaudiya Vaishnavas were founded by the poet-saint **Chaitanya**, it was the Goswamis who brought order and systematic thinking to Chaitanya's ecstatic devotionalism. The Goswamis were southern brahmins by origin, but their family had resettled in northern India. Their lives were transformed when Rupa and Sanatana met Chaitanya. Chaitanya dispatched the brothers to **Brindavan**, the village where the god **Krishna** is believed to have spent his childhood, with instructions to settle there and reclaim it as a holy place. The three Goswamis lived there for several decades, reclaiming the sacred sites (**tirthas**), having temples built, and above all providing the ideas and institutions that defined the Gaudiya Vaishnava community. Jiva was a versatile scholar who wrote on many different aspects of **Vaishnava** devotion, but is best known for his works on metaphysics, which provide the community's basic philosophical underpinnings. For further information see Sushil Kumar De, *Early History of the Vaishnava Faith and Movement in Bengal, from Sanskrit and Bengali Sources*, 1961.

Goswami, Rupa

(ca. mid-16th c.) A disciple of the Bengali saint **Chaitanya**, a pivotal figure in the establishment of the **Gaudiya Vaishnava** community, along with his brother **Sanatana Goswami**, and his nephew **Jiva Goswami**. Although the Gaudiya Vaishnavas were founded by the poet-saint Chaitanya, it was the Goswamis who brought order and systematic thinking to Chaitanya's ecstatic devotionalism. Records indicate that the Goswamis were **brahmins** whose families originally hailed from the **Karnataka** region. The family had settled in Bengal, where Rupa and Sanatana were in the service of a local Muslim ruler. However, their lives were transformed when Rupa and Sanatana met Chaitanya. Chaitanya dispatched the brothers to **Brindavan**, the village where the god **Krishna** is believed to have spent his childhood, with instructions to settle there and reclaim it as a holy place. The three Goswamis lived there for several decades, reclaiming the sacred sites (**tirthas**), having temples built, and above all providing the ideas and institutions that defined the Gaudiya Vaishnava community. Rupa was a passionate devotee (**bhakta**) of Krishna, but also had interests as a dramatist and a scholar. In addition to writing poetry as a vehicle for expressing devotion to Krishna, he also focused on analyzing **bhakti** as an emotional experience. He is most famous for enumerating the five **modes of devotion**, explaining the different possible ways to experience the love of God. For further information see Sushil Kumar De, *Early History of the Vaishnava Faith and Movement in Bengal*, 1961; and Shrivatsa Goswami, "Radha" in John Stratton Hawley and Donna Wulff (eds.), *The Divine Consort*, 1982.

Goswami, Sanatana

(ca. mid-16th c.) A disciple of the Bengali saint **Chaitanya**, and a pivotal figure in the establishment of the **Gaudiya Vaishnava** community, along with his brother **Rupa Goswami** and his nephew **Jiva Goswami**. Although the Gaudiya Vaishnavas were founded by the poet-saint Chaitanya, it was the Goswamis who brought order and systematic thinking to Chaitanya's ecstatic devotionalism. Records indicate that the Goswamis were **brahmins** whose families originally hailed from the **Karnataka** region. The family had settled in Bengal, where Rupa and Sanatana were in the service of a local Muslim ruler. However, their lives were transformed when Rupa and Sanatana met Chaitanya. Chaitanya dispatched the brothers to **Brindavan**, the village where the god **Krishna** is believed to have spent his childhood, with instructions to settle there and reclaim it as a holy place. The three Goswamis lived there for several decades, reclaiming the sacred sites (**tirthas**), having temples built, and above all providing the ideas and institutions that defined the Gaudiya Vaishnava community. Sanatana was more of a devotee (**bhakta**) than a scholar. This is evident in his written works, which tend to be either devotional songs or commentaries on religious texts. Sanatana's most famous text is the *Hari-bhakti-vilasa* ("The delight of devotion to Hari"), for which he wrote a commentary as well.

For further information see Sushil Kumar De, *Early History of the Vaishnava Faith and Movement in Bengal*, 1961.

Gotra

A word for exogamous lineages. Lineages are particularly stressed among **brahmins**, although the status associated with some lineages sometimes led other **twice-born** groups to adopt them as well. The word literally means "**cow** pen," and by extension the family is associated with a particular herd of cattle. Brahmins were believed to be descended from the seven sages—**Kashyapa**, **Vasishtha**, **Bhrgu**, **Gautama**, **Atri**, **Bharadvaja**, and **Vishvamitra**—with each family taking as its gotra the name of the sage believed to be its progenitor. The only situation in which it was really important was in marriages, since marriage within the gotra was forbidden. After marriage, a woman would adopt the gotra of her husband as part of her new identity. Since this practice was observed by brahmins, having a gotra became something of a status symbol. This led other twice-born groups to imitate the brahmins and adopt gotras as well.

Govardhan

Sacred mountain in the western part of the **Mathura** district of the state of **Uttar Pradesh**. According to Hindu mythology, this was the mountain that the god **Krishna** held up as an umbrella over the **Braj** region to protect its inhabitants from the storms generated by the wrath of **Indra**, god of the storm. According to the traditions of the **Pushti Marg**, a religious community founded by **Vallabhacharya** (1479–1531), a particular image of Krishna called **Shrinathji** was discovered by Vallabhacharya on Mount Govardhan, after Krishna revealed its location to the saint in a **dream**.

Govardhan Math

One of the four **maths** or sacred centers traditionally believed to have been established by the great philosopher **Shankaracharya**; the others are the **Sharada math**, **Shringeri math**, and **Jyotir math**. These four sacred centers are each associated with one of the four geographical corners of the Indian subcontinent; the Govardhan math is in the eastern quarter, in the city of **Puri** on the shores of the Bay of Bengal. Shankaracharya is traditionally cited as the founder of the **Dashanami Sanyasis**, the most prestigious Hindu **ascetic** order. The Dashanami ("ten names") ascetics are devotees (**bhakta**) of the god **Shiva** and are divided into ten divisions, each with a different name. These ten divisions are organized into four larger organizational groups—**Anandawara**, **Bhogawara**, **Bhuriwara**, and **Kitawara**— each of which has two or three of the ten divisions and is associated with one of the four sacred centers. Of these, the Govardhan math is associated with the Bhogawara group.

Govardhan Puja

Festival celebrated on the first **day** of the bright (waxing) half of the **lunar month** of **Kartik** (October–November), the day after the festival **Diwali**. The charter myth for this festival comes from the mythology of the god **Krishna**, and this festival is celebrated mainly in the **Braj** region south of modern Delhi, where Krishna is said to have lived. According to legend, this is the day that Krishna lifted up Mount **Govardhan** to protect the people of Braj from the storms sent by the god **Indra**. Indra was angry because Krishna had persuaded the village elders to make **offerings** to Mount Govardhan, rather than to Indra. Krishna held up the mountain as an umbrella for an entire **week**, after which Indra admitted defeat. On this day pilgrims circle Mount Govardhan on foot. The mountain is seen as a physical manifestation of Krishna himself, and because of Krishna's association with cattle, they also adorn and **worship cows** and **bulls**. In memory of the offerings given to Mount

Govardhan in that story, as well as the mountain of offerings (particularly milk-based sweets) that are prepared for celebration in modern times, the festival is also known as **Annakut** ("mountain of food").

Govinda

("gaining cows") Epithet of the god **Krishna**, referring to his childhood in **Braj** as a cowherd. See **Krishna**.

Govindswami

(late 16th c.) One of the poets of the **ashtachap**, a group of eight northern Indian **bhakti** (devotional) poets. The compositions of these eight poets are used for liturgical purposes by the **Pushti Marg**, a religious community whose members are devotees (**bhakta**) of **Krishna**. The Pushti Marg named all eight poets as members of the community and associates of either the community's founder, **Vallabhacharya**, or his successor **Vitthalnath**. Govindswami is believed to have been an associate of Vitthalnath. In his poetry, Govindswami writes from the perspective of a companion (**sakhi**) to Krishna's consort **Radha**, and in this voice not only gives a picture of the divine activities, but also an extremely detailed picture of everyday village life.

Grace

The notion of divine grace has been and remains vitally important in Hindu devotional religiosity (**bhakti**), although it is perceived differently among the various devotional movements in Hinduism. In the Tamil devotionalism that marked the earliest articulation of the bhakti movement, the two major religious groups, the **Alvars** and the **Nayanars**, both stressed the utter transcendence of their chosen god and the gulf between God and human beings. In this understanding, grace became something only God could give freely. Only God had the power to transform human beings and bring their souls to final liberation—a notion of grace not far removed from Christian ideas. Within the **Shrivaishnavas**, a later southern

The Grand Bassin, a mountain lake on the island of Mauritius. Just before the festival of Shivaratri, crowds of people gather at this lake and draw water to offer to the god Shiva.

Indian religious community, there was a debate whether liberation was primarily achieved through one's faith or one's works. The **Tengalai** school favored faith and argued that liberation came from God alone. In contrast, the **Vadagalai** school favored a person's works and countered that humans had to respond to divine grace in order for their souls to gain final liberation. The importance of divine transcendence and omnipotence, as articulated by Tamil devotionalism, has remained an important part of Hindu piety, even to the present time.

Southern Indian bhakti tended to express the **deity**-devotee (**bhakta**) relationship using images of master and servant. Northern Indian bhakti, particularly that which focused on the gods **Rama** and **Krishna**, stressed other images of this relationship: friend and friend, parent and child, lover and beloved. These differing conceptions necessarily influenced the notion of grace, ranging from the idea of God as other and saving power to the sacred quality coming from sharing everyday interactions. In the latter, grace is manifested through being able to take part in God's divine play (**lila**), to play with God, and thus take part in the divine world. In this model, God is immanent rather than transcendent, and divine activity comes in the guise of sharing the ordinary activities of human life. All of these models can be found in modern Hindu religious life, although certain ones are more strongly associated with particular groups or religious communities.

Grammarians

Philosophical school based in the teachings of **Bhartrhari** (7th c. C.E.). The Grammarians conceived of **Brahman**, the Ultimate Reality, as being manifested in sound, particularly the sound of the spoken word. They centered their cult around the word *Om*, a word that is described as the source of all things in the **Mandukya Upanishad**, an early speculative text. For further information see Harold Coward and K. Kunjunni Raja (eds.), *The Philosophy of the Grammarians*, 1990.

Grand Bassin

Mountain lake in the southern part of **Mauritius**, an island in the Indian Ocean 1,200 miles east of the east African coast. The Hindu population of Mauritius have established sacred sites (**tirthas**) in the landscape that often relate or correspond to sacred landscape features on the Indian subcontinent. Grand Bassin is a remote and high lake, which the Hindus on Mauritius call the **Ganges** River. In the days before the festival of **Shivaratri** (February–March), great crowds of people come to Grand Bassin. They bathe (**snana**) in the lake, **worship** at the temples surrounding it, and then draw pots of **water** from the lake and carry them on foot back to their homes. The pilgrims time their departures to arrive at their homes on the evening of Shivaratri, and the water is offered to the god **Shiva** in their local temple. This sort of rite can be found in several places in India, most notably at **Vaidyanath** in **Bihar**.

Grhastha

("householder") In the **dharma literature**, which gives instruction on religious practice and duties, a grhastha is a "householder." According to the dharma literature, the grhastha is the second of the four **stages of life** (ashramas) in the life of a man born into one of the three **twice-born** groups—**brahmin**, **kshatriya**, or **vaishya**—which have the highest religious and social status in Indian society. The householder stage is preceded by that of the **brahmacharin** or celibate student, and succeeded by the **vanaprastha** or forest-dweller, and the **sanyasi** or wandering **ascetic**. In practical terms, for most men the householder stage is the final stage of life, since most men do not choose to move beyond it. The householder stage begins with marriage, and leads to raising and supporting a family. This stage is an active and fruitful time of life, and the householder is indispensable to society since his labors and resources support those in the other three stages of life. This is also the only stage of life in which sexual intercourse is not explicitly forbidden, since the general fruitfulness of this stage of life is expressed through pro-

creation. A householder is permitted to pursue three of the traditional **aims of life** (purushartha): wealth (**artha**), desire (**kama**), and religious duty (**dharma**). Given the depth and richness of the householder's life, it is not surprising that many men have little inclination to move on to the two other stages.

Grhya Sutras

("aphorisms on domestic [rites]") The name given to texts that outline correct procedures for domestic religious ceremonies, in particular the daily rites connected with the domestic sacred **fire**, and the life-cycle rites known as the **samskaras**. The latter rites span the time before **birth** to the memorial **offerings** after death and are still observed by many pious Hindus, although the rites have been modified over time. In theory, a Grhya **Sutra** should be one part of a **Kalpa Sutra**, which should also contain prescriptions for Vedic rituals (**Shrauta Sutras**) and for appropriate human behavior (**Dharma Sutras**). In reality this doesn't always seem to be the case, since aside from the three complete surviving **Kalpa Sutras**, there are at least six other Grhya Sutras, indicating that these texts were composed independently. See also **Veda**.

Guardians of the Directions

A collection of eight **deities**, each associated with one of the four cardinal and intermediate directions. In their traditional order, the deities are as follows: **Indra** for the east; **Agni** for the southeast; **Yama** for the south; **Nirriti** for the southwest; **Varuna** for the west; **Vayu** for the northwest; **Kubera** for the north; and **Shiva** for the northeast. Most of these are deities who were important in the **Vedas**, the earliest Hindu religious texts. Except for Shiva, they were replaced as traditions changed and have become minor deities in modern

Hindu religious life. These eight deities protect the directions with which they are associated. Each direction also carries certain associations because of its presiding deity. For example, south is generally considered an inauspicious direction because it is associated with Yama, the god of death.

Gudimallam Linga

A particular **linga**, or symbolic form of the god **Shiva**. It is reliably dated from the second century B.C.E. and is arguably the oldest existing Hindu image. It is named after the place in which it is found, the village of Gudimallam, which is in the southeastern corner of the state of **Andhra Pradesh**, near the border with **Tamil Nadu**. Despite its venerable age, the linga is still enshrined in its original temple and remains an object of **worship**. The linga itself is a five-foot pillar of polished stone, which bears a four-foot-high carving of Shiva on its front side. The sculptural work is quite detailed and shows several surprising features. Shiva's **hair** is woven into a turban-like shape, rather than in the usual matted locks. Shiva has only two arms, rather than the multiple arms one commonly finds in later images. He carries a ram in his arms, rather than a **deer**—the only **sculpture** in which a ram appears. Finally, the figure of Shiva has no **sacred thread** (yajnopavit), which became commonplace later. The linga is also notable for the detailed work at the top of the pillar, which exactly models the head of an erect penis. This is also a departure from later iconography, in which the top of the linga is usually smoothly rounded. Although linga worship should be interpreted symbolically as an homage to the power behind the universe, the object's form is clearly phallic.

Guha

In the *Ramayana*, the earlier of the two great Indian epics, Guha is the king of the Nishadas, a tribe who lived on the banks of the **Ganges** River. When the god **Rama** goes into exile with his wife **Sita** and his younger brother **Lakshmana**, they pass through Guha's kingdom. Guha arranges for a boat to take them to the other side of the Ganges and personally conveys the three over to the other side. Although Guha is of very low social status, his humble services are accepted because of his sincere devotion to Rama. In the *Ramayana* of **Tulsidas**, a later vernacular rendition of the *Ramayana* that emphasizes the power of devotion, Guha symbolizes how sincere devotion can transcend all social boundaries.

Gujarat

Modern Indian state, located on the Arabian Sea at the border with Pakistan. Gujarat is one of the so-called linguistic states formed after Indian independence to unite government people with a common language and culture (in this case, **Gujarati**). It was formed in 1960 by splitting what was Bombay into the present states of Gujarat and **Maharashtra**. Gujarat's presence by the sea has given the area a long history as a trading center, beginning as the port of **Lothal** in the **Indus Valley civilization**, one of the earliest, highly developed urban cultures.

Most of the Indians who migrated to Kenya, Uganda, and other parts of East Africa are Gujaratis; substantial numbers of Gujaratis have migrated to the United Kingdom and the United States, especially New York City. Gujarat is also famous as the birthplace of **Mohandas Gandhi**. The **Sabarmati Ashram** near the city of Ahmedabad in Gujarat was his home base during much of the struggle for independence. Gujarat is also famous for several prominent holy places:

Guler was the birthplace of the Pahari style of miniature painting.
This Pahari painting depicts the god Rama killing a female demon.

Dwaraka, which is the site of **Krishna's** mythical kingdom, as well as the location of the **Sharada math** of the **Dashanami Sanyasis** religious community; **Somnath**, which is one of the twelve sites where **Shiva**, in his first manifestation as the **jyotirlinga**, came to **earth**; and **Girnar**, which is famous as a dwelling-place for **ascetics**. For general information about Gujarat and all the regions of India, an accessible reference is Christine Nivin et al., *India*. 8th ed., Lonely Planet, 1998.

Gujarati

One of the five southern **brahmin** communities (**Pancha Dravida**); the other four are the **Maharashtris**, **Karnatas**, **Andhras**, and **Dravidas**. As their name indicates, the core region for Gujarati brahmins is the modern state of **Gujarat**.

Gujjar

In traditional northern Indian society, the Gujjars were a **jati** whose hereditary occupation was herding cattle, buffalo, and other livestock. Jatis were **endogamous** subgroups in traditional Indian society that were organized (and their social status determined) by the group's hereditary occupation.

Guler

Historical site in the **Shiwalik hills**, the foothills of the Himalaya Mountains. In the eighteenth and nineteenth centuries these hills were the home to many small kingdoms, which served as important sites for the development of arts and culture. In Guler, the **Pahari** style of **miniature painting** first appeared in its developed form. The developed Pahari style differs from the earlier **Rajasthani** style in its emphasis on more linear drawing—perhaps influenced by

European art—and a more restrained use of color, both of which tend to give the paintings a more lyrical feel.

Guna

("quality") A fundamental concept that originated in the **Samkhya** philosophical school, but has become one of the key ideas in the Hindu worldview. The word *guna* literally means "strand," and by extension a "quality," of which there are believed to be three: **sattva** ("goodness"), **rajas** ("passion"), and **tamas** ("darkness"). According to the Samkhyas, in the time before the **evolution** of **prakrti** (primal matter), these three qualities were in perfect equilibrium. As mental activity began to disturb the balance, prakrti evolved into the subjective self and the objective world. All things and beings in the world have these three basic qualities, but their nature and tendencies differ according to the differing proportions. The quality sattva is always positive and carries associations with goodness, truth, wholesomeness, health, cognitive thought, and deep-rooted religious life. The quality tamas is always negative and is associated with darkness, ignorance, sloth, spoilage, and death. Rajas can be either positive or negative, depending on the context. It is negative when one becomes a slave to one's passions, blinding one to careful and conscious thought. However, one's passions can also help to engender activity and industriousness. Although much of Samkhya metaphysics has been long discredited, the notion of all things drawing their tendencies from the differing proportion of these three gunas has become an accepted part of Indian culture.

Gupta Dynasty

(ca. 350–550) Northern Indian dynasty whose ancestral homeland was in the lower **Ganges** River basin. The Gupta capital was initially at **Pataliputra**, identified with the city of Patna in the modern state of **Bihar**, but was later moved to the city of **Allahabad**, which lies at the confluence of the Ganges and **Yamuna** rivers. At its zenith under **Chandra Gupta II**, the Guptas controlled all of northern India and modern Pakistan, as well as the eastern **Coromandel** Coast all the way south to modern Madras. The Gupta reign is associated with an efflorescence of Indian culture, and with the revival of Hinduism in northern India. The force behind both of these trends was the royal patronage of the Gupta kings. According to tradition, one of their court poets was **Kalidasa**, who is considered the greatest **Sanskrit** poet. The Guptas are also characterized as ardent devotees (**bhakta**) of the god **Shiva**, a devotion they displayed through temple building and religious endowments. Aside from Chandra Gupta II, the dynasty's most famous rulers were his father **Samudra Gupta** and his grandfather **Chandra Gupta I**.

Guptakashi

("hidden **Kashi**") Village and sacred site (**tirtha**) in the **Himalaya** Mountains of the state of **Uttar Pradesh**. Guptakashi is located on the **Mandakini** River, one of the Himalayan tributaries that combine to create the **Ganges** River. The site's charter myth is connected to the **Pandavas**, the five brothers who are the protagonists of the epic *Mahabharata*. According to local legend, the **Pandavas** went to **Benares** (also known as Kashi) seeking an audience with the god **Shiva**, but Shiva slipped away and hid in Guptakashi. Guptakashi's two holiest sites are temples to Shiva. At one of these temples, Shiva is worshiped in his form as **Vishvanath**, the "Lord of the Universe," who is the presiding **deity** at the most important temple in Benares. The other is dedicated to his form as **Ardhanarishvara**, in which the left side of the image has female form, dress, and ornamentation, whereas the right side is male. The local claim that Guptakashi is a "hidden" Kashi shows the fluidity of the Indian sacred landscape, in which the sacredness of one place can be appropriated by another. This is a way to claim some of the splendor of Kashi as a sacred site and to attribute power to a much smaller and more remote site.

Gurjara-Pratihara Dynasty

(7th–11th c.) Northern Indian dynasty that filled the political void created by the collapse of the **Pushyabhuti dynasty** late in the seventh century. Like the Pushyabhutis, the Gurjara-Pratiharas initially had their capital at the city of **Kanyakubja**, on the **Ganges** River in eastern part of the state of **Uttar Pradesh**. At its peak early in the eighth century, the Gurjara-Pratiharas controlled most of the Indian subcontinent north of the **Vindhya Mountains**, and the Ganges basin well into **West Bengal**. The dynasty was weakened when the kingdom split in two in the mid-eighth century, with the Gurjaras reigning over the kingdom's western part from their capital at **Ujjain** and the Pratiharas remaining in Kanyakubja. Both kingdoms were engaged in constant warfare with the **Rashtrakuta** dynasty, which controlled central India south of the Vindhya Mountains; they were also harassed by Muslim raiders from modern day Afghanistan. The Gurjara kingdom was conquered by the **Chandella dynasty** in 1019 and became restricted to the lower Ganges basin. It finally disappeared about 1050 C.E.

Guru

("heavy") In its most commonly accepted meaning, a guru is a spiritual teacher or religious mentor; in an extended sense the word can refer to any teacher. The term is often used in the arts, where the relationship between master and disciple is still a vital part of learning. The relationship between guru and disciple (**shishya**) is one of the most fundamental and enduring facets of Hinduism and is the accepted model for the transmission of religious teaching, tradition, and authority. Aside from transmitting

knowledge, the guru-disciple connection also assumes a close and trusting relationship. The guru takes responsibility for the disciple's development, based on an assessment of the disciple's strengths, inclinations, and capacities, while the disciple faithfully follows the guru's direction. The literal meaning of the word guru is "heavy," indicating the impression they have on the lives of their students—weighty and marked. As a guiding presence, a guru is considered indispensable for true spiritual attainment. This is particularly true of secret traditions such as **tantra**, in which the guru's transmission of authority gives the disciple the necessary **adhikara** or "qualifications" for practice.

Guru

(2) **Sanskrit** term for the **planet Jupiter**. It is called Guru ("heavy") because it is considered the heaviest and most important planet in one's horoscope.

Guru Maharaj Ji

(b. 1957) Modern religious teacher and founder of the Divine Light Mission. In the early 1970s, Guru Maharaj Ji enjoyed phenomenal but fleeting success during a tour of the United States. Maharaj was the fourth **son** of Hans Ji Maharaj, a respected religious figure who founded the Prem Nagar **Ashram** in **Haridwar**, a sacred city on the **Ganges** River in the state of **Uttar Pradesh**. Maharaj's father died when he was eight, after which his mother announced that Maharaj had inherited his father's mantle. As with many modern Hindu missionary figures, Maharaj's religious message stressed the need for devotion to an enlightened master, which he claimed to be. At fourteen, he came to the United States to considerable success. It quickly dissipated when he and his mother disagreed over his lifestyle and his marriage to an American woman. He later reconciled with his family, but not before his mother had named his eldest brother Satpal as successor to the family line.

Guru Purnima

Religious holiday falling on the **full moon** (**purnima**) in the **lunar month** of **Ashadh** (June–July). Guru Purnima is a day of respect and reverence to one's **guru**, a word that has historically indicated a religious preceptor, but is used now for any teacher, adviser, or mentor. In the **dharma literature**, a young man is to spend his adolescence as a member of his guru's household, receiving room, board, and instruction. In return he renders to his guru obedience and loyalty. On Guru Purnima, a guru's students are directed to enshrine and **worship** their guru as a **deity**, giving their guru gifts and fees, according to their means. Modern Hindus celebrate this day in various ways, depending on the type of guru they have. Although some religious preceptors are enshrined and worshiped, this practice is not always performed. However, modern Hindus still celebrate this day by paying particular honor and homage to their teachers. This day falls on the full moon, which is associated with completion and perfection—the same qualities that gurus are considered to have. This day is also known as **Vyas** Purnima, since the sage **Vyasa** was renowned as a great guru.

Gurutalpaga

("going to the **guru's** bed") In the **dharma literature**, which outlined rules for religious duty and appropriate behavior, Gurutalpaga was one of the **four great crimes** that made one an outcast from society. This particular offense was committed by having sexual relations with the wife of one's guru or religious teacher. Since the disciple is considered a member of the guru's family and must treat the guru with reverence and loyalty, this was obviously a serious breach of trust. Since these disciples are adolescent men and many of their gurus may have had wives much younger than themselves, such proximity could have easily generated serious temptation and required a strict prohibition to maintain appropriate relationships. The gravity of this offense can be seen by the penances prescribed for its expiation (**prayashchitta**). According to the dharma literature, the offender could either tear off his genitals, or embrace the red-hot statue of a woman while lying on a red-hot iron bed. In either case it was expected that this expiation would result in his death, although the texts always note that death blots out the offense.

Guruvayur

Sacred site (**tirtha**) in the Thrussoor district in the southern Indian state of **Kerala**, a short distance inland from the Arabian Sea. Guruvayur is most famous for a temple to the god **Vishnu**, worshiped in his form as **Krishna**, and the temple's main image is of Krishna as a young boy just past toddler age. According to the temple's charter myth, the image at Guruvayur was originally at Krishna's mythic kingdom in the city of **Dwaraka**, on the Arabian Sea in the northern Indian state of **Gujarat**. When Dwaraka was destroyed by floods, the image was saved from destruction by **Guru**, the **planet Jupiter**, and **Vayu**, the god of **wind**. These two **deities** brought the image to Kerala, and in their honor the place was named Guruvayur. Guruvayur's mythic charter also describes the site's power to heal ailments such as rheumatism and leprosy. This healing power is a great attraction in modern times, not only for people with rheumatism, skin diseases, and other afflictions, but also for childless **women** seeking children and pregnant women seeking an easy delivery and a happy child.

Gyan Vapi

("well of knowledge") A well that is the sole part of the original **Vishvanath** temple in the city of **Benares**. The temple's name refers to the god **Shiva** in his form as Vishvanath, "Lord of the Universe," and was one of the most sacred Hindu sites in medieval India. In 1669 the armies of the Moghul emperor

Aurangzeb razed the temple and built a mosque in its place. Although the temple's destruction is usually portrayed as an act of Muslim iconoclasm, according to Gyan Vapi's account, Aurangzeb may have also intended it as a political message to punish local rebellion. According to local legend, the image of Shiva as Vishvanath was thrown into the well to protect it from desecration, and it remains there to this day.

Gyan Vapi, Battle of

Battle reportedly fought in **Benares** by the **Naga ascetic** warriors of the **Mahanirvani Akhara**. According to a handwritten book in the **akhara's** archives, in 1664 the akhara's soldiers won a great victory near the **Gyan Vapi** well. This document simply states that the **Sanyasis** were victorious against the forces of "the Sultan," although historians have inferred that this figure was the Moghul emperor **Aurangzeb**. If the story is true, this battle may have been a contributing factor in Aurangzeb's decision to raze the **Vishvanath** temple in 1669. In light of this claim, it is possible that the temple's destruction was motivated not simply by intolerant iconoclasm, but by the desire to inflict punishment for resistance and rebellion.

H

Hair

According to traditional Hindu notions regarding **purity** and impurity (**ashaucha**), head and facial hair trap and retain ritual impurity. In ordinary cases this impurity is removed by simple washing in running **water**, just as for the rest of the body. In cases of particularly violent impurity, such as that connected with death (**maranashaucha**), men will often conclude the period of impurity by completely **shaving** both their heads and beards. They may also have their nails cut, probably reflecting that conviction that any dispensable parts of the body should be removed as a way to get rid of any residual impurity.

Shaving the head is also the major feature in the **chudakarana**, the tonsure ceremony that marks the ritual conclusion of infancy to remove any residual impurities left from childbirth. Among adults such head shaving is usually restricted to men; **women** usually offer a token lock of hair as a symbol for the whole, although women may have their heads shaved to fulfill a religious vow. While shaving the head is fairly common, shaving the body hair is not—the **Sanskrit** language has different words for these two types of hair, and they are considered to be different things entirely.

Hala

("plow") In Hindu iconography, the branch of study concerned with the representation of various figures, the hala is an ordinary Indian plow, which represents farming; it is also considered a weapon. The hala is most often associated with the **avatars** of the god **Vishnu**, but the only figure who always bears it is **Krishna's** brother **Balarama**, for whom one of the epithets is **Haladhara** ("bearing a plow").

Haladhara

("bearing a plow") Epithet of **Balarama**, elder brother to the god **Krishna**. Balarama was given this name because of his strong associations with farmers and farming, and also because he occasionally used the plow itself as a weapon.

On one occasion he is said to have menaced the **Yamuna River** with his plow when he was displeased with the course she was taking. This threat to dig a new channel for her induced the Yamuna her to change her course to one with which Balarama was happier.

Halahala

In Hindu mythology, the name of the deadly poison produced when the gods and **demons** churn the Ocean of Milk. The gods and demons churn the ocean to produce **amrta**, the nectar of immortality. Yet their action produces not only the amrta, but also its antithesis, the halahala poison. This is an event of great peril, since if left unchecked this poison is so powerful that it will destroy the **earth**. The poison is neutralized by the god **Shiva**, who holds it in his throat without swallowing it. The poison turns his throat blue, hence one of his epithets is **Nilakanth**, "the blue-throated [one]." See also **Tortoise avatar**.

Halebid

Village in the southern Indian state of **Karnataka**, about sixty miles northwest of the city of Mysore. As at its sister city, **Belur**, Halebid is known for a magnificent collection of temples from the **Hoysala dynasty**, who ruled western Karnataka from the eleventh to thirteenth centuries C.E. The most notable site at Halebid is the magnificent **Hoysaleshvar Temple**,

Ruins of the city of Hampi. These structures were once a part
of the capital of the powerful Vijayanagar empire.

dedicated to **Shiva** in his form as Lord of the Hoysalas.

At both Belur and Halebid, the temples were built from a particular type of stone—variously described as chlorite schist, steatite, or soapstone—that is quite soft when newly quarried, but gradually hardens with exposure to air. This initial malleability makes the stone easy to carve, and resulted in the lush detail characteristic of Hoysala temples.

Architecturally speaking, Hoysala temples have certain unique features: a central hall connecting three star-shaped sanctuaries, and temple towers (**shikharas**) composed of well-defined horizontal tiers, rather than the continuous upward sweep characteristic of the northern Indian **Nagara** architectural style.

Hampi

Deserted city in central **Karnataka**, about 170 miles northwest of the state's capital, Bangalore. Hampi was the capital of the Vijayanagar empire (1336–1565 C.E.), which at its peak in the early sixteenth century controlled most of the Indian peninsula south of the **Narmada River**. The empire's wealth primarily stemmed from its control of the spice and cotton trade—both highly valuable commodities at the time—and the city of Hampi was built on a scale to reflect its importance. The empire came to an abrupt end after the battle of **Talikota** in 1565, when the last Vijayanagar king, Rama Raja, was defeated by a coalition of Muslim sultans from further north in the **Deccan**. The city was sacked by the invading sultans, and has been deserted ever since. See also **Vijayanagar dynasty**.

Hamsa

The name for the Barheaded Goose (*Anser indicus*), a bird with several important symbolic associations; the most significant is **purity** and transcendence, since the bird's color is largely white. It flies at very high altitudes, and it is reputed to nest in Lake **Manasarovar** in the high **Himalayas**, the region believed to be the land of the gods. Since it is popularly believed to be able to separate milk and **water**—

drinking for former, and discarding the latter—the hamsa is also a symbol for a discriminating person, who is able to take counsel from many different people, and to separate the good from the bad.

Perhaps because of these associations, the hamsa is also the name for a particular type of Hindu **ascetic**. The Hamsa ascetics were described as peripatetic—they were directed to stay no more than one night in a village or five nights in a town. They were also directed to perform different sorts of ascetic practices, such as subsisting on **cow's** urine or dung, fasting (**upavasa**) for a month at a time, or observing the **chandrayana** rite, a fast in which one increases and decreases one's food consumption according to the waxing and waning of the **moon**.

Hanuman

Monkey-headed Hindu god. Hanuman originally appears in the ***Ramayana,*** the earlier of the two great Indian epics, where he is described as a minister of the monkey king **Sugriva** and a devoted servant of **Rama**, the god-king who is the epic's protagonist. Despite Hanuman's seemingly minor place in the Hindu pantheon, he is an enormously popular **deity** in modern India, because he gives humans a god essentially like themselves (or as they would like to be) but on a greater scale and with greater capacity.

Hanuman is said to have been born of a union between the **wind**-god, **Vayu**, and the nymph **Anjana**. After his **birth** the infant Hanuman is continually hungry, and one day he attempts to eat the **sun**. **Indra**, the king of the gods and ruler of **heaven**, is incensed at Hanuman's action, and strikes the infant with a thunderbolt, breaking his jaw (hanu). Vayu becomes very angry upon learning of his **son's** injury and ceases to perform his usual activities. Since in Indian physiology winds are responsible for all internal functions—including digestion, respiration, and elimination—Vayu's

Image of Hanuman, a monkey-headed god who is a devoted servant of the god Rama. He plays a pivotal role in the Hindu epic the *Ramayana*.

strike means that no one can live a normal life. After a short time the gods realize their predicament and beg Vayu for forgiveness; he is placated when each of the gods promises to give Hanuman a divine gift.

By virtue of these divine gifts, Hanuman gains great powers. He is immensely strong, and his image portrays him with bulging muscles. He is also skilled as a healer, both through his skill with herbs and natural medicines, and his magical abilities to protect people from evil supernatural beings. Among his most unusual divine gifts are the power to live as long as he likes and to choose the time of his death.

His greatest virtue, and many would say the real source of his power, is his devotion (**bhakti**) to Rama. In the *Ramayana*, Hanuman plays a pivotal role in advancing the story. Hanuman is sent out with a troop of other monkeys to search for **Sita**, Rama's kidnapped wife, and after a long and arduous search finally finds her imprisoned in the kingdom of **Lanka**.

Hanuman plays an even greater role in the *Ramcharitmanas* (a vernacular version of the *Ramayana* written by **Tulsidas**), in which he is transformed from a powerful monkey servant to the devotee (**bhakta**), whose only aim is to serve Rama with loving devotion. This devotion precludes any type of worldly attachment, including marriage and family, and Hanuman remains a model for a religious lifestyle stressing celibate **asceticism**. In Indian culture, **celibacy** is perceived as a source of power, since it prevents the loss of a man's vital forces that takes place with ejaculation.

Yet for Hanuman's devotees, his greatest virtue is not his strength, but his ability to act as an intermediary to Rama, who is usually perceived as far more remote from human affairs. Because Hanuman is also a devotee, people feel an affinity and kinship with him, even though his powers are far greater than theirs. In fact, they believe that messages conveyed by Hanuman have a better chance of reaching Rama's presence and getting action. In a text aptly named the "Letter of Petition" (*Vinaya Patrika*), the poet-saint Tulsidas appoints Hanuman as his messenger, in the full confidence that his plea will be heard in the divine court. Hanuman's intimate access to **divine power**, his own undeniable strengths, and his perceived accessibility and sympathy have all combined to make him one of the most widely worshiped deities in India, and one who crosses sectarian boundaries.

Because of his service to Rama, he is usually counted as a **Vaishnava** or devotee of the **Vishnu**. Yet in an interesting twist, Hanuman is also considered to be an **avatar** or "incarnation" of the god **Shiva**, and is thus revered by the **Shaivites**, Shiva's devotees. As a protective deity, Hanuman is often worshiped on astrologically inauspicious days, to keep these inauspicious forces at bay. His prodigious strength, celibate lifestyle, and single-minded devotion have made him the patron deity of Indian wrestlers, who strive to imitate him as they train.

Finally, he plays an important role as a healer and sustainer. On one hand, he is famous as an exorcist, helping people get rid of evil spirits. On the other, he preserves life for those who know his special **mantra**, which gives them the power—as he had—to choose their time of death. Given his importance in modern Hindu life, Hanuman is only now receiving the attention he deserves. For more information see Sudhir Kakar, *Shamans, Mystics, and Doctors,* 1982.

Hanuman Chalisa

("**Hanuman's** forty") Forty poetic stanzas in praise of the god Hanuman, written in **Hindi**. A signature line (**bhanita**) at the end of the text attributes it as written by the poet-saint **Tulsidas** (1532–1623), best known as the composer of the **Ramcharitmanas**, a vernacular version of the epic **Ramayana**.

Short texts like the *Hanuman Chalisa* are often sung as a devotional act, or as an established part of **worship**, and in many cases people can recite the text by heart. The text is written in the **chaupai meter**, the predominant meter in the *Ramcharitmanas*.

The text begins with a description of Hanuman's physical features, then relates his devotion to **Rama** and his heroic deeds in the *Ramayana*. The closing verses reiterate Hanuman's power, promise benefits as a result of the recitation of the verses, and reclaim Tulsidas's wish that Hanuman will reside in his heart.

Hanuman Jayanti

Festival of the god **Hanuman's** birthday. In southern India, this is celebrated on the **full moon** in the **lunar month** of **Chaitra** (March–April), whereas in northern India it is more commonly celebrated on the fourteenth **day** of the dark (waning) half of the lunar month of **Kartik** (October–November). This latter date reflects the date of **Shivaratri**, the most important festival of **Shiva**, which is celebrated on the fourteenth day of the waning half of the month **Phalgun** (usually in February). The two festivals are associated because Hanuman is sometimes deemed an **avatar** or "incarnation" of Shiva, come to **earth** to serve the god-king **Rama**.

Although Hanuman's primary mythic importance is as a faithful and powerful servant of Rama, in everyday religious life Hanuman is a very important **deity**, with a wide following. His birthday has no prescribed celebrations, but usually his devotees (**bhakta**) often mark it with **worship**, festive processions, and devotional reading of religious texts, particularly the *Hanuman Chalisa* and the *Ramayana*.

Hara

("taking away," "Destroyer") Epithet of the god **Shiva**. See **Shiva**.

Harappa

Ancient city and archeological site on the Ravi River in Pakistan, about one hundred miles southwest of the modern city of Lahore. Harappa is one of the cities of the **Indus Valley civilization**, a highly developed urban culture that flourished in the Indus Valley region between the fourth and third millennia B.C.E. Harappa and **Mohenjo-Daro** have been the most extensively excavated of these cities, although archeological work is proceeding in some of the others, and the similarities between these different cities have revealed a great deal about this civilization's material culture.

Hare Krishnas

Colloquial name for the International Society for **Krishna** Consciousness (ISKCON). See ISKCON.

Hari

(probably derived from the **Sanskrit** verb *hr*, "taking away [evil]") Epithet of the god **Vishnu**, particularly in his avatar or "incarnation" as the god **Krishna**. See **Vishnu** and **Krishna**.

Haridasa

(ca. late 16th c.) Poet, singer, and devotee (**bhakta**) of the god **Krishna**, who founded the sect known as the Haridasis. According to tradition, Haridasa was the teacher of Tansen, the consummate musician at the court of the Moghul emperor **Akbar**. Most of the songs of Haridasa describe the love between **Radha** and Krishna. See also **Moghul dynasty**.

Haridwar

Sacred city (**tirtha**) on the **Ganges** River about 140 miles northeast of Delhi. Haridwar is one of India's **Seven Sacred Cities**. Dying in one of these cities is believed to ensure the final liberation of one's soul. It is located on the edge of the **Shiwalik Hills**, the foothills to the **Himalayas**, and is the place where the Ganges is believed to leave the mountains and enter the northern Indian plain. As with all the places where the Ganges makes some natural transition, Haridwar is considered especially holy, and has been a pilgrimage destination since at least the sixth century, when the Chinese pilgrim **Hsuan Tsang** reported enormous pilgrim crowds.

Haridwar's primary importance is as a bathing (**snana**) place, and it draws large crowds on festival days. For centuries it has been an important site for performing **asthi-visarjana**, the last of the funerary rites (**antyeshthi samskara**), in which the ashes of the deceased are immersed in the Ganges. Haridwar is also important as the gateway to the pilgrimage sites in the **Garhwal** region of the Himalayas, and during the pilgrim season (April–October) it serves as an important transit and supply point to places farther up in the mountains.

Finally, Haridwar has a long history as a dwelling place for ascetics. It is a major center for several **ascetic** groups,

Crowds gather in Haridwar to bathe in the Ganges River.

particularly the **Naga** class of the **Dashanami Sanyasis**, trader-soldiers who are devotees (**bhakta**) of the god **Shiva**. It also serves as the winter quarters for many ascetics who spend their summers in the Himalayas. The presence of so many ascetics has had a profound effect on the city's general character, both in the hundreds of **ashrams** that are spread throughout the city, and in the prohibitions on the sale of eggs, meat, and **liquor**.

Harihara

(early 14th c.) The founder of the Vijayanagar ("city of victory") empire, established in 1336, which ruled over much of southern India for the following two centuries. The empire took its name from the capital city that Harihara built near the city of **Hampi** in the modern state of **Karnataka**.

As a boy, Harihara was captured by soldiers of the Bahmani sultanate to the north, and had converted to Islam in captivity, which rendered him an outcast in the eyes of traditional Hindus. As a man, Harihara was sent to regain the southern region for the sultanate, but instead used the opportunity to establish his own kingdom. After gaining power, Harihara reconverted to Hinduism, despite having become an outcast through his acceptance of Islam. His example not only shows the fluidity of religious identity in early medieval India, but also Hindu pragmatism in relation to the ruling powers. Although Harihara had earlier become an outcast, his power as ruler gave him the authority to reconvert without orthodox opposition. See also **Vijayanagar dynasty**.

Harihara

(2) A **deity** seen as a combination of the gods Hari (**Vishnu**) and Hara (**Shiva**). Behind this hybrid deity lay the conviction that both of these divinities were differing manifestations of the same **divine power**.

This underlying unity was represented in several different ways. One way was to create a figure whose right half had the attributes of Shiva, and whose left half had those of Vishnu. Another method, found most often in modern poster art, is to display both Vishnu and Shiva in their full forms, riding on their respective animal vehicles. Vishnu's **elephant** and Shiva's **bull** are conjoined at the head, in a way that one can discern the heads of both **animals**, but only one can be perceived at any given moment. Both the elephant-bull and the divided figure show that Vishnu and Shiva are manifestations of the same divine energy, and that the particular deity one perceives depends on one's perspective at the moment. The joint Harihara figure presents an important religious truth, but this idea is far too abstract to become popular or widespread. In their everyday religious lives people have tended to **worship** one or the other of these deities, rather than their idealized union.

Harijan

("child of God") Name used by **Mohandas Gandhi** (1869–1948) to designate those social groups formerly known as **untouchables**. The name reflected Gandhi's conviction that these people were human beings like any others, and thus children of God.

Unfortunately, the word *harijan* can also carry a pejorative sense in modern India. It is used for any child whose father is unknown—with the child's paternity ascribed to God—and is thus a euphemism for "bastard." In modern times, the people whom Gandhi called Harijans prefer to used the name **dalit** ("oppressed"), since they feel that this more accurately describes their social status.

Hariray

(mid-17th c.) A noted disciple of **Gokulnath** (1551–1640 C.E.), the third **guru** of the **Pushti Marg**, a religious community founded by his grandfather **Vallabhacharya**.

Aside from being a disciple, Hariray is considered Gokulnath's scribe. He is the commentator on a text called the ***Chaurasi Vaishnavan ki Varta*** ("Account of eighty-four Vaishnavas"), and probably compiled the text itself under Gokulnath's direction. This text describes the lives of eighty-four **Vaishnavas**, or devotees (**bhakta**), of the god **Vishnu**, all associates and disciples of Gokulnath's father **Vitthalnath** or his grandfather Vallabhacharya. The text's real purpose is not to provide biographies of these figures, but to illustrate the importance of the Pushti Marg and its leaders. Besides the *Chaurasi Vaishnavan ki Varta*, a number of poems are also attributed to Hariray, but these may be the work of a later figure.

Harishchandra

In Hindu mythology, a king who is famous for his truthfulness and integrity. In modern Hindu culture, he has become the symbol for someone who patiently endures undeserved suffering.

Harishchandra's suffering is a result of the long-standing feud between the sages **Vasishtha**—his family priest—and **Vishvamitra**. When Vasishtha praises the virtue of Harishchandra, Vishvamitra becomes determined to prove him wrong. Disguised as an old **brahmin**, Vishvamitra conjures up an imaginary **son** using his magical powers and gets Harishchandra to promise that he will give whatever is necessary for the boy's wedding.

When the time comes to redeem this promise, Vishvamitra demands Harishchandra's kingdom. Vishvamitra expects that the king will balk at this demand, but Harishchandra immediately fulfills it. Vishvamitra then remarks that when giving a gift to a brahmin it is customary to give a gift of money (**dakshina**) and demands a large sum. To raise this amount, Harishchandra first sells his wife (**Chandramati**) and son into slavery and finally sells himself to an outcast, who puts him to work burning bodies at the **cremation ground**.

After enduring these miseries for some time, Harishchandra's son is bitten by a snake and dies. When Chandramati brings the body to be burned, he does not recognize her. He refuses to cremate the boy until the cremation fee is paid, since this will cheat his master of his rightful income. Chandramati has no money for the fee, and after listening to her lamentations Harishchandra recognizes her and becomes doubly miserable. The couple finally decides that **suicide** is their only escape from their misery and make a pyre on which to burn themselves. When Harishchandra is about to light the pyre, the gods appear before them, praising his righteousness and his commitment to his word, and Harishchandra's outcast master is revealed as **dharma** ("righteousness") incarnate. Harishchandra's son is restored to life, his kingdom is restored back to him, and everyone lives happily ever after.

Harivamsh

(d. 1552) Poet, singer, and founder of the **Radhavallabh** religious community, which is based on the figure of **Radha**. Initially portrayed as the god **Krishna's** human consort, she was later considered his adulterous mistress. The Radhavallabh community took a very different perspective, stressing Radha's nature as a **deity**, her equality and identity with Krishna, and her status as his lawful wife. The Radhavallabhs focused on the love (hit) of Radha for Krishna, and because of this emphasis the poet is also known as "Hit Harivamsh."

Harivamsh's poetry treats many of the traditional themes found in Krishna devotionalism, but from the perspective of a female companion (**sakhi**). He compiled a collection of eighty-four poems known as the *Hit-chaurasi*, which are notable both for their highly Sanskritized language and for their incorporation of the **alamkara** ("poetic ornamentation") tradition of earlier **Sanskrit** poetry. For further information see Charles S. J. White, *The Caurasi Pad of Sri Hit Harivams*, 1977.

Harivamsha

("lineage of Hari") A text traditionally considered to be an appendix to the *Mahabharata*, the later of the two great Hindu epics. The *Harivamsha* is one of the important **puranas**, which describe the mythology of the Hindu **deities**, as well as many other facets of popular Hindu life.

In particular, the *Harivamsha* is devoted to the mythology of the god **Krishna** (also known as Hari). It is especially important for the traditional stories connected with Krishna's childhood in the **Braj** region, for which it is the earliest identifiable source. The episodes described in the *Harivamsha* are further developed in the *Bhagavata Purana*, a later work that is considered the most influential text for the cult of Krishna.

Harsha

(r. 606–647) Ruler in the Pushyabhuti line, a dynasty whose capital was the city of **Kanyakubja** in eastern **Uttar Pradesh**. Harsha is generally considered the greatest Pushyabhuti ruler; he controlled a large part of northern India and to some extent restored the glory of the **Gupta dynasty** (350–550).

Historically, Harsha's reign is well-documented, in part by the Chinese pilgrim **Hsuan Tsang**, whose account gives invaluable information about Indian life at that time. Harsha was an able and energetic ruler who spent much of his later life evaluating the condition of his empire. He was also a cultured and literate man—he was the author of three **Sanskrit** plays—whose court was graced by significant literary figures, especially the playwright **Bana**. After his death, his kingdom quickly disintegrated when he died without an heir. See also **Pushyabhuti dynasty**.

Harshacharita

("The Deeds of **Harsha**") A drama written by the playwright **Bana** (7th c.), which chronicles the emperor Harsha's rise to power. Bana was a member of Harsha's court, and thus a contemporary; his tale contains some evident exaggeration, but also a great deal of historical detail. Bana was a careful observer, and the detailed descriptions in the *Harshacharita* give significant information about courtly and everyday life in his times.

Hartalika Teej

Hindu **women's** festival also known as **Teej**. See **Teej**.

Haryana

Modern Indian state that surrounds Delhi, the nation's capital, in every direction but the east. Haryana is one of the so-called linguistic states formed after Indian independence, to unite people with a common language and culture (in this case, **Hindi**) under one state government. Haryana was created in 1966, from the Hindi-speaking regions of the former **Punjab** state. It has traditionally been an important agricultural region, since the land is fertile and productive, but more recently it has also benefited from the attempt to create "satellite cities" around Delhi, in order to spread out the development in the capital region. These efforts have greatly raised the land values in the areas closest to the capital. Aside from this localized land boom, Haryana is a largely rural state.

Haryana's major religious sites, which are right next to one another, are **Kurukshetra** and **Thanesar**. The former is cited as the battleground for the war described in the epic *Mahabharata*; the latter is named as the place that the god **Shiva** was worshiped by the **Pandavas**, the *Mahabharata*'s protagonists.

From a true historical perspective, the level plains around the town of Panipat have seen three decisive battles that influenced the course of Indian history. In 1526, Babar, a central Asian monarch who had been displaced from his own homeland in Afghanistan, crushed the Lodis to end the Lodi dynasty and establish his own **Moghul dynasty**. In 1556 Babar's grandson **Akbar** decimated the Sur dynasty, which

had temporarily occupied the Moghul capitals at Delhi and Agra, and thus reestablished Moghul rule. In 1761 an invading Afghan army defeated the **Marathas**, ending the period of Maratha territorial expansion. For more information, an accessible reference is Christine Nivin et al., *India*. 8th ed., Lonely Planet, 1998.

Hashish

See **charas**.

Hasta

("hand") In Indian **dance**, **sculpture**, and ritual, a hasta is a particular hand position. In some cases, this hand position may have symbolic meaning, as in **varada** hasta or the "gift-giving" **gesture**; in other cases the hasta's name may simply describe the shape of the hand, as in **kataka** hasta, in which the tips of the fingers are loosely joined to the thumb. In the context of dance, all of these gestures have been given multiple symbolic meanings, and the dancer can use these gestures to tell a story through her gestures.

There is some overlap in meaning between the words hasta and **mudra** ("seal"), which are both used to describe hand gestures, and the two are sometimes used interchangeably. Of the two, mudras tend to be more strictly defined, and to be far more stylized than hastas. They stress the positions of the fingers, rather than of the entire hand; the fingers are always in very specific positions. Mudras always have very specific symbolic meanings.

Hastinapur

Archeological site about sixty miles northeast of Delhi. This site has yielded pottery and other artifacts believed to be from the ninth to sixth centuries B.C.E., which would make them contemporary with the latest parts of the **Vedas**, the earliest Hindu religious texts. In the *Mahabharata*, the later of the two great Hindu epics, Hastinapur is the capital of the **Kauravas**, a group of one hundred brothers who are the epic's antagonists. Although the name of the site and the place named in the epic matches, nothing has been found to provide a connection between these two.

Hatha Yoga

System of religious discipline (**yoga**) based on a series of bodily postures known as **asanas**. Practicing this yoga is widely believed to provide various physical benefits, including increased bodily flexibility and the ability to heal chronic ailments. Yet in the **Yoga Sutras** written by **Patanjali**, the earliest systematic treatment of yoga, these asanas are only one part of an eight-step program that also includes such practices as breathing exercises and meditation. The purpose of hatha yoga is to train and strengthen the body so that the practitioner can sit comfortably in meditation. Although Hatha yoga's emphasis is on the body, it assumes a spiritual and religious context that in contemporary times has often been either evaded or ignored—leading some Hindus to disparage such yoga as simply a technique to develop better sexual control.

A more esoteric meaning of hatha yoga comes from the **Nathpanthi ascetics**, who understand hatha yoga as referring to processes in the **subtle body**. The subtle body is an alternate physiological system believed to reside on a different plane of existence than the actual body, but with certain correspondences to the actual body. It is visualized as a set of six psychic centers (**chakras**) running roughly along the course of the spine; above and below these centers are found the two divine principles, **Shiva** (awareness) and **Shakti** (power), the latter as the latent spiritual energy known as **kundalini**. The aspirant aims to combine kundalini with the Shiva principle at the crown of the head; through this union, the physical body will become immortal.

According to the Nathpanthis, the phoneme *ha* refers to the **sun**, a symbol for Shakti, and the phoneme *tha* to the **moon**, which is a symbol of Shiva. Hatha yoga is interpreted as the union of the sun and moon—that is, these two centers of power are believed to exist in the subtle body.

Heavens

In Hinduism, there are believed to be many additional planes of existence besides the visible earthly realm. These other planes of existence include the heavens, which are realms of reward, pleasure, and enjoyment. Beings are born in heaven as a reward for their past good deeds, and the life of the gods living in these heavens is invariably described as long and pleasurable. Yet heaven is not permanent, and when one's karmic merit is exhausted and one's stay in heaven is done, one inevitably descends from heaven to take birth in a lower form.

In general, heaven is viewed as a distraction to serious religious life. Birth in heaven comes only through accumulating and expending an enormous amount of religious merit generated by past good deeds, and thus is a tremendous drain on one's accumulated spiritual resources. Furthermore, once one has been born in heaven, life is so easy and carefree that people generally feel no inclination to engage in religious life. For both reasons, life in heaven is considered a goal to which people should not aspire.

Hedgewar, Dr. K. B.

(1889–1940) Founder and first supreme leader (sarsanghchalak) of the **Rashtriya Svayamsevak Sangh** (RSS), which he formed in the central Indian city of **Nagpur** in 1925. The RSS is a conservative Hindu organization formed for the express purpose of providing leadership for a revitalized Hindu India; for most of its history it has characterized its mission as cultural, rather than religious or political.

The character of Dr. Hedgewar and the RSS are inextricably linked to the turbulent years immediately after World War I, and the profound dislocation in Indian society that came with the struggle for independence. In his youth, Hedgewar had been involved in the independence movement, and for some time even supported **Mohandas Gandhi's** Congress Party. But by the early 1920s, he had become disillusioned with Gandhi's methods. He had also been deeply influenced by the Hindu nationalist **Vinayak Damodar Savarkar**, whose central thesis was that the Hindus were a nation, despite their profound regional, social, linguistic, and religious differences.

On the festival of Vijaya Dashami (**Dussehra**) in 1925, Hedgewar formed the RSS to help create this Hindu nation by unifying Hindus previously separated by divisions of **caste** and class. This date is highly significant, since according to popular Hindu belief any endeavor begun on Vijaya Dashami will invariably succeed. Hedgewar led the RSS until his death, fifteen years after the organization was founded.

Aside from training a leadership corps, the RSS was also formed to protect Hindu interests. On one level, it endeavored to do this by developing more assertive, tough members, and by training them to use traditional weapons such as the wooden staff. On quite another level, the RSS has a long history of charitable work with refugees and victims of natural disasters, and one of its missions is service to the Hindu community.

In either case the RSS has often been perceived as anti-Muslim—until 1977, non-Hindus were barred from being members—and many of its members view the Muslim community as aliens in India, if not actual enemies. Throughout his life, Hedgewar kept the RSS strictly aloof from politics, and his insistence that it was a cultural and character-building organization helped keep it from being banned by the British. Under its banner as a cultural organization, the RSS spread from the state of **Maharashtra** to other parts of India, aided in part by deteriorating Hindu-Muslim relations in the years prior to independence in 1947. For further information see Walter K. Andersen and Shridhar D. Damle, *The Brotherhood in Saffron*, 1987; Tapan Basu et al., *Khaki Shorts and Saffron Flags*, 1993; and Christophe Jaffrelot, *The Hindu Nationalist Movement in India*, 1996.

Hells

In Hinduism there are believed to be many additional planes of existence besides the visible earthly realm. These alternate planes of existence include the hells, which are conceived of as places of punishment for one's past misdeeds.

Traditional Hindu accounts describe the hells in great detail, often linking particular sorts of punishments to particular sinful actions. Just as with **heavens**, life in a hell is ultimately an impermanent state, although the time of punishment is usually described as enormously long and incredibly painful. Still, when the time of punishment is done and one's bad deeds have been expiated, one will be reborn in a higher form.

Needless to say, **birth** in any of the hells is something to be avoided if at all possible, and for this reason people are urged to perform penances (**prayashchitta**) for their sins while they are still living, so that the consequences of these sins may not burden them in their next lives.

Hemp

Colloquial name for *Cannibus indica*, more commonly known as marijuana. In earlier times the plant's long fibers were used in the manufacture of rope and cloth. In contemporary times it is mainly used for its narcotic properties, either by crushing and processing the leaves to make **bhang** or by collecting the plant's resins as hashish (**charas**).

The use of hemp as a narcotic is illegal, except for specific places and times, including certain pilgrimage sites and festivals. However, many ascetics continue to smoke hashish regularly.

Hero-Stones

Monuments erected on the site where a person met a heroic death. These stones are known as **viragal**. See **viragal**.

Hetu

("reason") In Indian **philosophy**, this is an important part of formulating an inference (**anumana**). In this context, the word has two differing meanings, one general, the other more obscure.

The accepted form for an inference has three terms: a hypothesis (**pratijna**), a reason (hetu), and examples (**drshtanta**); each of these three have their own constituent parts. In its most general sense, the word *hetu* refers to the reason or evidence that supports the assertion in the initial hypothesis. For example, the hypothesis that a mountain is on **fire** would be supported by the reason that there is smoke on the mountain.

In a narrower sense, hetu can also refer to the part of a reason that proves the hypothesis. For example, if one proves the statement "the mountain is on fire" with the reason "the mountain has smoke," the part of the reason that indicates that there is smoke is the hetu.

Hetvabhasa

This is the term for a fallacious argument. For a valid inference (**anumana**), certain conditions must be met, or the inference will be invalid. The accepted form for an inference has three central terms: the first is a hypothesis (**pratijna**), which contains a subject class (**paksha**) and a thing to be proved (**sadhya**); the second is a reason (**hetu**) giving evidence for the hypothesis; and last come examples (**drshtanta**), which give further evidence for the hypothesis. In the stock example, the hypothesis that "there is **fire** on this mountain" is making a certain claim

(sadhya)—namely, that there is fire—about a certain class of things (paksha)—namely, this mountain. The inference's second part gives the reason (hetu) "because there is smoke on this mountain," which also makes a claim about the subject class—namely, this mountain.

One condition necessary for a valid inference is for the subject class to fall within the reason given, so that in all cases the reason would apply to it. The statement "there is fire on this mountain because there is smoke on that mountain" is an example where the subject class and the reason given are clearly separate.

Yet the most important condition for a valid inference is that the reason given must account for every case of the thing to be proved, such that it cannot be explained in any other way. This is known as pervasion (**vyapti**) and is a critical test for the hetu. For the Indian logicians, claiming that smoke implied the presence of fire was a valid inference, since smoke was always produced by fire.

On the other hand, the claim that fire implied the presence of smoke was invalid. This was because the logicians could name a case in which fire was not invariably accompanied by smoke, and thus failing this requirement of "pervasion"—the case of the red-hot iron ball, which was considered fiery, but not smoky. This counterexample is known as an **upadhi** ("obstruction"). It gives an example when one thing does not inevitably bring another, and thus shows that the hetu fails to pervade the sadhya, since there is a class of fiery things that do not smoke. For further information see Karl H. Potter (ed.), *Presuppositions of India's Philosophies*, 1972.

Hijra

Name for a class of male transvestites, most of whom have undergone self-**castration** as a ritual renunciation of their sexuality. Hijras often serve as homosexual prostitutes, and they are an established feature of the decadent underside in most Indian cities. Their

Panorama of the Himalayas in Nepal. Hindus consider the Himalaya mountains sacred since they are believed to be home to the gods.

most important social function is to sing and **dance** at houses in which a male child has been born, although they may also be called to perform on other auspicious occasions.

Their ritual role in connection with births shows a strong association with fertility, and at any function their presence is believed to confer health and prosperity on the sponsoring family, for which the hijras will demand appropriate compensation. At the same time, the life of the hijras seems fraught with contrary notions: Although they are ritually associated with fertility, they are themselves sterile, and their sexuality is nonprocreative. Though they are associated with **auspiciousness** and prosperity, they are a socially marginal group with very low social status. For the only reliable study to date, see Serena Nanda, *Neither Man Nor Woman*, 1999.

Himachal Pradesh

("Himalayan State") Modern Indian state located in the Himalayan region between the state **Jammu** and **Kashmir** and the kingdom of **Nepal**. Himachal Pradesh was created in 1966 when the former state of **Punjab** was divided into Punjab, **Haryana**, and Himachal Pradesh. As its name implies, Himachal Pradesh is a mountain state, with its lower regions in the **Shiwalik Hills** and its upper regions in the high **Himalayas**. Most of the state's people live in the long, fertile river valleys between the mountain ranges, and in the hot **season** its hill stations provide welcome relief from the scorching heat.

Himachal is the home for seven of the nine **Shiwalik goddesses**. These seven goddesses are all the presiding **deities** of a particular site, and some of them have become quite important in northern Indian religious life. Himachal Pradesh is also home to a spectacular **Dussehra** festival in the town of **Kulu**, at which all the gods in the Kulu Valley are brought to Kulu to honor the god **Rama** on his victory over the **demon**-king **Ravana**. For general information, an accessible reference is Christine Nivin et al., *India*. 8th ed., Lonely Planet, 1998.

Himalaya

A minor **deity** who is the personified form of the Himalaya Mountains. Although the Himalaya Mountains are one of the defining features of the Indian subcontinent, the deity Himalaya has a very insignificant place in Indian mythology. His most important role is as the father of the **goddess Parvati**, who when she reaches maturity is married to the great god **Shiva**. Himalaya is described as exceedingly wealthy, because of the mineral riches that the mountains contain. See also **Himalayas**.

Himalayas

("abode of the snow") Mountain range that arcs across the northern border of India, although the only Indian states with significant Himalayan regions are **Jammu** and **Kashmir**, **Himachal Pradesh**, **Uttar Pradesh**, and, further east, Sikkhim.

In a Hindu religious context, the Himalayan regions in the first three states are the most significant; the mountains in these three contiguous states are all part of an extended Himalayan cultural region, fronted by the **Shiwalik Hills**. They are considered sacred, both as the literal abode of the Hindu gods (in particular **Shiva**, who is believed to live on Mount **Kailas**) and also as the source of sacred rivers such as the **Ganges**, **Yamuna**, and **Indus**. These high mountains are also a traditional home for Hindu ascetics wishing to renounce the everyday world and search for personal spiritual realization; the physical hardships these **ascetics** must endure in the mountains are also believed to generate spiritual power.

Given their religious importance, the Himalayas are full of sacred sites (**tirthas**); among the most important are **Amarnath**, **Yamunotri**, **Gangotri**, **Kedarnath**, **Badrinath**, and **Nanda Devi**.

Hindi

Modern Indian language classified as a member of the Indo-European language family; Hindi is the "official" language of the Republic of India. Hindi is spoken throughout most of northern and central India as a second or "link" language and as a "mother" tongue in much of the states of **Uttar Pradesh** and **Madhya Pradesh**. It is also one of the broadcast languages for the television and radio networks run by the Indian government and by virtue of these mediums can be found throughout the nation.

As with many of India's regional languages, Hindi has a long history as a literary language, particularly in an earlier version known as **Braj Bhasha**, which was the dominant language in which northern Indian devotional (**bhakti**) poetry was written. The slow demise of **Sanskrit** in contemporary times has helped make Hindi an important language for fiction, learned scholarship, and writing on Indian culture.

In modern India, speaking a certain language often carries political implications, since an important factor in preserving regional identities has been the stress on maintaining one's regional language. For this reason, many people are not about to let Hindi replace their regional languages. This sentiment is particularly marked in southern India, where the imposition of the Hindi language is decried as a new form of imperialism.

Hindu Mahasabha

Hindu religious and political organization, formed at the 1915 **Kumbha Mela**, a gigantic religious festival. The Hindu Mahasabha was originally formed to help foster Hindu causes, such as a call for a complete ban on **cow slaughter**, promoting the use of the **Hindi** language in the **DevaNagari** script, and addressing the problem of **caste** discrimination.

In the early 1920s, the movement became more overtly political and by the early 1930s espoused an unabashed Hindu nationalism, exemplified by its leader, **Vinayak Damodar Savarkar**. The dark underside of this Hindu nationalist crusade was a pronounced animus toward Muslims, which was only strengthened by the deteriorating relations between the two communities in the years preceding World War II.

Although the Hindu Mahasabha was eager for official recognition by the ruling British government and sought to be recognized as the sole legitimate speaker for the Hindu community, these hopes were never realized. The British government included them in talks only after negotiations with the Indian National Congress Party had broken down, and cut relations with the Mahasabha after fences had been mended with the Congress.

After independence in 1947, the

party's image was damaged by its association with **Mohandas Gandhi's** assassin, **Nathuram Godse**. It continued to field political candidates until the early 1960s, but never gained significant political power. For further information see Kenneth W. Jones, "Politicized Hinduism: The Ideology and Program of the Hindu Mahasabha," in Robert D. Baird (ed.), *Religion in Modern India*, 1998.

Hindutva

("Hindu-ness") An idea first propounded by the political activist **Vinayak Damodar Savarkar**. It first appeared in a pamphlet titled *Hindutva/Who is a Hindu?* and is the fundamental basis of modern Hindu nationalism.

Savarkar's thesis was that the Hindus were a nation, despite their sharp regional, cultural, linguistic, and religious differences; furthermore, he defined a Hindu as anyone who considered India both fatherland and holy land. This loose definition was broad enough to encompass all of the variety found in Indian Hindu culture. But it was also clearly reaching for the lowest common denominator. For most Indians, identity is invariably based on concrete regional, linguistic, or sectarian grounds, rather than an abstract notions of being "Hindu."

Yet it is important to note who this loose definition excludes—Muslims and Christians, India's most visible **minorities**, who are marginalized by virtue of their "alien" holy lands. By this definition, Hindus "belong" in India simply by virtue of who they are, whereas Muslims and Christians, no matter how long their families may have lived in India, are always considered to be outsiders.

Hindutva ideology is a fundamental assumption of the **Rashtriya Svayamsevak Sangh** (RSS), a contemporary conservative Hindu organization, and the organizations that are affiliated with the RSS, particularly the **Vishva Hindu Parishad**, and to a lesser extent the **Bharatiya Janata Party**. Hindutva ideals are also a prominent feature of parties such as the **Shiv Sena**, which combine Hindu and regional identity. For further information see Christophe Jaffrelot, *The Hindu Nationalist Movement in India*, 1996.

Hinglaj

Sacred site (**tirtha**) located on the coast of the Arabian Sea in the Baluchistan Province of modern Pakistan. Hinglaj is one of the **Shakti Pithas**, a network of sites located throughout the subcontinent that are sacred to the **goddess Sati**. Each Shakti Pitha marks the site where a body part of the dismembered goddess fell to earth, and then took form as a different goddess; in the case of Hinglaj, the body part was the crown of Sati's head. Hinglaj is the furthest west of all the Shakti Pithas, and thus represents the furthest boundaries of the traditional Hindu cultural area.

The presiding goddess at Hinglaj is known by various names, the most common being Hinglaj Devi. She is considered an extremely powerful goddess—partly because of her dangerous location on the periphery of India, but also because the crown of the head (**brahmarandhra**) is considered the highest and most powerful part of the **subtle body**.

The subtle body is an alternate physiological system believed to reside on a different plane of existence than the actual body, but with certain correspondences to the actual body. It is visualized as a set of six psychic centers (**chakras**) running roughly along the course of the spine. Above and below these centers are found the two divine principles, **Shiva** (awareness) and **Shakti** (power)—the latter at the base of the spine, and former in the crown of the head.

Because of Hinglaj's association with mastery of the subtle body, a visit to her shrine was considered essential for anyone striving for perfection in **yoga**. By the 1800s the area around her shrine had become completely dominated by Muslims and thus well outside the Hindu culture area. To travel outside of this area is to risk loss of one's Hindu identity. To counter the danger of traveling outside this area, it became traditional for **ascetics** who had gone there on pilgrimage to be branded with her symbol on their return to India, as a way to purify them and remake them as Hindus. The political tensions between India and Pakistan since their independence in 1947 have made it almost impossible for Hindu pilgrims to visit the shrine. For further information see George Weston Briggs, *Gorakhnath and the Kanphata Yogis*, 1973. See also **pitha**.

Hiranyagarbha

One of the earliest Hindu cosmological myths. See **Golden Embryo**.

Hiranyakashipu

In Hindu mythology, Hiranyakashipu is a **demon** king who is killed by the god **Vishnu**, in his **avatar** or incarnation as a **Man-Lion**. As a result of his harsh physical **asceticism**, Hiranyakashipu gains a series of **divine powers**, which render him virtually invulnerable: notable of these powers is that he cannot be killed by man or beast, by day or by night, and neither inside nor outdoors.

Protected by these powers, Hiranyakashipu first conquers the entire **earth** and then drives the gods from **heaven**, growing prouder and more oppressive as his power increases. He particularly oppresses his **son Prahlada**, who despite his father's power remains a sincere devotee (**bhakta**) of Vishnu. Incensed at the thought that someone refuses to **worship** him, Hiranyakashipu finally gives Prahlada the ultimatum to worship him or die.

Prahlada calls on Vishnu for help, and Vishnu appears in the form of a Man-Lion—a man from the torso down, with the head and shoulders of a lion—which is neither man nor beast. The Man-Lion seizes Hiranyakashipu in the palace doorway, which is neither inside nor out, at twilight, which is neither day nor night, and uses his sharp claws to tear out the demon's entrails, killing him. The story of Hiranyakashipu is meant to illustrate the danger of pride, and the mythic reality that no power, however powerful, can keep one from the consequences of one's evil deeds.

Hiranyakeshin

(4th c. B.C.E.?) Sage, writer, and commentator, also considered a disciple of the writer **Apastamba**. Apastamba is the author of a type of text known as a **Kalpa Sutra**. He is only one of three authors, along with **Baudhayana** and **Hiranyakeshin**, whose surviving works contain all three elements prescribed for a Kalpa Sutra: prescriptions for Vedic rituals (**Shrauta Sutras**), for domestic rites (**Grhya Sutras**), and for appropriate human behavior (**Dharma Sutras**).

All three of these men belonged to the same school, the Taittiriya school of the **Black Yajur Veda**. According to tradition, Baudhayana was the oldest, Apastamba his disciple, and Hiranyakeshin Apastamba's disciple. This chronology is supported by the texts themselves, since Baudhayana's text is much less organized than the others, and more archaic in its language.

Hiranyaksha

In Hindu mythology, Hiranyaksha is a **demon** king who is killed by the god **Vishnu**, in the latter's **avatar** or incarnation as a **Boar**. Hiranyaksha has performed harsh physical **ascetic** practice (**tapas**) and as result, gained various **divine powers**. He eventually grows so powerful and proud that he spirits away the **earth** herself, hiding her at the bottom of the cosmic ocean. It is at such times of cosmic crisis that Vishnu takes form on earth, to restore the equilibrium of the cosmos through his actions. Vishnu takes the form of a giant boar and dives to the bottom of the ocean, where he slays Hiranyaksha, places the earth on the tip of his tusk, and lifts her from the waters. With the reappearance of the earth, the process of creation resumed. See also **Boar avatar**.

Hitopadesha

("beneficial teaching") A well-known moralistic story that is drawn from *Panchatantra*, a set of moralistic fables aimed at conveying practical and worldly wisdom. The *Hitopadesha* was compiled in the twelfth century as an introductory reader to **Sanskrit**.

The frame story for the both of these texts describes a king who is distressed by his **sons'** lack of learning and good moral character; these doubts lead to grave misgivings about their abilities to be good and fair rulers after his death. He resolves this problem by hiring a teacher who teaches the boys using fables, often with several shorter fables embedded in a longer tale. The *Hitopadesha* was intended to give pragmatic advice about how to be successful in the real world and maintains that caution and self-interest are the keys to success in life.

Holi

Major religious festival celebrated on the **full moon** in the **lunar month** of **Phalgun** (February–March), which in northern India comes very close to the end of the lunar **year**. Holi is essentially a festival of reversal and is celebrated with great enthusiasm throughout much of India. As the lunar year's final major festival, the celebrations for Holi mirror the pattern of cosmic dissolution found in other units of time, whether the solar **day** or the basic unit of **cosmic time**, the **mahayuga**. In this pattern, the order in the cosmos steadily deteriorates until all order finally disappears, but after a certain time is suddenly, completely, and perfectly reformed.

The festival of Holi is celebrated in two parts: a bonfire on the evening before Holi, and the "festival of colors" on the morning of Holi itself. Material for the bonfire is collected in the weeks before Holi and although the things put on this bonfire pile are supposed to be old and worn-out (with the symbolism of getting rid of the old), much newer things are often put on it as well, and this is a time in which people guard their **possessions** carefully.

The days before Holi see the breakdown of various social taboos. In his *The Divine Hierarchy*, author Lawrence Babb reports the use of **obscenity** and bawdy discourse during this time, including stamping the word "penis" all over town using stamps carved from potatoes. As Holi gets closer, pranks such as pelting passersby with water balloons become more and more common. Such behavior is ultimately harmless, but is still completely unacceptable in ordinary times and symbolizes the coming cosmic dissolution. On the night of Holi, the bonfire is lit, symbolizing the destruction of the old, and people may direct obscenities toward the **fire** as a vehicle for getting rid of enmities from the previous year. Mythologically, the bonfire comes from the burning of the **demon Holika**, who tries to trick her brother **Prahlada** into being burned on a bonfire, but is herself consumed by the flames.

The morning after the bonfire is the high point of Holi, the "festival of colors." For weeks before Holi, the shops in the markets display mounds of powders in various colors, most commonly in vivid greens, reds, and purple; the colors are used as powder, or are mixed with water. People play with the colored water using syringes or balloons. In the gentlest type of play, each person takes a small pinch of colored powder and gently applies it to the other person's forehead. Needless to say, the play with colors can often become much rougher, with people smearing and soaking each other with colors, dyeing each other's clothing in multiple hues, and often staining the skin for weeks afterward.

The evening before the festival of Holi, men in Delhi arrange
colored powders to prepare the site for a bonfire.

This and all other Holi-related antics are always described as "play" (khel), and the operating assumption is that one cannot become angry with the people with whom one is playing, no matter how outrageous the behavior or how pointed the insults. The festival of Holi is the one day in the year when the boundaries of the usual social hierarchy are completely disregarded, along with the taboos on physical touching that are primarily based on the inherent concern for ritual **purity**. Another characteristic of Holi is that it is one of the few occasions when socially respectable people consume **bhang**, an intoxicating preparation made from ground-up marijuana.

The morning passes in a welter of noise, confusion, and color, with (at street level) absolutely no rules, symbolizing the chaos of cosmic dissolution. Yet in the afternoon, cosmic (and social) order are suddenly restored. People take baths, change into new clothes, and go out visiting without fear of being colored, and any person bold enough to pelt someone with dyes at this time is subject to severe disapproval.

In recent times, particularly in the larger cities, the license associated with Holi has been taken as an opportunity for all sorts of antisocial behavior: public drunkenness, molesting **women**, destroying property, and the chance to settle old grudges by physically harming people. The chaos is so intense that in larger cities many people stay in their houses on Holi, "playing" with members of their immediate family in the gentler spirit that is characterized as "true" Holi.

Given the threat to public order, the government has taken some action, but the very nature of the holiday makes it difficult to regulate—since it is a festival of reversal, the government is one more force to be disregarded on that morning. Various government agencies have also tried to discourage the practice of making bonfires, although here the concern stems from worries about deforestation rather than the breakdown of social order. For further information see McKim Marriot, "The Feast of Love," in Milton Singer (ed.), *Krishna: Myths, Rites, and Attitudes*, 1966; and Lawrence Babb, *The Divine Hierarchy*, 1975.

Holika

In Hindu mythology, the wicked sister of the **demon**-king **Hiranyakashipu**. Holika helps Hiranyakashipu try to kill his son **Prahlada**, who is a steadfast devotee (**bhakta**) of the god **Vishnu**. Because of a **divine power**, she cannot be harmed by **fire**. She tricks Prahlada into sitting on her lap in a bonfire, expecting that she will be unharmed and he will die. Fortunately Vishnu transfers her power from Holika to Prahlada, and she is consumed by the fire, while he remains completely unscathed.

The myth of the burning of Holika is the model for the bonfires for the festival of **Holi**. On a mythic level, the bonfire symbolizes the triumph of good over evil; on another level, since the materials in the fire are supposed to be old and broken things, the bonfire symbolizes getting rid of one's baggage from the previous **year**, and starting anew.

Holkar, Ahalya Bai

(r. 1761–1795) Hindu queen in the Holkar dynasty. The family ruled one of the successor states resulting from the breakup of the **Maratha** empire, whose capital was in the central Indian city of Indore.

She came to power at a time when the influence of the **Moghul dynasty** had been greatly reduced and moved to fill the political vacuum that this created. During her long reign she managed to wield genuine political power over much of north-central India. She also served as a highly visible royal patron at several Hindu pilgrimage sites, including **Benares**, where she funded the reconstruction of the **Vishvanath** temple, and **Haridwar**, where she is said to have paid for the construction of a **ghat**, which is a structure that leads to a sacred bathing (**snana**) area. For further information see Govind S. Sardesai, *A New History of the Marathas*, 1986.

Homa

In its most specific meaning, homa refers to the "**sacrifice** to the gods" (**devayajna**), which is one of the Five Great Sacrifices (**panchamahayajna**) prescribed in the **dharma literature**, or texts on religious duty. Homa refers to the act of making **offerings** of clarified butter into a sacrificial **fire**, a rite that is directed toward satisfying the gods. Today, the word homa is often used with a far more general meaning, to refer to any religious rite in which offerings are placed in the sacred fire.

Homosexuality

Although homosexuality is not unknown in Indian culture, it has never had a very prominent presence. The *Kama Sutra* contains a brief account of homosexual oral sex and the classes of men who performed this, but it is little more than a passing mention.

In modern times, the male transvestites known as **hijras** often serve as homosexual prostitutes, and they are an accepted if marginal presence in Indian life.

Although according to the dominant Hindu ethos the search for pleasure—of any kind—is an **aim of life** (purushartha), other factors have channeled the expression of sexual desire in other directions, especially toward traditional marriage. One of these is the general desire for progeny, particularly **sons**; another is the notion of the family as the basic unit for social life. In addition, the traditional male concern with losing vitality through seminal emission is a reason to abstain from sexual relations. Finally, the cultural assumption that ultimate wisdom comes only when one has renounced all desires would have affected sexual desire of all kinds.

Hookswinging

One of the more extreme vows performed by devotees (**bhakta**) of the god **Skanda** during the annual pilgrimage at **Kataragama**, in the southern part of the island of **Sri Lanka**. This vow is performed in return for finding healing from physical ailments or deliverance from distress. Those keeping this vow inserted hooks into their back and thigh muscles; ropes are attached to these hooks, and the devotees are suspended over the heads of passersby.

These ardent devotees are reportedly rewarded for their suffering with a state of ecstasy in which they feel no pain and suffer no bleeding. In this state, they are also believed to be mouthpieces for the god Skanda, and other pilgrims seek their advice for every conceivable kind of problem. For further information see Paul Wirz, *Kataragama: The Holiest Place in Ceylon*, 1966; and Bryan Pfaffenberger, "The Kataragama Pilgrimage," in *Journal of Asian Studies*, Vol. 28, No. 2, 1979.

Horoscope
See **natal horoscope**.

Horse Sacrifice
See **ashvamedha**.

Hotr

Type of priest mentioned in the **Brahmana** literature, one of the later strands in the sacred literature known as the **Vedas**. The Brahmanas largely functioned as manuals describing how to perform sacrificial rites—which primarily involved burning **offerings** in a sacred **fire**. These rites were so complex that they required specialized ritual technicians: the hotr, the **adhvaryum**, the **udgatr**, and **brahman**. Of these, the hotr was the sacrificial priest who recited the verses from the **Rg Veda** that were used in the **sacrifice**.

House of Clay

Realm of punishment described in a verse in the **Rg Veda** (7.89), the earliest Hindu religious text. As described in this verse, the House of Clay is a place to which evildoers—particularly those guilty of speaking falsely—will be sent by the god **Varuna**, who is considered the guardian of righteousness and cosmic order (**rta**).

As its name indicates, the House of Clay is a gloomy and joyless place. What is notable in the original verse is the lack of any notion of reincarnation (**samsara**), which later became a central Indian assumption. At the time it was seen as an undesirable and permanent state after death.

House of Lac

In the *Mahabharata*, the later of the two great Hindu epics, this is one of the stratagems through which the epic's antagonist, **Duryodhana**, tries to kill the five **Pandava** brothers, who are his cousins and the epic's protagonists. Duryodhana builds the Pandavas a magnificent palace, without telling them that it is constructed completely of lac, a highly flammable substance. After the Pandavas have settled into the palace, Duryodhana has his minions set it on **fire** in an effort to burn them alive. The Pandavas are saved by the sagacity of their uncle **Vidura**, who not only warns them of the danger, but has constructed an underground passage allowing them to escape from the house and a tunnel to convey them far away without being discovered. When the house is set afire, the Pandavas escape through the tunnel and for some time are safe from Duryodhana, since they are presumed to have died in the fire.

Hoysala Dynasty

(11th–14th c.) Southern Indian dynasty that ranged over the southern part of the southern Indian state of **Karnataka**. The capital city was **Dorasamudra**, which is now called **Halebid**.

Sightseers at the Hoysaleshvar Temple in Halebid. The temple is known for the detailed and elaborate stone carvings that ornament its facade.

The Hoysalas were originally hill chiefs who were vassals to the **Chalukyas** (a central Indian dynasty that ruled from the seventh to eighth century C.E.), but who became independent in 1093. At their peak they ruled much of the states of Karnataka and northern **Tamil Nadu**, but by the beginning of the fourteenth century had seen their power decline. By the middle of the century, their kingdom had been annexed by the Sangamas, whose capital was at Vijayanagar.

The Hoysalas are most famous for the magnificent temples they constructed at the cities of **Belur** and Halebid, which are treasure-houses of medieval southern Indian **sculpture**.

Hoysaleshvar Temple

Largest and most magnificent of the Hoysala temples at **Halebid**, the dynasty's capital city; the temple itself was built in 1141–1182. The Hoysaleshvar Temple is dedicated to the god **Shiva**, in his form as "Lord of the Hoysalas."

Hoysala temples were built from a particular type of stone—variously described as chlorite schist, steatite, or soapstone—that is quite soft when newly quarried, but gradually hardens with exposure to air. This initial malleability makes the stone easy to carve and facilitated the lush detail characteristic of Hoysala temples. The Hoysaleshvar Temple is known for the quantity of lush detail, which surpasses other Hoysala temples. See also **Hoysala dynasty**.

Hrshikesha

("Lord of the Senses") Epithet of the god **Vishnu**, particularly in his **avatar** or incarnation as the god **Krishna**. See **Vishnu** and **Krishna**.

Hsuan Tsang

(605–664) Chinese Buddhist scholar and translator, whose account of his extended stay in India (629–645) provides one of the few reliable sources for Indian life in that period.

Hsuan Tsang's purpose in coming to India was to find reliable copies of the Buddhist scriptures, which had become severely garbled and corrupted during their transmission to China. He was a highly learned man and during his stay spent years studying in Buddhist educational institutions, particularly the Buddhist university at Nalanda. He traveled all over northern India and because of his piety and learning was honored by the kings he met, including the Emperor **Harsha**. For further information see his *Si-yu-ki: Buddhist Records of the Western World*, Samuel Beal (trans.), 1969.

Huhu

In Hindu mythology, Huhu is a particular **gandharva**, or celestial musician. He has the misfortune to displease a Hindu sage, when his amorous **water** play with some celestial damsels breaks the sage's meditation. The sage curses Huhu to become a giant crocodile, and he remains in this state for many years. The crocodile preys on the creatures in the lake, and one day seizes the leg of a giant **elephant**. This elephant is really King **Indradyumna**, who has also assumed this form as the

result of a **curse**. The elephant and the crocodile struggle for one thousand years, so evenly matched that neither can best the other. Huhu is finally released from his curse when the god **Vishnu** himself comes down from **heaven** and kills him. See also **Gajendramoksha**.

Human Sacrifice

The practice of human sacrifice was uncommon in the history of Hindu religious life, but not unknown. One of the common mythic motifs in the **worship** of certain fierce and powerful **deities** is for devotees (**bhakta**) to offer their own heads to the **Goddess** as the ultimate sacrifice and act of devotion, but experts are uncertain how frequently this rite was performed. One mythic example of this is the **demon**-king **Ravana**, who cuts off nine of his ten heads before the god **Shiva** grants him **divine power**. The resolve to commit this action is also attributed to the Bengali saint **Ramakrishna**, although the goddess **Kali** intervened before he could carry it out.

The one place where human sacrifice was undoubtedly a regular practice was at the temple of the goddess **Kamakhya** in **Assam**. This temple is one of the **Shakti Pithas**, a network of sites sacred to the Goddess that spreads throughout the subcontinent. Each Shakti Pitha marks the site where a body part of the dismembered goddess **Sati** fell to **earth**, taking form there as a different goddess. In this case, the body part was Sati's vulva, and the presence of such a highly charged part of the female body made Kamakhya a very powerful goddess.

When the new temple was dedicated in 1565, she was reportedly offered the heads of 140 men, and this practice continued until the British halted it in 1832. The men offered as human sacrifices were reportedly volunteers, who believed that they had been called by her to do this; in the time between announcing their intention to be sacrificed and their deaths they were treated as virtual divinities, since they were considered to have been consecrated to the goddess. For further information see E. A. Gait, *A History of Assam*, 1963. See also **pitha**.

Humors, Bodily
See **tridosha**.

Hundi

In earlier times, the name for a letter of credit issued from a mercantile house. By the early 1800s, these letters functioned as a virtual currency, since in some cases they would pass through twenty or thirty transactions before being returned for payment. Hundis are significant because they allowed families to transact business over large areas without having to actually carry large sums of money with them and thus helped to foster long distance trade.

In modern times, this is also the most common term for a temple collection box, where visitors deposit their **offerings**.

Hygiene

Orthoprax Hindus (that is, Hindus who stress correct religious practice) lay great stress on cleanliness of their bodies and their immediate environment. Although to the outside eye this scrupulous attention would seem to indicate a concern for hygiene, these actions are performed primarily to protect and retain religious **purity**.

In many cases, concerns for hygiene and purity overlap, as in the pervasive practice of bathing (**snana**) and the regulations concerning bodily cleanliness. Both of these simultaneously remove dirt and impurity (**ashaucha**), but in other cases these concerns clearly diverge.

One example of this divergence is the way that household refuse is often simply put out in the street—a prac-

tice that keeps the home pure and clean, but which fosters unhygienic conditions directly outside the home. Another example of this disjunction can be seen in the traditional use of **cow dung** as a purifying substance, or the way that the **Ganges** River is always considered pure, even in its lower reaches where it is full of sewage and industrial effluents. These examples clearly show that purity and hygiene are very different concepts and that, from a religious perspective, purity is by far the more important of the two.

Hypergamous Marriage

A marriage in which the wife comes from a group with lower social status than the husband. Although the ideal Hindu marriage is between a man and woman of equal social status, hypergamous marriage was admitted as a possibility in the **dharma literature**, although it was not encouraged. In most cases, it was specified that a man's first wife should be of equal social status, but that he was then permitted to marry **women** of lower status.

In modern India, where the predominant form of marriage is still **arranged marriage**, most marriages are still between men and women of equal status. However, a hypergamous marriage is likely to generate less opposition than a hypogamous marriage, where a woman marries a man from a lower status group. In the dharma literature, hypergamous marriage was known as anuloma, "with the **hair**" (i.e., in the natural direction).

Hypogamous Marriage

A marriage in which the wife comes from a group with higher social status than the husband. Such marriages were strictly forbidden in the **dharma literature**, and this prohibition illustrates the role of **women** in determining a group's social status.

It is deemed acceptable for women to marry people of higher social status (**hypergamous marriage**), because it is believed that they are improving the status of their group by becoming associated with a higher status group. Marriage to a man of lower status was strictly forbidden, since the exchange of women implies some sort of equality between the two groups, and thus drags the community's status down. In the dharma literature, hypogamous marriage was known as pratiloma, "against the **hair**" (i.e., in an unnatural direction). For further information see Jadunath Sarkar, *A History of the Dasanami Naga Sanyasis*, 1958.

I

Iconic Image

A pictorial or representational likeness of a **deity**, such as a statue or picture. This is in contrast with an **aniconic image**, in which there is no such representational image, and the connection between image and deity is symbolic.

Ida Nadi

One of the vertical channels (**nadi**) in the traditional conceptions of the **subtle body**. The subtle body is an alternate physiological system believed to reside on a different plane of existence than the actual body, but with certain correspondences to it. It is visualized as a set of six psychic centers (**chakras**) running roughly along the course of the spine, connected by three parallel vertical channels. Above and below these centers are found **Shiva** (awareness) and **Shakti** (power), the latter as the latent spiritual energy known as **kundalini**.

The ida nadi is the vertical channel on the left side of the body. As with the rest of the subtle body, the ida nadi has certain symbolic correspondences; in particular, it is identified with the **moon** and is thus visualized as being light in color.

Ikshvaku

In the *Ramayana*, the earlier of the two great Indian epics, Ikshvaku was a king who was the founder of the **Solar Line**. The Solar Line is one of the two great Indian mythic lineages in ancient India, along with the **Lunar Line**; the most illustrious members of the Solar Line were the god-king **Rama** and his brothers. Ikshvaku is the grandson of Vivasvan (**Surya**), the **sun**, and thus he and his offspring are descendants of the sun.

Ilangovadigal

Poet traditionally named as the author of the **Tamil epic** poem *Shilappadigaram* ("The Jeweled Anklet"). The poem highlights several themes important to Hindu culture, particularly the need for kings to be righteous in their judgments, and the power gained by a wife through devotion to her husband.

The main characters in the poem are a young couple, Kannaki and Kovalan. When Kovalan is executed because of a tragic misunderstanding, his wife Kannaki pronounces a **curse** on the city of **Madurai**, which causes many of the citizens to die before Kannaki retracts it at the behest of Madurai's patron **goddess**.

Ilangovadigal is believed to have lived in the first or second century C.E., a date that makes his authorship improbable, since the poem was probably written several centuries later.

Impalement

One of the favored means of execution that seems to have been particularly prevalent in ancient southern India. To impale someone is to kill them by piercing them with a sharp stake.

The most stunning instance is reported to have taken place in the city of **Madurai**, where 8,000 Jain **ascetics** were impaled by one of the kings in the **Pandya dynasty**, after the latter had renounced Jainism to become a **Shaiva**, that is, a devotee (**bhakta**) of **Shiva**. A tradition persists that the ultimate responsibility for this can be traced to the **Nayanar** saint **Sambandar**, who had converted the king and whose surviving poetry shows a deep animus for the Jains. If this report is true, it also indicates one of the rare cases of **religious persecution** in Hindu India, which on the whole has been remarkably tolerant of differing ways of religious life.

Depictions of this mass impalement can be seen in **murals** painted at the **Minakshi** temple in Madurai—whose construction far postdates the alleged event—as well as in popular art of different kinds.

Impurity
See **ashaucha**.

Inauspiciousness
This concept refers to events or conditions that in their very essence hinder or are inimical to life, prosperity, and general well-being. Along with **purity** and impurity (**ashaucha**), **auspiciousness** and inauspiciousness are fundamental categories in Hindu life.

Inauspicious conditions can be caused by a variety of factors. At times the inauspiciousness lies in the very moment itself—in an hour or **day** considered to be unlucky, in unusual events such as **eclipses**, or in astrological conjunctions that are considered inherently unlucky. In such "dangerous" times, one's activities should be severely curtailed, except for things that are absolutely necessary. Certain normally innocuous activities can become inauspicious in conjunction with particular times, and at these times such activities should be avoided.

Inauspiciousness can also arise from certain conjunctions in one's **natal horoscope**, or from erecting a home or building in an inappropriate place. As a quality, inauspiciousness is conceived of as a physical entity that is generated by certain conditions, and which then attaches to individuals, families, or larger communities.

Some of these inauspicious conditions can be avoided by refraining from certain activities at certain times, yet there are certain conditions that cannot be avoided—in particular, the inauspiciousness arising from eclipses or other astrological conjunctions. Whereas impurity (**ashaucha**) can be removed or destroyed through purification, inauspiciousness can only be transferred from one person to another, most often through the medium of gifts (**dana**). For more information see Gloria Goodwin Raheja, *The Poison in the Gift*, 1988; and David F. Pocock, "The Evil Eye," in T. N. Madan (ed.), *Religion in India*, 1991.

Independence Day
Indian national holiday celebrated on August 15—one of the few holidays celebrated according to the solar **calendar**—which marks the date in 1947 on which India gained independence from Great Britain.

Indigenous Aryan Theory
The theory that the **Aryans** were indigenous to the Indian subcontinent, rather than immigrants from other lands. The word Arya ("noble") is the name used for themselves by the people who composed the **Vedas**, the earliest Hindu religious texts.

Nineteenth-century European scholarship discovered structural relationships between **Sanskrit** and classical European languages and speculated that all these languages came from a common parent. Based on further analysis, these researchers hypothesized that people speaking this parent language originated in central Asia, somewhere near the Caspian Sea. From there, some went west to Europe, some went southwest to Turkey, and some went south toward Iran, and later to India. The conclusion that these Indian pilgrims came from Iran is based on comparisons between the Avesta and the Veda, the Iranian and Indian religious texts. These texts show broad linguistic similarities, and thus indicate that the people speaking the languages were closely related. This entire theory is thus based solely on the observed similarities between languages, and assumptions about how it changed.

Indigenous Aryan theory supporters reject this claim and maintain that the

Aryans are the original inhabitants of India, and as proof point to the artifacts found in the **Indus Valley civilization**, an ancient urban network in northeastern India. Both of these claims are highly tenuous and do not address the philological evidence behind the original Aryan theory. The Indigenous Aryan theory has political implications that have helped to spur its growth. Some supporters are reacting against the Aryan migration theory's perceived colonialist bias, since the theory was developed by Europeans and assumes that the dominant groups in modern India must have come from outside. Other supporters of this theory are the proponents of **Hindutva**, who claim that all Indians are "really" Hindus, and thus one social group, whatever their particular religious beliefs. This assertion has profound political implications in modern India, where Christians and Muslims are not only religious communities, but social and political ones. By connecting Hindu identity and good Indian citizenship, Hindutva proponents are marginalizing Christians and Muslims as outsiders.

Indira Ekadashi

Festival falling on the eleventh **day** (**ekadashi**) of the dark (waning) half of the **lunar month** of **Ashvin** (September–October). As with all the eleventh-day observances, this is dedicated to the **worship** of **Vishnu**, on this day in his form as the **Shalagram**. Most Hindu festivals have certain prescribed rites, usually involving fasting (**upavasa**) and worship, and often promise specific benefits. This ekadashi falls during the **pitrpaksha**, the fortnight dedicated to the ancestors, and faithfully observing this festival day is believed to result in the rescue of millions of one's forebears from woeful incarnations and bring them rebirth in **heaven**. The name "Indira" is an epithet of **Lakshmi**, Vishnu's wife.

Depiction of the god Indra, king of heaven and one of the eight guardians of the earth.

Indra

One of the oldest and most powerful Hindu **deities**. His status has changed over the years and this evolution shows how Hinduism has transformed.

In the earliest Hindu scriptures, the hymns in **Rg Veda**, Indra is the Vedic deity *par excellence*. As with most Vedic deities, Indra is associated with certain natural phenomena, in this case the power of the storm; he was seen as inhabiting the region (**antariksha**) between the **earth** and sky, the region where storms take place. In many ways Indra seems a paradigm for the virtues and powers celebrated in the Vedas, and (as many have inferred) celebrated as virtues by the Aryans themselves. Indra is the invincible warrior and the performer of great deeds.

One of the central hymns in the Rg Veda (1.32) describes Indra's battle with the serpent **Vrtra**, who is finally killed and cut into pieces, allowing the pent-up waters that Vrtra has blocked to flow freely over the land.

Indra is a drinker of the intoxicating beverage **soma**, whose influence leads him to expanded reveries on his own greatness; he is the ultimate man's man in a culture that is usually believed to have stressed manly virtues. Of the 1,028 hymns in the Rg Veda, nearly a quarter are devoted to Indra, who is described as the power encircling the earth.

Some of Indra's attributes and functions remain constant as the Hindu tradition changed and developed. In later Hindu mythology, Indra's realm is still the atmospheric region between the earth and sky, and he is still considered the god of the storm, the bestower of rain, and the wielder of the divine thunderbolt. Indra is also one of the eight **Guardians of the Directions**, holding sway over the eastern quarter.

Yet some things about Indra changed around the first millennium; most importantly, Indra has been "demoted" to being merely the ruler of the heavenly realms and the king of the gods. Far from being the supreme, unchallenged power in the universe, his position is much more precarious, for he is seen as affected by the workings of **karma**. Indra is actually subject to replacement when he is spiritually exhausted or when a challenger on earth grows spiritually strong enough to unseat him. Many of the stories in the classical **Sanskrit** texts have their plot advanced by Indra's throne becoming hot (a sign that a human being is gaining the power to replace Indra), and with Indra taking some action to counter this threat. In cases where the challenger is a celibate **ascetic**, whose source of power is the power of renunciation, Indra usually dispatches an **apsara** (divine nymph) whose heavenly charms can seduce the ascetic and by destroying his **celibacy** destroy his power as well. In other cases the threat can come from people completing one hundred great sacrifices; here Indra somehow forestalls the hundredth **sacrifice**, as he does by stealing the sacred horse of King **Sagar**. Indra is the lord and ruler of the gods, but his position can only be retained by keeping a sharp eye on all possible threats.

This loss of "divine" position is seen by the way Indra is portrayed in certain mythic tales. In the story of **Ahalya** he is portrayed as a lecher and an adulterer, seducing Ahalya by assuming the form of her husband, the sage **Gautama**. When Gautama discovers what has happened, he curses Indra to have a thousand vulvas on his body, although the **curse** is later modified to give Indra a thousand eyes. Indra's helplessness before his own lust and his inability to withstand Gautama's curse are sure signs that his divine position has slipped.

Although he is still regarded as the bestower of rain and the wielder of the thunderbolt, another indication of his diminished power can be seen in his encounter with the adolescent god **Krishna**. When Krishna persuades the village elders to cease making **offerings** to Indra, the latter sends torrential rains that threaten to destroy the village. In the face of this threat, Krishna calmly lifts Mount **Govardhan**, and for seven days and nights holds it over their heads to block the rain. Although Indra expends all his strength, he is unable to prevail against the adolescent Krishna, clearly demonstrating where the real divinity lies.

In the *Mahabharata*, the later of the two great Hindu epics, Indra is revealed to be the divine father of **Arjuna**, one of the five **Pandava** brothers who are the epic's protagonists. Arjuna shares his father's strengths and weaknesses; he is heroic and gallant, the archetypal warrior who relishes the clash of battle and is unceasing in defense of his personal and family honor. He can also be selfish, egocentric, and boorish, and has many extramarital liaisons, some of which produce offspring. Both are wonderful warriors, if that is what is needed at the time, but they lack other qualities to make them productive in times of peace. This story of Indra and Arjuna is further evidence that Indra has fallen from the most important deity to a minor one who is not an object of **worship**.

Indradyumna

In Hindu mythology, a righteous king who is a great devotee (**bhakta**) of the god **Vishnu**. He has been cursed to become a giant **elephant** by the sage

Agastya, who becomes angry when the king, deep in meditation, fails to greet the sage with proper respect. After much pleading, Agastya decrees that the **curse** will be broken when Vishnu touches the elephant on the back. As a result of this curse, Indradyumna roams the **earth** as an elephant for many years.

On one occasion when he is drinking at a lake, his hind leg is seized by a giant crocodile. The crocodile is actually a **gandharva** or celestial musician named **Huhu**, whom another sage had cursed to become a crocodile. Their struggle lasts for a thousand years, with the elephant unable to get free, and the crocodile unable to overpower the elephant. Finally Vishnu himself appears, kills the crocodile, and restores Indradyumna to his previous form. The release of Indradyumna from both the curse and the crocodile is known as **Gajendramoksha**, the "release of the elephant king."

Indrajit

("Conqueror of **Indra**") In the *Ramayana*, the earlier of the two great Indian epics, Indrajit is the **son** of the **demon**-king **Ravana** by his wife **Mandodari**. In some later versions of the *Ramayana*, he is portrayed as the son of the god **Shiva** himself, born after his mother had married Ravana. Like his father, Indrajit is a great devotee (**bhakta**) of Shiva, and because of his devotion Shiva teaches Indrajit how to make himself invisible. For a warrior, this power is obviously very valuable, and through it Indrajit is able to conquer Indra's heavenly realm and take Indra as a prisoner back to **Lanka**, hence his name.

The god **Brahma** goes to Lanka, the kingdom of Ravana, to arrange for Indra's release, in return for which Indrajit demands physical immortality. When he is told that this is impossible, Indrajit requests a different power—that when he performs a certain **sacrifice** he will receive horses and a chariot so that he can kill whatever enemy he faces, and while in the chariot he cannot be killed.

When the god-king **Rama** and allies are storming Lanka, in an effort to regain Rama's kidnapped wife **Sita**, Indrajit begins to perform this sacrifice. Warned about this danger by Brahma, Rama sends his brother **Lakshmana** to interrupt it. Lakshmana successfully disrupts the sacrifice, and in the ensuing battle kills Indrajit.

Indrani

(Feminine form of **Indra**) The wife of the god Indra, the ruler of **heaven**. Perhaps reflecting Indra's diminished status in later Hindu mythology, Indrani is not a prominent figure. Her only important role is as an object of desire in the story of **Nahusha**, who through his meritorious deeds has displaced Indra as the king of heaven. Nahusha assumes that he is entitled to Indrani as well as Indra's throne, and makes advances toward her. For his hubris, the sage **Agastya** curses Nahusha to be reborn as a giant serpent.

Indraprastha

The name given to the earliest of the cities built on the site now occupied by modern Delhi; Indraprastha was built on the banks of the **Yamuna River**, in the southeastern part of modern Delhi.

In the *Mahabharata*, the later of the two great Hindu epics, Indraprastha is named as the capital of the **Pandavas**, the five brothers who are the epic's protagonists. According to the epic, the city is built after their uncle, King **Dhrtarashtra**, has divided his kingdom between the Pandavas and his own **sons**, the **Kauravas**.

Although the epic is replete with descriptions of Indraprastha, there is little hard connection between the archeological site and events described in the epic.

Indus

River whose source lies in the high **Himalayas**, but which flows through

Pakistan for most of its length. The Indus is traditionally considered one of the seven sacred rivers of India—the others are the **Ganges**, **Yamuna**, **Godavari**, **Saraswati**, **Narmada**, and **Cauvery**—although in modern times this has diminished, especially since the creation of Pakistan in 1947 rendered it inaccessible to most Hindus.

Despite its diminished religious significance, the Indus remains important from a historical perspective, since many archeological sites from the **Indus Valley civilization** have been discovered on its banks.

Indus Valley Art

Despite the plethora of artifacts that have been recovered from the cities of the **Indus Valley civilization**, objects that could be interpreted as works of art are surprisingly sparse. No traces of decoration have been found inside or outside the buildings, nor has any monumental **architecture** been discovered.

The art objects that have been found in **Harappa**, a city on the Ravi River in Pakistan, have all been on a smaller scale: several stone statues of male torsos, the head and torso of a bearded man, a copper statue of a young woman naked except for bangles and jewelry (said to be a "dancer," because her arms and legs are lifted), statues of **women** with elaborate headdresses believed to be icons for a Mother **Goddess** cult, and the images of plants, **animals**, and humans carved on the **Indus Valley Seals**. The latter show delicate and quite realistic work, indicating a great deal of skill in working the stone, as well as the ability to make realistic figural images.

Indus Valley Civilization

(3000–2000 B.C.E.) An ancient and highly developed urban culture, so named because the first two sites discovered, **Mohenjo-Daro** and **Harappa**, both lie on the **Indus** River in what is now Pakistan. Further searching has uncovered other sites along much of the Indus, as well as a web of settlements stretching east to the upper **Ganges** basin, south through the modern state of **Gujarat** and into modern **Maharashtra**, and along the coast of modern Pakistan. The greatest concentration of these settlements has been found along the banks of the Ghaggar River, a small and seasonal watercourse that runs through the state of **Rajasthan**. Some historians claim that it is the bed of the ancient **Saraswati River**. Evidence from the sites seems to indicate that the sites further to the south developed later, but remained vital after the cities in the Indus River Valley, particularly Harappa and Mohenjo-Daro, had fallen into oblivion. The discovery of these sites in the early twentieth century prompted significant historical revision, since before then it had been generally assumed that the people known as the **Aryans** were the earliest developed culture in India.

The most striking feature of these cities is their uniformity—their general city plan was nearly identical from place to place (although they differed in scale), the bricks used throughout all the cities were exactly the same size, and there was a standardized set of weights and measures. Each of the cities also had a large central granary, which stored the grain necessary to feed such a sizable urban population. Such evident uniformity over such long distances bears clear witness to a strong and centralized government, which some analysts have speculated was religious in nature.

Another striking feature of all the cities was an advanced sanitation system. All the houses had channels for **water**, and an elaborate network of drains and sewers ran throughout the city, even in those sections where the houses were the smallest, and people presumably the poorest. Mohenjo-Daro also has a great tank built of brick and sealed with pitch, which the archaeologists have dubbed the "Great **Bath**." Why were the people who built these cities so concerned with sanitation and bathing?

Ruins in Mohenjo-Daro. These structures are some of the earliest discovered evidence of the Indus Valley civilization, a society believed to have emerged around 3000 B.C.E.

Some experts believe this reflected religious concern for ritual **purity**, rather than hygiene.

Many of the artifacts from these cities are remarkably well preserved, and give us a fairly comprehensive picture of their material culture: what they ate (wheat and barley were the primary food grains), what they wore (cotton), which **animals** they had domesticated (cattle, fowl, goats, sheep, pigs, donkeys, and dogs), and the implements of everyday life.

Archeological excavations have also found more than 2,000 small seals, which are assumed to have served as the insignia for mercantile families. Many of the seals bear writing, although it has never been deciphered, as well as realistic pictures of animals and human beings. Three of the seals display a horned figure sitting with his upper legs

splayed and his heels touching one another. Some viewers have cited the figure on these seals as proof that the Indus Valley culture is the ultimate source for the god **Shiva**, a figure who does not appear in the **Vedas**, the earliest Hindu religious texts, but who later becomes one of the primary Hindu **deities**. In the same way, recovery of several statues of **women** with grossly exaggerated female characteristics—breasts, buttocks, and genitalia—have prompted others to claim that this culture was the source for the later Hindu cult of the Mother **Goddess**.

One of the controversies connected with the Indus Valley culture is what people were living there and whether their descendants still live in India. The generally accepted theory among Western scholars describes a period of contact between the people in these cities and a pastoral group of outsiders called the Aryans. The language of the Aryans, **Sanskrit**, shows certain structural relationships with classical European languages and even closer connections to the Avesta, religious texts of ancient Iran. Based on an analysis of the relationships between these languages and the rate at which these languages have changed, scholars have inferred that all these languages came from a common mother language, and that people speaking this parent language originated in central Asia, somewhere near the Caspian Sea. From there, some went west to Europe, some went southwest to Turkey, and some went south toward Iran, and later to India. This entire theory is thus based almost solely on the observed similarities between languages and assumptions about the rate of linguistic change—some of which are necessarily arbitrary.

The one piece of material evidence for this theory comes in the remains of horses found at the Indus Valley sites. The horse was an established part of Aryan life, according to references based on the Aryan religious texts, the Vedas, whereas it seems to have been absent from the Indus Valley cities—it is not portrayed on any of the carved seals, which show many other animals, and the only bones that have been recovered from the Indus Valley cities are found in the most recent archeological strata. This theory describes a period of contact and possible conflict between the Aryans and Indus Valley peoples, after which the Aryan culture and religion became the dominant force in Indian life. The Indus Valley cities were completely forgotten until they were excavated in the early twentieth century.

The Aryan migration theory accounts for the dissemination of various languages, but is not universally accepted. Many modern Indians subscribe to the **Indigenous Aryan** (IA) **theory**, which contends that the Aryans are the original inhabitants of India, and as proof points to the artifacts found in the Indus Valley civilization. Some IA supporters are reacting against the Aryan migration theory's perceived colonialist bias, since the theory was developed by Europeans and assumes that the dominant groups in modern India must have come from outside. Other supporters are the proponents of **Hindutva**, who identify being Hindu with being an Indian. The IA theory allows Hindutva proponents to claim that all Indians are "really" Hindus and thus one social group, whatever their particular religious beliefs. This assertion has profound political implications in modern India, where Christians and Muslims are not only religious communities, but social and political ones. By connecting Hindu identity and good Indian citizenship, Hindutva proponents are marginalizing Christians and Muslims as outsiders.

Such claims are intriguing, but there is slim evidence for them. The real truth is that researchers have recovered lots of material objects, but what these things mean is open to interpretation. At the very least, we know that this culture flourished for about a thousand years. Its final collapse—because of a prolonged drought, according to one theory—took place around 2000 B.C.E. For further information see Walter Ashlin Fairservis, *The Roots of Ancient India,* 1975.

Indus Valley Religion

Although some experts have made definitive claims about the religion of the **Indus Valley civilization**, it must be remembered that all these claims are highly speculative, since they are solely based on the remains from the cities. Artifacts such as grains, animal bones, traces of fabric, and building foundations give us a good basis for knowing about the material life of this culture— what people ate, what they wore, and the types of dwellings they lived in.

The notion of religion, however, is far more abstract. It is thus not only harder to infer what types of religion were practiced from the artifacts that have been recovered, but these same artifacts can also be used as evidence for widely differing conclusions. The objects themselves are mute and can be interpreted in many ways. Still, among these objects are several artifacts that are intriguing.

Among the artifacts found at sites in the Indus Valley civilization have been ceramic female figures with grossly exaggerated female characteristics—breasts, buttocks, and genitalia. These figures strongly resemble the Bronze Age European image known as the "Venus of Willendorf," which has been associated with the **worship** of female fertility and procreative power. Given these similarities, it seems likely that a similar cult existed in the Indus Valley civilization. The statues give no indication of how widespread this cult was—whether it was related to fertility cults in other places or was simply a parallel development. There is no proof that this cult was the basis for the later Hindu worship of the **Goddess** as the supreme reality. Any such claims are making broader inferences from this limited material evidence—at best, such claims are highly speculative; at worst, they are irresponsible and driven by an underlying agenda.

The other intriguing artifacts from the Indus Valley civilization have come from seals, of which several hundred have been found. Many of the seals have pictures of **animals** or objects from everyday life, but three of the seals from **Harappa** bear the image of a horned figure sitting cross-legged on a small platform. Some viewers have described this figure as a "Proto-Shiva," since it has several features associated with the Hindu god **Shiva**—the sitting posture is associated with the practice of **yoga**, and the figure's horns indicate his form as Pashupati, the "Lord of Beasts."

Proponents of this theory point to the Indus Valley culture for the roots of Shiva, rightly noting that although Shiva becomes prominent in later Hinduism, he is virtually absent from the Vedic pantheon. Virtually the only place that Shiva appears is in the **Shvetashvatara**

Upanishad, one of the latest of the mystical texts known as the **Upanishads**, which describes the god **Rudra**—later identified with Shiva—as the supreme power in the universe.

Although it is possible that the worship of Shiva lies in the Indus Valley culture, anyone not inclined to believe this at the outset will be hard-pressed to find this particular evidence persuasive. There is also mysterious writing on the seals, and if and when this writing is deciphered these relationships may become clearer. See also **Veda**.

Indus Valley Seals

The most enigmatic objects from the **Indus Valley civilization** are small square or rectangular-shaped pieces of soapstone, which are believed to have been official seals for merchants and other individuals. Archaeologists have unearthed more than two thousand of these seals, which generally combine a pictorial image with an inscription. Most of the seal images are common domestic **animals**, particularly the **bull**, but a few portray mythical beasts such as a unicorn, or even more intriguing human figures. One well-known example of the latter shows a human figure—perhaps a mythic hero—strangling a **tiger** with each hand. Other figures include a horned man, in one case standing in front of a table and in another sitting in a **yoga**-like position. He is sometimes identified as an early form of the god **Shiva** and cited as evidence that this **deity's** cult came from the Indus Valley cities.

Far less is known about the seal **inscriptions**, since the writing system for these inscriptions has never been deciphered, although many different theories have been advanced. One reason for the disagreement is the division of opinion regarding the Indus Valley culture itself. Those who believe that Indus Valley culture preceded the arrival of the **Aryans**, and was distinct from it, tend to look for evidence in the **Dravidian** language family, which is linguistically distinct from the Indo-Aryan language family. Those who espouse the **Indigenous Aryan** view, which identifies the Indus Valley culture with that of the Aryans, tend to seek their evidence in the earliest **Sanskrit** texts known as the **Vedas**.

None of these theories have proved irrefutable, and part of the difficulty in deciphering this script comes from the inscriptions themselves. Linguists have identified 419 different symbols, which seems too many for the script to be alphabetic, but too few for each of these symbols to stand for a single word, as is the case in Chinese. The seals' small size also means that these inscriptions tend to be extremely short. Such brevity makes the text difficult to understand, since one lacks the contextual patterns that a longer text would supply. In their efforts to decode these inscriptions, linguists are working with a series of short and unrelated textual fragments. The script could probably be definitively deciphered with the discovery of a bilingual inscription, but in the absence of such a key, the problems may prove to be insurmountable. For further information see F. Raymond Allchin, *The Archaeology of Early Historic South Asia*, 1995; and Romila Thapar, *Interpreting Early India*, 1992. For the Indigenous Aryan viewpoint, see David Frawley, *The Myth of the Aryan Invasion of India*, 1994; and *Vedic Aryans and the Origins of Civilization*, 1997.

Infanticide

The practice of parents killing their child is uncommon and subject to sharp condemnation. In some cases these infants are illegitimate, and infanticide or abandonment is an attempt to avoid the social repercussions of what is considered an immoral act.

There are several examples of this practice in Hindu mythology, of whom the best known is **Kunti**. Kunti has been given a **mantra** by the sage **Durvasas**, which gives her the power to conceive and bear children by the gods. On a whim, Kunti impulsively uses the mantra to invoke the **Sun**, by whom she conceives and bears her son **Karna**. In her panic at unexpectedly becoming a mother—she was still unmarried, and understandably concerned about what people might think—she puts the child in a box and abandons him in the **Ganges**.

In other cases, infants are killed by their parents because of the family's desperate poverty. Almost without exception, the children killed in such cases are **daughters**. If caught, the parents would be subject to a murder charge. But infanticide is often hard to prove if a baby was not born in a hospital, where births are formally registered. For poor families, daughters are often seen as a tremendous financial burden, because the expense that will be necessary to arrange their marriages is often more than people can pay. This attitude toward daughters is also reinforced by the traditional Indian marriage pattern, in which a family's **sons** bring their brides into the family home, continue the joint family, and care for their parents in their old age. Since after marriage daughters become members of their husband's family, they are often seen as "temporary" residents in the homes of their parents. For further information see Elizabeth Bumiller, *May You Be the Mother of a Hundred Sons*, 1990.

Inference
See **anumana**.

Infinite Regress

In Indian logic, one of the **fallacies** to be avoided in constructing an argument. An infinite regress is not only an infinite series, but one in which there is no final cause to make it happen or not happen.

A standard Western example of an infinite regress is the man who informs the philosopher that the world is supported on the back of a giant tortoise. Upon being asked what supported the tortoise, the man replies, "another tortoise." Several similar queries bring the same reply, until in frustration the man bursts out "It's no use trying to trick me—after this, it is tortoises all the way down!"

In an Indian context, the infinite regress fallacy is seen as an extended case of the fallacy of **self-residence**, and equally objectionable.

Inherence

In the **Nyaya** philosophical school, inherence (**samavaya**) is the name for a weak relational force that is assumed to connect objects and their attributes—for example, connecting the color red with a particular ball, and thus making the ball red. See **samavaya**.

Inheritance

Traditional Hindu law has several different patterns for inheritance. A few communities in southern India practice **matrilinear succession**, in which inheritance is passed through the mother's line.

In much of the rest of India, inheritance is patrilineal. Patrilineal inheritance takes two major forms, according to the prescriptions found in two major legal texts: the *Dayabhaga* in the region of Bengal; and throughout much of the rest of India, variants on the *Mitakshara*.

The *Mitakshara* vests joint family property only in males born into the male line. All males have equal shares in the family property, although the head of the family is normally in charge of administering it. Under this arrangement, the death of a male heir automatically increases the share of all the other surviving males, whereas the **birth** of a male decreases this share. The *Mitakshara* gives **women** no right to inherit family property, although women generally have rights to personal wealth (**stridhan**) that was theirs to bequeath and inherit.

The *Mitakshara* system was based on the principle of survivorship, under which only living people could inherit property. The *Dayabhaga* model stresses succession, under which **sons** do not become shareholders of the family property at birth, but upon the death of their father. If a son happens to die before his father, the son's heirs (including his wife and **daughters**) become inheritors, not in their own right, but as representatives of the deceased heir.

Under the *Dayabhaga* model both **widows** and daughters could have a share in family property, and they are allowed to act as agents in their own right. In theory this seems far more advantageous to women, but in fact it is believed to have had some gruesome consequences. When the British first came to Bengal late in the eighteenth century, they were horrified by the prevalence of **sati**, the rite in which a widow would be burned on her husband's funeral pyre. Based on admittedly incomplete evidence, it seems that sati was not nearly so common in many other parts of India. One theory to explain this discrepancy is that sati was the family's way to keep their daughter-in-law—who was an outsider to the family—from being able to gain control over their ancestral property.

Initiation

In general, an initiation is a ritual in which a person is given certain new rights, capacities, and responsibilities. In a Hindu religious context, there are two important rites of religious initiation.

One of these is the **upanayana samskara**, an adolescent religious initiation performed on a "**twice-born**" male—that is, a member of the **brahmin**, **kshatriya**, or **vaishya** group—which is also known as the "second birth."

The other rite of initiation, **diksha**, is conferred on a person at the pleasure of a **guru** or religious preceptor and has no limitations on who or when it can be received.

Inscription of the edicts of Ashoka.

Inscriptions

The oldest Hindu inscriptions are the edicts of **Ashoka**, which were either carved on rock faces or on stone pillars; many of these inscriptions are still readable today, despite being more than two thousand years old. Inscriptions on pillars were ordered by rulers, and were concerned with more sweeping issues, probably due to the inscriptions' public quality and their often monumental nature.

Aside from stone, the inscriptions were often done on copper plates. These were often used to record land grants, deeds, and other sorts of bequests, since their permanence made them more preferable than paper for safeguarding property rights. In themselves such inscriptions generally contain very specific historical information, which can help to fill out more general knowledge about their time.

Installation

This is a general term that refers to the rites for both constructing and establishing the image of a **deity** in a temple setting (**devapratishtha**), and for ritually "awakening" the image so that it becomes a seat for the deity (**pranapratishtha**).

Intentional Language

General term for a cryptic and coded language (**Sandhabhasha**) intended to conceal information from people who have not been initiated into that particular religious group. See **Sandhabhasha**.

Intercalary Month

The Hindu ritual **year** is largely based on a lunar **calendar**, whose twelve **lunar months** are finished in about 354 solar days (as opposed to our 365-**day** calendar). This disparity with the solar calendar means that each lunar year begins eleven days earlier than the previous lunar year. The discrepancy meant that the two calendars would increasingly diverge, such that (for example) "spring" festivals could occur at any time of the year.

It has been resolved by the addition of an intercalary month about every 2½ years—more precisely, every thirty-two months, sixteen days, one hour and twenty-six minutes. This intercalary month can take place during any of the year's twelve lunar months and takes the name of the regular lunar month preceding it.

As an unusual phenomenon, the extra month is generally seen as a ritually dangerous time, and one of its common epithets is the "impure month" (**malamasa**). During this month it is believed that one should not initiate any new projects, or perform any religious ceremonies whose timing is fluid and can be postponed, particularly marriages. **Worship** is highly encouraged during this time and keeping religious fasts and giving charity (**dana**) are also thought to be highly efficacious.

All of these are means of countering the **inauspiciousness** of this calendrical time—fasts and worship are ways to gain divine favor and protection, while charity acts as a channel to remove any potential bad fortune, by transferring it to the recipient.

When this extra month comes in the lunar month of **Ashadh**, it is called **Purushottama Mas**, and especially marked by the devotees (**bhakta**) of the god **Vishnu** as a time for worship and other spiritual exercises.

Internal Sacrifice

In general, a type of **worship** in which concrete external actions have been replaced by internal and purely mental ones. See **antaryaga**.

Intoxicants

In general, Hindu culture condemns anything that could lead to loss of control, including intoxicants such as alcohol and mind-altering **drugs**. The level of disapproval associated with these substances depends on the substance itself and the circumstances under which it is consumed. For example, consumption of distilled spirits ("foreign **liquor**") is seen as a sign of adopting outside values, while consuming undistilled, fermented beverages such as "country liquor" and **toddy** is considered a low-class activity. However, there are a handful of Hindu temples at which liquor is the everyday **offering** to the **deity** and worshipers consume it as **prasad**, the sanctified food or drink that carries the deity's blessing.

The attitude toward intoxicating drugs is also complex. Although they are also subject to general disapproval, Hindu mythology portrays **Shiva** as regularly consuming both **bhang**, made from crushed marijuana, and the intoxicating **datura** plant. Some of Shiva's devotees (**bhakta**) do the same in emulation of their chosen deity, and many **ascetics** regularly smoke hashish (**charas**) mixed with tobacco, a habit interpreted by some as an intentional separation from the normal social system. Consuming bhang is a fairly common feature of certain religious festivals, such as **Shivaratri** and **Holi**, although there are many people who abstain.

Isha ("Lord") Upanishad

At eighteen verses, one of the shortest of the early speculative texts known as the **Upanishads**; the name of this upanishad comes from the first word of the text. It is believed to be one of the late upanishads due to its brevity, its composition in verse rather than prose, and the use of verses that appear in other upanishads. As with many of the later upanishads, the Isha Upanishad propounds a loosely defined monism, in which the source of all things is ascribed to a single power. This power can be discovered through a flash of mystic insight when the seeker is able to transcend the illusion that objects are unconnected and recognize the one real power in the universe. The insight is believed to give a definitive understanding into the workings of the universe and to bring the individual final release of the soul (**moksha**) from the cycle of reincarnation (**samsara**).

Ishitvam

("superiority") One of the eight superhuman powers (**siddhi**) traditionally believed to be earned when a person reaches a high degree of spiritual attainment. This particular power stems from the control over matter (**prakrti**), which along with **purusha** are the two principles of the **Samkhya** philosophical system. This control over primal matter allows one to create, destroy, and rearrange material objects.

Ishtadevata

("chosen **deity**") The specific Hindu divinity that an individual has chosen for more or less exclusive **worship** and devotion. In many cases, this choice is done without denying the existence of the other Hindu deities, although they are sometimes interpreted as secondary manifestations of the ishtadevata. On the whole, Hindus have been willing to acknowledge a plurality of divine names and forms, but each person generally directs attention and worship to only one of these deities. The particular deity one worships is ultimately a matter of personal choice, although family and regional loyalties usually play a strong role in this choice.

Ishvara

("lord") Primarily an epithet of the god **Shiva**, especially when the word is used at the end of compound names, such as **Rameshvar**, "the Lord of **Rama**," or **Mahakaleshvar**, "the Lord of Death." In its more general meaning as "lord," ishvara can also be part of the name taken by earthly rulers, such as the **Chalukya** monarch **Someshvara** (r. 1242–1268).

Ishvarakrishna

(4th c.) Indian philosopher who is traditionally cited as the author of the *Samkhyakarikas*, a collection of sayings that explain the basic position of the **Samkhya** philosophical school. The Samkhya school is one of the **six schools** in traditional Hindu **philosophy**, and its position is an atheistic philosophical dualism, in which two fundamental principles, **prakrti** ("nature") and **purusha** ("person"), are the source of all things.

Ishvara Puri

(c. 1500) Ecstatic devotee (**bhakta**) of the god **Krishna**, who is famous as the **guru** of the Bengali saint **Chaitanya**. Little is known about Ishvara Puri's background, although his surname "Puri" indicates that he took formal **ascetic initiation** in the Puri branch of the **Dashanami** Sanyasis. After meeting Ishvara Puri in 1508 in the pilgrimage town of **Gaya**, Chaitanya was fired with devotion to Krishna, and he began to perform the public ecstatic recitations of Krishna's name that have become an established element in the religious life of the community that claims him as its founder, the **Gaudiya Vaishnavas**. See also ISKCON.

ISKCON

Acronym for the International Society for **Krishna** Consciousness, a Hindu missionary community commonly known as the Hare Krishnas. This name comes from ISKCON's emphasis on the importance of repeating the divine name, particularly the formula known as the **mahamantra** ("Hare Krishna, Hare Krishna, Krishna Krishna, Hare Hare"). ISKCON was founded by A. C. Bhaktivedanta **Prabhupada**, and its religious roots lie in the **Vaishnava** piety of his native Bengal. The Bengali Vaishnava tradition has long emphasized the importance of publicly chanting Krishna's name, particularly in the **Gaudiya Vaishnava** community founded by the Bengali saint **Chaitanya**.

ISKCON comes out of this Bengali tradition, but in other ways it shows tensions that mark it as a twentieth-century phenomenon. Its strong missionary activities make it a highly unusual Hindu religious organization, as does its membership—Prabhupada founded ISKCON in New York City, most of ISKCON's members are Western converts from Judaism and Christianity, and the bulk of its missionary activities have been performed outside of India. The roots of ISKCON's membership, and the general fervor associated with converts, have led to some theological contradictions. On one hand, ISKCON doctrine tends to denigrate human capacity, putting the emphasis on the saving power of God's **grace**. On the other hand, ISKCON devotees (**bhakta**) believe that they gain religious merit by living a rigorously regulated lifestyle that mandates a strict vegetarian diet, abstinence from **liquor** and nonmedicinal **drugs**, sexual activity only for procreation, and a well-established daily religious routine; many devotees also adopt Indian clothing and **hair** styles. In these two opposing emphases—complete surrender to God's grace, and strict adherence to a prescribed "holy" lifestyle—ISKCON shows surprising parallels to evangelical Christianity. Since Prabhupada's death in 1977, the organization has been run by these Western converts, and thus ISKCON can be characterized as a "countercultural" Euro-American phenomenon, despite its Indian origins. ISKCON has a significant presence in **Brindavan**, the village celebrated as Krishna's childhood home, where the group has built a magnificent temple; they are also active in **Mayapur** in Bengal, which they claim as Chaitanya's birthplace. After a period of growth in the 1970s, ISKCON had serious legal problems in the 1980s, including losses in civil suits and allegations of money laundering and murder. For a sympathetic perspective on the movement, see Larry Shinn, *The Dark Lord*, 1987; and Robert D. Baird (ed.), *Religion in Modern India*, 1998. See also **vegetarianism**.

J

Jabali

A famous sage in Hindu mythology and **son** of the sage **Vishvamitra**. Despite his biological origins, Jabali eventually becomes associated with his father's sworn enemy, the sage **Vasishtha**. As a member of Vasishtha's group, Jabali becomes one of the advisers to King **Dasharatha**, the father of the god-king **Rama** in the epic *Ramayana*.

Jada

("inert," "insentient") In a philosophical context, the word *jada* is used to designate physical matter, which is inert and devoid of cognitive functions. In a more extended sense, the word can refer to any person completely lacking religious capacities, sensibilities, or interest, and who is, thus, from a religious perspective, simply inert.

Jagadamba

("Mother of the Universe") Epithet of the **Goddess**, highlighting her creative and generative capacities. See **Goddess**.

Jagadisha

("Lord of the Universe") Epithet of the regional **deity Jagannath**, and by extension the god **Vishnu**, to whom Jagannath has been connected as a form of **Krishna**, the eighth **avatar** or incarnation of Vishnu. Jagadisha is the name given to Jagannath in the **Dashavatara Stotra**, the opening hymn in the *Gitagovinda*, a lyric devotional poem composed by the poet **Jayadeva**. In modern northern India, the name Jagadisha is used in one of the most popular and best-known devotional hymns, the Jagadisha **Arati**, a hymn directed more particularly to Vishnu.

Jagamohan

In the temple **architecture** of **Orissa**, one of the major forms of the northern Indian **Nagara** style, the jagamohan is the entrance porch to the temple, which provides a transitional space between the outside world and the sacred space further in. In Orissan temples, the jagamohan tended to be low and squat, in sharp contrast to the **deul**, or main internal area, a beehive-shaped tower under which the image of the temple's primary **deity** resided.

Jagannath

("Master of the Universe") Presiding **deity** of the Jagannath temple in **Puri**. Puri is and has long been a major center for Hindu culture, a circumstance that has underlined and reinforced Jagannath's importance as the city's presiding deity. Although Jagannath is identified as a manifestation of the god **Krishna**, his roots lie elsewhere. He is generally considered to be an autochthonous ("of the land") deity, who was originally the local deity of Puri but who has been assimilated into the wider pantheon as a form of Krishna, and therefore, by extension, a form of **Vishnu**. This assimilation shows Jagannath's importance and influence in the local setting, since he could not be simply marginalized. It is also an example of the **Vaishnava** tendency for such assimilation, most often through the doctrine of the **avatars** or divine incarnations.

In the Puri temple and other iconographic representations, Jagannath invariably appears as a member of a trio: Jagannath (Krishna) appears on the right, his brother **Balabhadra** (**Balarama**) is on the left, and the smaller figure in the center is their sister **Subhadra**. This triadic grouping and the depiction of a female figure are very unusual in Krishna devotion, as is the form of these images, which clearly come from a folk or tribal tradition. All three deities are made from logs so roughly cut that the facial features are almost indistinguishable, their arms are unnaturally short and stubby, and the images are brightly painted. Each of these peculiar elements is seen as further evidence of Jagannath's indigenous roots. A final piece of evidence for his local origins is seen in his connection with his hereditary servants, the **daitas**, a tribal people who are considered virtually **untouchable**. Despite their marginal status in conventional society, the daitas are responsible for sculpting new images of the trio when they are periodically replaced. The daitas also consider Jagannath their blood relative, further pointing to his ambiguous roots.

The myth explaining these images is based on the virtuous King **Indradyumna**. Indradyumna has a vision of Vishnu in a **dream**, in which Vishnu directs the king to make an image of Jagannath from an enormous log that he has found. While the king is wondering how to do this, a mysterious man appears, who is actually **Vishvakarma**, the architect of the gods. The mysterious man offers to carve the statues, on the condition that he will not be disturbed until he is finished. He then disappears into his workroom for two weeks, but the people are mystified by what he is doing, since they hear no sounds of carving. This seeming inactivity piques the people's curiosity, and finally one of the queens prevails on the king to look inside. When the king opens the door, he finds no one there, and the statues only half-finished. In another dream that night, the king is ordered to paint and consecrate the statues as they are, and this form has reportedly remained the same ever since. For further information on the history and influence of Jagannath, by far the best source is Anncharlott Eschmann, Hermann Kulke, and Gaya Charan Tripathi, *The Cult of Jagannath and the Regional Tradition of Orissa*, 1978.

Jageshvar

Temple complex and sacred site (**tirtha**) in the village with the same name, located in the Kumaon foothills of the **Himalayas** in the state of **Uttar Pradesh**. The Jageshvar temple complex contains 124 different temples, concentrated in an area about the size of a football field. Virtually all of these temples are dedicated to some form of the god **Shiva**, and the few that house other **deities** are either temples to the **Goddess**—considered to be Shiva's wife—or in one case to the god **Hanuman**, who is sometimes considered an **avatar** or incarnation of Shiva. Most of these temples are extremely small—either an open image of Shiva's aniconic symbol, the **linga**, or a temple building no larger than a telephone booth. The three largest most important temples are to Shiva in his forms as **Kedarnath**, as **Mrtyunjaya** ("Conqueror of Death"), and as Jageshvar, from which the site gets its name. The name Jageshvar means "The Wakeful Lord" and signifies that this particular form of Shiva is always alert to the needs of his devotees (**bhakta**) and will quickly fulfill any request.

Local tradition claims that Jageshvar is one of the twelve **jyotirlingas**, a network of sites deemed especially sacred to Shiva, and at which Shiva is uniquely present. This claim is not supported by the traditional list of the jyotirlingas, but Jageshvar has been a pilgrimage site for more than a thousand years. The Mrtyunjaya temple has been dated to the eighth century C.E., while the Jageshvar temple was built about two centuries later. Since that time, further building at the Jageshvar complex has come through patronage by several different groups of hill kings, most recently those of the Chand dynasty, who ruled the region between the fifteenth and eighteenth centuries. The temple complex's indisputable antiquity, its association with royal power, and its identity as a place where Shiva readily grants one's wishes, have all combined to make it the most important pilgrimage place in the Kumaon region.

Sculpture of the goddess Ganga, the Ganges River, who is also known as Jahnavi.

Jahnavi

("**daughter** of **Jahnu**") Epithet of the **Ganges** River, which Hindus consider to be the physical form of the **goddess Ganga**. The name Jahnavi refers to an incident during her creation in which she encounters Jahnu, a great **ascetic** who has amassed great power through performing harsh physical **asceticism** (**tapas**). After the Ganges has been brought down to **earth** by the sage **Bhagirath**, but before she makes her way to the ocean, the playful river picks up and carries away Jahnu's belongings while the sage is meditating nearby. Jahnu is enraged at this disrespect; to punish Ganga, he drinks all of the **water** in the river. When the gods realize what has happened, they are very concerned. They somehow manage to placate Jahnu, and the sage agrees to release her. The problem then is how to release the Ganges in a way that will not defile her, since vomiting her up or voiding her as urine are both unacceptable. In the

end, Jahnu bypasses this dilemma by releasing her through his ear. She continues on her way to the sea, but acquires the name Jahnavi by virtue of being "born" from Jahnu.

Jahnu

In Hindu mythology, an **ascetic** who has amassed great power by performing harsh physical **asceticism** (**tapas**). One day while Jahnu is deep in meditation, his belongings are picked up and carried away by the river **Ganges** (believed by Hindus to be the physical form of the **goddess Ganga**), who has recently come down from **heaven** and is being led to the sea by the sage **Bhagirath**. Jahnu is enraged at this disrespect; to punish Ganga, he drinks all of the **water** in the river. When the gods realize what has happened, they are very concerned. They somehow manage to placate Jahnu, and the sage agrees to release her. The problem then is how to release the Ganges in a way that will not defile her, since vomiting her up or voiding her as urine are both unacceptable. In the end, Jahnu bypasses this dilemma by releasing her through his ear. She continues on her way to the sea and acquires the name **Jahnavi** by virtue of being "born" from Jahnu.

Jaimini

(4th c. B.C.E.?) Figure traditionally cited as the author of the **Mimamsa Sutras**, the central texts of the **Purva Mimamsa** school, one of the **six schools** of Indian **philosophy**. The Mimamsa school is most concerned with the examination and pursuit of **dharma** ("righteous action"). In their pursuit of dharma, the Mimamsa also believed that all necessary instructions were contained in the **Vedas**, the oldest Hindu religious texts. Given these twin assumptions, much of Mimamsa thought is devoted to the principles and methods of textual interpretation used to unlock the instructions that they were confident the Vedas contained.

Jajman

Common form of the **Sanskrit** word **yajamana**, "patron of the **sacrifice**." From the time of the earliest Vedic sacrifices, there was a sharp distinction between the people who performed the sacrifice (basically hired technicians) and the people who actually paid the money to sponsor it and were considered the rite's true beneficiaries. In contemporary times, *jajman* is the term used by **pandas**, the priests at pilgrimage places (**tirtha**), to refer to their pilgrim clients, with whom they have a hereditary relationship. This usage admits the reality that the pilgrims are their patrons, since the priests' livelihood comes from serving them, but the term also carries associations of mutual obligation. Pandas are entitled to fees from their pilgrim clients but must also render services to them, while pilgrims are bound to uphold this hereditary relationship but can depend on their pandas for help.

Jallianwala Bagh

A park (bagh) in the center of the northern Indian city of Amritsar at which several thousand people were killed or wounded in 1919. A crowd had gathered at this park despite a strict ban on public meetings established the day before. The British officer in charge, General Dyer, interpreted the gathering as willful defiance of the law and commanded his men to fire on the crowd. This incident was highly significant in the struggle for Indian independence (finally achieved on August 15, 1947), for it undercut British claims that their presence was necessary to keep the country from chaos and, in the minds of many Indian leaders, removed any moral authority by which the British could justify their rule.

Jamadagni

In Hindu mythology, a great sage and father of **Parashuram avatar**. Like many sages, Jamadagni is a man of explosive and incendiary temper. In one of the most famous episodes, when his wife **Renuka** returns home late because she has spent some time watching a king and his wife sport in the **water**, Jamadagni orders his **sons** to kill her. All of them refuse except Parashuram, who cuts off his mother's head. Jamadagni is pleased with Parashuram and tells him to choose whatever reward he wants. Parashuram requests that his mother be restored to life again, which she is.

Jamadagni is also famous as the owner of a divine **cow** that can provide all sorts of food on demand. The local king grows covetous of the cow and offers to buy it. When Jamadagni refuses to sell her, the king's men grow angry, kill Jamadagni, and take the cow back to the palace. It is in retaliation for this heinous act that Parashuram attempts to exterminate the kingly class (**kshatriyas**) from the face of the **earth**.

Jambhavan

In the **Ramayana**, the earlier of the two great Indian epics, Jambhavan is one of the ministers of **Sugriva**, king of the monkeys. Jambhavan is generally described as a bear, although in some sources he is said to be a monkey. In the search for **Rama's** kidnapped wife **Sita**, it is Jambhavan who convinces the monkey-god **Hanuman** to attempt to jump over the ocean to **Lanka**, reminding Hanuman of his **birth**, deeds, and the divine boons he has been given. Although at first Hanuman doubts his ability, he is convinced by Jambhavan's encouragement and, with a mighty spring, leaps over the sea to Lanka, where he eventually discovers Sita.

Jambudvipa

("rose-apple") In traditional mythic geography, the first and innermost of the seven concentric landmasses (**dvipas**) making up the visible world. At the center of Jambudvipa stands Mount

Meru, the center of the entire universe. Mount Meru is surrounded by mountain ranges, and the part of Jambudvipa south of Mount Meru is the land known as **Bharata**, the traditional name for the Indian subcontinent. See also **Cosmology**.

Jambukeshvar

Sacred site (**tirtha**) and southern Indian temple-town near the city of **Tiruchirappalli** in the state of **Tamil Nadu**, directly opposite the great temple complex of **Shrirangam**. The temple at Jambukeshvar is dedicated to the god **Shiva** in his role as "Lord of the Rose-Apple (jambu) Tree;" the image of Shiva is placed under one of these trees. Jambukeshvar is also one of the **bhutalingas** ("elemental **lingas**"), a network of five southern Indian sites sacred to Shiva. In each of these sites Shiva is represented as a linga, the pillar-shaped object that is his symbolic form, and at each site the linga is believed to be formed from one of the five primordial **elements** (bhuta)—**earth**, **wind**, **fire**, **water**, and **space** (**akasha**). At Jambukeshvar, Shiva's image is associated with water, and the linga is set into a pool created by a natural spring.

Jammu

One of the three distinct cultural areas in the modern Indian state of Jammu and **Kashmir**; the other two are western Kashmir and Ladakh. Jammu and Kashmir is a former princely state once ruled by the Dogras, a small regional dynasty. Although the Dogra kings were Hindus, they ruled over the **minority** populations of the mostly Muslim Kashmiris and the mostly Buddhist Ladakhis; this ethnic and religious division continues in modern times. The Jammu region is geographically part of the northern Indian plain, and the surrounding regions south of the **Shiwalik Hills** are Hindu majority regions. However, Jammu is also in close proximity to the

Punjab, the center of Sikhism, a monotheistic religion that combines elements of Hinduism and Islam; consequently Jammu is also home to a significant Sikh population. By far the most celebrated shrine in the Jammu region is the one dedicated to **Vaishno Devi**, a **goddess** who is reputed to grant all of one's wishes. In the eighteenth and nineteenth centuries, Jammu was also one of the centers for the **Pahari** school of **miniature painting**. Aside from being the name of this region, Jammu is also the name of the region's largest city, the state's traditional winter capital. For general information about Jammu and all the regions of India, an accessible reference is Christine Nivin et al., *India*. 8th ed., Lonely Planet, 1998.

Janabai

(d. c.1350) Female poet and saint in the **Varkari Panth**, a religious community centered around the **worship** of the Hindu god **Vithoba** at his temple at **Pandharpur** in the modern state of **Maharashtra**. According to tradition, Janabai came to Pandharpur with her parents when she was seven but refused to go home with them, saying that she wanted to remain close to the Lord. She became the servant of another Varkari saint, **Namdev**, who made her a member of his circle of devotees (**bhakta**). Janabai is famous for her devotional songs, which remain popular today. For further information see Justin E. Abbott and Narhar R. Godbole (trans.), *Stories of Indian Saints*, 1982; and G. A. Deleury, *The Cult of Vithoba*, 1960.

Janaka

The foster father of the **goddess Sita**. He discovered her one day while plowing a furrow in a field. In Hindu mythology, Janaka is the paradigm of the sage-king, a person who despite his wealth and position was as perfectly dispassionate as any **ascetic** living in the forest.

Janaki Navami

Festival falling on the ninth **day** (navami) of the dark (waning) half of the **lunar month** of **Phalgun** (February–March). This festival celebrates the **birth** of **Sita**, wife of the god king **Rama** and heroine of the epic *Ramayana*. Sita is not born in the usual manner, but is found by King **Janaka** in a furrow as he plows a field (hence the name Janaki, a female form of Janaka). As the wife of Rama, himself an **avatar** or incarnation of the god **Vishnu**, Sita is believed to be a form of **Lakshmi**, Vishnu's wife. In her absolute devotion to her husband, Sita is considered a model for Indian **women**; women performing the prescribed religious rites for this day are promised children and prosperity.

Janakpur

City and sacred site (**tirtha**) in the western part of **Nepal**, seven miles north of the border with the Indian state of **Bihar**. Janakpur is said to be the capital of King **Janaka**, a noted sage and the foster father of the **goddess Sita** in the *Ramayana*, the earlier of the two great Hindu epics. According to tradition, Janaka's capital was destroyed during the war described in the *Mahabharata*—the other great Hindu epic—and disappeared without a trace. The present site of Janakpur dates from the early eighteenth century and is said to have been discovered by two **Vaishnava** devotees (**bhakta**), Chaturbhuj Giri and Sur Kishor. Chaturbhuj Giri had a vision of the god **Rama** in a **dream** and was directed to dig beneath a banyan tree. When he did, he found four images of **Vishnu**, each in a differing divine manifestation. Sur Kishor was a great devotee of Sita, and through her agency discovered the spot as well. Other **ascetics** began to come to this site, which is still an important stop on the annual pilgrimage cycle of the **Ramanandi** ascetics. The ascetics were followed by shepherds and merchants, and the town of Janakpur gradually grew

Janaki Mandir in Janakpur, Nepal. This temple marks the site where the goddess Sita first appeared.

up from there. For extensive treatment of this site and the veracity of these stories, see Richard Burghart, "The History of Janakpur," in *Kailash*, Vol. 6, No. 4, 1978.

Janamjeya

In Hindu mythology, the **son** of King **Parikshit**; Janamjeya rules after his father's untimely death from the bite of the serpent **Takshaka**. Janamjeya has a pronounced hatred of serpents because of Takshaka's role in his father's death, and during his reign he performs a great **sacrifice** known as the Sarpasatra, through which most of the snakes on **earth** are killed. Takshaka manages to stop the sacrifice before all of the earth's serpents are completely wiped out by pleading with a **brahmin** to help him. The brahmin comes to Janamjeya's sacrifice as a guest and requests that the sacrifice be stopped. Since, according to tradition, a brahmin guest's request cannot be refused, Janamjeya is compelled to curtail the rite.

Janardana

("exciting his devotees") Epithet of the god **Krishna**. See **Krishna**.

Jana Sangh

Modern Indian political party, founded in 1951 by Shyam Prasad Mookerjee. Despite Mookerjee's earlier roots in the **Hindu Mahasabha**, a Hindu nationalist organization, the Jana Sangh's leadership largely came from workers dispatched by another conservative Hindu organization, the **Rashtriya Svayamsevak Sangh** (RSS). By the mid-1950s the Jana Sangh had become the political arm of the RSS, with RSS members filling most of the party's important positions. In its political platform the Jana Sangh espoused many populist Hindu causes, such as a ban on **cow slaughter** and the **prohibition** of alcoholic beverages, but the party was also noted for its sympathetic orientation toward farmers, who formed one of its important constituencies. The Jana Sangh's high point came in the 1977 general elections, when it won ninety-three seats in Parliament. It was the largest single party in the coalition of political parties that ousted Indira Gandhi's Congress Party and ended their two years of martial law. This triumph quickly turned to failure: the Janata government dissolved over the so-called dual-membership controversy, which was rooted in concerns over Jana Sangh members simultaneously being members of the RSS. Legislators from other parties saw this as creating a conflict of interest and were also wary of their government being directed by the RSS, which was considered a Hindu chauvinist organization. These outside legislators demanded that Jana Sangh members renounce all RSS ties, which the latter were unwilling to do. All attempts at compromise eventually failed, and after the Congress Party came back to power in 1980, the Jana Sangh legislators and other remnants of the Janata government formed a new party, the **Bharatiya Janata Party**. For further information

see Walter K. Andersen and Shridhar D. Damle, *The Brotherhood in Saffron*, 1987; and Bruce Desmond Graham, *Hindu Nationalism and Indian Politics*, 1990.

Janeu

The **sacred thread** worn by all "**twice-born**" (dvija) men, as a visible symbol of having undergone the adolescent religious **initiation** known as the "second birth." The janeu is a circular cord made of three strands (in which each cord also has three strands), which is worn over the left shoulder, crossing the body to fall on the right hip. See **sacred thread**.

Jangama

("moving") Priestly subgroup in the Virashaiva or **Lingayat** community, whose members are mainly concentrated in the southern Indian state of **Karnataka**. The Virashaivas are a devotional community who stress the **worship** of **Shiva** as the only real **deity**; aside from being essentially monotheistic, they have also rejected all forms of image worship except for Shiva's symbol, the **linga**. The Virashaivas were founded by the poet-saint **Basavanna**, partly in rebellion against the prevailing **caste** system, and he created the jangamas as a parallel priesthood to care for his community's members. The major function of the jangamas is to officiate at lifecycle ceremonies for the members of the community, such as **birth**, coming-of-age, marriage, and death. Jangamas may be married and raise families, but this Virashaiva subcommunity also serves as the major source of recruits for the celibate Virashaiva monks (**viraktas**), who have the highest status as religious leaders in the community.

Janmashtami

Festival on the eighth **day** (ashtami) of the dark (waning) half of the **lunar month** of **Bhadrapada** (August–September), which is celebrated as the god **Krishna's** birthday. As with all holidays connected with Krishna, this festival is particularly observed in the **Braj** region, where Krishna is supposed to have lived, although it is also celebrated throughout the country. Devotees (**bhakta**) often stay up late into the night, since Krishna is said to have been born at midnight, and the observances are often punctuated with singing, chanting, parades, and dramas enacting events in Krishna's life. It is during the month around Janmashtami that the dramas known as the Krishna **lilas** are presented in the town of **Brindavan**, traditionally believed to have been Krishna's childhood home.

According to tradition, Krishna is the eighth **son** of **Devaki** and **Vasudeva**. He is born in a prison in the city of **Mathura** in which his parents are held by Devaki's brother, the wicked king **Kamsa**. Kamsa has imprisoned the pair in an attempt to thwart the prophecy that he will be killed by his sister Devaki's eighth son. Kamsa has killed all of Devaki's older children at **birth** and intends to do the same with Krishna, but when Krishna is born wondrous things begin to happen: the jailers fall into a deep sleep, the locked prison doors miraculously open, and Vasudeva is able to spirit the infant out of the prison to the home of the couple who will become his foster parents, **Nanda** and **Yashoda**. Vasudeva returns that night, bearing Yashoda's new-born baby girl, who is really the **goddess Bhadrakali** in disguise. The next morning Kamsa kills the child by dashing her against a stone, but from the body arises a fearsome form of the Goddess, who taunts Kamsa by telling him that the person who will slay him has already escaped.

Japa

("muttering," "whispering") Individual recitation, usually the repeated utterance of a particular **mantra** or divine name(s), often while using a string of beads (**mala**) to perform a definite number of such repetitions. Such recitation is usually performed as an individual religious act, in a tone of voice audible to the reciter but not others who may be present. Japa is a particularly important practice in Hindu traditions stressing the benefits of reciting the divine name—such repetitions are believed to have gradual spiritual benefits. Japa is particularly stressed in the **Gaudiya Vaishnavas** community founded by the Bengali saint **Chaitanya**, where public recitation of the divine name is an important part of religious life.

Jaratkarava Artabhaga

One of the sage **Yajnavalkya's** interviewers in the **Brhadaranyaka Upanishad**, one of the earliest of the **Upanishads**. The third chapter of this upanishad presents a series of questioners, each trying to test Yajnavalkya's assertion that he is the best **brahmin** of all. Artabhaga finally questions Yajnavalkya about the human sense faculties and their realms of action, and eventually asks what happens to a person after death. Yajnavalkya draws him aside in private, and talks to him about **karma** ("action"), in what is generally regarded as the oldest reference to this fundamental Indian religious idea.

Jaratkaru

In Hindu mythology, a sage famous not only for his **asceticism** and knowledge but also because he illustrates the importance of male children in Hindu culture. Jaratkaru is a lifelong **ascetic** with no intention of marrying until he has a vision of his ancestors suspended over one of the **hells** by a grass rope, through which a **rat** (time personified) is gradually gnawing. His ancestors inform Jaratkaru that his failure to have a **son** means that the lineage will end with him, along with the rites performed for the deceased in that lineage, and that they will then fall into hell. To forestall this disaster, they instruct Jaratkaru to marry and beget a son.

Jaratkaru is initially hostile to this idea, but later specifies that if a woman also named Jaratkaru is found and given to him as alms, he will marry her. His conditions eventually reaches the **Naga** (snake) king **Vasuki**, who has a sister by this name. The marriage is performed under the condition that if she displeases Jaratkaru, he will leave her. Given Jaratkaru's ascetic past, it is not surprising that things did not work out between them. After being married several months, his wife has the dilemma of allowing Jaratkaru to sleep past sunset, which will make him late for his evening prayers, or to wake him and risk his displeasure. She chooses the latter; Jaratkaru is displeased with her and leaves despite her entreaties. Some time later the wife Jaratkaru gives **birth** to a son, Astika, and thus the sage's obligations are fulfilled.

Jat

One of the hundreds of subgroups of traditional Indian society known as **jatis** ("birth"). Each jati was associated with—and held a monopoly over—a particular occupation, and that occupation determined the social status of the jati's members; this system led to the modern **caste** system. The Jats are a northern Indian jati whose members are spread through many of the states of northern India, particularly **Haryana**, **Punjab**, **Uttar Pradesh**, and **Rajasthan**. In the Punjab the Jats are evenly split between Hindus and Sikhs, but in other areas the community is solidly Hindu. The Jats' hereditary occupation is farming, and they are often described as tough and resilient peasants; these qualities have also made them superior soldiers, both in the service of the British Empire and in independent India.

Jata

A long matted lock of **hair**. Ascetics often wear their hair in jatas for a number of religious and symbolic reasons. On one level, the uncut hair is a symbol of renunciation; its unkempt, matted quality demonstrates the **ascetic's**

distance from worldly concerns with order and propriety. On another level, ascetics wear jatas in imitation of the god **Shiva**, the paradigmatic ascetic, who is always portrayed wearing his hair in matted locks. Although jatas are most commonly worn by devotees (**bhakta**) of Shiva, some strict renunciants who are devotees of the god **Vishnu** also favor this hairstyle. Finally, from a nonreligious perspective, jatas are simply a very low-maintenance hairstyle. They are usually rubbed with wood ash to keep them relatively neat; as the hair grows the jatas simply become longer, and in many cases they can be neatly twisted into a crown, or **jatamakuta**, on the top of the head.

Jatakarma Samskara

The fourth of the traditional life-cycle ceremonies (**samskaras**). The first three were to be performed before and during **pregnancy**, while the jatakarma samskara was to be performed immediately after the **birth**. This ceremony had several elements, but the most prominent were uttering the word "vak" ("speech," a synonym for **Saraswati**) into the child's ear and feeding the child honey, ghee, and other items believed to bring good luck. This samskara is seldom performed in modern times, although there are many other rites connected with birth that are intended to protect the mother and child and to kindle the child's potential.

Jatamakuta

A crown (makuta) made of matted locks of **hair** (**jata**) twisted together and bound on top of the head. In Hindu iconography the jatamakuta is most closely associated with the god **Shiva**, who is the paradigmatic **ascetic** and always wears his hair in matted locks. In modern times, the jatamakuta is still a hairstyle associated with many ascetics, both **Shaiva** and **Vaishnava**.

An ascetic in Haridwar with his hair in matted locks (jata).
This hairstyle marks the wearer as a person who is detached from worldly concerns.

Jatayu

A virtuous vulture in the ***Ramayana***, the earlier of the two great Indian epics. When **Rama's** wife **Sita** is kidnapped by the **demon**-king **Ravana** and is being spirited away in Ravana's aerial chariot, Jatayu makes a valiant effort to rescue her. In his battle with Ravana, Jatayu's wings are cut off; the force of his subsequent fall left him near death. With his dying breaths he informs Rama and Rama's brother **Lakshmana** of what has happened, and identifies Ravana as Sita's kidnapper. Although Jatayu fails to rescue Sita, he is critical to the plot of the epic because he gives Rama the crucial information he needs to begin to searching for her.

Jati

("birth") A traditional social subgroup in Indian society. There were hundreds of these groups, considered exogamous because strict taboos existed against marrying outside one's jati—people belonging to different jatis were looked upon as different "species" of people. Jatis were usually defined by the subgroup's traditional occupation, which they and they alone had the right to practice. The jatis were hierarchically arranged in society, based on the perceived **purity** or impurity (**ashaucha**) of their occupations, and this hierarchy formed the basis for the traditional Hindu social structure known as the **caste** system.

Jatra

Vernacular form of the **Sanskrit** word **yatra** ("journey"). The word yatra is most often used to describe journeys to far-away places, whereas jatra is used to denote visits to spots within the immediate region.

Jauhar

A mass **suicide** in which **women** and children threw themselves on a bonfire to protect the family from dishonor when the men were defeated or killed in battle. Jauhar was considered the women's counterpart to death in combat. If their husbands and fathers were heavily outnumbered and faced certain death in battle, women would perform a mass suicide after the men left their fortresses. This phenomenon was most closely associated with the desert state of **Rajasthan**, which has strong martial traditions and a great stress on the importance of family honor. It is particularly associated with the **Rajasthani** city of Chittorgarh, where jauhars occurred in 1303, 1535, and 1568.

Jaya

In Hindu mythology, one of the gatekeepers of the god **Vishnu's** heavenly abode, **Vaikuntha**, who, with his brother **Vijaya**, is cursed to be born three times as a **demon** (asura) and to be killed each time by Vishnu. The sage **Sanaka** places this **curse** on them when they prevent him from seeing Vishnu. In their first **birth** the two are born as **Hiranyaksha** and **Hiranyakashipu**, who are killed by the **Boar avatar** and the **Man-Lion avatar** respectively. In their second incarnation they are born as **Ravana** and **Kumbhakarna**, who are both killed by Vishnu's **Rama avatar**. In their final birth they incarnate as **Shisupala** and **Dantavaktra** and are killed by Vishnu's **Krishna avatar**. After the conditions of the curse have been fulfilled, they return to their duties as Vishnu's gatekeepers.

Jayadeva

(12th c.) Poet and author of the *Gitagovinda*, a lyric devotional poem that uses the separation and eventual reunion of the lovers **Krishna** and **Radha** as a metaphor for the union of the human soul with God. According to tradition, Jayadeva lived at the temple of the god **Jagannath** in the city of **Puri**, where his wife Padmavati was a dancer. She is said to have been the first to **dance** to Jayadeva's songs as an **offering** to Jagannath, and the *Gitagovinda* has been sung and danced as a regular part of temple **worship** up to the present time. For further information see Barbara Stoller Miller (ed. and trans.), *The Love Song of the Dark Lord*, 1977.

Jayadratha

In the ***Mahabharata***, the later of the two great Hindu epics, Jayadratha is a king who is married to the princess Dussala. Dussala is the only sister of the **Kauravas**, a group of one hundred brothers who are the epic's antagonists. Jayadratha once sought the hand of **Draupadi**, and because of his bitterness at having lost her to the warrior **Arjuna**, he opposes Arjuna and his brothers, the **Pandavas**, for the rest of his life. During the Mahabharata war between the Pandavas and the Kauravas, Jayadratha takes the side of the Kauravas and is eventually killed by Arjuna. At Jayadratha's **birth** a celestial voice has prophesied that the head of the person who causes Jayadratha's head to fall to **earth** will split into a hundred pieces. Mindful of this, Arjuna, a peerless archer, cuts off Jayadratha's head with an arrow in such a way that it lands in the lap of Jayadratha's father, Brhatkaya. Brhatkaya is so startled that he allows the head to fall from his lap to the ground, and his own head breaks into a hundred pieces.

Jaya Ekadashi

Festival falling on the eleventh **day** (**ekadashi**) of the bright (waxing) half of the **lunar month** of **Magh** (January–February). As are all eleventh-day observances, this festival is dedicated to the **worship** of **Vishnu**, on this day particularly in his form as **Krishna**. Most Hindu festivals have certain prescribed rites, usually involving fasting (**upavasa**) and worship, and often promise specific benefits for faithful performance:

faithfully observing the "**jaya**," or "victory," festival is said to ensure that one's desired goal will be attained.

Jayapala

(d. 1001) One of the last kings of the **Pratiharas**, a northern Indian dynasty whose capital was in **Kanyakubja** on the **Ganges** River. By Jayapala's time the divided Hindu kingdoms in northern India were being threatened by the Turkish emirs, especially **Mahmud of Ghazni**, who had settled in modern-day Afghanistan. Jayapala was defeated and captured in battle with Mahmud and subsequently committed **suicide**; a short time later, Jayapala's **son Anandapala** suffered a crushing defeat, leaving a nearly complete collapse of power in northern India. Because of this absence of any effective opposition, Mahmud was able to indulge in almost yearly campaigns of pillage and plunder.

Jayarashi

(7th c.?) Author of the *Tattvopaplavasimha*, one of the only surviving texts of the **materialist** philosophical school. One of the philosophical peculiarities of the materialist school was that they accepted only perception (**pratyaksha**) as a reliable **pramana**, or means by which people can gain true and accurate knowledge. In his text, Jayarashi argued against the reliability of inference (**anumana**) as one of the pramanas by refuting the concept of cause and effect. To make an inference, such as inferring the result an action will bring in the future based on the result it brought in the past, one must believe that the cause-and-effect model is reliable.

Jejuri

Town in the Pune district of the central Indian state of **Maharashtra**, about forty miles south and east of the city of Pune. Jejuri is primarily noted as the site of the primary temple to **Khandoba**, an important Maharashtrian regional **deity** who has been brought into the pantheon of gods as an **avatar**, or incarnation, of the god **Shiva**.

Jhanki

("glimpse") A momentary "glimpse" of the divine, in which the devotee (**bhakta**) gains momentary access to the **world of the gods**. Jhankis are most often conveyed through the performing arts: through the mental images created when devotional poetry is read, recited, or sung, or through the images presented in religious **dance**, drama, or film. During these momentary encounters, the devotee comes briefly into the presence of the **deity**, sharing the deity's world. This stress on the opportunity to experience a brief physical presence in the deity's world is particularly strong in the **Vaishnava** devotionalism connected with the gods **Krishna** and **Rama**. **Worship** of these deities often stresses visualization of the deity's life and everyday actions as a way for devotees to gain access to that divine world. Devotees of both deities have created plays, or **lilas**, to aid them in this process: for Rama, they are the **Ram Lilas**, which are performed throughout India during the autumn festival **season**, and for Krishna, they are the Krishna Lilas, performed during the annual **monsoon** season in **Brindavan**, Krishna's childhood home.

Jimutavahana

(early 12th c.) Author of the *Dayabhaga*, a legal text primarily concerned with **inheritance**, partition, and the division of property. It eventually became the primary legal authority for the Bengal cultural region; areas outside Bengal were usually governed by a different legal text, the *Mitakshara*. One of the major differences between these texts concerns the nature of inheritance. The *Mitakshara* stresses inheritance by survivorship, in which only living males can inherit property, whereas the *Dayabhaga* stresses inheritance by succession, in which a dead man's heirs can inherit in his name.

Jiva

("life") In philosophical and **Vaishnava** (devotees of the god **Vishnu**) discussion, jiva is the name used for the embodied soul of a human being. In a more general sense, the word can refer to any living being.

Jivacchraddha

("**Shraddha** for a living [person]") A particular type of shraddha, or memorial service for the dead, although in this case it is performed for a person who is still living. In many cases, a person performs the Jivacchraddha for himself if he has no **sons** to fulfill the responsibility or if he suspects that the rite may not be performed properly after his death. The person performing this rite makes a small figure of sacred **kusha** grass, representing the person for whom the shraddha is being performed, and then proceeds with the normal shraddha ceremony.

Jivanmukta

In Indian **philosophy**, a person who has attained final liberation of the soul while still living (**jivanmukti**) and who continues to live in a state of liberation. The concept of the jivanmukta is essential in many branches of **Advaita Vedanta**, one of the **six schools** of classical Indian philosophy. The Advaita school upholds a philosophical position known as monism, which is the belief that a single Ultimate Reality known as **Brahman** lies behind all things, and that all things are merely differing forms of that reality. For Advaita proponents, the problem of human bondage is that human beings, blinded by **avidya** or mistaken understanding, do not recognize this ultimate unity, but mistakenly persist in seeing the world as made up of separate and diverse things. The possibility of attaining jivanmukta status is essential to the Advaita school because it supports their belief that bondage and liberation are attained not by doing or becoming anything, but rather by replacing a mistaken understanding with a correct one. After this has happened one will continue to live, but because of the radical change in consciousness one's life will never be the same.

Jivanmukti

("liberation while living") In later Indian **philosophy**, the notion that one can attain final liberation of the soul while still living and continue to live after that in a liberated state. The **jivanmukta** (one who is liberated while still living) is an important claim for many of the sub-schools of **Advaita Vedanta**, one of the **six schools** of classical Indian philosophy. The Advaita school upholds a philosophical position known as monism, which is the belief that a single Ultimate Reality known as **Brahman** lies behind all things, and that all things are merely differing forms of that reality. For Advaita proponents, the problem of human bondage is that human beings, blinded by **avidya** or mistaken understanding, do not recognize this ultimate unity. Liberation is not attained by "doing" anything or by becoming something that one is not, but by realizing what has always been the case, and thus exchanging a mistaken understanding for a correct one. Although this cognition forever changes how a person perceives the world, it brings no ontological changes, meaning that on a physical level one continues to exist as before, until the **karma** that has created one's present body is exhausted. For further information see Karl H. Potter (ed.), *Advaita Vedanta up to Samkara and His Pupils*, 1981.

Jnana

In Indian philosophical thought, a word with different meanings in different contexts. The word *jnana* is derived from the verb "to know," and one of its meanings, at least in a perceptual context, is "awareness." In a more abstract sense it stands for what it means to truly "know" something;

along with **karmamarga** and the **bhaktimarga**, the **jnanamarga** is one of the paths to liberation of the soul mentioned in the **Bhagavad Gita**. In this latter context, an appropriate translation might be "wisdom" or "realization," since this is not the sort of "knowledge" that comes from reading a book or receiving instruction, but instead reflects profound understanding gained through great effort.

Jnanakarmasamucchaya

("combination of awareness and action") Religious discipline for ending the bondage and reincarnation (**samsara**) of the soul, which was advocated by members of the **bhedabhada** ("identity-in-difference") philosophical school. According to this school, correct awareness (**jnana**) and ritual action (**karma**) were both necessary elements in gaining final liberation of the soul. The preparatory step was to perform meritorious ritual actions—fasting (**upavasa**), **worship**, and pilgrimage—to weaken one's negative karmic dispositions, such as greed, anger, and ignorance. These weakened dispositions were later completely destroyed through meditation. The assumptions behind this path were attacked by other philosophical schools, particularly the **Advaita Vedanta** school, which minimized the value of ritual action and claimed that final liberation came from awareness alone.

Jnanamarga

("Path of Realization") One of Hinduism's three generally accepted paths to gain final liberation of the soul, along with the Path of Devotion (**bhaktimarga**) and the Path of Action (**karmamarga**). While the bhaktimarga stresses devotion to God and the karmamarga emphasizes selfless action in the world, the jnanamarga stresses realizing the ultimate identity of one's individual Self (**atman**) and Ultimate Reality (**Brahman**). This realization is usually described as coming in a flash of insight, which may take years of effort to attain but which fundamentally shifts one's perspective on the world.

Jnana ("knowledge") Mudra

A particular symbolic hand **gesture** (**mudra**) in Indian **dance**, **sculpture**, and ritual. In the jnana mudra, the tips of the thumb and index finger are touching, with the palm and hand held across the region of the heart. As its name clearly shows, it is used to indicate a profound understanding of the basic workings of the universe.

Jnanasambandhar

Honorific epithet for the **Nayanar** poet-saint **Sambandar**. See **Sambandar**.

Jnanendriya

("organ of awareness") In Indian **philosophy**, jnanendriya refers to any of the sense organs, traditionally considered to be the eyes, ears, tongue, nose, and skin.

Jnaneshvar

(1275–1296?) Poet and saint who is the first great figure in the **Varkari Panth**, a religious community centered around the **worship** of the Hindu god **Vithoba** at his temple at **Pandharpur** in the modern state of **Maharashtra**. According to tradition, Jnaneshvar was an outcaste **brahmin**. He incurred this penalty because his father was a lapsed **ascetic**—he left his wife to become an ascetic, only to rejoin his family at his **guru's** command. Jnaneshvar came from a very religious family: His sister **Muktibai** is revered by the Varkaris in her own right, and his elder brother **Nivrttinath** is supposed to have been a "spiritual grandson" of the great ascetic **Gorakhnath**. Varkari tradition makes clear that Jnaneshvar lived much of his life in the town of **Alandi**, but the truth of the accounts of many events associated with his life is questionable—for example, he is said to have caused a buffalo to recite the sacred text known as the **Veda** in order to humble the pride of the local **brahmin** priests. Jnaneshvar's greatest work was the *Jnaneshvari*, a Marathi-language commentary on the **Bhagavad Gita**, one of the most influential Hindu religious texts. He is also famous for his songs in praise of Vithoba, which the Varkaris still sing today. For further information see G. A. Deleury, *The Cult of Vithoba*, 1960; and Justin Abbott and Narhar R. Godbole (trans.), *Stories of Indian Saints*, 1982.

Jnaneshvari

Marathi-language commentary on the **Bhagavad Gita**, one of the most influential Hindu religious texts. The *Jnaneshvari* was composed by the Maharashtrian poet-saint **Jnaneshvar**, whose intentions in writing it were to make the Bhagavad Gita accessible to the common people, who were not able to read the text in the original **Sanskrit**, and to give his own learned interpretation of the text's contents. This emphasis on giving ordinary people full access to religious life was one of the consistent themes in the (devotional) **bhakti** movement and, like many other figures, Jnaneshvar is reported to have faced considerable opposition from the **brahmin** priests, who thought that such advanced teachings should not be revealed to the common public.

Jogi

(variant of **yogi**, "adept") An epithet for various sorts of **ascetics**. It often refers to the **Nathpanthis**, followers of the teacher **Gorakhnath**. Their designation as "jogis" comes from the fact that the practice of **yoga**, particularly **hatha yoga**, is one of the major emphases in their religious life. The term may also refer to the **Aghoris**.

Joking Relationships

Within the traditional Hindu joint family, the types of relationships within a single generation differ markedly according to family status, particularly among the family's adult brothers and their wives. As the eventual head of the family, the oldest brother is usually portrayed as a serious and grave authority figure, toward whom everyone must act with respect. The eldest brother's wife is also given considerable respect, but she is also said to share a "joking relationship" with her husband's younger brothers, as do all wives with their husband's younger brothers. Whereas **women** are expected to behave decorously toward relatives with higher status, joking relationships have much greater freedom of expression. These are usually characterized as full of banter and casual conversation that would be inappropriate with a person of higher status.

Jones, Sir William

(1746–1794) Founder of the Asiatic Society of Bengal and one of the fathers of modern Indology. Jones came to Calcutta from England in 1783 as a Supreme Court judge during the governorship of Warren Hastings, considered one of the founders of the British Empire in India. He was employed by the East India Company, who, in its pursuit of trade and profit, acquired political power over regions of India. Jones immediately applied himself to the study of **Sanskrit**, in part to discover the particulars of traditional Hindu law, since the East India Company's general policy was to allow different religious communities to be governed by their own traditional laws. Jones was a linguistic genius who had mastered the current and classical European languages, as well as Persian. He immediately recognized Sanskrit as a distant relative of Greek and Latin, and through his influence the serious study of Sanskrit texts began. From a legal perspective, his most important work was a translation of the laws of **Manu** (**Manu Smrti**). This was one of the most important texts in the **dharma literature** and prescribed ideal rules and regulations for all sorts of human conduct. This translation was intended to give the British some idea of classical Hindu law, but they failed to realize that this text was composed not as a legal manual but as a guide to religious life. Jones died at age forty-eight from an inflammation of the liver. His translation was published posthumously.

Joshimath

Town and sacred site (**tirtha**) in the **Himalayas** on the banks of the **Alakananda River**, in the Chamoli district of the state of **Uttar Pradesh**. Joshimath is the location of the **Jyotir math**, one of the four **maths**, or dwelling places for **ascetics**, supposedly established by the philosopher **Shankaracharya**. The Jyotir math is home to **Dashanami Sanyasis**, or **twice-born** renunciant ascetics. According to local legend, the Jyotir Math is the place where Shankaracharya attained the ultimate realization and composed his commentaries on the Hindu scriptures. Aside from the Jyotir math, Joshimath is famous for its connection to a temple dedicated to Narasimha, the god **Vishnu's Man-Lion avatar**. This temple was also reportedly established by Shankaracharya and contains several stunning sculptural images. Joshimath is an important transit point on the road to the temple at **Badrinath**, and it is also the winter seat of Badrinath's presiding **deity**, where he (symbolically represented by a traveling image) resides and is worshiped during the winter months, when Badrinath becomes snowbound and inaccessible. See also **Narasimha avatar**.

Juggernaut

Anglicized form of **Jagannath**, who is the presiding **deity** of the temple with the same name in the eastern Indian city of **Puri**. The word "juggernaut," which in general English usage refers to anything that requires blind devotion or horrible **sacrifice**, comes from a widespread myth surrounding the procession of Jagannath, or Juggernaut, and his two siblings around Puri during the **Rath Yatra** each summer. The cars that carry them in the procession are enormous—Jagannath's measures forty-five feet high and thirty feet wide, and travels on sixteen wheels that are seven feet high—and are drawn by ropes pulled by hundreds of people. One of the staple fictions of British colonial lore described Jagannath's frenzied devotees (**bhakta**) committing **suicide** by throwing themselves under the car's wheels, in order to die in the sight of the god. Despite the legendary status of such stories, suicides of this sort were in fact extremely uncommon: most of those who died under the wheels of the Juggernaut procession were pulling the ropes when they lost their footing, fell into the cars' path, and were prevented from escaping by the crushing crowds.

Juna ("Old") Akhara

Name of one of seven subgroups of the **Naga** class of the **Dashanami Sanyasis**, renunciant ascetics who are devotees (**bhakta**) of the god **Shiva**. The subgroups are known as **akharas** and are similar to regiments of an army. Until the beginning of the nineteenth century the Nagas were primarily mercenary soldiers but were also active in merchandise trading; neither of these characteristics applies in contemporary times. Members of the Juna Akhara revere the sage **Dattatreya** as their "tutelary **deity**," the primary deity from which they learn; each of the akharas have different tutelary deities. Some accounts say **Bhairava** was the patron deity of the Juna Akhara in earlier times, which would explain the fact that the group is also known as the Bhairava Akhara. The literal meaning of the present name and its connection with Bhairava imply that it is very old. In contemporary times it is a large organization found only in northern India. In some places it is given low status for admitting members from the lower social classes.

Up until the middle of the present century, the Juna Akhara marched with the **Niranjani Akhara** in the bathing (**snana**) processions during the **Kumbha Mela** and was thus considered a subsidiary part of that akhara. For most of this century the Junas were upset that they held subordinate status despite the fact that they have far more members than any other akhara. The Junas began their attempt to gain the status of a separate procession with the 1903 **Haridwar** Kumbha Mela, but were not accorded this position until 1962. The akharas agreed that during a Haridwar Kumbha Mela, the Junas would lead the **Sanyasi** processions for the bathing on the festival of **Shivaratri**. However, the Niranjanis would be first for the other two major bathing days—the **new moon** in **Chaitra** and the Kumbha bath on April 14. This arrangement broke down at the 1998 Kumbha Mela in Haridwar, when the Junas demanded that they be allowed to go first at the Chaitra bath as well, based on their status as the largest akhara. On the day of the second bath, this disagreement erupted into a full-scale riot between **ascetic** groups and police in which many people were hurt. There was great worry that such violence would recur on the main bathing day, but the day came off without incident when the Juna Akhara boycotted the bathing processions.

Jupiter

In Hindu astrology, a planet associated with knowledge, power, and good character. In **Sanskrit**, Jupiter's name is **guru**, and its importance in Hindu astrology reflects the importance of the guru or religious figure in Hindu religious life. Jupiter is the most powerful of the benevolent **planets**—the others are the **sun, moon, Mercury**, and **Venus**—although for each person Jupiter's powers vary according to its place in the **natal horoscope**, or alignment of the heavenly bodies at the time of **birth**, and the influence of friendly or hostile planets. During the **week**, Jupiter presides over **Thursday** which, because of the planet's astrological powers, is considered an auspicious, or lucky, **day**.

Jutha

In its most general sense, jutha refers to any food that has come into contact with saliva. Such contact is believed to render that food impure and unfit for anyone else to eat. Since **eating** is traditionally done with one's fingers, any food on one's plate after one has begun to eat is considered contaminated by association, even if it has not yet been taken into one's mouth. As with all bodily fluids, saliva is considered particularly impure, a substance that "imprints" food with the nature of the person eating it. Eating food from the same plate is a sign of extreme closeness—most commonly done by husband and wife, but also by very close friends. Conversely, eating another's person's leftovers is a sign of extreme status difference—it is done only by people who are desperately poor, by disciples as a sign of devotion to their **guru** or religious leader, or by devotees (**bhakta**) receiving **prasad** or sanctified food, the vehicle for **grace** from their chosen **deity**.

Jwalamukhi

("flame mouth") Presiding **deity** of the Jwalamukhi shrine in the state of **Himachal Pradesh**, and one of the nine **Shiwalik goddesses**. According to the site's mythic charter, Jwalamukhi is one of the **Shakti Pithas**, a network of sites sacred to the **goddess** that spreads throughout the Indian subcontinent. Each Shakti Pitha marks the site where a body part of the dismembered goddess **Sati** fell to **earth**, taking form there as a different goddess; in the case of Jwalamukhi the body part was Sati's tongue. The human tongue is an extremely powerful part of the body—connected with speech, **eating**, and sex—and thus Jwalamukhi is considered a very powerful shrine. The cave containing the shrine has a small vent of natural gas, which has been lit for as long as people can remember. This flame is believed to be a self-manifested (**svayambhu**) form of the Goddess, here in the form of her tongue. For further information see David R. Kinsley, *Hindu Goddesses*, 1986; and Kathleen Erndl, *Victory To The Mother*, 1993. See also **pitha**.

The Mahakaleshvar Temple in the city of Ujjain. This site contains one of the twelve jyotirlingas, pillar-shaped images that mark places where the god Shiva is believed to have appeared in a shaft of light.

Jyeshth

According to the lunar **calendar**, by which most Hindu religious festivals are determined, Jyeshth is the third month in the lunar **year**, usually falling in May–June. This is considered the first month in the hot **season**: The weather in this month is scorchingly hot and bone dry. The major holidays in Jyeshth are **Achala Ekadashi**, **Savitri Puja**, **Ganga Dashahara**, and **Nirjala Ekadashi**.

Jyotirlinga

("**linga** of light") In several different mythic sources, the first manifestation of the god **Shiva** is described as a giant pillar of **fire**, which stretches above the **heavens** and below the **earth**. The gods **Brahma** and **Vishnu** try to find this pillar's top and bottom but cannot. When they admit their failure, the figure of Shiva emerges from the pillar of light and blesses them. Shiva's devotees (**bhakta**) believe that there are twelve sites in India where this jyotirlinga came down to earth; these twelve sites are deemed extraordinarily holy, and at each of them Shiva is believed to be uniquely present. At each of these sites the primary image is a linga, the pillar-shaped image that is a symbolic form of Shiva. Each of these lingas is considered a different manifestation of Shiva, and these twelve sites each take the name of the linga that is their presiding **deity**. The other eleven manifestations of Shiva and their locations are: **Somnath** and **Nageshvar** in the state of **Gujarat**; **Kedarnath** in the **Himalaya** Mountains; **Vishvanath** in the city of **Benares**; **Vaidyanath** in the state of **Bihar**; **Mahakaleshvar** in the central Indian city of **Ujjain**; **Omkareshvar** in the state of **Madhya Pradesh**; **Bhimashankar**, **Ghrneshvar**, and **Tryambakeshvar** in the state of **Maharashtra**; and **Rameshvar** in the state of **Tamil Nadu**.

Jyotir Math

One of the four maths or sacred centers traditionally believed to have been established by the great philosopher **Shankaracharya**; the others are the **Sharada math**, **Shringeri math**, and **Govardhan math**. These four sacred centers are each associated with one of the four geographical corners of the Indian subcontinent; the Jyotir math is in the northern quarter, in the town of **Joshimath** in the state of **Uttar Pradesh**, high in the Himalaya Mountains. Shankaracharya is traditionally cited as the founder of the **Dashanami Sanyasis**, the most prestigious Hindu **ascetic** order. The Dashanami ("ten names") ascetics are devotees (**bhakta**) of the god **Shiva** and are separated into ten divisions, each with a different name. These ten divisions are organized into four larger groups—**Anandawara**, **Bhogawara**, **Bhuriwara**, and **Kitawara**—each of which has two or three of the ten divisions, and each of which is associated with one of the four sacred centers. Of these, the Jyotir math is associated with the Anandawara group of the Dashanamis.

Jyotisha

In its most general usage, the word *jyotisha* refers to astrology. The word itself is derived from *jyotis* ("light," and by extension the heavenly bodies) and is concerned with the movement of the celestial bodies, their varying configurations, and the divisions of time that are derived from them. This attention to the **heavens** is a very old cultural concern, for jyotisha is one of the six **Vedangas**, the auxiliary branches of knowledge connected with the sacred scriptures known as the **Vedas**. As one of the Vedangas, jyotisha was concerned with identifying appropriate days and times to perform Vedic sacrifices.

Even in modern times, many traditional Hindus take astrology very seriously, based on the assumption that the results of one's previous **karma** lead one to be born at a particular moment. One's **natal horoscope**, or the positioning of the celestial bodies at the time of **birth**, thus provides a karmic "itinerary" indicating where one has been and what one might expect in the future. People frequently consider astrology when making important decisions, particularly in arranging marriages—to determine the couple's compatibility, to see whether any trouble is lurking ahead, and to arrange an auspicious or lucky time for the ceremony itself. In the same way, some Hindus will consult an astrologer before beginning any important undertaking, to be sure that the work will begin at an auspicious time and will therefore be more likely to succeed.

The basic principles of Indian astrology are very similar to those of Western astrology. The **zodiac** signs are nearly identical. However, the two systems have a different method for determining each sign's starting point, causing some discrepancies between the two systems. Aside from the **sun**, **moon**, and five visible **planets** in Western astrology, Indian astrology has two additional planets, **Rahu** and **Ketu**, which are both considered inauspicious and malevolent. In addition to the twelve signs of the solar zodiac, Indian astrology also has a lunar zodiac with twenty-seven "lunar mansions" (**nakshatras**), each of which has particular qualities. Although at the most basic level astrological reckoning is fairly simple, it can quickly become highly complex and is thus generally left to professional astrologers. This is still a viable profession throughout much of India, since the generally accepted belief that some times are **auspicious** and others **inauspicious** means that ordinary people will hire specialists to keep them informed of these times.

K

Kabandha

("headless trunk") A **demon** in the *Ramayana* (the earlier of the two great Hindu epics) who attacks the god-king **Rama**, the epic's protagonist, and Rama's brother **Lakshmana**. In a previous life Kabandha has been a king of the **gandharvas**, or celestial musicians; but in a battle with the god **Indra**, Kabandha's head is pushed down into his body. When Kabandha requests some means by which he can eat, Indra places a mouth in Kabandha's belly. Indra tells him that the **curse** will be broken when Rama and Lakshmana cut off his arms.

As Rama and Lakshmana travel through a forest, searching for Rama's kidnapped wife **Sita**, they are set upon by Kabandha, who grabs each of them in one of his long arms. Finding they could not escape, Rama and Lakshmana each slash off one of his arms, and with his dying breaths Kabandha asks the brothers to burn his body. As the body is burning, the gandharva king arises from the fire in his previous form and advises the brothers to seek help from the monkey-king **Sugriva**.

Kabir

(mid-15th c.?) A poet who is widely regarded as one of the greatest northern Indian religious figures. Kabir is among a group of central and northern Indian poet-saints known as **Sants** who shared several tendencies: emphasis on individualized, interior religion leading to a personal experience of the divine; disdain for external ritual, particularly image **worship**; faith in the power of the divine Name; and a tendency to ignore hierarchical distinctions between castes. Kabir strongly adhered to these beliefs—in his writings he uncompromisingly attacks any sort of religious practice based on habit or tradition, including **asceticism**, special modes of dress, fasting (**upavasa**), image worship, **caste**, and scripture.

In his poetry, Kabir identifies himself as belonging to a caste of weavers (julaha), and according to tradition he supported himself through this occupation. Kabir's history makes it difficult to link him with a particular religion. In Arabic, the name Kabir ("Great") is one of the names given to Allah in the Qur'an, identifying him as a Muslim. However, his poetry reveals his great knowledge of Hindu religious life. It is generally believed that the members of Kabir's julaha community were recent converts to Islam who had not yet been fully assimilated. Kabir's poetry, however, clearly shows that he considered himself neither Hindu nor Muslim. Part of Kabir's popularity undoubtedly stems from his blunt, passionate affirmation that real religious attainment is only gained by internal, individual experience of the divine, to which he gives the name **Ram**. This is not the god-king who is the hero of the *Ramayana*, but a name for the indescribable, absolute Supreme Reality. Both of these emphases reflect the influence of the **Nathpanthi** ascetics, who also stressed internal experience and **yoga**.

In one of his songs, Kabir once boasted that he had been so absorbed in the divine that he had never put pen to paper. His songs remain popular even today, and many of his shorter epigrams have become proverbial sayings. Kabir's oldest attested poetry survives in three major collections: one in the **Adigranth**, the Sikh scripture also known as the "Primal Book"; one collected by the **Dadupanth**, the religious organization founded by the Sant poet-saint **Dadu**; and the *Bijak*, which was compiled by the **Kabirpanth**, a religious community that claimed Kabir as its **guru** (religious preceptor). The significant differences among these collections indicate that they have no single source. For further information see Charlotte Vaudeville (trans.), *Kabir*, 1974; Linda Hess and Shukdev Singh (trans.), *The Bijak of Kabir*, 1983; John S. Hawley and Mark Juergensmeyer (trans.), *Songs of the Saints of India*, 1988; Nirmal Dass, *Songs of Kabir from the Adi Granth*, 1991; and David Lorenzen, *Kabir Legends and Ananta-Das's Kabir Parachai*, 1991.

Kabirpanth

Religious community whose members are followers of the northern Indian poet-saint **Kabir**. Some Kabirpanthis are **ascetics**, and some are householders. The group's most important center is located in **Benares** (where Kabir is believed to have lived) and houses an ascetic community. Although in his poetry Kabir rejects ritual, **worship**, and reliance on anything but one's own unmediated experience—a context implying the practice of **yoga**—the Kabirpanth has taken on all of these conventional religious trappings. The community's sacred text is the *Bijak*, a collection of poems and epigrams attributed to Kabir. Its sacred centers have pictures of Kabir, who has become an object of worship. Elaborate rituals are performed on certain prescribed days. This situation is ironic because it appears that many of the practices Kabir condemned have been adopted by the community professing to follow his teachings. Given Kabir's continual emphasis on the need for unmediated personal experience of the divine, the notion that he would be seen as the founder of a sect would itself have been outrageous to him. For further information see David Lorenzen, "Traditions of Non-Caste Hinduism: The Kabir Panth," in *Contributions to Indian Sociology*, Vol. 21, No. 2, 1987.

Kadambari

Sanskrit romance novel authored by the writer and dramatist **Bana** (7th c.), who was a contemporary of the northern Indian emperor **Harsha**. The love story between the main characters, a princess named Kadambari and a prince named Chandripida, is but one element of the book's complex plot. The *Kadambari* was left unfinished at Bana's death. It gives a detailed picture of Indian life during Bana's time.

Kadru

In Hindu mythology, the daughter of the divine sage **Daksha** and sister of **Vinata**. Kadru gives birth to a line of serpents, whereas her sister's children are born as eagles, the most famous of whom is **Garuda**. The well-known hostility between these species is attributed to a conflict between Vinata and Kadru: one day they are arguing about the tail color of a certain celestial horse, with Vinata arguing that it is white and Kadru asserting that it is black. The disagreement becomes more intense until they finally agree that whoever is wrong will become a slave to the other. To ensure her victory, Kadru persuades a number of her snake children to hang from the back of the horse. From a distance the tail appears to be black. (Some of her children disapprove of such dishonesty and refuse to participate. In revenge Kadru curses them to die in the snake-killing **sacrifice** performed by King **Janamjeya**.) When Vinata sees the black snakes, she believes she has been defeated and serves Kadru under extremely harsh conditions for many years. Vinata is finally rescued by her son Garuda, who discovers the fraud behind Vinata's defeat and embarks on a program of killing snakes that has never stopped.

Kaikeyi

In the *Ramayana*, the earlier of the two great Indian epics, Kaikeyi is the second wife of King **Dasharatha**, the mother of **Bharata**, and foster mother to **Rama**, the epic's protagonist. Kaikeyi is directly responsible for one of the most

Mount Kailas, overlooking the Chiu Monastery in Tibet. Kailas is considered to be the mythic Mount Meru, home of the god Shiva and the center of the universe.

villainous acts in the *Ramayana*: She forces Rama into fourteen years of exile in the forest, a major event in the epic's plot. Despite her evil action, she is not considered an evil person, but rather a person who acts out of love for her **son** yet who is burdened with extremely bad judgment and bad advice. When Dasharatha announces that he intends to anoint Rama as the heir to the throne, Kaikeyi is as happy as everyone else. Rama has always respected her as much as his own mother, **Kausalya**, and has treated Bharata as his equal. But as the day of the ceremony approached, Kaikeyi's mind is slowly poisoned by her maid, **Manthara**. Manthara convinces Kaikeyi that after Rama has been crowned the heir-apparent, she and Bharata will be treated as little more than chattel, or objects, if they are allowed to live at all.

Kaikeyi's concern for her son leads her to drastic action. Many years before, Dasharatha gave Kaikeyi two boons, or rewards, for her help in winning a great battle. She has never redeemed these boons, but now demands that Dasharatha exile Rama to the forest for fourteen years and crown Bharata as ruler in his place. Dasharatha pleads with Kaikeyi, but she does not change her mind. He is finally forced to grant her wish. Kaikeyi's request brings her disgrace not only from her husband, who curses her for separating him from Rama, but also from her son. Bharata rebukes Kaikeyi for depriving Rama of what is rightfully his, and refuses to rule until Rama orders him to serve in his place during the exile. The only person who does not condemn her is Rama, whom the epic portrays as serenely happy to obey his parents' commands, whatever they might be.

Kailas

Himalayan peak in southwestern Tibet renowned as a pilgrimage place (**tirtha**) for both Hindus and Buddhists. In Hindu mythology, Kailas is believed to be Mount **Meru**, the center of the universe. It is also believed that the top of

Mount Kailas is the place where the god **Shiva** makes his home. For both Hindus and Buddhists, the central act of pilgrimage to Kailas is to walk around the mountain, thus symbolically traversing the entire earth. The journey begins at **Manasarovar**, a lake near the mountain's base, which in Hindu mythology is esteemed as the lake of the gods. Many factors combine to make the sixty-five-mile circuit an extremely difficult journey: The area is extremely remote, the climate is harsh and unforgiving even in June (the customary pilgrimage time), and the circuit itself is physically strenuous, with its highest point over 19,000 feet above sea level. Storms can suddenly arise at any time of the year, and pilgrims who are unprepared can easily die of exposure. Given these difficulties, relatively few people perform this pilgrimage; it raises the status of those who do. For many years Chinese prohibitions on travel in Tibet made it impossible for people to undertake this pilgrimage. Since the early 1990s these rules have been relaxed and small groups of religious pilgrims are again making the sacred journey.

Kailasanatha

The largest and most famous of the rock-cut temples at **Ellora** in the state of **Maharashtra**; the temple is dedicated to the god **Shiva** in his form as the "Lord of Mount **Kailas**." The temple was constructed late in the eighth century by kings of the **Rashtrakuta dynasty** and completed during the reign of Krishna I. The Kailasanatha temple is modeled after other contemporary temples: its main elements are an outer gateway, an assembly hall, and a central shrine (**garbhagrha**) surrounded by a processional path (**pradakshina**) to smaller shrines. It is set on a high platform base topped with a ninety-six-foot-high spire representing Mount Kailas in the **Himalayas** and covered with decorative carving. The amazing point about this temple is that the entire structure is a **sculpture**—workers carved it out of a single rock outcropping, starting at the top and working down. It is estimated that during construction, the builders had to remove three million cubic feet of stone from the temple and the excavated courtyards surrounding it. See also **caves, artificial**.

Kaitabha

In Hindu mythology, one of two **demons** who attempt to kill the god **Brahma** (the other is **Madhu**). The story is recounted in several mythic sources, with some important differences among them. All versions agree that Madhu and Kaitabha are born from the god **Vishnu's** earwax during the period of cosmic dissolution (**pralaya**). As the creation of the world begins, a lotus sprouts from Vishnu's navel. It opens to reveal the creator-god, Brahma, who is immediately attacked by Madhu and Kaitabha. In all versions of the myth, Brahma appeals for help. Vishnu tricks the demons (who are strong but not too bright) and slays them. The difference comes in the **deity** to whom Brahma appeals for help. The story first appears in the mythology of Vishnu; here Brahma invokes that deity. Yet this same story also appears in the *Devimahatmya*, the earliest mythic source for the cult of the Mother **Goddess** as the supreme divine power. In this version, Brahma's hymn of praise is to the Goddess, who in her form as **Yoganidra** ("sleep of **yoga**") has lulled Vishnu into a cosmic stupor, rendering him unable to come to Brahma's aid. Pleased by Brahma's praise, the Goddess withdraws her influence over Vishnu; he awakens and slays the demons.

Kaivalya

("isolation") In **Samkhya** and **Yoga**, two of the **six schools** of Hindu **philosophy**, kaivalya is the state of final liberation. A person who has attained kaivalya has fully comprehended the difference between two important principles: the conscious but inert **purusha**, which is identified as the Self, and the active but unconscious **prakrti**. According to Samkhya metaphysics, confusion between these two eternally distinct principles triggers the **evolution** of subjective consciousness and the exterior world, in which the eternal Self becomes the witness to repeated rebirths. Of the two schools, Samkhya provides the theoretical explanation for bondage and liberation of the soul, whereas Yoga provides the method to liberation. The purpose in performing **yoga** is to help the person distinguish between these two principles, removing obstructions to understanding, particularly the karmic tendencies rooted in egoism. According to the **Yoga Sutras**, the foundational text for the Yoga school, those who can distinguish between these two principles and discern the soul's identity with the purusha attain independence from all external causes, mastery over all states of being, and omniscience. For further information see Gerald Larson and Ram Shankar Bhattacharya (eds.), *Samkhya: A Dualist Tradition in Indian Philosophy*, 1987; and Sarvepalli Radhakrishnan and Charles A. Moore (eds.), *A Sourcebook in Indian Philosophy*, 1957.

Kajari Teej

One of two festivals called **Teej**. See **Teej**.

Kala

In **Sanskrit** and its daughter languages, a word that can mean both "time" and "death." Kala is used as one of the alternate names for the god **Yama**, the lord of death and the master of all living beings.

Kalahasti

Temple and sacred site (**tirtha**) in the southern state of **Andhra Pradesh**, about fifty miles east of the town of **Tirupati** and 125 miles northwest of the city of Madras. Kalahasti is famous as one of the **bhutalingas** ("elemental lingas"), a network of five southern Indian sites sacred to the god **Shiva**. At each of these sites Shiva is worshiped as a **linga**, the pillar-shaped object that is his symbolic form, and at each site the linga is believed to be formed from one of the five primordial **elements** (bhuta)—**earth**, **wind**, **fire**, **water**, and **space** (**akasha**). Kalahasti's linga is associated with the element of wind, and the manifestation of Shiva there is Kalahasteshvar, the "Lord of Kalahasti."

Kalahasti is also one of the **Shakti Pithas**, a network of sites throughout the subcontinent that are sacred to the **Goddess**. Each Shakti Pitha marks the site where a body part of the dismembered goddess **Sati** fell to earth, taking form there as a different goddess; in the case of Kalahasti the body part was Sati's left shoulder. Kalahasti's sanctity is thus reinforced by having two highly powerful and sacred sites to two different **deities**. See also **pitha**.

Kalamukha

("black face") Extinct monastic sect whose members were devotees (**bhakta**) of the god **Shiva** and whose name may refer to their practice of marking their heads with a black streak. Little is known about their doctrines or practices. While there are contemporary literary references to the **Kapalikas**, another extinct Shaivite **ascetic** community, the only sources for the Kalamukhas are a series of **inscriptions**. From these inscriptions we know that the Kalamukhas were strongest in the **Karnataka** region, although they were also present in other southern Indian regions. They flourished between the ninth and thirteenth centuries.

Kalasha

("pitcher") In the **Nagara** style of temple **architecture** predominantly found in northern India, the kalasha is an inverted vase-shaped piece that crowns the temple towers (**shikharas**). In many cases, kalashas were made of gold to provide a decorative contrast above the stone. The kalasha on the highest tower typically has a banner fluttering from it. The architectural symbolism in Hindu temples corresponds to the structure of human body, so the kalashas stand for the crown of the head, the highest and purest part of the body. They are also a symbol of the highest human religious potential.

Kalhana

(12th c.) Kashmiri poet and author of the *Rajatarangini* ("River of Kings"), a poetic chronicle of the kings of **Kashmir**. Kalhana's chronicle is an unusually descriptive and accurate history of Kashmir and its political, social, and religious institutions. The text's only shortcoming is that it pays little attention to the outside world. Kalhana's historical emphasis is unusual for Indian writers, and his chronicle is one of the few indigenous Indian histories.

Kali

("black") Incomprehensibly fierce and powerful divine form of the Mother **Goddess**. Kali is the awful, uncontrolled power of the divine in its most terrifying aspects. She is consistently associated with images of **blood**, death, and destruction; her dwelling place is the **cremation ground**. Her iconography portrays her as clothed with severed heads and limbs, and her form is lean, gaunt, and haggard, with lolling tongue and lips smeared with blood. Paradoxically, millions of Kali's devotees (**bhakta**) refer to her as "mother."

Kali's roots are uncertain, but she is generally assumed to be an autochthonous ("of the land") **deity**. Her dark color—associated with low social status, her preference for dwelling in inaccessible places, and her **worship** by Indian aboriginal tribes and people at the margins of society, all seem to point to origins as a local goddess, perhaps of tribal people. Some early **Sanskrit** dramas, such as the poet **Bhavabhuti's** *Malatimadhava*, mention fierce goddesses who received **offerings** of blood from their devotees.

This same motif was a central element in the stories about the **Thugs** in the nineteenth century.

One of Kali's earliest descriptions comes in the *Devimahatmya*, the earliest known source for the notion that God is feminine. One of the *Devimahatmya*'s episodes describes the birth of Kali (in her form as **Mahakali**) as the anger of the Goddess incarnate. In the story, Kali first destroys the **demon** armies by stuffing them into her mouth and eating them whole, symbolizing her all-consuming power to destroy. Her other feat in this text is the destruction of **Raktabija**, a demon who receives the boon that any drop of his blood that falls to the earth will instantly turn into a clone of him—a boon that renders him practically unconquerable. Kali defeats him by drinking his blood as it is shed until it is completely gone. Both of these episodes reinforce her image as a terrifying and powerful goddess, her destructive capacity, and her associations with substances and practices normally considered to be defiling. As Kinsley notes, Kali can also be seen as a symbolic statement that human life is uncertain and that tragedy and misfortune can occur without warning, despite the best-laid plans.

Worship of Kali has followed two paths, one in agreement with these horrific images and one in contradiction to them. On one hand, Kali has been an important deity for practitioners of the secret, ritually-based religious practice known as **tantra**. The tantras describe reality as resulting from the interaction between polar opposites, symbolized in the deities of **Shiva** (consciousness) and **Shakti** ("power"). Shiva provides the ordering principle and is the Ultimate Reality, but Shakti provides the energy and dynamism that actually makes things happen. Consequently, goddesses take on an important role in tantric practice. Among these goddesses Kali stands preeminent, perhaps because she is the most radical articulation of feminine power and can thus be seen as bringing the greatest power to bear on

Image of the goddess Kali. Her fierce power is represented by the symbols of death and destruction that surround her: skulls, fire, her blood-smeared tongue, and severed heads and limbs.

behalf of her devotees. Her power over all things and Shiva's helplessness without this power is symbolized by the images of Kali standing over the prostrate Shiva, clearly in a dominant position. In this tradition, the tantric expert is seen as a heroic figure who gains power from the goddess.

The tantras also stress the reconciliation of opposites as a way to destroy all conceptual dualism and affirm the ultimate unity of the entire universe. To carry this out, tantric rituals may include practices involving substances normally forbidden, such as the so-called **Panchamakara**, or "Five Forbidden Things," as a way to affirm the provisional nature of all judgments of **purity** and impurity (**ashaucha**). Again, Kali is the quintessential tantric deity, since her iconography and mythology involve things normally considered impure: drinking blood and receiving **animal sacrifices**, living in the cremation ground, and clothing herself with severed limbs.

The other dominant image for the worship of Kali is as a mother. This image is preeminent in the Bengal region, and has become widely established there during the past few hundred years. This image of Kali is rooted in Indian images of motherhood, which are greatly idealized in terms of a mother's devotion to her children. The central belief is that if a devotee approaches Kali as a submissive child, ready to take whatever blows she gives, she will ultimately turn her awesome forces toward protecting her devotee. Kali's most famous devotees are the nineteenth-century Bengali figures **Ramprasad** and **Ramakrishna**; the former is famous for a poem in which he states that there are bad children but never a bad mother.

Religious adepts such as Ramprasad and Ramakrishna have been able to maintain this tension between Kali's horrific persona and her image as a mother, but in popular devotion this tension has been largely lost. Modern images of Kali tend to sweeten or ignore her horrific aspects, often portraying her as young, beautiful, and almost benevolent. For more information on Kali, see David R. Kinsley, *The Sword and the Flute*, 1975; and *Hindu Goddesses*, 1986.

Kalibangan

Archeological site in the western state of **Rajasthan**, a short distance from the border with Pakistan. Kalibangan is one of the cities of the **Indus Valley Civilization** and is part of cluster of cities in what many archaeologists believe was the **Saraswati River** valley, although at present the river disappears into the desert. The site at Kalibangan is nearly as large as the cities at **Harappa**, **Mohenjo-Daro**, and **Lothal**. The city plan is virtually identical to the others, thus revealing the scope of this mysterious ancient culture.

Kalidasa

(5th c. ?) Generally considered the greatest **Sanskrit** writer, noted both for his command of the language and his ability to evoke poetic emotion (**rasa**) in his listeners. There is little definite information about Kalidasa's life; even the dates of his birth and death have been widely debated. According to legend, Kalidasa was an illiterate village boy. As a joke he was presented as a suitor for a learned princess who had vowed that she would only marry a man who could defeat her in a silent debate—that is, a debate using gestures instead of words. Kalidasa "defeated" the princess through coincidence and mutual misunderstanding and became her husband. When the princess discovered the depths of Kalidasa's ignorance, she threw him out of the house, ordering him not to return until he had become educated. In desperation he went to a temple of the **goddess Kali** and was about to offer himself as a **human sacrifice**, when Kali appeared to him and gave him absolute mastery of **Sanskrit**. Upon his return, his wife is reported to have asked him, "Have you gained proficiency in [Sanskrit] speech?" ("Asti kascit vagviseshatah?"). Kalidasa gave his answer over time, using the three words in his wife's question as the first words of his three greatest works—*Kumarasambhava*, *Meghaduta*, and *Raghuvamsha*. He is also the author of the dramas *Abhijnanashakuntala*, *Vikramorvashiya*, and the *Malavikagnimitra*. These works reportedly gained him the patronage of king **Vikramaditya**, with whose court Kalidasa is traditionally associated.

Legend also recounts that Kalidasa's miraculous gift of learning caused his death. Since his wife had spurred his search for learning, Kalidasa thought of her as his **guru** or religious teacher. Out of respect, he refused all sexual relations with her. Enraged at his refusal, she cursed him to meet his death at the hands of a woman. Many years later, a king composed a line of verse and offered a large prize to the person who could compose the best ending. Kalidasa heard about this contest while enjoying the company of a courtesan and effortlessly composed the perfect ending. In her greed for the prize, the courtesan stabbed and killed Kalidasa. Although her crime was discovered and she was punished, this legend illustrates the Hindu belief in the unstoppable power of fate, particularly when driven by a **curse**.

Kalighat

Temple dedicated to the goddess **Kali** in the southern section of modern Calcutta. This temple is several hundred years old and is considered one of the most important temples in Calcutta. The city's name is supposedly an anglicized version of the temple's name. Local tradition claims that Kalighat is one of the **Shakti Pithas**, a network of sites sacred to the **Goddess**. Each Shakti Pitha marks the site where a body part of the dismembered goddess **Sati** fell to **earth**, taking form there as a different goddess; in the case of Kalighat the body part was one of Sati's toes. See also **pitha**.

Kalika Devi

Name of both a shrine in the **Shiwalik Hills** (foothills of the **Himalayas**) and of its presiding **deity**. Kalika Devi is one of the nine **Shiwalik goddesses** and is believed to be a form of the **goddess Kali**. The temple itself is in the town of **Kalka**, on the road between the cities of Chandigarh and Simla. As is the case with many of the other Shiwalik goddesses, the image of Kalika Devi is a natural stone outcropping. This is considered a self-manifested (**svayambhu**) form of the **Goddess**. Unlike many of the other Shiwalik goddesses, the **Hindi** literature on this shrine does not claim that the temple is one of the **Shakti Pithas**, a network of sites sacred to the Goddess, mythically connected as places where a body part of the dismembered goddess **Sati** fell to **earth**. Instead, the literature simply commends the temple for its power and majesty. The literature does note, however, that local priests claim it as the place where Sati's hair fell to earth. This illustrates both the influence that pamphlet literature can have in channeling pilgrim traffic and the need to tie one's site into the network of the Shakti Pithas.

The stone outcropping that forms Kalika Devi's image is considered to be her head. According to tradition, Kali took the form of a beautiful woman and came to the temple to sing festive songs during the festival of **Navaratri**. The local monarch was so smitten by her voice and beauty that he asked her to marry him. Enraged at this insult, Kali cursed the king to lose his kingdom. As a further sign of her displeasure, she caused the temple image to begin sinking into the earth. At the plea of an ardent devotee, she allowed the head of the image to remain visible. See also **pitha**.

Kalimath

("**Kali's** Dwelling") Village and sacred site (**tirtha**) in the **Himalaya** mountains of **Uttar Pradesh** state. Kalimath is located on a small tributary of the

Mandakini River about ten miles from the village of **Guptakashi**; the Mandakini is one of the Himalayan tributaries that combine to create the **Ganges**. According to local tradition, Kalimath is one of the **Shakti Pithas**, a network of sites sacred to the **Goddess**. Each Shakti Pitha marks the site where a body part of the dismembered goddess **Sati** fell to **earth**, taking form there as a different goddess. Local sources claim that Kalimath is the place where Sati's vulva fell to earth. It took form there as the goddess Kali, thus associating a highly charged female body part with a powerful and often dangerous form of the Goddess. The temple's image of the Goddess is extremely unusual—a brass plate a little more than a foot square, whose center is cut out in a small triangle, an aniconic symbol of the Goddess. This plate supposedly covers a pit—a clear symbol of the part of Sati's body which is supposed to have fallen there—but the area under the plate is deemed so sacred that looking under it is forbidden.

The claim that Kalimath is the place where Sati's vulva fell to earth illustrates the fluidity of the Indian sacred landscape. There is a much more widely accepted tradition associating this specific body part with the temple of **Kamakhya** in **Assam**. Such competing claims are not uncommon in the Indian sacred landscape, since people often make these claims to enhance their particular site's sanctity and prestige. It is notable that many Hindus seem little concerned with such apparent inconsistencies, perhaps stemming from the conviction that a single Goddess lies behind all her individual manifestations. See also **pitha**.

Kalivarjya

The name for a collection of about fifty-five acts "to be avoided in the **Kali** [Age]," the last age in the cycle of **cosmic time** after which it is believed the world will be destroyed and recreated. This was one of the strategies used by **brahmin** scholars to forbid certain religious practices that were prescribed in the sacred literature but were no longer acceptable because of changing ideas. The Kalivarjya prohibitions first appear in texts around the twelfth century C.E. Some of the practices considered acceptable in earlier times but prohibited during the Kali age include certain **animal sacrifices** prescribed in the **Vedas** (the earliest Hindu religious texts) and **suicide** by a person suffering from a terminal illness. For further information see Pandurang Vaman Kane (trans.), A *History of Dharmasastra*, 1968.

Kaliya

In Hindu mythology, a thousand-headed serpent who is defeated by the adolescent god **Krishna** in one of the earliest acts foreshadowing the god's future greatness. Kaliya has settled into a deep pool in the **Yamuna River**, rendering the pool and its surroundings uninhabitable because of the noxious poison he constantly emits. One day as Krishna and his companions tend the cows, Krishna decides to get rid of Kaliya. Despite his friends' pleas, Krishna climbs to the top of a tall tree and dives deep into the pool. A tremendous battle ensues. Krishna finally subdues Kaliya by dancing on his hoods, stamping each of the serpent's heads until blood runs out of Kaliya's mouths. Kaliya's wives beg Krishna to spare his life, and Krishna grants this request but banishes him to a more appropriate place. His mercy mirrors the Hindu world view that even beings such as Kaliya have a rightful place in the world. Although problems arise when such beings are in the wrong place, these can be corrected by sending them to a more appropriate one. For further elaboration of this idea, See John Stratton Hawley, "Krishna's Cosmic Victories," in *Journal of the American Academy of Religion*, Vol. 47, No. 2, 1979.

Image of the god Vishnu's Kalki avatar.
It is believed that Vishnu will appear in
this form at the end of the world.

Kali Yuga

A particular age of the world in one of the reckonings of **cosmic time**. According to traditional belief, time has neither beginning nor end, but alternates between cycles of creation and activity, followed by cessation and quietude. Each of these cycles lasts for 4.32 billion years, with the active phase known as the **Day of Brahma**, and the quiet phase as the Night of Brahma. In one reckoning of cosmic time, the Day of Brahma is divided into one thousand **mahayugas** ("great cosmic ages"), each of which lasts for 4.32 million years. Each mahayuga is composed of four yugas, the **Krta Yuga**, **Treta Yuga**, **Dvapara Yuga**, and Kali Yuga. Each of these four **yugas** is shorter than its predecessor and ushers in an era more degenerate and depraved. By the end of the Kali Yuga, things have gotten so bad that the only solution is the destruction and re-creation of the **earth**, at which time the next Krta era begins.

Kali Yuga is the last of the four yugas, lasting for "only" 432,000 years. It is also considered to be the most degenerate yuga, symbolized by its identification with iron—a metal that is sometimes useful, sometimes harmful, not particularly precious, and whose black color is associated with **Saturn**, the malevolent **planet**. Kali Yuga is considered the time when human wickedness runs rampant, virtue virtually disappears, and the world is inexorably falling into ruin. Hindus believe that the Kali Yuga began with the commencement of the great war described in the epic *Mahabharata*, and not surprisingly, it is the age in which we now live.

Kalka

Town in the Ambala district of the state of **Haryana**, about ten miles north and east of Chandigarh. Kalka is famous as the site of the temple of **Kalika Devi**, who is considered to be a form of the **goddess Kali** and is one of the nine **Shiwalik goddesses**.

Kalki Avatar

The tenth **avatar** or incarnation of the god **Vishnu**, and the only one of these incarnations who has not yet appeared. In traditional art, Kalki is portrayed as riding a white horse and brandishing a sword. It is believed that he will come at a time when the state of the world has completely degenerated. His arrival will signal its imminent destruction; his purpose will be to purify the world by destroying the wicked.

Kalpa

The largest unit of **cosmic time**, equivalent to 4.32 billion years. According to one concept, the kalpa is broken up into one thousand **mahayugas**, each lasting 4.32 million years. The kalpa, or **Day of Brahma**, is the longest conceived measure of time and is used to determine the duration of the universe. After the kalpa is complete, it is followed by an equally long "Night of Brahma," a period of universal dissolution (**pralaya**).

Kalpa

(2) ("proper," "fit") One of the six **Vedangas**, auxiliary branches of knowledge connected with the **Vedas**, the oldest Hindu religious texts. The Kalpa section prescribes the rites connected with the Vedic rituals and gives rules for performing ceremonial and sacrificial acts. The other Vedangas are **vyakarana** (**Sanskrit** grammar), **chandas** (Sanskrit prosody), **nirukta** (etymology), **shiksha** (correct pronunciation), and **jyotisha** (auspicious times for sacrifices).

Kalpa Sutras

("aphorisms on sacred law") An important class of **smrti** or "remembered [literature]." The Kalpa Sutras were first composed around the sixth century B.C.E. The sutras were collected to provide a unified religious and legal worldview. According to the general scholarly consensus, the theory used to associate these sutras imposed an appearance of conceptual order on what was more likely an organic development of Hindu religious law. The Kalpa Sutras are all attributed to famous sages. In theory each Kalpa **Sutra** contains three separate parts: prescriptions for Vedic rituals (**Shrauta Sutras**), prescriptions for domestic rites (**Grhya Sutras**), and prescriptions for appropriate human behavior (**Dharma Sutras**). The real picture is far more complex since only three sutras contain all three parts and are attributed to a single author. The three surviving Kalpa Sutras are attributed to the sages **Apastamba**, **Baudhayana**, and **Hiranyakeshin** and are all associated with the same school, the **Black Yajur Veda**. There are many other collections that have one or another of these parts, but not all three. Each of the Kalpa Sutras is also theoretically connected with one of the four **Vedas**, the earliest Hindu religious texts. However, it is likely that this claim was made to give authority to the collection.

Kalpataru

("wishing-tree") Extensive collection of writings on matters relating to religious law, compiled by the scholar **Lakshmidhara** in the middle of the twelfth century. The *Kalpataru* is one of the earliest examples of commentarial literature known as **nibandhas** ("collections"). The nibandhas were collections of Hindu lore, in which the compilers drew references on a particular theme from the **Vedas**, **dharma literature**, **puranas**, and other authoritative religious texts. Then they compiled these excerpts into a single volume. Each of the *Kalpataru*'s fourteen volumes is devoted to a particular aspect of Hindu religious life, including daily practice, **worship**, gift-giving (**dana**), vows, pilgrimage, penances (**prayashchitta**), purification, and final liberation of the soul (**moksha**). As one of the earliest nibandhas, the *Kalpataru* formed a model for later writers and was also an important resource for them. Lakshmidhara's writing is unusual because he used very few sources for his work—primarily the epic *Mahabharata* and a few of the sectarian collections known as puranas. Unlike later commentators, he does not cite the Vedas, the earliest Hindu religious texts, or the prescriptions found in the dharma literature. His text also consists mostly of these excerpted passages with very little commentary of his own, whereas later nibandha writers often give voluminous explanations.

Kalpavas

("residence for a **kalpa**") Strict religious vow taken during the annual **Magh Mela** festival in the city of **Allahabad** during the **lunar month** of **Magh** (January–February). Allahabad is located at the confluence of two sacred rivers, the **Ganges** and the **Yamuna**. The festival's primary religious act is bathing (**snana**) at this confluence. Although most people stay at this festival only a brief time, kalpavasis, or people taking the kalpavas vow, do not leave the site of the festival for the entire month. Kalpavasis also take vows to live a strict **ascetic** lifestyle, which includes daily baths in the Ganges, a restricted diet, particular dress and **worship**, and attendance at the religious gatherings known as **satsang**.

Kalpeshvar

Temple and sacred site (**tirtha**) in the **Garhwal** region of the **Himalayas**, about ten miles down the **Alakananda River** from **Joshimath**. The temple's presiding **deity** is the god **Shiva** in his manifestation as Kalpeshvar, the "Lord of the Cosmic Age." The Kalpeshvar temple is one of the **Panchkedar**, a network of five sites in the Garhwal region that are sacred to Shiva; the other four sites are **Kedarnath**, **Rudranath**, **Tungnath**, and **Madmaheshvar**. Shiva is believed to dwell in the Himalayas. This network of five sites is seen as a symbolic representation of his body. Kalpeshvar represents Shiva's matted locks (**jatas**).

Kalyanamandapam

("marriage hall") One of the common architectural features of southern Indian temples built in the **Dravida** style. The kalyanamandapam is a hall where the images of the temple's primary **deity** and that deity's spouse could be ceremonially united on festival days to symbolize their married state.

Kama

In Indian **philosophy**, one of the four purusharthas, or **aims of life**, with the others being **artha** (wealth, power, and prosperity), **dharma** (righteousness), and **moksha** (liberation). The most basic meaning of kama is "desire," with strong overtones of sexual desire, but kama can also refer to all types of attraction, including aesthetic pleasure from the arts. The most famous treatise on the fulfillment of kama is the *Kama Sutra*, which details the satisfaction of sexual desires. When pursued within the boundaries of righteous action, or dharma, desires and their satisfaction are recognized as a normal, acceptable part of life. It is when this governing force is absent that the search for pleasure becomes inappropriate and destabilizing.

Kama

(2) Minor **deity** identified as the personification of kama ("desire"). Kama is comparable to the Greek deity Eros and carries similar responsibility for igniting human sexual attraction and sensual desire. Kama is represented as a young man riding on a parrot, armed with a bow and arrows. The bow is a stalk of sugar cane, the bowstring a line of buzzing bees; his five arrows are five different flowers, each bringing a different emotional effect to the person it pierces. The five flowers and emotions are: lotus, infatuation; **ashoka**, intoxication (with love); mango, exhaustion; jasmine, pining; blue lotus, paralysis. Kama's iconography carries strong associations with spring, and the spring **season** (personified as another minor deity, Vasant) is perceived as Kama's friend and ally in awakening desire through the regeneration of the natural world and the showy display of spring blossoms.

The most famous episode in Kama's mythology begins with the ascent to power of a **demon** named **Taraka**, who can only be killed by a son of **Shiva**. Taraka seems impossible to defeat, since Shiva has no sons and is in deep meditation, grieving over the death of his wife **Sati**. The other gods ask Kama to shoot Shiva with an arrow of desire so he will marry the **goddess Parvati** and produce a son. Kama creeps up on Shiva and shoots him with an arrow. When Shiva realizes who has disturbed his meditation, he releases a stream of fire from the third eye in the middle of his forehead, instantly burning Kama to ashes. Through Shiva's **grace**, Kama is eventually brought back to life. One of Kama's epithets or alternate names is Ananga, or "bodiless," because of the loss of his body (and the fact that desire seems to strike in unseen ways). Despite being destroyed by Shiva and seemingly foiled, in the end Kama achieves his goal. His attempt to draw Shiva out of his meditation succeeds, and eventually Shiva marries Parvati. For more information on the interplay between Shiva and Kama, see Wendy Doniger O'Flaherty, *Siva*, 1981.

Kamada Ekadashi

Ekadashi, or eleventh-day, festival of the bright, waxing half of the **lunar month** of **Chaitra** (March–April). Most Hindu festivals have certain prescribed rites usually involving fasting (**upavasa**) and **worship**, and often promise-specific benefits for faithful performance. As promised by its name ("wish-granting"), faithfully observing this festival will fulfill one's desire (**kama**), whatever it may be.

Kamadhenu

In Hindu mythology, a **goddess** in the form of a **cow** (dhenu) who has the power to grant all one's wishes (**kama**). The Kamadhenu is considered the mother of all cattle. She is associated with giving gifts of food, and thus is an extension of the gifts of food given by all cows. In Hindu mythology, Kamadhenu is the property of the sage **Jamadagni**. Her theft by a local king prompts Jamadagni's son, **Parashuram avatar**, to circle the earth twenty-one times, in an attempt to wipe out the **kshatriya** (kingly) class.

Kamakhya

("desiring eyes") A particular manifestation of the Mother **Goddess**, whose temple on **Nilachal Hill** overlooks the Brahmaputra River just outside the city of Guwahati in **Assam**. This temple is one of the **Shakti Pithas**, a network of sites that spreads throughout the subcontinent and is sacred to the Goddess. Each Shakti Pitha marks the site where a body part of the dismembered goddess **Sati** fell to earth, taking form there as a

different goddess. The Kamakhya temple is the place where Sati's vulva fell to earth. Its image of the goddess is a natural cleft in the rock, around which the temple has been built. Since Kamakhya sprang from the most sexually charged part of the female body, it is no surprise that she is believed to be extremely powerful. Like many powerful goddesses, her productive capacity must be constantly recharged through receiving sacrifices, especially the **blood** of living beings. In modern times the usual **sacrifice** is a goat, but in earlier times the **offering** of **human sacrifices** is well documented. Kamakhya was reportedly offered 140 men when her present temple was consecrated in 1565. This practice continued until the British halted it in 1832. The men offered as human sacrifices were reportedly volunteers who believed that they had been called by her to do this. In the time between announcing their intention to be sacrificed and their deaths, they were treated as virtual divinities, since they were considered to have been consecrated to the goddess. For further information see George Weston Briggs, *Gorakhnath and the Kanphata Yogis*, 1973. See also **pitha**.

Kamakotipith

An important center for the **Dashanami** sect of **Sanyasi** ascetics, located in the southern Indian city of **Kanchipuram**. According to local tradition, the Kamakotipith was the first and most important of the **maths** or monastic centers, established by the philosopher **Shankaracharya**, who later established four other centers at **Joshimath**, **Puri**, **Shringeri**, and **Dwaraka**. This claim to primacy has generated fierce controversy. Opponents who support one of the other four maths, not only deny Kamakotipith's place as the first of the maths, but also assert that Kamakotipith is only a branch of the Shringeri math. Support for these claims can be drawn from the symbolism connected with the number four—the four cardinal directions, the four sacred texts known as

Vedas, and the four organizational groups of the Dashanami Sanyasis themselves. The number four symbolizes completion and totality, which makes a fifth sacred center problematic. Despite their possible merit, these contentions have not diminished Kamakotipith's status. It has a long history as an **ascetic** center, and its head monk is routinely considered one of the Shankaracharyas, the most important modern Hindu religious leaders. Kamakotipith's importance probably reflects the importance of Kanchipuram itself, which was such a significant sacred and political hub that any ascetic center located there could gain considerable authority.

Kamalakanta

(d. 1820) Bengali poet, devotee (**bhakta**) of the **goddess Kali**, and teacher and practitioner of the secret, ritually-based religious practice known as **tantra**. Kamalakanta spent most of his life as the **guru** and learned adviser (**pundit**) of the king of Burdwan, a region northwest of modern Calcutta, whose capital is also named Burdwan.

Kamandalu

A water pot traditionally used by **ascetics**, usually having a removable lid for ease in filling and a spout for pouring. Kamandalus may be made from various materials, such as gourds, wood, metal, or baked clay. They are generally wider than they are tall, making them stable and less likely to tip over. In India's climate, water is an obvious necessity. Even ascetics with very few **possessions** will generally have some means to carry and store it. Aside from satisfying their physical needs, water is an important element in ascetic religious life, since it is often an **offering** used in **worship** as well as the preferred medium for bathing (**snana**) and other rites of purification. This religious importance makes the kamandalu a powerful object in its own right. A kamandalu is considered especially significant when it has been used for years by a noted ascetic—objects kept in close proximity to such a person are believed to be charged with their spiritual power. In modern times, kamandalus are still important ritual objects, but their practical function has largely been replaced by screw-top plastic vessels.

Kama Sutra

("manual on desire") By far the most famous of the ancient **erotic** manuals, traditionally attributed to the sage **Vatsyayana**. This text is usually associated with an exhaustive catalog of sexual positions and pleasures, but in fact it goes far beyond this stereotype. Vatsyayana was interested in exploring desire in all its manifestations. The text begins with a consideration of the four **aims of life** (purushartha): worldly goods (**artha**), desire (**kama**), religious duty (**dharma**), and liberation of the soul (**moksha**). Vatsyayana argued that since desire was one of the established goals of human life, its pursuit was thus a good thing, as long as this pursuit did not interfere with the others.

Having established the legitimacy of desire, Vatsyayana then discussed how to foster it. The *Kama Sutra*'s second book contains the text's best-known material, the discussion and categorization of various types of sexual union. It begins by characterizing types of sexual endowment, both male and female. Next it describes different sorts of embracing, kissing, scratching, and biting as symbols of passion, along with sexual positions and oral sex. This is followed by chapters on gaining a wife, attracting other men's wives (which the text discourages, except in cases where one's passion is "too strong"), courtesans, and general remarks on the nature of attraction.

The text is a manual for all phases of erotic life in which sex can be refined into a vehicle for aesthetic experience as well as pure carnal pleasure. The *Kama Sutra* is also notable for its perspective on **women**, who are seen as having equal sexual desire and gaining equal pleasure. The ultimate aim is the sexual satisfaction of both partners, rather than one partner simply serving the other. The *Kama Sutra* has been translated many times.

Kamavasayitvam

("suppression of desire") One of the eight superhuman powers (**siddhi**), traditionally believed to be conferred by high spiritual attainment. This power gives one the ability to control desires. It also means that any declaration one makes, such as pronouncing a blessing (**ashirvad**) or a **curse**, will inevitably come to pass. The basis for this latter power seems to stem from the absence of individual desire in such a person, meaning that person will never be motivated by self-interest. This power reflects the pan-Indian belief that by renouncing everything, one can eventually gain power over everything.

Kamban

(9th c.) Southern Indian poet most noted as the author of the Tamil-language version of the *Ramayana*, the earlier of the two great Hindu epics. Kamban's text is known as the *Kamba Ramayana*, and remains popular in modern times. As with all vernacular translations of the *Ramayana*, Kamban did not simply translate **Valmiki's Sanskrit** epic from Sanskrit to a more common language, but adapted and even added to it as he saw fit. Of particular interest is his heroic portrayal of the **demon**-king **Ravana**, who is the villain in the original story. This shift may reflect feelings of regional pride, since Kamban was a southern Indian and Ravana's kingdom of **Lanka** is generally identified as the island of **Sri Lanka** in the Indian Ocean, southeast of the Indian mainland.

A kamandalu is used to hold water for use in religious rites.

Kamba Ramayana

Tamil language version of the *Ramayana*, the earlier of the two great Hindu epics. The *Kamba Ramayana* was written in ninth century by the southern Indian poet **Kamban**. As with all vernacular renditions of the *Ramayana*, Kamban did not simply translate **Valmiki's Sanskrit** epic, but adapted and added to it as he saw fit. Of particular interest is his heroic portrayal of **Ravana**, the **demon**-king, who is the villain in the original story. This shift may reflect feelings of regional pride, since Kamban was from southern Indian. Ravana's kingdom of **Lanka** is generally identified as the island of **Sri Lanka** in the Indian Ocean, southeast of the Indian mainland.

Kamika Ekadashi

Festival falling on the eleventh day (**ekadashi**) of the dark, waxing half of the **lunar month** of **Shravan** (July–August). As with all eleventh-day observances, Kamika Ekadashi is dedicated to the **worship** of **Vishnu**. Most Hindu festivals have certain prescribed rites usually involving fasting (**upavasa**) and worship, and often promise specific benefits for faithful performance. The name Kamika means "desiring," a theme supported by the charter myth. According to this story, the **brahmins** in a certain village refuse to perform religious rites for a landowner guilty of murdering another brahmin. The landowner is freed from that sin by observing the Kamika Ekadashi and is thus able to have the desired rites performed.

Kamsa

In Hindu mythology, the wicked king of **Mathura** who is considered the brother of **Devaki**, the god **Krishna's** mother, and thus Krishna's uncle. According to legend, Kamsa is born when a **demon** takes the form of **Ugrasena**, Devaki's father, and under this guise has intercourse with Kamsa's mother.

On Devaki's wedding day, a divine voice warns Kamsa that his sister's eighth child will eventually kill him. In an effort to prevent this prophecy, he kills all of Devaki's children as soon as they are born. Yet on the night Krishna is born, a deep sleep falls over the inhabitants of the palace, the locked doors magically open, and the infant is spirited away to the home of his foster parents, **Nanda** and **Yashoda**. When Kamsa finds out what has happened, he first sends his men to kill all the newborn children in the country. When that attempt fails to destroy Krishna, Kamsa sends various demon assassins, such as **Putana**, **Shakata**, **Trnavarta**, **Keshi**, and **Bakasur**. Krishna dispatches all of these with ease, and Kamsa eventually has to try other strategies. He announces a grand festival and dispatches his chariot to pick up Krishna and his brother **Balarama**, who by then have grown into adolescents. Kamsa's plan is to lure the brothers to the festival grounds where they can be killed in a "friendly" match with some experienced wrestlers. The two boys derail this plot by killing the wrestlers, after which Krishna leaps up into the royal box and kills Kamsa as well.

Kamya Karma

("desiderative [ritual] action") One of three general categories of ritual action, the others being **nitya karma** and **naimittika karma**. Kamya karma is a ritual performed solely for the performer's desire (**kama**) to obtain the benefits of this action. Unlike the other two categories, which must be performed at specific times or occasions, this one is completely voluntary and based solely on the desire for its benefits. One example of a kamya karma is religious pilgrimage, which one is not required to do but which is believed to generate religious merit. Another example would be performing a particular **vrat**, or religious vow, which might be done daily, weekly, monthly, or yearly.

Kanada

(2nd c. B.C.E.?) Philosopher who is traditionally named as the author of the **Vaisheshika Sutras** and founder of the Vaisheshika philosophical school, one of **six schools** of Hindu **philosophy**. Kanada's date is uncertain, but he is believed to have lived after the third century B.C.E. In its earliest form, the Vaisheshika school followed a doctrine of atomism, asserting that there are simple building blocks that cohere to form complex objects. This cohesion also attaches objects to their qualities. As Vaisheshika combined with the **Nyaya** school, another of the six schools, the Vaisheshikas gradually adopted the Nyaya idea of God as the regulating force behind these atomic relations.

Kanauj

Small city on the **Ganges** River, about fifty miles upstream from the city of Kanpur. Kanauj is now insignificant, but the city, formerly known as **Kanyakubja**, was once one of the most important in northern India. Its existence is documented as early as the sixth century B.C.E. The city was an important stop on the trade route running through the Ganges basin. It is referenced in Ptolemy's *Geography*, written around 150 C.E. Kanauj was also an important political center; in the early seventh century it was the capital of the **Pushyabhuti dynasty**, ruled by the emperor **Harsha**. In later centuries the **Pala**, **Rashtrakuta**, and **Gurjara-Pratihara** dynasties fought over the city, with the Gurjara-Pratihara eventually gaining control. After suffering an attack by **Mahmud of Ghazni** in 1017 C.E., Kanauj seems to have gone into permanent decline. Its modern legacy is being the location of the dominant branch of **brahmins** in the Gangetic Plain. They call themselves **Kanaujia** brahmins.

Kanaujia

One of the five northern **brahmin** communities (**Pancha Gauda**); the other four are **Gauda**, **Maithila**, **Utkala**, and **Saraswat**. Kanaujia brahmins trace their origin to the city of **Kanauj**. Kanaujia brahmins are found in greatest density in the eastern section of the state of **Uttar Pradesh**, near the city of Kanauj; subgroups can be found throughout **Bihar**, Bengal, **Madhya Pradesh**, and the inland regions of **Orissa**.

Kanchipuram

Temple-town and sacred site (**tirtha**) about forty miles southwest of the city of Madras in the state of **Tamil Nadu**. Kanchipuram is important as one of India's **Seven Sacred Cities**. Dying in one of these cities is believed to bring final liberation of the soul (**moksha**). At differing times Kanchipuram served as a capital for the **Pallava**, **Chola**, and **Vijayanagar** kings; each of these dynasties left its mark in the city's **architecture**. Kanchipuram is filled with temples, many of them magnificent examples of the southern Indian **Dravida** architectural style.

Kanchipuram's importance as a political center and its concentration of temples, brahmins, and scholars made it one of the greatest centers of Hindu life, learning, and religion.

Kanchipuram is also noted for its temples to each of the three major Hindu **deities—Vishnu**, **Shiva**, and the **Goddess**. The Vaikuntaperumal Temple is dedicated to Vishnu in his form as "Lord of **Vaikuntha**," his celestial realm. The Goddess is worshiped as Kamakshi ("desiring eyes"). Kamakshi is identified with the goddess **Kamakhya**, whose temple in **Assam** is the most powerful of all the **Shakti Pithas**.

Shiva is worshiped at the Kailasanatha temple, in his manifestation as the "Lord of Mt. **Kailas**," and at the Ekambareshvar temple. The image of Shiva at the former site is one of the **bhutalingas** ("elemental lingas"), a network of five southern Indian sites sacred to the god Shiva. In each of these sites Shiva is worshiped as a **linga**, the pillar-shaped object that is his symbolic form. At each site the linga is believed to be formed from one of the five primordial **elements** (bhuta)—**earth**, **wind**, **fire**, **water**, and **space** (**akasha**). The Kanchipuram linga is associated with the element of earth, the humblest but most essential of all.

Another reason for Kanchipuram's prominence is its long tradition as a center for **asceticism**. Kanchipuram's **Kamakotipith** is an ancient center for the **Dashanami** sect. Its leader is considered to be one of the **Shankaracharyas**, the most important contemporary Hindu leaders. According to local tradition the Kamakotipith was the first and most important of the **maths**, or monastic centers, established by the philosopher **Shankaracharya**, who later established four other centers at **Joshimath**, **Puri**, **Shringeri**, and **Dwaraka**. This claim to primacy has generated fierce controversy, with opponents not only denying Kamakotipith's place as the first of the maths, but also asserting that Kamakotipith is only a branch of the Shringeri math. Some

Vaikuntaperumal Temple in Kanchipuram.

support for these claims can be drawn from symbolism connected with the number four—the four cardinal directions, the four sacred texts known as **Vedas**, and the four organizational groups of the Dashanami Sanyasis themselves. The number four symbolizes completion and totality, which makes a fifth sacred center problematic. Kamakotipith reflects the importance of Kanchipuram as a significant sacred and political hub in which any **ascetic** center could gain considerable authority. See also **pitha**.

Kandariya Mahadev

The largest of the temples at **Khajuraho** in the state of **Madhya Pradesh**. It is dedicated to the god **Shiva** in his manifestation as "**Skanda**'s Lord"; Skanda is another **deity** who is considered to be Shiva's son, and the general of Shiva's army. The Kandariya Mahadev temple was built by the kings of the **Chandella dynasty** between 1025 and 1050. It was constructed at the end of the wave of creativity that produced all of the Khajuraho temples. It is the best-developed example of the Khajuraho branch of the **Nagara** architectural style, in which all of the temple's smaller towers lead to and culminate in one central tower directly over the sanctuary. Like most of the temples at Khajuraho, the Kandariya Mahadev temple is covered with **erotic sculpture**—perhaps as a symbol for union with the divine, perhaps as a religious affirmation of every aspect of human existence.

Kandarpa

Epithet of the god **Kama**, a minor **deity** identified as the personification of kama ("desire") who is comparable to the Greek deity Eros. See **Kama**.

Kangra

The name of a town and district in the state of **Himachal Pradesh**; the town was formerly the capital of a small hill kingdom with the same name. Kangra is famous for the temple of **Vajreshvari Devi**, one of the nine **Shiwalik goddesses**. In the eighteenth and nineteenth centuries, Kangra's status as a courtly center brought in patronage for the **Pahari** school of **miniature painting**.

Kanha

Epithet of the god **Krishna**. The name Kanha is actually a form of the name Krishna, modified in the transition between **Sanskrit** and vernacular language. See **Krishna**.

Kanhaiya

Epithet of the god **Krishna**. As with the name Kanha, Kanhaiya is actually a form of the name Krishna that has been modified in the transition between **Sanskrit** and vernacular language. See **Krishna**.

Kankhal

City and sacred site (**tirtha**) three miles south of the city of **Haridwar** in the state of **Uttar Pradesh**. Kankhal is most famous for the **Daksha Mahadev** temple, dedicated to the god **Shiva** in his form as "**Daksha's** Lord." This temple's charter myth is one of the most famous of all the stories of Shiva. Daksha is one of the sons of the god **Brahma** and the father of **Sati**, the **goddess** whom Daksha gives in marriage to Shiva. When Daksha feels that Shiva has not shown him proper respect, he plans a great **sacrifice** to which he invites all the gods, but purposely excludes Shiva. When Sati asks why her husband has been excluded, Daksha responds with a stream of abuse, denouncing Shiva as worthless and despicable. Humiliated, Sati commits **suicide**. Shiva is furious when he hears of Sati's death, and in his rage creates the fierce **deities Virabhadra** and **Bhadrakali**. He then comes storming with his minions (**gana**) to the sacrificial ground, completely destroying the sacrifice, and cuts off Daksha's head. Daksha is eventually restored to life, repents his foolish pride, and asks Shiva to remain at that site forever, which he agrees to do.

There are numerous smaller temples near the Daksha Mahadev temple, some of which are dedicated to figures associated with this story, such as Virabhadra. Across the street from the Daksha temple is a large **ashram**, or religious community, built by devotees (**bhakta**) of the Bengali mystic **Anandamayi Ma**. The ashram also contains her **samadhi shrine**, or **burial** place.

Kannada

One of the four **Dravidian** languages, along with **Tamil**, Telegu, and Malayalam; all four languages are spoken in southern India. Kannada is the predominant language in modern **Karnataka**, one of the "linguistic" states, formed after Indian independence in 1947 to unite people with a common language and culture under one state government. Despite its recent political significance, Kannada has a long history as a literary and cultural language and is particularly important as the language for the devotional (**bhakti**) poetry of the **Lingayat** religious community. See also **Tamil language**.

Kanphata

("split ear") Colloquial name for the **Nathpanthi** sect of **ascetics**, who are followers of the sage **Gorakhnath**. This particular name stems from the Nathpanthi's most characteristic feature: When a Nathpanthi ascetic is ready for final **initiation**, the cartilage in his ears is slit with a razor to insert the large earrings by which members of this group are easily identified. See **Nathpanthi**.

Kanvar

A bamboo pole with baskets or receptacles suspended from each end. In earlier times a kanvar would have been a natural way for people to carry heavy loads. Its major use today is for religious rites in which pilgrims carry **water** from one place to offer to a **deity** in another. The kanvar is the device by which the water is kept elevated the entire way. This keeps the water's original **purity** unbroken, preserving it as an appropriate **offering** for a deity. The most famous example of this rite is at the temple of **Vaidyanath** in the state of **Bihar**. It is also found at temples in **Haridwar** in **Uttar Pradesh**, **Tarakeshvar** in **West Bengal**, and the hills of **Maharashtra**.

Kanyadan

("gift of a virgin") In its most specific sense, the kanyadan is the part of the traditional wedding ceremony in which the bride's father (or guardian) formally transfers her to her husband's family. In a more general sense, the word refers to giving a **daughter** in marriage to another family. This "gift" is believed to be highly commendable for the father, since the bride is supposed to be given without

The city of Kanyakumari, at the confluence of the Indian Ocean, Arabian Sea, and Bay of Bengal.

asking for anything in return. At the same time, the status difference between the bride's family (as wife "givers") and the groom's (as wife "takers") can make this "gift" an extremely expensive proposition for the bride's family. See **Dowry**.

Kanyakubja

("[city of] humpbacked maidens") Ancient name for the site now known as **Kanauj**, which was the capital for several northern Indian dynasties in the latter half of the first millennium. The name *Kanyakubja* comes from a tale about a king who has a hundred daughters. One day the daughters' games disturb the meditation of a local sage who is filled with desire for them. The king worries about angering the sage and promises him one of his daughters in marriage. Ninety-nine of his daughters flatly refuse to marry the sage because of his advanced age and gruff demeanor, but the youngest agrees to do so in obedience to her father. The sage accepts the youngest daughter and curses the others to become humpbacked so they will never be able to marry.

Kanyakumari

("virgin girl") City and sacred site (**tirtha**) at the extreme southern edge of the state of **Tamil Nadu**, at the confluence of the Indian Ocean, Arabian Sea, and Bay of Bengal. Kanyakumari is important as a bathing (**snana**) place. Kanyakumari is also the name of the site's major **deity**, a local **goddess** who has been assimilated into the pantheon as a manifestation of the goddess **Parvati**. According to local tradition, Kanyakumari set her heart on marrying **Shiva**; when this was prevented she vowed to remain a perpetual virgin (kanya). Her manifestation here is clearly different from all the other forms of Parvati, who are invariably married to Shiva, yet Kanyakumari's unmarried status also gives her independent power.

Kapala

A human skull. In Hindu art, a skull is often carried by the god **Shiva**, who uses it as a vessel to hold his food and drink. As with many of Shiva's attributes, such as the snakes he wears as jewelry and the ash from the **cremation ground** with which he smears his body, the skull-bowl is a sign of Shiva's untamed nature and his aloofness from the standards and concerns of everyday life. Use of a skull-bowl has also been adopted by some **Shaiva** ascetics, both past and present, in imitation of this myth. The skulls are usually taken from cremation grounds; the upper skull is separated to be made into a bowl.

Kapalamochana

("releasing the skull") Bathing (**snana**) tank and sacred site (**tirtha**) in the northern section of the city of **Benares**. According to Hindu mythology, when the wrathful **deity Bhairava** cuts off the fifth head of the god **Brahma**, insulting the god **Shiva**, the skull sticks to Bhairava's hand as a visible sign of his crime. Bhairava visits all the holy places of the earth trying to get rid of the skull, but to no avail. When he arrives in Kapalamochana, the skull spontaneously drops from his hand, liberating him from his crime. This act indicates that Kapalamochana is the holiest place on earth.

Kapalika

Extinct monastic sect of Shaivite ascetics, or devotees (**bhakta**) of the god **Shiva**. Although none of the Kapalikas' own written records have survived, there are numerous descriptions of them by other **ascetic** groups and by dramatists of their time such as **Bana** (7th c.) and **Bhavabhuti** (8th c.). The sources describe the Kapalikas as worshiping the god Shiva in his wrathful form as **Bhairava** and as emulating Bhairava's characteristics: wearing their hair long and matted, smearing their bodies with ash (preferably from the **cremation ground**), and carrying a club and a skull-bowl (**kapala**). The Kapalikas are cited as indulging in forbidden behavior—drinking wine, eating meat, using cannabis and other **drugs**, performing **human sacrifice**, and enjoying orgiastic sexuality. Needless to say, most of the available sources do not approve of them.

David Lorenzen argues that despite the disapproval of their contemporaries, all the Kapalika practices must be seen in the context of **tantra**. Tantra is a secret, ritually-based religious practice that its initiates believe is far more powerful and effective than ordinary religious **worship**. One of its most essential themes is the ultimate unity of everything that exists. From a tantric perspective, to affirm that the entire universe is one principle—often, conceived as the activity of a particular **deity**—means that the adept must reject all concepts based on dualistic thinking. One way to do this is to partake of the "Five Forbidden Things" (**panchamakara**), consciously breaking societal norms forbidding illicit sexuality and consumption of **intoxicants** and non-vegetarian food. This is always done within a carefully defined ritual setting, in a conscious effort to sacralize what is normally forbidden.

Seen in this context, the Kapalikas' behavior is shocking but becomes more understandable. Lorenzen also speculates that in performing such behaviors (which may have only taken place during religious ceremonies), the Kapalikas were identifying themselves with their chosen deity, Bhairava. In the Hindu pantheon Bhairava is known for his uncontrolled excesses, particularly for cutting off one of the heads of the god **Brahma**, for which he has to perform severe penances (**prayashchitta**). In this understanding, the Kapalikas' practices are not motivated by hedonistic self-gratification but by the desire to imitate their chosen deity. The only developed source on the Kapalikas is David Lorenzen, *The Kapalikas and the Kalamukhas*, 1972.

Kapalin

("skull-bearer") The name for any **ascetic** bearing a human skull, either as a **begging** bowl or as a piece of ascetic paraphernalia. Such ascetics are devotees (**bhakta**) of the god **Shiva** in his terrible form. Their use of the skull is a symbol that, like Shiva, they have transcended all earthly concerns of **purity**, impurity (**ashaucha**), and conventional standards of what is and is not appropriate.

Kapha

("phlegm") Along with **vata** ("air") and **pitta** ("bile"), one of the three bodily humours (**tridosha**) in **ayurveda**, the traditional system of Indian medicine. Every person has all three of these humours, but usually one is dominant; this marks a person in certain ways, particularly with regard to health, digestion, and metabolism. Kapha is associated with the **elements** of **earth** and **water**, since phlegm has both liquid and solid characteristics. It provides solidity and fluidity. Those who exhibit this humor are said to be strong, healthy, and have great stamina. At the same time, this solidity can take the form of inertia and fatigue; "phlegmatic" people must do their best avoid these tendencies.

Kapila

A powerful and ornery sage in Hindu mythology. Kapila's most famous mythic exploit occurs in the story of the Descent of the **Ganges**. King **Sagar** is on the verge of completing his hundredth horse **sacrifice** (**ashvamedha**). This will give him enough religious merit to claim the throne of **Indra**, king of the gods. Indra forestalls this threat by stealing the sacrificial horse and tying it outside Kapila's **ashram**. Sagar dispatches his sixty-thousand sons to find the horse. When they finally locate it at Kapila's ashram, they find the sage deep in meditation. The sons assume that the sage's meditation is a ploy to keep from having to answer their questions, so they begin to abuse him physically. Kapila becomes extremely angry. The accumulated power generated by his long **asceticism** (**tapas**) is released like fire, burning the sixty-thousand sons to ash. Kapila later informs Sagar's sole surviving descendant, **Anshuman**, that the only way to

bring peace to the souls of the departed is to bring the Ganges down to earth and have their ashes touched by her waters. Fulfilling this condition galvanizes several generations of Sagar's descendants—Anshuman, **Dilip**, and **Bhagirath**—until the last is finally successful in bringing the river to earth.

Kapila

(2) Philosopher cited as the traditional founder of the **Samkhya** philosophical school, one of the **six schools** of Hindu **philosophy**. Little is known about him; much of what is known has a legendary tone that makes its value as historical data questionable. Kapila may have lived in the seventh century B.C.E. If this is true, Kapila would have lived about a thousand years earlier than **Ishvarakrishna**. The latter is the first Samkhya figure from whom we have a well-attested text, the *Samkhyakarikas*, which is the foundational text for the school.

Kapilavastu

Ancient city in southern **Nepal**, just over the Indian border from the state of **Bihar**. Buddhist sources identify it as the capital city of Buddha's father, King Suddhodhana of the Shakya tribe. Kapilavastu was part of the thriving urban network in that region of India during the fifth century B.C.E.

Kapu

Traditional Indian society was modeled as a collection of **endogamous**, or intermarried, subgroups known as **jatis** ("birth"). These jatis were organized (and their social status determined) by the group's hereditary occupation, over which each group held a monopoly. In traditional society, the Kapus were farmers. In much of modern **Andhra Pradesh**, particularly the region bordering modern **Tamil Nadu**, the Kapus are the dominant landholding group.

Karana

In Indian **philosophy**, the name for an instrumental cause, or the cause by which another thing is accomplished. An example often given by the **Nyaya** philosophical school states that when a potter connects two pot-halves using a stick, the stick is the instrumental cause for the creation of the pot. In **Sanskrit** grammar, the word karana has a parallel sense; it designates the word in a sentence that shows how the action is accomplished.

Karandamakuta

("basket-crown") A small crown in the shape of a basket, notable for its lack of ornamentation. In Hindu art, the karandamakuta is the head covering worn by a lesser **deity**. In contrast, the **kiritamakuta** worn by the god **Vishnu** is much larger and more elaborately decorated, in keeping with his status as one of the predominant deities in Hindu religious life.

Karka Sankranti

Date on the Indian **calendar** marking the **sun's** transition into the zodiacal sign of Cancer, and thus, the beginning of the **dakshinayana**, the six months in which the sun is traveling toward the south. In Western astrology this happens during the summer solstice (around June 21), but in Indian reckoning it occurs around July 14. The discrepancy arises due to the different ways in which the two systems mark the beginning of the astrological **year**. In Western astrology the beginning of the year is based on the sun's position in relation to the **earth** and occurs during the vernal equinox (around March 21). In Indian reckoning the starting point of the **zodiac** comes when the sun intersects the midpoint of a group of stars named Ashvini, and is based on the position of the sun with regard to fixed stars. Karka Sankranti is not marked by significant observances, unlike **Makara Sankranti,** which occurs six months earlier, marking the beginning of the sun's northward journey (**uttarayana**). The southern direction is associated with the god **Yama**, who is death personified. Thus, this southward movement is considered less **auspicious** than its northward counterpart.

Karma

("action") The notion of karma and its connection with reincarnation (**samsara**) are perhaps the most fundamental concepts in Indian thought and are ideas shared by all Indian religions: Hindu, Buddhist, Jain, and Sikh. Although the literal meaning of karma is "action," it is believed to encompass words and thoughts as well as deeds. The basic assumption behind the notion of karma is that of a dynamic universe, in which any action that one takes will have consequences that will eventually affect oneself. In the simplest explanation, good actions will have good consequences, and evil actions will have evil consequences, in an extended chain of cause and effect. Since thoughts are considered actions, this determination of "good" and "evil" actions also takes into account one's motives—a laudable action performed for an ignoble motive is still a laudable action, but will not generate as much merit as the same action performed for a pure motive.

Karma is seen as a purely physical process, much like the law of gravity. It does not require a divine overseer, although in devotional Hinduism, God is generally seen as having the power to nullify one's past karma. The effects of one's actions may come either in this life or in future lives. The former case is easy to believe, since most people accept that their actions have consequences, but the latter case is much more difficult to support with concrete evidence. Since the general tone of one's life is seen as more important than a few isolated acts, one might compare the idea of karma with the notion of a person's "character." Both are determined by one's habitual

The Himalayan town of Karnaprayag.

ways of thinking and acting, and entail an overall assessment of a person. For further information see Wendy Doniger O'Flaherty (ed.), *Karma and Rebirth in Classical Indian Traditions*, 1980; and K. S. Mathur, "Hindu Values of Life: Karma and Dharma," in T. N. Madan (ed.), *Religion in India*, 1991.

Karmamarga

("path of action") One of Hinduism's three generally accepted paths to gain final liberation of the soul (**moksha**), along with the Path of Devotion (**bhakti-marga**) and the Path of Wisdom (**jnana-marga**). Bhaktimarga stresses devotion to God, and the jnanamarga stresses the realization of the ultimate identity of one's individual Self (**atman**) and Ultimate Reality (**Brahman**). Karmamarga emphasizes selfless action performed for the benefit of others.

Karmendriya

("organ of action") In Indian **philosophy**, any of the five organs through which human beings act on their environment, traditionally considered to be: voice, hands, feet, and the organs of elimination and generation.

Karna

In the ***Mahabharata***, the later of the two great Hindu epics, Karna is the eldest of the **Pandava** brothers, although he is not aware of his true identity until a few days before his death. He is born when his mother, **Kunti**, in a moment of youthful impulsiveness, looks upon the **sun** while reciting a **mantra**, giving her the power to have a son by any of the gods. She is immediately visited by a shining figure, who leaves her with an equally shining son. Distraught and desperate at the birth of this child, which as an unmarried woman she feels she cannot keep, she puts him in a box and abandons him in the **Ganges**.

The child is adopted by the charioteer, **Adhiratha**, who raises Karna as his own son. Karna later comes to the court of King **Dhrtarashtra**, where he becomes friends with the king's son,

Duryodhana, the epic's antagonist. While at court, Karna begins a lifelong conflict with **Arjuna**, one of the five Pandava brothers. Arjuna's comments about Karna's unknown parentage are meant to deny Karna the recognition he deserves as Arjuna's equal. As do all the princes, Karna studies with **Drona**, the archery master. When Drona refuses to teach Karna the secret of the **Brahma** weapon Karna wants to use to kill Arjuna, Karna goes to the sage **Parashuram avatar** for this instruction. He presents himself as a **brahmin**, since Parashuram hates the **kshatriya** (ruling) class and refuses to accept any of them as students.

Parashuram teaches Karna all that he wants to know. During this period, however, Karna receives two **curses** that ultimately determine his fate. Karna kills a brahmin's **cow**, so the brahmin curses him to have his chariot wheel stick in the mud and be killed upon it by his enemy. The second curse comes from Parashuram. One day as Parashuram sleeps with his head in Karna's lap, a beetle bores into Karna's thigh, which in the epic is a euphemism for the genitals. Despite the pain and blood, Karna remains still so he will not disturb his sleeping **guru**. When Parashuram awakens, he realizes that Karna's tolerance for pain means that he is a kshatriya, thus Karna has gained instruction under false pretenses. Parashuram curses Karna that at the critical moment, he will forget everything he has learned. Both of these curses eventually come true; despite fighting with great valor in the Mahabharata war, Karna is killed by Arjuna when the wheel of his chariot is stuck in the mud.

On the eve of the great war, Karna's mother, Kunti, comes to him and reveals his true identity and implores him to return and fight alongside his brothers. Karna refuses, saying that things have gone too far for such measures, but promises Kunti that he will not harm any of his brothers except for Arjuna, whom he has sworn to kill. In his decision Karna is also bound by his loyalty to Duryodhana, whose friendship and support for many years overrides any obligation to a family he has just discovered. As a man willing to stand by his friends and his principles, even in a cause he knows to be flawed, Karna endures as one of the tragic heroes of the *Mahabharata*.

Karnaprayag

Himalayan town and sacred site (**tirtha**) at the confluence of the **Alakananda** and **Pindara** rivers, in the Chamoli district of the state of **Uttar Pradesh**. As with all the other river junctions in the **Garhwal** region, this is considered an especially holy place. Local tradition ascribes the site's name to the *Mahabharata* hero **Karna**, who is believed to have worshiped the **sun** at this place. In return he received a suit of armor that could not be pierced and a quiver of arrows that could never be exhausted.

Karnata

Southern Indian brahmins who make up one of the five southern **brahmin** communities (**Pancha Dravida**); the other four are **Gujarati**, **Maharashtri**, **Andhra**, and **Dravida**. The core region for the Karnata brahmins is the modern state of **Karnataka**.

Karnataka

One of the four southern Indian states, whose inhabitants speak a **Dravidian** language, in this case **Kannada**. Karnataka is one of the "linguistic" states formed after India's independence in 1947, intended to unite people with a common language and culture under one state government. The state was largely formed from the former kingdom of Mysore. In medieval times, Karnataka was the seat of important Hindu kingdoms, particularly the **Hoysala** and **Vijayanagar** dynasties; these dynasties built cities at **Belur**, **Halebid**, and **Hampi**, which are now important archeological sites. Karnataka is also the home of the **Lingayats**, devotees (**bhakta**) of **Shiva**, whose missionary work eventually squeezed out the thriving Jain community.

Sculptures decorate the Virupaksha Temple in Pattadakal,
one of many historical sites in the state of Karnataka.

Jain monuments, such as the massive statue at Shravanabelgola, still stand. Karnataka also contains important Hindu holy places, such as **Shrirangapatnam** and **Shringeri math**. Even though much of the state's economy is still highly agricultural, Karnataka's capital, Bangalore, is a worldwide center for computer software development. For general information about Karnataka and other regions of India, see Christine Nivin et al., *India*. 8th ed., Lonely Planet, 1998.

Karnavedha ("ear-piercing") Samskara

The ninth of the sixteen traditional life-cycle ceremonies (**samskaras**), in which an infant's ears were pierced. This rite was done not only for ornamentation but also for protective purposes. According to **Sushruta**, the author of one of the oldest Indian medical texts, piercing the ears protected children against certain ailments. Although in modern times most young girls have pierced ears, this practice is far less common for boys, suggesting that ornamentation has taken precedence over protection.

Karni Mata

Presiding **deity** of the temple by the same name in the village of **Deshnok** in the state of **Rajasthan**. Karni Mata is a local form of the Mother **Goddess**; her name refers to the place where an ear (karni) of the dismembered goddess **Sati** fell to earth. The temple is unusual in that it is inhabited by thousands of rats, which are considered Karni Mata's sons. According to the local tradition, Karni Mata's son drowned in a local pond. When she tried to influence **Yama**, the god of death, to give her son a favorable rebirth, she was told that he had already been reborn as a **rat**. At her request, Yama allowed all of her male descendants to be born as rats in the temple at Deshnok. Yama agreed that in the next life the rats would be reborn as family members of the temple's servants. According to this myth, the rats and the temple priests are all members of one extended family.

Karpatri Maharaj, Swami

A modern-day **ascetic** noted for the strictness of his ascetic practices. His name comes from his habit of using his hands (kara) as the vessel (patra) in which he received the food he took as alms. This is considered one of the strictest ascetic practices, since the amount of food one can receive in this way is fairly small. The lack of an **eating** vessel indicates complete renunciation of material **possessions**. Swami Karpatri was also known for his conservative political views. After Indian independence in 1947, he was one of the founders of the political party **Ram Rajya Parishad** ("Organization for Ram's Reign"). The party's basic assertion was that people had to follow the division of status and labor found in the traditional **caste** system in order to have a smoothly working society. Aside from this conservative social platform, the party also backed Hindu causes such as the demand for a total ban on **cow slaughter**. Despite being a **Sanyasi** who had renounced the world, Swami Karpatri still maintained some residual attitudes from his former life. He had been born a **brahmin**; even after renouncing the world, he would only take food from brahmin houses. Swami Karpatri exemplifies how many ascetics still retain connections with the "everyday" world—both in retaining some concern for their former status and in taking organized political action to promote causes reflecting deeply entrenched Hindu values.

Kartigai

Eighth month in the Tamil **year**, corresponding to the northern Indian solar month of Vrschika (the zodiacal sign of Scorpio), which usually falls within November and December. The existence of several different calendars is one clear sign of the continuing importance of regional cultural patterns. One way that the Tamils retain their culture is by preserving their traditional **calendar**. Tamil is one of the few regional languages in India with an ancient, well-established literary tradition. See also **Tamil months**, **Tamil Nadu**, and **Tamil language**.

Kartik

According to the lunar **calendar**, by which most Hindu religious festivals are deter-

mined, Kartik is the eighth month in the lunar **year**, usually falling within October and November. In northern India, Kartik coincides with the harvest when the weather is quite pleasant. Kartik is one of the most ritually important months of the year; its major festivals include **Karva Chauth**, **Rambha Ekadashi**, **Narak Chaturdashi**, **Diwali**, **Govardhan Puja** (**Annakut**), **Devotthayan Ekadashi**, **Tulsi Vivah**, and **Kartik Purnima**.

Kartik Purnima

Festival during the **full moon** in the **lunar month** of **Kartik** (October–November), celebrated as a bathing (**snana**) festival. During the festival, an early morning bath in the **Ganges** or any other sacred river is believed to provide the bather with exceptional religious merit. People often journey to sacred rivers to take advantage of this opportunity. Also on this day, Sikhs celebrate the birthday of their religious leader, Guru Nanak, born in 1469.

Karttikeya

("**son** of the Krttikas") Epithet of the god **Skanda**, considered the son of **Shiva**. Skanda is not born in the usual manner but develops when **Shiva's semen** falls into the **Ganges** River. The name *Karttikeya* comes from the six minor goddesses known as the Krttikas, who are the deified form of the constellation Pleiades. After Skanda is born, these goddesses become his foster mothers and nurse him, which in Indian culture is believed to create a mother-child bond. So that none of the goddesses will feel slighted, Skanda sprouts six heads, allowing him to nurse from all of them at the same time.

Karva Chauth

Religious vow (**vrat**) observed on the fourth (chauth) day of the dark, waning half of the **lunar month** of **Kartik** (October–November). Karva Chauth is taken by married **women** to ensure their husbands' health, prosperity, and long life. There are many such vows in which women's observances and sacrifices are channeled into maintaining the welfare and prosperity of the family. Although such vows are voluntary in the strictest sense, there is great social pressure for women to perform them, thus fulfilling their expected role as "good" wives. Karva Chauth is a very strict vow; women observing it neither eat nor drink until they see the **moon** rising that evening. When the moon appears, the women offer water to it and then are permitted to drink. On this evening, women may also **worship** the **deities Shiva** and **Parvati** (the divine example of a happily married couple) and **Karttikeya**, their son. Women also give each other small pots (karva) filled with sweets, hence the festival's name.

The charter myth for this observance tells how a young bride, while performing this fast at the home of her birth, grows faint and nearly lifeless. Her brothers are so worried about her health that one of them climbs into a tree with a lantern, while the others convince her that the light is coming from the rising moon. The young woman is greatly relieved, but as soon as she drinks water her husband falls down dead. Her brothers eventually have to confess what they have done. As the woman lays lamenting her newly gained widowhood, she is discovered by the **goddess** Parvati, who assures her that her husband will be restored to life if she faithfully observes Karva Chauth the following year. The young woman does as she is told and regains her husband.

This tale contains significant cultural information, particularly on people's differing obligations. A brother's duty is to protect his sister. A wife's primary duty is to her husband, and her efforts should be devoted to his welfare. As in many such tales, the consequences of failing to keep a religious observance are swift and severe, and the rewards from faithfully performing it are equally grand.

Kashi

("shining") One of the traditional names for the city of **Benares**. Benares is mentioned in the list of the **Seven Sacred Cities**, where death brings final liberation of the soul. In a more strict local sense, the name *Kashi* designates the largest of the three traditional sacred zones in Benares. It includes everything within the **Panchakroshi Yatra** road, a circuit around the city that marks the outer limit of the region. The name Kashi refers to the mythic story of the **jyotirlinga**, the "pillar of light" in which the god **Shiva** is said to have first appeared. According to tradition, the pillar of light did not just land in Kashi but was itself a form of Kashi, thus indicating the city's sanctity over all other places on **earth**.

Kashmir

One of the three distinct cultural areas, along with **Jammu** and Ladakh, in the modern Indian state of Jammu and Kashmir. Jammu and Kashmir is a former princely state, in which the Hindu Dogra kings also ruled over the **minority** populations of the mostly Muslim Kashmiris and the mostly Buddhist Ladakhis. Since Indian independence in 1947, this ethnic and religious division continues to be a source of trouble, and nowhere more than in Kashmir. At independence, Pakistan attempted to take the region by force and claimed a section of Kashmir. In the time since then, India and Pakistan have fought several wars over it; Pakistan claims it by virtue of their shared religion of Islam; India claims it by virtue of a document signed by the last of its kings, Maharaja Hari Singh. The Kashmiris themselves have been caught in this regional clash, and their demands for greater self-determination have been largely ignored. After the 1986 state elections, which were widely regarded as rigged, tensions in Kashmir came to a boil. Since 1990 the tension has turned into an open rebellion, assisted by covert aid from Pakistan.

Most Kashmiris became Muslims during medieval times. Before that time the region was a Hindu cultural area. Kashmir still has some stunning examples of early Hindu **architecture**, such as the **sun temple** at **Martand**, a temple to the god **Shiva** at **Pandrenthan**, and the shrine to Shiva at **Amarnath** cave which

Some pilgrims to the sacred site of Kataragama participate in extreme ascetic practices, such as swinging from hooks that are pierced through their backs.

is still an important pilgrimage site. Kashmir also has a minority Hindu population, known as the Kashmiri Pandits. Recent troubles have prompted many of them to migrate south to other parts of India. Although these two communities profess different religious beliefs, they share a common language and sense of Kashmiri identity and culture. For general information about Kashmir and regions of India, see Christine Nivin et al., *India*. 8th ed., Lonely Planet, 1998.

Kashyapa

In Hindu mythology, Kashyapa is the chief of the **Prajapatis** (a class of semi-divine beings) and the father of **Garuda**, the divine eagle who serves as the animal "vehicle" for the god **Vishnu**. Kashyapa is also one of the Seven Sages whose names mark exogamous clan "lineages" (**gotra**); the others are **Gautama**, **Bharadvaja**, **Vasishtha**, **Bhrgu**, **Atri**, and **Vishvamitra**. All **brahmins** are believed to be descended from these seven sages, with each family taking the name of its progenitor as its

gotra name. In modern times, gotras are still important, since marriage within the gotra is forbidden. After her marriage, the new bride adopts her husband's gotra as part of her new identity. See also **marriage prohibitions**.

Kataka Hasta

In Indian **dance**, **sculpture**, and ritual, a particular hand **gesture** (**hasta**), in which the tips of the fingers are loosely joined to the thumb, to create a ring (the word *kataka* literally means "bracelet"). This hasta is common in the images of Hindu goddesses, but also serves a useful purpose: a fresh flower may be inserted in her hand every day.

Kataragama

Sacred site (**tirtha**) located in the extreme southeastern part of **Sri Lanka** that is dedicated to the god **Skanda** in his southern Indian manifestation as **Murugan**. The site is notable for being outside of the Indian mainland and as an important place of **worship** for both Hindus and Buddhists. According to mythic tradition, the site was established when Skanda went hunting in the jungles of Sri Lanka, fell in love with a tribal woman named **Valli**, and vowed to remain forever in her home. As the son of the god **Shiva**, Skanda is a powerful **deity** in the Hindu pantheon. His relationship with Valli shows his accessibility and his love for his devotees (**bhakta**).

The annual Kataragama pilgrimage in July–August is a theater to demonstrate these qualities: Many people come seeking healing from physical ailments or deliverance from distress, while others come to fulfill vows for benefits already received. Such vows often take the form of extreme self-mortification—by carrying the **kavadi**, a yoke held in place by hooks piercing the flesh; by piercing the tongue or cheeks with tiny arrows, one of the symbols of Skanda; or by hanging from hooks embedded in the back and thighs. These ardent devotees are reportedly rewarded for their suffering with a state of ecstasy in which they feel no pain and suffer no bleeding. In this state of ecstasy, the devotees are also believed to be mouthpieces for the god Skanda. Other pilgrims seek their advice for every conceivable kind of problem, under the assumption that Skanda will give them the most appropriate answer. For further information see Paul Wirz, *Kataragama: the Holiest Place in Ceylon*, 1966; and Bryan Pfaffenberger, "The Kataragama Pilgrimage," in *Journal of Asian Studies*, Vol. 28, No. 2, 1979.

Katha

("conversation") Genre of public religious address based on recitation and exposition of a religious text. Katha is most often associated with the **Ramcharitmanas**, a version of the epic **Ramayana** written by the poet-saint **Tulsidas**, but may be used to explain other religious texts as well. Kathas may be delivered in a number of ways: The speaker may go through large parts of the text, give detailed analysis and commentary on a very small portion of the text, select passages from throughout the text to illustrate a particular theme, or present a completely spontaneous and free-floating exposition. For listeners, attending such events is not only aesthetically satisfying but also considered to be a form of **satsang** or religious association. Such gatherings were (and are) one of the major ways in which illiterate people memorize large parts of these primary texts. For further information see Philip Lutgendorf, *The Life of a Text*, 1991.

Kathak

One of the classical **dance** forms of India; some of the others are **Bharatanatyam**, **Orissi**, **Kuchipudi**, **Kathakali**, and **Manipuri**. Like much of traditional Indian culture, classical dances are identified with certain regions; Kathak is primarily found in northern India. Traditionally, Kathak descended from the **ras lilas** of **Braj**, devotional dances illustrating events from the life of **Krishna**. This claim has little historical support and may simply reflect the desire to root all of the Indian arts in religion. It is not disputed, however, that Kathak developed as an art form in the courts of the northern Indian princes, where it was performed for the entertainment of the monarch and his guests. In time, two major Kathak centers developed: Jaipur, famous for spectacular footwork; and Lucknow, known for its attention to acting. Stylistically, Kathak is marked by an upright posture, with the legs kept straight. The dance emphasizes rapid, rhythmic foot patterns, rhythms accentuated by strings of bells worn on the dancer's ankles and complemented by multiple turns; the torso is kept fairly immobile. As with all forms of Indian dance, Kathak includes a well-developed "vocabulary" of facial expressions and gestures of the arms and hands that allow the dancer to convey a great range of emotions to the audience. For further information see Mohan Khokar, *Traditions of Indian Classical Dance*, 1984.

Kathakali

One of the classical **dance** forms of India; some of the others are **Bharatanatyam**, **Orissi**, **Kuchipudi**, **Kathak**, and **Manipuri**. Like much of traditional Indian culture, classical dances are identified with certain regions; Kathakali is primarily found in **Kerala**. Unlike many of the other classical forms, Kathakali did not develop in a temple setting. It appeared as a developed style in the seventeenth century, although it is rooted in folk and religious dramas dating from centuries before. Kathakali has traditionally been danced only by men—the **women's** form in Kerala is **Mohini Attam**. A Kathakali performance is one of the most dramatic spectacles in the Indian arts. Part of this drama comes from the dancers' training, stressing controlled facial mobility to facilitate ease and power of expression. The dancers wear flamboyant costumes and headdresses. The most striking feature of all is elaborate makeup— the heroes' faces are painted a vivid green, with fluted ridges made of rice paste attached to their cheeks, while villains are painted in green and red and have knobs of pith attached to their chins and foreheads. Stylistically, the dance moves between athletic jumps and majestic turns, with religious texts forming the dominant source for stories. As with all Indian dances, Kathakali has a well-developed "vocabulary" of **gesture** and facial expression, which makes it possible for the dancers to engage in complex storytelling. As with all other classical dances, Kathakali has undergone certain changes in the past generation, spurred by a shift in the venue from temple courtyards to stage performance. For example, a planned stage performance requires a well-organized "program" and a designated time frame, whereas in earlier times Kathakali performances would often last all night long. For further information see Mohan Khokar, *Traditions of Indian Classical Dance*, 1984.

Katha Upanishad

One of the later and more developed **Upanishads**, the speculative religious texts that form the latest stratum of the oldest Hindu sacred texts, the **Vedas**. As with most of the Upanishads, the Katha Upanishad investigates profound questions, in particular the nature of the Self (**atman**). The text tells the story of a boy, **Nachiketas**, whose father sends him to Death in a fit of anger. Nachiketas goes to Death's abode, but finds no one. He waits for three days before Death returns. To make amends for ignoring a **brahmin** guest—which the text describes as a serious sin— Death gives Nachiketas three boons, or wishes. Nachiketas uses the first boon to be restored to his father's house and the second to receive instruction in performing a sacrificial **fire**. With the final boon, he asks what happens to a person after the death of the body. Death first tries to evade the question, then tries to bribe Nachiketas with other gifts. When the boy insists on an answer, Death begins to reveal his secrets; these revelations make up the bulk of the text. Death's secrets focus mainly on the reality of the Self, its eternal and indestructible nature, its subtle qualities, and the difficulties in realizing it. The Self is the ultimate truth, and to know it is to know the only thing that really matters.

Katyavalambita Hasta

In Indian **dance**, **sculpture**, and ritual, the name of a particular hand **gesture** (**hasta**) in which the arm hangs down beside the body and the hand rests on the hip in a relaxed manner.

Katyayana Smrti

One of the **smrtis** or "remembered" texts, a class of literature deemed important but less authoritative than the other textual category, the **shrutis** or "heard" texts. This smrti is attributed to the sage Katyayana and is an example of one of the **Dharma Shastras**, manuals prescribing rules for correct human behavior and ideal social life. Unlike the **Dharma Sutras**, which are ascribed to recognizable individuals, the Dharma Shastras are usually credited to mythic sages as a strategy to reinforce the authority of these texts. Katyayana's complete text has not survived, although more than one thousand verses have been compiled from later works. Katyayana's text was the first to focus on the rights of **women**: he gave particular attention to women's personal property (**stridhan**), both to explain their powers and to prescribe rules for its **inheritance** when a woman died.

Kaurava

In the *Mahabharata*, the later of the two great Hindu epics, the Kauravas are the hundred sons of King **Dhrtarashtra** and the epic's antagonists to the **Pandava** protagonists. The Kauravas receive their name as descendants of Kuru, an ancestor of King **Shantanu**. As in many cases in Hindu mythology, the Kaurava sons are born in an unusual manner. Their mother, **Gandhari**, receives a blessing (**ashirvad**) from the sage **Vyasa** that she will give **birth** to one hundred sons. Her **pregnancy** lasts for over two years. When she grows impatient and tries to hasten the delivery, she gives birth to a great lump of flesh. Vyasa advises Gandhari to divide the lump and place each piece in a pot of clarified butter (ghee). In due time, each of the 101 pots break open to reveal one hundred handsome boys, as well as a single daughter, Dussala. Of these hundred sons, the most important are the two eldest, **Duryodhana** and **Duhshasana**.

Kausalya

In the *Ramayana*, the earlier of the two great Indian epics, Kausalya is the first wife of King **Dasharatha** and the mother of the god-king **Rama**.

Kaustubha

In Hindu mythology, the gem that the god **Vishnu** wears on his chest. The Kaustubha jewel is one of the precious things produced by churning the ocean of milk. Other products include the **goddess Lakshmi**, the **Kamadhenu** or wishing-**cow**, and the nectar of immortality (**amrta**). Vishnu's **possession** of the Kaustubha jewel is a symbol of his power and his mastery over the universe. See also **Tortoise avatar**.

Kautilya

According to tradition, Kautilya was the author of the *Arthashastra* ("Treatise on Power"), a text which is a handbook on the exercise of royal power. The ruler portrayed in the *Arthashastra* cares little for ideals or **dreams**, but rather is willing to do whatever is necessary to remain in power. Aside from his authorship of the *Arthashastra*, Kautilya is also identified as the Machiavellian **brahmin** minister who orchestrated **Chandragupta Maurya**'s rise to power, but there are serious doubts that these Kautilyas are the same person.

Kavadi

A bamboo yoke topped with semicircular splints of bamboo that is carried on a devotee's (**bhakta**) shoulders during certain festivals devoted to the god **Murugan**. A kavadi is usually decorated with flowers, pictures, ribbons, and other ornaments. A devotee carrying a kavadi is inviting Murugan to descend and rest upon it, bestowing his **grace** through divine **possession**. Carrying a kavadi is usually done to fulfill a vow often made when asking Murugan for some favor, such as healing or deliverance from other distress. This can be an extremely strenuous rite: Fully loaded kavadis sometimes weigh one hundred pounds. The carriers sometimes secure the kavadis by using metal hooks stuck into the flesh of their backs and chests. Carrying the kavadi is seen as an act of devotion and can be found wherever the **worship** of Murugan is popular: in southern India, at **Kataragama** in **Sri Lanka**, in Malaysia, and in **South Africa**.

Kaveri River
See **Cauvery**.

Kavi

A word that most literally means "wise man," but more commonly refers to a "poet" or "bard." This secondary meaning comes from the pan-Indian assumption that the purpose of such poetic writers was not merely to entertain but to educate and to uplift.

Kavikarnapura

(mid-16th c.) Author of one version of the *Chaitanya-Charitramrta* ("Nectar of Chaitanya's Deeds"), an account of the life of the Bengali saint **Chaitanya**. Kavikarnapura's text was written in 1542, nine years after Chaitanya's death, when the effort to declare Chaitanya a saint had already begun. Kavikarnapura freely acknowledges his debt to an earlier biography of Chaitanya, written by **Murari Gupta**. He diverges from the earlier text by portraying Chaitanya as an incarnation of **Krishna**, descending to earth to bestow **grace** on ordinary mortals. As with the other traditional accounts of Chaitanya's life, the author does not claim this to be an "objective" biography but instead a hagiography written by a passionate devotee (**bhakta**).

Kavitavali

("series of poems") The final poetic work of the poet-saint **Tulsidas** (1532–1623?). In the *Kavitavali*,

Tulsidas gives a condensed version of the epic *Ramayana* as well as poems in which he clearly speaks in his own voice. Evidence in the text indicates that it was completed after 1615. The poems are written in the **savaiya** and **kavitt** meters, which are longer, more complex, and less accessible than the meters used in most of Tulsidas's earlier works. The *Kavitavali* is divided into seven sections, paralleling the internal structure of the *Ramayana*, but the bulk of the *Kavitavali*'s poems are in the last two sections. One of these is the "Lankakhand," which describes the climactic battle symbolizing the struggle between good and evil; in this section the kavitt **meter** is used to render vivid battle scenes. The final book is the "Uttarakhand," comprising more than half of the entire work. In this last section, Tulsidas has written some autobiographical verses and reiterates themes found throughout much of his work: the degeneracy of the present age (**Kali Yuga**), a stress on devotion as the only means of salvation, and the power inherent in God's name, through which any obstacles can be overcome. Parts of this latter section sound pessimistic, perhaps reflecting the trials of advancing age, but through it all comes a note of hope that the author's trust in God's saving power will not ultimately be in vain.

Kavitt

A particular **meter**, or rhythm pattern, in **Hindi** poetry. Verses composed in the Kavitt meter have four lines of thirty-one syllables each, with the break in each individual line often coming after the sixteenth syllable. This is an unusually long meter, thus lending itself well to extended descriptions employing alliteration; in his *Kavitavali*, the poet-saint **Tulsidas** uses this meter with great affect to describe battle scenes.

At an altitude of almost 12,000 feet in the Himalaya Mountains, pilgrims traveling to the sacred site of Kedarnath must climb a steep path and contend with unpredictable weather.

Kavya

("related to **kavis**") The most general name for courtly poetry or poetic prose, most often composed in the **Sanskrit** language. Such kavya was usually written and performed in a court setting, where innovative reworking of traditional forms was valued more highly than originality or self-revelation. The primary building block in such poetry was the two-line verse, which was a self-contained unit with regard to meaning. Verses were composed in meters ranging from four to twenty-six syllables per half-line, and were ornamented with various **alamkaras** ("figures of speech") in an effort to convey the mood (**rasa**) appropriate to the subject matter. Poetic forms range from single-verse epigrams, such as those of **Bhartrhari**, to extended epic poems (**mahakavyas**), most notably those of **Kalidasa**. Although such poetry contains frequent references to religious life, it was primarily intended for entertainment rather than moral encouragement, an emphasis which reflects the court atmosphere in which it was composed. The singular exception to this trend is the *Gitagovinda* of **Jayadeva**, a text said to have been composed at the **Jagannath** temple in **Puri**, which focuses on devotion to the god **Krishna** as lord of the universe.

Kayasth

Traditional Indian society was modeled as a collection of **endogamous**, or inter-marrying, subgroups known as **jatis** ("birth"). The jatis were organized (and their social status determined) by the group's hereditary occupation, over which each group held a monopoly. The Kayasths worked as scribes and recorders. They were mostly associated with maintaining business and mercantile records, accounting, and keeping businesses running smoothly and profitably.

Kedarnath

Village and sacred site (**tirtha**) in the **Himalayas** at the headwaters of the **Mandakini River**, one of the tributaries of the **Ganges**. The village is named for its presiding **deity**, who is the god **Shiva** in his manifestation as the "Lord of Kedar." Shiva is present at Kedarnath in the form of a **linga**, a pillar-shaped image. The Kedarnath linga is deemed one of the twelve **jyotirlingas**, a network

of sites deemed especially sacred to Shiva. Kedarnath's sanctity is only matched by the difficulty in getting to it. Its high altitude—close to 12,000 feet—means that it is only accessible between late April and October, a characteristic also of **Yamunotri**, **Gangotri**, and **Badrinath**, the three other major Himalayan pilgrim sites. A trip to Kedarnath preserves some of the difficulty formerly associated with Himalayan pilgrimage. Pilgrims travel the last ten miles on foot or horseback, during which the path climbs five thousand feet. Those braving the trek must contend with the unpredictable mountain weather, but may also be rewarded with spectacular vistas. The temple of Kedarnath is surrounded by mountain meadows and shaded by mountains capped with snow year-round.

The Kedarnath linga is a natural ridge of stone considered to be a self-manifestation (**svayambhu**) of Shiva, and is considered to be unusually powerful. The particular shape of this linga is tied to Kedarnath's charter myth. One version of this story is connected to the five **Pandava** brothers, who are the protagonists in the *Mahabharata*, the later of the two great Hindu epics. The Pandavas make their final journey into the Himalayas, searching for a vision of Shiva. They finally see him at a distance, but when they try to get closer, Shiva takes the form of a **bull** and begins running through the snow. The bull burrows into a snow bank. When the Pandavas follow, they find the body of the bull in the snow. The ridge of rock that forms the Kedarnath linga is considered to be the hump of this bull. The bull's head continues traveling over the hills, eventually stopping in **Nepal**, where it takes form as **Pashupatinath**.

A completely different charter myth draws on the traditional belief that Shiva makes his home high in the mountains. This myth identifies the **Panchkedar** (a network of five Shiva shrines in the **Garhwal** region) with five parts of Shiva's body, thus connecting the deity with the land itself and making the land holy. Of these five, Kedarnath is identified as Shiva's back, **Madmaheshvar** his navel, **Tungnath** his arm, **Rudranath** his face, and **Kalpeshvar** his matted locks (**jata**).

Kena ("By Whom?") Upanishad

One of the shorter of the early speculative texts known as the **Upanishads**, whose name comes from the first word of the text itself. The Kena Upanishad is unusual in that the first two sections are written in verse, and the third and fourth in prose. This change gives the text a somewhat disjointed feel, despite its brevity, and raises the possibility that it is a compilation of two earlier texts. As with many of the later upanishads, the Kena Upanishad propounds that the ultimate source of all reality is ascribed to a single power that can only be discovered through a flash of mystic insight. The verse sections describe this power: "It is conceived of by one who does not conceive of it, it is not conceived by one who conceives, it is not known by those who think they know it, it is known by those who think they do not know it" (verse 2.3). The prose sections are very different, narrating an encounter between a mysterious being (**Brahman** personified) and several of the primary gods in the earlier Vedic literature—**Indra**, **Agni**, and **Vayu**. Despite all their efforts, the gods are unable to exercise their respective powers of storm, fire, and wind, showing that their divine power is not independently theirs, but is derived from Brahman.

Kerala

One of the four southern Indian states, whose inhabitants speak a **Dravidian** language, in this case Malayalam. Kerala occupies the narrow strip of land between the Western Ghats and the Arabian sea, in the region formerly known as the **Malabar** coast. Kerala is one of the "linguistic" states formed after Indian independence in 1947, to unite people with a common language and culture under one state government. It was created from the Malayalam-speaking regions of the former Madras state, plus the princely states of Travancore and Cochin. Kerala has always been important as a trading center. The desire for its spices and sandalwood have brought merchants from the Middle East for thousands of years. In modern times it has had India's first elected communist government, and is the only Indian state to have 100 percent adult literacy. Kerala's most famous sacred site is the temple of **Aiyappa** at **Shabari Malai**. By custom the annual pilgrimage to the site is restricted to men as well as women past childbearing age. For general information about Kerala and other regions of India, see Christine Nivin et al., *India*. 8th ed., Lonely Planet, 1998.

Keshanta ("shaving the beard") Samskara

The thirteenth of the sixteen traditional life-cycle ceremonies (**samskaras**). The ceremony was performed by a young man in the **brahmacharin** (celibate student) **stage of life** and marked the first time he shaved his beard. According to tradition, this rite was followed by giving a gift to the teacher, ideally a **cow**. By ritualizing his first shave, the keshanta samskara was a way to mark the young man's changing status. After this he was responsible for remaining clean-shaven, as one more of the rules for maintaining ritual **purity**. In modern times this rite is no longer observed. See also **shaving**.

Keshava

([One with] "Flowing **Hair**") Epithet of the god **Krishna**. See **Krishna**.

Keshi

In Hindu mythology, Keshi is one of the assassins sent by **Kamsa**, the **demon-king** of **Mathura**, in an attempt to kill his nephew, the child-god **Krishna**. In the form of a savage horse, Keshi attacks

Krishna. Krishna easily fends him off and kills him, earning himself the name of **Keshimanthana**, "destroyer of Keshi."

Keshimanthana

("destroyer of **Keshi**") Epithet of the god **Krishna**. Keshi is one of the demon assassins sent by Krishna's uncle **Kamsa** to kill the child Krishna. Keshi appears in the form of a horse, but Krishna easily destroys him, as he does all the other **demons**.

Keshini

In Hindu mythology, one of the wives of King **Sagar**. Through a sage's boon, Keshini and her co-wife **Sumati** are given a choice in the number of children they will bear—one will bear a single son through whom the lineage will continue, whereas the other will bear sixty thousand **sons** who will die before they have any offspring. Keshini chooses the former, and through her son **Asamanjasa** the line of King Sagar is preserved. Her descendants are particularly important, since her great-great-grandson is the sage **Bhagirath**, who succeeds in bringing the river **Ganges** from **heaven** to **earth**.

Ketu

A malevolent "**planet**" in Hindu astrology (**jyotisha**), and was originally the body of a **demon**. According to the story, the gods and the **demons** join forces to churn the ocean of milk to obtain the nectar of immortality. The gods manage to trick the demons out of their share. While the gods drink the nectar, the demon **Sainhikeya** slips into their midst in disguise. As the demon begins to drink, the **sun** and **moon** alert **Vishnu**, who uses his discus to cut off the demon's head. Sainhikeya's two halves become immortal, since they have come into contact with the nectar. The severed body becomes Ketu, and the severed head becomes another malevolent planet, **Rahu**. Ketu is not regarded as a physical planet, but as the descending node of the moon, or the place where it intersects the ecliptic while passing southward. Ketu is also associated with comets and fiery meteors, generally considered signs of ill **omen**. See **Tortoise avatar**.

Khadga

("sword") In Hindu iconography, the sword is an object associated with a variety of **deities**. It carries strong associations with **Kali**, symbolizing the cutting off of her devotees' (**bhakta**) ignorance. Sometimes it is literally used to cut off heads of the **animals** sacrificed to her. The sword is also carried by other images of the **Goddess**, including **Durga** and **Santoshi Ma**, as well as certain images of **Shiva** and **Vishnu**.

Khajuraho

Small village in the Chattarpur district of the northern state of **Madhya Pradesh**, renowned for a magnificent collection of temples built about a thousand years ago by the **Chandella dynasty**. It is unclear why these temples were built in such an inaccessible place, although its remote location is believed to have spared the temples from iconoclasm during Muslim incursions. The most famous Hindu temples at the site are the **Kandariya Mahadev**, **Lakshmana**, and **Vishvanath**. There are many smaller temples to other Hindu **deities** and several Jain temples as well.

The temples at Khajuraho were built in the northern Indian **Nagara** style. The building replicates a sacred mountain with the highest point directly over the primary image. The outside of the temples were decorated with sculptural images, and the most famous of these depict women in various explicit sexual encounters. The significance of the **erotic** sculptures is much debated. Some claim that the sculptures sanction carnal pleasure as a religious path, while some interpret them to represent human union with the divine. Still others view them as teaching that the desire for pleasure must be transcended to attain the divine. For further information see Benjamin Rowland, *The Art and Architecture of India*, 1971.

Khandava Forest

In the *Mahabharata*, the later of the two great Hindu epics, the Khandava forest is consumed by **Agni**, a god whose material form is **fire** itself. According to the story, Agni becomes sick and is advised that he can only be healed by eating the creatures in the Khandava forest, many of whom are enemies of the gods. Agni makes seven attempts to "eat" the forest, but is always thwarted by the storm-god **Indra**, who rescues the forest by dousing it with rain. Agni is perplexed and solicits the help of the god **Krishna** and his companion **Arjuna**, the world's greatest archer. To help Agni, Arjuna is given the **Gandiva** bow and an inexhaustible quiver of arrows. When Agni again begins to burn the forest, Arjuna keeps off the rain by shooting a flight of arrows so thick that it forms a canopy over the forest. In this way Agni is cured of his illness.

Khandoba

Regional **deity** worshiped in the central Indian **Deccan** region, particularly in the states of **Maharashtra** and **Karnataka**. Originally believed to be a local deity, Khandoba is now considered to be an **avatar**, or incarnation, of the god **Shiva**; he takes this form to destroy two **demons** named Mani and Malla. After killing the demons he is persuaded to reside at a temple in **Jejuri**, Maharashtra, from where his **worship** spread throughout the region. Khandoba is an important popular deity because he is believed to grant people's wishes, particularly in response to vows. For further information see John M. Stanley, "Special Time, Special Power: The Fluidity of Power in a Popular Hindu Festival," in *Journal of Asian Studies*, Vol. 37, No. 1, 1977.

Khara

In the *Ramayana*, the earlier of the two great Indian epics, Khara is one of the brothers of the demon-king **Ravana**. With his brother **Dushana**, Khara tries to avenge the honor of their sister **Shurpanakha**, whose ears and nose have been cut off by **Rama's** brother **Lakshmana**. In a fierce battle, Rama destroys the demon army, killing Khara and Dushana. Seeing the failure of her two brothers, Shurpanakha goes to their brother Ravana to demand vengeance. Ravana realizes he cannot kill Rama in battle, but resolves to avenge his sister by kidnapping **Sita**, an action which drives the plot for the latter part of the epic.

Kharoshthi

("ass-lip") Name for one of the ancient scripts used in the **inscriptions** of the emperor **Ashoka** (r. 269–232 B.C.E.), the greatest figure in the **Maurya dynasty**. Ashoka's empire encompassed all of the subcontinent (except the deepest parts of southern India) and parts of modern Afghanistan. Ashoka's **Rock Edicts** and **Pillar Edicts** are the earliest significant Indian written documents, giving invaluable information about contemporary social, political, and religious life. The Kharoshthi script was used exclusively in the northwestern part of Ashoka's empire and was clearly derived from the Aramaic alphabet used in Achaeminid Persia. Although the script was modified to adapt it to the sounds of Indian languages, it clearly shows Persian cultural influence. It was far less pervasive than **Brahmi** script and had virtually disappeared from India by the early centuries of the common era.

Khatvanga

A club or staff topped with a human skull, it is one of the characteristic objects in Hindu iconography. At times the shaft of the staff was made from another human bone, such as a thigh or an arm bone. This symbol is most closely associated with the god **Shiva**. Its use reflects his marginal, uncontrolled nature and his utter disconnection with the conventional values of ordinary society. It is still sometimes carried by ascetics, for whom Shiva is the model **ascetic**, and a paradigm for emulation.

Khetaka

("shield") In Hindu iconography, the shield is associated with a variety of **deities**, including the **Goddess**, **Shiva**, and **Vishnu**. The shield is often found in images in which the figure carries a sword (**khadga**).

Kichaka

In the *Mahabharata*, the later of the two great Hindu epics, Kichaka is the brother-in-law of King **Virata**. King Virata is host to the five **Pandava** brothers (the epic's protagonists) during the year that they go incognito after twelve years of forest exile. During this time, Kichaka becomes attracted to **Draupadi**, the Pandavas' common wife, who serves as an attendant to one of the royal ladies. Kichaka continues his advances despite her protests and strikes her when she tries to escape. One of Draupadi's husbands, **Bhima**, is livid when he discovers what has happened. He tells Draupadi to arrange a secret meeting with Kichaka, on the pretense of surrendering to his desires. Bhima disguises himself as Draupadi and when Kichaka arrives, Bhima kills him with his bare hands.

Kimpurusha

Another name for the mythical **animals** known as **Kinnara**. See **Kinnara**.

Kindama

In the *Mahabharata*, Kindama is a forest-dwelling sage, whose **curse** on King **Pandu** advances the epic's plot. Although celibate in his human form, Kindama occasionally uses his **magic** powers to transform himself and his wife into animals, so that they can experience sexual pleasure. On one occasion,

as Kindama and his wife are in the form of deer, King Pandu shoots the copulating pair with an arrow. In their dying moments the sage and his wife revert to their human forms. The sage curses the horrified Pandu to die the moment he takes his wife in an amorous embrace.

Since Pandu is childless, he abdicates the throne in favor of his blind brother **Dhrtarashtra** and becomes a celibate renunciant. Pandu's wives, **Kunti** and **Madri**, eventually bear children through magical means. The struggle for power between their children and **Duryodhana**, Dhrtarashtra's son, is the epic's pivotal conflict.

Kinnara

("What, Man?") Mythical creatures described as either having the head of a horse and the body of a human being, or the head of a human being and the body of a horse. The Kinnaras are described as servants of **Kubera**, a minor **deity**. Kubera is one of the **Guardians of the Directions**, a group of eight deities believed to rule the cardinal and intermediate directions. He is the ruler over the northern direction, and thus identified as living in the **Himalayas**, where the Kinnaras also live. The Kinnaras are usually considered identical to the mythical creatures known as the Kimpurushas.

Kiritamakuta

A high crown, sometimes topped with a knob, studded with jewels and other ornamentation. In Hindu iconography the kiritamakuta is associated with the god **Vishnu**, particularly in his manifestation as **Narayana**. For Vishnu, the kingly imagery conveyed by this crown reinforces his claim to be ruler of the universe.

Kirtan

("repeating") A type of devotional singing or chanting of short verses which are usually different renditions of the divine name. This is often done in a

Ruins of the Sun Temple in Konarak. Built during the Ganga dynasty, the temple was designed in the shape of the chariot believed to carry the sun.

call and response fashion—the leader sings one line, and the listeners repeat it. The primary emphasis in this rite is the repetition of the divine name. As the identifying mark of the divinity, the Name is believed to contain the **divine power**, benefiting those who hear it as well as those who speak it. Kirtan is especially popular among the devotees (**bhakta**) of the god **Vishnu**, who historically have put greater stress on the theology of the Name. Kirtan is a common activity during congregational meetings known as **satsang**, the "company of good people," believed to have beneficial spiritual effects on those who take part in them.

Kirtimukha

("mask of glory") In Indian **architecture**, a kirtimukha is a decorative motif in the form of a devouring leonine monster. It often appears as the main decorative element on a temple tower or as a protective element over doorways.

Kishkindha

In the *Ramayana*, the earlier of the two great Indian epics, Kishkindha is a forest-kingdom ruled by monkeys. The monkey-king, **Bali**, rules when **Rama** (the epic's protagonist) first comes to Kishkindha with his brother, **Lakshmana**, searching for Rama's kidnapped wife **Sita**. Bali is killed by Rama, and is succeeded by his brother **Sugriva**, Rama's ally. Sugriva sends his subjects on a wide-ranging search for Sita. One of them, **Hanuman**, eventually discovers her being held prisoner on **Lanka**.

Kitawara

One of four major organizational groups of the **Dashanami Sanyasis**, renunciant ascetics who are devotees (**bhakta**) of the god **Shiva**; the other three divisions are **Bhuriwara**, **Bhogawara**, and **Anandawara**. Each of these groups has its headquarters in one of the four monastic centers (**maths**) supposedly established by philosopher **Shankaracharya**. Each of the groups are associated with one of the four **Vedas**, one of the "great utterances" (**mahavakyas**) expressing the ultimate truth, a particular **ascetic** quality, and several of the ten Dashanami divisions. The Kitawara group is affiliated with the **Sharada math** in **Dwaraka**, and is thus connected with the western quarter of India. The Kitawara's Veda is the **Sama Veda**. Their mahavakya is "tattvamasi" ("That thou art") and their ascetic quality is to eat very little. The Dashanami divisions associated with this group are **Tirtha** and **Ashrama**.

Koil

(also known as Koyal) One of the names for the Indian **cuckoo**. See **cuckoo**.

Kokila

One of the names for the Indian **cuckoo**. See **cuckoo**.

Konarak

Village on the Bay of Bengal in the state of **Orissa**, about forty miles east of the state capital, **Bhubaneshvar**. Konarak is famous for its **Sun Temple**. Now in ruins, the temple was built by king Narasimhadeva (r. 1238–1264), a monarch in the **Ganga dynasty**. The entire temple was intended to be a likeness of the sun's chariot. Twelve great wheels were carved on the sides at the temple's lowest level; in front of the temple are statues of several colossal horses. As at **Khajuraho**, the temple's lower levels are covered with **erotic** carvings, giving rise to diverse interpretations: Some claim the carvings sanction carnal pleasure as a religious path, while some interpret them allegorically as representing human union with the divine. Others view them as teaching that the desire for pleasure must ultimately be transcended to attain the divine.

The temple was built on a massive scale. According to one estimate, the massive central spire would have been over 200 feet high. It is uncertain whether this spire was ever completed, since the sandy soil at its base would have been unable to support the weight of such an enormous structure. This unstable soil has been the greatest contributor to the temple's increasing deterioration. The primary structure left at the site is the **jagamohan** (assembly hall). During the nineteenth century, the hall was filled with sand in an effort to prevent further collapse. For further information see Roy Craven, *Indian Art*, 1997.

Konkanastha

Another name for the **brahmin** community of the **Chitpavan**, a name that signifies their historical home on the Konkan coastline in the states of **Goa** and **Maharashtra**. See **Chitpavan**.

Korravai

Fierce form of the **Goddess**, worshiped in southern India and originally believed to have been an autochthonous ("of the land") **deity**. Korravai is associated with the hunt and the battlefield, and thus with **blood**, death, and carnage. Perhaps because of these associations, she was later identified with other fierce manifestations of the Mother Goddess, particularly the goddess **Kali**.

Koshala

In the *Ramayana*, the earlier of the two great Indian epics, this is the name of the region along the banks of the river Sarayu in which **Rama's** father, King **Dasharatha** rules.

Kota

City on the Chambal River in the modern state of **Rajasthan**, about 100 miles south of Jaipur. Before India's independence, Kota was the capital of a small kingdom with the same name. Kota was one of the centers of the **Rajasthani** style of **miniature painting**, a genre used to depict Hindu religious themes, particularly incidents in the life of **Krishna**. The Kota style is considered a derivative of the **Bundi** style because Kota was ruled by a junior member of the Bundi royal family. Both styles are marked by their attention to nature, shown by detailed depictions of trees surrounding the paintings' subjects. The

Kota style is marked by elements of the landscape looming out of proportion, giving the pictures a lush feel. For further information see W. G. Archer, *Indian Painting*, 1957; and *Indian Painting in Bundi and Kotah*, 1959.

Kratu

In Hindu mythology, one of the six **sons** of **Brahma**, all of whom become great sages. All are "mind-born," meaning that Brahma's thoughts are enough to bring them into being. The other five sages are **Marichi**, **Angiras**, **Pulastya**, **Pulaha**, and **Atri**.

Krauncha ("Curlew") Dvipa

In traditional mythic geography, Krauncha is the fifth of the seven concentric landmasses (**dvipas**) making up the visible world. See also **cosmology**.

Kraunchanishadana

("curlew-sitting") One of the sitting postures (**asanas**) described in commentaries to the **Yoga Sutras**. The Yoga Sutras are attributed to the sage **Patanjali** and give the earliest instruction of yoga. The Kraunchanishadana posture begins in **dandasana** or "stick-posture," in which one sits with the upper body erect, the arms straight with the hands flat on the ground and pointing forward, and the legs outstretched. From this posture one of the legs is folded back to the outside, with the heel pressed against the outer thigh. The other leg is raised straight up and pressed against the torso, with the hands clasped at the bottom of the foot.

Krishna

Hindu **deity** usually considered as the eighth **avatar** or incarnation of the god **Vishnu**; in certain religious contexts, however, as in the *Gitagovinda*, he is described as the ultimate deity and the source of all the avatars. In either case, Krishna is one of the major deities in the modern Hindu pantheon. Part of his popularity may stem from the extraordinary breadth of his manifestations, allowing his devotees (**bhakta**) to **worship** him in many different ways. His earliest appearance comes in the *Mahabharata*, the later of the two great Hindu epics, where he is a friend and adviser to the five **Pandava** brothers who are the epic's protagonists. His epic portrayal is highly complex, and his character is not always truthful or good. He is a regal king and heroic warrior, a cunning opponent, and a Machiavellian politician with his own underlying agenda. Here Krishna plays the role of a trickster, although late in the story, in the section of the epic known as the **Bhagavad Gita**, he eventually drops the mask to reveal himself as the supreme deity.

The later sectarian literature, particularly the *Harivamsha* and the *Bhagavata Purana*, virtually ignore this exalted, royal figure, preferring to concentrate on Krishna's birth, childhood, and adolescence. This latter stratum of Krishna's mythology has been clearly imposed on the earlier, heroic image, rendering Krishna a character with unusual mythic depth. Religiously speaking, the image of Krishna as child and lover has been far more important than the stern and somewhat amoral hero.

The characters in the story of Krishna's life, including his parents, friends, and companions, are not aware of his divinity, and throughout the story they confront many surprises and bewildering events. However, none of these plot twists surprise the readers, since they are aware that all of the characters are taking part in Krishna's divine play (**lila**). According to tradition, Krishna is the eighth **son** of **Devaki** and **Vasudeva**. He is born in a prison in the city of **Mathura**, where his parents have been confined by his uncle, the wicked king **Kamsa**. On Devaki's wedding day, a divine voice warns Kamsa that her eighth child will eventually kill him. In an effort to forestall this prophecy, he puts the couple in prison, and kills all of

Devaki's children as soon as they are born. Kamsa intends to do the same with Krishna, but when Krishna is born, a deep sleep falls on all the jailers, the locked prison doors are miraculously opened, and Vasudeva is able to spirit the infant out of the prison to the home of his foster parents, **Nanda** and **Yashoda**. Vasudeva returns that night, bearing Yashoda's newborn baby girl, who is really **Bhadrakali**, the **Goddess**, in disguise. The next morning Kamsa kills the child by dashing it against a stone. From the body arises the Goddess, who taunts Kamsa, telling him that the person who will slay him has escaped.

Krishna lives happily at Nanda and Yashoda's home. His mythic images from that early time stress either his persona as the adorable child or unexpected feats of strength and heroism. As an infant he is placed under a cart, which he strikes with his foot and kicks into the air; he also slays a variety of **demon** assassins sent by his uncle Kamsa, most notably **Putana**, **Keshi**, and **Trnavarta**. During all these feats his companions are amazed but never realize that divinity is in their midst. Nor, for that matter, do his foster parents. In one story Yashoda looks in Krishna's mouth when he has been eating some dirt and sees the entire universe inside it. Through the workings of Krishna's power of illusion (**maya**), she immediately forgets the whole incident. The themes of forgetfulness and hidden divinity are central to Krishna's childhood mythology. The people in **Braj** treat Krishna with easy familiarity, because they are unaware of his true identity. Krishna is said to prefer this sort of natural interaction over all other worship.

As a boy Krishna becomes known for his mischief, particularly his penchant for stealing butter from the **gopis** (milkmaids), although when he is caught he can usually manage to charm his way out of punishment. His adolescence is marked by two heroic episodes—driving off the serpent **Kaliya**, and defeating the storm-god **Indra** by holding up Mt.

Depiction of Krishna, an incarnation of the god Vishnu.

Govardhan—and by the development of his persona as a lover. On moonlit, autumn nights, he plays his flute **Murali** on the banks of the **Yamuna River**. Hearing its irresistible call, the village women rush to meet him, whiling away the night in the circle **dance** known as the **ras lila**. Although she is not mentioned in the earliest texts, **Radha** appears as Krishna's special companion and consort, symbolizing the relationship between deity and devotee using the imagery of lover and beloved.

Some parts of Krishna's mythology relate episodes from later in his life, including his return to Mathura, the slaying of Kamsa, taking his rightful place as ruler, and marrying **Rukmini** and a host of other wives. The earlier strands of his mythic identity—the king, hero, and cunning diplomat portrayed in the *Mahabharata*—can be tied in here, to make it seem like the account of a single life. Some of the most poignant devotional (**bhakti**) poetry details the exchange between Krishna's female devotees, the gopis, and **Uddhava**, Krishna's companion sent back from

Mathura. Uddhava reassures them that Krishna is the indwelling God and is omnipresent. For the gopis, this abstract concept is a poor substitute for the sweet boy they know so well. Their attention remains focused on the charming child of Braj, who never grows up, never grows old, and who invites his devotees to share his world.

The worship of Krishna emphasizes relationship and communion, both with the deity and one another. In the most elaborate forms of worship, Krishna's devotees envision themselves as entering Krishna's world and spending the day doing the ordinary activities of a village cowhand, such as getting up, eating, taking the cows to pasture, and bringing home the cows. Some devotional manuals give detailed daily calendars, for which the devotees can visualize themselves going to particular places and doing particular things at certain times—building a relationship with God through sharing the mundane parts of everyday life. Another common practice is communal singing, usually collections of the divine names known as **kirtans**, as a way to build relationships and communion among the devotees.

Another feature of Krishna's character and worship is the notion of lila or "play." As David R. Kinsley points out, the infant Krishna dispatches the demon assassins as a form of play, and they never pose any serious threat. His relationship with the people of Braj is also a sort of play. He comes as the divine presence in their midst, but keeps them completely unaware of this, occasionally hinting at it through his wondrous deeds, but unwilling to ruin their natural interactions with him by revealing their difference in status. In the same way, he is believed to be active in the lives of his devotees, always present, but dropping only teasing hints of his presence. Finally, lila is the name for a series of dramas performed during the **monsoon season** in the town of **Brindavan**. These productions, known as the ras lila, are not mere drama but combine both liturgy and drama. Krishna and his companions are played by local **brahmin** boys. While in costume, the boys are believed to have become the characters they portray. Part of the program is worship. The players, known as **svarups** ("own-forms"), gather on stage to give **darshan** to the audience. The most common religious act in modern popular Hinduism, darshan allows direct eye contact between the devotee and the image of a deity, which is considered to be a conscious, perceiving being. The second part of the program is the lila, a rendition of some episode in Krishna's mythology. The audience participates by virtue of its presence, making Krishna's lila part of present-day experience by performing or attending these productions. Given his stature as a Hindu deity, there are many works on Krishna. For further information see Milton Singer (ed.), *Krishna*, 1966; David R. Kinsley, *The Sword and the Flute*, 1975; Barbara Stoller Miller, *The Love Song of the Dark Lord*, 1977; and John Stratton Hawley, *Krishna: The Butter Thief*, 1983. See also **Vaishnavism**.

Krishnadas

(early 16th c.) One of the **ashtachap**, a group of eight northern Indian **bhakti** (devotional) poets. The compositions of these eight poets were used for liturgical purposes by the **Pushti Marg**, a religious community of devotees (**bhakta**) of **Krishna**. In the Pushti Marg's sectarian literature, all eight are also named as members of the community and as associates of either the community's founder, **Vallabhacharya**, or his successor **Vitthalnath**. Traditionally, Krishnadas is associated with Vallabhacharya. Little is known about Krishnadas, although traditional accounts hold that he was born in 1497. His poetry describes the physical beauty of Krishna as an object of aesthetic enjoyment. Within the Pushti Marg, he is remembered as a capable administrator and a defender of the sect's interests in **Brindavan**,

Krishna's childhood home, against the followers of **Chaitanya**.

Krishnadas Kaviraj

Author of the most influential version of the ***Chaitanya-Charitramrta*** ("Nectar of Chaitanya's Deeds"), an account of the life of the Bengali poet-saint **Chaitanya**, written about ninety years after Chaitanya's death. **Krishnadas's** text is the latest and most developed biography of Chaitanya and focuses mainly on Chaitanya's later life, particularly his visit to **Brindavan**, the northern Indian village were the god **Krishna** is supposed to have spent his childhood. This text is marked by the philosophical influence of the three **Goswamis—Rupa**, **Sanatana**, and **Jiva**—whose ideas played a major role in shaping Chaitanya's religious followers, the **Gaudiya Vaishnavas**. As with the other traditional accounts of Chaitanya's life, this text does not purport to give an "objective" biography, it is rather a hagiography (an idealizing and idolizing portrait) written by a passionate devotee (**bhakta**).

Krishna Deva Raya

(r. 1509–1530) Most important ruler in the **Vijayanagar dynasty**, the last of the great southern Hindu kingdoms. During his rule, Vijayanagar reached its zenith. Krishna Deva Raya defeated the Deccani sultans to the north, although he reinstated them as vassals. He conquered the eastern coast all the way to **Orissa** and maintained good trading relationships with the newly-arrived Portuguese, although he refused to become involved in their politics. His reign was a time of artistic achievement and general prosperity, evident in the artifacts of the time. His successors were not as successful, however. Less than forty years after his death, the coalition of the Deccani sultans defeated Rama Raja at the battle of **Talikota**. The Vijayanagar kingdom was completely destroyed.

Krishna Janam Bhumi

Site in the city of **Mathura** believed to mark the spot where the god **Krishna** was born. The present temple was completed in the 1960s, but the site itself is very old. One of the most religiously volatile sites in all of India, the new temple abuts the Shahi Idgah, a mosque built on the base of an earlier Krishna temple. According to one tradition, Muslim iconoclasts destroyed four successive temples at the spot now occupied by the mosque, marking the exact location of Krishna's **birth**. This claim seems doubtful since the mosque was built in 1661, and the temple it is said to have replaced was destroyed by the Moghul emperor **Aurangzeb** in 1669. In the 1980s the Krishna Janam Bhumi was one of the three sites selected by the activist **Vishva Hindu Parishad** to be reclaimed as a Hindu holy place, along with the **Vishvanath** temple in **Benares**, and **Ayodhya's Ram Janam Bhumi**. In all of these places, mosques were claimed to have been built on the site of an important Hindu temple, although only the first two have historical evidence that this occurred. During the 1990s there have been several campaigns to reclaim the Krishna Janam Bhumi, but to this point the campaigns have generated little support. Given the popular backlash after the 1992 destruction of the **Babri Masjid** in **Ayodhya**, the government has been far more restrictive on the activities it allows at such disputed sites. For further information see Christophe Jaffrelot, *The Hindu Nationalist Movement in India*, 1996. See also **Moghul dynasty**.

Krishnamishra

(late 11th c.) Author of the **Sanskrit** drama ***Prabodhachandrodaya*** ("Rising of the **moon** of wisdom"), an allegory celebrating the triumph of **Vaishnava** piety. The play is noted for the third act, in which four representatives of non-Vaishnava sects appear: a **materialist**; a Jain monk; a Buddhist monk; and a **Kapalika**, a member of an **ascetic** community who worshiped the god **Shiva**. The last is portrayed as depraved, indulging in meat, wine, and sexual gratification, as well as having a penchant for violence. Although the reader may safely assume that this is a biased perspective, it is instructive in the attitudes it reveals toward ascetics and all non-Vaishnava religious groups.

Krishnamurti, Jiddu

(1895–1986) Modern Indian thinker whose teachings centered on the necessity for personal realization through critical self-awareness. His teaching had strong roots in his own life experience. When he was fourteen years old, one of the leaders of the Theosophical Society, Annie Besant, proclaimed him to be an incarnation of the future Buddha Maitreya. He later repudiated these claims, and for the rest of his life stressed the need to examine and question all authority, including himself. Much of his life was spent in Europe and the United States, where his books and lectures found their primary audience. For further information see Pupul Jayakar, *Krishnamurti: A Biography*, 1986.

Krishna Paksha

The dark or waning half of a **lunar month**.

Krishna River

River running from west to east in south central India. Its headwaters lie in **Maharashtra** on the inland side of the Western Ghats. It meanders through **Karnataka** and **Andhra Pradesh**, fortified by the **Bhima River** and the **Tungabhadra River**, before entering the sea in the Bay of Bengal. The temple of the god **Vithoba** in the town of **Pandharpur**, considered the most important sacred site (**tirtha**) on the whole river, lies on the Bhima River.

Krittikas

In Hindu mythology, the Krittikas are a group of six minor goddesses who are the personification of the constellation Pleiades. Their important mythic appearance is as the foster mothers of the god **Skanda**. Skanda is considered the son of the god **Shiva**, but is born in an unusual way. When Shiva and **Parvati** are disturbed while making love, Shiva inadvertently spills his **semen** on the ground. In Indian culture semen is seen as a man's concentrated essence. Because he is a **deity**, Shiva's semen is inordinately powerful, capable of destroying the **earth**. The semen is first held by the god **Agni**, who is **fire** personified, but it proves too powerful for him. Agni puts the semen in the river **Ganges**. After 10,000 years, a shining child is discovered in the reeds along the riverbank. The child is discovered by the Krittikas, each of whom wants to nurse him. To oblige them, the child Skanda grows five extra heads. As a mark of their care, one of his epithets is **Karttikeya**.

Krpacharya

In the *Mahabharata*, the later of the two great Hindu epics, Krpacharya is a famous archer who teaches both the **Pandavas** and the **Kauravas**, the two competing families in the epic. Krpacharya is a supporter of the Kaurava leader **Duryodhana**. During the year the Pandavas spend in hiding, he sends spies to try to find them. In the Mahabharata war he fights on the side of the Kauravas. His most important act is setting fire to the Pandava camp during the night attack following the Pandava victory. All those trying to flee the flames are killed. After the war he stays for some time at the court of **Yudhishthira**, the eldest Pandava brother, but later renounces the world to live in the forest.

Krta Yuga

A particular age of the world in one of the reckonings of **cosmic time**. According to traditional belief, time has neither beginning nor end, but alternates between cycles of creation and activity, followed by cessation and quietude. Each of these cycles lasts for 4.32 billion years; the active phase is known as the **Day of Brahma**, and the quiet phase as the Night of Brahma. In one reckoning of cosmic time, the Day of Brahma is divided into one thousand **mahayugas** ("great cosmic ages"), each of which lasts for 4.32 million years. Each mahayuga is composed of four constituent yugas, named the Krta Yuga, **Treta Yuga**, **Dvapara Yuga**, and **Kali Yuga**. Each of these four yugas is shorter than its predecessor and ushers in an era more degenerate and depraved than the preceding one. By the end of the Kali Yuga, things have gotten so bad that the only solution is the destruction and recreation of the earth, at which time the next Krta era begins.

The Krta Yuga is the first of the four yugas, and at 1,728,000 years, it is by far the longest. It is also considered to be the best of all the yugas, symbolized by gold, the most valuable of all metals. In a dice game played in ancient India, the side designated Krta was the one for the winning throw, representing the best possible option. In the mythic descriptions of the Krta Yuga, people live extremely long times, are of tremendous physical stature, and by nature, are completely virtuous.

Kshanika ("momentary") Linga

A type of **linga**, the pillar-shaped object symbolizing the god **Shiva**. A kshanika linga is temporarily made for immediate **worship**, from whatever materials are at hand—whether earth, sand, grain, butter, or any other substance that can be heaped and molded. This use of temporary images reveals an important aspect of Hindu religious life—that although God is everywhere, many human beings tend to work better when they have a

The Krishna River runs across south central India, from Maharashtra to the Bay of Bengal.

concrete focus for their religious attention. This being so, God deigns to come into the humblest objects, if they are created with him (or her) in mind.

Kshatriya

In traditional Hindu social theory, the kshatriyas were the second most influential of the four major social groups (**varnas**). The kshatriyas' function was ruling, protecting, and creating social order so that the other varnas could carry out their tasks. This image is reflected in the creation story known as the **Purusha Sukta**. The kshatriyas are described as being created from the Primeval Man's shoulders and associated with strength and power. In actual practice, the kshatriya **varna** may have been the most permeable of all, since any person with the power to rule was usually given *de facto* kshatriya status, which could be solidified by a fictitious genealogy in the following generations. Perhaps the best example of this phenomenon is the subgroup known as the **Rajputs** ("king's **sons**"), who at varying times ruled large sections of northern and western India, but whose origins are unclear and obscure.

Kshemaraja

(11th c.) Kshemaraja was the primary disciple of **Abhinavagupta**, the Kashmiri writer famous for his works on poetics and aesthetics, and a pivotal figure in the development of **Trika** Shaivism. Based on a tantric philosophy, Trika Shaivism states that the sole true reality is the god **Shiva**, who is both supreme god and the source of the emanations that constitute the material of the universe. Final liberation of the soul (**moksha**) comes through a process of "recognition" (**pratyabhijna**) in which one realizes that the entire universe is all a manifestation of Shiva alone. Here one "recognizes" something that has always been true, but until that time has been obscured by a mistaken understanding. Kshemaraja continued the development of the Trika school. His most famous work is the *Svacchandatantra*. See also **tantra**.

Kubera

In Hindu mythology, a minor **deity** who is one of the eight **Guardians of the Directions**, serving as guardian over the northern quarter. Kubera is said to live in the Himalaya mountains, where he is served by mythical creatures such as **yakshas**, **nagas**, and **kinnaras**. He is enormously fat, and because of all the mineral wealth contained in the mountains, he is enormously wealthy. Kubera is the half-brother of the **demon**-king of **Lanka**, **Ravana**, and **Kumbhakarna** and **Vibhishana**. All four are sons of the demigod Vishravas, but Kubera has a different mother. Despite their relationship, Ravana steals Kubera's aerial chariot, the **Pushpak Viman**. Because of Ravana's notorious misdeeds, Kubera supports the god-king **Rama's** efforts to conquer Ravana.

Kubja

("hunchback") In the mythology of the god **Krishna**, Kubja is a hunchbacked woman whom Krishna meets while journeying to the city of **Mathura** to reclaim his kingdom. Kubja carries a jar of expensive salve that is meant for the king, but when Krishna asks her for some, she willingly gives it to him. As a reward for her generosity and devotion, Krishna straightens her spine, turning her into a gorgeous young woman.

Kuchela

("badly dressed") Another name for **Sudama**, one of the god **Krishna's** childhood friends. See **Sudama**.

Kuchipudi

One of the classical **dance** forms of India; some of the others are **Bharatanatyam**, **Kathak**, **Orissi**, **Kathakali**, and **Manipuri**. Like much of traditional Indian culture, classical dance shows strong regional identification; Kuchipudi is primarily found in **Andhra Pradesh**. As with much of Indian dance, Kuchipudi has its roots in religious life. It was developed in the village of Kuchipudi as part of a religious festival. The Maharaja of Golconda was so pleased with the dance that he awarded the village as a gift to the **brahmin** families there, with the condition that they continue to nurture the art, which their descendants have done. Stylistically, the dance shows the influence of Bharatanatyam, and like all Indian dance, it shows the well-developed vocabulary of **gesture** that is drawn from the classical manuals. At the same time, the form is softer and less geometric than Bharatanatyam, showing the influence of folk traditions. The language for the dance-dramas is Telegu, reflecting the local culture. As with all classical dances, Kuchipudi has undergone certain changes in the past generation, spurred by the shift to stage performance as the dance's primary venue. One of the most significant changes has been to open the dance to women. For further information see Mohan Khokar, *Traditions of Indian Classical Dance*, 1984.

Kulachara

("family practice") Any religious practice restricted to a family, either a group of blood relatives or people sharing a common religious or sectarian lineage. The authority given to kulachara allows for almost infinite variation in religious practice, particularly in the absence of any established religious hierarchy which has the authority to render judgments on such practices. For most Hindus, such family practice is the predominant influence shaping their individual religious lives.

Kuladevata

("family deity") The particular deity worshiped by a family, whether this "family" be blood relatives, or people who share the same religious lineage, sect, or region. In most cases, the kuladevata will be one's primary deity.

Kulashekhara

(9th c.) One of the **Alvars**, a group of twelve poet-saints who lived in southern India between the seventh and tenth centuries. All the Alvars were devotees (**bhakta**) of the god **Vishnu**, emphasizing passionate devotion (**bhakti**) to a personal god, conveyed through hymns sung in the **Tamil language**. According to tradition, Kulashekhara was the king of the Travancore region in modern **Kerala**. His religious commitment grew so strong that he eventually abdicated his throne. For further information see Kamil Zvelebil, *Tamil Literature*, 1975; and John Stirling Morley Hooper, *Hymns of the Alvars*, 1929.

Kulu

The most important city in the Kulu Valley in the state of **Himachal Pradesh**. The city of Kulu is famous for its **Dussehra** festival. Dussehra celebrates the victory of the god **Rama** over the **demon**-king **Ravana**; it is a celebration of the victory of good over evil. Kulu's festival centers around the figure of Rama from the Raghunathji temple in the nearby village of Dhalpur. When Rama is brought to the festival site in his temple car, he is celebrated by hundreds of **deities** who have come from temples up and down the Kulu Valley, as well as the people who have gathered to see the deities and the spectacle of their procession. The deities' actions are carefully choreographed according to well-established rituals.

Kumara

("youth") Epithet of the god **Skanda**, who is usually portrayed in the form of a young boy. See **Skanda**.

Kumara Gupta I

(r. 415–454) The fourth important ruler of the **Gupta dynasty**, who managed to keep his northern Indian empire intact for most of his reign. At the end of his reign, he had to contend with incursions in the west by the central Asians, known as the Hunas. While in battle with them, he was killed. Pressure from the Hunas continued in the years following Kumara Gupta's death and was one of the important factors causing the eventual collapse of the Gupta empire several generations later.

Kumarapala

(r. 1143–1172) Jaina king of the **Chalukya dynasty** in **Gujarat**, who was so committed to nonviolence that he imposed heavy fines on people who killed fleas and other vermin.

Kumarasambhava

("**Birth** of the Prince") One of the finest poetic works written by **Kalidasa**, who is generally considered the greatest classical **Sanskrit** poet. The *Kumarasambhava* is an epic poem based on a mythological theme. It begins by describing the ascendancy of a **demon** named **Taraka**, who receives a divine boon that he can only be killed by a son of **Shiva**. The poem describes the extended courtship of Shiva and **Parvati**, their marriage, and ends with an account of their lovemaking. The text ends before the birth of the god **Skanda**, who in other mythical accounts of this tale kills Taraka. This abrupt ending has led some interpreters to consider the play unfinished. Others simply view these later events as a foregone conclusion, by which the poet does not waste his hearers' time.

Kumarila

In Indian **philosophy**, one of the two great seventh-century commentators of the **Mimamsa** philosophy, one of the **six schools** of Hindu philosophy; the other great commentator was **Prabhakara**. The Mimamsa school was most concerned with the examination and pursuit of **dharma** ("righteous action"), for which members believed all necessary instructions were contained in the **Vedas**, the oldest Hindu religious texts. Consequently, much of Mimamsa thought is concerned with principles and methods of textual interpretation to uncover and interpret the Vedic instructions. Although both Kumarila and Prabhakara were committed to discovering the boundaries of dharma by interpreting the Vedas, there are significant differences in their philosophical positions, which show up most clearly in their **theories of error**.

Prabhakara begins with the assumption, similar to the **Nyaya** concept of **inherence** (**samavaya**), that there is a relatively weak correspondence between an object and its attributes. An example of this would be the relation of the color red to a particular ball, such that the ball is said to be red. According to Prabhakara, false beliefs result from **akhyati** ("nondiscrimination"). This occurs when a person observes two different things with the same attributes

and concludes that they are the same. Kumarila is closer to the **bhedabhada** ("identity and difference") philosophical position, which holds that all things have both identity and difference with all other things. Kumarila explains error as **viparitakhyati** ("contrary perception"), in which one mistakenly pairs up the similarities between two things, rather than noting their differences. For example, a person mistakenly believes that a shell with a silvery color is actually a piece of silver because he or she chooses to focus on the similarities between the shell and silver rather than the differences. People are impelled to make these choices by karmic formations, such as greed for silver.

Kumbhadas

(early 16th c.) One of the **ashtachap**, a group of eight northern Indian **bhakti** (devotional) poets. The compositions of these poets were used for liturgical purposes by the **Pushti Marg**, a religious community whose members are devotees (**bhakta**) of **Krishna**. In the Pushti Marg's sectarian literature, all eight poets are named as members of the community and as associates of either the community's founder, **Vallabhacharya**, or his successor, **Vitthalnath**. Kumbhadas is traditionally associated with Vallabhacharya. Little is known about Kumbhadas, although it is believed that he was born in 1469. His poetry describes the five **modes of devotion** described by **Rupa Goswami**, particularly the mode known as **madhurya** ("honeyed"). Madhurya describes the relationship between **deity** and devotee, using the language of lover and beloved, in which each has passionate love for the other.

Kumbhakarna

("Pitcher-eared") In the *Ramayana*, the earlier of the two great Indian epics, Kumbhakarna is the brother of **Ravana**, the **demon** ruler of **Lanka**. As his name indicates, his dominant facial feature is his prominent ears. Kumbhakarna is a reincarnation of **Vijaya**, **Vishnu's** gatekeeper, who has been cursed to be reborn three times as a demon, killed by the god Vishnu each time. Kumbhakarna and his brothers have performed harsh **asceticism** (**tapas**) in their youth to gain boons from the gods. When the god **Brahma** finally comes to give him boons, Kumbhakarna means to demand "nirdevatvam" (that he cannot be conquered by any of the gods). At the critical moment he is foiled by the **goddess Saraswati**, who has power over speech. She dances on his tongue and confuses his speech, causing him to request "nidravatvam" (sleepiness). Because of this slip of his tongue, Kumbhakarna will sleep for six months at a time, wake up to gorge himself with food and drink for a short time, and then fall asleep again. Some of the dramatic tension in the battle portions of the *Ramayana* pertains to the violent efforts to rouse Kumbhakarna, so that he can take part in the battle. Once awakened he fights valiantly, but is eventually killed by **Rama**.

As is true for all the **demons**, Kumbhakarna is not wholly evil. Before engaging in battle with Rama's army, he rebukes Ravana for kidnapping Rama's wife, **Sita**. He also notes that as the younger brother it is his duty to uphold the family honor. Here we find the demon Kumbhakarna upholding idealized Indian family values—the younger brother is supposed to support and defend his elder brother's interests as a way to keep the family intact. This same virtue is in Rama's younger brothers, **Lakshmana** and **Bharata**. Despite their enmity, the epic's "heroes" and "villains" have significant shared values.

Kumbhakonam

One of the many temple-towns in the **Tanjore** district of the state of **Tamil Nadu**, reflecting the district's importance as the home of the **Chola dynasty** kings. Kumbhakonam has several large temples. Built in the **Dravida** architectural style, the temple buildings are of modest height, cover an immensely large area, and are surrounded by a boundary wall with massive towers (**gopurams**) over each wall's central gateway. Kumbhakonam's most famous site is not a temple, but a temple bathing (**snana**) tank. A festival is held at the tank every twelve years, at which time the water in the tank is believed to become the **Ganges**. An estimated 400,000 people attended this event in 1992; tragically, forty-eight people were killed in a stampede. Outside the town is the **Swami Malai** temple, one of the six temples to the god **Skanda**.

Kumbha Mela

("Festival of the Pot") A religious festival celebrated in four different locations: **Haridwar**, **Allahabad**, **Ujjain**, and **Nasik**. The first two sites are by far the most important, with Allahabad considered the holiest of all. Attendance at these festivals is great. In 1998, ten million people were in Haridwar on the climactic day. Both of these sites also host an **Ardha** ("half") **Kumbha Mela**, generally six years after the full Kumbha Mela, which are smaller in scale, but can still draw millions of pilgrims. At Ujjain and Nasik, the full Kumbha Melas are not as well attended than at the other two sites.

The Kumbha Mela is a bathing (**snana**) festival; it is for this reason that all the Mela sites are found near rivers. The Kumbha Mela's primary actors are ascetics from all over South Asia who come to bathe in the sacred waters. According to tradition, the Kumbha Mela was organized by the great philosopher **Shankaracharya** to promote regular gatherings of learned and holy men, as a means to strengthen, sustain, and spread Hindu religious beliefs. The Kumbha Mela is also a time for these ascetics to display their status vis-à-vis one another. At each site, the order in which the different **ascetic** sects bathe is strictly enforced—the most important sects bathe first. In more recent times, this order has been

The bathing procession in Haridwar during the Kumbha Mela festival.
The differing ascetic orders proceed toward the holy waters according to a traditionally sanctioned order.

enforced by the government. In earlier times, it was the subject of much dispute, often degenerating into armed conflict as different ascetic sects vied with one another for the place of pride.

The time for each Kumbha Mela festival is determined astrologically, based on the positions of the planet **Jupiter**, the **sun**, and the **moon**. The Mela is held at Haridwar when Jupiter is in Aquarius (Kumbha) and the sun enters Aries; at Allahabad when Jupiter is in Taurus and the sun and moon are in Capricorn; at Ujjain when Jupiter is in Leo and the full moon appears in the **lunar month** of **Baisakh**; and at Nasik when Jupiter is in Leo during the lunar month of **Shravan**. These alignments occur about every twelve years.

The charter myth for the Kumbha Mela is taken from the story of Churning the Ocean of Milk. After the ocean has been churned and the nectar of immortality (**amrta**) has been extracted, the gods and their **demon** opponents begin to quarrel over the pot of nectar. The gods snatch the pot and make off with it, but the person carrying the pot grows tired, and in twelve days of carrying it sets it on the ground four times—namely, at the four sites where the Mela is held. In each place a bit of the nectar splashes on the ground, sanctifying the site. According to popular belief, at each Kumbha Mela's most propitious moment, the waters in which people are bathing become the nectar of immortality, and all those who bathe in these waters gain immeasurable religious merit.

Kumbha Mela is considered the largest religious festival in the world. Arrangements for the Melas at Haridwar and Allahabad are made by the government of **Uttar Pradesh**, coordinating transportation, drinking water, and sanitation for millions of pilgrims, as well as building temporary cities for the visitors. Ascetics come from all over the subcontinent, some staying for months. Many religious organizations set up booths in an effort to publicize their message.

Recently the government has begun using the Mela to promote ideas such as family planning and cleaning up the

Ganges, as well as promoting the Mela as tourism, spurring economic development. This combination of business and religion has roots in the past; in the early nineteenth century, the annual spring bathing fair at Haridwar was also a trading fair, particularly for horses. For many people, the opportunity to view the spectacle of the Mela is at least as strong an inducement as the promise of bathing away their sins. See also **Tortoise avatar**.

Kumhar

Traditional Indian society was as a collection of **endogamous** subgroups (in which marriage is decreed by law to occur only between members of the same group) known as **jatis** ("birth"). Jatis were organized (and their social status determined) by the group's hereditary occupation, over which each group held a monopoly. The Kumhars' hereditary occupation was making pottery.

Kunbi

Traditional Indian society was as a collection of **endogamous** subgroups (in which marriage is decreed by law to occur only between members of the same group) known as **jatis** ("birth"). Jatis were organized (and their social status determined) by the group's hereditary occupation, over which each group held a monopoly. The Kunbis' traditional occupation was farming. They were the dominant landholding community in **Gujarat**.

Kundalini

("spiral") Kundalini, the latent spiritual power that exists in every person, is one of the most fundamental concepts in **tantra**. It is the most vital element in the **subtle body**, an alternate physiological system believed to occupy a different plane of existence than gross matter, but which has certain correspondences to the material body. The subtle body is a set of six psychic centers (**chakras**), visualized as multi-petaled lotus flowers running along the spine and connected by three vertical channels. Each of the chakras symbolize human capacities, subtle elements (**tanmatras**), and sacred sounds. Above and below the chakras are the bodily abodes of the god **Shiva** (awareness) and the **goddess Shakti** (power), the two divine principles through which the entire universe has come into being. The underlying assumption behind this concept is the homology (or the similarity based on the common origin) of macrocosm and microcosm, an essential Hindu belief documented in the texts of the **Upanishads**.

The kundalini is an aspect of the universal Shakti present in all human beings; it is visualized as a snake coiled three times around the **muladhara chakra**, the lowest of the psychic centers. Although kundalini can be found in all people, it is usually dormant, symbolized by its coiled state. The object of the religious disciplines (**yogas**) involving the subtle body is to awaken and uncoil the kundalini, drawing it up through the subtle body's central channel (**sushumna**), piercing through the chakras on its way. Kundalini's ascent represents the awakening of spiritual energy. This awakening must be carried out under a **guru**'s supervision to prevent the aspirant from unknowingly arousing uncontrollable forces. As each chakra is pierced, it is believed to bring either the destruction of obstructions or the awakening of new capacities. When fully extended, the kundalini rises to the microcosmic realm of Shiva, the **sahasradalapadma** at the crown of the head, to unite with Shiva in perpetual bliss. For further information see Arthur Avalon (Sir John Woodroffe), *Shakti and Shakta*, 1978; Swami Agehananda Bharati, *The Tantric Tradition*, 1977; and Douglas Renfrew Brooks, *The Secret of the Three Cities*, 1990.

Kundalini Yoga

The religious discipline (**yoga**) focusing on the **kundalini**, the latent spiritual power that exists in every person. Through a combination of yoga practice and ritual action, it is believed that the kundalini is awakened and rises through the **chakras** in the **subtle body**. This action brings further spiritual capacities and, ultimately, final liberation (**moksha**) of the soul. One of the claims for kundalini yoga is that it is much quicker than other means of spiritual development, harnessing more powerful forces. For this same reason, it is viewed as more hazardous, and should be done only under the supervision of one's religious preceptor (**guru**). According to tradition, those who engage these forces without proper supervision risk unleashing forces they cannot control, possibly bringing on insanity or death.

Kunti

In the **Mahabharata**, the later of the two great Hindu epics, Kunti is the elder wife of King **Pandu**, and the mother of **Yudhishthira**, **Arjuna**, and **Bhima**. None of these children are actually Pandu's sons; they have been magically conceived through the effect of a **mantra** given to Kunti by the sage **Durvasas**. The mantra gives the woman who recites it the power to call down any of the gods and conceive a son equal in power to the god himself.

Kunti receives this mantra before her marriage. In a moment of youthful impulsiveness, she recites it while looking at the **sun**. She is immediately visited by a shining figure who leaves her with an equally shining son. Distraught and desperate at the **birth** of this illegitimate child, she puts him in a box and abandons him in the **Ganges** River. The child is adopted by the charioteer **Adhiratha** and grows up to be the heroic **Karna**.

Kunti's other three sons are born after her marriage, with Pandu's blessing: Yudhishthira from the god **Dharma**, who is righteousness personified; Arjuna from the storm-god **Indra**; and Bhima from the **wind**-god **Vayu**. Although these three grow up to be heroic and kingly figures, they develop a violent hatred for Karna because of his unknown parentage. One of the **Mahabharata**'s tragic themes is this bitter rivalry between men who do not know they are brothers. Their hostility is especially difficult for Kunti, aware of Karna's identity. She knows that the problems are rooted in her impulsiveness and cowardice. On the eve of the great Mahabharata war she goes to Karna, reveals his identity to him, imploring him to return and fight with his brothers. Karna refuses, saying that he has taken a vow to kill Arjuna, but he will not harm her other sons. After the war Kunti becomes a recluse, living in the forest with several other people of her generation. After living there for some years, she is killed in a forest fire.

Kurma Avatar

The Kurma avatar is considered the second **avatar** or incarnation of the god **Vishnu**. Taking the form of a tortoise, he helps the gods churn the Ocean of Milk so that they can obtain the nectar of immortality (**amrta**). See **Tortoise avatar**.

Kurmasana

("tortoise-posture") One of the sitting postures (**asanas**) used in **yoga**; also a posture in which images of the **deities** are portrayed in Hindu iconography. As described in commentaries on the **Yoga Sutras**, this posture has the legs crossed with the feet tucked under the thighs, and the crossed heels forming a cavity around the scrotum. In Indian iconography, the Kurmasana is sometimes represented at the base of a statue by an actual carving of a tortoise, forming the base on which the image is placed. In modern yoga manuals this posture is described as a sitting position in which the upper body is bent forward, with the arms extended sideways under the outstretched legs, so that person looks vaguely like a tortoise, with a head, "shell" (the trunk), and four outstretched limbs.

Kurukshetra

City and sacred site (**tirtha**) in the northern part of the state of **Haryana**, about ninety miles due north of Delhi. In Hindu mythology, Kurukshetra is the site of the climactic battle in the *Mahabharata*, the later of the two great Hindu epics. This battle is still discussed as if it was a recent event. Kurukshetra is also famous as a bathing (**snana**) place. A bathing pool attracts hundreds of thousands of pilgrims during **eclipses**, at which time it is believed to contain all the sacred waters of India.

Kusha

In the *Ramayana*, the earlier of the two great Indian epics, Kusha is one of the twin sons of **Rama**, the epic's protagonist. After their mother, **Sita**, has been cast into exile at the **ashram** of the sage **Valmiki**, Kusha is born in an unusual fashion. One day when Sita takes her son **Lava** to bathe in the river, Valmiki notices that the child is gone and fears that it has been seized by a wild animal. To spare Sita's motherly feelings, he creates an identical child out of kusha grass. When Sita returns with Lava, his twin is given the name Kusha. Later, Lava and Kusha go with Valmiki to Rama's court in **Ayodhya**. It is in Rama's court that they first recite the epic poem composed by Valmiki, the *Ramayana*. After Rama gives up his throne, he divides his kingdom between Lava and Kusha.

Kusha ("Kusha Grass") Dvipa

In traditional mythic geography, Kusha or "Kusha grass," is the fourth of the seven concentric landmasses (**dvipas**) making up the visible world. See also **cosmology**.

Kutichaka

("delighting in staying in the house") One the of four types of Hindu ascetics. The basis for these four types was their livelihood, which in practice has been much less important for **ascetic** identity than sectarian or organizational affiliation. The Kutichaka is the least prestigious of the four, with the others being (in order of increasing status) **Bahudaka**, **Hamsa**, and **Paramahamsa**. The Kutichaka is described as an ascetic who resides in a house (kuti) erected by himself or his sons and begs for food from his sons and relatives.

L

Laghava

("simplicity") In Indian logic, one of the general principles in constructing and pursuing an argument. According to the principle of "simplicity," when one is presented with two equally plausible theories, one should choose the theory that is easier to understand and makes the fewest assumptions. The primary criterion in evaluating an argument is the validity of the argument itself. Only after this has been satisfied may one raise objections based on complexity or simplicity.

Laghima

("lightness") One of eight superhuman powers (**siddhi**) believed to be conferred by high spiritual attainment. This particular power gives one the ability to become as light as one desires, bestowing the ability to fly.

Lajpat Rai, Lala

(1865–1928) Lawyer, reformer, and militant Hindu nationalist. Born to a humble Punjabi family, Lajpat Rai became wealthy from his legal work. By the age of thirty-five, he was able to devote all of his earnings to public work. He joined the **Arya Samaj** while still in his teens and supported Lahore's Dayanand Anglo-Vedic College, which was founded in 1889. At the turn of the century he was active in a variety of social and educational endeavors. He eventually entered politics. He actively resisted British rule, which brought him several prison terms. Unlike many of his contemporaries, he refused to advocate violence. His commitment to politics ultimately cost him his life; he died from injuries sustained in a beating by the police while leading a demonstration in Lahore.

Lakshmana

In the **Ramayana**, the earlier of the two great Indian epics, Lakshmana is one of King **Dasharatha's** sons by his wife **Sumitra**, and the younger half-brother of **Rama**, the epic's protagonist. Throughout the *Ramayana* Lakshmana is the model younger brother, existing only to serve and support Rama. When Rama is banished to the forest for fourteen years, Lakshmana follows him like a shadow for the entire time: first living as a forest **ascetic**, searching for Rama's kidnapped wife **Sita**, then fighting heroically in the battle with **Ravana's** army; finally he returns to serve Rama at his court in **Ayodhya**.

Many of the characters in the *Ramayana* are paradigms for Indian cultural values. Lakshmana (as with his brother **Bharata**) symbolizes the ideal younger brother. In northern India, brothers are the heart of the joint family. They remain at home, whereas after marriage, sisters live in their marital families. The eldest brother in every generation eventually becomes the head of the joint family. Carrying primary authority and responsibility for the family as a whole, the eldest cannot succeed without the cooperation of his younger brothers who must acknowledge and support his authority. In his service to Rama and his complete disregard for his own needs, Lakshmana is a dutiful younger brother.

Despite his bravery, valor, and total loyalty to Rama, Lakshmana is far from perfect. He lacks Rama's judgment and forbearance, and tends to act before he thinks. For example, when Bharata pursues the two brothers after they have gone into exile, Lakshmana leaps to the conclusion that Bharata is seizing the opportunity to kill them, to clear his own way to the throne. Lakshmana prepares to attack Bharata, but Rama's reasoning forestalls a potential tragedy.

Lakshmana's most serious lapse of judgment is with **Shurpanakha**, a **demon** princess and sister to Ravana, the demon-king of **Lanka**. When she makes amorous advances toward Lakshmana, he first ridicules her and then mutilates her. Ravana kidnaps Rama's wife, Sita, to gain a measure of revenge against the brothers. Like all of the characters in the *Ramayana*, Lakshmana is neither good nor evil—he has many virtues, but also some very real flaws.

Lakshman Jhula

Sacred site (**tirtha**) along the **Ganges** in the Tehri district of the state of **Uttar Pradesh**, roughly five miles upriver from the city of **Rishikesh**. The site takes its present name from a swinging footbridge (jhula) that spans the Ganges. The local charter myth describes Lakshman Jhula as the place where **Rama** and **Lakshmana** live as ascetics late in their lives, atoning for the sin of brahminicide, which they incurred by killing **Ravana** and his brothers (who are considered **brahmin demons**). Today, the area is famous for the Svargashrama of **Swami Shivananda**, part of a network of **ashrams** along its banks.

Lakshmi

("good fortune," "prosperity") Hindu **goddess** and wife of the god **Vishnu**. According to tradition, Lakshmi is created when the ocean of milk is churned to yield the nectar of immortality. Just as butter is the refined essence of milk, so Lakshmi is the refined essence of the primordial ocean, representing all the best things that come from it. Lakshmi is associated with wealth, good fortune, and prosperity, and is considered the embodiment of all these things. Images of Lakshmi usually depict her with the lotus and the **elephant**, both of which are associated with good fortune. Many images show gold coins falling from her hands, symbolizing wealth.

These potent associations make Lakshmi an extremely important force

Thirteenth-century sculpture of the goddess Lakshmi. She is considered the embodiment of wealth, prosperity, and fortune.

in Hindu life. Lakshmi exercises her power by her mere presence—when she comes, she brings prosperity and good fortune; when she leaves, these benefits leave with her. Given Lakshmi's power, people are understandably eager to please her, especially since she has the reputation for being capricious and fickle in her relationships with human beings—a reputation that reflects a realistic appraisal of life's vicissitudes. Lakshmi's capriciousness and her reputation for being somewhat spiteful make people extremely careful in their dealings with her, to avoid insulting her, even if unintentionally.

Lakshmi's primary annual festival is **Diwali**, when she is believed to roam the earth. People spend the days before Diwali cleaning, repairing, and white-washing their homes, making them suitable for welcoming the goddess. On the evening of Diwali, people open all their doors and windows (to facilitate her entry) and place lights on their windowsills and balcony ledges to invite her in. **Gambling** is a common practice during Diwali. Gambling is usually condemned as a pernicious habit, but during Diwali it reaffirms the connection between money and Lakshmi—here in her guise as Lady Luck.

Despite her capricious relationships with human beings, Lakshmi is considered to be the model wife, particularly in her devotion and subordination to her husband. When Lakshmi and Vishnu appear together, she is significantly smaller, signifying her subordinate status. Another common image of the couple shows Lakshmi massaging Vishnu's feet, and thus her wifely subordination. Lakshmi is not only the model for human wives but is also believed to be incarnate in each of them. Married **women** are believed to embody the good fortune of the household. It is generally accepted that households in which they are not honored will never be prosperous. For more information on Lakshmi and all the goddesses of Hinduism, see David R. Kinsley, *Hindu Goddesses*, 1986. See also **Tortoise avatar** and **ocean, churning of the**.

Lakshmibai
(d. 1858) Queen of the small kingdom of Jhansi in the southern part of the state of **Uttar Pradesh** and a leader in the 1857 struggle against the British, known as the "Mutiny" or the "First War of Indian Independence." Lakshmibai's kingdom was the victim of expanding British power. The British colonial government had pronounced the "doctrine of lapse" edict, annexing any kingdom in which the ruler had died heirless. Lakshmibai's husband died in 1853. Although he had adopted a son just before his death, the British refused to recognize the **adoption** and sought to annex the kingdom. Lakshmibai was one of the leaders during the 1857 rebellion; she died in battle.

She was eulogized as a patriot and proponent of Indian independence, and because of her power and martial ability, she is considered a manifestation of the powerful **goddess Durga**.

Lakshmidhara
(ca. mid-12th c.) Scholar, commentator, and author of the *Kalpataru*, one of the earliest examples of commentary literature known as **nibandhas** ("collections"). The nibandhas were compendia of Hindu lore, compiling themes from the **Vedas**, **dharma literature**, **puranas**, and other authoritative religious texts, into a single volume. Each of the *Kalpataru's* fourteen volumes is devoted to a particular aspect of Hindu life, such as daily practice, **worship**, gift-giving, vows, pilgrimage, penances (**prayashchitta**), purification, and liberation (**moksha**). As one of the earliest nibandhas, the *Kalpataru* served as a model for later writers. Lakshmidhara's work is unusual in that he uses very few sources for his work—primarily the epic *Mahabharata*, and a few of the sectarian compendia known as puranas. Unlike later commentators, he does not cite the **Vedas**, the earliest Hindu religious texts, or the prescriptions found in the dharma literature. His text consists almost solely of excerpted passages, with very little commentary of his own, whereas later nibandha writers often give voluminous explanations.

Lakshmi-Narayan Temple
A modern temple in Delhi just west of Connaught Place. It was built in 1938 by **Ghanshyamdas Birla**, the patriarch of a prominent industrialist family. Although the temple is dedicated to the god **Vishnu** and his consort **Lakshmi**, it is more commonly called the "Birla temple" after its patron. Since Lakshmi is considered the bestower of wealth, and the temple was built by a businessman, this dedication is hardly surprising. Aside from his religious endowments, Ghanshyamdas Birla was also the major

financial support behind the Indian National Congress, the political party led by **Mohandas Gandhi** which struggled to gain Indian independence. Since the day it was built the temple has been open to people of all castes and communities, upholding the denial of untouchability that was one of Gandhi's most important crusades.

Lakulisha

(2nd c.?) Legendary founder of the **Pashupata** religious community, a group of renunciant ascetics whose patron **deity** was the god **Shiva**. Lakulisha appears to have been an important influence in the development of other Shaivite ascetics, such as the **Kapalikas** and the **Kalamukhas**. He has been identified as an incarnation of **Shiva**. Many statues have been identified as Lakulisha's image; he is portrayed as a naked **yogi** with a staff in one hand and a citron in the other, with penis erect, either standing or sitting in the lotus posture (**padmasana**). For further information see David Lorenzen, *The Kapalikas and the Kalamukhas*, 1972.

Lal Ded

Another name for the Kashmiri poet-saint **Lalleshvari**. See **Lalleshvari**.

Lalitaditya

(8th c.) One of the few kings of the **Kashmir** region who was able to affect the politics of the northern Indian plain, partially due to the fragmented state of the Hindu kingdoms there. Lalitaditya's armies pushed into the **Ganges** River valley, successfully halting the advance of the Arab forces in the **Punjab** region. His successors were unable to retain these gains.

Lallavakyani

("Lalla's Sayings") Corpus of poetry ascribed to the Kashmiri poet-saint **Lalleshvari**, a devotee (**bhakta**) of the god **Shiva**. The poems in this collection allude to the difficult circumstances of her early life, and the domestic problems that induced her to leave her marital home. They also describe her encompassing devotion to Shiva, whom she describes as the only true source of happiness. These poems have been translated into English, but all the editions are quite old: see Sir George Grierson and Lionel D. Barnett, *Lalla Vakyani*, 1920; and R. C. Temple, *The Word of Lalla, the Prophetess*, 1924.

Lalleshvari

(14th c.) Devotional (**bhakti**) poet-saint also known as Lal Ded, who is one of the most popular poets in **Kashmir**. Lalleshvari was a devotee (**bhakta**) of the god **Shiva**; her songs focus on her devotion to him. Like many other female devotional exemplars, she had a difficult time integrating her marriage with her commitment to her chosen **deity**. According to tradition, her mother-in-law treated her quite cruelly. Her husband is described as an unfeeling man who neither objected to the abuse nor comforted his wife. After about twelve years of suffering she left home to wander as a religious seeker. To symbolize her renunciation of all attachments and earthly values, including feminine modesty, Lalleshvari wandered nude. During her wanderings she composed and sang songs of devotion to Shiva, which are still popular today.

Lanka

In the *Ramayana*, the earlier of the two great Indian epics, Lanka is the kingdom of the **demon**-king **Ravana**. Although Lanka is sometimes identified with the modern island of **Sri Lanka**, and though southern Indian sites such as **Rameshvaram** have been identified with events in the *Ramayana*, the epic's descriptions should be read as mythic and narrative accounts, rather than a geographical primer. The divine architect **Vishvakarma** had originally built Lanka for **Kubera** the minor **deity**, but

Kubera had been dispossessed by Ravana and his brothers.

Lankalakshmi

In the *Ramayana*, the earlier of the two great Indian epics, Lankalakshmi is the name of the guardian **deity** of **Lanka**, the **demon**-king **Ravana's** capital city. Lankalakshmi is also the rebirth of the **goddess** Vijayalakshmi, who has been cursed by the god **Brahma** to serve as Lanka's guardian deity. The **curse** will last until an intruder to the city manages to defeat her, foretelling the fall of Ravana. This defeat comes with the arrival of the monkey-god **Hanuman**, who leaps across the ocean in search of the goddess **Sita**, whom Ravana has kidnapped. Lankalakshmi recognizes Hanuman as an intruder and attacks him, fulfilling her duty as a guardian deity. Hanuman knocks her flat with a powerful blow, breaking the curse and signalling Ravana's fall.

Lasya

One of two general categories in Indian **dance**, which is soft, lyrical, and conveys a mood of love. Its contrasting form, **tandava**, is athletic, dramatic, and conveys violence and power.

Lava

In the *Ramayana*, the earlier of the two great Indian epics, Lava is one of the twin **sons** of **Rama**, the epic's protagonist. After their mother, **Sita**, has been cast into exile at the **ashram** of the sage **Valmiki**, Lava is born in the usual manner. His brother, **Kusha**, is magically created by Valmiki out of kusha grass. Later, Lava and Kusha go with Valmiki to Rama's court in **Ayodhya**. It is in Rama's court that they first recite the epic poem composed by Valmiki, the *Ramayana*. After Rama gives up his throne, he divides his kingdom between Lava and Kusha.

Leap Philosophy

("ajativada") Leap philosophy affirms that one can attain complete freedom from bondage—which in the Indian context is identified as the end of reincarnation (**samsara**) and final liberation of the soul (**moksha**)—but such freedom cannot be gained by a precisely specified sequence of causes and effects. Since gaining freedom is not a matter of cause and effect, there is no way to stimulate or influence this process through one's actions. Leap philosophers tend to denigrate the effectiveness of ritual action as a way to gain final liberation, except as a preparatory phase, stressing that liberation comes only through gaining inner realization. **Sureshvara** and **Shankaracharya**, members of the **Advaita Vedanta** school, dismiss ritual action, except as preparation for wisdom. Both philosophers believe that release from bondage comes through insight gained in a moment of realization, which radically and permanently shifts one's perspective on the world.

Leather

Considered an impure substance by many traditional Hindus, because it is the product of a dead animal. They believe that leather is an appropriate material for shoes, however, because the feet are deemed the lowest and most impure part of the body. For this reason, many people put on their shoes by slipping their feet into them without using their hands, thus avoiding touching the leather with a higher part of the body. Leather's associations with ritual impurity (**ashaucha**) make it inappropriate for other sorts of clothing—clothing which the hot Indian climate would render problematic—although now it is sometimes used for handbags and briefcases. In earlier times people who wished to avoid leather would wear wooden clogs instead; in modern times, footwear options also include plastic, rubber, and canvas.

Left Hand Tantra

A variation of the **tantra**; the rituals for this "left hand" variety include consciously violating taboos on nonvegetarian food, intoxicating drinks, and illicit sexuality. See **Vamachara**.

Levirate

An ancient practice, long condemned, in which a childless **widow** would have intercourse with her deceased husband's brother in an attempt to perpetuate his line. See **Niyoga**.

Lila

("play") A word whose broad literal meaning denotes any sort of play, game, or sport, but which in a theological context conveys a fundamental assumption about how God interacts with the world. According to this notion, the supreme **deity** engages in **creation** not from any sense of need, but for the sheer enjoyment and entertainment gained from creating and taking part in the world. This is particularly true for the god **Vishnu**, especially in his manifestations as **Rama** and **Krishna**. In this understanding, all divine interactions between God and his devotees (**bhakta**) are undertaken in this spirit of play, although in their ignorance human beings may not recognize the true nature of this encounter. Final liberation of the soul (**moksha**) comes when the devotee recognizes the true nature of this encounter, since after that moment of realization one's entire life is a series of playful interactions with God himself. One of the ways that contemporary devotees strive to enter Rama's and Krishna's divine world is through dramas that are themselves known as lilas. These lilas can be attended for entertainment, but viewing them can also be a deeply serious religious act. When child actors portraying the deities are in costume and in character, they are considered manifestations of the deities themselves. For ardent devotees, viewing these lilas is an avenue for gaining God's **grace**, and an entry-point into a privileged, divine world. For an excellent consideration of how Krishna's entire life is considered as play, see David R. Kinsley, *The Sword and the Flute*, 1975; for a description of the Krishna lilas, see John Stratton Hawley, *At Play with Krishna*, 1981; and Anaradha Kapur, *Actors, Pilgrims, Kings, and Gods*, 1990. See also **Ram Lila**.

Limitationism

Theory explaining diversity used by later branches of the **Advaita Vedanta** philosophical school, one of the "**six schools**" of classical Hindu **philosophy**. This school of thought upholds monism—the belief that a single Ultimate Reality known as **Brahman** lies behind all things, and that all things are merely differing forms of that reality. Proponents claim that reality is non-dual (**advaita**), that is, all things are nothing but the formless, unqualified Brahman, despite the appearance of difference and diversity. For the Advaitins, the assumption of diversity is a fundamental misunderstanding of the ultimate nature of things, and therefore is a manifestation of **avidya**. Although often translated as "ignorance," avidya is better understood as the lack of genuine understanding, ultimately causing human beings to be trapped in karmic bondage, reincarnation (**samsara**), and suffering.

Theoretically, if avidya is a defect that resides within an individual, and if many individuals can be afflicted with avidya at once, is there one avidya that afflicts everyone, or are there many separate avidyas? Limitationism asserts that there is a single avidya, afflicting many people at once. The theory proposes that avidya, in a person, is like the quality of color in an object. The color blue may be a single property of two coexisting objects; each instance of the color blue does not use up a finite "blueness" in the world. In the same way, many people may possess the single property of avidya.

The Lingaraja Temple in Bhubaneshvar. Built in the eleventh century,
the temple exemplifies the Orissan branch of the Nagara architectural style.

Linga

("mark," "sign") Aside from the word's literal meaning as any emblematic sign, linga is also the name for the pillar-shaped form of the god **Shiva**. Representing Shiva as the power of generation itself, from which men and women derive their procreative force, the linga is sometimes simplistically called a "phallic" symbol. An equally important part of the linga's image is the base (**pitha**) in which the shaft is placed, a base which represents the female organs of generation. The **Gudimallam** linga, the oldest known image of Shiva in this form, shows him as male and female, transcending the most basic defining factor of human identity.

Lingaraja Temple

Largest and most important of the temples in the city of **Bhubaneshvar**, dedicated to the god **Shiva** in his aspect as Tribhuvaneshvar, the "Lord of the Three Worlds." The temple was built in the eleventh century C.E., representing the high point of the Orissan branch of the **Nagara** architectural style. The temple building culminates in one single, highest point over the image of the temple's primary **deity**, with shorter subsidiary buildings leading up to it. The Lingaraja temple shows all the elements of the Orissan style: a beehive-shaped tower (**deul**) soaring 120 feet high, fronted by a dance hall (**natamandira**), traditionally used for performances, an entrance hall (**jagamohan**), and an outer entrance hall (**bhogamandapa**).

Lingayat

Kannada-speaking religious community whose members are devotees (**bhakta**) of the god **Shiva**, and who mainly live in the southern Indian state of **Karnataka**. Lingayat roots began in the seventh century with the **Nayanar** poet-saints in **Tamil Nadu** state, migrating northward. The community's founder was the poet-saint **Basavanna**; others included

Allama Prabhu and **Mahadeviyakka**. The community's founding members were driven by the hunger for God and were impatient with anything that got in its way—**worship** of images, **caste** distinctions, or the demands of family life. These early influences have continued to shape Lingayat culture. Lingayats do not use images in their worship. The only symbol they use is the **linga** of Shiva, which all Lingayats wear as a sign of membership in the community. The Lingayats have also largely retained their founders' egalitarian principles. Although the community eschews caste distinctions, there are higher-status priestly families known as **jangamas**, from whom the celibate monks known as viraktas are often drawn. In practice, this egalitarian emphasis has made the entire Lingayat community a **jati**, one of the **endogamous** social subgroups that make up larger Indian society; the difference is that the Lingayats are not marked by their occupation, but by their membership in a particular religious community. The Lingayats are the dominant community in modern Karnataka, both in terms of traditional landholding patterns and in their control over regional politics. For further information see A. K. Ramanujan, *Speaking of Siva*, 1973; and Sivalingayya Channabasavayya Nandimath, *A Handbook of Virasaivism*, 1979.

Lion

In Hindu mythology, a lion or a **tiger** is the animal vehicle of the Mother **Goddess**, as in her manifestation as the goddess **Durga**. Modern iconography shows the Goddess riding either of these animals, with no seeming difference between them, perhaps reflecting the fact that the **Hindi** word "sher" can refer to either the lion or the tiger. The fact that the Goddess rides such a dangerous animal is clearly a symbol of her power and capacity. In her mythology these animals are often described as her allies, engaging in battle at her command.

Liquor

Condemned by the traditional Hindus, although attitudes differ based on the type of liquor consumed. Consuming beer, wine, and distilled spirits ("foreign liquor") carries the stigma of adopting "foreign" Western values; whereas consuming undistilled, fermented beverages such as "country liquor" and **toddy** carry the taint of low-class behavior. Patterns of drinking tend to reflect and reinforce these negative attitudes. Since liquor is taboo in polite society, people who drink will often finish the bottle in one sitting and become intoxicated, thus "proving" that there is no such thing as responsible drinking.

Despite the general cultural disapproval, there are a few Hindu temples where liquor is the everyday **offering** to the **deity**. The worshipers also receive liquor as **prasad**, the sanctified food or drink that carries the deity's blessing. Alcohol has also been incorporated into religious rituals in certain types of tantric religious practice. **Tantra** is a secret ritual-based religious tradition, based on the belief that there is an ultimate unity of everything that exists. From a tantric perspective, to affirm that the entire universe is one principle means that the adept must reject all concepts based on dualistic thinking. One way to do this is to partake of the "Five Forbidden Things" (**panchamakara**), consciously breaking societal norms forbidding consumption of **intoxicants**, nonvegetarian food, and illicit sexuality. This is always done within a carefully defined ritual setting, in a conscious effort to sacralize what is normally forbidden.

Lohar

Traditional Indian society was modeled as a collection of **endogamous** subgroups (in which marriage is decreed by law to occur only between members of the same group) known as **jatis** ("birth"). The jatis were organized (and their social status determined) by the group's hereditary occupation, over which each

The lota is a vessel designed to allow one to drink from it without touching one's lips to its surface, which would render it impure.

group had a monopoly. The Lohars' hereditary occupation was blacksmithing and iron working.

Lohari

Festival falling on the night before **Makara Sankranti**, the day when the sun moves into the zodiological sign of Capricorn, which almost always falls on January 14. The central focus of this festival is a large bonfire. Celebrants collect fuel for weeks beforehand, lighting the fire on the evening of the festival. People **dance**, sing, and walk around the fire, giving the fire **offerings** of sweets, fried snacks, and peanuts; these same items are also given to those present as **prasad** or sanctified food.

Lohari is a seasonal festival, marking the passing of the coldest period of the winter and anticipating the return of warmer weather, symbolized by the fire. This festival is celebrated in the **Punjab** and in northern India where Punjabis have settled. This festival also serves as a public display recognizing some change within the family. Families that have recorded marriages or births in the past year celebrate with particular fervor, whereas families in which a person has died usually refrain.

Lokacharya

(ca. early 14th c.) Religious leader also known as Pillai Lokacharya, the founder of the **Tengalai** branch of the **Shrivaishnava** religious community. The Shrivaishnavas are devotees (**bhakta**) of the god **Vishnu**. The Tengalais have no faith in human capacities, emphasizing the need for the devotee's absolute surrender to the **grace** of God, which alone will save the devotee.

Lokayata

One of the traditional names for the **materialist** school of philosophy. See **materialist**.

Lopamudra

In Hindu mythology, the wife of the sage **Agastya**.

Lost Wax Casting

A method of metal-casting used to create the southern Indian **bronzes** during the **Chola dynasty** (9th–14th c.). The artisan makes a wax image of the statue, then covers the wax with layers of clay. The clay is fired and the wax vaporizes, leaving a clay mold into which molten metal is poured. Once the metal cools, the clay mold is broken, revealing the statue. Small imperfections are removed by hand, and the statue is polished to a high gloss. This casting method produces exquisite detail and subtlety of expression, but is extremely time-consuming because each wax image and clay mold can only be used once.

Lota

A vessel for holding water that usually narrows near the top (so that the vessel can be carried in one hand) with a flared opening to facilitate accurate pouring. The lota is used for drinking. Water can be poured directly into one's mouth without touching the vessel to one's lips, which would render the vessel and its contents impure. A lota is also often used in bathing (**snana**), to pour water over one's body, or for any other uses for which holding and pouring water are necessary.

Lothal

Ancient city and archeological site located near the Gulf of Cambay in the modern state of **Gujarat**. Lothal was one of the cities of the **Indus Valley civilization**, a highly developed urban culture that flourished in the Indus Valley region between the fourth and third millennia B.C.E. Lothal was a port city, although because of silting, the present site is now well inland. The size of the harbor indicates that it was a prominent port. Archaeological evidence suggests that Lothal continued to flourish for nearly 500 years after the decline of **Harappa** and **Mohenjo-Daro**, the two largest cities of the Indus Valley civilization.

Lotus

Flower with significant symbolism in Hindu culture. See **Padma**.

Lotus Position

See **padmasana**.

Love Marriage

In modern India, the name given to a marriage fixed by the bride and groom themselves, rather than an **arranged marriage** fixed by parents or guardians. Although Western romantic notions consider a love marriage the preferred method, many Hindus consider love marriages suspect. Love marriages carry the stigma of rebellion—children usurping the role traditionally played by their parents. It is sometimes thought to present the danger of inter-**caste** marriage and the likelihood that the marriage will be rooted in lust or infatuation, thus rendering it potentially unstable. The family is considered the foundation of society; anything undermining its stability is viewed quite dimly. Love marriages are becoming more common and accepted among modern Hindus,

especially in the larger urban areas. Arranged marriages, however, remain far more common.

Lunar Line

One of the two great mythic lineages in Hindu mythology, the other being the **Solar Line**. Kings in the Lunar Line traced their descent from **Soma**, the **moon**, who married the daughter of King **Ikshvaku** of the Solar Line. Soma and his wife begat an illustrious group of progeny, including most of the principal characters in the *Mahabharata*, the later of the two great Hindu epics.

Lunar Month, Structure of

Hindu festivals are determined according to a lunar **calendar**, in which a year is made of twelve lunar months. The lunar month is divided into two halves, each of which has fifteen **days**. In northern India the lunar month begins with the dark (krishna) half—when the **moon** is waning. This phase lasts fifteen days, ending with the **new moon**. This is followed by the light (shukla) half of the month—when the moon is waxing. This phase lasts fifteen days, ending with the **full moon**. The day after the full moon is the first day of the next lunar month, and so on. Any given lunar day is designated by the name of the month, the half (light or dark), and the lunar day (1 to 15). In southern India the pattern is reversed, with the lunar month starting with the light half and ending on the new moon.

The lunar month, as with all Hindu conceptions of time, represents changing times of **auspiciousness** and **inauspiciousness**, peaks and valleys marking times that are more or less propitious. The full moon, with its associations of fullness, abundance, and light, is always auspicious. It is believed that religious rites performed on this day generate as much merit as those performed for an entire month. The new moon, with its associations of darkness and emptiness, is a more ambiguous time. At times the new moon can be highly auspicious, as on the occasion of a **Somavati Amavasya** (new moon falling on **Monday**). Several major festivals (such as **Diwali**) fall on the new moon. Despite this, the new moon is less auspicious than the full moon. Within each fortnight various days are also associated with particular **deities**, and their devotees (**bhakta**) often do particular rites on those days: The eleventh day (**ekadashi**) is dedicated to the god **Vishnu**, the eighth day (ashtami) to the **Goddess**, the evening of the thirteenth day (trayodashi) and the fourteenth to the god **Shiva**, and the fourth day (chaturthi) to the god **Ganesh**.

As mentioned earlier, the lunar calendar is the basis for almost all Hindu holidays. To correct the discrepancy between the lunar and solar year (about eleven days), and thus keep these festivals at about the same time every year, an **intercalary month** is inserted every 2½ years. Although this extra month keeps the calendar in balance, it is considered highly inauspicious, perhaps because it is an unusual occurrence. During this month people take normal precautions to protect themselves during inauspicious times—basically putting off any new activities until the month is over, and propitiating protective deities until the end of the month.

Madhava

(from **madhu** "sweet") Epithet of the god **Krishna**, signifying the sweetness that he brings to the lives of his devotees (**bhakta**). See **Krishna**.

Madhava

(2) (14th c.) Author of the *Sarvadarshanasangraha*, a philosophical encyclopedia composed in the late fourteenth century. In this text, Madhava compiles the views of all existing philosophical schools, placing them in hierarchical order, based on his judgment of their value. According to the text, the **materialist** school is ranked the lowest and least reliable, since its proponents completely deny the virtue of any religious life. The **Advaita Vedanta** school, Madhava's own, is judged as the highest and most perfect expression of the truth. Although the *Sarvadarshanasangraha* is biased, it is one of the few extant sources which considers the perspectives of all the existing schools.

Madhima

("greatness") One of the eight **superhuman powers** (**siddhi**) traditionally believed to be conferred by high spiritual attainment. This particular power gives one the ability to become as large as one desires.

Madhu

In Hindu mythology, one of the two **demons** who attempt to kill the god **Brahma**; the other demon is **Kaitabha**. The story is recounted in several mythic sources with some marked differences between stories. All versions agree that Madhu and Kaitabha are born from the god **Vishnu's** ear wax during the period of cosmic dissolution (**pralaya**). As the creation of the world begins anew, a lotus sprouts from Vishnu's navel. It opens to reveal the creator-god Brahma, who is immediately menaced by Madhu and Kaitabha. In all versions of the myth, Brahma appeals for help, and Vishnu tricks the demons and slays them. The difference in the stories pertains to the **deity** to whom Brahma appeals for help. The story first appears in the mythology of Vishnu; here Brahma invokes Vishnu. Yet this same story also appears in the *Devimahatmya*, the earliest source in which the Mother **Goddess** appears as the supreme **divine power**. In this version, Brahma's hymn of praise is to the Goddess, who in her form as **Yoganidra** ("sleep of **yoga**") has lulled Vishnu into a cosmic stupor, rendering him unable to come to Brahma's aid. Pleased by Brahma's praise, the Goddess withdraws her influence over Vishnu; he awakens, and slays the demons.

Madhurya ("Honeyed") Bhava

The second of the five **modes of devotion** to God that were articulated by **Rupa Goswami**, a devotee (**bhakta**) of the god **Krishna** and a follower of the Bengali saint **Chaitanya**. Rupa used human relationships to describe the connection between devotee and **deity**. The five modes showed growing emotional intensity, from the peaceful (**shanta**) sense that comes from realizing one's complete identity with **Brahman** or Ultimate Reality, to conceiving of God as one's master, friend, child, or lover. The Madhurya Bhava is the last and most intense of the five modes of devotion. In this mode, devotees consider the relationship between themselves and the deity as that of lover and beloved. This mode appeared most prominently with regard to the god Krishna (in which the model devotees were the cowherd women of **Braj**), and

Radha (who is a symbol for the human soul.) This particular mode is seen as the most intense and demanding because of its emotional closeness. For that same reason, it is also seen as the sweetest.

Madhusudana Saraswati

(16th c.) A renowned member of the Sanyasi community, a group of renunciant ascetics who were devotees (bhakta) of the god Shiva. His last name reveals that he was a member of the Saraswati sect, one of the most prestigious of the ten Dashanami divisions; he is said to have lived most of his life in Benares, the greatest religious center of his time. According to ascetic legend, Madhusudana was responsible for the creation of a class of fighting ascetics, the Naga Sanyasis. According to tradition, Madhusudana created these fighters because he was distressed at the depredations the Sanyasis suffered at the hands of hostile Muslim faqirs. After consulting with Birbal, adviser to Moghul emperor Akbar, Madhusudana decided to form a fighting ascetic order dedicated to protecting other ascetics. Recruits came from the ranks of the shudras.

Madhva

(1197–1276) Philosopher and founder of the Dvaita Vedanta philosophical school, whose long life was largely spent in Udupi, a small town near the Malabar coast in the state of Karnataka. Madhva's basic philosophy was the utter transcendence of God. This conviction led him to develop the theory of dualism, which posits a qualitative difference between God in his transcendence and the corruptions of material things. According to Madhva, God is completely different from humans and the material world, even though both came from God and depend on Him for their continuing existence. Madhva differed sharply from the major school, Advaita Vedanta, which upheld the theory of monism—the belief that a single Ultimate Reality (called Brahman) lies behind all things, which are merely differing forms of this single reality. Whereas Advaita collapses all things into one thing, Madhva firmly insists on maintaining differences.

Madhva's emphasis on dualism led him to articulate these differences, known as the "fivefold difference": the difference between God and Self, between God and the world, between individual Selves, between Selves and matter, and between individual material things. Even though each Self contains an aspect of God, fundamental difference gives the Self only limited capacity for religious life. This limited power means that final liberation of the soul comes solely through the grace of God, who alone has the power to effect it. Final liberation was conceived both as freedom from rebirth and as the soul's opportunity to remain in the divine presence forever.

Madhya Pradesh

("middle state") Modern Indian state located in the geographical center of the subcontinent. Madhya Pradesh was formed after Indian independence in 1947 from the former Central Provinces, Berar State, and several princely states. Large parts of the state are inaccessible and relatively undeveloped, particularly in the Vindhya Mountain and Satpura ranges. Madhya Pradesh also has a large percentage of adivasis (indigenous tribal people), many of whom are very poor. Madhya Pradesh contains many important archaeological sites, including the Chandella temples at Khajuraho and the caves at Udayagiri. Sacred sites (tirthas) include the Narmada River, one of the seven sacred rivers of India, and the holy city of Ujjain. For general information about Madhya Pradesh and other regions of India, see Christine Nivin et al., *India*. 8th ed., Lonely Planet, 1998.

The Vishvanath Temple at Khajuraho, Madhya Pradesh, dates back to 1002 C.E.

Madmaheshvar

Temple and sacred site (**tirtha**) in the **Garhwal** region of the **Himalayas**, about twenty miles north of the village of **Ukhimath**. The temple's presiding **deity** is the god **Shiva** in his manifestation as Madmaheshvar. Madmaheshvar is one of the **Panchkedar**, a network of five sacred sites in the Garhwal region; the other four sites are **Kedarnath**, **Rudranath**, **Tungnath**, and **Kalpeshvar**. This network of five sites is seen as a symbolic representation of **Shiva's** body; Madmaheshvar is believed to be Shiva's navel.

Madri

In the *Mahabharata*, the later of the two great Hindu epics, Madri is the junior wife of King **Pandu** and the mother of **Nakula** and **Sahadeva**. Neither of these children are actually Pandu's **sons**, since he has been cursed to die the moment he holds his wife in amorous embrace. Rather, they have been magically conceived through the effect of a **mantra** given to Pandu's other wife, **Kunti**, by the sage **Durvasas**. The mantra gives the woman who recites it the power to call down any of the gods and to have a son equal in power to that god himself. With Pandu's blessing, Kunti teaches the mantra to Madri, who recites it to the twin gods known as the **Ashvins**. Thus she bears twins. They live happily until springtime comes to the forest. Under the intoxicating influence of spring, Pandu embraces Madri; the **curse** takes effect, and Pandu falls down dead. Because of her role in Pandu's death, Madri consigns her children to Kunti's care, and ends her life on Pandu's funeral pyre.

Madurai

Temple-town and sacred site (**tirtha**) on the Vygai River, in the state of **Tamil Nadu** in southern India. Madurai is most famous for the large temple dedicated to **Minakshi**, the **goddess**, and her consort Sundareshvara. Minakshi is a local **deity** who has become a major regional goddess, whereas Sundareshvara is considered a form of the god **Shiva**. After the fall of the Vijayanagar empire late in the sixteenth century, southern India was ruled by the **Nayak dynasty**, with the capital at Madurai. Much of the Minakshi temple was built by **Tirumalai Nayak** (r. 1623-1659); his palace is another of the city's attractions. The streets around the temple form four concentric processional circuits, with the temple directly in the middle. The town was planned as a lotus with layers of petals, with the image of Minakshi at the center, around which all things revolved. Symbolically, the Minakshi temple was not only the center of the city, but the center of the earth. See also **Vijayanagar dynasty**.

Madya

("wine") In the secret ritually-based religious practice known as **tantra**, wine is the first of the Five Forbidden Things (**panchamakara**). Since "respectable" Hindu society strongly condemns the consumption of alcoholic beverages, its ritual use in tantra must be understood in the larger tantric context. One of the most basic tantric assumptions is the ultimate unity of everything that exists. From a tantric perspective, to affirm that the entire universe is one principle means that the adept must reject all concepts based on dualistic thinking. One way to do this is to partake of the "Five Forbidden Things," consciously breaking the societal norms forbidding the consumption of **intoxicants**, nonvegetarian food, and illicit sexuality—making sacred that which is normally forbidden. Tantric adepts cite such ritual use of forbidden things as proof that their practice involves a more exclusive qualification (**adhikara**), and is thus superior to common practice. In its ritual use—which is usually in very small quantities—the intoxication produced by wine is an approximation of the bliss of realization. For further information see Arthur Avalon (Sir John Woodroffe), *Shakti and Shakta*, 1978; Swami Agehananda Bharati, *The Tantric Tradition*, 1977; and Douglas Renfrew Brooks, *The Secret of the Three Cities*, 1990.

Magh

According to the lunar **calendar**, by which most Hindu religious festivals are determined, Magh is the eleventh month in the lunar **year**, usually falling within January and February. During Magh there is a month-long bathing (**snana**) festival, the **Magh Mela**, at the confluence of the **Ganges** and **Yamuna** rivers in **Allahabad**. The other major festivals in Magh are **Sakata Chauth**, **Shattila Ekadashi**, **Mauni Amavasya**, **Vasant Panchami**, **Bhishma Ashtami**, **Jaya Ekadashi**, **Ravidas Jayanti**, **Makara Sankranti**. In southern India, **Pongal** and the **Float Festival** are celebrated during Magh.

Magha

(7th c.) **Sanskrit** writer whose best-known work, the drama *Shishupala-vadha*, describes the death of **Shishupala** at the hands of the god **Krishna**. In Hindu mythology, Shishupala is a form of **Jaya**, **Vishnu's** gatekeeper, who has been cursed to be born as a **demon** three times and killed each time by Vishnu. Shishupala is the last of these births, after which the **curse** is broken. Aside from its mythic theme, the play is noted for a number of unusual verses, designed to show the poet's skill. These include verses that are perfect palindromes and ones that use only one or two consonants.

Magh Mela

Religious festival celebrated every **year** during the entire **lunar month** of **Magh** (January–February) in the city of **Allahabad**. According to the Hindu **festival calendar**, Magh is one of the months in which bathing (**snana**) in sacred rivers is highly praised. This is particularly significant because Allahabad lies at the confluence of two sacred rivers, the **Ganges** and the **Yamuna River**. During this month, pilgrims set up an encampment at the confluence, which becomes a bustling religious center. During their stay, pilgrims live a strict and disciplined religious life. This includes a morning bath, followed by gift-giving (**dana**) and **worship**; **eating** a restricted diet, and evenings spent singing hymns (**kirtan**) and listening to religious discourses. Some pilgrims even take a strict vow, known as **kalpavas**, to remain there for the entire month, a vow which also entails a strict **ascetic** lifestyle. More than a million pilgrims attend this festival. Every twelfth year, when the Magh Mela becomes the Allahabad **Kumbha Mela**, attendance increases. In 1989 an estimated fifteen million pilgrims came for a single day, with millions more coming during the rest of the month.

Magic

In Hindu tradition there are many different powers in the universe, and many ways of influencing them, both seen and unseen. The emphasis on magic goes back to the **Atharva Veda**, one of the oldest Hindu religious texts, which is mostly a collection of spells. Even today many Hindus accept that certain powerful religious adepts have the power to command unseen forces, as well as the power to counteract the spells levied by others. People who have gained high levels of religious attainments are also believed to have superhuman powers (**siddhi**), allowing them to do things that ordinary people cannot. These superhuman powers are not seen as magical, but rather as the normal exercise of a level of understanding higher than most people have attained. Indian culture also has a long tradition of illusion, sleight of hand, and other sorts of trickery, baffling and entertaining onlookers for centuries. For an extensive account of these powers, see Lee Siegel, *Net of Magic*, 1991.

Mahabalipuram

Village on the Bay of Bengal in **Tamil Nadu**, about thirty miles south of Madras. Although famous as a beach resort today, during the **Pallava dynasty** (6th–9th c.) Mahabalipuram was a major port, second in importance only to the capital at **Kanchipuram**. Mahabalipuram has several impressive religious monuments, erected during the reigns of **Narasimhavarman I** (630–668 C.E.) and **Narasimhavarman II** (700–728 C.E.). One of the monuments is a rock-cut **sculpture** depicting the myth of the Descent of the **Ganges**, using a natural vertical fissure to lay out the river's path. Other notable constructions are the "Rathas," a series of free-standing temples carved from one giant boulder, dedicated to the **Pandavas**, the protagonists in the epic *Mahabharata*. The most recent attraction is the temple along the shore, built during the reign of **Rajasimhavarman** (early 8th c.). The temple's major **deity** is the god **Shiva**; a smaller shrine also holds an image of the god **Vishnu**. Although all of these have been weathered by time and the elements, they remain some of the most visited sites in southern India.

Mahabharata

One of the two great **Sanskrit** epics, traditionally ascribed to the mythical sage **Vyasa**. The *Mahabharata* is much longer than the other great epic, the *Ramayana*. At almost 100,000 stanzas, the *Mahabharata* is the world's longest epic poem. If the *Ramayana* can be characterized as the tale of the "good" family, in which brothers cooperate to support and preserve their family, the *Mahabharata* describes the "bad" family, in which hard-heartedness and the lust for power in an extended royal family ultimately cause its destruction. The epic is set in the region west of modern Delhi and describes a fratricidal civil war. A greatly abridged account can be given as follows:

Shantanu is the king of the Kurus. He dies an untimely, heirless death. In a desperate attempt to preserve the royal line, Shantanu's wife, **Satyavati**, calls upon her elder son, the sage **Vyasa**, who fathers children by Shantanu's two wives. The elder son, **Dhrtarashtra**, is born blind, and thus the rights to the throne fall to his younger brother **Pandu**. Pandu later abdicates his throne because of a **curse**, and goes to live in the forest with his two wives, **Kunti** and **Madri**, leaving his elder brother to rule in his place. In time Dhrtarashtra's wife, **Gandhari**, magically gives birth to one hundred sons, of whom the oldest is **Duryodhana**; the hundred sons are called the **Kauravas**, and are the epic's antagonists. In the forest Kunti has three sons, **Yudhishthira**, **Bhima**, and **Arjuna**, while Madri has the twins **Nakula** and **Sahadeva**. These five sons are the **Pandavas**, the epic's protagonists. None of these children are actually Pandu's sons, since he has been cursed to die the moment he holds his wife in amorous embrace. Rather, they have been magically conceived using a **mantra** given to Kunti by the sage **Durvasas**, giving the woman reciting it the power to call down any of the gods and have a son equal in power to that god himself. When Kunti first receives the mantra, long before her marriage, she impulsively recites it while gazing upon the **sun**, and gives birth to a shining child. Distraught and desperate, Kunti puts him in a box and abandons him in the **Ganges** River. The child is adopted by the charioteer **Adhiratha**, and grows up to be the heroic **Karna**.

As the result of his curse, Pandu dies an early death, and Kunti (his wife) and his sons (the Pandavas) return to the court at **Hastinapur**, where the boys are raised as princes. From the beginning there are bad feelings between Duryodhana (the eldest of the Kauravas) and his cousins, largely because Duryodhana desires the throne, which rightly belongs to Yudhishthira (one of the Pandavas). After foiling several attempts to kill them, the Pandava brothers leave the kingdom to become mercenaries. On one of their journeys, Arjuna wins the hand of the princess **Draupadi**, who becomes their common wife (their mother commands that Arjuna share whatever he wins with his brothers). After some time Dhrtarashtra (father of the Kauravas) renounces the throne and divides his kingdom. The Pandavas build a new capital at **Indraprastha**, identified near modern Delhi.

For a little while things are quiet, but Duryodhana is not content to share his kingdom. He invites Yudhishthira for a game of dice, matching Yudhishthira against **Shakuni**, the most skillful gambler alive. Although Yudhishthira is a model for truthfulness and virtue, his fatal flaw is his love of **gambling**. In the match Yudhishthira loses his kingdom, all his possessions, his brothers, himself, and finally his wife. In one of the epic's most powerful scenes, Duryodhana's brother, **Duhshasana**, drags Draupadi by her hair into the assembly hall, her clothes stained with her menstrual blood. Draupadi's humiliation moves Dhrtarashtra to set them free, but also sparks the enmity that helps drive the rest of the plot. After some bargaining, the parties agree that the Pandavas will spend twelve years in exile and a thirteenth incognito. If they can remain undiscovered during the thirteenth year they will regain their kingdom. If they are discovered, however, the cycle of exile will begin again.

After thirteen years, Yudhishthira and his brothers approach Duryodhana for their rightful share, but are haughtily rebuffed. All efforts at conciliation fail; Duryodhana claims that he will not give them enough land in which to stick the point of a needle. Pushed to the wall, the Pandavas prepare for battle. On one side are Yudhishthira and his brothers, aided by their counselor **Krishna**. On the other are Duryodhana and many respected figures, such as **Drona**, **Bhishma**, and Karna. For eighteen days the battle rages, until most of the important people are dead. Yudhishthira and his brothers survive. Yudhishthira is crowned king and rules righteously for many years. Late in life he installs his grandson, King **Parikshit**, on the throne. With his siblings he takes a final journey into the **Himalayas**. During the journey his brothers fall dead, one by one;

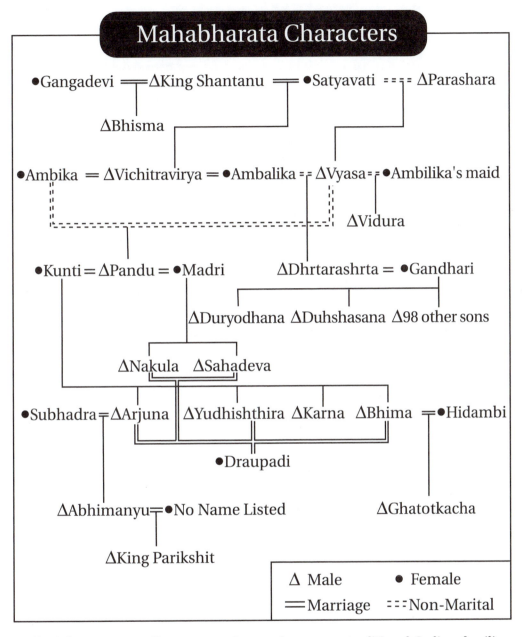

Mahabharata Characters

•Gangadevi ═══ ΔKing Shantanu ═══ •Satyavati ┅┅ ΔParashara

ΔBhisma

•Ambika ═ ΔVichitravirya ═ •Ambalika ┅ ΔVyasa ┅ •Ambilika's maid

ΔVidura

•Kunti ═ ΔPandu ═ •Madri   ΔDhrtarashrta ═ •Gandhari

ΔDuryodhana ΔDuhshasana Δ98 other sons

ΔNakula ΔSahadeva

•Subhadra ═ ΔArjuna ΔYudhishthira ΔKarna ΔBhima ═ •Hidambi

•Draupadi

ΔAbhimanyu ═ •No Name Listed   ΔGhatotkacha

ΔKing Parikshit

Δ Male	• Female
═ Marriage	┅ Non-Marital

Yudhishthira eventually enters the divine realm.

The complete epic is more complex than this summary. One of the features of the epic is that it contains many unrelated tales, for which the main story acts as a frame. Aside from being a tale of a dysfunctional family, the *Mahabharata* also contains a great deal of cultural wisdom, making the names of characters symbolic even today. A televised serial of the text, which ran for more than a year in 1989–90, was wildly popular throughout India. It is also interesting to note

that many traditional Indian families will not keep a copy of the text in the house, since it is believed that to do this will foster discord in the family.

Mahabhashya

("Great commentary") A commentary on the *Ashtadhyayi* of **Panini**, written by **Patanjali**, the grammarian, in the second century B.C.E. Panini's text gives a complete and accurate description of all the forms of the **Sanskrit** language and set the standard for the language after his time. Although the *Ashtadhyayi* is considered a masterpiece, it appears to invite more detailed commentary because it is written in a series of aphorisms or **sutra**. Each of these aphorisms provides the basis for those which follow. Panini's ultimate purpose is to give a complete account of the language in the briefest possible space. Aside from expanding and expounding Panini's grammar, Patanjali also gives some useful information of his own. The *Mahabhashya* contains the earliest known reference to the Greeks.

Mahabrahman

("Great **Brahman**") In traditional Indian society, a debased class of brahmins who officiate at rites for the dead, especially at the rites performed immediately after death. In many of these rites the Mahabrahman is identified with the deceased person and is fed and given gifts that are intended to help satisfy the soul of the deceased. These acts are seen as transferring the **inauspiciousness** of death from the family to the Mahabrahman. Such constant association with death and its inauspicious qualities is seen as a highly undesirable way to make a living; Mahabrahmans have extremely low social status, despite being brahmins by birth. As compensation for taking on such inauspiciousness, Mahabrahmans usually demand high payment from a family. For further information see Jonathan Parry, "Ghosts, Greed and Sin: The Occupational Identity of the Benares Funeral Priests," in *Man*, Vol. 15, 1980.

Mahadeva

("great God") Epithet of the god **Shiva**. See **Shiva**.

Mahadeviyakka

(12th c.) Poet-saint and religious leader in the **Lingayat** religious community, a **bhakti** (devotional) community centered on both the **worship** of **Shiva** as the single supreme god and on the rejection of all **caste** regulations. The Lingayats were formed in the southern Indian state of **Karnataka**, where they still have a considerable presence. The collections of poetry that form their most important religious texts are composed in the **Kannada** language. Mahadeviyakka was a contemporary of **Basavanna** and **Allama Prabhu**; her status in the community is marked by the suffix akka ("elder sister"). According to tradition, she was devoted to Shiva at a very young age and considered him to be her true husband. This caused great problems during a brief, unhappy marriage, a mismatch between a carnally inclined man and a woman who would have no human lover. She eventually left her husband, wandering naked as a sign that she had cast away all attachments. She later became associated with the Lingayats, known as the "Lord's men." The theme running through most of her poetry is love for Shiva, sometimes as her husband and sometimes as her adulterous lover, both portraying her struggles with the world. For further information see A. K. Ramanujan, *Speaking of Shiva*, 1973.

Mahakaleshvar

Temple and sacred site (**tirtha**) in the sacred city of **Ujjain** in the state of **Madhya Pradesh**. The temple is named for its presiding **deity**, the god **Shiva** in his manifestation as the "Lord of Death." Shiva is present at Mahakaleshvar in the form of a **linga**, a pillar-shaped image. The Mahakaleshvar linga is one of the twelve **jyotirlingas**, a network of sites at which Shiva is uniquely present. The linga is in an underground room, reached only by traversing a long, dark passageway. This passage may symbolize the darkness and terror of death. **Worship** at Mahakaleshvar is believed to protect one from an early or untimely death, and at death, bring liberation of the soul (**moksha**).

The city of Ujjain has a long history as a sacred, economic, and political center. One of the **Seven Sacred Cities**

(Saptapuri), it also has other important religious sites. Historically, Ujjain is said to have been the capital of King **Vikramaditya**, founder of the **Vikram Era**. Trade routes that passed through it made it economically prosperous.

Mahakali

In the *Devimahatmya*, the earliest and most important source for the mythology of the **Goddess**, the three parts of this text describe the goddess in three different manifestations: **Mahasaraswati**, **Mahalakshmi**, and Mahakali. All of these manifestations are extremely powerful, but Mahakali is the most ferocious of all. She is said to have sprung from the forehead of the Goddess, as a physical manifestation of the **deity's** rage when insulted by the **demon** generals **Chanda** and **Munda**, who denigrate her fighting ability because she was a woman. According to the story, Mahakali is black in color, thin, and haggard, with long teeth and nails, and utters terrifying cries. She defeats the demon armies by picking them up and stuffing them into her mouth, consuming them whole. She later kills Chanda and Munda by cutting off their heads. Her final adversary is **Raktabija**, who has received the boon that any drop of his blood falling to the earth will instantly turn into a copy of him, rendering him practically unconquerable. **Kali** defeats this demon by drinking his blood as it is shed, until finally it is completely gone. For more information on Mahakali and all the goddesses of Hinduism, see David R. Kinsley, *Hindu Goddesses*, 1986; and John Stratton Hawley and Donna Wulff (eds.), *Devi*, 1996.

Mahakavya

An epic poem in **Sanskrit** literature. According to tradition, there are six such mahakavyas: the *Kumarasambhava*, *Meghaduta*, and *Raghuvamsha* by the poet **Kalidasa**; the *Shishupala-vadha*

by the poet **Magha**; the *Kiratarjuniya* by the poet **Bharavi**, and the *Naishadacharitra* by the poet-king **Harsha**.

Mahalakshmi

In the *Devimahatmya*, the earliest and most important source for the mythology of the **Goddess**, the three parts of this text describe this goddess in three different manifestations: **Mahasaraswati**, Mahalakshmi, and **Mahakali**. Unlike the goddess **Lakshmi**, who is a sedate and propitious married goddess, Mahalakshmi is seen as a powerful warrior goddess, the premier divine power on the earth. She is formed from the collected radiance (tejas) of all the gods, in order to kill a **demon** named **Mahishasura**, against whom the gods have been unable to prevail. Her climactic act in the *Devimahatmya* is killing Mahishasura, despite his desperate attempts first to defeat and then to elude her. For more information on Mahalakshmi and all the goddesses of Hinduism, see David R. Kinsley, *Hindu Goddesses*, 1986.

Mahamandaleshvar

("Great Lord of the Region") Term of respect given to a **Mandaleshvar** when one of his disciples is chosen a Mandaleshvar while the preceptor is still living. Mandaleshvars are the learned ascetics who lead the **Naga akharas** of the **Dashanami Sanyasis**, a practice that began in the nineteenth century. The Dashanami Nagas are renunciant ascetics who are devotees (**bhakta**) of **Shiva** and who formerly made their living as traders and mercenary soldiers. Their rough-and-ready qualities made them effective soldiers, but gave them little preparation for formal argument with Christian missionaries. Mandaleshvars were chosen from among the more learned **Paramahamsa** ascetics, so that the latter could provide a more coherent and telling opposition; he also serves as the Nagas' teacher and spiritual adviser. The enshrinement of

Mahant Bhagwan Das, renowned sadhu, attends the Kumbha Mela religious festival in Allahabad.

a Mandaleshvar's disciple is thus seen as boosting his teacher's prestige to an even more rarefied state.

Mahamandapa

The mahamandapa is an architectural feature found in the **Khajuraho** variation of the **Nagara** architectural style. Usually found in northern India, the Nagara style emphasizes verticality, with the whole temple building culminating in a single highest point; in the Khajuraho variant, the entire structure gradually leads up to the central tower, as foothills lead up to the mountains, with the peak of this central tower directly over the temple's primary image. In this style, the mahamandapa is the name for the temple's main entrance-hall, which was separated from the main sanctuary (**garbhagrha**) by a short vestibule named the **antarala**.

Mahamantra

A thirty-two syllable **mantra**, or sacred formula, the recitation of which is the primary religious act for devotees (**bhakta**) belonging to ISKCON (International Society for Krishna Consciousness), a group more popularly known as the Hare Krishnas. The mantra itself is "Hare Krishna, Hare Krishna, Krishna Krishna, Hare Hare; Hare Rama, Hare Rama, Rama Rama, Hare Hare."

Mahamaya

("[she whose] power of illusion is great") Epithet of the **Goddess** in the *Devimahatmya*, the earliest and most important textual source for the notion that God is female. This epithet reflects her position as the sole and supreme power in the universe, wielding the power of illusion that obscures this fact from human awareness. See **Goddess**.

Mahanirvani Akhara

The name of a group of the **Naga** class of the **Dashanami Sanyasis**, a type of renunciant **ascetic**. The Dashanami Nagas are devotees (**bhakta**) of the god **Shiva**, organized into different **akharas** or regiments on the model of an army. Until the beginning of the nineteenth century, the Nagas' primary occupation was as mercenary soldiers or traders; both of these have largely disappeared in contemporary times. This akhara is described as taking part in a battle with the forces of the Moghul emperor **Aurangzeb** in 1664, and are credited with saving the city of **Benares** from being sacked.

The Mahanirvani Akhara is one of the seven main Dashanami Naga akharas and remains one of most influential. The principal center of the Mahanirvani Akhara is in **Allahabad**, site of the largest and most important bathing (**snana**) festivals, known as the **Kumbha Mela**.

Their strength in Allahabad has allowed them to assume the most desirable spot at the head of the bathing procession during the Kumbha Mela. Each of the akharas has a (guardian) **deity** who defines their organizational identity; the tutelary deity of the Mahanirvani Akhara is the great sage **Kapila**.

Mahant

("great") Honorific title given to an **ascetic** who is the leader of a monastery. Mahants are chosen by their predecessors and designate their successors. While they are living, they have virtually total control over the monastery and its assets, even though they do not own them. In any given ascetic establishment, the mahant has very high status, since he is the absolute ruler of his small domain.

Mahanubhav

("Great Experience") A regional religious community, whose members are devotees (**bhakta**) of the god **Vishnu**, and who are found mainly in the central regions of the state of **Maharashtra**. The Mahanubhavs were founded by Chakradhar in the thirteenth century. Under his influence the community has rejected many aspects of "mainstream" Hindu religious life: social distinctions based on **caste**, the **worship** of images, and the religious authority of **brahmins**. The community is also noted for espousing an **ascetic** way of life. Although the Mahanubhavs are considered **Vaishnavas**, they acknowledge only one God, whom they call Parameshvar ("Great Lord"), and whom they conceive as having had five incarnations. Two of these incarnations are established figures in the Hindu pantheon, the god **Krishna** and the deified ascetic **Dattatreya**. The other three are sectarian figures: their founder Chakradhar, Chakradhar's **guru**, and his guru's guru. Their modern practice stresses pilgrimage, vows, and almsgiving. Nevertheless, through much of Maharashtra there is a

The state of Maharashtra is home to the sculpted caves of Ellora.

legacy of suspicion and mistrust of the Mahanubhavs, perhaps rooted in their anti-authoritarian history. For further information see Anne Feldhaus, *The Religious System of the Mahanubhav Sect*, 1983.

Mahapataka

("Great Sinner") In the **dharma literature**, a person who has committed one of the **Four Great Crimes**, namely murdering a **brahmin** (**brahmahatya**), stealing a brahmin's gold (**steya**), drinking **liquor** (**surapana**), or committing **adultery** with the wife of one's **guru** (**gurutalpaga**). These crimes were considered so heinous that the performer became an outcast from society. Another indication of the gravity of these acts was that their expiations (**prayashchitta**) were so severe that they normally ended in death; in some cases this outcome was specifically prescribed. Aside from prescribing such punishments for the actual offenders, the dharma literature also prescribed similar outcaste status for anyone who knowingly associated with such people for more than one year.

Mahapatra

("great vessel") In parts of northern India, the name of a debased **brahmin** group whose members gain their livelihood primarily through receiving gifts, particularly those given following a death. Such brahmins do not actually perform the rites for the dead, although they are seen as symbolically representing the dead person. Their low status stems from this connection with the dead; the gifts they accept transfer the **inauspiciousness** of death from the family to the Mahapatra. This latter assumption is reflected in the group's name—they are "vessels" into which one can deposit such inauspiciousness, and thus be rid of it. Such constant association with death and its inauspicious qualities is seen as a highly undesirable way to make a living, giving this group extremely low social status, despite being brahmins by **birth**. Despite their debased status, they are a necessary part of traditional society, in that they serve as the means through which such inauspiciousness can be removed.

Mahar

Traditional Indian society was a collection of **endogamous** subgroups (in which marriage is decreed by law to occur only between members of the same group) known as **jatis** ("birth"). These jatis were organized (and their social status determined) by the group's hereditary occupation, over which each group held a monopoly. The Mahars were an **untouchable** jati in Maharashtrian society, performing various services and labor for the landlord communities. The Mahars are famous for two figures: the medieval **bhakti** poet **Chokamela**, and the modern jurist and social reformer **Dr. B. R. Ambedkar**.

Maharashtra

Modern Indian state along the Arabian Sea, stretching east over the Western Ghats to encompass the northern part of the **Deccan** Plateau. Maharashtra is one of the "linguistic" states formed after Indian independence in 1947; these states were created to unite people with a common language and culture (in this case, Marathi) under one state government. It was formed in 1960 by splitting the former state of Bombay into the present states of **Gujarat** and Maharashtra. Bombay, the capital, is the financial and industrial center of modern India. The western regions are heavily industrialized; the eastern regions are more agricultural, dominated by sugar plantations. Historically, Maharashtra is the homeland of the **Marathas**, a group whose eighteenth-century empire stretched across much of northern India. The **Rashtriya Svayamsevak Sangh** and the **Shiv Sena**, two Hindu nationalist organizations that have both tried to influence Indian politics, were founded in Maharashtra. Along with its economic and political importance, the state contains many important historical, cultural, and religious sites. Historical and cultural sites include the rock-cut caves of **Ellora**, a UNESCO World Heritage Site; the Buddhist caves at Ajanta; and the cave temple at **Elephanta** in the Bombay harbor. Places of religious importance include the **Godavari** and **Bhima** rivers and their attendant sacred sites (**tirthas**); the sites associated with the saints of the **Varkari Panth** religious community, particularly the temple to the god **Vithoba** at **Pandharpur**; and three of the **jyotirlingas**, which are sites particularly holy to the god **Shiva**: **Bhimashankar**, **Ghrneshvar**, and **Tryambakeshvar**. For general information about Maharashtra and other regions of India, see Christine Nivin et al., *India*. 8th ed., Lonely Planet, 1998.

Maharashtri

Southern Indian brahmins who make up one of the five southern **brahmin** communities (**Pancha Dravida**); the other four are **Gujarati**, **Karnata**, **Andhra**, and **Dravida**. As their name would indicate, the core region for Maharashtri brahmins is the modern state of **Maharashtra**. The Maharashtri brahmins are themselves divided into two subgroups: the **Chitpavan**, or Konkanastha brahmins, who live in the coastal regions, and the **Deshastha** brahmins, who live further inland in the **Deccan**.

Maharishi Mahesh Yogi

(b. Mahesh Prasad Verma, 1911) Hindu teacher and founder of the religious technique known as **Transcendental Meditation** (TM). The Maharishi ("Great Sage") was trained as an engineer, but eventually renounced the world after meeting one of the **Shankaracharyas**, a name given to the most important modern Hindu religious leaders. He stayed with Shankaracharya for the next twelve years, in pursuit of spiritual knowledge. He established an **ashram** at **Rishikesh** but was relatively unknown until his association with the Beatles, the British musical group who came to India with him on pilgrimage. In the early 1970s, TM instructors traveled throughout American college campuses, touting the physiological and spiritual benefits of meditation and providing people (for a fee) with a **mantra** or sacred sound that would bring them these benefits. According to TM proponents, meditation is also supposed to have pacific effects on the larger environment, and result in reduced crime, tension, and hatred. During this period Maharishi International University was established at the former Parsons College in Fairfield, Iowa, as a center to teach TM. In the late 1970s, Maharishi University instituted a program training people to develop the six classical **superhuman powers** (**siddhis**). Since then several disappointed patrons have won lawsuits against the organization.

Mahasaraswati

In the *Devimahatmya*, the earliest and most important source for the mythology of the **Goddess**, the text describes this goddess in three different manifestations: Mahasaraswati, **Mahalakshmi**, and **Mahakali**. The opening story begins at the creation of the cosmos. As the god **Brahma** emerges from the lotus sprouting from the god **Vishnu's** navel, he is beset by two **demons** named **Madhu** and **Kaitabha**, who try to kill him. Brahma tries to elude the demons, but because Vishnu is fast asleep, overcome by the power of the Goddess, he cannot give Brahma any help. It is only when Brahma praises the Goddess that she leaves Vishnu, letting him awake. She then clouds the demons' minds so that they can be tricked (and killed) by Vishnu. In the pantheon, **Saraswati** is the goddess associated with art, learning, and culture—anything involving the life and activity of the intellectual and aesthetic faculties. Mahasaraswati is also connected with intellect, emphasizing her ability to control people's perceptions. For more information on Mahasaraswati and the goddesses of Hinduism, see David R. Kinsley, *Hindu Goddesses*, 1986.

Mahat

("great one") In the account of **evolution** found in the **Samkhya** philosophical school, mahat is the first evolutionary stage. It consists of the initial disturbance of **prakrti** (primal matter) transforming from its original state of equilibrium. Mahat is called the "great one" because prakrti remains unchanged. Mahat is also known as **buddhi**, the mental faculty for awareness, apperception, and decision making that is believed to be at the root of mental processes. The mental processes facilitated by buddhi spur the development of the next stage in the evolution, **ahamkar** or subjective consciousness, after which the division of the world into subjective and objective spheres proceeds.

Mahavakya

("great utterance") Short statements from the speculative texts known as the **Upanishads**, called "great" because they reveal the true nature of reality and of the Self. One of the most famous mahavakya is **tat tvam asi** ("that thou art"), expressing the unity of the Self with **Brahman**. Other well known utterances are **ayamatma Brahman** ("This Self is Brahman"), **sarvam idam khalu Brahman** ("Truly, this universe is Brahman"), **aham brahmasmi** ("I am Brahman"), and **prajnanam Brahman** ("Knowledge is Brahman"). These great utterances are most important in the **leap philosophy** propounded by the philosopher **Sureshvara**. Leap philosophers believe that complete freedom is possible, but out of our immediate control, in that it cannot be gained by a precisely specified sequence of causes and effects. According to Sureshvara's understanding, when a person whose understanding has been purified hears one of these mahavakyas, the profound truth in the utterance brings the flash of insight that brings final liberation of the soul (**moksha**).

Mahavidyas

A collective name for ten fierce and powerful manifestations of the **Goddess**. According to tradition, the goddess **Sati** assumes these forms one after another, in an attempt to persuade her husband, the god **Shiva**, to allow her to attend a **sacrifice** given by her father **Daksha**. These ten forms are all frightful and fearsome, even to Shiva, showing the ultimate superiority of the Goddess over Shiva. These ten forms are **Kali**, Tara, **Chinnamasta**, Bhuvaneshvari, Bagala, Dhumavati, Kamala, Matangi, Shodashi, and **Bhairavi**. Some of these forms, particularly Kali, have become important **deities** in their own right. For further information see David R. Kinsley, *Hindu Goddesses*, 1986.

Mahayuga

A unit of **cosmic time**. According to traditional Hindu reckoning, time has neither beginning nor end, but alternates between cycles of creation and activity, followed by cessation and quietude. Each of these cycles lasts for 4.32 billion years, with the active phase known as the **Day of Brahma**, and the quiet phase as the Night of Brahma. In one reckoning of cosmic time, the Day of Brahma is divided into one thousand mahayugas ("great cosmic ages"), each of which lasts for 4.32 million years. Each mahayuga is composed of four eras, named the **Krta Yuga**, **Treta Yuga**, **Dvapara Yuga**, and **Kali Yuga**. Each is shorter and more evil than its predecessor; by the end of the Kali Yuga, things have gotten so bad that the only solution is the destruction and recreation of the **earth**, at which time the next Krta Yuga begins.

Mahendravarman

(r. 600–630) Ruler in southern India during the **Pallava dynasty**, when it was a stronghold of Tamil culture. According to tradition, Mahendravarman was born a Jain, but became a devotee (**bhakta**) of the god **Shiva** under the influence of the poet-saint **Appar**. Mahendravarman was a cultured man and a patron of the arts, as well as the author of the play *Mattvavilasa* ("Sport of Drunkards"), which was popular throughout southern India. The rock-cut temples at **Mahabalipuram** were built during his reign. He fought with the surrounding monarchs, especially the **Chalukya** king **Pulakeshin II**; it was in battle with Pulakeshin's forces that Mahendravarman met his death.

Mahesh

("Great Lord") Epithet of the god **Shiva**. See **Shiva**.

Maheshvar

("Great Lord") Epithet of the god **Shiva**. See **Shiva**.

Mahipati

(1715–1790) Writer and hagiographer of the devotional (**bhakti**) poet-saints, particularly those saints connected with the **Varkari Panth**, to which Mahipati himself belonged. The Varkari Panth is a religious community centered around the **worship** of the Hindu god **Vithoba**, whose temple at **Pandharpur** is in the modern state of **Maharashtra**. According to tradition, Mahipati was a civil servant in his home town. One day he was summoned to his job without being able to finish his daily worship. Mahipati did the business at hand, but then resigned his position, vowing never to use his pen except in the service of the saints. Mahipati freely admitted that much of his material on the saints was drawn from earlier works, particularly the ***Bhaktamal*** written by the poet-saint **Nabhadas**. As with Nabhadas, he presents each of his subjects as a paradigm of devotion; the stories reinforce and validate the power of devotion to overcome all obstacles. His major works are the ***Bhaktavijaya*** and the ***Bhaktililamrta***; the former has been translated by Justin E. Abbott and Narhar R. Godbole as *Stories of Indian*

Saints, 1982; parts of the latter by Justin E. Abbott as *The Life of Eknath*, 1981, and *The Life of Tukaram*, 1980.

Mahishasura

In the ***Devimahatmya***, the earliest and most important source for the mythology of the **Goddess**, Mahishasura is the buffalo-**demon** who is responsible for the birth of the Goddess. Mahishasura receives the boon that he cannot be killed by any male and is able to vanquish the gods. They are driven from their heavenly realm and take shelter in the mountains. While they are there, the assembly of the gods let forth their collected radiance (tejas), coalescing into the figure of the Goddess, who represents all their collected power. The Goddess rides off on a **lion** to challenge Mahishasura. He falls in love with her, but when he proposes marriage, she declares she will only marry the man who can defeat her in battle. A fierce battle ensues; Mahishasura is defeated. He tries to elude the Goddess by changing his form several times, but she keeps striking each one with her sword, finally killing him by cutting off his head.

Mahishi

In Hindu mythology, the name of a buffalo-demoness killed by the god **Aiyappa**. Mahishi receives the boon that she can only be killed by a person not born from the union of male and female. To circumvent this boon, Aiyappa is born of a union of the gods **Shiva** and **Vishnu**, when the latter takes the form of the enchantress **Mohini**. When Mahishi is killed, the female figure of **Lila** rises from her body. Lila wants to marry Aiyappa; he agrees that he will marry her in the year a celibate pilgrim does not come to visit him at **Shabari Malai**. Since **women** of childbearing age are forbidden to visit Shabari Malai, and those men who come are required to be celibate, Lila is still waiting for this vow to be fulfilled.

Mahishmati

Ancient city on the **Narmada River** in central India. During the fifth century B.C.E., Mahishmati was the outer boundary for the expansion of the **Aryan**.

Mahmud of Ghazni

(998–1030) Turkish ruler whose capital was at Ghazni (now in modern Afghanistan). Between 1001 and 1027, Mahmud made seventeen raids into India, lured by the tales of India's fabulous wealth. His plundering was aided by the fragmented political life in northern India, which prevented Hindus from forming any effective opposition. Mahmud struck at many of the centers in northern India, particularly pilgrimage centers, which were renowned for their wealth: Multan, **Mathura**, **Thanesar**, **Kanauj** (which never recovered after being sacked in 1018), and finally **Somnath**, from which he reportedly took tremendous booty. Although these raids often entailed iconoclasm (the destruction of religious imagery), as at the **Shiva** temple in Somnath, Mahmud's fundamental motives were economic—replenishing his coffers with as much plunder as possible, and returning to Ghazni before the advent of the hot **season**. As such he is different from some of the later Muslim kings, such the Moghuls, who actually exercised political sway over much of India. Aside from his pillaging raids, Mahmud is associated with the scholar **Alberuni**. Alberuni accompanied Mahmud on one of these expeditions, later using his observations to write an account of Hindu life and culture. See also **Moghul dynasty**.

Maithila

Northern Indian **brahmins** who make up **Pancha Gauda**, one of the five northern brahmin communities; the other four communities are **Kanaujia**, **Gauda**, **Utkala**, and **Saraswat**. Maithila brahmins are a small community, found only in the **Mithila** region in the northern part of modern **Bihar**. Despite the community's size, Maithila brahmins are well known for their commitment to learning and culture, as exemplified by their most famous member, the poet **Vidyapati**.

Maithuna

("copulation") In the secret ritually-based religious practice known as **tantra**, sexual intercourse is the fifth and last of the Five Forbidden Things (**panchamakara**); the panchamakara are used in their actual forms in "left hand" (**vamachara**) tantric ritual, whereas they are represented by symbolic substitutes in "right hand" (**dakshinachara**) tantric ritual. Many traditions in Hindu tantra describe ritualized sexual intercourse as a symbol of the ultimate union of the god **Shiva** and his wife **Shakti**. Ritual sexuality must be seen in the larger tantric context. One of the most pervasive tantric assumptions is the ultimate unity of everything that exists. From a tantric perspective, to affirm that the entire universe is one principle means that the adept must reject all concepts based on dualistic thinking. The "Five Forbidden Things" provide a ritual means for breaking down duality; in this ritual the adept breaks societal norms forbidding consumption of **intoxicants**, nonvegetarian food, and illicit sexuality in a conscious effort to sacralize what is normally forbidden. Tantric adepts cite such ritual use of forbidden things as proof that their practice involves a more exclusive qualification (**adhikara**), and is thus superior to common practice. In some forms of this ritual the woman is the initiate's wife, who is worshiped before intercourse as a manifestation of the **Goddess**. In other cases this ritual intercourse is portrayed as adulterous, usually with a woman of very low status, to magnify the social boundaries being transgressed. This latter practice is uncommon now, at least in southern India, where Brooks describes it as virtually

unknown. For further information see Arthur Avalon (Sir John Woodroffe), *Shakti and Shakta*, 1978; Swami Agehananda Bharati, *The Tantric Tradition*, 1972; and Douglas Renfrew Brooks, *The Secret of the Three Cities*, 1990.

Makarasana

("crocodile seat") In Indian iconography, a base on which an image may be placed. The base is a figure of a crocodile, with a flat part on its back for the image.

Makara Sankranti

Religious festival that falls on the day the sun makes the transition (**sankranti**) into the zodiacal sign of Capricorn (**makara**). According to Western astrology, this occurs around December 20, but in Indian astrology (**jyotisha**), this occurs on January 14. This is one of the few celebrations in the festival **year** marked by the solar rather than the lunar **calendar**. On Makara Sankranti, the sun is reckoned as beginning its "northward journey" (**uttarayana**). This will continue until **Karka Sankranti** six months later, when the sun enters Cancer, and begins its "southward journey" (**dakshinayana**). Since the uttarayana is believed to be more auspicious than its counterpart, the day marking this transition is deemed particularly auspicious. Makara Sankranti is primarily a bathing (**snana**) festival; great numbers of people come to bathe in rivers on that day, especially the **Ganges**. The largest bathing festival on the Ganges is at **Sagar** Island in state of **West Bengal** (also known as **Ganga Sagar**), celebrated as the place where the Ganges empties into the sea at the Bay of Bengal.

Mala

("garland") This word denotes any sort of necklace. Garlands made of flowers are ubiquitous throughout India, both as **offerings** to a **deity**—around whose neck they are placed as adornment—or

Ascetic wearing a mala of sacred wooden beads.

given in the same way to any honored guest as a sign of welcome and respect. Garlands or necklaces made from more permanent materials are important pieces of religious paraphernalia, and in some cases carry clear sectarian associations. Many **Shaivas** wear malas made from **rudraksha** beads, an aniconic form of their patron deity, **Shiva**. In the same way, many **Vaishnavas** will wear a mala made from the wood of the **Tulsi** plant, since this plant is said to be a form of the **goddess Lakshmi**, the spouse of their patron deity **Vishnu**. Although these materials serve as sectarian markers, malas used for ritual purposes can be made from virtually any material. Most favored are substances such as amber, rock crystal, coral, semiprecious stones, and **gemstones**—materials which are durable, valuable, and not formed by human hands.

For ritual purposes, malas are used to keep count during **mantra** recitation (**japa**), by moving one bead through the finger and thumb with each recitation. Such malas are usually strung with 108 pieces. Each mala has one bead set apart from the others; mantra recitation always begins with this bead. This bead symbolizes Mount **Meru**, the mythical mountain that is the cosmic pivot supporting the entire created order. According to established practice, when one has reached the end of the mala and has come back to the Meru bead, one should reverse directions. By virtue of never passing over the Meru bead, one is thus symbolically circling Mount Meru as the center of the universe.

This connection with daily religious practice makes malas powerful religious objects, believed to be charged by their owners' spiritual energy. For this reason, malas are almost never exchanged— except for a mala given by a **guru** to a disciple. Most malas are touched only by the owner. People doing recitation will often keep the hand and mala concealed in a cloth bag (known as a gomukh or "**cow's** mouth"), as a barrier to potentially corrupting outside forces. The conviction that a mala absorbs its owner's spiritual energy also lies behind the taboo on repairing and reusing a broken mala. According to popular belief, a mala breaks because it gradually draws off its owner's negative spiritual forces. Once broken, a mala should therefore be discarded, to prevent the owner from coming back into contact with this potentially damaging energy.

Malabar

Traditional name for the southern Indian coastal region bordering the Arabian sea, in the modern states of **Kerala** and **Karnataka**.

Malamasa

("Impure month") An **intercalary month** inserted into the lunar **calendar** about every 2½ years, to correct the discrepancy between the lunar and the solar calendars. Although this month is necessary to maintain the correspondence between the two calendars—and thus, for example, to keep the spring festivals in the spring—it is considered an unusual event, impure and ritually dangerous.

Malatimadhava

Play written by the **Sanskrit** dramatist **Bhavabhuti** (early 8th c.), who was particularly noted for his ability to express and transmit the play of emotions through language. The play's general plot is the triumphant love between Malati and her beloved Madhava (an epithet of the god **Krishna**), despite numerous obstacles along the way. The drama is noted as an exquisite poetic work, but also because the primary villain is an evil **ascetic**, generally believed to be a member of the extinct ascetic sect known as **Kapalikas**. The Kapalikas were devotees (**bhakta**) of **Shiva**, emulating him in his wrathful form as **Bhairava**: wearing the hair long and matted, smearing the body with ash (preferably from the **cremation ground**), and bearing a club and a skull-bowl (**kapala**). The Kapilikas are cited as indulging in forbidden behavior—drinking wine, eating meat, using cannabis and other **drugs**, performing **human sacrifice**, and orgiastic sexuality—which made them feared. Bhavabhuti's description is one of the earliest references to **Shaiva asceticism**, and thus historically significant. The play has been translated into English by Michael Coulson and published in an anthology titled *Three Sanskrit Plays*, 1981.

Mali

Traditional Indian society was a collection of **endogamous** subgroups (in which marriage is decreed by law to occur only between members of the same group) known as **jatis** ("birth"). The jatis were organized (and their social status determined) by the group's hereditary occupation, over which each group held a monopoly. In traditional northern Indian society, the Malis' hereditary occupation was tending gardens, growing flowers, and making flower garlands (**mala**).

Mallikarjuna

Temple and sacred site (**tirtha**) on the holy mountain **Shrishaila** in **Andhra Pradesh**. The temple is named for its presiding **deity**, the god **Shiva** in his manifestation as the "[Lord] White as Jasmine." Shiva is present at Mallikarjuna in the form of a **linga**, a pillar-shaped image. The Mallikarjuna linga is one of the twelve **jyotirlingas**, a network of sites at which Shiva is uniquely present. Mallikarjuna's charter myth is based on a competition between Shiva's two sons, **Ganesh** and **Skanda**, who agree that the first one to circle the earth will be the first one to be married. Skanda mounts his **peacock** and takes off, sure that he is faster. Ganesh, however, simply walks around Shiva and his wife **Parvati**, as a symbol that they are the entire universe. When Skanda returns, he is very angry to discover that he has been beaten. He leaves **Kailas**, the Himalayan mountain believed to be Shiva's abode, and goes to southern India. Parvati is very upset at the absence of her son, but none of the envoys they send can persuade Skanda to return. Finally, Shiva and Parvati go themselves, landing on Shrishaila mountain. Skanda has already departed for a nearby mountain. Before following after him, his parents consecrate the first site as Mallikarjuna.

As with all the jyotirlingas, Mallikarjuna is deemed a very powerful site. Worshiping this jyotirlinga is said to bring the increase of wealth, freedom from disease, well-being, and any other desired end. The site itself is a difficult place to reach, deep in the jungle on the top of Shrishaila mountain. For this reason, the major festival celebrated here is **Shivaratri**, the most important festival to Shiva during the entire year, when devotees (**bhakta**) come and stay for several days.

Mallinatha

(14th c.?) **Sanskrit** scholar and commentator noted for his commentaries on the plays written by the poet **Kalidasa** (5th c.?); these commentaries have become sources for interpreting the texts. Although the subject of his commentary was largely "secular" poetry, Mallinatha himself was a Jain, and may have been a monk. His work illustrates the important role that the Jains played in the preservation of Indian literary culture. In addition to their commentaries, they copied and recopied the manuscripts, a never-ending task due to the fragile nature of the **palm leaves** on which they were written.

Malviya, Madan Mohan

(1861–1946) Hindu activist and founder of **Benares Hindu University**. Malviya belonged to the first generation of Hindus seeking to reclaim India from British rule; these men were well educated, politically active, and passionately committed to traditional Hindu culture. Benares Hindu University was founded in 1916 to uphold Hindu cultural and philosophical traditions, as well as to educate students in the sciences, preparing them for the modern world. Aside from his work in education, Malviya organized and supported Hindu religious causes, in particular a ban on **cow slaughter** and opposition to a proposed dam on the **Ganges** River at the pilgrimage city of **Haridwar**. The dam would have restricted the free flow of the Ganges, so in 1914 and 1916, he spent considerable energy organizing opposition so that a compromise with the government could be found. For a glowing account of his life, see M. A. Parmanand, *Mahamana Madan Mohan Malviya*, 1985.

Malwa

Traditional name for the plateau in **Madhya Pradesh** centered around the city of **Ujjain**, the region's traditional capital. During the seventeenth and eighteenth centuries, the Malwa region was one of the centers for the **Rajasthani** school of **miniature painting**. The Rajasthani style is generally characterized by a flat perspective. Visual power is derived from bands of vivid colors that often serve as a backdrop to the painting.

Mamsa

("meat") In the secret ritually-based religious practice known as **tantra**, meat is the third of the Five Forbidden Things (**panchamakara**); the panchamakara are used in their actual forms in "left hand" (**vamachara**) tantric ritual, whereas they are represented by symbolic substitutes in "right hand" (**dakshinachara**) tantric ritual. "Respectable" Hindu society strongly condemns the consumption of nonvegetarian food; its ritual use therefore must be seen in the larger tantric context. One of the most pervasive tantric assumptions is the ultimate unity of everything that exists. From a tantric perspective, to affirm that the entire universe is one principle means that the adept must reject all concepts based on dualistic thinking. The "Five Forbidden Things" provide a ritual means for breaking down duality; in this ritual the adept breaks societal norms forbidding consumption of **intoxicants**, nonvegetarian food, and illicit sexuality in a conscious effort to sacralize what is normally forbidden. Tantric adepts cite such ritual use of forbidden things as proof that their practice involves a more exclusive qualification (**adhikara**), and is thus superior to common practice. For further information see Arthur Avalon (Sir John Woodroffe) *Shakti and Shakta*, 1978; Swami Agehananda Bharati, *The Tantric Tradition*, 1977; and Douglas R. Brooks, *The Secret of the Three Cities*, 1990.

Manas

("mind") In the metaphysics of the **Samkhya** school, one of the **six schools**

Pilgrims circling Mt. Kailas traditionally begin the journey with a bath at Manasarovar.

of Hindu **philosophy**, manas is one of the stages in the devolution of **prakrti** (primal matter), resulting in the world that we see around us, in which human souls are subject to reincarnation (**samsara**). Manas evolves from the step known as **ahamkar**—the stage marked by the first sense of Self and subjectivity. The mind (manas) develops as the source of intellectual activity which, colored by this feeling of subjectivity, creates the notion of an individual identity. According to the Samkhyas, concurrent with this mental identity comes the development of the individual's sense organs (**jnanendriyas**) and the organs of action (**karmendriyas**), as well as the subtle elements (**tanmatras**) that are the source for the world's material objects. Although later philosophical schools largely rejected Samkhya **cosmology**, manas became generally accepted as one of the five human sense organs. As the eye perceives sight and the ears perceive sound, the manas perceives mental objects (ideas), allowing the subject to experience them.

Manasa

Manasa is a regional goddess considered to be a form of the **Goddess**. She is worshiped mainly in eastern India, and is primarily associated with snakes and snakebites. As with **Shitala**, the goddess, whose divine presence was considered to be revealed by infection with smallpox, Manasa's divine presence comes violently with snakebites, considered a form of divine **possession**. This conception shows the ambivalent nature of many regional goddesses who are both powerful and dangerous. When Manasa appears, it is always traumatic, and sometimes tragic; such is the nature of human interactions with divinity. Manasa is worshiped both to keep people free from snakebites—a very real concern in an agricultural country with highly venomous snakes—or for the recovery of a person who has been bitten. Her **worship** is marked by annual festivals at which people sing songs in her honor, and which are often marked by divine possession and snake-handling.

Manasarovar

Lake and sacred site (**tirtha**) close to the base of Mount **Kailas** in Tibet. Pilgrims walking around Mt. Kailas traditionally begin their circuit with a bath in the lake before proceeding to the mountain. The lake is traditionally thought to be one of the **Shakti Pithas**, a network of sites

Mandalas can be depicted as complex concentric designs.

sacred to the **Goddess** that spreads throughout the subcontinent. Each Shakti Pitha marks the site where a body part of the dismembered goddess, **Sati**, fell to earth, taking form there as a different goddess; Manasarovar was the palm of Sati's right hand. See also **pitha**.

Manava Dharma Shastra

Another name for the text on religious duty (**dharma**) and social order ascribed to the mythical sage **Manu**. See *Manu Smrti*.

Mandakini River

Himalayan tributary of the **Ganges** River, which joins with the **Alakananda River** at the hill town of **Rudraprayag** in the state of **Uttar Pradesh**. As with all the Himalayan tributaries of the Ganges, the **Mandakini** is considered sacred. Important pilgrimage places (**tirtha**) along it include **Kedarnath**, which is at its headwaters, **Guptakashi**, and Rudraprayag.

Mandala

("circle") As with many **Sanskrit** terms, a word with different meanings in different contexts. In the context of geography it can imply a region, as in the case of the **Braj** region, known as the Braj Mandala. In the context of the **ras lila**, the circle **dance** between the god **Krishna** and his devotees (**bhakta**), mandala refers to the group of devotees as well as to the shape of the dance itself. By extension, mandala can refer to any group of people, although it carries the connotation of people who have gathered for some serious religious purpose. In the context of the secret ritually-based religious practice known as **tantra**, mandala refers to a symbolic diagram used as an aid to meditation, as a ritual accessory, or as a symbolic road map of the spiritual quest. In this context, mandala is more characteristic of Buddhist tantra, with Hindu **tantrikas** more frequently using the terms **yantra** and **chakra**.

Mandaleshvar

("Lord of the Region") Term of respect for the ascetics chosen to head the **Naga** class of the **Dashanami Sanyasis** in their disputations with Christian missionaries. The Dashanami Nagas are groups of renunciant ascetics who are devotees (**bhakta**) of **Shiva** and who formerly made their living as traders and mercenary soldiers. Their rough-and-ready qualities made them effective soldiers but gave them little preparation for formal argument. The Mandaleshvars were chosen by the Nagas from among the more learned **Paramahamsa** ascetics, providing a more coherent and telling opposition to Christian missionaries. An **ascetic** who becomes a Mandaleshvar becomes the spiritual adviser and the teacher of the Dashanami Naga members of the **akhara**, who deem him a spiritual preceptor as much as their own gurus.

Mandana Mishra

(early 9th c.) Founder of the **Bhamati** school of **Advaita Vedanta**, who is traditionally held to be a contemporary of **Shankaracharya**, the Advaita school's greatest figure. The Advaita school upholds a philosophical theory known as monism—the belief that a single Ultimate Reality lies behind all things, which are merely differing forms of that reality. Advaita proponents claim that reality is non-dual (advaita)—all things are nothing but the formless, unqualified **Brahman** (the highest reality in the universe), despite the appearance of difference and diversity. For the Advaitins, the assumption of diversity is a fundamental misunderstanding of the ultimate nature of things, a manifestation of **avidya**. Although often translated as "ignorance," avidya is better understood as the lack of genuine understanding that ultimately causes human beings to be trapped in karmic bondage, reincarnation (**samsara**), and suffering.

Mandana suggests the vivarta ("illusory manifestation") causal relationship to show how the unchanging Brahman is connected with the world as it is perceived. The concept of superimposition (**adhyasa**) shows how humans project a mistaken understanding onto the correct understanding. For example, a piece of rope is mistaken for a snake. Although this judgment is erroneous, one is actually perceiving something real, in this case the rope, but "superimposing" a different and mistaken identity on it, thus "transforming" it into something it is not. In the same way, it is argued, human consciousness begins with the existent reality (Brahman), which is actually there, but superimposes onto it something which is not (the judgment of a diverse world).

Mandana also differed from Shankaracharya on several points, posing problems for his later followers. One of these judgments was that the locus of ignorance was in the Self, since it was absurd to conceive of Brahman as subject to ignorance; another was that there were multiple Selves, since the liberation of one person did not cause the liberation of all. Mandana's comments presuppose the existence of a common (if illusory) world, upon which he felt called to render a judgment; he ended up describing it as anirvachaniya—"that which cannot be described." In his analysis, Mandana also distinguished between two kinds of ignorance—a primal "covering" that keeps one from perceiving the truth, and a "projective" ignorance through which human beings actively obscure things.

Mandapa

("pavilion") The mandapa is an architectural feature found in the **Khajuraho** variation of the **Nagara** architectural style. Usually found in northern India, the Nagara style emphasizes verticality, with the whole temple building culminating in a single highest point. In the Khajuraho style, the entire structure gradually leads up to the central tower, as foothills lead up to the mountains, with the peak of this central tower directly over the temple's primary

Rupmati's Pavilion, Mandu.

image. In this style, the mandapa is the name for a hall of the temple that is usually between the entrance hall (**ardhaman-dapa**) and the main hall (**mahamandapa**).

Mandara

In Hindu mythology, the name of a sacred mountain where the minor god **Kubera** and his court reside. In the myth of the **Tortoise avatar**, Mount Mandara is identified as the churning-stick used to churn the ocean of milk (the mountain's tremendous size makes it an effective churn).

Mandir

("home") In northern India, the most common name for a temple in which the image of a **deity** has been installed and consecrated for **worship**. Although such temples often have facilities for congregational worship, social life, or cultural events, the building's primary function is to serve as the home for the deities assembled there and considered the temple's real owners.

Mandodari

In the ***Ramayana***, the earlier of the two great Indian epics, Mandodari is the wife of the **demon**-king **Ravana**, and the mother of **Indrajit**, **Atikaya** and **Akshakumara**. Despite being a loving and loyal wife to Ravana, Mandodari continually advises him that he has done wrong in kidnapping **Rama's** wife **Sita**. She pleads with him to come to terms with Rama before it becomes necessary to fight. Ravana refuses to do so, because of his pride and his deter-mination to avenge the insult to his sister **Shurpanakha**, who has been mutilated by Rama's brother **Lakshmana**. In the end, this stubbornness costs Ravana his life.

Mandu

Hilltop fort in southwestern **Madhya Pradesh**, about seventy miles south of Indore. Although Mandu is deserted today, it was the capital of a small king-dom until the sixteenth century, and was eventually assimilated into the Moghul empire as a vassal state. During the early seventeenth century Mandu was one of the important centers for the **Rajasthani** style of **miniature painting**. The Rajasthani style is generally characterized by a flat perspective. Visual power is derived from bands of vivid colors that serve as a backdrop to the painting. See also **Moghul dynasty**.

Mandukya Upanishad

One of the speculative religious texts known as the **Upanishads**, which form the latest stratum of the **Vedas**, the oldest Hindu sacred texts. The Mandukya Upanishad's underlying concern is to investigate ultimate questions, in particular the nature of the Self (**atman**). The Mandukya Upanishad is generally considered one of the latest upanishads, based on its brevity—a mere twelve verses—and on its concise articulation of philosophical monism. The first verse praises the sound *Om*, calling it the essence of the entire universe. The second verse identifies the world with **Brahman**, the Self (**atman**) with Brahman, and characterizes the Self as having four quarters. The succeeding verses describe the four quarters of the Self, each of which removes another layer of egoism: The first layer is described as waking consciousness, characterized by perceptions of subject and object; the next is **dream** sleep, which is sheer subjectivity; then deep sleep, which has neither subject nor object; and finally a mysterious state simply called "the fourth" (**turiya**), which is the Self itself.

Further verses identify these first three states as corresponding to the three parts of the sound *Om*: the vowels "a" and "u" (which combine to form the vowel "o"), and the letter "m." The fourth state is said to be "beyond all letters" and without duality. The upanishad explicitly states that to know this brings one final liberation, in which one spontaneously merges with the Self.

Mangalam

("auspicious") Term whose root meaning can be applied to anything believed to bring good fortune: a benedictory formula, a favorable **omen** or portent, an auspicious ceremony such as marriage. It may apply to an object, such as the **mangal sutra**, a necklace worn by married **women** primarily in southern India as a sign that they are married and that their husbands are still living.

Mangal Sutra

("auspicious thread") Symbol worn by married **women** primarily in southern India indicating their married status. Married women are considered to be inherently **auspicious**, since their potential generative power can be expressed through socially sanctioned procreation. Accounts from several centuries ago describe this symbol as a simple thread, often colored yellow with turmeric; in contemporary times the mangal sutra is often an elaborate necklace. Wearing a mangal sutra indicates that a woman has a living husband, thus she is a vessel of auspicious qualities. For these reasons, a woman must remove her mangal sutra upon being widowed, as she must remove all the other symbols of marriage.

Manikarnika

("Jeweled earring") Sacred site (**tirtha**) in the city of **Benares** on the **Ganges** River in the state of **Uttar Pradesh**. The site takes its name from the Manikarnika Kund, a bathing (**snana**) tank supposedly dug by the god **Vishnu**, and into which fell an earring of the god **Shiva**, thus sanctifying the tank by its presence. In modern times the site is better known for the **cremation ground** at Manikarnika **Ghat**. In most Indian cities the cremation ground lies at the margin of the settlement, since its association with death makes it an inauspicious place. However, the Manikarnika cremation ground is in the center of Benares. Despite the normal human desire to ignore and to deny the reality of death, in Benares it is paraded in full view—not to distress or depress people, but to make them confront this reality. Awareness of death has traditionally been considered a great spur to religious life. Since Benares is also one of the **Seven Sacred Cities**, death within the city also carries the hope of ultimate liberation.

Manikkavachakar

(9th c.) Tamil poet-saint who was a devotee (**bhakta**) of the god **Shiva** and the author of the *Tiruvachakam* ("holy utterances"). He is considered the fourth great figure in the Tamil Shaivite tradition, along with the **Nayanar** poet-saints, **Appar**, **Sambandar**, and **Sundaramurtti**. Manikkavachakar's hymns bear witness to the intensity of his individual religious experience and are seen as the culmination of the earlier devotional (**bhakti**) tradition. These hymns are also the basis for the development of the **Shaiva Siddhanta** philosophical school, making him a pivotal figure in southern Indian Shaivism. For further information see Glenn Yocum, *Hymns to the Dancing Siva*, 1982.

Manimegalai

Tamil epic poem which was written as a sequel to "The Jeweled Anklet" (*Shilappadigaram*), connecting its characters with those of the earlier play. The story focuses on a young woman named Manimegalai who, although wooed by the local prince, becomes a Buddhist nun. Manimegalai has numerous debates with people from competing religious traditions, thus giving a picture of sixth century southern Indian religious life.

Manipura Chakra

In many schools of **yoga**, and in the secret ritually-based religious practice known as **tantra**, the manipura chakra is one of the six psychic centers (**chakras**) believed to exist in the **subtle body**. The subtle body is an alternate physiological system, existing on a different plane of reality than gross matter, but corresponding to the material body. The six psychic centers are visualized as multi-petaled lotus flowers running roughly along the spine, connected by three vertical channels. Each of the chakras has symbolic associations with various human capacities, different subtle elements (**tanmatras**), and different seed syllables (**bijaksharas**) formed from the letters of the **Sanskrit** alphabet, encompassing all sacred sound. Above and below these centers are the bodily abodes of **Shiva** (awareness) and **Shakti** (power), the two divine principles through which the entire universe has come into being. The underlying assumption behind the concept of the subtle body is the homology of macrocosm and microcosm, an essential Hindu idea since the time of the mystical texts known as the **Upanishads**.

The six chakras are traditionally enumerated starting from the bottom; the manipura chakra is the third. It is visualized as a ten-petaled lotus, located in the region of the navel. The petals each contain a seed, in this case the consonants from retroflex "dha" to "pha." The manipura chakra is identified as the bodily seat for the subtle element of **fire**, the power of which is believed to bring about digestion. For further information see Arthur Avalon (Sir John Woodroffe), *Shakti and Shakta*, 1978; and Philip S. Rawson, *The Art of Tantra*, 1973.

Manipuri

One of the classical **dance** forms of India; some of the others are **Bharatanatyam**, **Orissi**, **Kuchipudi**, **Kathak**, and **Kathakali**. Like much of traditional Indian culture, classical dance shows strong regional identification; Manipuri is found only in the state of Manipur, nestled between Burma and **Assam** in eastern India. Developed in the eighteenth century, Manipuri reflects the importance of **Vaishnava** devotionalism. One of the principal dance genres involves acting out episodes from the life of the god **Krishna**, especially the **Ras lila** and his dalliance with his lover **Radha**. In other genres dancers play a two-headed drum or cymbals, leaping dramatically during the performance. This form has roots in devotional Vaishnavism, particularly the ecstatic singing and dancing associated with the **Gaudiya Vaishnava** community in Bengal. For further information see Mohan Khokar, *Traditions of Indian Classical Dance*, 1984.

Man Lila

A divine play (**lila**) between **Krishna** and his devotees (**bhakta**). In this lila, one of Krishna's female companions feigns wounded pride (man), usually because he makes some sort of error, such as calling her by another woman's name. For some time she pretends to be angry, but is eventually won over by his charm and undivided attention. This motif of a woman feigning anger—to make her lover flatter and fawn over her, and to sweeten the joy of the eventual reconciliation—has a venerable history in **Sanskrit** poetry. In modern times, this lila is often presented in devotional theatrical presentations, which are themselves known as lilas ("plays"), since their function is to reveal the work of the divine.

Man-Lion Avatar

Fourth **avatar** or incarnation of the god **Vishnu**; the man-lion's form is usually rendered as the head and shoulders of a **lion**, and the torso and legs of a man. As with all the avatars of Vishnu, the Man-Lion avatar comes to restore the cosmic balance, which has been thrown out of equilibrium by the disproportionate power of some individual. In this case the source of trouble is the **demon**-king **Hiranyakashipu**, who by the power of his **asceticism** (**tapas**) has gained three boons from the gods: that he cannot be killed by man nor beast, by day or by night, and neither inside nor outdoors.

Portrait of the god Vishnu's Man-Lion avatar. Vishnu takes this form to defeat a demon who has conquered heaven and earth.

These boons render him virtually invulnerable; Hiranyakashipu proceeds to conquer the earth and drive the gods from **heaven**. He oppresses his son **Prahlada**, who despite his father's power remains a sincere devotee (**bhakta**) of Vishnu. The more devotion Prahlada shows to Vishnu the more abuse his father gives him, until finally Hiranyakashipu, maddened at the thought that someone refuses to **worship** him, is at the point of killing Prahlada.

Prahlada calls on Vishnu for help, and the Man-Lion, a being which is neither man nor beast, bursts forth from a pillar in the palace. The Man-Lion seizes Hiranyakashipu in the palace doorway, which is neither inside nor out, at twilight, which is neither day nor night, and uses his sharp claws to tear out the demon's entrails, killing him. Once Hiranyakashipu has been killed, Vishnu installs the righteous Prahlada as the king of the realm. This action reveals an important truth about the Hindu view of reality. Although Prahlada is a "demon" (asura), he is not inherently evil, nor is he simply a being to be exterminated. All kinds of beings have their rightful place in the Hindu cosmos—problems come when they gain disproportionate power and use it to their own ends.

Manmatha

("churning the mind") Epithet of the **Krishna**, reflecting his ability to bewitch and beguile his devotees (**bhakta**). See **Krishna**.

Mansa Devi

Presiding **deity** in the village of Manimajara, located in the **Shiwalik Hills**, a short distance from Chandigarh, and one of the nine **Shiwalik goddesses**. According to local tradition, this is one of the **Shakti Pithas**, a network of sites sacred to the **Goddess** that spreads throughout the subcontinent. Each Shakti Pitha marks the site where a body part of the dismembered goddess **Sati** fell to **earth**, taking form there as a different goddess; Mansa Devi was Sati's head. The word *mansa* means "wish," and it is claimed that Mansa Devi will grant whatever wish the devotee (**bhakta**) brings to her. There is another temple of Mansa Devi on the hill above the bathing (**snana**) ghats in the sacred city of **Haridwar**; here, too, the officiants claim that the presiding deity will fulfill all one's wishes.

The charter myth for the Manimajara Mansa Devi, set in the time of the Moghul emperor **Akbar**, illustrates her power and concern for her devotees. Akbar appoints a **Rajput** chieftain to manage the land around Manimajara. One year the chieftain is unable to pay his taxes because bad weather has ruined the crops. The chieftain is put in prison, but his plight moves one of Mansa Devi's devotees, who implores her to intervene in his behalf. The chieftain is released and the taxes waived; when the chieftain discovers how this has happened, he is so grateful that he erects a temple in honor of the goddess. See also **pitha** and **Moghul dynasty**.

Manthara

In the *Ramayana*, the earlier of the two great Indian epics, Manthara is the hunchbacked maid of King **Dasharatha's** wife, **Kaikeyi**. Manthara's whisperings against Dasharatha's son **Rama**, the god-king who is the epic's protagonist, slowly poisons Kaikeyi's mind. She succeeds in convincing the queen that after Rama has been crowned Dasharatha's heir, she and her son **Bharata** will be little better than slaves, if they are allowed to live at all. Goaded by Manthara, Kaikeyi decides to demand two boons Dasharatha gave her years before. With the first boon she dictates that Rama be sent in exile to the forest for fourteen years, and with the second she stipulates that her son Bharata be crowned heir in Rama's place.

The epic's oldest version, the *Ramayana* of **Valmiki**, paints Manthara as a genuine villain. There is little explanation for her actions, although given the belief in **karma**, her physical disabilities would have been seen as revealing moral and spiritual deformity as well. In the *Ramayana*, written by the poet-saint **Tulsidas** (1532–1623?), Manthara's behavior is ultimately attributed to the gods who send the **goddess Saraswati** to confound Manthara's mind, setting in motion the chain of events leading to the **demon Ravana's** death. In typical fashion, Tulsidas puts a more charitable spin on the event, relating it to Rama's ultimate purpose for being born on earth.

Mantra

In its most basic sense, sacred sound. A mantra is a collection of phonemes that may or may not have syntactic meaning as actual words, since their importance comes not from the meaning of the utterances, but from the very sounds themselves. Mantras are believed to confer power and varying spiritual capacities on those who have been given the qualification (**adhikara**) to use them. The qualification comes from being given the mantra by one's teacher, believed to transmit not only the sounds of the mantra, but the power associated with it. This living transmission is considered an essential feature in "possessing" the mantra; for this reason mantras learned in other contexts are believed to be ineffective. The idea of mantra as sacred sound is traced back to the **Vedas**, the oldest Hindu religious texts. One of the most common mantras, the **Gayatri** mantra, is actually a verse from the **Rg Veda** (3.62.10). The use of mantras is emphasized in the secret ritually-based religious practice known as **tantra**. For further information see Arthur Avalon (Sir John Woodroffe), *Shakti and Shakta*, 1978; Swami Agehananda Bharati, *The Tantric Tradition*, 1977; and Douglas Renfrew Brooks, *The Secret of the Three Cities*, 1990.

Mantraraja

("king of mantras") Name given to a particular eight-syllable **mantra** associated with the god **Vishnu**, in which he is addressed as **Narayana**. The mantra itself is "**Om** Namo Narayana" ("Om, homage to Narayana"). This mantra is particularly important in the **Shrivaishnava** religious community, which developed in southern India in the twelfth century. The mantra is especially associated with the community's founder, **Ramanuja**. Faithful recitation of this mantra is said to bestow residence in Vishnu's heavenly abode, **Vaikuntha**.

Mantrashastra

The name for the body of learning that focuses on **mantras** or sacred formulae: their classification, meaning, and use. Some of this learning exists in textual form, but given the secret nature of the subject matter, and the traditional insistence on oral, personal transmission from a religious teacher, much exists only in oral form.

Manu

In Hindu mythology, the Manus are fourteen semidivine kings, perceived as the progenitors of the human race and rulers over the universe. According to traditional belief, time has neither beginning nor end but alternates between cycles of **creation** and activity, followed by cessation and quietude. Each of these cycles lasts for 4.32 billion years; the active phase is known as the **Day of Brahma**; the quiet phase is known as the Night of Brahma. In one instance of **cosmic time**, each Day of Brahma is divided into fourteen equal periods, each ruled by one of the fourteen Manus.

Manu Smrti

("Laws of **Manu**") One of the **smrtis** or "remembered" texts, a class of literature deemed important, but less authoritative than the **shrutis** or "heard" texts. This smrti is ascribed to the sage Manu and is an example of one of the **Dharma Shastras**—manuals prescribing rules for correct human behavior and ideal social life. The Dharma Shastras are usually ascribed to mythic sages, reinforcing the authority of these texts. Manu's text is by far the most influential of the Dharma Shastras and is believed to have been composed just before the beginning of the common era.

Manu's text shows the break between the **Dharma Sutras** and the Dharma Shastras, for it is plainly intended as a blueprint for an entire society, rather than a set of rules for a particular **brahmin** group. The introductory chapter details the **creation** of the world and the consequent social order; the chapter ends by summarizing the rest of the volume's contents. The next five chapters focus on the four major social groups (**varnas**) and the four **stages of life** (ashramas), using material from the Dharma Sutras.

Manu's themes in chapters seven through nine sharply diverge from earlier sources. Chapter seven defines the duties of a king. Chapters eight and nine treat various legal matters that might come before the king for adjudication. Manu attempts to put all of these under eighteen thematic headings. The material in these chapters encompasses all manner of criminal and civil law, from assault and theft to contract law and marital duties laying down a legal framework for the stable governance of society.

The remaining chapters are less original. The tenth chapter discusses occupations that members of the different varnas may follow in times of distress (**apaddharma**), when normal social rules no longer apply. The eleventh talks about gifts to brahmins and rites of expiation (**prayashchitta**), remaining faithful to the Dharma Sutras. Manu's final chapter has a more abstract and speculative nature, focusing on the workings of **karma** and describing the consequences of various good and evil acts. The text has been translated numerous times; see Wendy Doniger O'Flaherty and Brian K. Smith, *The Laws of Manu*, 1991.

Manvantara

Manvantara is the name of an era in one instance of **cosmic time**. According to traditional belief, time has neither beginning nor end but alternates between cycles of creation and activity, followed by cessation and quietude. Each of these cycles lasts for 4.32 billion years; the active phase is known as the **Day of Brahma** and the quiet phase is known as the Night of Brahma. In one instance of cosmic time, each Day of Brahma is divided into fourteen equal periods, each ruled by one of the fourteen Manus. Manus are celebrated as the sovereigns of the **earth** and are perceived as semidivine beings who are the progenitors of the human race. Currently we are living in the seventh age, with seven yet to come. The **Manu** of this present age, Vaivasvata, was saved from **pralaya** (universal destruction) by **Vishnu** in his form as the **Fish avatar**. Vaivasvata is regarded as the progenitor of the **Solar Line** of Kings.

Maranashaucha

The ritual impurity (**ashaucha**) caused by death (marana). All bodily effluvia (**hair**, spittle, pus, **blood**, etc.) are considered to be sources of impurity, but a **corpse** is the most impure thing of all. Any death immediately causes the most violent impurity, affecting the entire family. For the family's safety, this impurity must be carefully contained and managed through the funeral rites (**antyeshthi samskara**). Here one sees the significant ritual difference between **birth** and death. Although birth also brings impurity (**sutakashaucha**) on the family, because of the bodily products attending it, this impurity is considered less violent, because the birth of a child is an auspicious, life-affirming event. Death, on the other hand, is seen as bringing bad fortune, and thus the family must not only take care of this impurity, but must also get rid of the **inauspiciousness** caused by the death.

Maratha

Traditional Indian society was a collection of **endogamous** subgroups (in which marriage is decreed by law to occur only between members of the same group) known as **jatis**. Jatis were organized (and their social status determined) by the group's hereditary occupation, over which each group held a monopoly. The Maratha jati was one of the dominant landholding communities in the **Maharashtra** region, along with the **Kunbis**. They were most concentrated on the Konkan coast and the inland region around the city of Pune. The Marathas were tough peasant farmers who by the middle of the eighteenth century had forged a large but short-lived empire, the Maratha confederacy, extending over much of northern and central India. By the latter part of the eighteenth century, the confederacy had fragmented into various smaller states.

Maratha Dynasty

(17th–19th c.) Central Indian dynasty in the region of the western state of **Maharashtra**, particularly along the Konkan coast of the Arabian Sea. The dynasty was founded by the Maratha chieftain **Shivaji**, who spent most of his life locked in a bitter struggle with the Moghul empire. At Shivaji's death in 1680, the Marathas controlled only a small strip of land in western Maharashtra. After the death of the Moghul emperor **Aurangzeb** in 1707, the Moghul empire began to disintegrate; the Marathas filled the political vacuum. At its peak in the mid-1700s, the Maratha Confederacy controlled northern and central India from coast to coast, stretching as far north as Delhi and the **Ganges** River basin. Expansionism was halted in 1761, when the Maratha army was defeated by the Afghans at Panipat in the state of **Haryana**, a short distance north of Delhi. Both groups of combatants sustained major losses in the battle, rendering them unable to contest the arrival of the British. A little more than a decade later, the Maratha Confederacy had fragmented into constituent states, each with its own capital. Of these, the Bhonsle dynasty had its capital in the city of **Nagpur**, the Holkar dynasty had its capital in the city of Indore, the Gaikwad dynasty had its capital in the city of Baroda. The Scindia dynasty had capitals in Gwalior and **Ujjain**, while the **Peshwa** dynasty had its capital in Pune. All except for the last survived as princely states until Indian independence in 1947. See also **Moghul dynasty**.

Margali

Ninth month in the Tamil solar **year**, corresponding to the northern Indian solar month of Dhanush (the zodiacal sign of Sagittarius), usually falling within December and January. The existence of several different calendars is one clear sign of the continuing importance of regional cultural patterns. One way that the Tamils retain their culture is by preserving their traditional **calendar**. Tamil is one of the few regional languages in India with an ancient, well-established literary tradition. See also **Tamil months**, **Tamil Nadu**, and **Tamil language**.

Margashirsha

According to the lunar **calendar**, by which most Hindu religious festivals are determined, Margashirsha is the ninth month in the lunar **year**, usually falling within November and December. Margashirsha is generally considered an inauspicious month; the only major festivals in Margashirsha are **Bhairava Jayanti**, **Utpanna Ekadashi**, and **Mokshada Ekadashi**.

Maricha

In the *Ramayana*, the earlier of the two great Indian epics, Maricha is the uncle of **Ravana**, the **demon**-king of **Lanka** who is the epic's antagonist. After Ravana's sister **Shurpanakha** has been insulted and mutilated by **Rama** and **Lakshmana**, the epic's protagonists, Ravana decides to take revenge by abducting Rama's wife, **Sita**. He enlists Maricha's help to kidnap Sita. Maricha takes the form of a golden **deer**. When Sita sees the deer, she asks Rama to kill it for her. Rama pursues the deer into the forest, giving **Lakshmana** strict instructions to stay with Sita no matter what happens. Rama pursues the deer some distance from their home and finally gets close enough to shoot it.

With his dying breath, Maricha cries out Lakshmana's name in a voice that sounds like Rama's, intending to draw Lakshmana away and leave Sita unprotected. Given his orders, Lakshmana is at first unwilling to leave. He finally leaves when Sita, in an uncharacteristic display of suspicion and anger, accuses Lakshmana of withholding help to Rama because he wants to have her to himself. At this unjust allegation, Lakshmana is spurred into action. Before he leaves he draws a magical protective circle around Sita, instructing her that no harm can befall her as long as she stays in the circle. Ravana, in the form of an old **ascetic**, approaches Sita, **begging** for alms. Out of respect for an ascetic, Sita steps out of the circle to offer the alms. Ravana reveals his true form and carries her away.

Marichi

In Hindu mythology, one of the six **sons** of **Brahma**, all of whom become great sages. All are "mind-born," meaning that Brahma's thoughts are enough to bring them into being. The others are **Kratu**, **Angiras**, **Pulastya**, **Pulaha**, and **Atri**.

Mariyammai

Originally a local **goddess** in southern India, whose cult has become a regional phenomenon. Mariyammai embodies many of the contradictions and tensions associated with Hindu conceptions of the Goddess in general. According to her charter myth, Mariyammai is originally a **brahmin** woman, who is beheaded because of her husband's jealousy. She is brought back to life, but not before her body has become switched with that of another woman, this one an **untouchable**. Mariyammai's brahmin head and untouchable body symbolize the imperfect joining of brahminical Hindu and southern Indian culture, as well as the nebulous status of brahmins as the "head" of southern Indian society.

Markandeya

A sage in Hindu mythology. Markandeya is best-known for two mythic exploits, one of which is associated with the god **Shiva** and the other with the god **Vishnu**. According to tradition, Markandeya is a very intelligent and religious boy who is devoted to Shiva and proficient in all the branches of learning. This seemingly unlimited potential is even more poignant because he learns that he is fated to die at sixteen. Shortly before his sixteenth birthday, Markandeya begins to **worship** Shiva with even greater fervor. Because of the boy's accumulated religious merits, the servants of **Yama**, the god of death, cannot get near him. So Yama himself has to go for Markandeya. When Yama throws his noose over Markandeya to draw out the boy's soul, it also loops over the statue of Shiva to which Markandeya is clinging. Shiva arises from the image and kills Yama, although he later relents and brings him back to life.

Markandeya's other mythic exploit is a vision of **pralaya**, the universal dissolution of the cosmos. One evening as he is meditating, the sky grows dark, the wind rises, and rain falls until the earth is inundated with water. Markandeya is swept this way and that, until he comes to an enormous banyan tree with an infant sitting in it. Markandeya is drawn to the child and sees that the entire universe is inside this infant boy. He wanders inside the child for some time until he falls out of the child's mouth; then he sees the infant and the banyan tree again. Markandeya realizes that the infant is Vishnu, but before he can reach him again, the child has disappeared.

Markandeya Purana

One of the eighteen traditional **puranas**, the sectarian compendia of mythic stories and sacred lore that are among the most important sources for modern Hinduism. **Markandeya** is said to have been an ancient sage, but he was not intimately connected with any particular **deity**. In this respect, the *Markandeya Purana* is different from most of the others, which have a clear sectarian bias. This purana is noted for one of its subsections, the *Devimahatmya*. Describing the ultimate power behind all things as female, the *Devimahatmya* is the earliest and most important textual source for the mythology of the **Goddess**. Scholars contend that although this text is the first place that this theological conviction appears, it must have existed earlier, since it appears in this text fully developed.

Marriage, Eight Classical Forms

Dharma literature (texts prescribing rules for correct human behavior and ideal social life) recognizes eight forms of marriage: **Brahma**, **Daiva**, **Arsha**, **Prajapatya**, **Asura**, **Gandharva**, **Rakshasa**, and **Paishacha**. The first four forms were approved (**prashasta**). In each case, the father of the bride was responsible for arranging the marriage: in the Brahma form, he gave his **daughter** as a gift without conditions; in the Daiva form, she was given as a sacrificial fee; in the Arsha form, in exchange for a pair of cattle for **sacrifice**; and in the Prajapatya form, with the condition that the husband and wife perform their duties together.

The other four forms were considered reprehensible forms of marriage (**aprashasta**). Two of these four were tolerated: the Asura form, in which the bride was exchanged for money, and the Gandharva form, in which bride and groom plighted their troth by mutual consent—that is, through consensual sexual intercourse. The final two forms were strictly forbidden: Rakshasa, in which the bride was forcibly abducted; and Paishacha, in which a man took sexual advantage of a woman who was insentient—the result of drunkenness, a deep sleep, or drugging. It is interesting to note that all of these forms were deemed to create a valid marriage—even the two that were forbidden. The aim in sanctioning such forbidden marriages was not to encourage such actions, but to give the woman the legal status of a wife. In contemporary times most of these forms of marriage are no longer practiced except for the Brahma marriage, which carries the highest status, and the Asura marriage. For further information see Pandurang Vaman Kane (trans.), *A History of Dharmasastra*, 1968; and Raj Bali Pandey, *Hindu Samskaras*, 1969. Despite

In many traditional Hindu marriage ceremonies, the groom's turban is attached to the bride's sari, binding the couple together.

their age, they remain the best sources for traditional Hindu religious rites.

Marriage Ceremonies

In India, virtually everybody gets married. Marriage is a religious duty for **twice-born** men, satisfying one of their **Three Debts**, in this case the debt to their ancestors. Twice-born men are householders born into one of the three "twice-born" groups in Indian society, **brahmin**, **kshatriya**, or **vaishya**. Such men are eligible to receive the adolescent religious **initiation** known as the "second birth." For most Hindu **women**, being wives and mothers defines their identity. Marriage is also the event by which families are formed and grow. Since the family is considered the bedrock of Hindu society, for most people, marriage is the single most important event in their lives.

The great significance of marriage in Hindu culture means that this life-changing event is attended with potential peril because there is no certainty of success. Other potential dangers come from the inauspicious nature of certain times, people, and the belief that this **inauspiciousness** may bring bad fortune for the future. Finally, given that the bride and groom are the center of attention in the days before the marriage, there is the danger that other people's ill will and envy may unleash malevolent and unseen forces. As with many of the other life transitions, Hindu marriages are attended with considerable attention to discerning the unseen forces that could have a negative affect on the couple's future life and protecting the bride and groom from them. The wedding is always performed at an astrologically auspicious time, to start the marriage on the best possible note. In the days before the wedding, the bride is often secluded, keeping her from coming in contact with people or things deemed inauspicious. On their wedding day both the bride and groom are anointed and adorned similar to the **deities** in a temple—according to popular belief, on their wedding day, the couple become **Lakshmi** and **Vishnu**, god and **goddess**. This heightened status puts them in ritual danger when they are outside in the world, both from the legion of sources for ritual impurity (**ashaucha**), and because they are believed to be more susceptible to the evil eye (**nazar**) and other forms of **witchcraft**. These dangers are countered by amulets and various **rites of protection** when the bride or groom must be in the public eye, such as when the groom and his group of friends travel in triumphal procession to the wedding hall, as is common in northern India. Once inside, the danger is less pressing, since they are in a closed and ritually structured environment, surrounded by family and friends.

There is no single Hindu marriage ceremony, as is clear from the eight classical forms of marriage recognized in the **dharma literature**. Of these eight, the two forms generally practiced today are the **Asura** form, in which the groom's family gives money as a **brideprice** to obtain the bride; and the **Brahma** form, in which the bride's family gives their daughter to the groom, without making any conditions on him at all (although in contemporary times the groom's family can usually expect a **dowry** with the bride). The Brahma marriage carries much higher social status and is the most popular form. Although in such a marriage the wedding ceremonies have regional and sectarian variation, certain common rites reveal important cultural assumptions.

The two major themes in a Hindu marriage are the transfer of the bride from her family to her husband's family, and the indissoluble merging of bride and groom into a new entity, the married couple. The transfer of the bride is done in the **kanyadan** ritual, the "gift of the virgin" performed by the bride's father. The bride and groom's marital union is symbolized by several common rites, including **panigrahana**, in which the groom takes the bride's hand as a sign of their union. Another such rite, considered the defining point of the marriage, is the **saptapadi**, the "seven steps" which the bride and groom take together. The seventh step completes the bride's transfer to the groom's family; it is at this point that the marriage becomes indissoluble. In modern times the saptapadi is often performed in conjunction with another ceremony, the **agnipradakshinam** ("circumambulating the fire"). Instead of taking seven steps, the bride and groom make seven revolutions around a small fire. On one hand, the presence of fire shows that marriage is a **yajna** or Vedic **sacrifice**. On the other, since the fire is considered to be the Vedic god **Agni**, he becomes the divine witness to the marriage. During the circumambulations the bride and groom are often physically joined by tying part of his turban to the edge of her sari. This visible bond between them is yet another sign of the inner union that has just been formed.

As described, in marriage the wife's identity is "assimilated" to her husband's, rather than some sort of mutual transformation. In northern India, the bride lives with her husband's family after the marriage; her new identity stems solely from her relationship with her husband, whereas his identity remains essentially unchanged, although augmented by marriage. For further information see Pandurang Vaman Kane (trans.), *A History of Dharmasastra*, 1968; and Raj Bali Pandey, *Hindu Samskaras*, 1969. For information on modern practice, see Lawrence Babb, *The Divine Hierarchy*, 1975. See also **marriage, eight classical forms**.

Marriage Prohibitions

As in other cultures, Hindus have well-defined rules and prohibitions regarding whom one should and should not marry—marriages should be **endogamous**, that is, between members of the same social subgroup (in this case, the **jati**). Within this larger community, it is generally accepted that the bride and groom should not come from the same **gotra** or the same **pravara**—both mythic lineages detailing relationships with ancient sages. The other strong prohibition was on marrying those with whom one had a **sapinda** relationship—common ancestry. According to one well-known code of law, the *Mitakshara*, the sapinda relationship ceases after the seventh generation on the father's side, and the fifth generation on the mother's. People with common ancestors beyond those boundaries may contract a valid marriage.

This sapinda formula was routinely ignored, particularly in parts of southern India, where marrying one's maternal uncle's daughter was not only permitted, but considered commendable. While some of the texts in the **dharma literature** condemn the practice as an abomination, others note that this is a practice peculiar to the south, where it is permitted only as part of the family's customary practice (**kulachara**).

There is a long history for cross-cousin marriage in southern India; it is a common practice even today. Among southern Indian brahmins, there is some speculation that their relatively small population—about four percent of the total—made it impossible to find **brahmin** spouses under the strict criteria. Given the competing imperatives to marry other brahmins and to observe the lineage restrictions, this custom was deemed less important.

The village of Martand is known for its ruins of an eighth-century temple built to the sun god.

Mars

In Hindu astrology (**jyotisha**), a **planet** associated with activity, war, and misfortune. Due to these associations, Mars is considered a strong yet malignant planetary force. **Tuesday,** the **day** of the **week** ruled by Mars, is considered an inauspicious day, a day on which people often perform **rites of protection** to safeguard themselves from Mars's baleful influence.

Marshall, Sir John

Director General of the Archeological Survey of India (ASI) from 1901 until his retirement in 1931. During his tenure as director, Marshall discovered then excavated the cities of the **Indus Valley civilization**, for which he received his British knighthood. He also carried on the work of his predecessors at the ASI, particularly **Sir Alexander Cunningham**, documenting and cataloging India's archeological artifacts.

Martand

Village in the state of **Jammu** and **Kashmir** about forty miles southeast of Shrinagar, the capital. Martand is noted as an architectural history site, best known for its temple to the **sun** god, built during the eighth century. The temple ruins are in a mountain meadow, offering spectacular views of the surrounding mountains.

Marut

Class of minor **deities** considered to be the companions of **Indra**, god of the storm. The Maruts are described as having a flashing color, armed with golden weapons symbolic of lightning, and roaring like **lions**.

Marwari

Northern Indian trading community named after its place of origin, the Marwar region surrounding Jodhpur in **Rajasthan**. The Marwaris have spread all over northern India; many of them have become extremely wealthy. The Marwaris are stereotyped as ruthless and cutthroat in their business practices, yet at the same time, they are munificent in donations to religious causes, reflecting traditional religious piety. The most successful Marwari families, such as the **Birlas**, still control large parts of the Indian economy. Marwari support and patronage is an important consideration for all northern Indian political parties.

Masi

Eleventh month in the **Tamil year**, corresponding to the northern Indian month of Kumbha (the zodiacal sign of Aquarius), usually falling within February and March. The existence of several different calendars is a sign of the continuing importance of regional cultural patterns. One way that the Tamils retain their culture is by preserving their traditional **calendar**. Tamil is one of the few regional languages in India with an ancient, well-established literary tradition. See also **Tamil months**, **Tamil Nadu**, and **Tamil language**.

Materialist

The name for a philosophical school espousing the belief that the individual and the physical body are identical. The body is composed of certain physical elements, so with the death of the body, the individual ceases to exist. Since the materialists believed there is no life after death, they also believed there is no reason to engage in religious activities in the hope of a better afterlife. The materialist believes that one should live well, enjoy life to the fullest, and then die. This viewpoint was first espoused by **Ajita Keshakambalin**, who was a contemporary of the Buddha. Its later adherents were called both Lokayata ("worldly") and Charvaka (after the supposed founder). The materialists were universally reviled by the other philosophical schools, all of whom considered their rejection of religious life dangerous. One of their philosophical theories, and a sign of their rootedness in concrete experience, was their position on the **pramanas**, the means by which human beings can gain true and accurate knowledge. Most schools admitted at least three such pramanas—perception (**pratyaksha**), inference (**anumana**), and authoritative testimony (**shabda**). In contrast, the materialists accepted only perception, denying the validity of the other two. Emphasis is placed on experience and the belief that what is directly before one's eyes is indisputable.

Math

(often translated as "monastery") A dwelling place for **ascetics**; usually a large, well-settled dwelling for a number of ascetics belonging to an established order. The four most famous maths are believed to have been established by the philosopher **Shankaracharya**: the **Jyotir Math** in the Himalayan town of **Joshimath**; the **Govardhan Math** in the city of **Puri**, on the Bay of Bengal; the

Sharada Math in the city of **Dwaraka** on the Arabian Sea; and the **Shringeri Math** in the town of **Shringeri** in southern India. These maths are the headquarters for the four major groups in the **Dashanami** sect **Sanyasis**, renunciant ascetics who are devotees (**bhakta**) of the god **Shiva**. Although most maths do not have the status of these four, they all serve as ascetic and religious centers.

Mathura

City and sacred site (**tirtha**) in the **Braj** region of the state of **Uttar Pradesh**, about ninety miles south of Delhi. Mathura is known as the town in which the god **Krishna** was born. The **Krishna Janam Bhumi**, purportedly the site of his birth, can still be seen today. Krishna was spirited out of Mathura on that same night because his wicked uncle **Kamsa**, who was king of Mathura, had killed all of Krishna's older siblings at birth. When Krishna came of age he returned to Mathura, killed Kansa, and claimed his patrimony. As with sites in the Braj region, Mathura is full of associations with Krishna's earthly life; these allow his devotees (**bhakta**) access to him, in that they can visualize the places he visited, and thus through imagination take part in his mythic deeds themselves.

Mathurakavi

(10th c.) The last of the **Alvars**, a group of twelve poet-saints who lived in southern India between the seventh and tenth centuries. All the Alvars were devotees (**bhakta**) of the god **Vishnu**, and their emphasis on passionate devotion (**bhakti**) to a personal god, conveyed through hymns sung in the **Tamil language**, transformed and revitalized Hindu religious life. According to tradition, Mathurakavi was the disciple of **Nammalvar**, to whom he was led from northern India by a great light in the southern sky. By asking a question about the supreme spirit, Mathurakavi was able to rouse Nammalvar from a yogic trance in which the latter had spent much of his life. From that point Mathurakavi served Nammalvar as his **guru**. Whereas the other Alvars were quite prolific, Mathurakavi wrote only ten songs, all in praise of his master. For further information see Kamil Zvelebil, *Tamil Literature*, 1975; John Stirling Morley Hooper, *Hymns of the Alvars*, 1929; and A. K. Ramanujan (trans.), *Hymns for the Drowning*, 1981.

Matrilinear Succession

(Marumakkatayam) Most of Hindu society is overwhelmingly patrilineal (organized around the father's familial line). However, the **Nayars** of the state of **Kerala** in southern India base society on matrilineal succession (the mother's familial line). Matrilineal succession was practiced from very early times, although it had largely disappeared by the middle of the twentieth century. Under a matrilineal system, both descent and **inheritance** are passed on through the mother's line, which is center of the family. The woman's husband lives in her family home, but has no claim upon their children, and no claim on any of their marital property. A man has a certain amount of control over his own family's ancestral property—which he is often called to manage—but the property ultimately is inherited by his sister's children, rather than his own. In many cases the woman's "official" husband never actually consummates the marriage, and the woman is free to form long-term liaisons with other men, according to her choice.

Matsya

("fish") In the secret ritually-based religious practice known as **tantra**, fish is the second of the "Five Forbidden Things" (**panchamakara**), which, in "left hand" (**vamachara**) tantric ritual, are used in their actual forms, but are represented by symbolic substitutes in "right hand" (**dakshinachara**) tantric ritual. "Respectable" Hindu society strongly condemns the consumption of nonvegetarian food, so this ritual use must be seen in the larger tantric context. One of the underlying tantric assumptions is the ultimate unity of everything that exists. From a tantric perspective, to affirm that the entire universe is one principle means that the adept must reject all concepts based on dualistic thinking. The "Five Forbidden Things" provide a ritual means for breaking down duality. In this ritual the adept breaks societal norms forbidding consumption of **intoxicants**, nonvegetarian food, and illicit sexuality in a conscious effort to sacralize what is normally forbidden. Tantric adepts cite such ritual use of forbidden things as proof that their practice involves a more exclusive qualification (**adhikara**), and is thus superior to common practice. For further information see Arthur Avalon (Sir John Woodroffe), *Shakti and Shakta*, 1978; Swami Agehananda Bharati, *The Tantric Tradition*, 1977; and Douglas Renfrew Brooks, *The Secret of the Three Cities*, 1990.

Matsya Avatar

The first of the ten **avatars** or incarnations of the god **Vishnu**, which all took place at moments of crisis in the cosmos. See **Fish avatar**.

Matsyagandhi

("[she whose] smell is fish") In Hindu mythology, another name for queen **Satyavati**. Matsyagandhi is a fisher-girl who stinks of fish. She attracts the eye of a powerful sage, who later uses his **magic** powers to give her a pleasant scent. See **Satyavati**.

Matsyendranath

According to tradition, the **guru** of the sage **Gorakhnath** and the founder of the **Nathpanthis**, a group of renunciant **ascetics** who are devotees (**bhakta**) of the god **Shiva**. He is also known as Minanath. According to the Nathpanthi tradition, Matsyendranath received his teaching from Shiva himself, by taking the form of a fish (in **Sanskrit**, the words *matsya* and *mina* both mean "fish"), and eavesdropping while Shiva was teaching his wife **Parvati**. For further information about Gorakhnath and the **Nath** tradition, see George Weston Briggs, *Gorakhnath and the Kanphata Yogis*, 1973. See also **tantra**.

Matter, Primeval

The general translation given to the **Sanskrit** word **prakrti**, one of the two first principles in the **Samkhya** philosophical school. See **prakrti**.

Mauni

Derived from the word *muni* ("sage"), mauni designates a person who is observing a vow of silence as a religious act. Just as members of certain Christian monastic orders observe a vow of silence to turn their thoughts inward and enrich their inner lives, in the same way Hindu **ascetics** have taken vows of silence as a tool for spiritual development. At times these vows may be for a finite period of time (a week, a month, and so on), but even now there are ascetics who have not spoken in decades, communicating through expression, gesture, and writing on a piece of paper or a slate.

Mauni Amavasya

This festival falls on the day of the **new moon** (amavasya) in the **lunar month** of **Magh** (January–February). Those observing this holiday pass the day in silence. The word **mauni** (speechless) is derived from the word **muni** (sage); silence is seen as one of the religious practices helping to promote spiritual awareness. During the entire month of Magh, bathing (**snana**) in the **Ganges** (or another sacred river) is seen as meritorious. Bathing on the day of the new moon offers greater sanctity. A well-known spot for this rite is at the city of **Allahabad**, at the confluence of the Ganges and the **Yamuna** Rivers.

Mauritius

Island nation in the Indian Ocean, 1,200 miles east of the African coast. Mauritius has a significant Hindu **diaspora population**. As in many other cases, Indians were first brought to Mauritius as indentured agricultural laborers, in this case as workers on the sugar plantations. Currently, they comprise nearly 75 percent of the island's population, running the nation's political system. The Hindus on Mauritius have transferred India's sacred geography to their new land: A southern lake named **Grand Bassin** is claimed to have an underground connection to the River **Ganges**, and the lake has become a significant pilgrimage site.

Maurya Dynasty

The earliest of the great Indian empires. At its zenith, the Maurya dynasty ruled over most of the Indian subcontinent, except in the deep south. The dynasty was founded by **Chandragupta Maurya** in the fourth century B.C.E., but reached its peak under his grandson **Ashoka**, who reigned from 269–232 B.C.E. The kingdom was centered in the lower **Ganges** basin, with its capital at **Pataliputra**, near the modern city of Patna in the state of **Bihar**. The Mauryan empire is the first historically documented centralized Indian empire; it was operated and maintained by a large governmental bureaucracy. Despite its size and organization, the empire was short-lived. It began to disintegrate on Ashoka's death; fifty years later it had virtually disappeared.

Maya

A **Sanskrit** word. Maya's literal meaning is "**magic**" or "illusion"; the connotation it carries is a magic show or illusion in which objects appear to be present, but are not. In the Hindu philosophical tradition, maya describes how human beings become confused about the true nature of the world and themselves. Such illusion keeps them enmeshed in bondage to their desires and continues the cycle of reincarnation (**samsara**) that comes from this; at the same time, however, such people are unaware that they are in bondage.

In Hindu theism—in which the highest power is conceived as a **deity**—maya is generally described as one of God's powers, through which the deity can accomplish his or her purposes; in this understanding, maya is seen as an existing entity. The analysis of maya is a little different in the **Advaita Vedanta** school, which propounds a position known as monism. Monism claims that a single Ultimate Reality, called the unqualified **Brahman**, lies behind all things. Despite the appearance of difference and diversity, the only thing that really exists is this formless, unqualified Brahman. For the Advaitins, the assumption of diversity is a fundamental misunderstanding of the ultimate nature of things. The Advaita school accepts that God wields maya as a power, but since God (as a being with particular qualities) is considered lower than the highest, ultimate Brahman, both God and maya are part this lower reality. Thus, both are ultimately not real. The Advaitins describe maya as confusion from the lack of correct understanding; the confusion disappears when perfect liberation has been reached.

Maya Devi

Local **goddess** considered to be a form of **Durga**, whose home is in the northern Indian town and sacred city of **Haridwar**. According to local tradition, the site where her temple is built is one of the **Shakti Pithas**, a network of sites sacred to the Goddess which spreads throughout the subcontinent. Each Shakti Pitha marks the site where a body part of the dismembered goddess **Sati** fell to earth, taking form there as a different goddess; Maya Devi was Sati's navel. Although this claim is not attested in other literature on the Shakti Pithas, the site itself is believed to be very old. One of the oldest names for the Haridwar region is **Mayapur**, the "city of Maya." See also **pitha**.

Mayapur

City in **West Bengal** on the western side of the Hugli River across from the holy city of **Navadvip**, about sixty-five miles north of Calcutta. Although both cities claim to be the birthplace of the Bengali saint **Chaitanya**, Navadvip's claim is older. However, the claim that Mayapur was the birthplace of Chaitanya is supported by the International Society for Krishna Consciousness (ISKCON), more popularly known as the Hare Krishnas, who have built a magnificent temple complex at Mayapur as the headquarters of the organization. For extensive information about this site, see E. Alan Morinis, *Pilgrimage in the Hindu Tradition*, 1984.

Mayashiva

("illusionary **Shiva**") In Hindu mythology, a **demon** named Jalandhara assumes the form of the god Shiva in an attempt to trick **Parvati**, the **goddess**, into having sexual relations with him. Jalandhara has been unable to conquer Shiva on the battlefield, so he hopes that he can diminish Shiva's power by compromising the faithfulness of his wife. Jalandhara comes to Parvati in Shiva's form, but she is so suspicious that Jalandhara is unable to fulfill his desires. Jalandhara's power is eventually broken in the same way, when **Vishnu** (in the form of Jalandhara) manages to seduce Jalandhara's wife, Vrnda.

Meat Eating

An accepted part of the diet for most Hindus. A 1996 poll of urban Hindus found that only a quarter of the respondents were vegetarians. However, this figure may be higher in villages, where people tend to be more traditional and conservative. As the product of a dead **animal**, meat is seen as impure, and those who are concerned about religious **purity** (particularly **brahmins**) will generally avoid it for that reason. Even nonvegetarians recognize a hierarchy of animal foods. Some people will eat only eggs; others will also eat chicken and/or fish, whereas others will also eat mutton. Pork is generally avoided by all but the lowest-status people; pigs are considered scavengers and deemed unclean. Beef is taboo for religious reasons, except for a very small Hindu community in southern India. Even those who eat meat generally do not eat it in large quantities. Because of its relatively high cost, it is generally prepared as one dish among many, rather than the central part of the meal.

Medhatithi

(mid-9th c.) Author of the most authoritative commentary on the *Manu Smrti*, also known as the "Laws of **Manu**." Medhatithi was schooled in the techniques of textual interpretation developed by the **Purva Mimamsa** school, one of the **six schools** of Hindu **philosophy**. Due to his interpretive abilities, his commentary quickly became the accepted standard.

Medicine

See **ayurveda**, *Charaka Samhita*, and *Sushruta Samhita*.

Megasthenes

(3rd c. B.C.E.) Ambassador sent to the court of **Chandragupta Maurya** by Seleucus Nicator, a general in Alexander the Great's army who ruled the eastern part of the empire after Alexander's death. Megasthenes lived for many years in the Mauryan capital, **Pataliputra**. His reports of life there are the first European accounts of India. His original account no longer exists, but the fact of its existence is attested to by the many references to it in the works of later Greek writers; these writers, however, often voice doubts about his credibility and veracity. See also **Maurya dynasty**.

Meghaduta

("Cloud-Messenger") One of the great poetic works by **Kalidasa** (5th c.?), generally considered to be the greatest classical **Sanskrit** poet. The Meghaduta is a short poem consisting of one hundred verses, written entirely in an extremely long **meter** called mandakranta—seventeen syllables to each quarter verse. The poem tells the story of a **yaksha** (nature sprite) who has been temporarily banished to the southern part of India. Separated from his beloved wife, who is at their home in the kingdom of **Kubera** in the **Himalayas**, the yaksha sees a **monsoon** rain cloud moving northward in its annual journey. He implores it to carry a message of love to his beloved. The yaksha describes the regions through which the cloud travels. This description gives a vivid picture of everyday life and the cultural centers of Kalidasa's time. In some sources the poem is called *Meghasandesha*, "The Message [carried by] a Cloud."

Meghanada

("roaring like thunder") In the *Ramayana*, the earlier of the two great Indian epics, Meghanada is one of the epithets of **Indrajit**, son of the **demon**-king **Ravana**. See **Indrajit**.

Meher Baba

(b. Merwan Sheriar Irani, 1894–1969) Modern religious figure who was born a Parsi, but whose teachings draw on Islamic mystical thought and Hindu devotional (**bhakti**) teachings. Meher Baba ("Divine Father") claimed to be an **avatar** or "incarnation" of the divine, and his followers accept him as such. In 1925 he took a vow of silence, which he kept for the rest of his life, communicating through gestures and an alphabet board. Despite his silence, he compiled his teachings in a five-volume set of

Pilgrims in Allahabad gather in a mela tent to listen to a guru.

discourses titled *God Speaks*. Like many contemporary Hindu missionary figures, Meher Baba emphasized the need for devotion to one's **guru** or religious preceptor, through which the disciple would gain all things. For further information from a devotee's (**bhakta**) perspective, see Jean Adriel, *Avatar*, 1947.

Mehndipur

Village in the state of **Rajasthan** in the southern region between the cities of Agra and Jaipur. The village is best known for the temple to the god **Balaji**, considered to be a form of the monkey-god **Hanuman**. People possessed by malevolent spirits come to Balaji to be cured through his power. For a thorough discussion of the language of **possession** and exorcism, see Sudhir Kakar, *Shamans, Mystics, and Doctors*, 1991

Mela

("meeting") In the widest sense, the word *mela* can refer to any type of large gathering, usually for some specific purpose. In a religious context, the word mela is generally translated as "festival" or fair. Melas include commercial interests, religious activity, and entertainment. Melas are usually attended by vast numbers of religious pilgrims, traveling to the site of the festival. By far the largest of these melas is the **Kumbha**

Mela at **Allahabad**. In 1989, the Kumbha Mela drew 15 million people on a single day, and millions more during the month of the festival.

Mena

In Hindu mythology, the wife of the minor **deity Himalaya**, and the mother of **Parvati**, the **goddess**. Mena christens her daughter, **Uma**, through her exclamation "U Ma!" ("Oh, don't!") when Parvati announces her desire to make the god **Shiva** her husband. The *Shiva Purana* details Mena's initial discomfiture with her unconventional **son**-in-law, yet later suggests Shiva as the paradigm for the ideal husband, since he is completely devoted to his wife.

Menaka

In Hindu mythology, a beautiful celestial maiden (**apsara**), who is a minion of **Indra**, the king of the gods. Menaka's primary function is to seduce sages threatening to replace Indra as the ruler of **heaven**. In traditional Indian culture, **semen** is seen as the concentrated essence of a man's vital energies; **celibacy** is a means to conserve and retain these energies. Menaka's powers of attraction are used to seduce these **ascetics**, diminishing their accumulated spiritual powers. Her most notable partner is the sage **Vishvamitra**, who is twice smitten by her charms. Their first liaison results in the **birth** of the maiden **Shakuntala**, celebrated in the drama *Abhijnanashakuntala*, written by the poet **Kalidasa**. During their second liaison, Vishvamitra lives with Menaka for ten years, before leaving her for renunciant life in the forest.

Menstruation

In traditional Hindu culture all bodily discharges are considered to be a source of ritual impurity (**ashaucha**). Women are considered ritually unclean during their menstrual periods; menstrual fluid is considered a source of impurity. However, menstruation is also considered a sign of **auspiciousness** or good fortune, since it indicates women's reproductive capacities. The ritual observances and taboos for menstruating women vary widely between differing social groups. In some groups, women are subject to only a few restrictions, such as a ban on entering temples during that time. In other groups, women are expected to confine themselves to certain parts of the house and to refrain from everyday activities such as cooking. Although such strict practice sounds oppressive, for many women this interval was prized as a monthly respite from their everyday duties, which would be performed by the other women in the household.

Mercury

In Hindu astrology (**jyotisha**), a planet associated with mental quickness, memory, and education, based on its short orbit around the **sun**. Despite these generally positive features, Mercury is considered a weak planet, easily influenced toward benevolence and malevolence by other **planets**, or by its position in the **natal horoscope** (janampatrika). Mercury's association with the mind suggests that the mind's powers can be harnessed for either good or evil ends. During the **week**, Mercury is said to rule over **Wednesday**; this day is not heavily marked as auspicious or inauspicious, reflecting the planet's light powers.

Mercury

(2) Elemental mercury is a pivotal substance in Indian **alchemy**. Hindu alchemy analyzes the world as a series of bipolar opposites in tension with one another. Unifying these opposing forces brings spiritual progress and end of reincarnation (**samsara**). This model of uniting or transcending opposing forces is shared with Hindu **tantra**, a secret, ritually-based religious practice. This theme is shared with **hatha yoga**, which is based on a series

of physical exercises that are also believed to affect the **subtle body**.

The governing metaphor for this combination of opposites is the union of **sun** and **moon**. Both the sun and the moon are connected to other opposing principles through an elaborate series of associations. In keeping with this bipolar symbolism, mercury is conceived as the **semen** of the god **Shiva** and thus full of healing power. It is also identified with the moon (perhaps through its bright silvery hue), with healing and restorative power, and with the nectar of immortality. Elemental **sulfur** is identified with the **goddess Shakti's** uterine **blood**. When mercury and sulfur are mixed and consumed, the aspirant's body is purified and refined, eventually rendering it immortal. Modern descriptions of this practice warn that it should only be carried out under the direction of one's **guru** (spiritual teacher); otherwise these combinations will be harmful, since by itself mercury is a deadly poison. For further information see Shashibhushan B. Dasgupta, *Obscure Religious Cults*, 1962; and David Gordon White, *The Alchemical Body*, 1996.

Meru

Mythical mountain in the center of the continent of **Jambudvipa**, the innermost of the concentric landmasses that make up the visible world in traditional Hindu **cosmology**; Mount Meru is the center of the entire world, the pivot of the entire created order. It is said to extend far up into the **heavens** and have its roots far beneath the earth, and on its crest is a divine city which is the home of the gods. The mythical Meru is often identified with the Himalayan mountain known as **Kailas**. For this reason Kailas has been an important pilgrimage place (**tirtha**), despite its inaccessible location.

Meter, Poetic

Indian poetry has well-developed metrical forms, basically following two dominant patterns. The first metric pattern is based simply on the number of syllables in a line. In the second pattern, each line contains a certain number of metric beats, based on the distinction between "heavy" and "light" syllables. A heavy syllable is any syllable with a long vowel or a consonant cluster and is given two metric beats; all other syllables are considered light and counted as one beat.

Sanskrit poetry tends to stress the former pattern, and has codified meters ranging from four to twenty-six syllables per half-line, yet even within these syllabic constraints each meter usually has a prescribed sequence of light and heavy syllables as well. Two different Sanskrit poetic meters may thus have the same number of syllables, but vary in their syllabic patterns. Although such subtle differences could generate vast numbers of meters, in practice there were only about a hundred. The vast majority of Sanskrit texts are written in a single meter, the **anushtubh**, which has eight syllables per half-line.

Later devotional (**bhakti**) poetry, particularly in northern India, tend to favor poetic forms based on the number of metric beats. The most popular forms are the **doha**, which has twenty-four metric beats in two lines, and the **chaupai**, which has four lines of sixteen beats each. Although there are several poetic forms based on the number of syllables in each line, particularly the **savaiya** and the **kavitt**, these were used less often.

Mewar

In the time before Indian independence in 1947, Mewar was a princely state in southern **Rajasthan**, the capital of which was in the city of Udaipur. In the seventeenth and eighteenth centuries, Mewar was one of the important centers for the **Rajasthani** style of **miniature painting**. The Rajasthani style is characterized by a flat perspective. Visual power is derived from vivid bands of colors that often serve as a backdrop to the painting.

The east gate of the Minakshi Temple in the city of Madurai. The temple is dedicated to the goddess Minakshi, the city's guardian.

Mimamsa Sutras

The founding text of the **Purva Mimamsa** school, one of the **six schools** of traditional Hindu **philosophy**. The *Mimamsa Sutras* are traditionally attributed to the sage **Jaimini**, who is believed to have lived in the fourth century B.C.E. The Mimamsa school was most concerned with the investigation of **dharma** ("righteous action"), believed to be revealed in the **Vedas**, the earliest Hindu religious texts. Much of Mimamsa thought is concerned with principles and methods for textual interpretation, to discover and interpret the instructions contained in the Vedas. The *Mimamsa Sutras* were elaborated in numerous commentaries, the most famous of which were written by **Kumarila** and **Prabhakara** in the seventh century. For further information and text, see Sarvepalli Radhakrishnan and Charles A. Moore (eds.), *A Sourcebook in Indian Philosophy*, 1957.

Minakshi

("fish-eyed") Presiding **deity** of the Minakshi temple in the city of **Madurai** in the state of **Tamil Nadu**. Her name refers both to the shape of her eyes (long and oval), and to their fluttering movement, both of which are considered marks of feminine beauty in classical India. Minakshi was originally a local deity, the guardian for the city of Madurai. As Madurai became important, by virtue of being the **Pandya dynasty** capital, so did Minakshi. According to her charter myth, Minakshi is born with three breasts—already a sign that she is unusual—and is raised by her parents as a man. As she accedes to the throne in Madurai, she vows that she will only marry a man who can defeat her in battle. She fights and conquers all the kings of the earth, but when she approaches the god **Shiva**, she is suddenly stricken with modesty and transformed from a powerful warrior to a shy and bashful girl. At this moment her third breast disappears, further signifying the loss of her special status. Minakshi and Shiva (in his manifestation as Sundareshvara) are married. Their wedding is celebrated every year in Madurai during the **Chittirai** festival.

Despite her transformation in the charter myth, Minakshi is still an unusual **goddess**. The wedding of a goddess usually marks her domestication and implies subordination to her husband. Minakshi, however, remains the more important deity in Madurai, perhaps reflecting her previous status as the city's guardian deity. For more information see Dean David Shulman, *Tamil Temple Myths*, 1980.

Minanath

Another epithet for **Matsyendranath**, traditionally cited as the spiritual teacher (**guru**) of **Gorakhnath**, the great **yogi**. See **Matsyendranath**.

Miniature Painting

The origins of Hindu miniature painting lie in the royal art of the Moghul court, where miniature painting and portraiture were well-established genres. In the seventeenth century other centers for miniature painting began to arise, perhaps spurred by Moghul artists seeking patronage in Hindu vassal kingdoms. Although portraiture and court scenes continued to be important, the miniature genre expanded to include other themes such as the illustration of the musical modes known as **ragas**, which are associated with particular times and/or **seasons**. Another prominent theme was Hindu religious imagery, reflecting the influence of the devotional (**bhakti**) movement, which was in full flower in northern India. Religious themes first concentrated mainly on the mythic exploits of the god **Krishna** and portrayals of the god **Shiva**. At times, these two major themes were combined. Miniature paintings were also used to illustrate manuscripts, thus integrating literature, art, music, and religious images.

The development of Hindu miniature painting can be broadly divided into three schools, each corresponding to a geographical area: **Rajasthani**, Deccani, and **Pahari**. The earliest developed school was the Rajasthani, which flourished in seventeenth and eighteenth centuries in the **Malwa** region of the state of **Madhya Pradesh** and the small kingdoms that surrounded the region. The Rajasthani style is characterized by a flat perspective; visual power is derived from vivid bands of colors that often serve as a backdrop to the painting. The Deccani style was established in central India and showed little variation from Moghul court art. The Pahari ("mountain") style flourished in the eighteenth and nineteenth centuries in the small kingdoms in the **Shiwalik Hills** north and west of Delhi. The Pahari style first appeared in **Basohli**, where the influence of the Rajasthani school is evident, and later developed in **Jammu**, **Guler**, **Garhwal**, and **Kangra**. The developed Pahari style differs from the Rajasthani style in its emphasis on more linear drawing—perhaps influenced by European art—and a more restrained use of color, giving the paintings a more lyrical feel. For further information see W. G. Archer, *Indian Painting*, 1957. See also **Moghul dynasty**.

Minorities

In any society, minority groups are defined according to a particular social context. In India the two most prominent minority groups are Muslims and Christians. Muslims—about twelve percent of the population—are viewed with suspicion, due to India's troubled relations with Pakistan. Christians and Muslims are viewed as having religious loyalties that lie outside of India—Mecca for Muslims, and Rome or Jerusalem for Christians. These two communities have been perceived very differently from other religious communities, such as the Sikhs and the Jains, who are part of the Indian cultural tradition. Cultural and political organizations espousing forms of Hindu nationalism (**Hindutva**), particularly the **Rashtriya Svayamsevak Sangh** and its affiliates, have often stressed the "otherness" of these communities. Such organizations have as their express purpose the unification of Hindus from all regions, castes, and backgrounds, but do so through criteria that exclude these minorities.

Mirabai

(early 16th c.?) A poet-saint who was a devotee (**bhakta**) of the god **Krishna**. Although little is known about her, Mirabai's songs remain some of the best-known devotional (**bhakti**) poetry. According to tradition, Mirabai was born into a royal family in a small kingdom in **Rajasthan**. From her earliest days, she was passionately devoted to Krishna. Although her parents arranged a marriage with the scion of another ruler, she considered Krishna to be her true husband. After extended conflict with her in-laws—in which they reportedly attempted to poison her—her release came with the death of her husband, after which she was allowed to leave her marital home. She spent her later years visiting places associated with Krishna and sharing in the "good company" (**satsang**) of other devotees. She went to **Dwaraka**, the city over which Krishna is said to have ruled, and met her end by being absorbed into the image of Krishna at his temple there.

Mirabai's poetry is marked by her expressions of longing for Krishna. She often speaks of herself either as his wife or his waiting lover, seeking physical and mystical union with him. Her poetry is an intensely personal expression of her religious fervor; the power of this longing has made her a symbol of religious devotion. For scholars, Mirabai's poetry raises perplexing questions of authorship, for the earliest manuscripts are several hundred years older than when she is supposed to have lived, but for common people the songs bearing her name are widely popular even today. She has also been featured in at least ten feature films, showing the staying power of devotion even in the modern age. For further information see A. J. Alston (trans.), *The Devotional Poems of Mirabai*, 1980; and John Stratton Hawley and Mark Juergensmeyer (trans.), *Songs of the Saints of India*, 1988.

Mitakshara

A voluminous commentary on the **Yajnavalkya Smrti**, written early in the twelfth century by the scholar **Vijnaneshvara**. This particular commentary played a pivotal role in the British colonial administration of India. The British were content to have their Indian subjects governed by their traditional religious laws, but to do so they needed to know what these laws were. For large sections of British India, the *Mitakshara* was given the status of traditional law, functioning as a legal code.

The only major part of India in which the *Mitakshara* did not hold sway was in Bengal, where the legal authority was the **Dayabhaga**. One of the major differences between the two was in matters of **inheritance**. The *Mitakshara* stresses inheritance by survivorship, in which only living males can inherit property, whereas the *Dayabhaga* stresses inheritance by succession, in which a dead man's heirs can inherit in his name.

Mithila

In the **Ramayana**, the earlier of the two great Indian epics, Mithila is the kingdom ruled by King **Janaka**, foster father of **Sita**, the **goddess**. The region is known for its wealth, as well as for the righteousness of its rulers; it is identified with the Mithila region in the northern part of the state of modern **Bihar**.

Mithuna

("pair") In **architecture**, the name for what has been described as a "loving couple." A more candid characterization is that of sculptures of men and **women** engaged in sexual activity, either as a pair or a larger group, with the occasional animal thrown in for variety. The most famous examples of such sculptures are at the temples at **Konarak** in the state of **Orissa**, and at **Khajuraho** in the state of **Madhya Pradesh**. The meaning behind such explicit sculptures has been variously interpreted. Some people claim that they sanction carnal pleasure as a religious path, some interpret them as representing human union with the divine, and still others view them as teaching that the desire for pleasure must ultimately be transcended to attain the divine. Any of these may be true, or the sculptures may simply reflect an affirmation of life on all its levels.

Mitra Mishra

(early 17th c.) Author of the **Viramitrodaya**, a compendium of Hindu lore. The *Viramitrodaya* is an example of a class of commentarial literature known as **nibandhas** ("collections"). The compilers of the nibandhas culled references on a particular theme from the **Vedas**, **dharma literature**, **puranas**, and other authoritative religious texts, placing these excerpts into a single volume. Each of the *Viramitrodaya*'s twenty-two sections is devoted to a particular aspect of Hindu life, such as daily practice, **worship**, gift-giving (**dana**), vows, pilgrimage, penances (**prayashchitta**), purification, death rites (**antyeshthi samskara**), and law; the final section is devoted to final liberation of the soul (**moksha**). In addition to citing the relevant scriptural passages, Mitra Mishra also provides extensive commentary of his own. His work became an important source for later legal interpretation, particularly in eastern India.

Mleccha

Sanskrit word traditionally used to designate a foreigner or a non-**Aryan**. The word *mleccha* is also used to indicate a person who has become an outcaste and thus has no place in established society. The verb from which the word *mleccha* is derived means "to speak confusedly or indistinctly," indicating someone who has not yet mastered the language.

Mnemonics

The best-known example of a mnemonic system comes in the study of the **Vedas**, the oldest Hindu religious texts. Traditionally, the power of the Vedas is not derived from the meaning of the words, but in the very sounds themselves. It was imperative for the text to be conveyed without error. This posed a significant challenge. The Vedas have been orally transmitted by an elaborate system of learning strategies, keeping the text unchanged for over three thousand years, identical in all parts of India. This remarkable feat was achieved by memorizing the text in differing patterns: as verses, as the individual words,

as pairs of words in sequential succession (ab, bc, cd, and so forth), and according to some reports, backwards. The ultimate aim of all of these patterns was to render the text into sheer sound, rather than phrases with definite syntactic meaning, since the latter could be subject to substitutions. Although this effort has succeeded in preserving the sacred sounds, in many cases the meanings of these words have become unclear, especially for words which appear only once. This problem was evident as early as the fifth century B.C.E., when **Yaska**, the **grammarian**, wrote the *Nirukta*, explaining the meaning of many of these words.

Modes of Devotion

Devotion to God (**bhakti**) has been the most important force in Hindu religion for more than the past millennium. However, the form and tone of this devotion have varied considerably in different times and places. The most thorough articulation of different possible modes of devotion was done by **Rupa Goswami**, who lived in the mid-sixteenth century. Rupa was a devotee (**bhakta**) of the god **Krishna** and a member of the **Gaudiya Vaishnava** religious community founded by the Bengali saint **Chaitanya**. Devotion to Krishna is characterized by the emphasis on relationship, particularly the visualization of mythic incidents from Krishna's life, through which one can enter his divine world, and thus take part in his divine "play" (**lila**) with the world.

Rupa distinguished five such modes, which were characterized by growing emotional intensity. The first was the "peaceful mode" (**shanta bhava**), in which the devotee found mental peace through the realization of complete identity with **Brahman**. This was seen as an inferior mode, since the **deity** was seen impersonally, and the devotee had no personal relationship with God. The other four modes were based on human relationships, from the most distant to the most intimate and loving: master

Ruins at Mohenjo-Daro. This archeological site contains some of the earliest discovered remains of the ancient Indus Valley civilization.

and servant (**dasa bhava**), friend and friend (**sakha bhava**), parent and child (**vatsalya bhava**), and lover and beloved (**madhurya bhava**). Although all of these modes were legitimate forms of relationship with the divine, the last was considered the highest because it generated the most intense emotions.

Moghul Dynasty

(1525–1857) Muslim dynasty that ruled large parts of India for almost 200 years. The dynasty was established by Babar (r. 1625–1630), a central Asian monarch who had been displaced from his own homeland in Afghanistan and defeated the Lodi dynasty rulers at Panipat in 1625. Babar's son Humayan (1508–1556) acceded to his father's throne but spent much of his life fighting an Afghan threat. He finally recovered his kingdom, but within six months died from injuries sustained in a fall. Humayan was succeeded by his son **Akbar** (1542–1605), considered the greatest of the Moghul emperors, both for his long reign of forty-nine years and for his efforts to include his Hindu subjects as equal citizens, not simply as conquered infidels. Akbar was succeeded by Jahangir (1569–1627), and Jahangir by Shah Jahan (1592–1666). The last of the great Moghuls was **Aurangzeb** (1618–1707), who added parts of the **Deccan** region to the Moghul empire. During Aurangzeb's reign, the **Krishna Janam Bhumi** in the city of **Mathura** and the **Vishvanath** temple in the city of **Benares** were destroyed. Such incidents have caused much speculation as to whether the destruction was the result of anti-Hindu religious sentiments (the Moghuls were Muslims) or an expression of Moghul political dominance. After Aurangzeb's death the Moghul empire broke apart, but the dynasty continued to wield diminishing influence until the 1857 rebellion against the British, when it was definitively removed.

Mohan

("beguiling," "bewildering") Epithet of the god **Krishna**, which may refer either to his overwhelming attractiveness, which is believed to beguile the mind, or to his ability to wield **maya** or the power of illusion, and thus cloud people's minds. See **Krishna**.

Mohenjo-Daro

Archeological site on the **Indus** River in modern Pakistan, about two hundred miles north of Karachi. Mohenjo-Daro is one of the cities of the **Indus Valley civilization**, a highly developed urban culture that flourished in the Indus Valley region between the fourth and third millennia B.C.E. **Harappa** and Mohenjo-Daro have been the most extensively excavated of these cities, although archeological work is proceeding at others. Similarities at these different sites reveal insights into this civilization's material culture. One of the features at Mohenjo-Daro is the "Great Bath," a large water-tank built of brick and sealed with pitch. Scholars speculate that it was connected with ritual **purity**. See also **bath, Mohenjo-Daro**.

Mohini

("bewitching") In Hindu mythology, a rapturously beautiful, divine enchantress, seen as a manifestation of the god **Vishnu**. Vishnu takes this form to trick the **demons** into giving her their share of the **amrta**, the nectar of immortality, which has been churned from the Ocean of Milk. Through her charms, Mohini succeeds in getting the amrta from the demons; she gives it to the gods, thus depriving the demons of their chance at immortality.

In most versions, the story ends here, but the charter myth for the southern Indian god **Aiyappa** adds an interesting twist. According to the story, when **Shiva** sees the enchanting figure of Mohini, he cannot resist her. The product of this union is Aiyappa, who is considered the son of Shiva and Vishnu. Yet Aiyappa's unusual parentage occurs with good reason, as with most such stories in Hindu mythology. Aiyappa is born to kill a **demon** named **Mahishi**, who has

received the boon that she can only be killed by a person not born from the union of male and female. Mohini's "true" identity (Vishnu) satisfies this condition, and when Aiyappa comes of age he kills the demon. See also **Tortoise avatar**.

Mohini Attam

The youngest form of classical Indian **dance**, found mainly in the modern state of **Kerala**. Mohini Attam was developed in the early eighteenth century at the royal court in Travancore in Kerala. This style of dance shows traits of both **Bharatanatyam** and **Kathakali**, a Keralan dance form. The dance is named after the mythical enchantress **Mohini** and projects a coquettish sensuality. Some of the dance's physical poses are taken from Bharatanatyam, whereas the stylized hand gestures (**mudras**) come largely from Kathakali. For further information see Mohan Khokar, *Traditions of Indian Classical Dance*, 1984.

Mohini Ekadashi

Festival falling on the eleventh day (**ekadashi**) of the bright, waxing half of the **lunar month** of **Baisakh** (April–May). The festival is dedicated to the **worship** of **Vishnu** in his **avatar** as **Rama**. Most Hindu festivals have certain prescribed rites usually involving fasting (**upavasa**) and worship, promising specific benefits for faithful performance; observing this festival frees one from the results of one's evil acts.

Moksha

In Indian **philosophy** moksha is one of the four purusharthas, or **aims of life**; the others are **artha** (wealth, power, and prosperity), **kama** (desire), and **dharma** (righteousness). Moksha literally means "release"—the human soul's (**atman**) final liberation from the cycle of reincarnation (**samsara**). The quest for liberation involves questioning and ultimately detaching oneself from pursuits of normal social life. Although all four purusharthas are legitimate and sanctioned, liberation is usually seen as the ultimate goal, the last goal to be pursued after fulfilling the pleasures and pains stemming from the other three. Moksha is also unchanging, bringing one complete and absolute freedom, whereas the other three are ultimately transient, for they are pursued within the ever-changing world of desires.

Mokshada Ekadashi

Festival falling on the eleventh day (**ekadashi**) of the bright half of **Margashirsha** (November–December). As for all the eleventh-day observances, this is dedicated to **Vishnu**. Most Hindu festivals have certain prescribed rites usually involving fasting (**upavasa**) and **worship**, and often promising specific benefits for faithful performance. Faithfully observing this festival is believed to bestow final liberation (**moksha**) of the soul.

Monday

(Somavar) The second **day** of the Hindu **week**, whose presiding **planet** is the **moon**. The moon is associated with coolness, healing power, and **Soma**, the Vedic **deity**. The Hindu god **Shiva** is manifested as **Somnath**, the Lord of the Moon. Monday is considered one of the most powerful and auspicious days of the week. Worship on certain Mondays is believed to bring even greater religious benefits, such as on a **Somavati Amavasya**, (a **new moon** falling on a Monday), and on the Mondays in **Shravan** (a **lunar month** specially dedicated to Shiva). The Sixteen Mondays Vow (**Solah Somvar Vrat**) is performed on sixteen consecutive Mondays. Like other such vows, the Solah Somvar Vrat entails reading the vow's charter myth in a ritual setting, combined with worship and a regulated diet.

Moneylending

An important element in the economic activity of the traditional and modern Indian merchant families. Since farmers have profits only after the harvest, they must be able to borrow during the other times of the year. In modern times many farmers borrow from banks, but in earlier times their only resource was these merchant families. Their interest rates usually reflected the borrower's credit worthiness: unsecured loans might have interest rates as high as 30 to 50 percent per year because there was a good chance for default, whereas the interest on loans secured by collateral might be as low as seven percent. To some extent, these moneylending merchants were economically bound to their farmer-creditors, with one providing the capital and the other providing the labor. Moneylenders could not refuse credit to farmers after a bad year, since this would have removed any hope of future repayment. For further information see Christopher Alan Bayly, *Rulers, Townsmen and Bazaars*, 1983.

Monsoon

A season of torrential rains, whose name comes from an Arabic word meaning "season" (mausam). The monsoon is preceded by a period of intense heat; daily temperatures go over one hundred degrees Fahrenheit. As the hot air rises, it draws in a vast current of moisture-laden air from the coastal regions of southern India. The monsoon is one of the year's three major **seasons** and is a vital part of people's daily lives. Because much of India's farmland is not irrigated, the monsoon rains are vital to agriculture. The coming of the monsoon is much awaited in real life; it also has a prominent place in Indian culture. One image of the monsoon comes from love poetry, in which a woman is anxiously scanning the sky, watching the clouds roll up as she awaits her returning beloved. In earlier times the rains made travel almost impossible, making it a bitter time for separated lovers but a sweet and happy time for united couples. The poet **Kalidasa's** epic *Meghaduta* describes a man exiled in southern India, who addresses one of the monsoon clouds, giving it a message to convey to his beloved. The monsoon rains are also associated with the god **Krishna**. His dark skin color is compared to a rain cloud. Also, his birthday is celebrated at the end of the rainy season, and his divine persona appropriates the image of the lover associated with the rains.

Moon

In Hindu astrology (**jyotisha**), a **planet** associated with fecundity (fertility), although its aspect can be either benevolent or malevolent—benevolent with the waxing moon, and malevolent with the waning moon. During the **lunar month**, the **full moon** is considered the most auspicious time of all. The **new moon**, however, is considered a ritually ambiguous time, and thus potentially dangerous. During the **week** the moon presides over **Monday**, generally considered an auspicious **day** and one that is sacred to **Shiva** as **Somnath**, the Lord of the Moon.

Morari Bapu

(b. Muraridas Prabhudas 1946) Modern commentator and expositor (kathavacak) on the *Ramcharitmanas*. Written by the poet-saint **Tulsidas**, the *Ramcharitmanas* is a vernacular version of the *Ramayana*, the earlier of the two great **Sanskrit** epics. As with all vernacular renditions of the *Ramayana*, Tulsidas did not simply translate **Valmiki's** Sanskrit epic, but adapted it to address his own religious concerns, particularly the importance of devotion (**bhakti**) to God, one of the text's central themes. Morari Bapu claims no supernatural powers or ability; his religious fame rests solely on his commitment to the text, and his power in expounding it. At times he speaks to audiences of more than 100,000 people, giving **katha**

(discourse) to the Hindu **diaspora populations** in Europe and North America, as well as in India.

Mrcchakatika

("The Little Clay Cart") Drama written by the playwright **Shudraka**, probably in the early fifth century. The play describes the flowering of love between a poor but noble **brahmin**, Charudatta, and a wealthy and virtuous courtesan, Vasantasena, set in the context of a complicated political intrigue. The play is noted for its portrayal of everyday urban life, exemplified by the little clay cart—a child's toy. It has been translated into several languages and is periodically performed for modern American audiences.

Mrtyunjaya

("Conqueror of Death") Epithet of the god **Shiva**. The mythic charter behind this particular name comes from the story of the sage **Markandeya**. Devoted to Shiva, Markandeya is an intelligent and religious boy who is proficient in all branches of learning. His story is poignant because he is fated to die at sixteen. When Markandeya learns of this, shortly before his sixteenth birthday, he begins to **worship** Shiva with even greater fervor. On the appointed day, **Yama**, the god of death, comes to claim Markandeya. When Yama throws his noose over Markandeya to draw out the boy's soul, it catches the statue of Shiva to which Markandeya is clinging. Shiva arises from the image and kills Yama, saving Markandeya's life. Although Shiva relents and restores Yama to life, this particular form of Shiva illustrates his power to protect his devotees (**bhakta**) from all things, including death.

Mudra

("seal") In Indian **dance**, theater, and iconography, a mudra is a stylized hand **gesture** that conveys a specific meaning, ranging from concrete things such as animals, everyday objects, and the Hindu **deities**, to abstract things such as emotions. In the context of the performing arts, particularly dance, performers tell detailed stories through gesture alone. In the context of iconography, many of these gestures are traits associated with particular deities. There is some syntactic overlap between the terms *mudra* and *hasta* ("hand"); one of the distinctions between them is that some of the hastas simply describe the position of the hand, and others have symbolic meaning, whereas mudras always have very specific symbolic meanings.

Mudra

(2) Fermented or parched grain. In the secret ritually-based religious practice known as **tantra**, fermented grain is the fourth of the "Five Forbidden Things" (**panchamakara**), which, in "left hand" (**vamachara**) tantric ritual, are used in their actual forms, whereas in "right hand" (**dakshinachara**) tantric ritual they are represented by symbolic substitutes. Fermented grain may have intoxicating effects, but it is also reputed to be an aphrodisiac. "Respectable" Hindu society strongly condemns the use of intoxicants and/or sexual license. Thus the ritual use of this substance must be seen in the larger tantric context. One of the most pervasive tantric assumptions is the ultimate unity of everything that exists. From a tantric perspective, to affirm that the entire universe is one principle means that the adept must reject all concepts based on dualistic thinking. The "Five Forbidden Things" provide a ritual means for breaking down duality. In this ritual the adept breaks societal norms forbidding consumption of **intoxicants**, nonvegetarian food, and illicit sexuality in a conscious effort to sacralize what is normally forbidden. Tantric adepts cite such ritual use of forbidden things as proof that their practice involves a more exclusive qualification (**adhikara**), and is thus superior to common practice. For

further information see Arthur Avalon (Sir John Woodroffe) *Shakti and Shakta*, 1978; Swami Agehananda Bharati, *The Tantric Tradition*, 1977; and Douglas Renfrew Brooks, *The Secret of the Three Cities*, 1990.

Mudrarakshasa

("**Rakshasa's** Ring") The only surviving **Sanskrit** drama written by the playwright **Vishakhadatta**, who is believed to have lived in the sixth century. The play chronicles the rise of **Chandragupta Maurya**, founder of the **Maurya dynasty**, and the machinations of his cunning **brahmin** minister, **Chanakya**. The drama's plot is highly complex, as with many Sanskrit plays, but its climax comes when the principal characters are dramatically rescued from execution at the last moment. Although the play is based on actual events, historians feel that the portrayal of Chandragupta Maurya as a weak king is inaccurate. The play has been translated into English by Michael Coulson and published in an anthology titled *Three Sanskrit Plays*, 1981.

Mueller, F. Max

(1823–1900) Linguist, translator, editor, and ardent student of comparative religion and mythology. Mueller was an important figure in nineteenth-century intellectual history. His primary contribution was introducing Indian ideas to Western audiences by translating primary texts into the *Sacred Books of the East* series. His work allowed Hindu and other Asian religious traditions to show the sophisticated thought often concealed by popular religious practice. Mueller began developing a "science of religion"— a field of knowledge that could be pursued as any other. As a professor at Oxford, he helped to change scholarly views on Hinduism and other Asian religions, moving Western minds from simply dismissing them as polytheistic "idolatry" to taking them seriously as coherent and compelling pictures of the world.

Muhurta

In traditional timekeeping, a muhurta is a period of forty-eight minutes, of which there are thirty during each day. The **Brahma Muhurta** is the most auspicious time period, coming directly before dawn. The time before the Brahma Muhurta is considered the least auspicious in the day. This cycle exemplifies a pattern in the Indian view of time. A period of inauspiciousness is typically followed by a sudden regeneration of fortune.

Mukhalinga

A form of the **linga**, the pillar-shaped object symbolizing the god **Shiva**. A mukhalinga has one or more faces (mukha) sculpted on the shaft of the linga. According to the manuals detailing the form and construction of Hindu images, the number of faces on the linga should not exceed the number of doorways in the temple. Thus, a temple with one doorway should have a mukhalinga with one face, and so on, up to four. The manuals also specify that these faces should be placed facing the entrances. For further information see T. A. Gopinatha Rao, *Elements of Hindu Iconography*, 1981.

Muktananda

(1908–1982) Modern Hindu teacher, proponent of a religious path named **siddha yoga** ("discipline of the adepts"), and founder of the organization named SYDA (Siddha Yoga Dham America). Muktananda left his family at age fifteen to search for spiritual enlightenment. His spiritual master (**guru**) was an **ascetic** named Nityananda, who was widely believed to be an **avadhuta** (a person who has shaken off all attachments). Siddha Yoga's metaphysics are a modified form of **Kashmir** Shaivism. The organization's signature teaching is that the guru's spiritual power can immediately awaken the disciple's latent **kundalini**, hastening the process of spiritual development. This doctrine emphasizes the importance of the guru, reinforced by Muktananda's charismatic presence. Although his home base was an **ashram** just outside of Bombay, Muktananda traveled throughout the world, establishing ashrams and meditation centers in North America, Europe, and Australia. He was succeeded by **Swami Chidvilasananda**. For further information on Muktananda's teaching, see his autobiography, *Play of Consciousness*, 2000.

Muktibai

(1279–1297?) Poet and saint in the **Varkari Panth**, a religious community centered around the **worship** of the Hindu god **Vithoba**, at his temple at **Pandharpur** in the modern state of **Maharashtra**. According to tradition, Muktibai was the sister of the great Varkari teacher **Jnaneshvar**.

Muktinath

Temple and sacred site (**tirtha**) at the headwaters of the Kali Gandaki River in **Nepal**; the temple sits at nearly 13,000 feet at the foot of Annapurna, one of the highest mountains in Nepal. Muktinath is a sacred site to both Hindus and Buddhists; each has a temple there. The Buddhist temple is built over a vent of natural gas, which produces a flame when lit. The Hindu temple, dedicated to the god **Vishnu**, is built over a natural spring that is channelled outside the temple through 108 spouts shaped like heads of **cows**. The Kali Gandaki River is also religiously important because the river bed is one of the major sites of fossilized black **ammonite**. Known as the **shalagram**, this ammonite is considered a self-manifestation (**svayambhu**) form of Vishnu.

Muktiyoga

In the **Dvaita Vedanta** philosophical school propounded by **Madhva**, a

A man's head is shaved in the traditional Hindu practice of mundan. Removing one's hair is believed to be purifying.

muktiyoga is a person who is predestined to attain liberation. See also **Dvaita Vedanta**.

Muladhara Chakra

In many schools of **yoga**, and in the secret ritually-based religious practice known as **tantra**, the muladhara chakra is one of the six psychic centers (**chakras**) believed to exist in the **subtle body**. The subtle body is an alternate physiological system existing on a different plane of reality than matter, but corresponding to the material body. The six psychic centers are visualized as multipetaled lotus flowers running roughly along the spine, connected by three vertical channels. Each of the chakras has symbolic associations with various human capacities, various subtle elements (tanmatras), and different seed syllables (**bijaksharas**) formed from the letters of the **Sanskrit** alphabet, encompassing all sacred sound. Above and below these centers are the bodily abodes of **Shiva** (awareness) and **Shakti** (power), the two divine principles through which the entire universe has come into being. The underlying assumption behind the concept of the subtle body is the homology of macrocosm and microcosm, an essential Hindu idea since the time of the mystical texts known as the **Upanishads**.

The six chakras are traditionally enumerated starting from the bottom; the muladhara chakra is the first. It is visualized as a four-petaled lotus, located in the region at the base of the spine. The petals each contain a seed syllable, in this case the consonants from "va" to "sa." The muladhara chakra is associated as the bodily seat for the subtle element of **earth**, to which excretions are compared. The muladhara chakra is also considered the locus for the **kundalini**, the latent spiritual energy present in all human beings, visualized as a serpent wound three times around the muladhara chakra. Despite its associations with the most mundane element and the most impure bodily function, the muladhara is also the source of potential for religious attainment. For further information see Arthur Avalon (Sir John Woodroffe), *Shakti and Shakta*, 1978; and Philip S. Rawson, *The Art of Tantra*, 1973.

Mulamantra

("root mantra") A mulamantra is a sacred sound or sounds (**mantra**) that are considered to be the most subtle form of a **deity**. Every Hindu deity has a mulamantra. Different manifestations of the deity usually have different mantras, which are associated with them alone. The mulamantra is usually considered to be the highest and truest form of the deity, since it is nothing but sacred sound.

Munda

A **demon** general killed by the **Goddess** in the *Devimahatmya*, a **Sanskrit** text which is the earliest and most important mythic source for the cult of the Goddess. This text describes the Goddess in several different manifestations. The seventh book tells how the goddess **Ambika's** anger takes form as the terrifying goddess **Kali**. Kali attacks the demon armies commanded by Munda and his companion **Chanda**. After destroying the armies, Kali beheads the two generals. As a memorial of this mythic deed, the Goddess is worshiped by the name **Chamunda**, the slayer of Chanda and Munda.

Mundan

("**shaving**") In general terms, mundan refers to any type of haircutting or shaving done for religious purposes, such as the head-shaving traditionally done at certain pilgrimage places (**tirtha**). In **Tirupati** in southern India, the hair is given as an **offering** to the presiding **deity**; shaving is also a means of ritual purification, as in the rites for the dead. In a more specific sense, mundan is often used as a synonym for the **chudakarana samskara**, a life-cycle rite in which a young child's head is shaved, removing the last residual impurities from **birth**. See also **hair**.

Muni

A term of ancient provenance, dating back to the **Vedas**, the earliest Hindu religious text. In the Vedas this term is used to denote an **ascetic**, sage, or seer, particularly one keeping a vow of silence.

Murali

In Hindu mythology, murali is the god **Krishna's** flute. As recounted in sectarian texts such as the *Bhagavata Purana*, and countless vernacular devotional (**bhakti**) poems, the sound of this flute has an enticing quality that is irresistible to Krishna's devotees (**bhakta**). When they hear its melody, they rush to Krishna's presence. The flute and its siren song are seen as an extension of Krishna's own enticing presence.

Murals

Sanskrit literature contains numerous references to mural painting. In early medieval times, these were common forms of decorating both temples and the homes of the wealthy. The heat and moisture of the Indian climate have not been kind to such artwork; few examples remain today. The most famous murals are at Buddhist sites—Ajanta in central India and Sigiriya in **Sri Lanka**. These murals convey themes about everyday life. There are also traces of painting in the caves at **Ellora**. Paintings from the Chola era were recently discovered at the **Rajrajeshvar temple** in **Tanjore**; they are being restored. See also **Chola dynasty**.

Murari

("Mura's enemy") Epithet of the god **Krishna**. Mura is an extremely powerful **demon** who conquers all of the gods. He is eventually killed in battle by Krishna. See **Krishna**.

Murari Gupta

(16th c.) Author of the earliest version of the *Chaitanya-Charitramrta* ("Nectar of Chaitanya's Deeds"), an account describing the life of the Bengali saint **Chaitanya** (1486–1533). Murari Gupta's text focuses on Chaitanya's early life up to his southern Indian pilgrimage ending in 1513. The last part of the text briefly mentions his pilgrimage to **Brindavan** in 1514 and his final return to **Puri**, where he lived for the rest of his life. Like the other traditional accounts of Chaitanya's life, this does not purport to be an "objective" biography; it is rather a hagiography (idealized portrait) written by a passionate devotee (**bhakta**). Nevertheless, Murari Gupta was a contemporary and companion of Chaitanya; his text reflects first-hand experience and is the most reliable of these traditional sources.

Murti

("shape," "form") The most common name for a sculptural image of a Hindu **deity** fashioned by human beings, rather than those that are self-manifested (**svayambhu images**) forms of the deity.

Murugan

("fragrant, beautiful") Hindu **deity** primarily worshiped in southern India. Murugan originally appears in the Tamil **Sangam literature**, where he is a hill deity associated with the hunt and wild, unsettled places. One of Murugan's characteristic objects is the lance, symbolizing the hunt. As brahminical Hindu culture gradually came to southern India, Murugan was drawn into the established pantheon as a form of the god **Skanda**, who is the son of the god **Shiva**. By the tenth century Murugan's identity had evolved as that of a philosopher and exponent of the **Shaiva Siddhanta** philosophical school and as the patron deity of **Tamil language** and literature. For southern Indians, especially in the state of **Tamil Nadu**, worshiping Murugan becomes a vehicle to affirm their traditional culture. This has been particularly true since Indian independence in 1947, when the attempt to impose **Hindi** as the national language was seen as northern Indian cultural imperialism and was met with incredible resistance. The cult of Murugan has five major pilgrimage centers—**Palani**, **Tiruchendur**, **Tiruttani**, **Tirrupparankunram**, and **Swami Malai**. All of these sites are located in different parts of Tamil Nadu. This network of sacred sites (**tirthas**) is a way in which the cult of Murugan has come to symbolize Tamil identity. For further information see Fred Clothey, "Pilgrimage Centers in the Tamil Cultus of Murukan," in *Journal of the American Academy of Religion,* Vol. 40, No.1, 1972.

Musala

("pestle") A musala is a grinding pestle, used with a mortar to husk and grind grain. Miniature versions were used to grind spices. Aside from its utilitarian use, the musala's long, club-like shape could easily serve as a weapon. It is one of the characteristic objects in Hindu iconography, appearing with images of various **deities**—the **Goddess**, **Shiva**, and **Vishnu**.